D1403797

PISTOLS

A
MODERN
ENCYCLOPEDIA

PISTOLS

A MODERN ENCYCLOPEDIA

Henry M. Stebbins
Albert J. E. Shay
Oscar R. Hammond

THE STACKPOLE COMPANY
HARRISBURG, PENNSYLVANIA

Copyright © *1961*

By

HENRY M. STEBBINS

All Rights Reserved

Library of Congress Catalog Card Number 60-14560

Printed and Bound in the United States of America
by THE TELEGRAPH PRESS, *Established 1831*
Harrisburg, Pennsylvania

PREFACE

I N a world that labors mightily for peace, but which has been plagued by armed conflict somewhere on its surface since recorded history was first chiseled on the walls of caves in southwestern Europe, handguns are still the individual's last-ditch weapon.

Aside from a few champions in specialized fields of rifle shooting, who must devote all their available free time to earnest practice in their specialty to stay in the top ten—be they smallbore, bench-rest, Olympic or military-rifle artists—*every rifleman I've ever known uses handguns in the off-season.* Taking these people together with other men—police, plant guards, mailhandlers, bank guards, members of the armed forces, hunters and just plain folks who shoot a pistol or revolver for recreation—there is a huge number of handgunners in our United States who are vitally interested in the use of one-hand weapons, professionally, semi-professionally or recreationally.

Many fine volumes have been written about pistols, but the specialized approach of most of them covers particular types or phases of pistol usage. It is fortunate, for example, that volumes are devoted to the evolution, history and description of particular models or types for identification by the advanced student or collector.

It is also fortunate that when Harry Stebbins and his friends wrote this book they made sure that it was of basic use to the novice by assuming comparatively little familiarity with handguns on the part of the reader and giving the fullest possible coverage to types and models currently in use. The beginner can read this book intelligently and decide what best suits his own gun and ammunition needs.

Since Harry's own use of pistols covers a long life, he was also able from that experience, and from the experiences of his old shooting friends in many fields of pistol usage, to develop the text so that the widely experienced handgunner will find much in it that is new and useful to him.

Harry's background being that of a target shooter, hunter and woodsloafer, with some fifty years at it, he has a wide experience with pistols. His previous books have been on the rifle, but, as he would say, it simply happened so. He likes and uses all kinds of personal firearms—rifles, pistols and shotguns.

His old friend Oscar Hammond, whose avocation when a youth lay in the fields and woods, has since his boyhood days been a user of every type of pistol he could get his hands on, not to mention the long guns, too. He was born and reared on a farm in central New York, where the density of population was so light that a Colt Single Action Army .45 was a safe and recognized working tool in his hands. Ock Hammond thus gives the reader his considered judgments from a lifetime of practical use under conditions that have all too nearly disappeared in our Country. He, like the other two on this three-man writing team, has owned and extensively used an enormous variety of handguns.

Albert J. E. Shay, Harry's friend of long standing and the third contributor, is one of the few links between the black powder era of handguns and the present. Bert enlisted in the Navy and spent his life in it. When he was a member of the landing party at Vera Cruz in 1914, the Model 1911 .45 Colt Auto Pistol had just been adopted by our armed forces. He has been shooting it and anything else in the way of personal, one-man firearms ever since. Bert hasn't confined his work with the pistol to strictly professional Naval lines! He has shot on Navy teams, coached them, and for recreation has founded and coached many civilian pistol clubs wherever he has made his home ashore. Early in his shooting career, he became a handloader to get the amount and variety of firing he craved. In that field his experiences have embraced everything from casting and loading more types of bullets than a modest-sized pamphlet could list. He designed several fine target bullets which are still available from the mold makers. Bert's experimental work with handguns—not to mention that with other firearms—has covered the line from the old .50 caliber Navy Remington single-shot through the most modern types of police, target and military guns, including the development and chronography of loads for use on target or game. When I first met him, over twenty-five years ago, he was consuming some 10,000 pistol primers a year! And he is still at it, for the sheer love of the game.

Such backgrounds assure the readers of this book a practical coverage of handguns, written by and for shooters. It fills a great need in the literature on the subject, so that the game may grow as the typically American sport of handgun shooting should.

THOMAS C. FLORICH
White Plains, New York

FOREWORD

~~ ~~~~~~

THIS book is for pistol users—the potential, the more or less active, and the deeply and hopelessly addicted!

It discusses currently-made American arms, the European productions of practical value to us here, and many of the most useful, interesting, and sometimes downright challenging oldtimers that deserve to be put into service again.

Any long-time shooter with even a moderately upstanding bump of curiosity must find ammunition as fascinating as the guns that fire it, and we are no exceptions. It must be correct for the gun, which is always an individual and must be humored to bring out its best—and it must be entirely safe. We are enthusiasts, but we are cautious enthusiasts, particularly in making recommendations to others.

In our writing about handguns and cartridges we have used, we admit, "catalogue dope." Much can be learned from it. But as we had our own experiences and judgments to record, too, we compressed it, usually in tabulated form. Naturally we tried to be impartial, for there are all sorts of needs and all sorts of tastes, and a lop-sided writer or speaker is often tiresome, and sometimes misleading.

Any book of this sort can be outdated, and perhaps rather soon. With this in mind we endeavored throughout to make clear the basic principles of what makes a good handgun or cartridge, and what doesn't. We wanted to lay the sort of background that would help any reader, even a novice in the pistol game, to find it not too hard to evaluate new products as they appear.

We didn't build this book alone and unaided. Tom Florich and his son, Tom, Jr., contributed a chapter that we think is outstanding in its field, as well as an equally useful section in the chapter on basic handloading. Arms and ammunition manufacturers, gunsmiths, engravers, and importers helped us with photographs and information we needed. Many, like Fred T. Huntingdon of R.C.B.S. Gun & Die Shop, Dave Bushnell the importer of optical equipment, and Max E. Thompson of Western Cartridge, went to special pains to provide material for our use. Throughout the years, dozens and dozens of friends, on the range and in the field, have shared their experiences and findings with us in that easy interchange that outdoorsmen know so well. We are grateful to them all for their help, and to the editors of *The American Rifleman, Gun Digest, Guns* and *Precision Shooting*. Every one of these individuals understands that "the right of the people to keep and bear arms" is part of the American birthright, and what's more, one of the bulwarks of our Country's strength.

HENRY M. STEBBINS

Middletown, Virginia

CONTENTS

FOR millions of us Americans the handgun—revolver or semi-automatic pistol—holds a unique, compelling fascination. It grips our imagination in a way that no other weapon can. It has made history and it continues to make it. Rich in the romance of pioneer days, the pistol is redolent of ten thousand desperate fights—fights for worthy or for pitifully trivial causes.

Never before has it been so popular in our Country, the most pistol-conscious in all the world. Oldtimers in the shooting game have been amazed, sometimes amused, at the flood of new or revised models that have come to market since Word War II ended. Yet these guns have sold in the huge quantities that modern production plans call for, and European arms makers have cashed in on our demand for handguns and our ability to pay for them.

The neat, unobtrusive pistol is impressive in its potential might. It is no toy, but a trusted ally in the lawless spaces of land, sea and air. Small, short and comparatively light, it can go with us law-abiding citizens on occasions when the long rifle or even the stubby carbine must be left behind. It can be fired with one free hand, and carried with both hands free. So it is a useful weapon, and an intimate one. Long practice makes it almost as much a part of us as our fists.

But as civilians we shall own pistols only as long as we can prove actual need of them, and use them safely. No longer.

For military personnel and law enforcement officers, the handgun is more useful now than ever before. I've known a certain young lieutenant of Infantry since he was a red-headed five-year-old firebrand with, even then, a blazing spirit of inquiry. He writes: "Pistols have ceased to be just nice souvenirs. Experience in Korea . . . As a result they issued out a lot more .45s than the prescribing Table of Organization and Equipment calls for. Further, many of the soldiers took to buying a pistol out of their own pocket. Certainly a testimonial to the usefulness of handguns."

But some law enforcement officers, and some members of the judiciary, too, feel that pistols have no place in the hands of private citizens. This opinion is understandable. Trained for their job, true specialists, they want no interference in it, no "amateur" help.

There's the key word. A resolute, law-abiding citizen, expert with the handgun, is no amateur. He becomes the finest kind of deputy, whether he's formally enrolled or merely ready to do his part when emergency breaks.

It can break in places remote from prompt police control, and nearly always it breaks with suddenness and surprise. What about the widow in the dirt-road farmhouse, about the woman stranded alone when her car coughs and quits by some cliff-darkened turn on the highway, or anywhere far from help? Don't they need the legal right to own a pistol, to learn to be

CHAPTER 1

HANDGUNS FOR CIVILIANS? WHY?

A well regulated Militia, being necessary to the security of a free State, the right of the people to keep and bear Arms, shall not be infringed. —CONSTITUTION OF THE UNITED STATES OF AMERICA, Amendment 1.

efficient with it, to carry it on "lawful occasions?" Men, too, have proper and sometimes frequent need of a handgun as one of the tools of their jobs. Only representative—there's no need to try to list them all —are the truckdriver, operator of a small boat, cattle-rancher, sheep-herder, farmer with "mean stock," banker, payroll carrier, store proprietor, far-traveling salesman, forest ranger, timber cruiser and fire warden.

Some law officers distrust the pistol because they know, often at first hand, of many crimes committed with it. This distrust is natural. Yet it's natural to forget that other weapons, less startling on casual view, are quite as deadly. Such an arsenal-in-disguise contains, among other instruments, the ice-pick, hammer, monkey-wrench, hatchet, axe, loaded cane, kitchen knife, ski pole, stair-rod, stick of firewood and of course the automobile. Thirty minutes and a hacksaw convert a single- or double-barrel shotgun into a pistol with which it's almost impossible to miss. This obliging feature delights the criminal, who seldom goes in heavily for target practice! He usually lacks determination, the sense of fun and the social instinct. You find these sunny qualities on the pistol target range.

Never more obviously than now did loyal American civilians need cooperation and understanding. Law

1

officers are not a breed apart, either in high-handed privilege or in devotion to the maintenance of order and decency. Most of them are ordinary human beings, men with families and a budget, the hopes and worries, the dreams and dreads that are common to us all. After the automobile operator's exam—afterwards, mind you—many of us civilians have found the officer an approachable fellow and enjoyed a chat with him. He leads a life of varied activity, with a great opportunity to observe human nature in the brash or trembling raw. Frequently his reflections on what he has seen are illuminating, and humorous, too.

Sheriff Neal Lewis of Chenango County, New York, was one of my great friends. I enjoyed his heartiness, shrewdness and unfailing good humor. We had many talks in his office and afield—I never heard anyone else speak crow language as convincingly as he did. Under his kindliness lay a hard courage. Once or twice the time had come to shoot it out, and he hadn't backed down. Knowing well what makes a criminal, he never spoke of these occasions. The bitter memory was buried deep. As many of his kind wear a badge, I do not despair of eventual cooperation between wearers of uniforms and wearers of civilian clothes.

There are less serious uses for a handgun, and often they are recognized by understanding men who issue licenses. The fisherman may turn one on a rattlesnake, a copperhead, a bobcat or a weasel. A few of us— mighty few—are expert enough to be justified in hunting with a pistol. The collector has good reasons for owning them, and by no means is he always ordered to deactivate his specimens. The target shooter learns muscular coordination and self-control with this weapon that's so difficult to master, and in competition he can and usually must develop valuable mental and moral qualities. The plinker and the casual shooter have fun and the relaxation so badly needed in stressful times. If all of us are careful about where our bullets land we can do the sport no harm. Definitely we contribute to that precious intangible called "national preparedness."

The fact that we can still own and use a pistol is due in considerable part to the foresight and labor of one man. C. B. Lister, secretary of the National Rifle Association and editor of its magazine, *American Rifleman,* was tireless in fighting to maintain our constitutional right to keep and bear arms. He died on the job.

OFTEN the seasoned pistoleer is as undecided as the beginner as to what handgun will serve his purpose best. To make decision still more difficult, the shooter frequently wants a gun that's a specialist in several different jobs!

Still other considerations crowd in. How good a shot is he, what is at stake, how reliable must the weapon be? Hunting frogs in a sun-drenched marsh can be pleasant sport; hunting a saboteur in a factory yard some moonless midnight, can be a man's most vital and exacting experience in life, or his last.

Who is qualified to pronounce finally on gun choice, and who would assume the responsibility of doing so? Why, guns themselves, like the people who use them, are individuals. Some specimens of the same make, model and caliber are more reliable, more accurate, or more smoothly tuned up for good shooting than others. On the counter chronograph, two apparently identical pistols, fed the same run of ammunition and fired alternately shot-for-shot, can flash up quite different figures to be translated and averaged into bullet velocity.

But let's look at gun choice more broadly. Type of mechanism, weight, barrel length, safety devices, grip fit, trigger pull, sight equipment, caliber, brand name and other big or little details appeal differently to different people, no matter how logical they all may be in—well, in normal life. These matters build or destroy confidence. A workman who likes and respects his tools is a long piece down the road toward efficiency.

We can classify pistols as pocket guns, holster or work guns, plinkers, target arms and home protection weapons. By "pistol" or "handgun" we mean all types: revolver, single shot, double- or multi-barrel, hand-operated repeater (perhaps the last was the Fiala .22 of about thirty years ago; it looked much like the Colt Woodsman of that time), and semi-automatic. Like other shooters in camp, den, gunstore or clubroom, we call the latter an "automatic." We know—but disregard the fact—that the term implies continuous, machine-gun-type fire when the trigger is held back, a delivery that we pistolmen certainly do not want! Some of us have seen a semi-automatic with worn sear do just that, its muzzle climbing up and up as the magazine vomited. We remember the dazed look of the shooter after that dismaying burst of fire had ended.

The pocket gun should be light and short enough to ride comfortably all day in the pocket that holds it. Some pockets are bigger, more strongly stitched, and better placed to avoid showing an obvious bulge than are others. In general, a nine-inch overall length and a weight of 2 or 2¼ pounds come close to the convenient or even permissible maximum. Perhaps the minimum is a personal matter. Just how well can we direct a small chunk of lead from a really little gun? Today 2-, 3- and 4-inch barreled pocket revolvers are commonly acceptable, and to these barrel lengths we add a cylinder length of roughly 1¼ or 1½ inches. The automatic or autoloader has its chamber in its barrel.

CHAPTER 2

BEWILDERING CHOICE— WHAT GUN?

Browning-type autos, with their recoil spring under the barrel requiring a fairly heavy slide, fit and balance well in the pocket, and their muzzle weight helps in steady aiming, too. The old Pocket Model .38 Colt, 31 ounces unloaded, 4½-inch barrel, rode smoothly and was worth the sag if you wanted lots of penetration. This could pay off in an emergency occurring in the wilderness maybe once or twice in a lifetime, and this model had pretty fair smack, too. The modern Colt Commander and Smith & Wesson autos are lighter, catalogued at 26½ ounces apiece, and almost as smooth and snag-free in outline. Colt choice includes the .45 caliber, and S.&W. choice a double-action trigger mechanism for a quick first shot. Compared with these three, a butt-heavy, 4-inch barreled Luger of about the same weight as the old .38 is as smoothriding a pocketful as a six-weeks-old kitten. Its chief advantage over the oldtimer is its positive and fairly convenient thumb safety, less handy than those on the two moderns mentioned, but not bad. I remember my Pocket Model Colt with affection and respect, for it was true to its class and never failed me in a lot of shooting in the woods and on improvised target ranges. However, it had no safety lock, and its hammer, though neatly spurred for the thumb as were all but the earliest issues, could not be cocked fast with a one-hand grip.

The "belly gun" falls into the class of pocket arms, even though it can be heftier and of the largest caliber. This short-barreled fellow goes into a waistband holster or is tucked in between trousers and shirt, unholstered. It isn't classed as a holster gun, ordinarily, though it could serve as such.

Holster or work guns are made for heavy duty, often for long-range shooting—in long woods ranges, at least. Caliber, weight and barrel length are limited by the outdoorsman's endurance and his sense of the practical as opposed to a *sometimes* irrational delight in lugging lots of hardware. In the wilderness mere quickness of draw seldom means much. When speed does figure in the gun's line of duty, the barrel often measures only 4 inches. In the cities, that is a popular length for police revolvers; shooting is usually at very short or at least fairly short range and speed of draw is critical. Unless a criminal or a suspect is known to be desperate and ready to kill, he gets the privilege of first shot. The state policeman operating in rural districts, like the Mountie in Canadian wilds, can use a longer barrel and a heavier caliber than the .38 Special. They often need the longer sure-hitting range and extra power. Sometimes they have to kill large animals in their line of duty, a job that seldom comes to the city or village officer.

To carry a heavy gun comfortably, and to protect any pistol as well as possible, the shoulder holster seems preferable to the belt type when you travel afoot or in a car. On horseback or aboard a canoe, a belted-on gun seems natural, easy and convenient. Certainly a short but heavy gun like a Super .38 or .45 automatic, or a 4- or 4½-inch barreled .44 or .45 revolver, can be carried in the pocket, but its weight is a nuisance, and shortening the barrel of the big sixgun doesn't help much except in making it quicker to draw.

The plinking gun is any kind for which you can get plentiful ammunition to turn on tin cans, blocks of wood, stumps peering warily through brush and other inanimate but still challenging targets. The .22 makes little noise if it has a reasonably long barrel and, in revolver form, a decently close fit between cylinder and barrel. Some handloads of .32 and even .38 caliber are pretty quiet. At a distance they sound like a .22 rimfire closer by; they don't blast. When you can go over the hill to wilderness or a close facsimile of that delightful region, noise can hardly get you into trouble. You may even find a place so devoid of habitation, so far from human haunts at some times of the year, that you can fire overhead—not at a low, long-traveling angle—at targets hurled aloft, or cut loose at bits of wood out on a pond or hurrying down fast water. Shooting into an incoming wave can give the lead a return ticket straight back to you, and a bullet skipped off smooth water may travel hundreds of yards before it comes to rest, you know not where. We know that gunpowder and alcohol don't mix safely. Water can be as dangerous an element as alcohol. Just for an example, a wooded shore-line of a pond or lake may look like an excellent

backstop. But it also can screen people you don't know are there.

Plinking is fascinating from the start, and that start often has led to the development of capable target, game and military shots. To keep up the interest it should be varied. After you've gained reasonable hitting ability with the handgun, the matter of timing comes in to add to the challenge and to your pleasure. Drawing the gun and firing one quick, accurate shot have practical value. Later you put the stop-watch on the delivery of several shots, but you still want hits. Fire-power depends on two elements, accuracy and volume or rate. See that the gun really fits your hand and that it's heavy enough for steadiness.

Target guns are specialized if scores are our main objective. They should be, for in all practical shooting only the hits count, and nothing else gives pleasure. Weight, balance and the fit of the gun in the hand are the deciding factors. Hardly less important are the type of action, caliber and sighting—not only the design of those sights but also their "radius," the distance between front and rear as determined by barrel and action length and by the mounting of the sights. There are several classifications of target shooting, the chief designations being slow or deliberate firing and the delivery of shots within a time limit. Our choice should never be based on the maker's name stamped on the barrel. We want the gun that helps us bring out our best shooting.

Since target arms have the weight and balance for steady holding, they often double as holster or work guns and go to far places in the woods and mountains or on the plains. Except for the European style single-shot "free pistols"—fitted with set or "hair" triggers sometimes so light that a breath can trip them, and often with extension rear sights for longer radius, set back in harm's way—almost all target handguns are rugged enough for outdoor service if they get reasonable care.

And their adjustable sights pay off in the field! It isn't that we'd be likely to add a click or two of windage or elevation for a try at some fairly distant and decidedly obliging critter. It's the ability that these sights give to zero in for any heavy or light load we care to use, and for the hold we prefer on game, either dead center or just below the exact spot we want to hit. Probably a majority of target shots hold at six o'clock, just at the bottom of the round black bull's-eye, and the sight elevation pitches the bullet high enough to puncture the bull's center, when all goes well. Obviously this method wouldn't work in the hunting field. Adjustable sights are so big a help that some experienced shooters demand them on any type of pistol they care to own. When two or more people past the novice stage use the same gun, they must have such sights, just as on a rifle. Few of us hold, grip, aim or even see alike.

Home guns have been referred to rather slightingly as "bureau drawer specials." Unfortunately most of them are. They seldom see a practice range often enough, though lives depend on them.

Since they are left loaded for long periods of time, revolvers seem decidedly better than automatics. A revolver has no magazine spring to be weakened or possibly "set" by long tension, and its hammer never needs to be left at full cock to be ready for instant service. For it, we can buy ammunition that is effective, yet not so high in penetration as to endanger nice old Mrs. Brown in the next apartment but one down the line. Absolute reliability and simplicity of operation are essentials: it isn't only a gun crank who may depend on it for his or her life.

The bedside table or a holster slung to the bedpost is a more practical garage for it than the bureau drawer is. If young children are in the house, however, it must be out of their reach. But they're seldom six feet tall, and their ability to stack chairs and climb has limits. An automatic with a stiff recoil spring and a loaded magazine handy is safe around the smallest kids, though to pick up a stuffed magazine and use it for a sledgehammer would be a perilous practice.

Each gun and each type of gun have their ideal purposes and their limitations. Yet most of the good ones can serve more than one purpose. Weight, size, length, grip, balance, sighting and even caliber are fairly flexible qualities as we use them. We all have our ideas of the pistol that doesn't exist but almost does, unless our needs are extensive. So *the all-round gun* takes many forms.

Perhaps a majority of thoughtfully cast votes would go to the 4-inch barreled .38 Special on a medium-weight frame. The Smith & Wesson Combat Masterpiece or the Colt Trooper would qualify, if we insist on having sights adjustable for distance, the effect of wind on the target range, our vision and manner of holding and loads of different power or various bullet weights. Yet such sights can snag on a pocket lining; so the 4-inch barreled Colt Official Police or S.&W. Military and Police might be better. Still (as the gun crank's brain keeps churning) a 5-inch .38 Special is pleasanter to shoot, doesn't seem to crack quite so loudly, and we might do better work with it. But maybe that caliber won't do—too light or possibly too heavy. Sooner or later we'll have to give up, pick the nearest we can get to the all-rounder, and learn to shoot it straight and get it into action fast, too.

To prove nothing, but simply to give an example that certainly interested me, here's the choice of a friend of mine. Bob has had a great deal of experience with arms, as a civilian and as a serviceman in combat. He's an unusually sharp pistol shot, maybe a bit unusual too in that his ability with the handgun is, comparatively, a good deal better than it is with the rifle. He's no slouch with either, and, as you'd expect, he's a really capable offhand rifleman. Pistol shooting taught him trigger control. The only handgun he has or even seems to want is a 2-inch barrelled Colt Detective Special, a 21-ounce job. Since this is a .38 Special, he gets approximately the blast and recoil of a heavily loaded .44 or .45 of some twice the weight and three times the barrel length. These ructions don't seem to disturb him. He has placed and sometimes won in matches, not big events, but still fast company. Perhaps more important, he enjoys shooting that little gun. He fires it whenever he can and is thoroughly familiar with it.

The "one gun" may be an automatic. Analysis of its values and disadvantages alongside those of the revolver feeds the flame of an old argument that can roar to bonfire heat when shooters get together. Here are some well-charred sticks for that fire:

REVOLVER

1. Reliability. Seldom indeed is it locked by molten, shaved lead or by half-burned powder grains that prevent full closing of the cylinder or full descent of the ejector into its home in the cylinder. A misfire halts us for only an instant, for another chamber lies ready.

2. The usual heavy-duty revolver carries only six shots and is slow to reload without three-shot clips like those for the 1917 Colt and Smith service guns. (At this writing there are three modern S.&W. descendants of the 1917 of that make. Easy loading must have had something to do with that.)

3. Most of us find the sixgun easier to master, except for half-decent accuracy in fast double-action fire. Recoil does seem heavier with the same ammunition, lots of us think, but in long sessions at target it doesn't set up vibrations in our hand quite as quickly—when we use the .45 Auto rounds in each type of gun. Its barrel lies higher above our hand than does that of the automatic, a slight disadvantage.

4. The cylinder gives it a waistline bulge, but the gun can be shorter and lighter than an auto of considerably less killing power.

5. Its operation is simple, quickly understood by almost anyone who may need to use it. If the gun gets into unfriendly hands, this could be too bad!

6. Cleaning it is a fairly long job, for each chamber as well as the barrel needs attention. However, a mild case of rust doesn't put its action out of commission, and its usually heavier hammer is more likely to fire the cartridge in cold that might affect the auto more seriously in firing and in handling its ammunition.

7. Quick for the first shot, at least if it's double-action; slow for well-aimed succeeding shots. Yes, some have mastered accurate double-action, and in less time than most of us might think.

8. Ammunition choice is wide. Then too, it handles bullets with far better sectional density (weight in proportion to caliber) than the self-loader does, as normally loaded, both arms being for centerfire cartridges. It functions with extremely light charges and with those well above standard power, at least when the gun is of good quality. Yes, factory Magnum loads

are pretty close to the workable, safe power, but they aren't made for the autoloaders, up to this writing.

9. Wear affects it only slowly if we treat it right.

10. It is difficult to reassemble if we tear it down, which we'd want to do if it fell overboard into water, for example.

11. If a small, rounded grip is needed by a small hand, this is the type of pistol to consider first. In normal deliberate firing, the wrist is locked as the hand is extended.

12. The bullet must jump from the cylinder into the rifled barrel. This would seem to cost accuracy and power, but tests indicate no serious velocity loss from snugly fitted revolvers, and nearly all models used for target have their barrels much more rigidly assembled than most centerfire automatics do. So they shoot better on the average.

13. If you're a handloader, the revolver saves its empty brass for you. Your reloads can vary from very light squib or "whisper" doses to full standard power, and sometimes above that.

AUTOMATIC

1. The best makes, and particularly those models with a short-recoil or locked action instead of a simple blowback, rarely jam when kept in good condition and fed with high quality ammunition. If the shooter trusts no factory or arsenal he can handload his cartridges, inspecting each component. But if a misfire occurs, both hands must be used to chamber another cartridge. With a double-action automatic—like the Smith & Wesson, several foreign models, and probably numerous future models of American make—you can pull the trigger instantly for another try, and then the defective primer may fire, or may not.

2. The auto is reloaded rapidly with extra magazines, which must be in nearly perfect shape and free from excessive sand or grit if they're to work surely.

3. It spits out its bullets smoothly, but its trigger pull in heavier caliber arms is usually coarser, less suitable for accurate work. As a rule, in centerfire its recoil seems lighter, its report sharper.

4. Flat and compact, it's easily toted.

5. Its more complicated action means little to the specialist, who may be a lone wolf with no wish to share his gun. He knows how to adapt it to arctic or tropic conditions, or almost anything earthly.

6. The guncrank can easily keep it in beautiful shape except when things are really rough. Reasonable care is necessary if it's to be reliable—ready when wanted.

7. Double-action autos deliver a quick first shot.

There's no safety that *must* be released, no hammer that *must* be cocked with the thumb. Few autos except some .22s have a really fine trigger pull.

8. Loads must be fitted to its action. Ultra power gives serious wear, may cause a breakdown, or worse. Reduced power can be too low to operate the self-loading mechanism. Not all automatics handle the deadly soft-lead bullets reliably, but require either hard-alloy or jacketed bullets. Comparatively few operate well with flat-ended "wad-cutter" or even with home-cast hollow-point bullets. The standard factory-made centerfire ammunition is more compact than corresponding revolver cartridges, but never as deadly, except when lots of penetration is needed, but not the wider wound path given by a blunter, soft-lead bullet.

9. A long, Browning-type slide with floating barrel assembly needs rather loose tolerances, which open wider with use. To maintain a .45 automatic for exacting target work requires, as a rule, more frequent attention than a target revolver must have.

10. After a dunk in the creek, it's easy to dismount, dry, and oil most self-loaders, with cleaning rags and over a fire.

11. Most of them have fairly large grips, except those with grips for no more than, say, 1½ fingers. Some prefer the rather flat grip to the more rounded grip of the revolver. When you fire the usual auto, your wrist is not locked as it is with the revolver; it's in a neutral position. To many this seems more natural, but on the target range it's responsible for an occasional wild shot if you relax your vigilance. For instinctive pointing, a shooter with no preconceived ideas probably would prefer the auto style of grip. However, grips of both types of pistol vary so much that generalizations are risky, as usual!

12. The bullet sits close to the rifling lands, which should contribute to accuracy—and does, at least in theory. But most auto-pistols, like most auto-rifles, are chambered loosely to make operation surer, and this doesn't help. When the rear sight is mounted on the receiver or a barrel extension instead of on a more or less loose-fitting slide or breechblock, the finest grade of accuracy isn't going to be cut down by the lack of cooperation of the aiming notch!

13. Objections to handloading for the automatic probably are voiced most loudly by sixgun fans. You do have to shag the twirled-out brass, but you can reload it to whisper power and the brass stays in the gun, ready for you to shuck out by hand. It is *not* always necessary to resize auto cases full-length, either, as some think.

THIS subject can cover a field too wide to come within the range of common sense! One could start with miniature foreign-made automatics created as noise-makers and watch-charms. Their caliber is so small that one could almost use a toothpick as a cleaning rod, and their greatest threat is blood-poisoning.

At the other extreme might stand the gun of a famous oldtime Eastern dentist whose doctor warned him that his life was to be short. Doc Holliday took himself westward to enjoy what time was left, with the idea that he might hasten the end, and thus started one of the most notable gunman careers in the history of the West. It is rumored that one of his oddities was to carry, on occasion, a sawed-off shotgun slung from his belt by a piece of rawhide and stuck down his pants-leg. Although this was a far-fetched version of a pocket gun, we must admit that it was a concealed weapon.

Let's concede that these extremes are impractical, and stick to revolvers and semi-automatic pistols with barrels little, if any, longer than 4 inches. Longer guns won't ride in the average pocket, and they're slower to draw, other things being equal.

THE .22s

There's the thought of caliber. Everyone agrees that the larger bores are by far the best in the stopping power that's all-important in a defense weapon. But before going on to the far more respectable centerfire pocket guns, we do want to give the .22s a fair break in this chapter's discussion.

Most of us would rather be missed by a .45 than hit by a .22, and today's .22 bullet, well placed, is something we can do without. The high velocity long-rifle load is a hard-hitting deal, with lots of penetration even with the mushrooming hollow-point bullet, though the nerve shock and knockdown power of the big-shots are sadly lacking. At today's cost of cartridges, most of us find we can't afford to fire larger calibers as much as we'd like to unless we reload our empty centerfire cases. A good—and attractive—.22 pocket gun is likely to have a lot of lead poured through it. Its lighter report helps in finding informal ranges where we can shoot.

That pocket .22 goes with us on the hunting trip, blends well with the fishing rod, is almost a necessity on the trapline. It fits nicely in the glove compartment of the car, in our pack-basket or rucksack, or in the feminine pocketbook. We even take it to the club pistol range to "try it out," although we may have a heavier, longer-barreled, target-sighted gun with large, hand-filling grip for our serious shooting. Yet always the little gat is an enjoyable companion for those fortunate enough to live where they can spend a holiday afternoon exploring the outdoors. One never knows when he must be protected from a particularly sly-looking knot in a dead tree, a tin can paratrooped out of a car, a leaf sneaking down some remote back-

CHAPTER 3

POCKET GUNS

BY OSCAR R. HAMMOND

woods creek, or a rat raiding a garbage dump. We usually come home only when our ammunition is all gone. Every shot has made us that much surer of hitting something with the next one, *and if we are always careful of the background,* no harm at all has been done to the shooting fraternity's reputation.

More seriously, there are many communities where rabid foxes are far too numerous, and they are a menace not only to animals but to humans as well. A shot from our .22 pocket pistol—and it certainly must be well placed—could easily be a life-saver if one of these sick varmints should show up. Poisonous snakes also can be taken care of with the .22, when it's pointed right.

So the .22 needn't be overlooked, even when viewed strictly as a defense weapon. Quite possibly the added accuracy and gun-handiness gained in such economical shooting would offset the greater penetration and shock power of larger calibers. It also appears that the average person is more likely to have his .22 within reach than one of the larger, heavier sizes.

Pocket arms for sport and for defense are numerous in this country, thank goodness, and to try to point out the best one is a formal invitation to a pointless argument. Each of us has his own ideas, and they can be based on experience and individual need, not simply on taste or whim—which can be rational, too. Let's scan the current line of American arms, and look at some no longer made, too, but still available on the used-gun market.

Smith & Wesson have a beauty in their *Kit Gun*. It has a 2- or 4-inch barrel, adjustable sights, weighs about 22½ ounces in 4-inch and is safe and reliable

Smith & Wesson round-butt .22 Kit Gun with 4-inch barrel. Counter-bored chambers enclose each cartridge head.

in every way. Rounded stocks make it ideal for the pocket; and for holster use, there's the square-butt model and better shooting, too, most of us would agree. If lightness is wanted, there's the 14¼-ounce Airweight with 3½-inch barrel.

One possible objection is the rear sight, which sometimes catches in the clothing, even if its edges are beveled down, as were those of some pre-1953 Kits. The target fan, who for reasons of his own doesn't care for the usual long heavy gun, finds it almost perfect, weight considered—with grips perhaps larger and more hand-filling than the square factory type, and an adapter like the Pachmayr to fill some of the space behind the trigger guard. Kit accuracy isn't sneered at on the range; like the Stradivarius violin, it has more music in it than most of us can hope to bring out. This is true of most of our top grade guns.

S.&W. make the *Combat Masterpiece* .22, weighing 36½ ounces loaded, in most ways the same as the .38 Special in that model. Rugged in every way, the .22 has a 4-inch barrel, adjustable sights, and larger, square-butt grip that makes it hard to conceal. Accuracy is excellent. Law officers and others who habitually carry its counterpart in .38 find it superb for low-cost practice. The slightly heavier 4-inch *Colt Official Police* .22 has solid, non-adjustable sights, and some would prefer it for that reason, though the Smith's front sight, at least, is just as snag-proof in the pocket.

Colt's had—and we wish they still had—a fine little gun in the *Banker's Special,* a 2-inch barrel job on the old short Police Positive frame. The grip was rounded, and the weight of 23 ounces hardly burdensome; yet the gun showed surprising accuracy. The later 3-inch *Courier* went 19½ ounces in .22, and few objected to that extra inch of barrel. The ramp front sight was easy to draw and to see, and the fully checkered stocks were of walnut, like those on the Banker's.

Obsolete like these two, the *Harrington & Richardson New Defender* with 2- or 3-inch barrel was hard to beat. It was a popular early entry in the snubnose .22 class that was really shootable. Grips came in a

wide choice of shape, it had adjustable sights, and its trigger pull wasn't bad at all. Accuracy was satisfactory, and the top-break cylinder opening made cleaning and loading easy. H.&R. now offer a handy little piece in the *922 Bantamweight,* with 2½-inch barrel, 20-ounce weight, and 9-shot capacity. Its coil-spring action is an improvement over many older guns in the class, and the ejection of empties is simplified: you push them out all at once with the cylinder pin. Sights are clear, though not adjustable, and they don't tend to catch in the pocket. Accuracy is satisfactory, though the small space between upper grip and trigger guard may afford a poor grip for a big hand.

Iver Johnson's Protector Sealed Eight with 2½-inch barrel made a fine pocket gun, its counterbored cylinder adding to safety in case of a burst cartridge rim. The older *I.J. "Hammer-the-Hammer"* and *"Safety Hammerless"* were reliable arms at moderate prices. They offered three grips, including a rounded one for the pocket, and barrel lengths from 2 to 6 inches. In spite of their small narrow sights, some pretty good shooting was done with these light guns. Solid frame I.J.s like the inexpensive old *Model 1900* didn't have the hammer-the-hammer safety block that prevented firing except when the trigger was deliberately pulled. It's well to carry such old guns with the hammer down on an empty cartridge, to reduce the risk of the cylinder turning in our pocket and bringing a live round under the hammer. Old *"Triple Action"* models that bring the hammer to a sort of half cock position as the trigger goes forward don't lock their cylinders against turning; and they need care in the carrying, as do other makes and models of the type. But then, all guns need care.

The modern *Iver Johnson Target Model 57* and *Cadet Model 55S* have 2½-inch barrels, weigh 27 and 24 ounces, respectively. Perhaps their greatest improvement is the flash-control cylinder. It's recessed up front to steer gases, grease, and possible lead shavings away from a bystander. Just now, the Cadet is about the least expensive .22 in this class, among the old-line makes.

We have few U.S.-made .22 automatics that are short and light enough for day-in-day-out pocket use, and some would say that we haven't any, or even that we don't need any, considering the smallbore's lack of power. The Colt Woodsman Match Target, Woodsman Sport Model and Huntsman come with 4½-inch barrels, like the recent Hi-Standard Supermatic, Olympic .22 short, the Field-King, and current Flite-King .22 short, Sport-King and Duramatic. There are also the 4¾-inch standard Ruger and 4½-inch J. C. Higgins Model 80. But at the moment only the *Whitney* is a special pocket job. Its sights are low and smooth, its grip is flat and certainly not over-sized, and though its 23-ounce weight and 9-inch overall may keep it out of the ideal pocket pistol class, it is balanced for such carrying. The long receiver encasing the 4⅝-inch barrel puts weight and bulk fairly well forward for easy riding. It's definitely designed as a combination plinking and pocket .22, and its grip slants back to make "natural" pointing a less difficult goal to reach.

But like the others so far considered, it's "only a .22." Fond though we are of those little guns, we willingly join the majority who prefer more dependable power in a pocket arm. Now we get into the centerfires, ranging from the little and often disregarded .32 S.&W. long or Colt New Police to the .45 Auto, and including also the tiny Colt .25.

COLT AGENT

Caliber: .38 Special. The usual .38 line, from the mild short and long Colt through the Special wadcutter target, the Special standard, and the high velocity.
Weight: 14½ ounces; ½ ounce less than the 2-inch Cobra .38.
Barrel: 2 inches.
Overall: 6¾ inches.
Sights: Fixed, non-adjustable, glare-proofed. Front sight is of ramp type, .10 inch wide. Square rear notch is .135 inch.
Stocks: Checked walnut, rounded butt.
Finish: Blue.

A six-shooter, like the other Colt revolvers made in modern times, the Agent is the smallest and lightest .38 Special of that make. Its grip is shortened for easier carrying; hence its lighter weight compared with the Cobra. Note that though the grip is rounded for the pocket, it's still square enough for a firm grip. It's true that these two, and the Detective Special and Police Positive Special, need adapters for comfort. With almost any .38 load the second finger usually takes a beating when these close-coupled guns are fired. The top front of the grip is just too close to the trigger guard, many of us find.

When the change from the small to the heavier frame Police Positive and Police Positive Special was made a generation ago, this matter got no attention. The Positive was made for the .32 Colt New Police, or the S.&W. long, and for .38 N. P., or the short .38 S.&W. The Colt bullets were flat, not round-nosed variants, usually a bit heavier, but interchangeable with those of S.&W., which came out earlier. Even heavy .32 handloads were pleasant to shoot, and so of course were the .22 short, long and long-rifle sizes, or the .22 Winchester Rim Fire, adapted to the old Police Positive Target, a 6-inch gun with adjustable sights. It came in .32 also, originally, it seems, for the short .32 S.&W., and for short and long .32 Colts. All this .32 ammo is still made, at this writing; but the Colt short and long are not interchangeable with the S.&W. short and long. Colt rounds can be dropped in, but their smaller-diameter cases don't always expand fast enough on being fired to keep gas from rushing back and perhaps slapping the shooter's hand.

The Agent is improved for strictly pocket use by the *Colt Hammer Shroud,* which can be installed on old or new guns drilled and tapped for its holding screws. A smooth-backed hammerless revolver results, and you still can thumb-cock the hammer for de-

Colt Agent.

liberate firing, an impossibility with the conventional hammerless, which fires double action only.

The other three current Colts in this class—Cobra, Detective Special, and Police Positive Special—also can take the shroud, and so can the discontinued Banker's Special and Police Positive. The moderns are small-framed, but derived from the second, heavier version of the Police Positive Special, which has a *longer* frame than that of the Banker's or Police Positive. The name "Special" referred to the .38 Special chambering of the long cylinder, and the .32-20 Winchester rifle cartridge was included in this model until World War II.

Old guns in good condition can be sensible secondhand buys. They are safe with modern factory ammunition, except the high-velocity 80-grain .32-20s and, probably, the speeded-up .38 Specials—just to be on the safe side and considerate of oldtimers never meant to take such pressures.

COLT COBRA

Caliber: .32 New Police, .38 New Police (on special order). .38 Special.
Weight: 15 ounces in 2-inch, 17 in 4-inch .38 caliber. The .32 is heavier; less steel is bored out of its barrel and cylinder.
Barrel: 2, 3, 4 and 5 inches.
Overall: 6¾ inches with 2-inch barrel.
Sights: Fixed, glare-proof, ramp-style front; square notch rear.
Stocks: Checked walnut, round butt.
Finish: Blue.

The use of light-alloy metal caused this now long-established gun to become a great pocket favorite. Barrel and cylinder are of steel, and like other modern Colt .38 Specials it is listed as satisfactory for the heavy high-velocity factory loads. As I see it, they are for service use. For all ordinary shooting, I prefer the mid-range wadcutters, factory loaded, or handloaded to similar power. And unless you need a lot of penetration this charge is really effective. The flat-nosed bullet packs a wallop even though it's lighter and slower than the standard-velocity round-nosed bullet. You still know you're shooting something respectable,

Colt Cobra with 2-inch barrel.

and those big, clean-punched holes, even in target paper, are pretty impressive. One objection to the wadcutter shape is that it does lead some guns at the breech or leade of the barrel. With modern non-corrosive ammunition we don't have to worry about destructive primer fouling hiding under the lead smears and making trouble. And slight leading at the breech of a sixgun doesn't seem to interfere with the sort of accuracy most of us can work up with a pocket arm as short and light as this one. If you ask around, you'll probably find that a good many sharp pistolmen take this fouling in their stride. Occasionally they clean it out, but a *little* of it doesn't seem harmful. A lot of us older shooters have noticed that we get more of this leading than we used to. Some have thought that modern lead-alloys are responsible, not possibly better workmanship on guns made long ago. They sometimes have this trouble, too, with modern bullets. All this is pretty much speculation.

My Cobra, a 2-inch .38 Special, gets a lot of travel, and a fair amount of firing, too. It's so short, light and handy that it goes along when even a 4-incher would be left behind. It is one gun that fits in an unconventional and, you might say, unexpected pocket—right *side,* not hip, of the trousers. The grip is long enough for a quick reach, and rounded enough to minimize the bulge.

As for caliber, it's obliging, too, for it takes the short and long Colt and all the Special .38s. Yes, light bullets like the short do print a little lower on target than the heavier stuff the gun's sighted for. A good gunsmith can ream out .38 Special chambers just far enough to take the fatter-bodied, short .38 S.&W. and Colt New Police cartridges. This results in rather odd-looking, slightly bottle-necked empties when you fire the longer rounds, and some reloading dies would need the reaming, too. But if you travel to odd places this chambering might be worth a lot. The old, short .380 British cartridge with outside lubricated bullet is much like our .38 short Colt and would fit in unaltered Special chambers.

COLT DETECTIVE SPECIAL

Caliber: Same as for Cobra, preceding.
Weight: 21 ounces.
Barrel: 2 inches.
Overall: 6¾ inches.
Sights: Same as for Cobra.
Stocks: Same as for Cobra.
Finish: Blue or nickel.

The chief difference between this gun and the 2-inch Cobra is its all-steel frame. The extra weight makes holding steadier and reduces the upchuck of recoil. The absence of aluminum-alloy parts pleases some people—not all of them oldtimers, either—who want no such material in a gun, regardless of proved durability.

The Detective has been on the market for well over twenty years in .38 Special caliber, and the chief differences between present and first models are the shape of the front sight and the fact that the trigger is now grooved instead of checkered. A grooved or otherwise roughened trigger is standard on most American handguns of today, and it does feel good. If you are one of those who always squeeze with the tip of the forefinger, not with the first joint or still farther back, a smooth, slick trigger surface is plenty annoying on a gun that's so small-framed that you must put a bend in your trigger finger to get that front pad into position. Or so lots of us think.

The old front sight was rounded, almost a true semi-circle; and the modern one is in the so-called "ramp style," a shade longer but still a short, compact sight. Riflemen used to a 2½- or maybe 3-inch front sight base on their pet high-powers might wonder if this Colt job is a ramp at all. The alleged purpose of a rifle-sight ramp, with its long, inclined rear surface, is to guide the eye in quick aiming. It also makes a rifle a hair steadier in holding, and it's so much the correct and accepted thing that most sporting rifles except some low- and medium-priced .22 rimfires have one. Now handguns are getting the treatment, too. That rearward slant can help in quick handgun alignment, and the clean-cut top edge of this Colt sight

Colt Detective Special.

shows up a little more sharply in aiming than the old half-moon front does. After the finish is worn off, either type needs to be blackened for target. Weight makes the Detective less punishing to fire through a number of ten-shot strings than is the Cobra, although the small space for the second finger still calls for an adapter's fill-in, or for a low grip on the gun—which some shooters do use successfully. Obviously, fast follow-up shots can come more readily from a 21-ounce gun than from a 15-ouncer, other things being as equal as they are in these two Colts.

It's plain, too, that these 2-inch sixguns are made as much for quick, second-nature pointing and firing as for any sort of aimed fire. Weight matters here, too, simply because it affects balance and feel. But you choose the weight you prefer, and stick to that gun. It takes hours of conscientious steady practice both in dry-firing with an empty gun and with live ammunition—and if you count them you'd best keep it secret if you value such reputation for sanity as you have. Like the old Westerners with their medium- or long-barreled .45s and .44-40s, you still "throw" the gun into alignment, whether or not you raise it high enough to see the sights.

COLT POLICE POSITIVE SPECIAL

Caliber: Same as for Cobra and Detective Special, preceding.
Weight: 23 ounces in 4-inch .38.
Barrel: 4 or 5 inches.
Overall: 8¾ inches with 4-inch barrel.
Sights: Same as for Cobra and Detective Special.
Stocks: Checked walnut. Both round and square butts have been listed.
Finish: Blue or nickel.

About a half-century of good service stands behind this pocket gun, which used to come, in both the original and the later heavier-frame models, in .32-20 as well as .38 Special. Today it fills the place of the discontinued Police Positive, .32 and .38 New Police calibers. For these rounds the cylinder is too long, calling for a longer than normal bullet jump from the cartridge case into the chamber. Still, practically every fine .22 target revolver has a too-long cylinder. It looks as though they all had dreams of being fur-

Colt Police Positive Special with 4-inch barrel.

Colt Trooper.

nished, some day, in .32 S.&W. long or New Police, if not .38 Special. This is just one of the odd facts in production that we have to humor, or forget.

Long ago, this model was about the least expensive .32-20 or .38 Special revolver you could buy, and still have a good make. Sure, it was light for those loads, and it kicked, especially with black powder Specials. But this ammo cost considerably less than the smokeless, and in most revolver sizes it was more powerful, too, with perfectly safe pressures. Six-inch barrels were available then, even on the little round-butt .32 Pocket Positive, a small-frame, round-butt sixshooter weighing about a pound.

COLT TROOPER

Caliber: .38 Special and .22 long-rifle.
Weight: 34 ounces in .38, 37 in .22.
Barrel: 4 inches.
Overall: 9¼ inches.
Sights: Quick-draw ramp-type front ⅛ inch wide; adjustable rear.
Stocks: Checked walnut, square butt.
Finish: Blue.
Wide hammer spur for quick cocking and large target style stocks affording a rest for the second finger are available.

This is a fairly heavy gun, but others of about its weight have seen pocket use by those who like steadiness and recoil-absorption as in a .38 Special, and willingly put up with the drag in carrying one. Popular examples are the 4-inch Colt Official Police and the 2- or 4-inch Smith & Wesson Military & Police, all with choice of round or square butts.

The Trooper, as its name suggests, probably is intended more as a law officer's holster gun than as a pocket arm. Then there's the .22 Trooper for plenty of economical target training. The weight and the upstanding rear sight would disqualify the Trooper in the minds of some pocket gun users, but others would value these features as an assistance in accurate shooting. For that matter, the 41-ounce, 3½-inch barreled S.&W. .357 Magnum has traveled many miles in well-stitched pockets, though doubtless many more ride in shoulder or belt holsters.

A recently discontinued Colt .38 Special, the *Marshal,* was meant especially for the pocket. Weights were 29 and 31 ounces with 2- and 4-inch barrels. The sights were solid, non-adjustable, the front smoothly ramped for good definition combined with easy draw, and the checked walnut stocks were rounded at the bottom to minimize the bulge in a pocket.

Both Trooper and Marshal are easy to cock, thanks to the new-type Colt mainspring. They aren't short-action guns with short hammer fall, like the S.&W. Military & Police types, the K target guns, and the 4-inch Combat Masterpiece. They give a full hammer blow (not that the Smiths aren't adequate), and some of us find them softer in thumb-cocking than the short actions.

But this is only one detail among many. The feel of the particular make and model in your hand is at least equally important. It certainly means enough to make the brand name a trivial thing.

The Junior Colt

Caliber: .25 Colt Automatic.
Weight: 12 ounces; a bit heavier in .22 Short conversion.
Barrel: 2¼ inches.
Overall: 4⅜ inches.
Sights: Fixed, low-lying, typical .25 auto-pistol type.
Stocks: Checked composition.
Finish: Blue.
Magazine capacity: 6. An extra can be preloaded into the chamber.

Unlike most of the other handguns described in this chapter, this is not an American-made arm. It is made in Spain for the Colt Patent Fire Arms Manufacturing Company, to that firm's standards. There's nothing unusual about this. Most of the barrels for the fine old American double shotguns were made abroad, though at least one company had the tubes made here, by an outfit that few of us ever heard of. It was common, too, for complete shotguns made abroad to be sold under American brand names. Until recently, most British high-power bolt rifle actions were of German Mauser make, and who thought any-

Junior Colt .25 Autoloading Pistol.

thing of it? Some of our American guns, made here, are sold under names other than those of the firms who built them.

The Junior takes the place of the American-made Colt .25 hammerless auto that was discontinued some fifteen or more years ago. It has hardly any resemblance to the old gun, though it is of general Browning design. As .25 autos go, it is of better-than-medium grade, though at present it retails for less than half the price of the Colt .45, Super-.38, or light-weight Commander. About the same ratio held for the pre-war .25 and .45-.38 guns—the Commander wasn't around then.

This new .25 has a barrel a quarter-inch longer than the old one, and overall is one-eighth inch greater, weight an ounce less, differences that mean one-sixteenth spoonful in practical ways. The big differences are in the exposed hammer and the slightly more seeable sights. Any of us would welcome the higher sights, but the presence of the exposed hammer is of debatable value. It's in style, however, on small automatics.

Most of us who used the old .25 Colt found no fault with its hammerless design. All the slip side safeties I've seen on these guns, my own and others I have examined, were pretty secure, not liable to scuff off to "Fire" position in pocket carry. If they did, there were still that heavy trigger pull and the grip safety that really had to be gripped before the gun could fire. Yet a person learned to slide the safety off pretty fast. If the safe could be put on, the hammer—or striker, really, as there was no swinging hammer inside the gun—was cocked. Hammerless design and a less sharp protrusion of the frame just above the grip made the old gat a bit smoother to draw than many designs. Old Browning .25s were similar to the hammerless Colt, which of course was made on Browning patents. Some of us, I for one, thought they were made even better, though they never were well-known in this country. If you want a hammerless Colt .25, there are a good many in used or sometimes practically new condition to be had. As far as I know, they are not priced as collectors' items, though that could happen to them. We need not worry about their strength, for the .25 Auto cartridge still has close to original ballistics.

That means it's a peewee, as most shooters well know. However, the vest-pocket guns that shoot it have, time and again, saved the day for those who carried them. A .25 isn't much, but it has the penetration to cause deadly wounds. Only with a brain shot, I suppose, could it be expected to act as an instant stopper. But you could wisely be armed with a .25 on occasions when heavier hardware would be out of the question.

Colt Derringer No. 4

Late in 1959 Colt announced the No. 4 Derringer .22 short single-shot pistol. It is intended for the collectors' market, as it is a close copy of the 1872 No. 3 Colt, which fired the .41 short rimfire cartridge, and presumably the long, too, with its own blunt-nosed, man-stopper style of bullet and a heavier black powder charge to drive it. The name of Henry Deringer, who was famous for his short, muzzle-loading pocket pistols of large caliber, came to apply to the whole type and was usually spelled "Derringer," with or without the capital letter, in such general references.

No. 3 Colt Derringers (the double *r* was used in the old catalogues) are so scarce and expensive that few collectors own one, even though they were made pretty well into the twentieth century and were popular as single guns or as pairs for right and left pockets. Many were cased, neatly, as these new guns are.

The modern Colt Derringer is "in colors," like some snub-nosed revolvers, some shotguns and .22 revolvers, and who knows how many more to come? But these Colt colors are meant to duplicate those of the No. 3. The barrel is blued, the hammer and the sheathed or encased trigger are also darkish, in "Dulite" finish. The frame is gold-colored, and the stocks walnut-toned.

Perhaps the wide popularity of .22 single-action revolvers, and of double-actions also made to resemble the Colt Single Action Army, sparked this Derringer development. The .22 sixguns are useful as shooting-irons, and they satisfy the urge to own something like the Peacemaker, which old or new sells at high prices. The serviceable old sixgun of the wild places has become a collectors' item, at least when it has or seems to have a bit of history behind it. (It's still all gun, of course.)

Much the same thing happened to the Remington double "Derringer" .41 rimfire (with one barrel above the other), called the Model 95 and made from 1888 to 1935. Its scarcity and cost (even in battered, unserviceable old specimens) have been offset by more or less close new copies in other makes, in calibers .22 rimfire, .38 S.&W., and .38 Special. Mechanically, the Great Western in the .38 calibers is an improvement on the original. It's stronger, and needs to be for such ammunition. The .41 rimfire bullets weighed only 130 grains, and the black powder charges 10 and 13, or 16 in .41 long. These bullets do make big holes, but they're weak in penetration.

The new Colt is tiny, as Derringers are. Weight is only 7¾ ounces, and overall length 4 15/16 inches. Since it's so short, we must use great care in handling it, seeing that its muzzle points in a safe direction and cautiously lowering its well-spurred hammer from full to half cock over a loaded round in the barrel. The .22 short cartridge is no toy.

So the gun does have some defense value even though it's a single-shot, and so small that to some people it might look harmless. Almost proverbially, Derringers are hard to shoot at arm's length with any sort of accuracy. They aren't meant for it. Their expected effective range is a few yards, a few feet, or

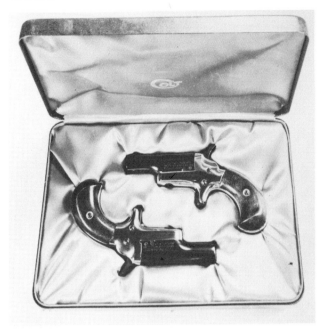

Cased set of .22 short caliber 1959 model Colt No. 4 Derringers.

even a few inches. One could be shucked out of the coat-sleeve, for example, and fired from under a card table. It isn't so much the recoil that makes them tough shooting—the .22 Colt has little recoil, though .41s buck a bit—but the tiny grip. This is typically curved, as on familiar Colts and Remingtons, and could hardly be of poorer shape for shooting. It does make for easy packing in pocket, muff, handbag or what you will. I'm afraid the little heater would drop out of a waist-band! But there have been even worse grips, such as that on the No. 1 National "Derringer." On this one, the sheathed trigger came as low as the bottom of the stock.

Colt Commander

Caliber: 9 mm. Luger, .38 and .45 Colt Automatic.
Weight: 26½ ounces.
Barrel: 4¼ inches.
Overall: 8 inches.
Sights: Fixed, ramp-style glare-proofed front; square notch rear sight movable for lateral correction.
Stocks: Checked Coltwood.
Finish: Blue.
Magazine capacity: 9 in 9 mm. and .38, 7 in .45. An extra can be preloaded into the chamber.

Pausing only long enough to give a respectful preliminary salute to a pocket gun made in a caliber as potent as the rimless .45 Colt Auto, let's digress for a brief sum-up of autoloaders as pocket guns. It is rather wonderful to have a smallish .45 that's both shootable and reasonably convenient for shoving into a pocket, to be toted for miles on end. Except for special customized revolvers, amputated in barrel length and butt-trimmed to suit the individual, we had hardly anything like it in the past. There were stubby little foreign guns like the .44 and .45 Webleys,

Colt Commander .45.

but those "bulldogs" weren't really powerful. The .44 B.D. took 15 grains of black powder and 168 of lead, the .44 Webley 18 and 200, and the .45 Webley 20 and 230—old Winchester loadings. Our American Harrington & Richardson did put out a bulldog for the two .44 rounds, and there were other American makes. These dogs were light, all right, and bitchy to shoot with any sort of accuracy. (No end of fun, however, with that bark and that belch of smoke.) Comparison of the Webley .45 cartridge with the .45 auto is painful to that once popular British load. The bullets are of equal weight, and the Web has the advantage of plain soft lead composition, a deadly bullet substance for a handgun. But the velocity was as low as a snake's shiny bottom, though it did give penetration enough for most emergencies—a standing man, unlike most four-footed animals, has all his vital spots exposed when he faces you. Still, eight faster, much more easily aimed rounds, with unquestioned power at almost any possible pistol range, add up to a secure feeling.

In the .22 rimfire auto-pistol line we have, perhaps, only the Whitney of U. S. make that could qualify as a pocket gun for those who are content with this small caliber. Most of the others are butt-heavy and muzzle-light; they don't ride well in a shallow hip or side pocket. They do get around as pocket guns because they're so dog-goned attractive and nicely balanced for quick-pointing, practically instinctive aiming.

By the end of World War II our little centerfire pocket automatics were out of production. Although it was felt that they were too small to be effective, they still are in fair demand as used guns, especially by those who are familiar with them. *Colt* guns of this type were hammerless Browning designs, the .25 weighing but 13 ounces and handicapped by almost invisible sights, hard trigger pull, and about a one-finger grip. But it got around, and the 23- to 24-ounce .32 and .380 model, 3¾-inch barrel against 2 of the .25, actually was a rather popular woods

and plains gun. You could shoot it pretty well, and like nearly all other automatics except the Luger, it was flat and compact compared to revolvers of similar calibers. The small *Harrington & Richardson* .25 is almost forgotten, a collector's find.

Remington Model 51 hammerless .32 and .380 autos are a bit rare, and usually prized. Grips were so cleverly designed that they seemed to feel right in almost any hand, and the low but clear, square Patridge type sights were fine for the pocket. (The type is named for its designer, a famous match competitor of the past. The square front sight fits into the notch of the square-cut rear sight, leaving a little light showing on each side, and the line-up of the flat-topped front and rear sights on the same horizontal level is an easy job for normal eyes.) The Remington was a compact performer in the pocket gun class, 3¼-inch barrel and 21-ounce weight. It was not a straight blowback semi-automatic; it had an ingenious locked-breech mechanism. Did a slew of anti-pistol laws account for its brief period of manufacture, 1918-1927?

Savages were locked-breech, too. The breech-block (or slide) was held in place by the torque of the bullet as it worked against the rifling lands in the barrel. This is really a considerable effort, especially with jacketed bullets, and it uses a fair amount of the energy developed by the powder gases. Savage models differed mostly in fullness and rear-slope of grip and in shape of hammer spur, though a few were hammerless. None of their hammers were as easy to cock, by any means, as that of a handy revolver, but the thumb safety was positive. It locked the hammer (really the cocking lever of the long firing pin or striker), not just the trigger or sear. Except for the confoundedly heavy trigger pull so common on this make, the Savage was easy to shoot with pocket-gun accuracy, and easy to point-shoot in the dark, a generously and justly advertised feature. The grip of the later models was fuller at the bottom, giving a slant much like that of the Colt 1911-type autos, including the *Commander,* and this may have improved the pointing still more. Some of us with small hands found the straighter-gripped early Savage just as good—and that was really good. Savage .32 and .380 magazines were hearty feeders—ten and nine rounds, respectively. The small but ungainly Savage is rare indeed among .25 caliber autos.

None of these small centerfire autoloaders were as reliable as the big .38 and .45 Colts have been in just about all models and individual specimens. I don't mean that they were chronic jammers, except for the rare lemons that turn up, but they did require care and good ammunition. And magazine springs of any type can weaken after being fully-loaded for months without reprieve. This goes for main-springs on hammerless types that always are kept cocked and ready. Savage and Remington both made experimental .45s—collectors' gold today, not war veterans.

Special Commander Advantages

Returning to the current Colt Commander, we find that it has every right to be considered carefully as a pocket gun. Its calibers are formidable. Even the .38s—to call the 9 mm. Luger or Parabellum such, as we can with reason—are long in penetration compared to most other handgun loads, including the .45s. It's reasonable to suppose that they have more shocking power than the .380 Automatic with its much lighter and slower bullet, even though that stubby slug formerly did have a bluffly rounded point. All these auto bullets, except for the imported Norma 9 mm. (and the 93-grain .30 Luger of that make) and a few special custom jobs, are generally unavailable now in expanding types. Soft points can mushroom to some extent at Luger, Mauser, or .38 Auto Colt velocities, but hollow points rarely, if ever, split their jackets and open on impact. A handloader could use the Norma 9 mm. soft point in a .38 Auto, .38 Special or .357 Magnum. The common full-jacketed or hard-point slides through flesh with less destruction than blunt- or flat-nosed lead bullets of similar caliber and weight ordinarily give.

But the flat, compact Commander is easily carried, holds a lot of cartridges compared to bigbore revolvers, and is quickly reloaded with extra magazines, if need ever arises—as it has, of course. Considering the gun's overall length, the intersight distance is greater than those of most pocket revolvers, and this helps in accurate aiming. Except for a small hand, the gun is easy and natural to grasp.

Even though the hammer spur is of the old Mauser 7.63 mm. military type—a bit like those of early Colt autos, too, rounded and rather small—it is grooved on top for the thumb. The thumb safety that locks the firing action when the hammer is cocked is nice for a right-hander. For a southpaw it's horrible, but aren't they all? The safety is positive, though pocket carry can scuff it into the "off" or firing position—or it just could. However, the trigger pull is heavy; a mere touch certainly won't fire the gun! As with all current Colts except the Single Action Army, the trigger is roughened for better control. The gun is easy enough to handle under the recoil of the smaller calibers, and a man or woman used to the standard Army .45 auto ought to master this light-weight .45 in a short time. Naturally it would hardly go along for a day of match competition. It wouldn't take a skilled handloader long to find the softest recoiling charge that would function his own particular Commander reliably, and he'd still have the advantage of a fast-firing pocket gun that heaves out .45 caliber bullets.

For compactness the Smith & Wesson 9 mm. automatic is superior, with its shorter grip. Because of this, it holds one round less than the Commander in that bore. This might or might not be one of the decisive factors he'd mull over in making up his mind

Great Western double derringer for the .38 S.&W. cartridge.

on the choice between the two weapons. There are so many other details to ponder and compare that I'm thankful to own what I own, and be satisfied with it. This doesn't mean that I haven't the greatest respect for the two guns just mentioned. I have.

Great Western Derringer

A double-barrel, 13-ounce over-and-under pocket gun of reasonable power has obvious protective value. This Great Western .38 qualifies. It's a close external copy of the Model 95 Remington .41, 1888-1935, but it's chambered for the short .38 S.&W. or for the .38 Special. Coil-spring action eases hammer cocking, and chrome molybdenum steel parts give strength.

The barrels are 3 inches long, like those of the old 11-ounce, 4⅞-inch overall Rem. The new derringer is still easy to pack and simple to operate: the breech opening and closing, the loading and extraction, and the firing, too, for the single hammer touches off the barrels alternately as you cock and then release it. The non-guarded "sheath-type" trigger has a pull heavy enough for safety. A derringer isn't for precision shooting, and it must be extra safe to handle, as these two doubles are. You buy a Remington where you can find one to suit you; the G. W. is distributed by Stoeger Arms Corporation, 45-18 Court Square, Long Island City 1, N. Y. That firm is at least nationally known.

The small, one-and-a-half-finger grip and the sketchy sights really are good enough for the purpose. At close quarters these guns can do the work without any particular skill behind them. They are likely to be on hand when wanted because they're so small, short, light and well-rounded.

The derringer family is an old one—named from Henry Deringer, and note the difference in spellings—

and the Remington was a comparatively late member. The early Colt, National and others had served well as single-shots, commonly for the same .41 rimfire round, though derringers went back to muzzle-loading times. Besides the Great Western there is another on the market, in .22 caliber. It too could figure as a "conversation piece" for collectors of the new and odd. But since derringers give us few thrills of marksmanship, we do rather insist on the delights of respectable blast and hearty muzzle-lift in recoil! Anyone who depends on .22 rimfire power for self-defense had best get himself a gun he can shoot about as straight as he can look. Instantly vital targets on man or beast become small as bullet smack shrinks. Certainly, a .22 derringer would be fun to play with, and far better than no gat at all in a rough situation.

There's no doubt about the derringer's eclipse having been caused by the pocket automatics, which had by comparison not much more in their favor than a grist of cartridges housed in the magazine. The .41 rimfire load was less reliable than the Remington double itself, misfires having been common in the old days. This was probably a good reason why these guns—and the singles, too—were often carried in pairs. At least one of the four Remington barrels would surely fire! Good, fresh .41 ammo has been handled for quite a long time by Male-Town, Inc., 317 Central Ave., White Plains, N. Y.

The .41 rimfire has a longtime reputation for close-range power, and surely the sight of such a big black muzzle (or .38 muzzles) would terrify a not-too-desperate attacker. But it isn't a husky caliber. Before the smokeless, non-corrosive ammo came in, the .41 short packed from 10 to 13 grains of black powder behind a rather pointed 130 grain bullet, hardly a fast load. The .41 long, a collector's piece for lo! these many years, was more respectable. It cost more, kicked harder, and wasn't as popular. Sixteen grains of black powder boosted the same 130 grain bullet weight, but the slug was decidedly blunt up front, a true "man-stopper," at least in shape. These bullets, and the heavier .41 short Colt *centerfire,* all of them outside-lubricated, measure about a .402 inch diameter, some .045 larger than most .38 S.&W.s and .38 Specials.

But the .38s carry more stuff: the old dose for the short S.&W. was 14 or 15 grains of black powder and 145 or 146 of lead, and the Special's ration was 21 or 21½ and 158. The flat-pointed Colt New Police, interchangeable with the much better known short .38 S.&W., is still available, and there's a raft of .38 Specials. The most reasonable and most effective defense load for the Great Western in .38 Special would be the 148 grain wadcutter target round. Its "point" is as flat as a barrel-head, and the reduced powder and lead weights make easier shooting than full-charge Specials. The G. W. would take the heavier loads, but the old flat-nosed Colt Special is gone from the stores, and round-points aren't the choice for defense purposes—against human enemies, at least.

Harrington & Richardson Model 632 Guardsman

Caliber: .32 S.&W., S.&W. long, or Colt New Police.
Weight: 19 and 24 ounces.
Barrel: 2½ and 4 inches.
Overall: 6⅞ inches in 2½-inch barrel.
Sights: Fixed ramp front; square notch rear.
Stocks: Tenite "Cling-Fast," round butt on 2½-inch, square on 4-inch.
Finish: Blue. Model 633 2½-inch is chromed, at extra cost.

As the name indicates, this is a six-shot .32. In grip styles and frame it is similar to the 922s, nine-shot .22 calibers. These are solid frame guns, no swing-out or tip-up cylinders, but you simply pull out the cylinder pin, remove the cylinder, and eject all the empties with one push of the pin. Naturally, reloading is slower than with swing-outs or tip-ups, but thorough cleaning is a little easier.

This sixshooter is definitely the choice, just now, for the buyer who wants a moderate-priced, new, not second-hand revolver for the .32 cartridges—which have much more practical value for defense purposes than the rimfire .22s and still are comfortable to shoot. Whether other .32s in the price class will come out soon is a question; the caliber has gone through its second or third wave of great popularity and is taking it easy now.

The short, rounded grip of the 2½-inch gun is cramped, much less roomy than even that of the little old .32 Colt Pocket Positive, which was ⅜ inch shorter overall in the same barrel length, and 3 ounces lighter. This small 632 is for the pocket or cash-register drawer or tackle box stowage as thug insurance, and little else. Those who want to do good shooting with the fine .32 long cartridge would choose the 4-inch model in place of it.

And it is a fine cartridge, though not highly popular now, even though the S.&W. K target gun is made for it still. Smith & Wesson used to call it "the sweetest shooting revolver cartridge ever made," and a lot of us said, "That's right!" Actually, this claim was staked out when primers were corrosive. Then it was almost impossible to keep a .22 rimfire from rusting when you fired smokeless rounds in it. The black powder cartridges, or those loaded with semismokeless— King's, Du Pont's Lesmok, or Western's Nublend— were no problem in any caliber, but they smoked up indoor galleries. To build such a choking fog was a poor way to become the club's most beloved member! However, you could use smokeless in any of the .32 to .45 calibers, or in the vest pocket Colt and Browning .25s for that matter, and clean your gun carefully, with 100% happy results. So the .32 became the smallest practical gallery size, and in centerfire classifications it holds a following because of its mild report and recoil, although the great majority in the later years have used .38 and .44 centerfires. Their wider bullets could nip a 10-ring when a .32 might rate only a 9 when let loose with an equal degree of marksmanship. The 632 doesn't pretend to be a target revolver, but in the longer style it can turn in satisfying shooting. If some of that pleasure comes simply from using a bigger bore than .22, and a bullet well over twice as heavy, what of it? The enjoyment is real.

The 632 descends from a long line of inexpensive .32s—pocket guns mostly, though many of them could be had with 6 inch barrels, and some with oversize, square-butt stocks. They came in solid frame and in the handier, more costly tip-up designs. The light-frame guns took five short .32 S.&W. cartridges, the heavies, six of the longs. Sights were fixed, non-adjustable, and front blades were about 1/50 inch thick, early fadeouts in failing light.

Yet a lot of us enjoyed them. Black powder rounds cost much less than the smokeless—or "nitro," as some oldtimers called them—and they gave a fine flash and bang. The .32 long almost paralleled the later .38 Special in powder-and-lead ratios and wasn't overloaded for smack. You could fire quite a few of them before your barrel choked up with black mud and sent your bullets out cartwheeling. These revolvers were worth taking care of, and when they were well kept they shot pretty well. They were common in H.&R. and Iver Johnson makes, the most enduring of the type and class. In six-shot .32 Long tip-up, with big grips, they went to about 22 ounces, a bit more in the hammerless variety, which with its long heavy pull, was certainly not for target-punching. But a 3¼-inch .32 Long hammerless sixshooter, smooth to draw, had its uses. In five-shot .38 S.&W., an ounce lighter in this barrel length, it was still more practical. It would be, even yet.

Harrington & Richardson 732

In general appearance this 1958 model is like the H.&R. 632 just described. The important difference is its swing-out cylinder that makes ejection of empties and reloading so much easier and faster than with the solid-frame 632. In spite of its name, *Seven Thirty-Two*, it holds six .32 S.&W. Longs. Initially it costs the same as the new .22 caliber 929, a nine-shot gun, from which it is patterned. It comes at present only in 2½- and 4-inch barrel lengths, not in 6, and is intended more for protection than for field use. Its heavy, flatsided barrel raises 4-inch gun weight to a comfortable 26 ounces.

But since the rear sight can be driven from side to side to adjust the shooting fairly closely to a person's individual hold and manner of aiming (we don't all *see* sights alike), it could give pretty warm satisfaction outdoors. For those who want to try this interesting old caliber, it's an inexpensive little gun. With flat-nosed bullets like those in factory-loaded .32 Colt New Police rounds, interchangeable with .32 S.&W. Long, it is deadlier than a .22 rimfire pistol in spite of lower velocities. Home-cast wadcutter or semi-wadcutter bullets are still better. The front sight is ramped and fixed, solid, but with most of us, elevation is less a problem than windage adjustments.

Harrington & Richardson 732 Guardsman, which succeeded the 632 solid frame .32.

The snub-nosed 2½-inch gun can be had in chrome finish at a slight extra cost. It is known as Model 733, and for carrying in a possibly sweat-soaked pocket or for use in drippy climates, it's to be preferred. You can aim better with a blued-finish pistol, but not so many of us have the skill that lets us do good shooting with a snub-nose.

If this model could be and were produced in five-shot .38 S.&W. caliber, it would be a decidedly better protection weapon. I remember some lonely but still pleasant nights in the woods with only a .32 long Smith or Colt as guard-dog. At least I felt much better than I should have with a .22. The only times I felt insecure were when I camped within spitting distance of a road sometimes traveled. It was the human animals I wondered about; the other kinds were old friends.

Smith & Wesson Centennial

Caliber: .38 Special, 5-shot cylinder. Short and long Colt cartridges fit, but the factory doesn't recommend this gun, or any of its .38 Specials lighter than the .357 Combat Magnum and the heavier .38-.44s and .357s, for high velocity .38 Specials.
Weight: 19 ounces; 13 ounces in Airweight.
Barrel: 2 inches.
Overall: 6½ inches.
Sights: Fixed, non-adjustable; 1/10-inch wide, serrated ramp front, flat-topped; square notch rear.
Stocks: Smooth, uncheckered walnut, Magna type, wide at top for comfort in shooting.
Finish: Blue or nickel.

By the end of World War II, the *"squeeze-handle Smith" or "lemon squeezer" hammerless* was gone. It came in various models and in calibers .32 and .38 S.&W. Like the Centennial, these guns were of true hammerless type, couldn't be cocked by hand, and the trigger pull was purposely made long and hard. The plate at the rear or backstrap of the grip had to be squeezed in, by an adult's natural hold, before the trigger could begin its rearward travel. Even on the tiny .32 the distance from this backstrap plate to trigger was so great that very small children could hardly fire the gun. The Centennial has this feature,

Smith & Wesson hammerless Centennial is probably the smoothest drawing pocket revolver to be had. It comes in .38 Special caliber.

Old S.&W. New Departure Safety Hammerless for the short .38 S.&W. cartridge. A much smaller model took the short .32 S.&W. round. The oldtimer is not quite as smooth as the Centennial because the checkered barrel latch at the breech (for opening) protrudes slightly. The Centennial, having solid frame with swing-out cylinder, opens with pressure on the thumb latch at the left side of the frame. However, the oldtimer needs no apologies. Both models hold five cartridges.

which in effect adds to overall length; so the Bodyguard S.&W., lacking it, is ⅛ inch shorter.

The .38 S.&W. cartridge still is considered good for defense—many call it the minimum—but the short .32 never rated high as a man-stopper. The .38 squeeze-handle maintained production longer. Yet the short .32s had admirers, for they weighed only about 14 ounces, holding just five rounds. A good friend of mine, a police chief, carries a 2-inch barrelled Iver Johnson hammerless .32, much like the Smith in design but with no squeezer safety, and so far he's felt well-armed. Ability to place a bullet where it's needed usually means more than caliber alone.

The I. J. "Safety" gun, by the way, had an exposed hammer, easy to cock for deliberate firing. The name came from its hammer block, a steel bar that made discharge impossible from a blow on the lowered hammer—unless the trigger was held back, and who'd do that? Colt and Smith hammer guns

have similar devices, except for a few made long ago. If the hammer slips from your thumb when cocking, it doesn't fire the gun.

S.&W. hammerless revolvers feature a sort of "pause" in the trigger pull. You can feel it, just before the trigger has gone back far enough to trip the concealed hammer. Then the gun could be fired much like a very-heavy-triggered, hammer-cocked revolver. This took practice, and plenty of it, but at last you'd learn to disregard the buildup of tension and be able to pop some fairly difficult targets.

Unlike the old hammerless S.&W.s—and the 1888 New Departure really was good—the Centennial is a solid frame gun, not a tip-up barrel-breech type but with swing-out cylinder. This strong frame is naturally longer for the .38 Special cartridge. Heavy-caliber tip-ups never have been popular in this country, as they have in England, except for still-cherished oldtimers like the S.&W. .44 Russian and .44 American.

The Centennial kicks, even the all-steel model; and the Airweight more seriously, with that light-alloy frame. So the new-style cylinder latch is welcome on it and on the other .38 Special Smiths of this class—Bodyguard and Chief's Special—and on the longer-framed Military & Police Airweight. The latch is flat and grooved, not hollowed and checkered, more comfortable to those who rest their right thumb on it when they fire. Many of us do that, with both Colt and S.&W. double-action, solid-frame guns, or with *the 1909-1920 .38 S.&W. Perfected,* a fine old arm that had a double cylinder lock, the thumb-latch and the lift-up extension of the top rib, too, like the one on most modern Harrington & Richardson or Iver Johnson tip-ups. The hollowed latch has had to go, handy though it was for a quick thumb-thrust in opening the gun, and the new flat latch is on the later .22, .32 and short .38 S.&W. Smiths, from the soft-shooting .22-.32 target arm to the bucking little Terrier .38.

Smith & Wesson Bodyguard

Caliber: .38 Special, same as the Centennial, preceding.
Weight: 14½ ounces; 20½ in all-steel model, which came later.
Barrel: 2 inches.
Overall: 6⅜ inches.
Sights: Same as on Centennial.
Stocks: Checked walnut, Magna style.
Finish: Blue or nickel.

The grip looks small for a .38 Special gun, but it's actually similar to that on the Centennial except that there's no squeezer safety. This is really a hammer gun. The high housing of that hammer helps to account for the appearance of too small a grip. In usual S.&W. fashion, there's plenty of grip room for the second finger; it isn't cramped against the trigger guard.

The hammer spur shows at the top of the housing, and you can cock the bodyguard with your thumb, though hardly fast enough for rapid-fire target competition! For a deliberate shot it's fine. You can draw the gun smoothly from your pocket, as you'd slide out a true hammerless.

To some of us the bodyguard may look odd, but for its purposes it's efficient. The high housing is an answer to Colt's hammer shroud, which converts light-framed hammer guns into the semihammerless pocket-type. On the Colt the housing is detachable, and a little less hump-backed, but some would say that the Smith is the choice because the housing is part of the gun and not an afterthought. You don't need logic in some arguments, or even in liking some particular gun, and for that reason doing better with it.

Smith & Wesson Chief's Special

Caliber: .38 Special, same as Bodyguard and Centennial, and like them, a five-shot revolver.
Weight: 2-inch barrel, round butt, 19 ounces. 12½ in similar Airweight.
Barrel: 2 and 3 inches. For many of us the latter makes a good medium choice.
Overall: 6½ inches with 2-inch barrel and round butt stocks.
Sights: Same design as on Centennial and Bodyguard.
Stocks: Checked walnut, Magna, round or square butt-type.
Finish: Blue or nickel.

It resembles the .38 Regulation Police five-shot gun except for the longer frame and cylinder for the .38 Special cartridge. For extreme lightness the Airweight is the S.&W. to choose. It weighs less than the Colt Agent and Cobra of 14½ and 15 ounces, which hold six rounds, but pay for that firepower with more cylinder bulge. Whether or not the extra weights are worth carrying is for the individual to decide. Much more important is the fit of the gun in his hand. Which make will he shoot better?

Don't overlook the .38 Special wadcutter target load, factory or home-brewed, in choosing defense ammunition. Classed as "mid-range," it is less powerful and milder in recoil than standard Specials, and the blunt, sawed-off nose of its bullet is deadly.

S.&W. Bodyguard semi-hammerless.

Round-butt S.&W. Chief's Special with 2-inch barrel.

Square-butt S.&W. Chief's Special, Airweight, 3-inch barrel.

Smith & Wesson .32 Hand Ejector

Caliber: .32 S.&W. long; takes also the short .32 S.&W. and the long .32 Colt New Police (sometimes called Police Positive).
Weight: 18 ounces in 4-inch barrel.
Barrel: 2, 3 or 4 inches.
Overall: 8 inches in 4-inch.
Sights: Fixed, 1/10-inch serrated ramp front; square notch rear.
Stocks: Checked walnut, Magna-type.
Finish: Blue or nickel.

This little sixshooter has been successful and always more or less popular since it came out in 1903. A plain round barrel with semicircular front sight blade was the old standard, and lengths were 3¼, 4¼ and 6 inches. The latter, as a holster gun, would have been worth fitting with the long, full "Target" stocks originally standard on the 1911 .22-.32. A little filing of the backstrap would have done it. These stocks went up high, then came back in a lip about ⅜ inch deep—from the rear of the grip frame, that is. They increased trigger reach and made the little .22 fill a good-sized hand. Before people realized the value of fillers like the Pachmayr grip adapter, or the one S.&W. formerly made for their own big guns, these "oversize" grips satisfied a lot of target shooters. They were made also (a fact little known) for the medium-

The S.&W. Hand Ejector is a round-butt gun for the .32 S.&W. Long. This one has a 3-inch barrel.

Four-inch barrel S.&W. .32 Regulation Police. The "square" butt is rounded for easy carry, unlike those on earlier Regulation Police guns.

frame Military & Police S.&W. with round butt. The modern S.&W. grip adapter, like the Pachmayr in shape but lacking the stiffening, grip-hugging reinforcement of steel all the way down, is a good gadget, unfortunately not well known.

Magna stocks on the Hand Ejector are unlike some modernizations of one-hand and two-hand artillery: they don't spoil the looks of a formerly beautiful model. They look good on all the Smiths, according to my personal opinion. In old times the Hand Ejector was furnished with both hard-rubber and walnut stocks, sometimes one kind, sometimes the other.

With 2-inch barrels the H. E. and the .38 Terrier are the smallest, most easily carried of all S.&W.'s with the conventional, fully exposed hammer spur. In pocket size this type goes right up to the 2- and 4-inch Military & Police .38 Special, and even to 4-inch bigbores, the .44 Special and the still heavier .44 Magnum, some would say when considering heavy pocket guns.

A few people still trust the .32 S.&W. long or the New Police cartridge for defense, and these loads are at least as deadly as the .32 auto-pistol round. Many prefer the simple-to-operate sixgun to an automatic for pocket use. Consequently, there's still room in the market for a little revolver of this type. Colt makes guns in this caliber, though in the unnecessary .38-Special-length cylinder to simplify production.

Smith & Wesson Regulation Police

Caliber: .32 S.&W. long, like the preceding Hand Ejector, also the short .38 S.&W. or Colt New Police. The .38 has a 5-shot cylinder.
Weight: With 4-inch barrel, 18¾ ounces in .32, 18 ounces in .38.
Barrel: 2, 3 or 4 inches in .32; 4 inches in .38.
Overall: 8½ inches with 4-inch barrel, either caliber.
Sights: Same as on Hand Ejector, preceding.
Stocks: Checked walnut, Magna. These are of the so-called "square butt-type," formerly flat on the bottom but now rounded for the pocket.
Finish: Blue or nickel.

There was no doubt of the .32 Hand Ejector's accuracy, but folks with medium or oversize hands often

found it hard to shoot that round-butt model as well as they knew it deserved. So finally this model, not really new, came out, and as a surprise to most of us it appeared in .38 caliber also. The Colt Police Positive .38 was familiar, and with 5- and 6-inch barrels as well as the popular 4-inch, but we'd realized that it would take a magician to change the .32 Hand Ejector into a .38 sixshooter. The frame just wasn't big enough, even with paper-thin chamber walls. A slight change in lockwork and cylinder ratchets made a 5-shot, .38 possible, and practical, too, we found out when we began to shoot this model. Weight was about the same 18 ounces as in today's make-up, and though that seemed light for a .38 *then,* the Regulation Police proved shootable, not a target gun but really good as a pocket revolver. It was comfortable to fire.

In spite of the square butt, this .38—noticeably lighter and less bulgy amidship than the Colt opposite number—became a favorite of many law officers, home-owners, yachtsmen, campers, and so on—people who wanted a light gun with fair wallop and good shootability. The .32 model also was lighter than the Police Positive Colt, and some chose it for this, among other, reasons. Both makes sold well, and the real differences between them were small.

Smith & Wesson Terrier

Caliber: .38 S.&W. or Colt New Police.
Weight: 17 ounces.
Barrel: 2 inches.
Overall: 6¼ inches.
Sights: Same as on Hand Ejector and Regulation Police.
Stocks: Checked walnut, Magna, round butt.
Finish: Blue or nickel.

The Terrier is simply a 2-inch Hand Ejector at last made in .38. It has the rounded butt of the H. E. and the 5-shot cylinder of the .38 Regulation Police.

By comparison, the 2-inch Colt Agent, Cobra and Police Positive Special weigh about 14½, 15 and 23 ounces, and measure 6¾ inches overall. They take six of the longer .38 Special cartridges (high-velocity types sanctioned by factory catalogue data), and the

Five-shot .38 S.&W. Terrier on the Hand Ejector frame.

S.&W. .38 Special Military & Police with 2-inch barrel and round butt.

last two models also come in long .32 and short .38 New Police calibers. Colt's discontinued .38 Banker's Special, New Police caliber, weighed 19 ounces and went 6½ inches overall, with the short cylinder. It came in .22 caliber also, and the same 2-inch-length barrel. A nice gun.

Smith & Wesson Military & Police

Caliber: .38 Special, .38 long or short Colt, but the factory does not recommend high speed Specials. The frame is medium-size, not large, though it's longer than that of the five-shot .38 Specials—Centennial, Bodyguard, and Chief's Special. None of these guns should be unsafe with factory high-velocity loads. We've used a few in this M. & P. model. But in time they can make the cylinder chatter; things get loose, even with that fore-and-aft locked S.&W. cylinder.

Weight: 30½ ounces in 4-inch barrel, all-steel frame type, with square butt; 26 ounces in 2-inch barrel, round butt; 18 ounces in 2-inch Airweight with round butt.

Barrel: 2, 4, 5 and 6 inches in both standard and Airweight.

Overall: 9¼ inches in 4-inch barrel, round butt; 6⅞ inches in 2-inch barrel, round butt.

Sights: At this writing the square butt model has a serrated ramp front sight, the round butt a semi-circular "service-type" front, and the Airweight with round butt a serrated ramp front. These fronts are 1/10 inch wide, and rear sights are of the square-cut Patridge-type. Sights are fixed or "solid."

Stocks: Checked walnut, Magna, round or square butt.

Finish: Blue or nickel.

These revolvers have the short-action, shortened hammer fall, which proved so popular with most shooters on the .22, .32 and .38 K target models. They have the new-type hammer, too. Some oldtimers call it the "cap pistol hammer," and perhaps with justification. Its spur is longer and more deeply curved than that of the old sort. To start with, it is fine; but a shooter who's had maybe dozens of earlier Smiths and used them a lot finds his thumb overreaching the new spur, and he must learn to take a shorter reach. Then in time he'd probably appreciate the cocking ease of the new models.

For a while S.&W. had a special-job "Hump-back

Hammer," the old-type with most of the curve ahead of the spur filled in, and from it you easily trace the modern development. Only the tip of the thumb, not the whole pad, goes to work in cocking the modern Smith hammer. For a quick-draw pocket gun the new spur may not suit everyone.

The large frame, the large cylinder, and the weight of the M. & P. disqualify it as a pocket gun, some would decide, though the 2-inch Airweight with round butt is only three ounces heavier than the much smaller framed Colt Cobra .38 Special, also a sixshooter. So the M. & P. is more often an outside holster-rider, even though the 2-inchers with round butt fit handily into a hideaway holster under the arm (shoulder holster) or in a waistband holster for the trousers. Three ounces' extra weight don't make the lightest M. & P. much more comfortable to shoot than the short Cobra; but the grip does, for it makes room for the often-abused second finger, whether or not an adapter fills unwanted space between the trigger guard and the upper part of the grip front—the front strap, as it's called. The S.&W. achieves this fit at the cost of only ⅛ inch

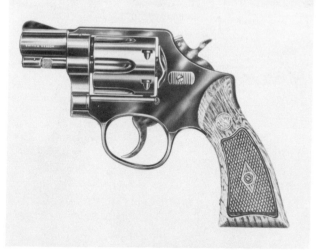

Military & Police Airweight with square butt.

greater overall length than the Cobra's, partly because the bottom of the grip is more rounded. It looks like, and is, a considerably bigger gun all-around, and the chamber walls in the cylinder are thicker.

But three ounces extra weight in a pocket gun do mean something to many of us, as it is about the heft of an extra half-dozen .38 Special cartridges. Choice between Cobra and Military & Police, when a six-shot gun is wanted, can about shake down to the question as to which we prefer. Probably that's what the usual decision is.

Smith & Wesson Combat Masterpiece

Caliber: .38 Special, as in Military & Police model. On order this gun comes in .22 long-rifle caliber, and shorts and longs can be used.
Weight: .38 caliber, loaded, 34 ounces. Less steel bored out of the .22 adds weight. In K-target models, loaded weights are balanced in .32 and .38 guns by wider barrel ribs than the .22 has.
Barrel: 4 inches.
Overall: 9⅛ inches.
Sights: ⅛-inch-wide Baughman design front, streamlined for quick draw, on a plain ramp; rear, S.&W. micrometer target-type, which gives audible clicks as you adjust for windage (lateral deflection) or elevation. Generally, a square-backed front sight is more liable to catch in quick draw than a rear sight; so this gun can qualify for pocket use even though most of those who own one probably tote it in a holster. For some shooters' eyesight, a 4-inch-barreled target revolver like this is better than a 6-inch.
Stocks: Checked walnut, Magna, square butt.
Finish: Blue. Since this is essentially a target-type gun, nickel finish isn't offered; it would cause too much glitter for accurate sighting. Nickel is more rust-resistant than standard blue, and a pocket gun may be exposed to sweat. Some police officers, and others, like nickel because it shows in dim lights and announces that the gun-holder really is armed, and no fooling.

This fine revolver resembles the K-Masterpiece target family except for its quick-draw front sight and 4-inch barrel. Like most U. S. handguns now made, it has a trigger grooved for better control, and in addition the front and back straps are grooved. When the oversize target stocks go on it as an extra, the front strap steel is covered with walnut and the gun is hardly of pocket size any more.

S.&W. Combat Masterpiece with quick-draw front and finely adjustable target rear sight.

The Combat Masterpiece is at home on the target range, in a woods holster, or even in a pocket. It would do almost anywhere, subject to caliber limitations, and would be many shooters' idea of the nearly perfect all-round handgun. With any safe loading this .38 would hardly be the equal of *the S.&W. 3½-inch .357 Magnum,* long proved in both police and F.B.I. service. That is a 41-ounce gun, unloaded, which sags almost any clothing but an Eskimo's. Although we don't classify it here as a pocket gun, it could be worth the lug. With Maggie loads, the muzzle blast is terrific and the recoil quite something. But some people wouldn't mind either, and the two are akin. Blast increases apparent recoil. Maybe you remember that when *the heavy .38-.44 Smith* came out, people said it seemed less noisy—and only a 5-inch barreled gun, too, when they were used to a 6-inch. Of course it kicked less than standard weight .38 Specials. But with Specials the Magnum is one of the sweetest shooting revolvers you could ask for. The extra weight and the nearly ultra-short barrel do the trick.

Lots of us have wanted a 4-inch K-.22, and some have had a 6-inch amputated to that length. Here is one factory-made. A friend of mine had a fore-runner of it years ago—gunsmith's cut-off job. He liked the handiness and the still steady hang that short Smith had. But he couldn't make quite so good a score as he had with the old 6-incher. So a dealer got it, who sold it promptly and easily. The short inter-sight distance didn't suit my friend's eyesight, and he knew that with any such arrangement the alignment must be extra precise.

Smith & Wesson Combat Magnum

Caliber: .357 Magnum; .38 Specials and the short and long .38 Colt can be used, too.
Weight: 35 ounces, unloaded.
Barrel: 4 inches.
Overall: 9½ inches. This gun regularly carries the oversize Target stocks, which could be altered or changed.
Sights: Same as on Combat Masterpiece.
Stocks: The Target stocks give this gun a ⅜-inch greater overall length than that of the Combat Masterpiece.
Finish: Bright blue (a special polish) or nickel.

Although this is a medium-frame gun like the Combat Masterpiece .38 Special, it is adapted to the still-powerful .357 Magnum. (The .357 didn't automatically shrink when the .44 Magnum came out.) Both have the short action of Military & Police type, and the grooved front and back straps and trigger of the K target guns.

This rather light .357 gets a little extra weight from the underbarrel housing for the ejector rod, a design used long ago on the Triple Lock .44 Special, then dropped for a while during and after World War I years, and later brought back. The ribbed barrel is heavy, getting weight out front where you can use it.

The barrel breech projects only a short distance from the rear of the frame, as compared with the K guns, target or service, or compared with the heavier frame Smiths—except the extremely rugged .44

S.&W. .357 Combat Magnum with Target stocks.

Magnum. It is less likely to be bulged by heavy loads or by oversized hard bullets than a longer breech of equal size would be. A .357 Magnum revolver does not *need* a long cylinder for factory ammunition. Some factory rounds are shorter overall than .38 Specials, though the Magnum cases are longer. But a long cylinder gives leeway to a handloader who dislikes one factory method of loading .357 lead bullets, with the brass crimped over the bullet's front shoulder, not into a groove. Yes, the Magnum kicks, and over-shoulder crimping is a good way to keep the lead from moving forward under recoil—or really staying put when the gun goes back. A broken crimp lowers the sixgun's bullet velocity, and the lead can move up enough to protrude from the cylinder and lock the gun temporarily. A good crimping groove, beveled, not square at the rear, can hold lead bullets in place under pretty stiff jumpback of the gun, provided the loading tool makes good use of that groove.

Here again is a revolver that could qualify as an all-rounder, not too heavy or bulky and surely not too puny in the power it delivers. For the latter reason, it might be the choice over the .38 Combat Magnum. But it could be that neither would be chosen, as American gun-lovers are a breed of free men who put some value on individual choice.

Smith & Wesson 9 mm. Automatic

Caliber: 9 mm. Luger or Parabellum.
Weight: 26½ ounces without magazine. About ¼ pound lighter than a German Luger 9 mm. with 4-inch barrel.
Barrel: 4 inches.
Overall: 7 7/16 inches.
Sights: Fixed, 1/10-inch serrated ramp front; square-notched Patridge--type rear, adjustable for windage. Top of slide is matted to prevent light reflection from disturbing aim.
Stocks: Checked walnut.
Finish: Blue.

This isn't Smith & Wesson's first venture in automatic pistols, but without doubt it was the most successful until the .22 target auto came along. Both are of high quality. So was the little *.35 pocket gun of 1913,* superseded in the early 1920s by a revised model for the easy-to-find .32 Colt Auto cartridge.

That .35, underloaded and less powerful than the 32, was still a sensibly designed round. The bullet bearing that contacted the barrel's rifling lands was of soft lead prompt to upset and fill the rifling grooves, thus cutting off the hot powder gases that shorten barrel life. It came in metal point or soft point, the latter being merely a lead bullet with a tin-plated copper or gilding metal band around its front! Bullet weight was 76 grains compared to 71 or 74 of the .32 Auto, and diameter was only about .008 inch larger than the Colt's. ".35" was an advertising name. You can fire .32 Autos in the .35, for the loose bullet fit lowers pressure—though it doesn't help power or accuracy!

The S.&W. .35 was a beautifully made pistol. It had a unique trigger safety that you set to ready, if you were right-handed, by simply squeezing a button in the top front of the grip and shifting it to the left and in. So the gun was a bit like the squeeze-handle Smith, the double-action hammerless revolver, which also has a safety (the plate on the backstrap or rear of the grip) which goes in and is readied for firing as you grip the gun—intentionally. In case the auto's safety should seem to be poor risk insurance, S.&W. fitted a recoil spring disconnector so that a person with weak, even feeble hands could leave the barrel empty and still have no trouble in jacking in a cartridge from the magazine with a quick, easy pull and release of the slide.

The S.&W. 9 mm. automatic of today is no retread of any earlier U.S. model. It comes in two styles, single and double action. You thumb-cock the single's hammer, just as with a Colt .38 or .45. The double action, though it costs a little more, is the choice for a pocket gun meant for that business first of all. It's like some foreigners, such as the 9 mm. Walther or the militarized P-38, small pocket Walthers, and the Mauser H Sc. .32. For the first shot, you needn't cock the hammer: a pull on the trigger does that, just as with a double-action revolver. Yet this gun is suit-

S.&W. Model 39 auto-pistol with double-action trigger. This 9mm. Luger caliber gun has been made in single-action, too, but most people choose the d. a. for defense use.

able for leisurely, accurate shooting. When you thumb-cock the hammer, the trigger comes back to a normal auto-pistol position, and in the Smith that's within reach of a rather short forefinger. Those who choose the S.&W. as a woods gun probably would be perfectly content with the single-action model.

The action is of Browning type, the barrel housed in the slide and coming back in recoil, for a short distance, locked to that slide. Then the barrel breech drops, the barrel stays put, and the slide goes on back. It may be imagination, but the idea pops up that this dropping of the barrel, S.&W. and big Colt fashion, assists in extracting a fired case that might want to stick.

In this type of action, generally most reliable though it is, there's always some looseness between the slide and the frame or receiver. Snug, precise fitting, we all know, produces splendid accuracy in a match quality Colt. To add to snug alignment, an S.&W. guide rod runs clear up through the barrel bushing at the muzzle.

Just as on the modern heavy-caliber Colts—and some of the old ones too, but not the Pocket Model .38—the slide stays open after the last shot, telling you it's time to put in a loaded magazine and thumb down the slide stop to toss a cartridge into the chamber. When the magazine is out, you can't fire the S.&W. This is for the forgetful, who sometimes take out the mag and overlook the loaded chamber, but if you lose the mag, all you have left is a short, heavy club. Time to pull off the trail and whittle a perfect dummy mag of wood so you can still use the gun as a single shot!

The S.&W. is compact. It's thin, and for a powerful autoloader it's easily carried. The grip is built around a short, thin cartridge, doesn't have to hold a supply of .45s. The slide tapers from front to rear, adding to appearance and reducing bulk.

It isn't a tiny gun, but it's small enough for a rather small hand, and the short trigger reach—short for an automatic—is a definite help. The grip slants well to the rear, assisting toward the so-called instinctive pointing that really comes from long conscientious practice, with any gun. It flares forward at the lower front to position the hand, and it flares back at the upper rear to save the web of the hand from being chewed by the hammer spur when the slide flies back in recoil.

There is no squeeze-grip safety on this S.&W. auto, as there is on modern Colt centerfires and some Lugers. There is an arched housing at the rear of the grip, in modern Colt .45 service and .38 auto fashion, and the lack of a grip safety would please some folks. Twigs have been known to work in and make a gun temporarily unshootable. And the grip safeties on the .25, .32 and .380 Colts require such a husky squeeze that a target shooter who favors the light, easy hold, as some still do, is lost when trying to use one of these pocket guns.

That little loop at the bottom of the grip, in .45

Colt Government Model style, is for a lanyard. Such an attachment in use can be worth as much as the gun when you're in a boat; and on horseback it means something, too. It is not only policemen who see good sense in tying a pistol to the pistoleer.

Perhaps the operation of the S.&W.'s thumb safety is a fault. It is up, not down, in firing position. The downthrust of a Colt safe has become quick and easy to a lot of us. (Lugers vary: some up, some down.) The double-action Smith can be carried with its hammer down and still more easily be put into fighting readiness than any of the now obsolete (are they?) single-action automatics, both kinds being carried safely. The S.&W. safe disconnects the trigger and puts a bar between the hammer and firing pin. You can *load or unload* this automatic pistol with the safety lock on.

Those of us who know war-production P-38 Walthers needn't be alarmed at the way in which pressing the thumb safety drops the Smith hammer. It does it safely; there are no brittle parts to break, no danger of the gun's going boom when we do this. The S.&W. is strictly quality-made, and some people would call it the perfect military auto-pistol.

Others would deride any such claim because of the cartridge it shoots. Yes, it's easier to train recruits with a moderate-powered 9 mm. or .38 than with a .45, and the lightness of gun and ammo would help supply-men and foot-sloggers. But how many recruits get liberal pistol training? Some hadn't even a decent smattering of rifle practice before they went into the lines. If a pistol is for short range, you want one with plenty of smash, don't you, one that will knock out an enemy even with a rather poorly placed hit? To carry on the argument is pointless. Perhaps the balance between accuracy and power is an adjustment that each civilian who uses a pocket gun, or any other one- or two-hand firearm, must make for himself.

Having a rear sight easily adjustable for windage is good on a service-type automatic, like this one, provided it is used correctly. Most pistol shooters seem to vary more in horizontal than in vertical deflection of shots: some shoot a fixed-sight gun to the right, some to the left. And an enemy soldier is generally more vertical than horizontal, isn't he, when he rushes you? Just the opposite of a black mamba or a boa constrictor! For those critters we'd be more fussy about our elevation than our windage.

The S.&W. front sight is described as "fixed." At least some were adjustable up or down for elevation, at the factory, by a screw inside the slide—so Elmer Keith explains in that fascinating book, *Sixguns.* Putting elevation on an absolutely solid front sight is easy, sometimes too easy: you file it down. To lower bullet impact you cut down the rear sight, if you can, or if the front bead is detachable you take it out and substitute a higher one.

HOLSTERS

Although we have stressed pockets throughout this chapter, holsters and their value need emphasis, too. They protect our gun from perspiration, and they keep out the dirt, lint and tobacco crumbs that line the average pocket and might cause a disastrous jam of an automatic or even of a revolver with finely fitted parts. A holster greatly helps quick draw, too, especially of guns with exposed hammer and target sights. One can add really very little to a handgun's bulkiness, and when made for a pocket arm its weight is scarcely noticeable.

The belt holster doesn't show beneath the coat-tail when the bottom is stuffed into the hip pocket, and some holsters are made especially for that pocket. The shoulder-type is handy, particularly when we ride in an automobile. It's a godsend to the unfortunate truss-wearer who doesn't crave extra weight around the belt. The waistband variety, worn inside belt and trousers, is highly accessible. Carried in front, it permits fast draw of bulky-cylindered revolvers or guns with target sights, and it is nearly as efficient as the upside-down kind of shoulder holster. Incidentally, our good wife will appreciate it if we do not oil the leather.

The combination of the tanning chemicals and oil makes a non-removable stain on clothing.

The pocket gun, usually so small and light, in time becomes a familiar part of our hand, and it is easily waved around in emphasizing conversation! Among friends it's best to leave it right in the pocket or holster. Few people are accidentally shot by a gun that isn't pointed at them!

Certainly one of the super pocket guns is the Sheriff's Model recently made by Colt for the Centennial Arms Corporation, 3318 West Devon Avenue, Chicago 45, Illinois. It's a 3-inch barreled .45 job, Single Action Army type. With no ejector rod, it's slow indeed to reload, but perhaps the philosophy is that five shots— an empty chamber lined up under the hammer in usual SAA practice—should be enough for any emergency. Finish is blue and color case-hardened, grips of smooth, uncheckered wood, a businesslike appearance. No pinweight, it is nevertheless short enough to carry and draw well. This gun costs a little more than the standard Colt SAA, but pairs with consecutive serial numbers can be had at no extra charge above the usual Centennial retail. This fact would appeal to collectors, but other people, too, will want this slinger of 250 and 255 grain lead bullets.

IT'S NOT only the military and the police who carry a handgun on the job. Factory guards, night watchmen, private detectives, bank guards and others who may need to show, or even use, a pistol will pocket or holster one when going on a tour of duty. Many a bank teller has one within easy reach, and some—too few—have been trained or have taught themselves to fire it instantly and accurately in case an emergency breaks.

Usually less subject to sudden need is the handgun that the rancher, forester, prospector or trapper may belt on as part of his working capital. He could feel naked without it. Frontiers still exist, though they may be enclosed within civilization's borders. The farmer seldom needs a pistol but may carry one just for the fun of it. Or he may work in snake country or have mean stock. A .45 Colt slug behind the jaw, coursing upward into the maddened brain of a bull, saved the life of an Upstate New York farmer who believed in owning a sixgun and knowing how to use it. His was a single-action Colt, "the old hog-leg," so named from its outline.

The soldier, sailor, marine, airman and coastguardsman are issued weapons, one of which may be a pistol. The .45 automatic or 1917 revolver, or the .38 Special revolver, is common. Men or women going into combat areas have bought and packed along a handgun when none was issued to them. It was sensible life insurance when it was reliable and powerful. An *American Rifleman* story told of a Smith & Wesson .44 Special and a supply of ammunition packed inside a ham—a gift, Korea-bound.

Nations, like individuals, disagree on the quality of reliability and the quantity of power they must have in the pistol they adopt. Looked at impartially, our 1911 .45 Colt (or the 1911-A later version with short trigger and arched housing at the rear of the butt) stands at peak reliability among military automatics. It may be entirely alone on that peak, though the odd-looking, straighter-stocked *.455 Webley & Scott* the British Navy used was a good gun, and its metal-cased bullet had a blunt, almost man-stopper style nose. With almost any decent automatic as much depends on the care given it and the grade of its ammunition, as on its design or even its individual quality. The magazine must be in good condition, reasonably clean, and its feed lips not battered out of shape. A dry gun *can* perk, but light lubricating oil on the moving parts is a help.

Our .45 Colt has power, more than any other service caliber in common use. It has blast and recoil, too, that make it harder to master than .38s and smaller calibers. Britain rarely has chosen an automatic for her servicemen. She went from the .455 revolver and its 265 grain bullet to a .380 cartridge interchangeable with our short .38 S.&W. Its 200 grain lead at a velocity of about 600 feet per second gave place to full-jacketed 176 to 181 grain bullets when our enemies began executing prisoners in possession

CHAPTER 4

WORK GUNS

of plain lead bullets that could be construed as dumdums. Many governments use the 115 to 125 grain 9mm. Luger load, and Russia stepped down the velocity of the 85 grain 7.62 mm., practically a .30 Mauser, and interchangeable, from some 1400 to 1100 f. s. But then, Russia believes in a lot of shooting, and the lives of her soldiers and the feelings of her home folks are cheap.

Most police forces in our country use revolvers rather than automatics—though a generation ago a big Connecticut city standardized for issue the .32 Colt automatic. The Colt or Smith .38 Special with 4-, 5- or 6-inch barrel and weighing about two pounds is as much "general issue" (or approved) as any. Not too heavy for an all-day or an all-night ride in a properly slung holster, these guns are large enough to hold rugged, long-wearing component parts. They also have the steadying weight that makes good shooting possible with standard ammunition or even with stiffly-charged metal-piercers. Police pistol teams are numerous, enthusiastic and skilled. Although a .38 Special target gun is the prized possession of many of these shooters, the sturdy old service gun with fixed sights usually travels the beat. Men shoot it well with skill achieved through a companion model dressed up for range competition. Many advanced departments long ago saw the wisdom of training their men with .22s of the Official Police, K-.22, or Officer's Model type, and of supplying plenty of .38 handloads for practice, too. But many sluggard departments didn't. In between is the casual, occasional practice where no civilian witnesses are allowed. Sometimes these cops forget to burn their targets on leaving the scene of disillusionment, and then it's the duty of the first right-minded civilian who finds them to take care of

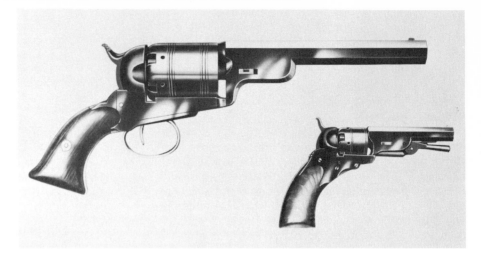

Paterson experimental Colt models, cap-and-ball, in .47 and .28 calibers. The .47 seems big enough for any "work," and the Baby Paterson looks efficient, too. Note the long cylinders on most large front-loading revolvers, to breech up the load and to hold, in some of the big ones, as much as 50 grains of black powder.

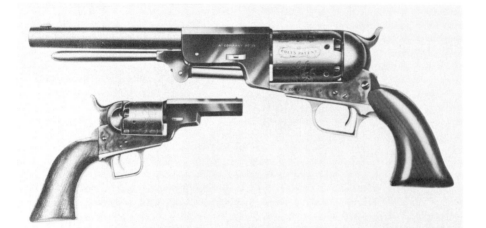

Colt "Walker" or First Dragoon .44, a four-pound gun, and the Wells Fargo or Baby Dragoon. Both of these Colts—and others, too,—grew with United States history in the conquest of the West and in bringing services to it.

that detail. Keep the bad news from getting out where it could do harm!

It seems reasonable that men and women who guard the public should get every encouragement and facility to master their weapons. If the cost appears unreasonable to village boards and city councils, let these people think of the value of life. A visit to the hospital or the morgue might stimulate thought. And remember that an ill-aimed bullet can find the wrong human target.

To resume: Heavier calibers than .38 Special are used, and lighter ones too. The policeman's intent is to disable an antagonist, not kill him, unless his own life is at stake. He deserves a fair chance for that life, and almost always the nature of "law and order" gives a thug the privilege of first shot. So you don't see as many .32s and stubby little .380s in police use as you did in years past, though the .38 S.&W. still gets around. In 2-inch barrel pocket style it's sometimes a "second gun," stashed away out of sight, a life-saver if the big gun is torn from the officer's hand or snatched from his holster. Well cared for, neither type of revolver is liable to fail.

That old .38 S.&W. with 145 or 146 grain bullet

is giving way steadily to general use, by law officers, of the .38 Special with 158 or 200 grain lead, or the 110 or 150 grain metal-piercers. Light, handy pocket guns for the Special are available, such as the 14½-ounce Colt Agent, 12½-ounce S.&W. Chief's Special, or 13-ounce S.&W. hammerless Centennial. Small frame Colts can wear a hammer shroud to prevent the hammer spur from catching in the pocket. These featherweights mean much to plainclothes men who formerly chose a Colt Banker's Special or S.&W. Terrier for the short .38 to keep weight to 1¼ pounds or under. Some of them use automatics, even a .25. A nickel finish is less prone to rust than the standard blue, makes rough aim easier in poor light, and shows up formidably in those dark places that "cry aloud for a murder."

A .45 is issued to some officers who may or may not ride a horse or a motorcycle. The Colt automatic has been used a lot, but a sixgun is quicker for the first and usually most important shot. If the fast reloading of clip-held .45 auto rimless rounds meant less than power, the long, heavy .45 Colt revolver cartridge got the call, when the Colt New Service was still made. Just the impressive look of those big hulls in the belt loops can make a bad actor think, and think again. The .44 Magnum is far more powerful, and the medium-caliber .357 Magnum's good velocity makes it effective enough for most service, including the penetration of car bodies.

Alas for legends of the Old West! In these days many a cow-puncher objects to the tonnage and bulk of a big, competent sixgun and totes a .22 or .32 automatic, or no gun at all. What he needs is a shooting-iron that will make a noise above a hoof-beat for signaling, bop the head off a snake, or humanely finish a sick calf or cow with a head shot. The latter task can require pretty fair penetration. The cowpoke will need more power, and greater skill, if he hopes to scupper some moronic coyote that blunders into pistol range. Such prairie wolves are getting scarce!

In this chapter we are concerned with guns of considerable power. We mention .22s and .32s only in passing, even though all of us know that they have done good work, so good that they have become the mainstay of seasoned outdoorsmen. Target arms go to a later chapter. Some of them are too heavy for the average shooter to make good scores with, and as a matter of fact you see few of that kind on the firing lines in hot competition. The fact that they have adjustable sights doesn't mean, to us, that they are too delicate for wilderness use. On the contrary, they are much the better for those sights, although they do need a little extra care.

Usually the outdoorsman, like the policeman, chooses a revolver instead of an automatic. The revolver is not necessarily more reliable, but its center-fire ammunition costs less, comes in more varieties, and caliber for caliber is more deadly—except that in medium sizes the auto's penetration is much greater. Sometimes that quality is wanted, as in taking the life of some large animal.

The double-action sixgun argument is an old one: which of the two long-established makes is superior? Here is a brief add-up of some of the points commonly made in camp or den or rumpus-room.

S.&W. 1891 single-action could be fitted with a .22 rimfire barrel for single-shot target use. This gun, for the short .38 S.&W. cartridge, was used to some extent in the West.

Double-action S.&W. with tip-up cylinder, like that of the 1891 .38, came in .44 caliber. Note the rear of the trigger guard, with reverse curve to go easy on the second finger during recoil. The old Colt Walker's guard is somewhat similar, and so is the one on the latest Ruger Super Blackhawk in .44 Magnum caliber.

THE COLT VS. SMITH & WESSON HASSLE

The Colt versus Smith argument is about a century old—and is still fun to get into! We could summarize it before we start by stating that the gun to choose is the one that fits your hand and gives the balance and hang you like.

Team members on each side are the double-action, side-swing-ejection sixshooters, although with the .38 S.&W. Regulation Police Smith began production of fiveshooters. There are two other types that more or less compete, or have competed: the single-shot target pistol and the automatic. The *S.&W. 1891* single

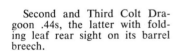

Second and Third Colt Dragoon .44s, the latter with folding leaf rear sight on its barrel breech.

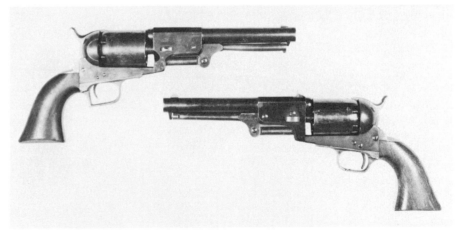

shot, made in .32 and .38 calibers as well as .22 was for years the only common entrant in serious target competition, except for the better grade of Stevens single shot .22s. It was made on a single-action .38 revolver frame, but the *Perfected .22* that superseded it was for no good reason except thrift built on a double-action frame. Still, it was a better gun, most shooters seem to have admitted: there was no noticeable kick-back of the double-action trigger after you'd eased off a shot, and the larger grip suited most people except for, probably, those who wisely doctored the grip of any .22 target gun to suit their individual hands. The *Straightline S.&W.*—so named because the striker (not a hammer) plunged straight forward to fire the .22 long-rifle cartridge and therefore was supposed to disturb the aim less—was no financial success. People disliked its auto-pistol grip style and couldn't made such good scores with it. The barrel swung to the side, and there was no automatic ejector

like that on the tip-up Perfected. With the breech opening exposed at the right it was not hard for a right-hander to extract and reload, but the southpaw was reminded again that he was a forgotten man. Many efforts in special stocking were made to cause this gun to turn in the scores, but few were successful.

Colt's Camp Perry Model .22 of 1926-39, especially in late versions, had a fast hammer fall compared with the Straight-line. This was because it was built on a revolver frame, the old favorite Officer's Model .38, a famous winner in centerfire matches. But it didn't displace the S.&W. Model 1909 Perfected, or the Harrington & Richardson single shot of more modern design—built on the frame of the current 999 Sportsman, a nine-shot .22 revolver. Already the strictly slow-fire matches were dropping out, except in the good and earnest ranks of the United States Revolver Association. This Colt was light-barreled with a beautiful taper that didn't help scores. First a 10- and then

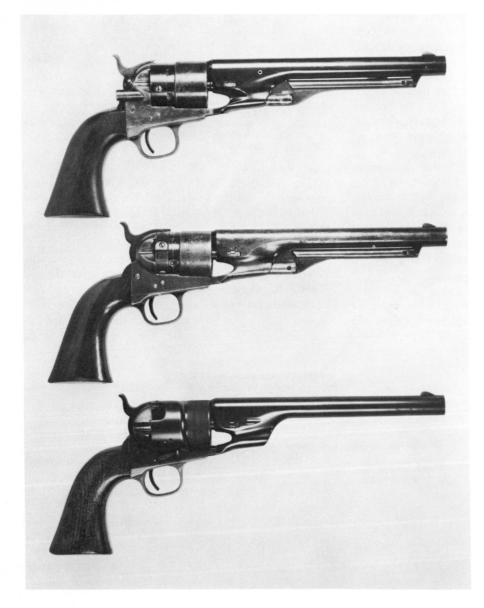

Metallic cartridge conversions of 1860 Colt Army .44 cap-and-ball revolvers. The 1851 Navy Colt was a .36.

an 8-inch barrel were standard, and gun weight was 34 ounces, the same as that of the 6-inch .38 Officer's at that time. It would have been easy to fit a heavier custom barrel, much more so than to a Stevens or S.&W. frame. This barrel was attached to a sort of dummy cylinder, flattened but fluted like a sixgun's, and it swung out to the left with the crane when you opened the gun.

Colt's Patent Firearms has never gone in for break-open, tip-up cylinder revolvers, like those once made by Smith & Wesson. But both *have been* in the auto-pistol field, Colt's steadily since 1900, S.&W. now and then. Comparison is difficult here, and perhaps foolish. Generally, the Colt has dominated the American scene. But in .22 caliber it's had its trouble, or spur, from competitors, target model Hi-Standards and Rugers, and even before the H.S. there was competition from the light but well-built little *Reising,* which was stocked and balanced very much like the old 6-inch .38 Colt Military auto. *The single-shot Hartford,* with blowback ejection of empties, resembled the Colt Woodsman except for its cheaper appearance.

Smith versions of the autoloader have been few. The .35 and the revised model in .32 were too expensive for sharp competition against the established Colt and *Savage* .32s and .380s, although they were indeed beautifully finished guns. Then too, there were the foreign imports to fight. The modern 9mm. military or pocket Smith and the .22 target auto are serious contenders against anything else in the world.

Now we can get to the main hassle: which is better, the Colt or the Smith & Wesson double-action solid-frame revolver?

Cost? Comparative prices have fluctuated through the years. In general, Smiths used to cost more; now it's the other way. But the differences are rather small, and few of us—I sincerely hope—would be obliged to make this detail the all-important one in deciding.

Quality of finish, too, has varied through the years. Since times long past, a powerful Smith argument has been that these guns have by far the better finish. Then someone would haul out a finely polished and blued or nickeled Colt, with beautifully checkered grip, too, pehaps; and where were you except frustrated? Wartime guns don't count. Those were commonly gray, not lustrous blue, and so much the better! Less gleam to give us away. Crack target models always were superb. Oh, were they? Well, if some weren't, that was just too bad. The slump in workmanship after World War II was to be expected, with rising production costs, and both these makes were affected, like almost everything else except optical goods. The resultant howls had some results, and we can anticipate more.

The weights of similar competitive models don't vary enough to make much sensible difference, as a rule. The S.&Ws. are generally lighter in plain service models with non-adjustable sights. Slimmer barrels account for some of the difference. There are, or were,

three standard frame sizes, not counting the old, light *Colt Pocket Positive .32,* formerly offered in Colt short and long calibers as well as Smith & Wesson sizes. The S.&W. light frame is built around the .32 caliber, like the early and still made Hand Ejector; but the Colt is of .38 size, and a sixshooter at that, not a five-round gun like the Smith .38 Regulation Police. There were .22s on these frames, and the S.&W. .22-.32 Target and Kit Gun survive. Next came the .38 long and .38 Special frames. The Special was the largest caliber in Smiths, whereas the Colts were made for .41s with narrower rims than the early and differently loaded .41s for the big Single Action Army and Bisley. The largest regularly made guns were the S.&W. Military in .44 Special, .38-40, .44-40 and .45 Colt calibers, also the .455 British in World War I, and the *Colt New Service,* now discontinued. We have reasonable hope that the last will be revived, as the Single Action Army was. It took those calibers just mentioned, also the stubby .450 British, and went on up to the short but still rather monstrous .476 British —or Eley, as these three British calibers often were called. Many of both makes were produced for the .45 Auto Colt rimless in World War I, when we couldn't make the .45 Colt 1911 model fast enough.

Cylinder rotation has been a grand field for argument. Colts turn right, clockwise, most Smiths the reverse. Some early Colts were left-hand, it's true, and this was thought to be rather sad, for the cylinder swung out to the left. Wouldn't that left-hand rotation tend to loosen the alignment? The Smith fancier's reply is that *his* pet's cylinder is anchored fore and aft, not just at the rear. I think we can let that ride. In a worn Colt you may notice that the hand—that thrusting arm that comes out of the breech face when you cock the gun—fails to align the cylinder on cocking; but when the trigger is pulled, it does, and what's more, it holds the cylinder more tightly than a worn Smith does. Anyway, that's my experience, but I don't mean that every Smith I ever had, and there were a lot, had such poor alignment that it shaved bullets. That's uncommon in either make.

Now here is a theory, and it may be a fact. As the chambers empty big, heavy .44 or .45 caliber cartridges, the gun grows lopsidedly lighter, either right or left, and this tends to make it shoot to the lighter side. To add to this mix-up, Colt rifling is to the left, S.&W. to the right, as on most American arms. How delightful, for this should balance the effect, if any, of the emptied chambers! I remember one very cheap revolver that had perfectly straight rifling, no twist, but I've forgotten its cylinder rotation, and that's too bad, and too late now to do anything about. Right-hand rifling does drift a bullet slightly to the right, lefthand rifling to the left, and these effects mean something in long range military target shooting with rifles.

Rifling twists in pistol barrels normally are a bit faster than in rifles firing the same cartridge, to keep bullets point-on, even at the lower handgun velocities. Colt rifling is six-groove, with a complete turn in each 16 inches of barrel, except for the .22s and late model .38 Officer's Model match guns, which make the turn in 14 inches. The change in the .38 was made, Charles Askins, Jr., explained in his *Pistol Shooter's Book,* to handle the .38 Special wadcutter target bullet better. That keg of lead, deeply hollowed at the rear, has a long bearing surface, which goes well with quick rifling. (Riflemen have found that quite light varmint hunting bullets can be used in a fast twist, like .30 caliber ten-inch, when the jacketed bullet has a deep, wide hollow point—the front third or so of the jacket containing no lead core at all. That permits lengthening the overall and still keeping bullet weight low.) Smith & Wesson rifling is five-groove except for .22 and .45 Auto calibers' six-groove. Twists vary: 18.75-inch in .32, .38 and .357; 12-inch in the old .32-20 (rifles use 20); 20-inch in .44 Special; 14.6 in the 1950 .45 target gun for the .45 Auto. The old .22-.32 revolver used 10-inch, as did early, experimental .22s on the K frame, long before the present K-.22 target-sighted gun came out, and 15-inch in the single shot. Rifle twist for the .22 long-rifle cartridge is usually 16-inch, and 10-inch in the pistol proved to be too steep, especially with fast modern bullets in the heavier .22 1-r loadings. This is true, even though the .22-32 made championships in any caliber revolver competition, back when it was new.

These twist variations seem to matter little, even to the most skilled pistol shooters, and this goes for rifling groove diameters, too. These are measured from the bottom of one groove to that of the opposite groove —and good luck be with you and your micrometer when you measure a lead slug driven through a five or any odd numbered grooved barrel. Colt groove diameters are smaller in almost all calibers, though the grooves are wider. Individual guns vary, too, and the handloader who wants the best accuracy, or top power with safe pressures, should measure his barrel and size his cast lead bullets to groove diameter, or not more than .001 inch larger. The factory loads are safe in the guns meant to use them: no need to worry about that:

The durability of working parts is a fine field for feuding. With reasonable care, and without abuse, either make of gun should stand up for thousands of shots. Large or medium frame revolvers can carry heavier, stronger parts, and on the average they make fewer trips to the gunsmith or to the factory service department. One big gun that looks rugged but really isn't, inside, is the Colt Single Action Army: its parts often break, though we'd certainly not call it a chronic invalid. Among the fifty-odd handguns I've owned (not really many, I know) and used a lot under all sorts of conditions, I remember only one breakdown that wasn't my fault. (I broke two firing pins by dry snapping, not putting an empty case into the chamber

to cushion the pin.) This one unpreventable mishap occurred on a canoe trip. Gordon and I had been shooting a good many black powder cartridges in the little .32 S.&W. Regulation Police, for they were more powerful than the smokeless rounds then, and cost a sensible chunk less. No doubt the gun was heavy enough for them, and I took care of it every evening; but one fine, bright morning we found that the hand wouldn't revolve the cylinder. We could still line up the chambers by human hand and fire slowly and carefully. When we got home I sent the gun to the factory and it came back in perfect and lasting working order. I doubt that they even charged for the work in those far-off days, but they might have. When you use handloads, as I do now for some 95% of my centerfire shooting, you're on your own; and if they're heavy you can expect a breakdown now and then. Still, such loads definitely have their purposes.

To digress a bit, it burns me to hear or read of folks' criticizing Elmer Keith for having blown up guns with stiff handloads. Reason 1: he was honest enough to admit it. 2: that's how ammunition progress is made. It stinks, I think, to use for yourself loads just under the danger line he and others like him have pointed out after trial and blow-up, and then deride such pioneers as knotheads.

Ease of primary dismounting, I think, goes to the S.&W. "Primary" means just to take out the side-plate and cylinder for cleaning and oiling the readily exposed working parts, or leaving them dry or graphite-dusted for the Arctic. Further dismounting requires some gunsmithing skill. Also, with the Colt you may run into trouble in replacing the side-plate after what you meant to be no more than primary dismounting. (From this it's plain to see that I'm a mechanical dub. Well, I have some company.) To cock the Smith hammer when the cylinder is swung to the side, draw back on the cylinder latch. This makes cleaning the firing pin hole easy.

Ease of loading is about the same in the two makes. With the Smith you thrust the cylinder latch forward to open the gun; with the Colt you draw it back. The forward thrust is easier, at least if your hand is cold. But couldn't it happen inadvertently under recoil if your thumb rests on the latch, as most thumbs do? In this wonderful world of shooters and shooters' arguments almost anything can occur. If you value your Colt, and you should, hold back the latch when you return the cylinder.

Ease of cocking develops, I think, for the make you favor and use so much that it becomes most familiar. For double-action firing the great Ed McGivern seemed to favor the S.&W. definitely, but some shooters think the newer short-action Smiths, fine though they are for single-action work, were not improved as to double-action. In thumb-cocking, the Colt is definitely obliging: tension seems to lessen as the hammer nears the end of the arc. The long-action S.&W. is just the opposite. In the short-action, you do not have to draw the hammer back so far, and if you like or learn to like the new-style hammer's spur shape your gun is handy. S.&W.s, before the new U-shaped mainspring went into some models, had a mainspring strain screw near the bottom front of the butt. You could ease it off for softer cocking—and perhaps hangfires, misfires, or ragged ignition that a good accuracy test might reveal. In the same classification is the narrowing or thinning of a mainspring: not good.

Sights do much to ensure attainable accuracy of any gun, even a shotgun. Modern fixed sights of both makes are square-cut, Patridge-style, easy and exact to see if there's light enough on both sides of the rear notch to let the front sight stand out to the individual shooter. If the notch is to be widened, then is the time to put on right or left windage if you need lateral adjustment. Both S.&W. and Colt have experimented freely, almost desperately, with rear sights in recent years. (Old Colt target guns had elevation in the front sight, excepting the earliest, for which there were blades of different shapes and heights.) The rather high Coltmaster two-way rear sight was followed by the more compact Accro, also two-way. The early S.&W. rear sights had opposing screws for windage and one top screw for elevation. Sometimes this top screw would loosen, particularly with centerfire loads of some consequence; so an additional locking screw went in. With the handgun's short inter-sight distance, and often with more than one barrel length in a shooter's battery, adjustments weren't particularly easy to figure out right on the firing line (where some shooters do change sighting and profit by it, though some don't, and still profit); and a better sight came along. This S.&W. Micrometer Click sounds off for each change intentionally made, isn't a pest by giving free, unintended changes, and is doing well. As Keith pointed out in *Sixguns,* it's similar to a good one made earlier by the King Gunsight Company.

But do not think that the matter of sights is important in choosing between Colt and Smith. It isn't, at least to most of us. A target shooter may have his preferences between issue sights on these makes, but it's about equally likely that he'll consider custom sights. I *do* like the 1/10-inch wide front sight, and the 1/8-inch even better. They show up well for me and it still is possible to overhold with them for a long shot afield. The old narrow, rounded-top front and U-notch rear, and the bead front too, I used to like because we did not have much else then, and I knew no better. You still find beginners who think "fine sights are more accurate." Then the thing to do is to be kindly and try to prove to them that it just ain't so. One way is to remind them that in the dimness of a cedar swamp you want a visible set of sights!

Here we leave this discussion, but generous margins on these pages provide room for the reader's further comments, or for his rebuttal of these statements.

Colt Official Police

Caliber: .22 rimfire short, long and long-rifle; .38 Special standard and high velocity, also .38 short and long Colt.
Weight: .22, 38 ounces; and .38, 35 ounces—both with 6-inch barrel.
Barrel: 4, 5 and 6 inches in .38; 4 and 6 in .22.
Overall: 11¼ inches in 6-inch barrel.
Sights: Fixed, glare-proofed, Patridge-style. Front is ramped.
Stocks: Checked walnut, square butt. Rounded butt on special order. Plastic "Coltwood" stocks, formerly used on this and other Colt revolvers, have been discontinued.
Finish: Blue or nickel.

Two calibers useful to the outdoorsman, .32-20 Winchester and .41 Short and long Colt, have been dropped. The great popularity of the .38 Special among police officers and target shooters made their going inevitable with the modern streamlining of production. The .32-20 was and still is a flat-shooting load up to pistol distances that are practical for most of us, and the bluff-nosed .41 long is a better killer than the round-nosed .38 Specials the factories load, including those with boosted velocities. The .41 revolver, not the ammunition, went out with the preceding, and similar, Army Special Colt, but the .32-20 hung on for a while in the Official Police.

Handloads can make the .38 Special deadly on most game below the size of deer, and the low-velocity, flat-fronted midrange wad-cutter factory hull does well on all but the smallest small game, on which it can be pretty rough.

The .22, with solid, fixed sights like those on the .38—except that the front sight is much lower, to give elevation—was meant as a police trainer. For this, it's excellent. But it's also a good game gun, within the mighty narrow limits of the caliber, for weight makes it steady to hold and less frustrating than some in a cross-wind that pulls at the shooter's arm and gun. Held with both hands, it's nearly as easy to hit with as a little .22 rifle about twice as heavy, provided your eyesight allows you to aim with it as well as you could with the rifle—open-sighted, of course, as they so tiresomely come from the factories.

Two perhaps zany ideas sprout from this practical .22 field pistol. Have it rechambered for .22 W.R.F. or Special, a cartridge much more powerful than the

Colt Official Police, 4-inch barrel.

.22 long-rifle. This could be done safely, though the Winchester sachems who designed the 1890 W.R.F. had the barrels bored oversize, to fit oversize bullets. But many other rifle-makers didn't; and results were satisfactory, the shooting good, the pressures low and safe. Once I had a Colt Police Positive Target in .22 long-rifle, and thinking a spare cylinder for W.R.F. would be nice in the woods (and it was!) I asked Colt's about it. They supplied and fitted it, and I—well, I should have had sense enough to keep that outfit forever and a day. Resighting for the heavier load was easy, and W.R.F.s are oilproof and waterproof as well as respectably powerful, compared to long-rifles. So is the .25 Stevens rimfire cartridge. And here is the second idea, not original of course, or even unacted upon, I believe. Conversion to .25 would require a relocating of the firing pin or hammer nose to make it strike clear across the .25's rim. A great many .25 rifles failed to do this and the cartridge got an unearned bad name for stringing its shots up and down on the target. Poor ignition caused it. Although the .25 was loaded only experimentally in high speed type, its bigger bullets made it better than standard, not magnum, .22 rimfires, as owners of old Stevens single-shot pistols found. Now the .25 ammo is discontinued, and even .22 W.R.F. handiness in .22 rimfire magnums may not save that excellent old smallbore from similar oblivion. The .22 Official Police, chambered, bored and rifled to .22 rimfire mag, could be a mighty useful woods gun with 6-inch barrel. Simply rechambering it wouldn't do the job.

If these remarks have failed to imply that the Official Police is a fine outdoorsman's pistol, I've failed to make my point. It is, for it's a rugged gun with enough weight for good shooting, qualities that have made it so popular with law officers. With rounded butt and 4-inch barrel it's a usable pocket gun, a bit heavy, but worth the weight on a serious occasion. A rounded butt would suit some of us in wilderness carry and shooting, though out there we'd probably want the 6-inch. It's easier to aim, less noisy, and with most loads a little more powerful. For a heavier .38 Special double-action field gun we'd choose a .38-.44 Smith & Wesson, the target-sighted Outdoorsman or the solid-sighted Heavy Duty, unless we preferred a Colt but didn't want the target-sighted Python .357, which uses .38 Specials, too. For the Colt New Service is gone, dropped in World War II, along with a lot of other old favorite pistol, rifle and shotgun models. It was a good time to stop, some manufacturers must have thought, and perhaps in some instances it was! It came in .38 Special as well as .357 Magnum, and like the bigbore New Service of the later years it had square or rounded grips. Instead of the familiar bigbore barrel lengths—4½, 5½ and 7½ inches—it offered the Official Police lineup of 4, 5 and 6. But the barrel was heavier at the breech than that of the O. P., though not adding too much weight, and providing a really beautiful taper. In 6-inch this

.38 went to 43 ounces, an ounce under today's Python on the medium-size O. P. frame. Forty-odd is near the limit for a practical outdoorsman's revolver.

Any New Service in top-flight shape is a bit of a used-gun rarity, and the .38 might be one of the hardest to find. There is a rather tireless little rumor that the New Service will be revived, and let us hope there are enough of us to bring this to pass, even if it's re-christened and looks a little different on the outside.

Probably the easiest New Service to find is the 1917 .45 made for the rimless auto cartridge. A good many of them got around and a few should still be in first-class condition. Don't get one of the early vintage with chambers bored to the same diameter straight through—without the shoulder for the square, uncrimped mouth of the case to abut on. With that one you must use the three-shot, half-moon clips to hold rimless cartridges for the firing pin to whack, unless you get the special .45 Auto-rim loads for it—which do have the merit of being pretty rugged at the base for reloading. The rim—or flange, as the British say, and correctly enough—is exceptionally thick to fill the wide space between cylinder face and the recoil plate, the breech, the bushing of the firing pin. The throated-chamber .45 1917s often have been converted to ."45 long Colt" (as we must say, to make ourselves clear to many who never used or heard of the old cartridge). Even in the old balloon-pocket .45 Colt cases, not solid-head to make a stronger base and home for the primer, there's just about enough brass at the head to make separations unlikely at the cylinder-recoil plate gap. Such bursts were common when non-corrosive primers were new and contained mercury. On firing, mercury made the brass brittle for reloading, and before long something had to give. As far as I know, this was harmless. But a long thumb stretched across the gap could be burned, and perhaps such thumbs and such ammo did get together. Unless the brass had been swollen badly from reloads, and not sized down, it usually wasn't hard to get the remains out of the chamber and go on firing from it. As I recall, a car key pulled out .38 Specials. Now practically all those mercuric non-corrosive primers are gone. I threw quite a few into Round Pond, myself. Down and down they bubbled through those depths browned with leafmold, and no one mourned.

Colt Three-Fifty-Seven

Caliber: .357 Magnum; also takes the .38 Special family and their first cousins a generation removed, the short and long Colt .38s.

Weight: 36 ounces in 4-inch, 39 in 6-inch.

Barrel: 4 and 6 inches.

Overall: 9¼ inches in 4-inch barrel.

Sights: Quick-draw ramp-type front, ⅛ inch wide. Rear sight adjustable for windage and elevation.

Stocks: Checked walnut, square butt.

Finish: Blue.

This revolver can be had at extra cost with the large target-style stocks and target hammer with wide

Colt "Three-Fifty-Seven," 4-inch barrel.

cocking spur, and it is commonly so illustrated. With standard stocks and 4-inch barrel it could qualify nicely as a heavy pocket gun, for it weighs only an ounce more than the Smith & Wesson Combat Magnum .357. Both of them have the quick-draw type of front sight that can hardly catch in the clothes. But the Colt comes in 6-inch barrel, too, which the S.&W. does not at this writing. The extra barrel length is well worth while in .357 for the added velocity it gives, and the reduction of muzzle blast.

So it makes a good belt gun in 6-inch, not really heavy, and perfectly safe and suitable for Magnum rounds, as the S.&W. Combat Maggie is, too. These are medium-size-frame sixguns, a quarter pound or more lighter than the heavy .357 double-action Smiths, and for that reason they are noticeably less burdensome along about 4 p.m., with dark nearer to you than is camp. For many target shooters this 6-inch Colt would be of ideal size and weight for .38 Special ammunition, say mid-range for 25 yards and full-charge for 50, if they believe in switching. A different front sight might or might not seem necessary. Whereas the S.&W. Combat .357 is rather promising as an "all-around revolver" in the pocket-possible class, the longer Colt merits consideration as an all-purpose gun that rides in a holster or part of the time in a target shot's carry-all.

Colt Single Action Army

Caliber: .357 Magnum, .38 and .44 Special, .45 Colt.
Weight: .45 caliber, 36 ounces in 4¾-inch, 37 in 5½, 39 in 7½. .38 caliber, 41 ounces in 5½-inch, 43 in 7½. Buntline has 12-inch barrel and weighs 43 ounces in .45.
Barrel: 4¾, 5½ and 7½ inches, 12 inches in Buntline. Special long barrels of the past went from 8 to 16 inches, and short barrels, without ejector rod, were 3½ and 4 inches.
Overall: 11½ inches with 5½-inch barrel, 18 inches in modern Buntline.
Sights: Fixed, non-adjustable. The early type of front sight, curving gently to the front and steeply to the back, is still standard on the regular gun. The modern Buntline front has been made in this shape and also as a near semicircle.
Stocks: Checked black rubber. Walnut at extra cost. The durable walnut stocks, less liable to chip or break from a fall on rock, or to warp in great heat, are common on old Peacemakers, Army issue or commercial.
Finish: Case-hardened frame; blued barrel, cylinder, trigger guard and backstrap. Nickel finish formerly offered.

The wind-seamed outdoorsman who rides the plains is only one of many who respect the Single Action Army Colt. It was dropped from 1946 to 1955, ironically enough, because too few thousands per year had been sold. Those guns last! They're right for horseback because they're so safe. If a shot fired from a double action or automatic makes your horse shy, your grab for the reins—or for more stabilizing leather! —may loose off another shot, into the horse as likely as not.

The S.A.A.—like its buddy the Bisley Model with higher, longer, more-curved grip—was famed for ruggedness. Unquestionably these guns have been in more rough spots afield than most other pistols. Yet they need intelligent treatment, for some parts are small and liable to break. Still, they generally keep on shooting until you get to a gunsmith. You may have to turn the cylinder by hand, but you seldom need to fire by whacking the hammer with a rock, which has been done. Half- and quarter-cock notches break at times; so wise users load only five chambers and set the hammer clear down on the empty one. If set *between* two neighboring cartridges, the cylinder can turn and bring a primer under the hammer nose. Unless the bolt is out of order the empty chamber under the fully-down hammer can hardly shift.

Few if any other revolvers were made for so many different rounds. In rimfire there were the .22, .32 and .44. Old Winchester catalogues list the ".44 Flat, Winchester and Colt," brought out about 1873 when the S.A.A. came out (the Bisley was an 1897 model) and in this rimfire caliber the Colt could be called "Frontier Six Shooter" along with .32-20, .38-40 and .44-40 sizes. All were rifle-and-revolver sizes popular in the early and later West because one beltful of identical rounds (not the High Velocity Winchesters in a revolver, of course) took care of both long and short gun. Model 1860 Henry and Model 1866 Win-

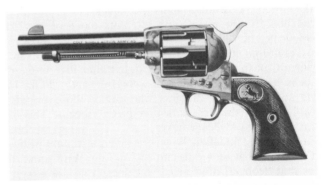

The Model 1873 Winchester .44-40 rifle and carbine's long hunting day is almost over, except in places too wild and remote for most of us to see; but the Colt Single Action Army, born at about the same time and once chambered for all the '73 Win cartridges, hangs on as serviceable and efficient. This one has the 5½-inch barrel.

chester rifles took this .44 Flat, also a .44 Pointed for longer range, though 200 grains of lead eased out by 26 to 28 grains of black powder scarcely made a high-speed load. Centerfire S.A. Colt calibers included the .32 and .38 S.&W., .32 and .38 long or short Colt, .32-.44 S.&W. target size, .41 long or short Colt. (There was also a wide-rimmed .41 carrying 20 grains black and 130 of pure lead, midway in length and loading between the 14-160 short and 21-200 long, made usually with narrower rims for the Army Special that preceded the Official Police, and for still earlier medium-frame guns like those swing-out cylinder .38s adopted by the Navy in 1888 and the Army in '92. Beg pardon for this gun-crank wandering.) Other calibers were .44 Russian, .44 Colt (for converted cap-and-ball guns too), and .450, .455 and .476 Eley. Late popular sizes were .32-20, .357 Magnum, .38 and .44 Special, .38-40, .44-40, .45 Auto and .45 Colt.

Guns with serial numbers below 160,000 were for black powder only, and those below 340,000 for pressures under 15,000 pounds per square inch—like Smith .44 Specials below 16,500. Treat all old guns considerately. I saw a Bisley Colt .45 chamber that had been burst by a sensible dose of handloaded smokeless and 250-grain lead bullet. When the round before the fatal one was fired, the latter's bullet shucked forward (or stayed put while the gun went back) and stuck out the front of the cylinder. This temporarily locked the gun. My friend pushed the lead back, but too far, and the reduced powder room ran up excessive pressure. It would have needed a very careful shooter to remove the round and inspect it before loading it in again. I don't believe I'd have done so, either.

The 4¾, 5½ and 7½-inch barrels went on both Army and Bisley guns. The latter came in target style for many years as a regular item, though S.A.A. target guns are rare, factory-made. Sights were adjustable, the top-strap flat, and barrels almost always 7½ inches long. Pocket guns in 3½ and 4-inch, without the ejector rod, were furnished in really old times.

The ten-year eclipse of single-action Colts boosted the price of second-hand specimens to astounding heights. It also resulted in attempts more or less to duplicate the oldtimer, the S.A.A., that is, for most of us preferred its grip and hang to those of the Bisley. Since Colt in reviving the gun didn't alter it to modern ideas and the other makers were free and willing to do so, you'll find shooters who prefer those brands. Still, there's the "conversation piece" idea—"This is just like the old Peacemaker that . . ." and so on: one can continue indefinitely in praising the thumb-buster Colts for what they did, and still can do. With some of us that "conversation piece" bit doesn't go down well. Let the gun do the talking. Still, any good American who loves a gun is on our side, and *that* is something for us hard-shells to remember. Those who are against us would legislate the pistol out of the hands of civilians; then the rifle and shotgun would have their turn.

Please don't think that this idea is fanciful; I wish it were!

The Bisley Colt is rarer than the Single Action Army. Many fewer were made, and they hadn't the almost natural hand-feel of the S.A.A. It is more like a double-action Colt or Smith without a grip adapter; that is, the hand rides high up behind the trigger guard. And the grip is definitely of saw-handle type. But it always had and held admirers. I like them both. I find the Army more natural to point, of course, and the Bisley more comfortable to shoot with heavy loads. But neither of these guns is at all a punisher, for the grips are wide and full at the top, a natural sort of Magna style. In firing, the Bisley grip doesn't tend to slide down in your hand as the Army grip does. Yet somehow I believe I'd take the Army for a run of rapid fire; I don't know why. As far as comfort goes, both are superb. Some prefer the long hammer spur of the Bisley, though both are easy to get at after you know them. There is one thing, though, that the un-accustomed must look out for; that is, to keep his thumb out of the path of the falling hammer. If too close, it can be blood-blistered promptly. This seldom happens more than once to the same person!

In his *Sixguns* Elmer Keith describes fully the technique of fanning a single action with the edge of the palm, also of slip-shooting, letting the hammer slip from the thumb instead of pressing the trigger. He tells too how hammers and triggers were adapted, the latter being sometimes put out of service entirely. Naturally a double-action revolver is the one for fast shooting, (and it takes plenty of practice, too, before real accuracy comes). But fanning and slip-shooting weren't only for emptying a gun fast. Fanning could be a life-saver in quick work close-up, where no aim is taken, and slip-shooting can be precision work.

The Buntline Special isn't the only Colt to have a super-long barrel. Special factory jobs are the despair or the delight of collectors. When I was a kid I saw some pretty little Colt Police Positive .32s or .38s in a Portland store. Probably some Maine trappers found good use for them on their lines, and a gloved hand could reach out and steady the barrel without being burned by the hot gas escaping from the cylinder-barrel joint. Such guns, the heavy Buntline included, can be fired one-handed, too. Since the rear sight is ahead of the hand—not almost behind it as on Lugers fitted with long barrels and the rear sight 'way back instead of in the more common position on the barrel —the weave of the sights isn't so terribly frustrating. The Buntline, too, is called a "conversation piece" but it doesn't deserve it; it could be too practical for any of that. The long barrel should develop some interesting velocities with slowburning Du Pont 4759 in sensible, safe handloads. With black powder, too, we could expect higher speeds than standard barrel lengths give. Many of us enjoy reloading for the Single Actions with that propellant, in spite of the extra work in cleaning the guns and the fired cases. Black powder gives

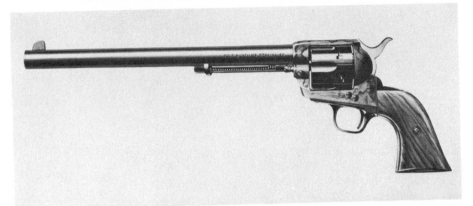

Colt S.A.A. Buntline, 12-inch barrel.

a much less sharp report than smokeless does, though recoil is heavier, if slower to arrive. With the Buntline's long barrel both noise and kick are reduced, and quite likely this gun is the pleasantest shooting, really powerful .45 now on the market.

The "Dope Bag" story in the July '58 *Rifleman* explains the derivation of this long gun's name. Edward Judson, a colorful oldtime showman, who wrote under the pen-name of Ned Buntline, helped popularize these special Colts, which had come out at least as early as 1888. In those years, and even as early as 1876, Colt had furnished a skeleton shoulder-stock on order. Now any such attachment on a pistol results in a "firearm" under the Federal Firearms Act, and the arm must be registered with the Alcohol and Tobacco Tax Division of the Treasury Department. This is expensive and bothersome, so much so that few law-abiding citizens even consider owning a "firearm." The same rule applies to .22 caliber rimfire rifles with barrels under 16 inches in length, and other rifles, by a revised ruling, with tubes under 16 inches.

Colt Government Model .45 Automatic

Caliber: .45 Automatic.
Weight: 39 ounces.
Barrel: 5 inches. (Longer custom barrels have been made for special uses.)
Overall: 8½ inches.
Sights: Fixed, except that rear sight can be driven back and forth for windage, glare-proofed, in modern production of square Patridge design. Today's front sight slants forward, "ramp-style," to catch the light and still keep the gun easy to draw.
Stocks: Checked "Coltwood" plastic on today's commercial models. At this writing the checked walnut stocks have not been restored to the automatic Colts, as they have been to the revolvers.
Finish: Blue or nickel.
Magazine capacity: 7.

An enthusiast could call this pistol the most useful weapon in the world. He'd have to plant numerous hedges around any such claim, such as its limitation to one person's use. It is for one fist, not for a squad, a regiment, an army, or a whole nation—if that monstrosity, streamlining, should ever finally come to pass. Since it is only a pistol, its power, fire capacity, accuracy and range are limited. But except in wartime, more men are killed by other men close-up and individually than from a distance and wholesale. For day-in, day-out, night-in, night-out (dark-street or lonely-dirt-road) individual or family protection, the pistol still stakes out a claim to be king of weapons.

What, then, does this pistol have that makes it outstanding, and what does it lack?

Power. Since the chunky, almost obsolete British Webley & Scott automatic using the effective blunt-nosed .455 bullet is a collector's item in our country, the Colt .45 is the deadliest auto-pistol generally available to us. We can sacrifice the penetration we don't need as concerns a human enemy, and add to shocking power, by handloading the .45 with semi-wadcutter cast lead bullets like those made and loaded by Western Cartridge for target use. First, we'd want to develop the load for our gun and prove it relentlessly, through hundreds of shots, for sure functioning. But the standard Service cartridge, using that round-nosed, full-jacketed bullet, has demonstrated times without number that it's enough. Or it is nearly always. Sometimes it has been inadequate when rather poorly placed, though as a rule any solid hit does all that's needed—even a hit in the arm or leg. The standard .45 Auto has nothing like the long, deep penetration of the .30 Luger or Mauser, .38 Auto, .357 or .44 Magnum, and it doesn't have the wounding and knock-down ability of large caliber hollow-point lead bullets at high or

Colt Government Model .45 Automatic.

even fair velocity. The factory-loaded .45 "long" Colt, though its solid 250 or 255 grain lead bullet is almost of pointed shape because of that narrow little flat up front, proves decidedly a better killer. Yet for almost any occasion the .45 Auto cartridge is enough.

Fire capacity of the 1911 Colt is considerable. Fully loaded, it holds two more rounds than a sixgun, and the 7-shot clips or magazines go in and out of the gun handily. Between the shots of a clipful there is no click of a thumb-cocked hammer, a sound much more easily located at fairly close quarters than the blast of firing, as some hunters who use the semi-automatic rifle or shotgun have found out. The clicks and clanks are swallowed up in the report. And for logistics, getting there with what's required, the .45 A.C.P. is a short, compact and light bigbore handgun cartridge, easy to carry in quantity.

But fire capacity depends on gun reliability, too, and any autoloader must have reliable ammunition, even a .22 rimfire rifle meant to digest obligingly the short, long and long-rifle rounds separately or mixed. A weak load can fail to blow the breechblock back far and fast enough to eject an empty and feed a fresh round, and a grossly overcharged handload can blow the magazine right out of an automatic pistol. A misfire halts the firing, and a second or third snap of the hammer—comparatively easy and non-disconcerting with a double-action Smith & Wesson or Walther, etc. —doesn't invariably fire that cartridge. You must take time out to haul back the slide for a new one. With a revolver you just go on to another chamber.

Still, a revolver can be locked by a primer that flows back into the firing pin hole, by a poorly crimped-in bullet that jumps out the front of its chamber, or by lead fusing. All these causes are rather uncommon, glory be. The latter happened only once in my experience. The gun was a pirate- or goon-rebuilt Colt Single Action Army .38 Special. It perked 100% with store-bought rounds, but semi-wadcutter handloaded bullets that were absolutely reliable in a well-cared-for Smith & Wesson fused at the Colt's barrel and cylinder joint, and it was "Cease firing!" right then and there.

In justice to the .45 Colt we can say that it has probably the most reliable of all auto-pistol systems, the locked-breech, short-recoil Browning. My own Colt .38s and .45s failed only with ancient and grossly defective ammunition, and hardly ever then. With even fairly fresh commercial stuff, or with good handloads, they never failed so far as I can remember.

The accuracy of individual .45s varies so widely that it's hard to believe they are all of the same design. We could be cheerful—and not plain foolish—and say that nearly every .45 Auto shoots as well as it needs to! Although the military jobs are not for sniping, in the ever-unpredictable business of war the .45s have made long shots, and sometimes obliged, too, when they had to, or else. But in trench or foxhole, in basement hallway or from behind a bush, a pistol can be life-saving quicker than a rifle, and reach the necessary greater distance faster than a knife or bayonet. Commercial .45s are generally better fitted and therefore more accurate than the gray-blue wartime production, and match guns, factory or custom, sometimes approach the unbelievable, for the long and carefully developed and improved .45 cartridge, including the best service grades, is highly accurate. Tests with barrels set into rifle-type bolt actions, and machine rest firing, proved that long ago, and today's best ammunition is even better.

The range, the reach-out of the .45 auto and its ammunition are longer than most of us can expect to use. The big, short, but still heavy bullet isn't meant to shoot flat but to hold its punch so well that it can do serious damage at rather great distances. For killing at long range, it isn't in the class of the Magnums, though it has smack that is lacking in the pin-prick .30 caliber pistol bullets of high velocity. The .38 Automatic, high-speed .38 Special, and 9 mm. Luger are more easily brought on target 'way out, but they are only medium calibers in killing power.

HISTORY

In the Spanish-American War of 1898 the .38 long Colt service cartridge seems to have been effective enough, but it was not effective against the Filipinos in the war that followed. They were savage men, or, if you prefer a different viewpoint, men who were fighting for such freedom and such a fatherland as they knew.

Our Army learned in the hard and tragic way that a bigger caliber was needed, at least in some kinds of in-fighting. There is more than one side to this question. Smaller calibers are easier to carry and to shoot accurately without so much training, but there are times in war, and in the wilderness too, when nothing would seem too big.

The 1905 Military and the new rimless .45 cartridge were commercially available. Therefore, they got plenty of amateur field testing as well as the grueling go-over the military gave them. The Colt won the 1906-07 trials, the Savage (now a collector's prize) coming in second. Three or four more years of weed-out led to the 1911 Colt's final adoption. It was much as we see it frequently today except that the present or 1911-A1 has the arched and checkered mainspring housing at the rear of the grip. This is an attempt to reach the natural-pointing slope of the slant-gripped Luger, a gun that was tried out, too, by our Government in small caliber and in .45. The A1 trigger is set farther back than the original; it's better for short or medium length forefingers. The frame behind it is beveled, and that helps, too.

The 1905 Colt, too rare today, has its points as an outdoorsman's pistol. In 1908 the hammer was given a cocking spur long enough to be much handier than the old rounded hammer-top, but not long enough to be a catch-all. In fairness, I must admit that none of the Colt autos were snaggers, at least in my experience.

Since it was sold so largely to outdoor men, the 1905 had as an extra a detachable holster-stock, Luger or Mauser fashion but better looking. Hitched on the rear of the butt, it made holding steadier for some shooters; the free hand could steady the stock or the firing hand. It was a super-short stock. It brought the muzzle blast close to the ears, but some fortunate people always seem to be able to ignore that. Note the popularity of short-barreled custom-made magnum rifles today; some of those barrels are down to the old minimum of 18 inches. A stocked pistol is now a "firearm" subject to special Federal tax, and in general that's a good thing.

Yes, the grip of the 1905 is like those of other early Colt autos, pretty straight down, not slanted like the 1911's handle; but it's not hopeless. Plenty of practice, dry or with live ammo, will—it really will—enable you to keep from dropping a snapshot a yard low at 50 feet! Some of us like these old Colts enough to learn about them. The 1905 is smoother in the pocket or at the top of the holster than the 1911 is; it's a somewhat handier piece of duffle.

Since it was made for the 200 grain bullet load with velocity of about 900 f. s., it should be handloaded instead of fired with rounds of the modern 230 grain stuff. This is an opinion that stems from an affection for the smooth-lined pioneer Colts in .38 and .45 Auto. Since we can expect an overweight pistol bullet to shoot high at short ranges, a cast-lead bullet of about 200 grains is right for the 1905. And let's work up the powder charge slowly. A .45 slug makes a big hole, anyway. Does it need supersonic speed to be deadly?

1911 Evaluation

So many outdoorsmen and military men have counted the .45 1911 as their first favorite that it deserves careful consideration. We've discussed its reliability, power, accuracy and so on. What is it like to shoot?

Since it's a bigbore and primarily for killing, not for superb long-range accuracy like the .44 Special, it has some recoil and blast. So does the .44, even with the rather mild factory loads, and so do other modern bigbores worth consideration. But in beginning to shoot we fire only a few rounds. After a gunful or two, your hand may be trembling from the peculiar recoil of the .45 Auto: the slide comes slamming back; the gun may seem at first to come apart in your hand. But how many shots would you fire during a day in woods or mountains or on the plains, or in a month's trip in those lovely longed-for places? Not many, except in plinking. The recoil isn't painful.

But the bite of the hammer is, when and if you get it. The horn at the top of the grip safety is made rather long, now, to prevent the bite, and the hammer spur isn't excessively long. The web of my right hand took

some chewing when I began to shoot the .45, but I changed my grip and avoided that trouble. It wasn't difficult.

Muzzle blast of the .45 1911 is something else; it seems sharper than that of a fairly heavily charged bigbore sixgun, and many times sharper than the thudding boom of black powder. There are ear-plugs available; and if you value your hearing, it's smart to use them with any handgun above .22 rimfire or .32 S.&W. long. The *Colt Conversion Unit* gives you .22 rimfire practice with almost the same gun. Only slide, barrel, recoil parts, sights, magazine, etc., are different. You use the same grip and the same trigger, the parts that count so much in your familiarity with a pistol. And then of course there are .45 handloads under full power, even the useful squibs that don't operate the action but convert the auto into a repeater and allow you to toss your empty brass into a box instead of hunting for it.

Yes, the .45 is hard to learn to shoot; most people call it more difficult than a revolver of similar caliber. But some of us do better with its flat grip than with the rounded handle of a sixgun—less chance for the gun to turn in the hand, under heavy recoil. The standard auto trigger pull is long and creepy, compared to that of even a standard, non-target model of first-class revolver. Still, it isn't hopeless, except maybe in the most exacting target competition, where you'd want a match grade .45.

That flat grip and the absence of a big, bulging cylinder make the .45 compact; it is one of the best consequential-caliber pistols to pack in a shoulder holster, out of the way in brush or even aboard a canoe, but handy to get at when you need it. It rides well in a belt holster, too.

After the day is over, supper cooked and eaten, you will find in the short evening's leisure before you hit the sack or the blankets, that one barrel is sooner cleaned than seven of them—counting a sixgun's chambers. (Fine argument, that one! You and I know that six well-burnished chambers are as easy and almost as quick to clean as one good barrel, and the .45 fouled with jacketed bullets can be a bit obstinate.) If the .45 has fallen into the drink you can easily strip it for drying and oiling without need of a rackful of screwdrivers and drifts.

The caliber is well established even among us civilians. You can generally buy the ammo, even in places where your particular choice among a half dozen other splendid huskies just might not be on the shelves—such hulls as .38-40, .44-40, .44 Special or Magnum, .45 "long" Colt or .357. But it doesn't equal the .22 rimfire or even the .38 Special in ready availability.

The Government Model .45 does well as a wilderness gun if you like and learn how to use an automatic. And with the Single Action Army it divides the honor of being our Country's most history-making pistol since modern times brought standardization of arms and ammunition.

Colt Super .38 Automatic

Caliber: .38 Super Automatic. Most of these Colts handle also the lower velocity .38 as made (until perhaps recently) for early model Colt autos.
Weight: 39 ounces.
Barrel: 5 inches.
Overall: 8½ inches.
Sights: Same as on Government Model .45, but adjusted for the .38 cartridge.
Stocks: Checked "Coltwood" plastic. Walnut discontinued at least at this writing.
Finish: Blue or nickel.
Magazine capacity: 9.

The .38 Colt Automatic has been an outdoorsman's gun from the start. Around 1900 the first model came out, the first of all Colt auto-pistols available commercially. Even then a .38 caliber was a little too late for the Army's most serious consideration. But this medium caliber became popular with wilderness wanderers from desert to forest, and has remained so, to a considerable degree, through half a dozen Colt models.* The guns were flat-shooting, more than reasonably accurate until the slides wore loose (which oiling could have postponed), gave deep penetration, and were as reliable in functioning as the Mauser and Luger had been uncertain. The ammunition cost a lot but it was compact and light. Recoil was moderate and the report of the old 1100 f. s. velocity load from a 6-inch barrel was not unpleasantly sharp. The 4½-inch *Pocket Model* was noisy, and its bullet velocity was quoted at 1070 f. s.—not enough different to matter, for you might get that much variation in one boxful of cartridges fired on the same day.

Most of the old .38s are reliable even today, used with factory or hand-loaded cartridges in their velocity class. Super rounds are liable to jam these guns, blow out the magazines, even crack the slides. The 6-inch *Military* is easier to shoot than the compact Pocket,

*The early Sporting (7-shot magazine) and Military (8-shot) with 6-inch barrels, and the 4½-inch (7-shot) Pocket; the more modern 5-inch Super and recently discontinued Super Match, and the 4¼-inch Commander (all with 9-shot mags) for today's powerful Super .38 Auto loads.

which like the very old *Sporting* has a short grip, but all of them have been to far places. Modern Colts usually do well with the old light loads and are practically as effective with them. Soft and hollow-point bullets have gone with the tide of time. The latter were too thickly jacketed at the nose to expand as long-exposed soft points usually did. A handloader could use 116 grain Norma 9 mm. Luger soft points, or cast lead bullets like the Ideal 125 grain 360271, or probably the 115 grain 360345 (which I never tried), both semi-wadcutters with taper and flat-nosed point above a square bearing shoulder. The former did splendidly in my Military in both full and gallery charges. The gallery load was too weak to operate the action; it wasn't for timed or rapid fire. The standard .38 Auto Ideal 125 grain 358242 round-nosed bullet could be hollow-pointed. Perhaps because of the nice fit of the 360271 in my barrel's throat there was no trouble from leading, no wish for a copper gas-check cup on that bullet's base—which isn't heeled down to receive one, anyway. At velocities much over 1100 f. s. it might have been needed, though I doubt it, in this combination.

The report of the Super loads from the 5-inch barrel is sharp enough to disturb many of us during target sessions. The gun could qualify as "centerfire," like the revolvers generally used in that class; its recoil is lighter than the .45's, and self-loading action helps in timed and rapid fire if you like the fit, trigger pull, balance and sights of the gun. Some Super .38s have been customed over to .38 Special, using the mild midrange wadcutter cartridge with bullet nose flush with the case-mouth. There have been rumors of factory production, and now they're here.

Although the ten-shot Super .38 penetrates as far as next pay-day and its juicy cartridges are certainly compact, most woodsmen who want a powerful automatic probably get a .45 instead. It is too rough only for really small game, on which the .38 can fail miserably, and it has far more knock-down power if "deer-meat" is wanted. At practical pistol ranges, this bigbore shoots flat enough for most of us. This doesn't mean that the man or woman skilled in woodcraft, stalking and marksmanship needs something bigger than a .38 Auto. Quite often any centerfire cartridge seems to *some* of them excessive in power for their kind of shooting—or they'll say so! A person must go far to meet any large, dangerous American animal unless he blunders into a pasture or barnyard where a bull enjoys strong proprietary interest. If the gritty little squirrel or woodchuck were large enough to fight back, we'd be bored less frequently with tales of squirtgun enthusiasts who leave unrecorded cripples along the trail. The really expert can kill almost anything with a .22, but most of them pack something bigger, from choice.

Super .38 Colt Auto.

A 7½-inch barreled Great Western .44 Special.

Great Western Frontier Sixshooter

Caliber: Rimfire, .22 long-rifle; centerfire, .357 Magnum or "Atomic," .38 and .44 Special, .44 Magnum, .45 Colt.

Weight: 40 ounces in 5½-inch barreled .22 caliber.

Barrel: 4¾, 5½ and 7½ inches. Deputy model has 4-inch barrel, and Buntline Special 12½-inch. Other lengths have been furnished.

Overall: 11⅛ inches in 5½-inch barrel.

Sights: Fixed, original Colt type except that front sight is made high so that it can be filed down to add the elevation the shooter wants. Deputy has ramp-type fixed front sight, rear sight adjustable for windage and elevation. Adjustable target sights can be fitted at extra charge on fixed-sight models.

Stocks: Frontier model has imitation stag designed to resist warpage from heat or exposure. Genuine stag, pearl, or ivory at extra cost. Deputy has smooth walnut stocks as standard.

Finish: Blue. Case-hardened frame at extra cost, but standard on .44 Magnum. Polished but unblued guns may be sent out for plating if the customer so desires.

It was announced in February of 1958 that exclusive distribution of Great Western guns had gone to Stoeger Arms Corporation, 45-18 Court Square, Long Island City 1, New York. This famous old jobbing and retailing firm evidently has confidence in the new line of Great Western arms. Some years ago their general quality and performance were poor. That is not true of recent production. G.W.s are American-made; there seems to have been a rumor that they aren't.

We classify the Great Western Frontier as a work gun, an outdoorsman's revolver, because in regular issue it has the fixed sights of Colt Single Action Army type. The .357 and .44 Magnum Rugers are target-sighted. They have gone into the target guns chapter, even though you and I and most certainly Uncle Jim over at Beaver Meadow know that adjustable sights belong on any outdoor handgun we hope to hit with. They have gone on—automatically, by special design, or by tinkering—just about every model of American-made revolver, automatic, or single-shot pistol carried afield by a person who valued accurate shooting. In far and wild places they have served well, and few of them have had sighting equipment too "delicate" to stand up under reasonably careful use. Some target sights, and not only oldtimers, don't hold their

adjustments reliably under the jolt of lots of shooting. Look at them now and then.

If the Deputy G. W., standard with 4-inch barrel, were a little longer it could have gone into the target guns chapter. Some use it as a pocket revolver! It comes in .22 long-rifle, .357 Magnum, and .38 Special, at this writing. With an index in the back of this book we needn't stew over chapter classifications, anyway.

That .357 Atomic Great Western caliber perhaps needs explanation. It's a special, non-factory load in standard .357 Magnum brass. The charge is 16 grains of Hercules No. 2400 rifle powder (often handloaded

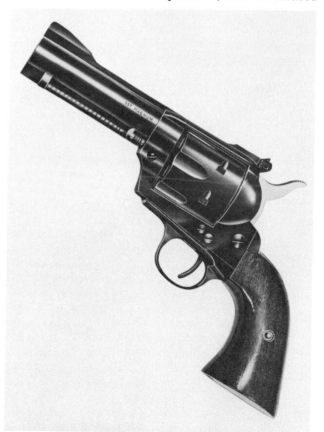

Great Western "Deputy," 4-inch barrel, adjustable target-type sights.

in big sixgun cartridges) and the standard 158 grain lead bullet. A long barrel is said to give about 1600 f.s. velocity. No responsibility for any handload listed in this book is assumed by the publishers or the authors. There are too many variables involved. *Any* experienced handloader recommending a charge nearly always would like to add the proviso, "when I'm right at your elbow, watching everything you do." About the only exception is during the interchange of data among friends, when each one knows and respects the others' sense and ability.

Prices of Great Western revolvers vary a good deal, according to extra features and to calibers, too. An unusual offering is the "Do-it-yourself Kit" in all calibers but the .44 Magnum. It saves twenty dollars, as of today, but it isn't for amateurs. The machine operations are done, and instructions come with the kit, but the de-burring, fitting, polishing and finishing are for the buyer to do or have done. This calls for gunsmithing skill. The parts come in a neat case, which you can exhibit later to show where you started.

This kit reminds me (skip this paragraph if you like) of some of my bug-eyed, wistful reading as a ten-year-old. A two-cent stamped request had brought a Colt catalogue, one of those 3x5 booklets that a collector might drool over today. It showed the 1905 .45 auto and its shoulder stock, the Bisley and the Bisley Target, and the great old line-up of cartridges, including the squatty .450, .455 and .476 Eley. There were gun parts, too, and I thought of buying them

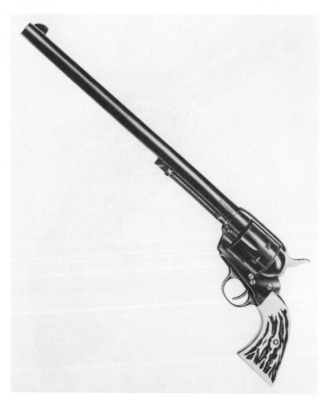

The 12-inch barreled Great Western Buntline .357 Magnum. These barrels have been listed also as 12½-inch.

piece by piece with my spending allowance of ten or fifteen cents a week. Then I'd put 'em together and have a gun! Just a dream; I couldn't have mended a mouse-trap then; and even now I'm no candidate for the G. W. kit. I had the wish and the anticipation, and still have them—most thankfully.

Unlike the Colt Single Action, the Great Western hasn't stood still. Improvements have brought an efficient, modernized single-action revolver. The stiff cocking of early G.W.s is eliminated in current models. The mainspring is still flat, as we'd expect in this fairly close copy of the Colt; but cocking is now softer than with the first Great Western models. For durability, the hand, cylinder-bolt and trigger have been made of shock-resistant beryllium copper. No aluminum-alloy parts are used as in some Rugers, and the hammer is of No. 6150 chrome vanadium steel. Anticipating the demands of handloaders who want guns that will stand the utmost in permissible pressures (and some that aren't permissible), the company uses No. 4140 chrome molybdenum steel— 185,000 pounds per square-inch strength—in cylinders of .357, .38 and larger calibers. In good Colt style, the barrel breech extends only a short distance from the frame and is less likely to be bulged by an over-size, over-powered bullet than a longer and thinner barrel projection. Not all handloaders stick to the .001-inch over rifling groove diameter that's about maximum for heavy charges.

Some G. W. parts are interchangeable with the Colt's, or practically so. Hammer, trigger and bolt screw are different, and the firing pin is a separate part, mounted in the breech of the frame and struck by the falling hammer. It isn't a hammer nose, in Colt fashion. After a session on the range, many Colt Single Action Army or Bisley users habitually check screws for loosening, but there is less of this in the new G. W. gun. Probably all Colt shooters who take up the G. W. will continue the habit of loading only five cartridges, leaving an empty chamber under the fully lowered hammer. The strongly made hammer and trigger of the G. W. should practically eliminate the breaking of parts that plagued the old Colt; and the gun should, apparently, be safe to carry at quarter-cock with a live round in line with the hammer. However, this gun has no steel hammer block of the modern Smith & Wesson or Colt double-action type, to rise between hammer and cartridge when the hammer is lowered—or even when it slips from the thumb and the trigger is not held back. For absolute safety, it might be sensible to continue the five-round cylinder loading of any Colt-type single action. A revolver is much more liable to falls and knocks than a rifle is. A Winchester or Marlin exposed hammer, for example, is hardly ever struck accidentally. Even if it is, the parts are big and the half-cock notches strong enough to take almost anything.

The G. W. hammer spur seems especially long and rakish, easy to cock with a thumb as you pull the

Great Western .38 Special, 4¾-inch barrel.

Smith & Wesson Military and Police

Caliber: .38 Special standard or reduced velocity. Formerly made for standard velocity .32-20 Winchester rifle cartridges also, and sometimes called the "Winchester model."

Weight: 30½ ounces in 4-inch barrel; 18 ounces in 2-inch Airweight when fitted with round butt.

Barrel: 2, 4, 5 and 6 inches. Long ago 6½-inch barrels were made. Can we expect an 8⅜ with rib, as added to the M.&P. Target line in 1959?

Overall: 9¼ inches in 4-inch barrel, square butt type; ⅜ inch shorter with rounded butt.

Sights: 1/10-inch serrated ramp front, square notch rear. The semicircular "service-type" front is going out on this medium frame Smith, and on the small frames, too.

Stocks: Checked walnut Magna, round or square butt.

Finish: Blue or nickel.

gun down after recoil. For some shooters with large hands, it may be too long, reaching too far down over the back-strap. It could be filed back, just as some Colt .45 and Super .38 spurs have been for a different reason, i.e., because they bit the web of the hand when they were shoved back, lightning-fast, by the autoloader's recoiling slide.

The Great Western Arms Company is ambitious and progressive. It's perfectly possible that they will build a single action that's of better quality than present or past Colts, as well as of more durable modern design. Some would even say, without qualification, that they now make the best.

Furthermore, they seem unusually willing to undertake special work. Various calibers, barrel lengths and sighting equipments have been put on in addition to those catalogued. Of course they do apply special ornamentation to their guns to please individuals, but that is even less unusual.

They seem anxious to please the customer who isn't satisfied with streamlined offerings. You may have heard the story of the 4-inch barreled Colt Police Positives in .22 rimfire caliber, not the target-sighted Police Positive Target, which for years came standard in .22 and .32—four choices: .22 long-rifle and W.R.F., .32 long Colt and S.&W. long. These were solid-sighted police service guns. Only one order of these 4-inchers was made, according to good authority, and it was sold fast. Then no more came, in spite of requests.

There is a third general grade of firearm, in addition to standard production and the individualized custom job. It's the semi-custom. G. W.'s 4-inch Deputy is a good example. It is a standard revolver but with the custom features of a full-length barrel-and-topstrap rib, target sights, and smooth, un-checkered walnut stock. The rib is for-sure special, and usually you see it only on a straight custom gun. It is reasonable to expect almost anything that's progressive or new, if this company keeps up its second-wind start. It should, following its rather severe raking-over in print, and very likely too by correspondence and word-of-mouth. Customers were doing exactly what they should have done, improving the quality of U. S. production.

Like the Colt Official Police, formerly the Colt Army Special, this Smith & Wesson has been a standard part of police equipment since calibers such as the .32 S.&W. long and .38 S.&W. short became generally regarded as too light for service use. They are still standard except in departments that go to some heavier caliber. Throughout the years—generations, in fact—they have stood up well on the job. After all, they started as Army, Navy and Marine models for the .38 long, and they saw at times even more exacting service than the average policeman is likely to experience—the extremes of cold, heat, desert dust, snow and ice storms, where men lived as well as they could in the outdoors, in tents pitched wherever or whenever they could be. On such active service, barracks and ship's quarters are often far away, but the policeman has his station to return to when his tour of duty ends. However, the rigors of police work can be severe, like those of the professional or the grab-the-chance outdoorsman. All these classes of shooters have used and liked the sturdy, medium-size .38s. They are big enough to have large, long-wearing working parts; no one could call them dainty.

Smith & Wesson do not recommend the Military & Police for high velocity .38 Specials, and they are wise. There's no question of the guns' strength to stand the heaviest factory charges, but light and medium-weight .38 Specials are likely to develop a chattering of the cylinder after many of these rounds

Smith & Wesson Military & Police, square butt, 4-inch barrel.

have gone through them. I once used a boxful of these loads, early Winchester Superspeeds, in an M.&P. I had in the early 1930s. It wasn't a smart thing to do, but that didn't stop me! They were loaded with the old flat-point 158 grain Colt Special bullet, a better killer than the round-nosed S.&W. variety. But this form of .38 Special factory bullet has gone down the drain. Too few people seemed to know about it and ask for it. However, those 50 rounds of Superspeeds did no harm to my gun, as far as I could see.

The Super-Police type of 200 grain blunt-nosed .38 Special apparently isn't forbidden for use in the M.&P. revolver, since it's a relatively low-pressure load. I doubt that it should be used freely in these medium-weight guns. In featherweight .38 Specials of any make, it would be a beaut! Those who love recoil would adore it. Against criminals it has built a good reputation for stopping power, nearly equaling the .41 long in this respect. In fixed-sight .38s about all you can do with the Super-Police at short ranges is to underhold; it shoots higher than 158 grain stuff.

S.&W. guns in this caliber have standardized barrel groove diameters of .356-.357 inch; Colts, .353-.355. In most other calibers, too, Smiths have larger diameters than Colts normally do, and always there are individual differences, as we'd expect. Handloaders who want the best accuracy, or wish to use the heaviest charges safely, should measure their barrels, micrometering a lead slug driven through them, and in sizing bullets keep within the .001 inch maximum tolerance. But factory loads are satisfactory in either make of gun, as far as bullet diameters go.

Choice between the two makes of revolvers depends, sensibly, on which grip, hammer and trigger action (including double-action pull if you plan to learn that more than useful technique), weight, balance and other practical considerations suit you the better. As a rule the S.&W. had the finer outside finish, and until lately it usually cost more than the Colt gun. The latter runs a few ounces heavier, built on a .41, not a .38, size of frame. Military models in more recent times were not meant to be finished as glossily as commercials.

Probably the two makes are about equal in resisting wear, or the abuse which so many good guns get, but don't deserve. The Smith cylinder is locked at front and rear, the Colt only at the rear; yet if you hold the trigger back, the cylinder of a somewhat worn Smith usually can be turned slightly, while the Colt's seldom can, for the "hand" that revolves it pushes up hard on the cylinder ratchet. If you think much of your Colt, however, it's best to take time to draw the cylinder thumb-piece or latch back as you close the gun. This doesn't seem necessary with the S.&W. On neither one, should the cylinder be slammed shut. This may look smart, but it isn't. An old Colt may not line up its chambers as you cock the hammer, but when you pull the trigger it does. And see that it does, if you think of buying it. Either

or any kind of revolver can shave its bullets from poor adjustment. This is bad for accuracy and for the disposition of bystanders. It happens that I have never experienced it with either of these two competitive models, but I've had it with others. I was standing offside, it was true, but as I thought, far enough to the rear. Still, the splatter came back and hit me. If one of those lead shavings should strike an eye, the results could be most serious. Stand way back, for they don't all splash out to the side. I was actually about four feet to the rear of the gun.

The square Patridge sights we have today are a big improvement over the rounded notch rear and rounded top front of the past. Correctly speaking, a Patridge design front has a straight up-and-down rear face, not a slanted ramp. With the new ramp front it's easier to get a clear sight picture than with the old half-moon type.

Choice of barrel length depends on the kind of use that's expected. The 2-inch is a pocket or hide-away holster length, and very handy for a soldier's foxhole gun, his personal weapon. The 4-inch is a pocket favorite, too, as well as a holster length, not too long for easy carrying almost anywhere, walking, or riding a car seat. For a one and only revolver the 5-inch is good, noticeably less noisy than the 4, and quiet compared to the blasting 2-inch. It gives good sight radius, fits a fairly short holster, and as a rule develops slightly higher velocity. But even with the 4-inch you get a pretty steady-holding gun. A few of us might find the 6-inch a little unsteady, or apparently so, on first trial, for these Smith barrels are lighter than those on Colt opposite numbers. People with middle-aged or older vision sometimes turn in a better performance with a 4-inch than with a 6-inch, though more care is needed in aligning sights so close together.

In this chapter we have had the outdoorsman pretty steadily in mind, rightly or not. His choice generally would be the 6-inch, which is long enough for good aiming, balance out front, and ballistics, but not too long. My first Military & Police was a 6-inch. By mistake it came with the rounded instead of the square butt. It was such a beautiful gun, though, that I couldn't bear to send it back for exchange, and I kept it a long time. After all, the grip was long enough for my rather small hand, for I didn't use an adapter to fill that unfortunate space up top and just behind the trigger guard. I'd never heard of an adapter and at that time they weren't commonly made. I carried that .38 very often under a heavy winter mackinaw, and at least the round butt did reduce the bulge.

It is too bad that the .32-20 revolver went out of production so long ago—well before World War II. That was a light and comfortable-shooting magnum, of small bore, it's true, but the best of all standard .30 or .32 caliber handguns for small game. Even with standard factory loads it shot flat and fast, and the report from a 6-inch barrel wasn't unbearable.

This Smith and the Army Special Colt will take fairly heavy .32-20 handloads, though not the stuff that can be safely crowded into the much bigger cylinder of the single-action Colt. Recoil of standard loads is light but quick, and the small-game-killing power of the flat-nosed but fast bullet is competent.

The .38 Special recoil in one of the older Smiths has been called downright uncomfortable by a good many seasoned shooters, but the present Magna stocks, wide at the top, take most of the punishment instead of passing it to the web of the hand. We refer to target shooting, when many shots are fired in a session. For twenty rounds or so my .44 Military with the old thin-topped stocks, loaded with charges reduced but still much heavier than .32-20, is no bother. Some like these old stocks because the lines flow nicely into the flat plane of the frame. Some find the Magna stocks a bit too full on top for their shooting. They get better trigger reach with some of the walnut thinned away. All these considerations are important, even good lines and good looks. We choose our guns for our pleasure.

Smith & Wesson Highway Patrolman

Caliber: .357 Magnum. Also takes .38 short and long Colt and .38 Special.
Weight: 41¾ ounces in 4-inch barrel, 44 ounces in 6-inch.
Barrel: 4 and 6 inches.
Overall: 11¼ inches in 6-inch barrel.
Sights: ⅛-inch Baughman Quick Draw front on plain ramp; S.&W. micrometer rear sight which clicks off windage and elevation adjustments as you make them.
Stocks: Checked walnut, Magna. Target stocks, which fill the upper part of the space behind the trigger guard, are available at extra cost.
Finish: S.&W. Satin Blue. Anti-glare sandblast stippling on barrel top and frame edging.

This is the moderate-priced or service job in a heavy-frame S.&W. .357 Magnum. When it came out it was slightly heavier than the original and more expensive .357 Magnum model, but now in equal barrel lengths the guns weigh the same, or near it. The original .357 ribbed barrel was heavy enough for the cartridge. A motorcycle patrolman carrying one of these revolvers in either model wants no more weight in his holster. Actually he doesn't need it for shooting unless he chooses a heavier caliber, like the .44 Magnum.

Grooved tangs and trigger (both tangs show, when the standard stocks are used) are target aids, and just as useful to the outdoorsman. Most of our current American-made pistols now have the grooved trigger. The grooved tangs, or front and back straps of the grip, go back to the days when Smith & Wesson crowed over them in comparing them with the cross-hatched or checkered straps of old Colt target models. S.&W. referred to "the file-like action on the hand," and the implication as to guilt was clear enough! A checkered back-strap can do it when you shoot heavy loads.

S.&W. Highway Patrolman .357 Magnum, 4-inch barrel. Recessed chambers enclose the case-heads.

In price, the Patrolman is in close competition with the Ruger Blackhawk .357 Mag. Most police officers would choose, I think, the double-action Smith for its much faster ejection and replacement of fired cartridges. If they had mastered even the elementals of the art of fast, effective double-action shooting, there would be even less doubt.

However, there are other things to ponder, like the feel of the gun in the hand. The Ruger, patterned after the Colt Single Action Army, though modernized and streamlined for low-price-tag production, has a grip and pointing feel that many prefer to those of a big double action. A grip adapter or Target-style stocks in effect, bring the trigger of the double action up where it belongs for straight-out extension of the trigger finger when the hammer is cocked. But this shortens the grip. Some people whose job just might include gun-fighting dislike a short grip, because it permits an assailant to wrench the gun away easily. Naturally no unhandcuffed crook cares for intimate closeups, in theory. But actual events can be different. This objection to the double action's adapter may sound small. I think it is, but it should be mentioned.

To many of us outdoorsmen, the Highway Patrolman has been a boon from sweet Lady Luck in a good mood. We wanted an S.&W. .357 of good weight but read the price story of the standard and still rather original Magnum. "Bright blue" or nickel is the finish of the old pioneer and the Combat .357s, but the Highway boy comes in the less expensive, more easily applied "Satin Blue," and that is typical of the small details that make the big dollar difference. The Highway Patrolman is a fine gun, one to give pride and satisfaction to owners and users. If we go to a supermarket instead of a top-flight delicatessen we still can buy nourishment, can't we?

For the outdoorsman who likes the caliber and the type of gun, the Patrolman in 6-inch barrel length rides handily in a holster and can be relied on to do its part of a good job when it is hauled out of the leather. Forty-four ounces, plus the moderate heft of six .357 cartridges, make a belt holster gun heavy for many of us. But there's the shoulder holster, which with reasonably wide shoulder strap can ease the burden. If you live in a state where the ordinary civilian can legally carry a handgun only in plain sight—as I do—get the hitching strap long enough to reach back comfortably around your heaviest winter coat. You'll want the gun along on most outdoor holidays you get. It's plain suffocating to wheeze up a slippery hillside with your chest strapped tight.

In 6-inch barrel this gun qualifies for target use, shooting sweetly with .38 Special rounds as it's in the heavy class—too tiring for some of us. If your club stages a long-range match, over 50 yards, you may want high velocity Specials or even Magnum rounds, though most of the oldtime long-shooting records went to .38 and .44 Specials of what we'd call today standard velocity, or near it. The chamber-filling Magnum case may not be the best .38 (.357 inch bullet) case in the world for handloading squib loads meant to puncture 25 or 50 foot Standard American pistol targets. But it still has a wide range of practical use for those of us who load our own ammunition. Some object to using any too-short case, but it's always been done, and modern primers and powders give only small and slow erosion in modern steel cylinders. *Usually* a full-length case is one of the many factors that make for accuracy. A lot of us think that if we're going to get a heavy .38 revolver for all-round use, it might as well be a .357. Then, if ever we want to use Magnum rounds, we can. It's true that in heavy-cylindered guns the .38 Special can be handloaded to right brisk velocities with permissible, entirely safe pressures.

Smith & Wesson .38-.44 Heavy Duty

Caliber: .38 Special, including high speed rounds. Also .38 short and long Colt.
Weight: 40 ounces in 5-inch barrel.
Barrel: 4, 5 and 6½ inches.
Overall: 10⅜ inches in 5-inch barrel.
Sights: Fixed, 1/10-inch service-type front, semicircular, not ramped; square notch rear sight.
Stocks: Checked walnut, Magna.
Finish: Blue or nickel.

At this writing the Heavy Duty .38 costs just five dollars less than the Highway Patrolman .357 with adjustable sights. It has been changed little since it came out in 1930 in 5-inch length. The present model has the new type hammer with deeply curved spur. When it first was known and used, shooters were enthusiastic about this big revolver's lack of recoil, even with the high-velocity factory rounds that came out for it. They still can gloat over this dispensation, though with the passage of time mighty few could be found now to say that it seems to make less noise than a medium-frame .38 Special of similar barrel length!

The 4-inch model I had was sharp-sounding

S.&W. .38-44 Heavy Duty, 5-inch barrel. Much like the .44 Special except for its lower front sight.

enough even with standard loads, as .38 Special guns of that length naturally are; but at least it was no 2-inch howitzer. In pocket carry it gave me a low-degree slew to the right, and for me it just wasn't a hideaway gun. It could be, in a shoulder holster. The recoil was light, and the big, heavy cylinder made steady holding easier than any 4-, 5- or 6-inch medium-weight .38 Special had ever done. It was the only length available then in the Smoky Mountains, right after World War II. If I were getting one to-day, it would be the 6½-inch. Except for the lack of adjustable sights, which could be customed on, it would be a swell outdoorsman's gun, within the power limitations of .38 Special. Many experienced shooters say that's far enough to go in a .38 because that comparatively mild caliber is much easier to master than any magnum or big bore. They have a point. For small game a properly loaded Special is enough. Proper loading could run from a round-ball, 1½- or 2-grain powder charge squiffum for bullfrogs to a full-weight flat or hollow-pointed bullet at good velocity.

But the name "Heavy Duty" suggests police work, and the gun is rugged enough to stand up to it—with the care that they all need. With metal-piercing bullets, the .38 Special does a fair job on car bodies, though not to compare with the performance of a .357 or a .44 Magnum. The gun is so heavy that few officers would care to tote it afoot. In a car or on a motorcycle it would be different. Yet the .38-.44 is so easy to shoot with useful accuracy that some would gladly carry it on any assignment—unless more power were absolutely needed. It has its place as a house pistol, too. For most people with really small hands, hands that do most of the housework, a smaller-framed revolver, or an automatic if it's wanted, would be better. With them the reach to the trigger would be shorter, easier and more natural. An exception would be the .38 Super auto, and the .45, especially if the big-boy had one of the original style of triggers, not shortened as on the 1911-A1. Two-handed, what a gun the Heavy Duty is! Its weight settles it into steadiness.

Smith & Wesson 1950 .44 Military

Caliber: .44 S.&W. Special. Also shoots the shorter .44 S.&W.
Russian, no longer loaded by our factories.
Weight: 39½ ounces in 6½-inch barrel.
Barrel: 4, 5 and 6½ inches.
Overall: 11¾ inches in 6½-inch barrel. So listed.
Sights: Same rounded, flat-topped front as on Heavy Duty .38,
but higher for the heavier caliber; square notch Partridge-
type rear sight.
Stocks: Checked walnut, Magna.
Finish: Blue or nickel.

S.&W. New Century or Triple Lock, which introduced the
.44 Special cartridge. Third lock shows at front of the swung-
out crane.

The present .44 Military got its start with the still
famous New Century or Triple Lock of 1907. Generally speaking, there are six main variants. These are
the Triple Lock, the 1914 British Service .455 Mark II
of World War I, the 1917 U. S. Service, the post-war
gun, the 1926 model, and the present 1950. We are
counting big-bore, fixed-sight revolvers, not .38s and
.357s and target models. The family has taken some
large calibers: .44 Special, .450 Eley, .455 Eley or
Mark II Service, and .45 "long" Colt. Apparently some
were made for the .38-40, .44-40, and .455 Colt or
Canadian, the last having a longer case than the Mark
II's, and, by the way, chambering neatly in S.&W.
1917s made for the .45 Auto Colt cartridges. The
Winchester commercial .455 Colt carried a soft lead
265 grain bullet (same weight but less pointed than
the usual American-made Mark II) ahead of 17 grains
black powder or its weak equivalent in smokeless.
Comparatively low power allowed the lead to be sized
down safely in the '17's barrel of smaller bore and
groove diameter. This load shot high in the .45 because
of its heavy bullet—heavy in almost any modern pistol.

The Triple Lock has the usual S.&W. front and rear
locking of the ejector rod, and a third lock where the
cylinder crane and under-barrel lug meet when the
gun is closed. This heavy, strong lug or build-up en-
cases the side of the ejector rod when the cylinder
goes home. It may not actually stiffen the assembly—
for that would require watchlike fitting, which this
old Smith misses by something less than a terrier hair
—but it protects the ejector rod from being bent, and
adds weight where most of us like it, out front.

At midnight of August 4, 1914, when "the lights
were going out all over Europe," England declared
war on Germany. To what we'd call the more democratic, the freer part of the world, that was a tremendous relief even though England was an ill-armed nation. Except for her superb navy (our own bulwark for
nearly three years to come, which we should remember when sacrifices for national preparedness arise!)
and her tiny but marksmanship-trained army, she was
unprepared. To supplement the Webleys she called on
us for .455 revolvers. Then the ejector rod housing
and third cylinder lock were dropped to ease production, though some Triple Locks did come out much
later, as Elmer Keith points out in *Sixguns* (page 40).
There was some question, too, about the clogging of
the housing with mud in trench service. Maybe you
remember having seen Bruce Bairnsfather's cartoon

depicting some of the minor discomforts of that war.

After the Armistice the Military was made much in
the 1914 British fashion, but in .44 Special caliber;
with the 1926 model, the ejector rod housing came
back. The 1950 is similar except for its shorter action,
Magna stocks, and new type hammer spur. Smith &
Wesson naturally have used improved steels as they
appeared, and heat-treated alloy steel cylinders beginning with serial 16,600.

Today's 1950 Military weights are like those of the
1926. Mine is earlier, without the ejector rod housing.
It has the 5-inch barrel, and the scales read 36 ounces
empty and 41 loaded. It seems not to be muzzle-light;
it's just fine, though when I got it, soon after World
War II, I was looking for a 6½-inch job.

It's surprising how many well-informed men want
a bigbore revolver with 4-inch barrel for quick draw.
Here is a standard gun in that length, much lighter,
and less powerful too, than the .44 Magnum S.&W.
Still, it's no popgun with flat or hollow pointed bullets,
and scarcely a frog-hunting pistol with round-nosed
factory loads.

Probably the average outdoorsman would pick the
6½-inch barrel, and the target-sighted model, too, if
he could have his likin's. The .44 Target comes regularly only in this length, but the catalogue print doesn't
follow that specification with "only," as it does in
describing some others. Special jobs have been made
up by all our factories, it seems, even in rather flush
times.

The 5-inch barrel could be, and is, a happy medium
for some of us. The specimen in the next room is one
of my keeping guns. I grew to like it because it's so
handy and not really much noisier than the 6½ was.
Or is this just a camp-follower of increasing deafness?

Except for the .44 Magnums—Smith, Ruger, and
Great Western—the S.&W. Military and Target guns
of recent vintage are favorites with .44 Special handloaders who want to improve the factory cartridge's
mild ballistics. The recent cylinders are strong. Perhaps the strongest strictly .44 Special cylinders are

those with the large-diameters on Colt New Service sixguns, made not too long before that model went out in World War II. Single Action Army and Bisley cylinders aren't as large as those of the New Service. The main thing, to some of us, is that we can get a Smith & Wesson on order if it isn't in the gunstore.

Smith & Wesson 1950 Army

Caliber: .45 Auto Colt rimless, or .45 Auto-Rim.
Weight: 36¼ ounces.
Barrel: 5½ inches.
Overall: 10¾ inches.
Sights: 1/10 inch wide service-type front; square notch rear.
Stocks: Checked walnut, Magna.
Finish: Blue.

Like the .44 Military without ejector rod housing, this revolver started as a war baby, one of the 1917 emergency productions. We couldn't make .45 automatic Colt pistols fast enough for our World War I forces; so the big Smith and the still heavier Colt New Service were adapted to the rimless .45 Auto cartridge. This made for quick loading with three-shot "half-moon" clips designed for the '17s.

After the war, Colt let the war model die, as far as commercial production went, but Smith & Wesson continued theirs. It came out as a commercial gun with checked walnut stocks and a fine blue job instead of the smooth grips and grayish-blue 1917 finish. Enough people to keep up demand seemed to be buying it, wanting a new gun and one made under the best of conditions.

Clip-loading helped keep the S.&W. 1917 going; it was so practical. It was not a new idea; a similar system had been tried in England, long before. As I recall, it is pictured in Greener's old classic, *The Gun and Its Development.* But our style of clips is simpler, and more easy to manufacture. A recent S.&W. catalogue lists them at five cents each, minimum order 50 cents.

Soon after World War I the Auto-rim cartridge was brought out for revolvers, and it's still made. The rim or extracting flange is about twice the average normal thickness, to fill in between cylinder and breech face as the flange of the rimless auto-pistol round plus the clip does. The Auto-rim case-head is strong, good for handloading, and the thick rim positions the case even-

ly in the gun for uniform ignition. Once-fired rimless rounds, without the clip, are easy to pick out with your fingernail. The clips aren't necessary with them unless your Colt '17 is an early one with cylinders bored straight through, having no shoulder for a stop to the case-mouth.

Many 1917s have been rechambered to .45 Colt. The headspace or positioning of the case-head in the chamber must come from the abutment of the case-mouth up front and the long .45 Colt's case-mouth is turned over or crimped into the lead bullet. But the system still can work. With the Auto case in the unaltered gun this front-fashion headspacing is easy: the brass is thicker at the mouth and is left square, not crimped. The long .45 can't be headspaced by its rim in the '17 because the cylinder is cut back at the rear to give room for the "rimless" cartridge's rim or flange plus clip system. Some long .45 cylinders have been fitted to the war guns, too. Conversion of both kinds has been worth-while to many sixgun shooters who wanted the extra power of the long load, though with the heavy 250 and 255 grain bullets these revolvers sighted for the 230 grain Auto bullet shoot high at close ranges.

The Colt is about four ounces heavier than the Smith, and the chamber walls in its larger cylinder are thicker. Strength of modern steels in late S.&Ws. is to be considered, too. Both guns have taken heavy handloads, but such feeding is for the individual to determine, as always. The 250 and 255 grain Colt bullets, or any others, should be sized to no more than .001 inch over barrel groove diameter for heavy loads and the best accuracy. It pays to measure cylinder throat diameter, too. There's danger in letting a lead bullet be upset to fill it, and then asking it to be sized down abruptly by barrel throat and rifling. Elmer Keith has pointed this out rather often.

The butt swivel on 1917 guns was handy in rough carrying. You could anchor the gun to you with a lanyard. On Colt New Service arms, except the target model, it was standard until the rounded-butt model (at first only in .357 Mag. and .38 Special) came in the 1930s. This one didn't regularly have it. Smith continued it in the commercial 1917, but it isn't standard on the 1950 Army.

The chief external differences between the '17 and '50 commercials are the Magna stocks as regular fitting and the new shape of the hammer spur on the current arm. Late commercial '17s were sighted like the '50, with square-cut rear and flat-topped front, much superior to the original sights because they're quicker and more accurate.

Which is easier to shoot with our Service .45 cartridge, the sixgun or the autoloader? The revolver has a fine, clean trigger pull, which can be made very light and still be safe. For most beginners it's better for slow-fire accuracy, and also because it shakes up the hand less than the auto does with that recoiling slide. Under a short time limit the tyro might do better with

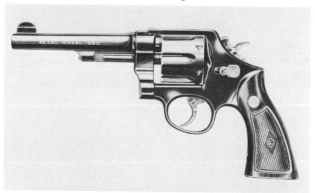

S.&W. 1950 Army Model .45.

the auto because he has only to aim, fire, recover from recoil, and go at it again. If his hand is big and easy to wrap around the auto's flat grip, and his trigger finger long enough to squeeze off the shots without having to lie along the side of the gun (which is bad for accuracy except with a special hand-fitting stock like those on some customized single shots, etc.), he might take to the automatic. Liking a gun has much to do with mastering it.

To cock the revolver's hammer fast and smoothly enough for even-cadence and at least decent-scoring rapid fire, takes a lot of practice. Much of this can be in dry fire, no ammunition burned up. To learn accurate double-action shooting is still harder. There is, too, a tendency for a heavily loaded, round-, not flat-gripped revolver to twist in the hand when recoil slaps back.

Because and in spite of all this, the sixgun is probably easier for most of us to master, unless the shooting must be pretty fast. As for reliability, the two gun types are much on a par. For long-sustained rapid fire, which seldom comes up, the auto can be fired faster than the clip-loaded sixgun, but not much. Here, familiarity with the chosen model would be the chief thing.

Lugers

This being so much an outdoorsman's chapter, the familiar, though no longer regularly manufactured, Luger gets in. Its popularity in this country began in the early 1900s, and even today you probably see more of them than of any other foreign handgun doing outdoor work. They are cleaner-lined and easier to shoot than the heavy, clumsy, round-gripped 7.63 mm. or .30 caliber Mauser militaries that were fairly common years ago. There were good, serviceable British Webley bigbore revolvers, really stocked better for shooting than our Colt and Smith double actions, but that was about their only advantage. Our double actions took more powerful and more easily available cartridges.

The 7.65 or .30 and the 9 mm. or .35 Lugers were attractive because of their flat trajectories and deep penetration, which practically equaled those of the Mausers. The slanted grips made pointing easy, at least in medium-size or large hands, and the guns were closely fitted and accurate to great distances. With long barrels, they are great two-hand pistols. Although their light, small caliber bullets have little shocking power, they killed big game by exact placement, for those little pills sank in deep. In .30 caliber the soft-point bullets with long lead exposure could muss up things a bit more, but only excellent shooting or blazing good luck made Lugers effective on sizable game.

In styling and quality Lugers have varied more than any other pistols that come to mind. Common barrel lengths ran from 3⅝ to 8 inches, and there were longer-barreled carbines for specially hot loadings, not for pistol powder charges. Some safeties go up for

A .30 caliber Luger with 4⅝-inch barrel. A fine specimen, shown here by courtesy of Stoeger Arms Corporation.

ready; some go down, which is more convenient. By the way, these safeties really lock the firing mechanism. Many Lugers had grip safeties, soft and effortless to compress with the hand, like those of the .45 Colt Auto, Super .38, and a few of the old 1905 .45s. At the rear of some butts is a lug for attaching a shoulder stock; this would convert the pistol into a Federally-taxed "firearm." The lanyard loop so common at the rear of the breech is really for two-hand shooting. Grip the strap with the free hand and bring it around your shoulder, pulling rather hard against the tension of the out-stretched firing hand.

The early model Luger with flat recoil spring in the butt can be identified by the shape of the thumb-and-finger grips for opening the breech, near the rear of the toggle-locked breech-bolt. They are milled for grasping only up front. In the 1908 and later guns they are built, and milled, full-circle, and these pistols have the better form of recoil spring, coiled. However, with many manufacturers and dates there are almost endless variations in Lugers.

Individual quality is judged partly by outside finish; the best are a glossy blue with some depth to it. Knowing the date of manufacture helps, and many are stamped with the year. Wartime guns sometimes got through too-easy inspections as things got tough for the *Vaterland.* Lugers assembled from differently numbered parts *may* be good, but not many are, in general.

I had two Lugers, which I used a lot. They were decidedly different. The World War I relic 9 mm was at least safe to fire; some post-war specimens weren't. Its trigger pull weighed 14 pounds, seven times as much as the empty gun, and it was full of creep. This gun occasionally jammed, a fact that has been exaggerated somewhat. It wasn't entirely reliable, either with factory rounds or with handloads using the 125 grain 356402 Ideal cast lead bullet.

The other, a .30 caliber, was also a used gun, though almost new, and definitely perfect in condition. I bought it from Abercrombie & Fitch in New York, and had their gunsmiths (Griffin & Howe, probably, even then) work on the trigger pull, also checker the face of the trigger. The result was by odds the best Luger pull I ever squeezed, a slight takeup of the complicated mechanism, then a clean let-off of about five pounds. This gun had the American eagle on the top of the breech—or receiver ring, as we'd call it on a bolt action rifle—and had been made for export, probably before World War I started. It took the increased-velocity American ammunition that came in the 1920s, didn't seem to mind a bit.

Its barrel length was 4⅝ inches, and the taper was so substantial that this smaller-calibered pistol was little, if any, heavier than the 4-inch 9 mm with more metal bored out of the barrel. Both guns were muzzle-light and harder to shoot than 6-inch Lugers. Bert Shay's 8-inch .30 with barrel made from a section of .30-06 Springfield tube has good muzzle weight and is less subject to tremor than any other Luger I've shot.

I was interested in the reliability of my .30. From stories I'd heard, it looked like a good one. I kept the slide-ways well oiled, the whole gun in good shape. My friends and I fired it over 2,000 shots without a single jam from reasonably fresh cartridges, as I recall. There may have been a bobble or two, however, from some old, corrosive-primer ammo I bought as a bargain after non-corrosive stuff had come. (That was a tough time for non-fast-talking dealers.)

At the end of all this shooting the barrel showed no signs of wear that I could see, and no chamber burning from split case-necks in the ancient fodder. Good stuff in that D.W.M.-manufactured barrel! After some further use I sold that Luger, and it still seemed to be perfect inside. Evidently it had a precision, close-tolerance bore and chamber, the latter not too common in automatic pistols. They would have reduced the rate of erosion from firing.

With this truly hammerless automatic (a plunger or striker fires the cartridge), I had an experience I never heard of elsewhere with a Luger, though it's fairly common with Colt .45s. Some particle, possibly a flake of primer metal, came back and struck me as I fired. With Colt .45 primers that tend to crater when punched by the firing pin, this can happen understandably. The barrel-breech drops down across the face of the breechblock (the slide) in the unlocking action of short-recoil; and thus a protruding bit of primer cup can be sheared off. The Luger's short-recoil unlocking action is different: barrel and slide go back, locked together until the toggle lock of the breechblock opens. That barrel is screwed solidly into the Luger's tuning-fork receiver; it goes back without dropping. How can primer metal be sheared off? As a rule a good Luger handles its cartridges so smoothly that there's small chance of case metal being scraped away.

All in all, the Luger seems as mechanically safe as any other automatic pistol, if you get a good specimen. Poor ones have been blown up by standard ammunition. Such happenings are rare, but it doesn't pay to overload a Luger, or any gun. And the hot sub-machine gun stuff is not for it. U. S.-made ammo is satisfactory in the sound ones. For us, there's little sense in using imported rounds, for our own factories have made both Luger sizes for a half-century and more— the .30 having come in 1900, the 9 mm in 1908.

Old Klucks Will Do Nicely

It was on a family outing to Signal Mountain, one of the beautiful though unpublicized peaks in New York's Adirondacks, when on the trail to the fire-tower we met the ranger. He seemed to be a native —anyway, he didn't wear high-top shoes in country where poisonous snakes were almost unknown—and he appeared woodswise, in spite of the fact that he carried a revolver, usually the mark of a tenderfoot, then and there.

This fellow's gun was even then obsolete, a double-action Colt Lightning with the odd-shaped "bird's-head" grip, humped at the top to keep it from climbing in recoil then slanting back nicely in its roundness, with a long reach to the trigger. Its holster hung from a belt stuffed with .38 longs and, I believe, a few .38 shorts. A ranger's salary does not allow expensive ammo, though he has his fun, being outdoors enough to know what goes on there.

There was no need for all that ammunition, no need even for the gun, as the Adirondacks are safe for people of sense. He carried it for his own pleasure. Some people don't understand that; so the excuse could have been the north-woods "hedgehog" or porcupine, and in autumn the ruffed grouse or "partridge." Hedgehogs girdle trees, annoying the lumberman; and in still-wild parts of that forest, the "patidges" will sometimes sit on a limb and just look a little concerned. Father and the guides, but few others in those parties, would quite often catch a grouse in that mood, and clip his head off with a big rifle bullet. A body shot from a .38 short or long wouldn't absolutely ruin one.

You and I choose our own kluck pistols, shoot and care for them well, and have our rewards, too. They improve on acquaintance.

IT'S FUN to shoot target. Something happens: you hit or you don't. You make definite and sometimes all too easily remembered scores, which you can compare with those of others. You can play this game all your life and never reach perfection, for even our best shooters have their limitations.

A well-run match moves right along, businesslike and brisk, no lagging. The competitive spirit soars. Why, even the lone pistoleer tries to beat himself, to better his previous efforts. That too is the fun and frustration mixture that keeps a person alive.

We have a great many target shooters in the United States, the majority no doubt being casual and unorganized, but still keen for at least a while, or perhaps for a lifetime. Any sort of competition keeps and whets that keenness. Sure it's fun to shoot at target, *and with the right start, which is understanding and encouragement, almost anyone likes it.*

The solid rewards—over and above the unfailing fun—are many. Relaxation from the stress of life's daily business, meeting the other shooters (so friendly) and learning from them, the sense of achieving something that isn't softened to infantile efforts, and the growing confidence that in an elemental brutal emergency you could take care of yourself and those who depend on you. What other skill-sport can equal shooting?

Our three American arms of the personal, individual sort are the rifle, shotgun, and pistol. All require different techniques, and you rather seldom find a shooter who's good at all three. Yet their techniques conflict, I think, less than is commonly stated. (We must always allow a percentage discount for excuses to avoid hard work and disciplining the mind to one job at a time.) We like them all and champion none to the downgrading of the others.

HAS FORMAL COMPETITION GOT IT?

We need more shooters, and so—much more important—does our Country. All that is obvious.

As far as scoring is concerned, forever aiming at a possible 100 or whatever, the pistol is our most difficult arm. It has its peculiar compensations, though. It is the most intimate and personal of the three, because it's easily carried, or set in a handy, accessible, inconspicuous place. Grade for grade, it costs a little less than the rifle or shotgun, and its ammunition very much less when you get into the more powerful sizes. It's easily toted to the practice and/or competitive range, and you can shoot it all day without dressing especially for the occasion; blue jeans or business suit, it makes no difference.

But the complaint is often heard that our present formal firing setup isn't practical. You stand erect, in a position carefully calculated to enable you to give your best. You have fitted the pistol into your hand so that it will be a straight extension of your arm, and you shoot it at full arm's-length, one-handed, because you aren't allowed to use the free hand to steady the

CHAPTER 5

TARGET ARMS

firing hand. There is time enough for deep breathing and a carefully held part-lungful, and for exact or nearly exact sight alignment even in rapid fire. In slow fire, if you can't ease off the shot during the seconds of held breath, you bring the gun to "Raise pistol," or to "Ready," a safer and still fairly restful position, and start the process again just about when you choose. Except for the one-hand hold and the erect stance you have a good deal on your side in formal target shooting.

But the trap or skeet shot with the scattergun, and the rifleman in four-position events—prone, sit, kneel, and offhand standing—they too have their formalized aids. All three of us know the target locations, the distances, and the time to the tick, or near it, when we're to fire at those targets. So formalized rifle and shotgun are impractical, too?

The "learn on the game" shooters—now, thank Heaven, disappearing from the scene, for they start as bloody bunglers—called target shooting a waste of powder and lead. In a way, anyone could admire a fool for being *so* wrong; it's super-human stupidity and therefore rates some kind of award!

If as a beginner you hunted with a fellow who'd been through the target mill—rifle or shotgun—and still enjoyed going back to it, you at least had the advantage of seeing good shooting done. Your companion had benefited from the right start because his work had been scored and he hadn't been allowed to "forget the misses!" And a well-powdered clay bird or perforated paper target ten-ring had been real, concrete encouragement, not to compare with a reassuring generality—so much swamp gas, to put it politely.

Target training pays. I'll always remember—at least as long as I have my buttons—the day I first saw a Camp Perry trained shooter snap in a second round from a bolt action Winchester Model 54 rifle. The first shot was placed, but a second was needed. The four-motion (really two) flick of the bolt handle was nearly as fast as the down-and-up of a lever, practically a blur. But this youngster, Jim White, knew the importance of the first shot on game. Rapid fire was for those times when the first round wasn't enough.

All right, so our pistol competition is formalized. It's still a start, and the best, for as you go on you lose that who-am-I feeling and hope with reason to place somewhere near the top. That's competition. It sharpens skill partly because it induces buck fever, the pressure of unsureness of yourself, and gives you a chance to lick it.

The leisurely rate of slow fire teaches things like stance, sighting, breathing, holding, and that so important trigger squeeze. With timed fire of two five-shot strings of 20 seconds each, you start the mastery of recovering from recoil, cocking the hammer unless you shoot double action or use an automatic, and the smooth cadence—a name for calm self-control—that gets you through nicely and effortlessly under the time limit, in 18 seconds, perhaps. Rapid fire cuts you to 10 seconds for each five-shot string. All these stages come slowly, each getting several months or whatever's needed before the next hurdle looms up. All this time you have been gaining pistol familiarity. There's nothing mysterious about that phrase. You know how easily you sign your name. That's pen familiarity.

Now, a handgunner who can hit a man's chest almost every time at 50 non-shrinked paces is rather well able to take care of himself when he has distance to separate him from one who can't do that well. When he can quickly riddle an enemy at 25 yards, a range at which many are missed completely with a pistol, he's doing all right, too. A shooter who's learned formal rapid fire can speed it up if he needs to, and still make hits.

So an even reasonably good target shot has justifiable self-confidence. He has also the basic handgun familiarity that leads to more practical defense training, from close-up hip* or cross-draw or side-draw clear up to long-range firing from a sitting or back or prone position. One extreme means lightning offense at short distances; the other can sometimes keep a hostile rifleman face down in cover or even lay him out.

But target shooting, more or less formalized, comes first and for many of us is as much as we can readily get, with safety to all concerned. We get it as civilians on a municipal range, perhaps, though there's a growing public realization that what we might call "shooting games" are practical elsewhere and can be per-

fectly safe. Good at target, and not poky, we'd be able to handle almost any situation in which we might find ourselves with "only a pistol" for protection.

The formalized style is made safe by range discipline for the many who want to learn to use a handgun with deadly effect, just in case they ever need to. When it's generally known that they can shoot, there'll be less likelihood of their ever needing to shoot.

The more practical forms of pistol shooting, some of them at least, are taught to various fortunate law-enforcement officers. Even a long-continued, faithful course in formalized shooting is much to be thankful for. Such training has brought about migrations of the criminal element—to less intelligently protected cities, who had only themselves to blame. Often a great many innocent civilians must suffer from crimes of violence before intelligent protection comes to pass. However, mass intelligence isn't always that slow.

In this chapter we talk about American-made handguns for formal target shooting. This implies adjustable sights, and reasonable weight for the particular shooter. The guns included are mostly of quality grade, but not always, for not all of us who want to become skilled with a handgun can afford the best, even in a used gun. A few that would qualify have been discussed before. It is plain enough that almost *any* currently made U. S. target arm is useful outdoors and not too delicate to be a work gun. The adjustable sights plus normal common sense in using them make the handgun all the more competent outdoors, where vital pistol targets are usually *small* and must be hit right.

Some of the less expensive handguns, fitted with good or at least middlin' adjustable sights, have got into this chapter. I've seen too many fine targets shot with them to have any wish to keep them out. They actually can give more than "a good start," helped along with intelligence and persistence. So far in life I've hardly seen a gun or a shooter to sneer at, have you?

Colt Woodsman Match Target

Caliber: .22 long-rifle.
Weight: 36 and 40 ounces.
Barrel: 4½ and 6 inches.
Overall: 9 and 10½ inches.
Sights: Rear sight adjustable for windage and elevation; ramp-type ⅛-inch square front (1/10-inch on order) with removable blade, undercut or slanted back to avoid light reflection. Slanted forward on 4½-inch gun, for easier pocket draw.
Stocks: Checked black Coltwood plastic with thumb-rest. In 1960 all Colt .22 autos became available with checked walnut stocks at no extra cost.
Finish: Blue.
Magazine capacity: 10.

With Hi-Standards and Rugers of corresponding top quality, these Colts are still popular on smallbore firing lines. Few contestants use a .22 revolver in important matches because of the handicap of thumbing back the hammer in the rapid-fire time limit, though they may have chosen a .38 revolver for cen-

---

*Not really from the hip, for the hand is extended forward in a poking sort of jab.

Colt Woodsman Match Target, 6-inch barrel.

terfire events. You see plenty of earlier model .22 autoloaders in skilled hands, but sixguns, old or new, are scarce. If the art of double-action shooting comes into its own, the picture may well be different.

Up to this writing, the Colt .22 has been marketed only for the long-rifle cartridge, a heavy-odds favorite over the short even at 25-yard and shorter ranges. Although the Olympic course of rapid fire calls for the lighter recoil and consequent shorter recovery time offered by the short, some Colt Woodsman target guns have been used in those international events with good success.

In a .22 caliber revolver we can fire almost as many modern shorts as we like, for economy's sake, or for lighter report, without much danger of burning out the chambers. The erosion rate would be divided by five, or by as much as nine with a Harrington & Richardson or a Hi-Standard, or a J. C. Higgins as made by the latter for Sears, Roebuck and Company. It would come to I don't know how many thousand rounds. I do know that in one of my K-.22 S.&Ws. I fired over 2,000, counting a few BB and CB caps, and at the end of it all I couldn't see even the slightest harm done to those beautifully burnished chambers. But in an autoloader, the use of shorts is perhaps not advisable. One chamber must take all the wear, and there's a possibility of the short, or the long, kicking back the slide just far enough to let it slam forward on the jammed case and, by ill luck, injure the extractor hook.

Still, few ambitious shooters complain much about the cost of long-rifles. They often buy them at club rates or from the Army's Director of Civilian Marksmanship, if they're National Rifle Association members, at about what they pay a dealer for shorts. Using the same ammunition always helps to simplify sighting problems!

The Woodsman is of old and honorable ancestry, and the present model is not the first to be specially built and adjusted to target competition by the factory. Any number have been refined by gunsmiths and individual shooters. Then there was *the previous Match Target*—which you still see at the ranges. It was lighter, only 36 ounces with the "new 6½-inch heavy

barrel," and most of us would say it wasn't as good-looking as today's gun. The barrel was flat-sided, rounded at top and bottom, but the underslung integral section was carried only a little way ahead of the receiver. Since this model used the original short-gripped frame, and people with big hands had complained about the lack of grip length on the standard Woody, the checked walnut stocks were carried below the steel grip, and there was a rather simple-minded looking gap you had to reach into to release the butt-locked magazine. The arrangement looked susceptible to breakage and generally was a mess, compared to other Colts. The modern longer grip, on all current Woodsmen, is adequate for almost any hand, and it's solid, not ventilated.

Bringing out the improved match gun in two barrel lengths was intelligent. It hadn't been done before, regularly at least, in this grade. The old Woodsman offered 4½- and 6½-inch barrels in standard grades, but when the M.T. came out, most match shooters preferred its extra weight and long sight radius. It happens that some of us with middle-aged or more venerable eyesight see pistol sights best when they're fairly close together. And just last Saturday I found that my reading glasses made the sights seem as black and sharp as store-bought steel tent-pegs. Then too, the heavy match .22 auto is a swell outdoor gun, in its caliber, and a reasonably short one might be carried when a longer one would be left at home. Since World War II, the pistol's popularity has increased as a fun gun for him and her, young and old, weak and no-end virile to use and enjoy. All these folks are painlessly learning things that would help in really rough times, if such times are ahead. They are certainly *behind* us Americans. One factor in our national survival was firearms familiarity, wasn't it?

The new, weighted barrels give the modern Match Woodsmen an appearance somewhat like that of the old 6-inch Military and 4½-inch Pocket .38 auto Colts. Those who know *them* respect them as businesslike. They were harder to shoot than the racy, slantgripped modern .22s, but many woods and mountain men shot them with telling effect.

The present Colt sights are neater and more low-lying than those of the early Match Target. There is no doubt that the old Kelly front sight was a good target job. Its square rear face was straight up and down. When it was blackened, it stood out clearly against target paper on a six o'clock hold, just at the bottom of the black bull's-eye, where so many target shots aim. (True, some of the best hold dead center in the black, and if your eyesight allows you to do this efficiently, that's fine. It's the natural hold for game or defense shooting.)

However, much can be said for an undercut front sight on either rifle or pistol. But you want to keep your hands away from that knifelike edge, or you may be saying much that isn't nice. My friend Frank Sheary once made a front sight for his .38 Special K-Target

S.&W., using a white metal that was easy to work and already in his kit-box. Outdoors under the sun that sight did not glitter, because it was so deeply undercut. Holster wear is not exactly harmless to your undercut Colt front (so nicely and durably blued). But that unwanted polishing from leather may be less harmful than one would think, thanks to the undercutting.

Here is a reluctant bit of advice, not a gripe. With today's labor costs, particularly for hand work, not all high grade guns are what they should be. Nor were they even in "the good old days."

So it pays to inspect even a brand-new gun before we buy it. Getting it on a special order from a dealer may not be good; and doesn't he know that, and regret it!

Fine finish is good to look at and to show to others. We hardly expect a new match grade gun's barrel and receiver to double for a nail-file, and we're seldom asked to. But there can be, and often are, finishes inferior to the best standard work of twenty years ago.

What really annoys the particular target shot—he's learned to be particular about *his own* work, the marksmanship angle, as well as about the tool, the gun—is a bad trigger pull. The autoloaders are harder to refine than the revolvers, and the punishment of their recoiling parts doesn't help a bit.

We want three things good about a trigger pull. Its weight of pull-off must suit us, mustn't be inordinately heavy. A wide trigger face, as on all new Woodsmen, makes the pull seem lighter than it is, and gives better control. The pull must be clean, without creep, drag, hitch or temperamental coyness. And when it's through, it should quit.

A good gunsmith can adjust these details on almost any pistol. The second two should be right when they leave the factory—in target grade—but somehow I've found that few are, among autoloaders. There is often some takeup (to use a pleasant word) before the release of the hammer; and just about always, dog-gone it, there seems to be backlash. That is perceptible movement backward after the hammer has been turned loose to go to work on the firing pin. Backlash in almost any rifle I can ignore—when in a tolerant, kindly mood, that is—concentrating more on sight picture and steady hold than on the mechanics of a trigger that trips off at perhaps a third or a quarter the weight of the rifle. It is not always easy or helpful to ignore it. With a handgun, backlash throws me, and it's doubtful if I am alone in getting sore about it.

The foregoing comment applies to practically all our commercial .22 auto-pistols, not by any means just to the Colts. The Woodsman section happened to come first in this chapter, but it was not intended to be down-graded in any way, in this unloading of cargo.

Colt Woodsman Sport and Target Models
Caliber: .22 long-rifle.
Weight: 30 and 32 ounces.

Barrel: 4½ and 6 inches.
Overall: 9 and 10½ inches
Sights: Two-way adjustable rear, ramp-type front with removable blade to allow the owner to substitute other designs, such as gold-, white-, or red-faced blades, if he wishes to.
Stocks: Checked black Coltwood with thumb-rest.
Finish: Blue.
Magazine capacity: 10.

The first Woodsman pistols weighed only 28 ounces, as I recall, but after a few years the 6½-inch barrel was made heavier, up to a 29-ounce gun total. Much later came the 4½-inch Sport Model of 27 ounces. The present jobs are heavier. They have longer grips, slanted about the same as the old ones but with plenty of length to the back-strap.

Check that back-strap if you have an old model Woodsman. You may know already, of course, that if the angle where you press your thumb in dismounting these guns is cross-hatched checkered you have a really old one, which was not intended for high velocity .22 long-rifle cartridges. On the later models, improved for use with this ammo, the curve of the mainspring housing is barred, not cross-hatched. Many old guns were modernized, safely, by installation of the newer style of housing.

When the Woodsman first appeared, it was an eye-opener to many of us, as it was so easy to shoot at least fairly well. It pointed like a Luger—and of course had the barrel lightness, the muzzle-weave, of that gun. Fast firing was easy—this was our first .22 auto-pistol, remember—and it seemed to shoot with almost

Colt Woodsman Target Model, 6-inch barrel.

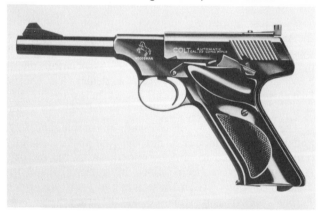

Colt Woodsman Sport Model, 4½-inch barrel.

rifle accuracy and flat trajectory, which was no surprise to those familiar with the long-barreled single shots. As a matter of fact, it was just about as accurate and powerful as two .22 target revolvers that had been with us for a long time, the S.&W. .22-.32 and the Colt Police Positive Target, six-inch barrel sixguns with equally good sights and a steadier hang out front. It was the slick working of the Woodsman that befuddled us. Later some of us thought it was easier to master in slow fire accuracy than the old, familiar .22s had been, and of course it was a whiz in rapid fire. When Smith & Wesson brought out the heavy K-.22 revolver—much later, after little known experiments—we began to learn what easy, effortless, pretty darn good shooting was, within the limits of common sense, I mean! There had been heavy single shot .22s before, by Stevens; but mostly they'd been used by the few elite of target shots.

Our modern Woodsman has gone about as far as a medium-weight, two-pound automatic .22 can go, it now seems. But years from now, some student browsing in library dust may read this and properly call it one of the twentieth century's most stupid remarks.

That remark is no plug for Colt Patent Firearms. There are several pistols of this class, much alike in the less important matters of length, weight and price, but importantly different in the way they suit you, the individual. A good way of choosing might be to grip the lot, one by one, with your eyes closed and not trying to figure out which company made which.

Colt Woodsmen have been to far places because they've been available for many years. Now they have serious rivals, but in early times only the *Reising* autos contested them. The *Fiala* was built like a Woodsman, externally, but it was a hand-operated repeater, not an autoloader.

The present Woodsman pistols have come far since the earliest models. Heavier barrels make holding easier, and more exactly adjustable sights also help us achieve precision. The first Woodsman sights had the long-used but never satisfactory elevation system in the front sight; i.e., raise it to lower bullet strike, screw it down to add elevation. The windage adjustment in the rear sight had a better scale in its base, and you could read it fairly well. But the two-way rear sight, so long used by Smith & Wesson, is the modern favorite, with good reason.

Maybe the biggest improvement was the change in trigger location. At first it was almost in the middle of the guard, a tight fit for a gloved finger. (We rarely see gloves worn at matches, for competitors value their sensitiveness of trigger control, but in northern winters outdoor folks need protection. Who can shoot well when he's shivering?) Then on special order a few triggers were set close to the guard, more in Luger fashion. Finally the close-coupled trig became standard at about the time when the gun acquired more barrel weight—or a little later. Short-fingered shooters did better with it.

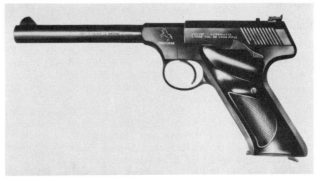

Colt Targetsman Autoloader, 6-inch barrel. Rear sight is simpler than the Accro sights on Woodsman models, but it's serviceable and useful to the target shot.' Stocks feel much like those on modern Woodsman pistols.

Colt Targetsman Autoloader

This spring-of-1959 Colt .22 auto is practically a Huntsman with an adjustable rear sight. That useful, low-cost variant of the standard Woodsman is described in the next chapter. It is already familiar as successor to the Challenger. Fixed sights (except for the drive-over-and-try of the dovetailed-in rear sight, not by any means a hopeless sort of windage adjustment, at that) and less costly fitting and finish set the Huntsman price, at this moment, at $28 less than the Woodsman. It's what some would call "a good knockabout gun" and others would rate as a good gun, anyway, once they'd sighted it in for windage.

Except for its two-way adjustable rear sight on the end of its receiver, and the Colt medallions in the stocks, the Targetsman is much like the Huntsman. It has been advertised as the lowest-priced .22 target automatic, and such it seems to be. Right now the Ruger Mark I Target with Micro-click rear sight costs a dollar more. To stimulate sales, The Targetsman, at least at first, had a holster thrown in for its $56.50 price. The holster was valued at $7 retail and looks about like that, a closed-end belt job with snap-down retaining strap.

There is *no* sarcasm in any of the foregoing remarks. Choice between Colt and Ruger target guns in this price stage depends on which you think you could shoot better. The Ruger with 6⅞-inch barrel, compared to 6½ Colt length, weighs 43 ounces, more than a half-pound over the Colt heft. Its feel and handling qualities are entirely different. Almost always these Mark I Rugers have a clean trigger pull. They may or may not have noticeable backlash after the hammer has been released. Try the pulls on both guns, if you can, and on several specimens of each. Almost all target-gun pulls can be gunsmithed into good shape, with varying cost.

The important news about the Targetsman is that it's a medium or low-priced .22 auto with two-way rear sight, and of medium weight, too, for easy field carry if that's its job. Perhaps its sighting will stimulate other manufacturers to produce rivals.

Colt Officer's Model Match

Caliber: .22 long-rifle or .38 Special. The shorter cartridges can be used. The 1959-designed .22 Magnum Rimfire was added to the Officer's Model line.

Weight: 39 ounces in .38, 43 in .22. The earlier Officer's Model.

Target: .38 6-inch weighed 34 ounces, or 36 with heavy barrel. The .32 with heavy 6-inch barrel went to 37 ounces, the 6-inch .22 to 38 ounces.

Barrel: 6 inches. Early O.M.Ts. had 6- or 7½-inch barrels, with 4-, 4½- and 5-inch added later, in the .38 caliber.

Overall: 11¼ inches with standard 6-inch barrel.

Sights: Two-way adjustable rear; ramped, undercut ⅛ inch front, with choice of 1/10 inch on order.

Stocks: Large Target style, fully checked walnut, square butt.

Finish: Blue.

The Officer's Model is another of those half-century guns that have deserved to stay in production—and it has done it! It's one of the greatest score-making sixguns. In early times, it was the highest refinement of standard grade, over-the-counter Colts, except possibly for the bigbore New Service Target. Both had hand-finished actions as a regular thing. About the only difference was that the New Service grip straps, both front and rear, were checkered for sure hold, whereas only the rear one of the O.M.T.—or of the much less expensive little Police Positive Target .22 and .32 in the last issues—was regularly so treated.

The Officer's Model Match is the third general type of this fine arm. Though it looks lighter than *the post-World War II Officer's Model Special,* it weighs the same. The latter, with its untapered barrel, looked huge, but it balanced well. It didn't come in .32 New Police or S.&W. long caliber, as the O.M.T. had for a while—or at least it wasn't made so regularly. I've never heard of an Officer's Model .32-20, though Smith & Wesson made their Military & Police Target for it when the cartridge had the popularity it still deserves for woods use. Both these makes of medium-weight target revolver have been outdoors a great deal, over millions of pleasant miles.

The Special was the first really heavy-barreled Officer's the factory put out. Gunsmithed jobs, like the

Colt Officer's Model Match, 6-inch barrel, target-type stock. A heavier-barreled gun than the old Officer's Model Target, and with far more finely adjustable sights, many would say. Some shooters do better with extra weight; some don't. Smith & Wessons get added weight mainly by means of heavy barrel ribs, and by encased ejector rods on some models.

prized and high-scoring one owned and used by Bert Shay, preceded it. The advantage was good weight out front to steady the hold, not so much heft in the frame and cylinder as with the big New Service Target or the later Shooting Master—which was practically the same except for its rounded butt. In .38 Special the S.M. weighed 44 ounces with standard 6-inch barrel, and in .45 Colt the N.S.T. 7½-inch job went to 42. Note the difference due to small caliber, with less steel bored out of barrel and chambers. The .38 barrel was much more tapered, too, than the .45.

It is true that some target shooters do like a large caliber *and* a heavy gun. These they can get today in S.&Ws. and in single-action Great Westerns and Rugers. A big bullet clips a wide-diameter hole in target paper, and, with equally good placement, sometimes scores a ten when a .38 would have settled for a nine. The bigbores are few at today's matches, except those that call for the .45 Government Auto caliber. They used to be well-liked for indoor center-fire competition, with light loads. Glance through a mold catalogue like those pages in the *Ideal Handbook* now published by Lyman Gun Sight Corporation, and note the short, light-recoiling (and softer-sounding) patterns for short-range work with big guns. Factories produced such ammunition ready-loaded. Here are some: .44 Russian 105 grain round ball and 115 grain "conical" with 6 grains of black powder, or with the smokeless equivalent behind the latter; .44 Russian or .44 Special 145 grain wadcutter, smokeless "mid-range" for the 20-yard galleries so common then.

But now the .38 Special is the nearest to standard caliber we have in target centerfires. The .32 long comes and goes in flurries of popularity, and it certainly has its advantages—light report and recoil, and some shooting economy, too. But the Officer's Model is not at present made for it, leaving the field clear to Smith & Wesson, although another revival of this caliber could bring it back to Colt target-gun listing.

For those who want a heavy .22 target revolver—as issued, not built up—the Officer's is the thing. It is 4 ounces over the S.&W. K-.22 Masterpiece. Naturally there are other considerations, such as grip fit, balance, and the design of lockwork and sighting equipment.

The modern Officer's Model .38 Specials, and all those made for twenty years or so past, are safe to use with high velocity factory ammunition. For emergencies this would be all right, and Smith K models could be safe with the stuff, too. But it's hard on cylinder fittings and in time makes the lineup loose. The resultant chatter is a high price to pay for such convenience. For target use up to the standard old 50-yard slow fire, the regular .38 Special ammo has the ballistics required, easily. It's also much less disturbing, which results in better scores.

Some regret the passing of the 7½-inch barrels. They certainly were attractive for an outdoorsman's use, with their long sighting radius and their steady hang in spite of the comparative slimness of those tubes. (For that matter, many of us find the 12-inch-barreled Colt Buntline Special .45 single action really steady-holding.) With black powder or with a load of fairly slow-burning smokeless, they gave high velocities, and the report was lighter and "farther away from you." But the modern heavy 6-inch barrels are steadier yet to hold, when weight is wanted; and they are nicely calculated in sight radius—enough for most of us and too much only for those whose eyes have lost a good deal of the accommodation they used to have.

Colt Python .357

Caliber: .357 Magnum. Uses also .38 Special and short and long Colt. Gun can be chambered especially for the .38.
Weight: 44 ounces.
Barrel: 6 inches.
Overall: 11¼ inches, same as Officer's Model Match.
Sights: Similar to those on Officer's Model except that the ⅛-inch-width front sight only is offered, and the ramp for it is replaced by a full-barrel-length ventilated rib, the ventilation being meant to dissipate heat waves that interfere with accurate aiming.
Stocks: Fully checked walnut, square butt, large Target-type.
Finish: Colt Royal Blue.

Grooved, wide trigger and wide hammer spur add to this target gun's convenience, as on the Officer's Model. The contact points of the lockwork are hand-honed, as we'd expect at the price.

The revolver is Colt's big effort at a splendid target arm that needs no more than the individual fittings and adjustments which the most meticulous competition shot demands. Or rather, most of them; some shoot as well with practically as-issued guns.

The Python has the weight of a big-bore target arm, thanks to the barrel rib and the under-barrel addition to give steadiness. It is not a big-frame revolver, but an Officer's Model, Official Police or old Army Special in design. It's strong enough for the .357 Magnum, or it wouldn't have been put out in that caliber. Still, the chamber walls are a good deal thinner than those of a heavy-frame .357 like the big Smiths or the discontinued Colt New Service, New Service Target or Shooting Master, or the Single Action Army when made for this powerful load. The handloader who likes husky charges, sometimes above the factory Magnum and still safe when put up right, should remember this fact.

If we ever have a .40 caliber revolver cartridge from the factories, the Python should be a good target model to handle it. The frame is the old .41 caliber, like that of the Army Special, and now it's made of modern steel. The .41 was an actual .40. Excellent though it was, so few regrets were registered when the gun dropped from production that a revival or replacement seems unlikely. The .41 long ammo is still made, as it deserves to be. But comparatively few new shooters know much, if anything, about it, and the gap between .38 and .44 guns still yawns. People are so used to the gap that they hardly know what they're missing!

Colt Python target gun, ventilated rib barrel to help dissipate heat waves. Note the smooth cylinder latch, like that on other Colt sixguns, to make life easy for the right thumb when recoil comes.

The choice between the two Python calibers depends on the purposes it is to fulfill. For all-round shooting, including long range and wilderness travel, most of us would want the .357. Not all, however, for .38 Special loadings, hand or factory, include excellent small game jobs. Some of us are conservative and see no need of any "ultimate" in any caliber. For straight target shooting up to 50 yards, the gun chambered for .38 Special could be expected, with fair good sense, to be the most accurate with those cartridges, though differences should be slight.

The gun is smooth, even in double-action firing, and it has enough muzzle-weight to suit almost anyone. It's a long way in refinement from the 1908 Army Special, which itself in more basic ways was a decided improvement on the New Army and New Navy .38s which it replaced. These were service, not target models, but they did have one splendid characteristic, old-time careful workmanship. To get that quality now you have to pay a good deal, usually. You'll see some of it in fine target jobs like the Python. This is written impartially, not with any sentimental longing for the past!

Colt National Match .45 Gold Cup

Caliber: .45 Auto Colt rimless, full charge, or the factory midrange loads with 185 grain metal patched or 210 grain lead bullets of semi-wadcutter shape.
Weight: 37 ounces, 2 ounces less than the Government Model .45 or the .38 Super Automatic.
Barrel: 5 inches.
Overall: 8½ inches.
Sights: Front sight with vertical rear face in standard Patridge style; improved two-way adjustable rear sight.
Stocks: Checked walnut with gold plated Colt medallion.
Finish: Colt Royal Blue, as on Python revolver.
Magazine capacity: 7.

Many shooters remember the National Match .45 and Super Match .38, refined for target shooting. Actions were hand-smoothed, barrels were selected for fine boring, rifling and chambering, trigger pulls worked over, and adjustable sights fitted. You could get them also with fixed, non-adjustable sights (except

Colt National Match .45 Gold Cup. The highest standard factory refinement of a bigbore target autoloader.

for windage, by moving the rear sight to and fro) of the same square-cut-Patridge shape. As straight factory jobs these autoloaders were good; the price difference between service and target guns was only about 20%. But they couldn't be expected to perform like the best custom target jobs. Now, with loose spending money more generally spread out than it was in the 1930s, a factory has a better chance to turn out high-quality work in volume. This particular morning's price-tags of the two models are $78.25 and $125.00— a substantial difference between service and standard grades.

If the Super Match .38 had been given the costly refinements that make a superb target gun, it might have been startling. It is eligible in centerfire matches except those confined to .45 Auto ammunition; and at about 1100 f.s. velocity the .38 is pleasant-shooting, with only moderate recoil. The Super's big advantage over .38 revolvers is its self-loading action. With no hammer cocking, the ten seconds of five-round rapid fire are ample time for a good shot, and this stage is important in total scoring. I've never fired clean-cutting semi-wadcutter cast bullets in the Super; but they worked nicely in the .38 Military, and in .45 Auto use they're common on the ranges. So it is to be expected that the Super, too, would handle them reliably. Ideal 358480 should be good when seated correctly for overall length.

The Gold Cup .45 is not simply an improved Government Model; it's practically a new and different pistol. An article in the December, 1957, *American Rifleman* by staffman M. D. Waite is properly entitled "A New Colt .45." He describes the gun concisely and clearly.

When gunsmiths, no matter how great their skill, worked over the .45 to improve its accuracy, they could do little more than remodel the basic service arm. At first they assembled factory parts, mating them for close tolerances in fit. Then specially made parts came. The factory had done little more than the first sort of job, which did, of course, help.

Lots of us remember, and maybe still use, the 1911-A1 improvement, with (or without) the arched mainspring housing at the rear of the grip to help fill the hollow of the hand and cause the gun to point straighter out when held naturally. That is essentially the Government Model of today. Those of us who had short forefingers rejoiced in the new, set-back trigger and the cutaway of the frame on each side of it to help us get our finger on the trigger without its touching the frame. This contact tends to cause shooting to the left, for a right-hander. So much for the first main factory improvement.

The 1933 National Match .45s, and Super Match .38s, were refined with closely fitted parts, select barrels, and adjustable target sights. They had not been built as match pistols. Even so, many thought they were worth the price; and the custom jobs by J. D. Buchanan, Jesse Harpe, A. E. Berdon and other fine pistolsmiths seemed worth what *they* cost, too, because of their excellent hand-work and the hours of highly developed skill.

The Gold Cup trigger is skeletonized, grooved of course, over .35 inch wide, and with an adjustable, spring-loaded, capstan head stop to cut backlash. Short-fingered shooters may not like it, and possibly a new design for them will come from the factory. Pull weight of the N.R.A.-tested sample gun was just under five pounds, and the pull was clean, as we'd expect in this grade of target pistol. The width of the half-cock notch in the hammer is about one-third that of standard, to prevent wear on the sear. This is a fine feature. Actually a half-cock notch on a strictly target .45 might seem unnecessary. The big, exposed-hammer Colt autos use a short firing pin of the flying type. It goes forward to punch the primer only from the momentum it gets from the hammer blow. With the hammer fully down, at rest, the short pin can't touch the primer. *But* if the hammer should slip from your thumb, you'd be glad, naturally, of that notch to stop its fall! That is what it's for. It works, if you release the trigger in time.

Model 1961 Colt National Match .38 Gold Cup for the .38 Special midrange wadcutter cartridge only. Its internal design is entirely different from those of the .45s and the Super-.38s made for the rimless, high velocity .38 Auto Colt round.

The Gold Cup sights stand between a flat, grooved slidetop rib 7/16-inch wide, but the rear sight is more low-lying and compact than that of the .45 National Match, a gun not regularly made for several years past. Sight radius is not quite as long as that of the N.M., but it's more than that of service guns. To cut glare, the top of the slide is sand-blasted, though the flat sides of slide and receiver or frame are highly polished and blued. The rear sight clicks for adjustments, and the front sight has the popular ⅛-inch target width.

This pistol is easier and more accommodating to open than earlier .45 issues because the slide grooves that you grimly grasp (as a beginner, anyway) slant forward, as on the Mauser H SC .32 and some others. They are not up-and-down. This is a simple example of thoughtfulness, too rare in this world! The slide is lighter than that of the .45 predecessors. It's steel and cut away inside where it can stand it. This pistol is specially made to handle reduced factory mid-range loads, though it takes the standard ammunition, too—both kinds without your having to change recoil springs. And to digest the steel G. I. cases better, its extractor has been reshaped. Many of the boys and girls use such cases for economy. It takes a good deal of shooting to boss the .45 automatic, even one as well tailored for target as this one.

Next to the trigger adjustment against backlash, the tying-down of the hand-fitted barrel is probably the biggest help toward scores. The recoil spring plug, that checkered button under the muzzle which you depress when dismounting the gun, is *fitted* into the bushing at the muzzle. It is chamfered for snugness in entering the chamfered bushing. This feature helps to bring the barrel back into battery in the same position, shot after shot. You can grip an old, worn .45 and rattle it with an easy shake. Not this one.

The standard Gold Cup mainspring housing is flat, much like those of the first 1911s. It is grooved for grasp, and so is the front strap. The arched housing comes on special order, for shooters with big and long-fingered hands.

There seems to be nothing delicate or fragile about this .45. Some care should go into keeping dust and woods duff from entering the trigger slot. Otherwise, it's much like any other well-sighted outdoorsman's pistol. Those who like the gun and the cartridge should find it serviceable afield, and they should make more hits with it than with Government Model guns. The ejection has been improved, and spur of the grip safety is long. These features ought to restrain the Gold Cup from throwing empties into your face occasionally, or from biting the web of your hand when the slide, flying back, cocks the hammer for you.

Colt National Match .38 Gold Cup

Caliber: .38 Special midrange wadcutter with bullet seated flush with the case-mouth. Not intended for use with full charge .38 Specials, and the magazine will not handle full standard-length rounds with bullets projecting well beyond the brass.

Weight: 37 ounces, same as that of the .45 Gold Cup.
Barrel: 5 inches.
Overall: 8½ inches.
Sights: Similar to those on .45 Gold Cup, Partridge style front with vertical rear face, two-way adjustable rear sight.
Stocks: Checked walnut, gold-plated Colt Medallion.
Finish: Colt Royal Blue.
Magazine capacity: 5. Just right for timed and rapid fire stages; no danger of over- or under-counting.

Ingeniously accurized to compete with target revolvers in the "centerfire" class (.32s, .38s, and less commonly .44s and .45s) this type has two great advantages. It chambers that great favorite, the .38 Special midrange wadcutter cartridge—factory rounds or closely equivalent handloads—and you don't have to spend any of the precious ten seconds in five-shot rapid fire in thumbing back its hammer, as practically all of us still do with a double-action revolver.

A third advantage, many will say, is its ready availability as a factory job. Custom pistolsmiths have altered many .38 and some .45 Auto Colts to .38 Special midrange, usually adding their own touches of refinement in accuracy, sighting equipment and trigger work. Necessarily these were rather expensive jobs, built more or less to order, and that takes time. Probably all straight factory-made target arms get from some of the more particular brothers the "damn with faint praise" treatment, "It's a good do-it-yourself kit." Although we can't expect this one to escape such comment, we can expect fine performance from it. Colt went all out on it, I believe.

Trigger action and sights are much as on the .45 Gold Cup; so they should satisfy all but the far and few, the perfectionists. A second thought tells us, of course, that it's those people, more than any others, who are responsible for firearms and ammunition improvements. Some are civilians; some are military personnel.

Its inherent, built-in accuracy is a result of design and workmanship. Like the .45 Gold, it has a special barrel bushing up front to provide even pressure between barrel and slide. Other fittings are of tight target grade, too. All its own is Colt's new type of floating barrel. Since it's not mounted on a link, as on Colt .45s and Super-.38s, it doesn't drop at the rear during recoil, but goes straight back a mere ⅛ to 3/16 inch. Although barrel and slide are never locked together as on the other two types, the barrel is pulled to the rear that fractional inch, along with the slide, by the friction of the expanded fired cartridge case against the chamber. The pressure falls, and the case is free to be drawn back and ejected. This isn't a new principle, but it's new in this application and purpose. The .45 and .38 Auto need their locked breech system to help the mass of recoiling parts to resist heavy recoil. The .38 wadcutter is mild.

A natural question is: "What's wrong with the standard .38 Auto Colt case in regard to accuracy?" Why, nothing's wrong. Like most sizes, it's capable of very great accuracy when it's loaded for the job and fired in a top-notch gun. Recoil springs could be lightened to take comfortable shooting reduced loads for 25 and 50 yard work, and semi-wadcutter bullets can be made to feed reliably in the oldest and newest models of .38 Colt autos. This takes work—if handloading is work—and .38 Special wadcutters are both factory-loaded and custom-loaded in huge quantities. Some of the folks who shoot these Specials a lot never handload a single round.

What about this new gun's practical value? Could it qualify for a one and only handgun? Not if you want to get into "forty-five" competition as distinct from "centerfire," but otherwise it could be a good choice. Magazine capacity is low, but you can slip in a fresh mag and thumb down the slide stop much faster than you can reload a revolver. The wadcutter .38 has quite fair stopping power because of its bullet's blunt shape and usually soft lead composition. For boring to the life of a big animal with one well directed shot—no time to take more, perhaps—it's a poor competitor against nearly all husky rounds.

Colt Conversion Unit

This kit makes a .22 rimfire out of a .45 or Super .38—though not the short Commander type—at a little over half the price of those guns in standard grade. The special magazine holds ten .22 long-rifle cartridges, and you use the same grip and trigger pull with both calibers, big and small. The slide carries the special .22 parts, including the target sights.

Our Government experimented with .22-.45 conversions well before the first Colt Ace came out, but most of us shooters knew little about this. General Hatcher describes the experiments in his *Pistols and Revolvers and Their Use.* The sub-caliber insert barrel for the Luger was well established, and in general was good. It fired a small round ball through a rifled barrel. Now there are .22 Luger inserts.

The first Colt Ace was a complete .22 pistol and could not double as a centerfire. It weighed an ounce less than the .45 or Super .38 and was ¼-inch shorter in barrel and overall. The slide, and of course the recoil spring, had to be light to handle the .22 ammunition. This gun had good sights, for its day, though hardly the equal of those on S.&W. target revolvers. It felt like a .45 in your hand until you fired it. Then not only the light report but also the weak recoil were decidedly different.

With "Carbine" Williams' invention of the floating, recoiling chamber, the second model Ace felt about like a .30 Luger in recoil; not much more, but that extra kick made better training for forty-fivers. The same system was used in developing the Remington Model 550 .22 auto-rifle to shoot shorts, longs and long-rifles without adjustment, and mixed in the magazines if you wanted to play the musical scale. Gas getting in ahead of the separate, floating chamber shoves that floater back hard against the breechblock and increases back-thrust of .22 shorts.

For a long time *the second model Ace* was offered as a complete gun, or as half a gun, the conversion unit. Now only the latter, the topside part, is catalogued. As a complete pistol it had the same 5-inch barrel length as the .45, but it weighed 3 ounces more, or 42 ounces. If your .22 ammo was old and a little feeble, the floating chamber still allowed it to function the gun, usually. Few of us care to use high velocity .22s for practice when we can get the generally more accurate and always less noisy standard speed type, or the match grade long-rifles of similar power.

Harrington & Richardson Sportsman 999

Caliber: .22 short, long and long-rifle.
Weight: 30 ounces.
Barrel: 6 inches.
Overall: 10½ inches with modern stocks. Over 11 inches with some of the early stocks offered as optional equipment.
Sights: 1/10-inch square Patridge type; front adjustable for elevation, rear for windage.
Stocks: Checked walnut with small thumb-rest. Trigger guard extension serves as filler or adapter, providing a rest for the second finger.
Finish: Blue.

For years the Sportsman has been known as the best value—or certainly very near it—in moderate-priced .22 revolvers. To beat it, you generally had to know enough about used guns to buy a second hand Colt or Smith & Wesson at about the same price. Even then you might have preferred the H.&R., for it was and still is a good gun. The present well-earned popularity of .22 autoloaders in matches that include timed and rapid fire has made the going a bit tough for .22 target revolvers. General prosperity, too, has contributed to the Sportsman's less common appearance on the firing lines. But some of us still prefer a revolver, and if our all-round handgun shooting includes the bigbores that are built for business, for the greatest possible killing power, we just about have to go to the revolvers. The large grip and wide hammer spur of this .22 help make it a trainer for .44s and .45s; yet the 30-ounce weight isn't too much for a husky teenager or woman just learning to shoot a handgun. The Sportsman, as its name implies, is a fine outdoorsman's gun, too, within .22 rimfire limitations.

The cylinder of this tip-up frame revolver holds

Harrington & Richardson Model 999 Sportsman, 6-inch barrel

nine rounds, in usual H.&R. fashion. Its handling shorts just as well as long-rifles is an advantage that up to this minute no one-barrel-assembly .22 auto-pistol has, although some .22 autoloading rifles do. There's the amusing thought that an automatic-ejecting revolver fouled with shorts will keep on hauling out long or long-rifle empties after an autoloader would have quit. Of course, it pays to keep a gun clean, but not all of us do it! And when you divide the number of plinking or short range target rounds you've fired by nine, the day when you're driven to use the cleaning rod is just that much postponed! So is the erosion of the chambers by the short rounds, although with modern ammunition any such damage is slow in coming, compared to the promptness in the old days. Longer empties stick in chambers burned out by shorts. At first the ruination reaches only just in front of the short cases' length, but it's enough.

At its moderate price, this gun hasn't the finely adjustable sights of the best target arms, or the beautiful, smooth trigger pull, either, except by luck. All that is to be expected. The pull can be refined if it needs it. The job of re-tempering glass-hard case-hardened parts, as on the Smith & Wessons, is for the factory or a skilled gunsmith, not for an amateur who lacks such ability. Soft metal wears.

The Sportsman still offers good value, still helps a beginner or allows an accomplished shot do good work. Coil springs add to its considerable durability, though in the overall look it may not have the practically human-lifetime endurance of the very best. That could not be expected, but I shouldn't say it hasn't happened. It probably has.

It used to come with single-action lockwork, too. That form was the favorite of target shooters, but lack of demand, largely due to autoloader popularity, killed it. You had also a choice of eleven different stocks varying in shape, thickness, and the presence or lack of a thumb-rest. Included were a couple of grips of foreign free-pistol type, with a spur or extension of the walnut at the bottom rear of the grip.

In single-shot pistol style, named *the U.S.R.A.* after the United States Revolver Association which did so much slow fire precision shooting, it competed against the best foreign free pistols (free from Standard American restrictions in lightness of trigger pull and length of sight radius and barrel), and it did well, too. As I recall, General J. S. Hatcher used in this competition a special 7-inch barreled H.&R. single shot. That length later became standard, along with the 8-inch and the original 10. From time to time, there were various weights of barrel. There was no question of the accuracy of these arms.

This single shot cost a great deal less than the long-established *Smith & Wesson Perfected or Olympic single shot.* Yet its balance and grip styles often permitted better shooting, even when that beautiful old Smith was specially stocked for the owner, and perhaps barrel-weighted, too.

A 10-inch barrel was standard on the Perfected, but I liked mine so much as a woods gun that I had the factory cut it to 7-inch. (The double-action trigger—taken from a revolver action, and for no good reason except economy—didn't bother me with its trigger-return spring, as the kick-back was light.) The S.&W. folks told me the muzzle would be off-center from the cut-off, for the assembly had come from a centerfire revolver, originally; but that didn't faze me, either. It made an extremely handy little woods pistol, accurate, of course, and easy to clean. To me, the holding tremor seemed less than it had in 10-inch.

The H.&R. Sportsman also came in snub-nosed barrel, round-butt pocket type. In World War II, the frame was used for the five-shot *Defender* handling .38 S.&W. and Colt New Police rounds. Plastic grips replaced walnut, but the sights were still adjustable, and the good weight of 25 ounces made this one of the easiest-shooting guns for those cartridges—although the barrel was only 4-inch, a popular pocket length then. The big grip was unhandy in some forms of stowage, but it helped in drawing from a holster.

Through all changes and adaptations, today's Sportsman is much like the early ones that did so well as to be startling as "cheap guns." A recent change is the flattening of the barrel sides. This is in the manner of the new and less expensive Side-Kicks, but to a much smaller, even timid, extent. The Sportsman always had a heavy barrel rib for good balance at target, though not quick "point" shooting. There, a short barrel and more weight in the hand help most of us.

Harrington & Richardson Ultra Side-Kick 939
Caliber: .22 rimfire, short to long-rifle.
Weight: 33 ounces.
Barrel: 6 inches.
Overall: 10½ inches.
Sights: Patridge-type fixed front; rear sight adjustable for windage.
Stocks: Checked walnut, thumb-rest for right hand, or at extra cost for left hand. Trigger guard extension for second finger to rest on.
Finish: Crown-Lustre blue.

The nine-shot 939 is less expensive than the Sportsman, but the price difference is small. It has the solid-frame, swing-out cylinder action so popular now in low and medium price .22s. It does not have the hinged, tip-up barrel and cylinder of the Sportsman. When the guns are of equal quality, we could expect longer lifetime from the solid frame. For the heaviest centerfire loads above military requirements, it's the big favorite. Whether we get longer life from an inexpensive .22 solid frame is questionable. With good care, either sort should give generous accuracy life—up to many thousands of shots.

Some General Liabilities

Since this is the first inexpensive revolver to be treated formally in this book, we should pause to look over some of its assets and liabilities.

H.&R. Ultra Side-Kick, Model 939, 6-inch barrel. See cylinder release at rear of hammer.

The greatest asset is that it makes pistol shooting available to many of limited means, and to others, also many, who take up the sport so tentatively, merely dipping their toes into the pool, that they don't care to invest much in a first gun. This means a lot. It is important to the sport, to the discouragement of crime that always comes when it's suspected that victims might be armed and shoot back, and to our Country's defense. A .22 can kill. It also leads to firearms familiarity, and often to bigger, more effective arms.

The liabilities are perfectly natural when you think of cost accounting. It takes expensive, skilled work to produce the flawless—and a great deal of time.

One liability is a creepy, rough, much-too-heavy trigger pull. This sort is common under today's manufacturing conditions, and not alone in inexpensive arms.

Another is the uncertain alignment of chambers and barrel. Off-center, it shaves lead. So a good many low-priced revolvers are and have been made with excessive throating out of the barrel breech, to catch a misdirected bullet from an off-center chamber.

With this may go a wide gap between cylinder and barrel, even more than .01 inch in some specimens. Either defect is bad enough, and the combination cheats you of power—or so some Potter counter chronograph tests implied. We fired two .32 S.&W. long caliber revolvers with a gallery load, 1.4 grains Du Pont 5066 and the 98 grain Ideal cast bullet. The snug Colt Police Positive Target with barrel cut to 3¾ inches averaged 535 f. s. instrumental velocity, a shade under the theoretical "muzzle" velocity, and a 4½-inch barreled nameless revolver turned up only 311 f. s. Both guns are in excellent shape, not pitted or badly worn. The temperature that January morning was 32° Fahrenheit, the humidity bone-piercing.

The orphan had a considerable gap between barrel and cylinder and an excessively coned barrel breech. It also had chambers lazily and economically bored straight through, not shouldered down to afford a bullet seat. This is fine with .22 rimfires using the long-rifle cartridge with its case-diameter bullet, heeled down at the base to enter the brass, and with old .32, .38 and .41 Colt rounds with the same bullet type.

But the .32 S.&W. long is a more modern design of centerfire, with the bore-bearing lead enclosed in the case. Consequently, a lot of gas rushes out and is wasted if it's fired in a straight-through chamber. Yet the difference in velocity between these two guns was so great, that we felt sure the loss was partly due to the cylinder-barrel gap and the overdone barrel throating.

Excessive revolver barrel throating can be dangerous to bystanders. I've been hit by flying fragments from such guns. Naturally I didn't stand alongside the cylinder, for even the best revolvers can leak out hard particles directly to the side. I was about 45 degrees to the rear. Fortunately I wore glasses, but these hot, fast fragments of lead stung my skin.

If you want to spot your companion's shots on a safe background, best stand about six feet to the rear, almost directly behind him. If he had a glass head, that would help. He doesn't, but even so you can tell pretty well from this position whether his shots strike left, right, high, low, or on. Recoil blots out his view; so he depends on you.

Do *not* think that this particular make or model of medium-price .22 is particularly susceptible to these faults. Far from it! The weaknesses are all too general. Watch for these things when you're in the buying mood for either new or old guns.

Also watch for stiff actions. Some of them are really tough to open or close. No gun should leave a factory in such uncooperative shape, but believe me, a surprising number of them do! They include pistols, rifles and shotguns; they are of many makes; and some of them sell for plenty of money. The natural question comes up: how much use am I expected to give a gun before it's fit to use? I wish I could say.

This 939 Ultra deserves more special comment. It's a gun that's striking in appearance, and by and large that won't hurt its sales. The flat-sided barrel suggests, in a way, the Colt Match Woodsman .22 auto, and the ventilated barrel rib suggests the Colt Python revolver, both fine and costly target arms. The sides of the barrel on the Ultra I used were polished nicely and blued well.

One might wonder if .22 target shooting, even rapid-fire strings, would warm up a heavy barrel enough to generate heat waves that could interfere with precise aiming. Maybe it would, with the sun an ardent helper. At any rate, the rib is businesslike. And the gills or vents—or interstices, as Dr. Samuel Johnson would have dignified them (bless his kindly heart!)—these slots are not merely something more for a real gun-lover to keep clean and oiled against rust; they do the big part of dissipating heat waves too.

The thrust-knob behind the hammer is to unlatch the cylinder for swing-out, and it's fun to explain and demonstrate it. Empties are ejected by an easy shove on the cylinder rod, Colt or S.&W. fashion. In the old Harrington & Richardson Sportsman you keep tipping the barrel down on its hinge until they come out. With either system anyone soon learns to let gravity help, so that the cases fall clear.

Hi-Standard Supermatic Trophy Automatic

Caliber: .22 long-rifle.

Weight: 49, 51 and 53 ounces.

Barrel: 6¾, 8 and 10 inches. Extra interchangeable barrels for the same receiver can be had, in modern H-S fashion.

Overall: With 10-inch barrel, 15½ inches with stabilizer, 14½ inches without it.

Sights: New design. Rear sight is dovetailed into the barrel (or the slide of a 6¾-inch gun) and the rear face is wide, quick to see, and slanted back. This leaf is spring-loaded to prevent looseness, and windage and elevation screws are, also. Adjusting knobs are slotted wide enough to take a dime's edge, the sight clicks for each change, and you can read and record the settings. Detachable front sight is also of square-cut Patridge design, and undercut or slanted back.

Stocks: Checked walnut with thumb-rest. Front and back straps are grooved for non-slip hold.

Finish: Lustrous blue. Gold trigger and safety button, gold inlaid lettering.

Magazine capacity: 10.

The High Standard Manufacturing Corporation, forgivably, congratulated themselves for having had the courage to produce this entirely new 1958 line, the Trophy and the less expensive Citations. At first glance, they look like weapons from Mars, or from the mysterious side of the moon, but the guns are handling and shooting well. That counts.

The usual rear sight location—let's discuss the space-world look later—on the longer-barreled models is appreciated instantly by those who have fired a long-billed Luger. The 6-inch Luger often has its elevating rear sight on the breech-block, but barrel location is standard on the 8-inch, and it is welcomed. With such a long barrel—and remember the Luger barrel is set farther forward—there is all too much weave, front and rear and everywhere, with a rear sight mounted 'way back. This must be experienced to be realized!

Permissible sight radius in Standard American pistol shooting is ten inches. With the 6¾- and 10-inch barrels, you get 9⅜ inches, and with the 8-inch barrel, 7½. These guns obviously aren't made, at present, in anything like pocket size, and some would say that no holster would fit them neatly and provide smooth riding. This gun-crank's bet is that plenty of them will be carried afield, even so, because they are easy to shoot.

The trigger pull on this grade is a matter for pride, and its quality ought to be maintained. The weight adjustment screw is in plain view at the rear of the receiver, and there's also anti-backlash adjustment, that screw at the right of and above the trigger. The trigger's face is wide, and serrated, as we'd expect; and the chrome-nickel-molybdenum steel hammer and sear are carburized, skin-hardened like action parts of the Model 52C Winchester .22 rifles, to give long wear without change in feel or weight. If you look askance at the demountable barrel, remember that the spring which holds it in place is stiff, and the contact surfaces closely fitted. This is a quality gun. Finally, ten inches is enough barrel length to give respectable pistol velocity to the .22 long-rifle bullet. Only a little extra, but it helps, even though a rifle barrel can't make the .22 l-r more than a puny little load.

The barrel is grooved along the sides for attachment of the two weights of 2 and 3½ ounces. Factory literature states that these deep cuts dampen barrel vibration, and that sounds reasonable. The underside of the barrel has detents at stations ⅝-inch apart for the Allen screw lockup of the weights' clamping plates. Thus a great variety of balances can be had with one gun and one barrel, to suit the individual user. Without the weights the gun is of course lightest and least muzzle-heavy, and the barrel taper is attractive. The enlarged muzzle end of the barrel is, undeniably, unusual in appearance, and some wouldn't care for it at all. It has to be big to take the detachable recoil stabilizer or muzzle brake, which reduces upchuck in the manner so familiar on tommy guns—or submachine guns. Gas rushing up through the vent in the stabilizer does, in effect, push the muzzle down, jet-fashion. In the Olympic course of rapid fire, this recoil reduction means a great deal: you can have a barrel of weight that you can handle, not a section of drilled crowbar, and it still drops back into line of aim without too much effort on your part. And in our more liberal Standard American time limits, the muzzle-vent system is so helpful that it's extremely popular, both built-in—as on the recently discontinued Hi-Standard Supermatic, Olympic and Field-King with 6¾-inch barrels—and detachable, like this one and the Ruger and Smith & Wesson versions.

One of the most important details in any pistol for any use is its grip fit and trigger reach, a combination that makes or mars scores. An autoloader with its magazine inside the grip—and practically all in common use except the old military Mauser have it—is limited in adaptability by the metal frame that holds the magazine and often some working parts, too. The grip frame of most revolvers can be cut down considerably, if a special small grip or a differently shaped one is required. With either gun, the stocks can be formed to fit the individual hand, subject to the metalwork under them.

A great criticism of auto-pistols is that the reach from the rear of the grip to the face of the trigger is too long for small hands, except on pocket-size guns. These new Hi-Standard models have a short reach, less than 2½ inches, which will please a good many pistoleers.

These grips also have considerable backward slant, which makes for natural pointing, Luger fashion, in the practice or application of defense shooting. But at target you do a lot more than point. You hold on the aim in slow fire, or any fire, trying to squeeze out the most points. With a revolver, your wrist is more or less locked. Naturally back-slant helps in shooting the auto. Almost any modern .22 self-loader is easier to

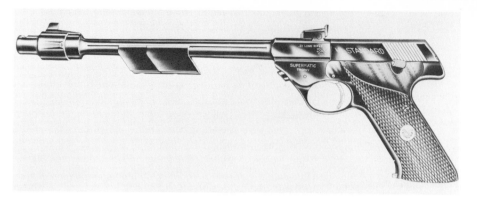

Hi-Standard Supermatic Trophy.

shoot than the rather straight-gripped .45 Colt, the muzzle of which must be held up deliberately, to keep from ripping up a divot half way to the target. Practice smooths out curable difficulties, but practice is eased by the right grip in the first place. The way to find the right gun, for you as an individual, is to try all the different grips you can find, even if you become something of a pest. Those who are versed in shooting will understand.

And that is only a start, for grip alteration and getting used to the gun may both become necessary. Few people have ever closed their fingers around a grip that seemed perfect on first contact.

Conversion Kits

The Trophy and the Supermatic Citation are for .22 long-rifle rounds, the Olympic Citation for .22 shorts. Human nature wants one gun for both, but neither cartridge shoots its best with the other's rifling twist, and long-rifles won't enter a short chamber. Unless simplicity is sacrificed, .22 short recoil won't operate long-rifle autoloading actions, and long-rifle recoil is rough on a .22 short auto-pistol's action balanced for the light shove.

So the factory offers conversion kits for these Trophy and Citation triplets, and insists that the fitting be done by their own people. For about one-half more money you get the use of two guns, not at the same instant, but promptly. The kit contains the slide, barrel, barrel weights, and magazine. You stick to the familiar trigger pull continuously, which is good, even though these guns have fine and adjustable pulls.

Old Models

High Standard has been in the auto-pistol race for about thirty years, so long that repair parts for some models earlier than 1942 are not on hand at this writing. This fact is not surprising, or in any way extreme, as some of us know too well. The Corporation has made a great many models. The most recent of interest to target shots are the 43-ounce Supermatic, the 41-ounce Olympic for .22 shorts, and the somewhat lighter Field-King. All have 6¾-inch barrels with built-in recoil stabilizer, and there are also unstabilized 4½-inch models, more for field use in themselves,

though interchangeable barrels could be had. Some do better at target with short barrels because the shorter intersight distance suits their eyesight better.

These models are no longer to be made, it seems, but we shall see them on firing lines for years to come. The heavier two have detachable barrel weights for either length. On these guns the stabilizers are simply cuts through the barrel, right and left of the front sight. A few people didn't care for them because they are a little troublesome to clean. The detachable stabilizer of the current guns is easy to get at, and a cleaning tool comes with the outfit. A great many shooters don't or won't clean either kind except on a dull rainy afternoon with no fishing trip in sight. But modern ammunition is tolerant.

Some of us remember or even still use fine old H.-S. target or field automatics with exposed hammers, the H line. They came in many weights and styles, one of the latest having been the HDM (Military), popular just after World War II. These hammers lay so far back that a quadruple-jointed thumb was necessary to cock them on quick-draw, but they were reassuring to look at. You knew whether or not the gun was cocked, and if you relied on a .22 auto for home defense you could have a chambered round ready to go, with no strain on the mainspring. Any such instant preparedness depends very much on who lives in your home and what he knows about safe gun-handling.

Hi-Standard Supermatic Citation

Caliber: .22 long-rifle.
Weight: 50, 52 and 54 ounces.
Overall: Same as Trophy.
Sights: Same as on Trophy.
Stocks: Checked, laminated plastic, walnut colored, with thumb-rest.
Finish: Like that of Trophy except that trigger, safety and lettering are not gold plated or inlaid, and the blue may be less lustrous, for the price difference is considerable.
Magazine capacity: 10.

From a practical point of view, there is little choice between this model and the Trophy. Either gun, and the companion Olympic Citation, can be had with walnut stocks, with or without a thumb-rest for either hand. The extra cost of these stocks seems reasonable, considering the material and workmanship.

Hi-Standard Supermatic Citation,
caliber .22 long-rifle.

Many shooters prefer for rough field use (this roughness is related to the care we are able and willing to give) a perfectly plain gun, not ornate in any way. Even with no thought of resale, such folks "hate to take a fine arm into the woods," or to any place where doing the immediate job is more important than the tool. Of course this attitude is debatable. Honest service wear looks good to some; and I am among that perhaps odd lot. Some dislike any embellishment on a fine weapon, though excellent bluing or browning or whatever the finish is, or is called, is welcome. It may be a dull but still beautiful and functional finish that doesn't wink out sun-ray reflection to alert the game!

The Trophy certainly isn't garish in finish, at least in the manner of some arms that knock our eyes out. Some of us always insist on having the best, whatever our notions of that ideal may be. It's worth noting that the .22 short Olympic model in the following discussion comes only in the Citation grade at present, though of course a conversion kit would make the Trophy handle shorts for Olympic and our own rapid-fire courses.

Hi-Standard Olympic Citation

Caliber: .22 short.
Weight: 46, 48 and 50 ounces.
Barrel: 6¾, 8 and 10 inches.
Overall: Same as Trophy and Supermatic Citation.
Sights: Same as on Trophy and Supermatic Citation.
Stocks: Plastic, as on Supermatic Citation.
Finish: Like that of the Supermatic Citation.
Magazine capacity: 10.

The Olympic weighs less than its Supermatic Citation companion because its slide is of dural, not steel, to facilitate the blowback self-loading action with the light recoil of the .22 short cartridge. Since there's a limit to alibis, a rapid-fire target pistol must be close to 100% reliable in tossing out empties and chambering fresh loads.

Lightening the stock and even the action of a rifle or shotgun in effect makes it more muzzle-heavy because a greater proportion of weight is out front, for the forward hand to support. This doesn't mean much in the handling of these .22 auto-pistols except that in trying them a person might naturally wonder why a

quarter-pound lighter gun didn't feel lighter, held out in aiming.

It is surprising, perhaps, how much use .22 short pistols get at target ranges well over 50 feet, or even 25 yards. On a calm day, there's nothing much to prevent a little old 29-grain bullet from finding the Standard American 10-ring at 50 yards, provided it gets a good start in its brief career.

Hi-Standard Supermatic Tournament

Caliber: .22 long-rifle.
Weight: 42 and 46 ounces. All these H-S weights are as catalogued. Most of them differ from those given in the fine coverage article, "New Target Pistols," by the N.R.A. technical staff in the August, 1958, *American Rifleman.* I have no explanation.
Barrel: 4½ and 6¾ inches, tapered; old standard H-S lengths.
Overall: 11¼ inches with 6¾-inch barrel.
Sights: Rear sight similar to those on the three preceding models; ramped, square front.
Stocks: Similar to those on Supermatic Citation and Olympic Citation.
Finish: Blued.
Magazine capacity: 10.

The Tournament has a heavy round barrel of the familiar old H.-S. type, and at present it is not furnished with any stabilizing vent. A custom muzzle stabilizer could be fitted, if wanted; but the heavy barrel brings the gun weight nearly, if not quite, up to that of the .22 short Citation of the same length. It's a good weight and length for handling the heavier recoil of the .22 long-rifle cartridge, except when time of recovery is most important in making fast hits. The gun is reasonably priced, and for $10 more (just now) it comes with a set of two barrel lengths. In weight and general styling, it is much like the recently discontinued Supermatic for the same ammunition.

The front and back straps of the grip are not grooved, but a gunsmith could groove them. The gun has the wide target trigger that improves the shooter's control, usually, and makes the pull seem lighter than it is. This trigger has the anti-backlash screw for adjustment of over-travel, after the hammer has been tripped, down to nothing or near enough to it. The magazine has the same sort of "controlled" release as the more expensive grades have, at the bottom of the butt. It is out of the way, even if less convenient than

Hi-Standard Supermatic Tournament gets its muzzle weight from a heavy round barrel much like those on earlier H.-S. models. In modern H.-S. style, its barrel is detachable.

the Colt .45 1911 or one-time .22 Woodsman type, with a button up behind the trigger. It is possible to shed a badly wanted magazine from the latter kind, though luckily that is one blunder I have never yet committed.

This is a companionable, easily holstered pistol, with nothing much about it to explain to people who know guns either fairly well or as the scribes and prophets do. Shooting a .22 short automatic is so much plain fun, when you shoot just for fun, that it would please many folks if this model came out in that caliber, too. Some of us like a little heavier and more expensively made pop-pistol than the 35- or 37-ounce Hi-Standard Flite-King, in the same barrel lengths as this long-rifle gun. Unless the possible invaders from outer space are small and easily scuppered, I'd prefer something more effective than a .22 short for protection. The .22 long-rifle isn't much, but it's still a lot more than the short.

Hi-Standard Free Pistol

Service and civilian shooters of international match ability, and we other Americans, are getting pretty tired of so many Olympic shooting wins going to Russia. Our competitors deserve not only honor, but also the best possible backing.

This single-shot, .22 long-rifle caliber pistol was planned for American use in the 50-meter slow-fire 1960 Olympic matches at Rome. It's in the "free pistol" class, free because such guns come under so few restrictions in weight, barrel length, sights and trigger pull. This type is meant to make the highest possible scores in one-hand firing.

Years ago, our shooters took along their refined, American-made single-shots, such as the Smith & Wesson and Harrington & Richardson, and even autoloaders, and often did well against the European free pistols. As time passed, competition grew hotter, and the guns they shot against were so good that they often bought pistols like them, foreign-made.

For the convenience of Americans in or hopeful of entering the game, and for the pride of us all, free pistols made right here became more and more desirable. Early in 1960 the Hi-Standard project was

announced. Mass production—or at least quantity production—should compete with European prices plus our import duties without sacrificing the quality of performance.

Much of the credit for development goes to our Army's Advanced Marksmanship Unit, Fort Benning, Georgia. Master Sergeant Herman Gano, designer and gunsmith, in particular suggested many of the gun's details of construction. The High Standard Manufacturing Corporation and the Benning Unit teamed up well against the monotonous drift of foreign victories. With our own guns, and with our own excellent ammunition as a matter of course, our folks will have a better chance to reverse it.

At this writing the work is not completed, but here are some general specifications. Barrels are to come in 8, 9 and 10 inch lengths, and the heaviest model is to weigh 50 ounces. Rotary sear and sear connector minimize possible gun tremor in the tiny interval between trigger touch-off and the bullet's leap from the muzzle. They also add to safety.

An electro-magnet's pull, not a steel-to-steel trigger contact, releases the striker. Two 6½ volt batteries lie in the grip, much as the magazine of an autoloader does. (For a comparison that may not be sensible, the big "B" battery of a venerable Beltone hearing aid

Model 1960 Hi-Standard .22 single-shot Olympic.

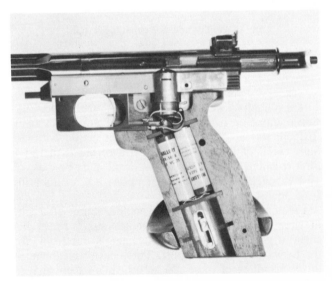

Cutaway of Hi-Standard Olympic's firing release mechanism.

that I still use occasionally has 22½ volt power, and the little powerhouse of my later transistor Zenith, smaller but not nit-sized, has 1½ volt energy.) The electrical tripping of the H-S primer-smacker should reassure beginners who fear that a set trigger may cut loose at a cross word or even an uncharitable thought. Triggers of some conventional free pistols can mistake a light jarring of the gun, or even a change in temperature, for the command to fire. Even so, the H-S trigger can be set as low as one-tenth ounce.

The grips on the new gun are oversize because most free pistol shots like them so, in the beginning. Fitting them by degrees to the hand is an individual job, one for each shooter to perform or have done for him alone. The grips shown in the illustration are therefore only a start, although they do have the basic details, the rests for the bottom of the hand and for the thumb—a forefinger groove is commonly used on the other side—and the buildup under the trigger guard, which positions the second finger to take most of the gun's weight as does the applied or integral filler or "adapter" that most of us want on most double-action revolvers. Perfect fitting of the stocks, for the individual, makes the gun almost go to bye-bye in his hand, and his grip tends to become consistent far more easily than does one on an unfitted handgun. Even a twenty-pound bench rest rifle must be held the same for each shot; and it's very much heavier, is well supported, and is hardly "held" at all, in the usual sense.

The tentative price of the H. S. Olympic is something under $300. Free rifles for 50-meter rimfire or 300-meter centerfire are costly, too. We must remember that the targets' scoring rings are small, and that we need shootability as well as accuracy for Olympic conditions.

Iver Johnson Trailsman 66

Caliber: .22 short, long and long-rifle. A .32 and .38 caliber "Snub," five-shot, came out in 1960.
Weight: 34 ounces, or 27 ounces in 2¾-inch "Snub" style.
Barrel: 6 inches; "Snub" 2¾ inches. Chrome lined to resist corrosion and give long accuracy life against erosion. Hard to rust or burn out, as proved in high power rifle barrels.
Overall: 11 inches. "Snub," 7 inches, with rounded grip.
Sights: Square Patridge type. Front is adjustable for elevation, rear for windage. Sighting plane has non-glare mat finish, as would be expected.
Stocks: Checked plastic with thumb-rest. Rounded or square target stocks on "Snub."
Finish: Blue.

This is an unusually low-priced but well designed 8-shot revolver. It has the tip-up, not the swing-out cylinder action, and the hinge is large and sturdy for long wear. There are useful target extras, such as those listed above, and a wide, well grooved hammer spur and grooved trigger face. The muzzle end of the cylinder is counterbored, like those of other current I. J. revolvers, to deflect hot gases and flying particles forward and down, for the safety of bystanders. This one feature can mean much on the firing line, par-

Iver Johnson Trailsman 66.

Another view of the Trailsman. Note chrome-lined barrel.

ticularly in rather informal practice where there may be no wise, experienced range officer on hand to see that every last, fine detail of safety is observed—as it should be, always!

About the only serious criticism of Trailsman design is the lack of a rest or filler piece for the second finger. The curve behind the guard comes high enough to make it necessary, as it is on most as-issued S.&W. or Colt double-action revolvers. The *I. J. Champion,* a single-action target revolver, and the lately discontinued *Armsworth* that resembled it, both had it in the form of a curved metal plate, screw-anchored to the front strap of the grip and adjustable in height.

The Trailsman's low price is not a give-away. The old and well regarded Iver Johnson firm isn't in business as a charitable organization, although it certainly has done its part in arming America and keeping her gun-conscious by producing inexpensive but sound revolvers, shotguns, and .22 single-shot rifles. No one can expect perfect workmanship in a target revolver at $39.95 during a long period of inflation. For that matter, an informed and critical gun-lover can find faults in too many specimens of our best, or at least near-best, production, particularly if he's acquainted with the superb standard-run jobs turned out a generation ago. But this 1958 I. J. is to be considered seriously by the beginner who does not have a big wad of currency allocated for his first target revolver.

A gunsmith can smooth the trigger pull or do other jobs—if any come up. The approximately two-pound weight of the Trailsman is about right for the average beginner; and after he graduates to a finer target arm, the old I. J. still should be serviceable for field use. It's rugged. Of course this .22 revolver, like practically all others now made, has the embedded cylinder breech; each case-head is enclosed by a countersink to protect the thumb in the event of defective brass bursting.

In this class and caliber, the difference between swing-out cylinder and tip-up barrel and cylinder doesn't seem important. Each is handy, once you become familiar with it, and ammunition pressures are so low that the tip-up locking system is strong enough. When the .38 S.&W. cartridge came out with the overweight Super Police 200 grain bullet, the news soon got around that it wasn't smart to use it in tip-up guns. British tip-ups, finely and expensively made, do handle heavy, large caliber bullets. But these are distinctly low velocity loads by modern standards.

Thorough cleaning of a cylinder is easier if it comes out of the revolver with no crane attached. That helps particularly if we use black powder, as so many do in the early single action Colts. The smooth nonfluted cylinders of recently discontinued I. J. revolvers—like the *Armsworth* and slightly less expensive *Supershot* target arms, and early issues of the still current Model 55 plinker with non-adjustable sights—were in theory easier to keep free from powder stains than fluted cylinders are. But to a modern eye, they looked odd, and that styling has been discontinued. Some new or revived features about firearms catch on; some do not.

Early I. J. Target Guns

Long ago, the standard "Hammer-the-Hammer" revolvers could be had with 6-inch barrels and the

Iver Johnson Trailsman, snub-nosed 2¾-inch barrel, round butt. Not a target gun, but shorties, too, need adjustable sights unless they're for pocket carry and draw.

large "Western" walnut grips (or the slightly lighter hard-rubber "Perfect") with long, square butt. The former had a decided lip or curl-back at the top, to position the hand in holding and against recoil. The greatest standard weights were 17½ ounces in .22 and 22 ounces in .32 S.&W. long or .38 S.&W. short. The sights were fixed, as we'd expect. These guns, like similar Harrington & Richardson and Hopkins & Allen models, were about the least expensive target revolvers, and good at their price. They were discontinued many years ago, and second-hand specimens should be in good condition if we are to buy them, for many old parts are no longer around.

The .22 *Supershot Sealed Eight* was a double action with target sights and a finger rest too, if wanted, at extra cost. The *Supershot Nine* held one more cartridge in its cylinder, which was not counterbored for the case-heads. The *Champion* was really a better gun, though it weighed the same 28 ounces, because it was a single action with a nice, straight trigger face (which some like on a pistol) and usually a really good pull. Its barrel contour resembled that of the Harrington & Richardson Sportsman, before the sides were milled off flat.

Late Supershots had the flash control cylinder, recessed up front, and so did the *Armsworth*. In final production both had the smooth, unfluted cylinder. Both carried one-piece walnut grips. The Super wood was checked at the rear, the Armsworth along the sides.

Iver Johnson 57 Target

Caliber: .22 short, long and long-rifle.
Weight: 27, 29 and 30½ ounces.
Barrel: 2½, 4½ and 6 inches.
Overall: 10¾ inches with 6-inch barrel.
Sights: Patridge-type; front adjustable for elevation, rear for windage.
Stocks: Checked plastic with thumb-rest.
Finish: Blue.

Only the 6-inch, or possibly the 4½-, would be the natural choice for target or accurate field work. Short-barreled .22 revolvers, like small .22 automatics, are extremely popular today for plinking, as auxiliaries (mostly for fun) to a rifle or shotgun, and for pocket use. We can be glad that they are, for every sound and serviceable type of arm in use does its bit to make Americans—men, women and kids more gun-conscious and gun-familiar.

The 57 is lighter and less expensive than the Trailsman, with many of its good features: wide hammer spur, scored trigger, big and rugged sights, flash control cylinder and case-head enclosure. It differs mainly in being a solid frame gun, not a tip-up, which makes reloading slower, though eight shots should be enough for most uses or minor emergency afield, even with a .22. The Iver Johnson Arms and Cycle Works deserves a crown for putting out such a moderately priced revolver with adjustable sights, and for making the less expensive 55 model, too—similar but with fixed sights. Our future top shots are young, and some

Iver Johnson solid frame Model 57 with 4½-inch barrel and adjustable sights that qualify it for a beginner's target use. He can adjust them to help center his shots.

do have to count their quarters and half-dollars, though hardly their pennies any more, before they arm themselves.

These 55 and 57 revolvers have the weight and hang that make them attractive to plenty of older shooters. Some like what they call a "knock-about gun," even though they may have the sense to give any firearm decent care—perhaps because they enjoy doing this on principle, or more to have the weapon ready and reliable whenever it may be needed.

Ruger Mark I .22 Automatic

Caliber: .22 long-rifle.
Weight: 39 and 42 ounces.
Barrel: 5¼ and 6⅞ inches. *The former seems to have been discontinued permanently.*
Overall: 9¼ and 10⅞ inches.
Sights: Patridge type ⅛-inch front, undercut on long barrel to prevent glare, straight-faced on short barrel model, which can qualify as a pocket or handy holster gun. Micro click two-way adjustable rear sight.
Stocks: Black Butaprene type hard rubber, checked.
Finish: Blue.
Magazine capacity: 9.

The Mark I Target came several years after the standard Ruger auto, and it too sold at a surprisingly low price, thanks to good engineering and acceptable short-cuts in manufacture. It won the 1953 National .22 championship at Camp Perry, Ohio, where the best shots and the best guns assemble to shoot it out. For target, the long barrel is the usual choice, though custom refinements may include heavier barrels and hand-made-to-fit-the-hand stocks. As it comes from the factory box it's a good target pistol, although like most others, especially autoloaders, it may need to have its trigger pull freed of backlash. (It seems at this writing that the 5¼-inch barrel model has been definitely discontinued. Demand might bring it back.)

There's a special advantage here, perhaps partly theoretical when you study the close competition between men and between guns to reach the winner's pinnacle. The receiver carries the rear sight, but this receiver is not a breech-block. That part slides through it; so the sight does not ride back with it in recoil, in common auto-pistol fashion. Tolerances of breech-block fit aren't passed on to the rear sight. The Ruger receiver is a simple tube that holds barrel and breech-block, and it's separate from the grip and magazine frame.

A Mark I muzzle brake or stabilizer is available for rapid fire. It is a simple, dependable thing. In dry practice the hammer can be snapped indefinitely, for it's meant to be practically unbreakable. The safety, very much in German Luger position, but a button instead of a long lever, locks sear and bolt. It can hold the bolt open when you're behind the firing line, as rules demand.

This splendid target arm is suitable for field service, too, and we needn't be suspicious of it because of its low price. But it is a gun for a rather long hand, just as the Luger is, or the Colt .45 auto, or any number of others. Try it for fit before you buy it, as with any other handgun. Your forefinger, squeezing the trigger, should be long enough to do so without riding along in contact with the frame. Side pressure there, in spite of effort to adjust, tends to vary enough to cause irregular shooting—away from that pressure. Perhaps this should be remembered particularly in this case, for the gun is very attractive in appearance and in price-tag.

Since I'm one of those who need a fairly muzzle-heavy pistol (or rifle) to help dampen the tremors, I prefer the long Ruger for scores, although for woods-handiness the shorty is one of the most alluring. Ruger has given us good guns in this and other models. He also gave some manufacturers fits, I presume, in the dollar value he offered. Many competitors of the standard, lower-priced Ruger automatic came along. His Single-Six .22 revolver in old Colt Peacemaker single-action styling led something of a parade, too. In these days of inflation, the consumer could sit back and grin. He needed to.

The use of stampings and an electrically welded

Ruger Mark I .22 automatic with 6⅞-inch barrel. The less target-popular 5¼-inch Mark I seems to have been discontinued.

frame isn't important. What counts is good performance at economical price, bringing joy to many hearts and bringing more converts to the pistol shooting game, from plinking to sharp competition.

The 5¼-inch Mark I seems to beg to go to the wild and unspoiled places, either in the pocket or in a holster. The adjustable sights and good weight help to make it easy to shoot well, and it's a far more compact package than the 6⅞-inch job. With so much weight in the butt of the shorty, hip-pocket carry isn't too good, unless that pocket is about as deep as a well, but in a big side pocket in a hunting coat, it's different toting. This rear-end heft makes a retaining strap desirable on a belt holster for this gun, so it can't possibly fall out in gymnastic wilderness travel. A snap strap that can be scuffed off with an upward nudge of the side of the hand causes little delay in getting the gun out. The times when we need quick draw in the wilderness are comparatively few, though they can be important! Some of us would prefer the longer barreled gun afield because we could shoot it enough better to pay for the extra bulk.

Ruger Blackhawk .357 Magnum

Caliber: .357 Magnum. Also takes .38s from short Colt to Special.
Weight: 39 ounces with 4⅝-inch barrel.
Barrel: 4⅝ inches, tapered from ¾ to 11/16 inch. 6½ and 10 inch barrels added in 1959.
Overall: With 4⅝-inch barrel, 10⅛ inches.
Sights: Patridge type. Ramped front post ⅛ in wide, matted against glare and set close to muzzle to increase sight radius. Micro rear sight, two-way adjustable, well behind cylinder to cooperate with the long-radius front sight mounting.
Stocks: High impact-resistant hard black rubber, checked. Walnut made standard in 1960. Genuine staghorn or ivory at extra cost.
Finish: Blue.

This followed the Ruger .22 revolver, which also is a six-shooter. It was the first generally available .357 sixgun at moderate cost. Using a close replica of the Colt Frontier grip, frame and general build was good business. The old Peacemaker was then still in Limbo, out of production and much longed for and romanced about, and even so-so used ones cost plenty. Almost everyone knew that the Colt grip is obliging, fits nearly any hand and gives little punishment with even the heaviest loads. Choosing .357 Mag instead of a big-bore like .44 Special or even the storied .45 Colt made sense, too, for high velocity sells many guns today, both pistols and rifles. Factory subloads for the .357 are common—.38 Special on down. These do not include the fatter-bodied .38 S&W Short and Colt New Police.

For economy, the grip straps and trigger guard are a one-piece aluminum-alloy casting. The barrel length first offered is one of the best for a heavy-barreled, medium-bore Single Action Army type.

Some few moments ago, the kind of reader that any careful writer likes to have would have asked

Ruger Blackhawk .357 Magnum, 4⅝-inch barrel.

an embarrassing question: "Why list this powerful shorty among target guns and pitch the finely made and modern Great Western into the chapter on work guns?" After a preliminary "Ahem!"—not expected to be impressive—this writer explains that the Ruger comes regularly with target sights, not as extras; and the extra, if any, could go into smooth tuning-up, if it were needed. Then too, he has small use for a target arm that can't do field work. Furthermore, he plans to sweat out an index of models and other things. It's for the back of the book, just as we carry our useful car tools in the back of the car—or at least wish we had them somewhere with us on the road.

If you want a moderately priced .357 just now, you choose between this Ruger, the Colt "Three-Fifty-Seven," and the heavier S.&W. Highway Patrolman. You decide between single and double action, and more important, the fit and balance of the guns in your hand. The Colt is on a .41 caliber frame, but how many .357 users shoot .357 exclusively, with light .38s available for it? The finely target-sighted Patrolman got in among work guns because it costs less than the standard .357 S&W Mag. A person might then not cry bitterly if it picked up scratches in service!

The .357 is excessive for 50-yard targets made of paper, and some like to try longer ranges. What's so terrible about loading Magnum brass with subloads? Yes, there's too much air-space, but the long case sets the forefront of the bullet closer to the barrel breech than .38 Special brass does. That means less jump for the lead, and superior accuracy because of it.

Ten-inch sixgun barrels are not for target, for that length, *including* cylinder, is the maximum allowable. Figure on about 2¼ to 2⅝ inches for cylinder. The over-long barrels, fine in the field, are here because of the Buntline craze; but we can be glad that they are here, because they certainly have their advantages, just as the other extremes, the snubnoses, have.

This strong Ruger with chrome-moly steel frame and cylinder, and only a short barrel breech projecting from the frame, isn't liable to be hurt by any sensible handload. Having the firing pin mounted in the frame, not attached to the hammer, is a fine thing. It is just one of those modernizations that the Ruger and Great Western have and the still conventionally made Colt Single Action Army hasn't. The coil mainspring makes cocking pretty smooth, too, though it seems a bit pointless to criticize the Army or the much different Colt Bisley in this respect—at least if you like these old guns as much as I do, and millions of others, too.

The six-groove rifling and 16-inch twist are fine for the 158 grain bullets used, regardless, largely, of high or low velocities. There is nothing startling about them. The flat top-strap, as used on old target model Colts, is of course just fine. This Ruger has been and is popular, and it's already stood up under enough use to be proved durable. In testing, 150% proof loads are used. It is true that there is no base pin bushing as on the Colt. But if the base pin wears, a new cylinder or else a fine gunsmith job could come up. Firing heavy loads does wear the usual base pin, but Ruger material is strong, meant to take wear.

Even for a one-gun pistoleer this medium-caliber Blackhawk is worth consideration, although it's a bit heavy, perhaps, if that man has a nice wife and kids who also want to shoot pistol. However, last week when I had the pleasure of shooting with a young couple, I wish you could have seen the lady handle his K-.38 Smith. That one weighs 38½ ounces, loaded, obviously less than the 39-ounce Ruger, empty, but not a great deal less. She had fired it off and on for a few years, and she was absolutely deadly with it. In long target strings it would tire her, she said, but that of course depends largely on how much training you go in for. A very good way for anyone to start with a too-heavy pistol is two-handed, but she was far and long beyond that.

You and I know that good modern guns are made of durable steel. There have been tragic accidents with old single-action revolvers that fell on rock, hammer spur first, and discharged because quarter-or half-cock notches or sears broke out. Human intelligence got to work, and now the warning to carry a single-action always with the hammer clear down on an empty chamber is commonly, but not always heard. If you rest the hammer nose on the fired primer of an empty case, with at least some guns the cylinder still can shift and by patient ill-fortune bring a live round under that striker, all ready for a fall and a discharge. The warning still holds. Ruger could have made a short, spring-loaded separate firing pin that would reach the primer only by the momentum given it by the fall of the hammer—in exposed-hammer Colt automatic style. But with such a short firing pin, hopping back into its house the instant after doing its work, there would be the chance of primer metal flowing back into the firing pin's home, at least when heavy loads were used. That would tie up the gun, perhaps for just as long as it would take a free hand to give the cylinder a wrench, perhaps longer. A multi-shot handgun is for instant repeating action, upon which we depend in case of need.

Ruger Blackhawk .44 Magnum

Caliber: .44 Magnum. Also takes .44 Specials, but if we shoot up the still shorter .44 Russians in it, we break a cartridge collector's heart.

Weight: 40 ounces with 6½-inch barrel. Pretty heavy for many target shooters, but not all of them, by any means.

Barrel: 6½ inches, tapered from 25/32 to 45/64 inch. 7½- and 10-inch barrels followed in May, 1959 announcement.

Overall: 12⅛ inches with 6½-inch barrel.

Sights: Similar to those on .357 Ruger, and low-mounted, too. Front ramp is more square than the .357's, as this is a holster gun, and not for any pocket but a mighty special one.

Stocks: Smooth, unchecked walnut in standard issue. Easier on the hand under heavy recoil. Uncheckered, selected wood stocks can be had at extra cost for S.&Ws. in Magna or Target style.

Finish: Blue.

For a target shooter who wants a heavy bigbore especially for long range, this is one to consider. Its primary purpose is business: hunting, defense, police use when smash and penetration are needed, as against car bodies or motors. Barrels are long enough to give steady hang and good velocities, the 6½ packing pretty well, and faster to draw than the others. The 7½ fits woods work and the 10 isn't only for two-hand shooting. This gun appeared promptly after the .44 Mag cartridge came out, and it costs a good bit less than the Smith & Wesson.

A heavily charged sixgun with Colt Single Action Army grip style, like this one and the Great Western .44 Maggie, slides back in your hand with recoil. In this respect it's comfortable. The hammer spur is down there for you to thumb it back—it may even be too long, and need filing. Cocking the hammer and getting back on target take practice, and so does thumb-cocking a double-action, which by comparison stays put in recoil and hands the punishment, if it is that, back to you.

In shooting a heavily loaded rifle you also have to recover from recoil; but with either type of arm, "practice does it," unless you are over-gunned. After some shooting with milder, introductory loads you may no longer be over-gunned. It is true that even experienced shooters do feel the sting of .44 Magnum recoil. It's considerable, but it can become endurable. *Starting* with it would bring experience fast!

Ruger Blackhawk .44 Magnum, 6½-inch barrel.

A single-action can be used very well in timed and rapid fire competition. With a double-action, some of us find, after long experience, that we start the hammer back with a *short* pull on the trigger—try this first with an empty gun. Some others find the s. a. hammer handier than any on a double-action. It depends partly on shooting background and on your particular gun enthusiasm. The single-action has the fascination of romance—even, or perhaps most particularly, to the saltiest old characters, because they know its reputation and achievements. What harm is there in all that?

Smooth walnut or ivory grips seldom become slippery, even in a moist hand, though one would expect them to. With good color and finish they are attractive. Once my buddy and I ordered a pair of plain, smooth walnut stocks from Smith & Wesson for our .38 Regulation Police pocket gun. They were far better-looking than factory-checkered jobs. If anything, they seemed to give a better hold on that small five-shooter—which really could kick a bit with the 200 grain Super Police Western or Winchester loads that came out when we had it.

The 20-inch twist of the Ruger .44 Mag's rifling is fast enough for the fairly short standard bullet, or for heavier ones. It is the same as used for years by S.&W. for the .44 Special. And you know that the .44-40 Winchester rifle, with a stubby 200 grain bullet, got by with a 36-inch spin rate.

The cylinder is 1.749 inches long. On the S.&W. .44 Mag it is nearly identical, 1.75, and on the .357 Ruger it is 1.604, but on the S.&W. .44 Special frame it is 1.57 inches. The length allows long loading of .44 Magnum brass, with rather long-pointed bullets set well out. Shooters appreciate these long .44 cylinders.

A perhaps zany thought arises: how would this long case perform with the mild-cracking, still fairly powerful black powder? The mild old .44 Special factory load was only 26 grains of it, whereas the longer, thin-brassed .45 Colt case could accept 40 grains, both crammed in under standard bullets. It might make a most interesting and sweet-shooting mean between those two old black powder rounds. The Magnum case is ⅛ inch longer than the Special, but of course it is solid-headed. Many Specials, like a boxful I bought the other day, still have the balloon pocket for the primer, which gives them more capacity but less head strength than solid-web Specials. Ruger .44 chamber walls are thick, a matter important to handloaders who put up heavy charges.

Like the Ruger .357 and most other single-actions, this gun probably should be carried with an empty chamber under the hammer. This may seem an extreme safety measure, but anyone who's seen an even fairly bloody firearms accident is likely to go whole-hog on safety!

There has been some loosening of Ruger .357 and .44 frame screws under recoil, and it's common with

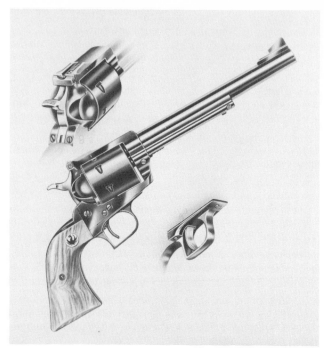

Ruger Super Blackhawk .44 Magnum, 7½-inch barrel, 48 ounces gun weight. Especially designed for heavy (but sensible) loads. Reverse curve of trigger guard is to make life pleasanter for the second finger when recoil comes back heartily.

old Colts. A touch of varnish under the screw-heads, or perhaps only a bit of linseed oil, ought to stop it. Late Blackhawks have "Nylok" screws with a Nylon plug in the threads.

The 1959 Super Blackhawk .44 Mag is a larger, heavier gun, 48 ounces with 7½-inch barrel. The steel, not light-alloy, frame is bigger. An unfluted cylinder and a heavier top-strap add weight and strength. To help reduce recoil discomfort, the rear of the guard has a reverse curve, or is, in fact, almost straight. Therefore it's less likely to belt the second finger when the gun rears up and back. This gun costs but little more than the standard Ruger .44 Mag, yet it's really for specialists who want the greatest ballistic performance from handloaded ammunition. Or is it? Husky pistolmen, or those who shoot two-handed afield, would like it for standard or reduced charges because of its weight and barrel length. Other lengths may come, and the big steel grip frame is to be available for standard Ruger .44 Blackhawks.

Smith & Wesson .22 Automatic, Model 41

Caliber: .22 long-rifle.
Weight: 43 ounces with muzzle brake attached and a ⅜-ounce aluminum weight in recess under the barrel. Set of three adjustable Olympic counterweights at extra cost. With 5-inch barrel, not adapted to S&W muzzle brake, barrel weight, or counterweights, the gun weighs 37½ ounces.
Barrel: 7⅜ and 5 inches, interchangeable and complete with sights, at extra cost.
Overall: 12 inches with muzzle brake attached. Short model, which at this writing has no muzzle brake, about 8 9/16 inches.

Sights: ⅛-inch undercut Patridge style front; S.&W. micrometer click rear, slanted back at an angle similar to that of
  the front sight face. The five-inch Model 41 has a straight-
  profile front sight, making it more suitable for pocket
  carry. Sight radius, 9⅜ inches, or 7 inches on short model.
  Sights mounted on barrel and barrel extension. As with
  the Ruger auto, the rear sight does not move back with
  the breech-block's recoil. On long barrel, elevation clicks
  give ⅜-inch change at 50 yards, windage clicks ¼-inch.
  On the short gun you get more.
Stocks: Checked walnut, modified thumb-rest adaptable to
  right- or left-handed shooters.
Finish: Blue. Sandblasting, matting and serrations break up
  light reflections around aiming areas.
Magazine capacity: 10. Will this gun be supplied in .22 short
  caliber? Yes, 1961 brought it.

S.&W. Model 41 .22 automatic, 7⅜-inch barrel interchangeable with the 5-inch. Recoil compensator, for the long barrel,
is not included in the measured barrel length.

Difference in balance and in sight radius made the
little-brother 1959 shorty welcome to some target
shooters who either dislike much muzzle weight or who
find their eyesight does better with more close-coupled
handgun sights. For outdoorsmen it is almost a pocket
gun in spite of its considerable weight, and certainly
a handy-riding holster pistol. Since it has practically
all the household equipment the long gun has, except
the brake and barrel weight, it sells at the same price.

Long awaited, and long years in preparation, Smith
& Wesson's .22 autoloading pistol disappointed few if
any particular shooters—and almost no open-minded
shooters who know that we all have our preferences in
little as well as big details of a target handgun. Like all
other firearms, it isn't and can't be everyone's dish of
tea. Weight, grip fit, balance and sight radius are matters of individual choice, not just to please a person
but to enable him to develop his highest potential
ability. This is corny comment, but let it stand as a
reminder to be tolerant.

The S.&W. .22 auto has modern features; it is progressive, neither conservative nor radical. Take the
sights: close click adjustments; visibility assured by
matting or grooving every area of the gun that might
throw reflections on them, including the sandblasted,
matté finish of the back of the slide and frame; rear
sight mounted on a long barrel extension instead of on
a moving breech-block. The shelf of the left grip is
for a right thumb, the one on the right grip for a right
forefinger. In reverse, this suits the left-handers. Still
many target shots have any score-gun restocked to
fit them. This almost always pays off, especially *after*
long experience and acquired skill have built an individual shooting style. The front strap of the grip and
the face of the trigger are grooved, and the back strap
is practically covered by the checkered stock wood.

An automatic slide stop holds the breech open after
the last round has been fired. With the magazine removed, the gun can't be fired at all. This is a fine
safety device in the home, but if the magazine is lost,
and no spare available, you're really up the creek without a paddle.

In modern style the gun has a muzzle brake for less
disturbance in rapid fire, and counterweights to add
muzzle-heft, also to help the brake reduce muzzle

upchuck. The aluminum alloy brake weighs about
½ ounce, slides over a narrowed section of the gun's
muzzle, and is screwed into the 2 11/16-inch aluminum (or steel at extra cost) counterweight that itself
screws into the fluted recess under the barrel. The steel
counter goes to about 1½ ounces, four times the
weight of the regularly furnished light one.

There are three other counterweights at extra cost.
The long top one goes in the underside of the barrel,
up front, and it and the middle one have 13 and 6
stations, respectively, to give more than ample choice.
The bottom section goes on the middle one in a single
location—probably to no one's great disappointment.
The weights of these counters, from the top one on
down, are some 7¼, 4¼, and 4 ounces, which add up
to as near as never-mind a full pound. They are made
available for trained shooters who can use and profit
by them. They were not born in a nightmare.

The ⅜-inch wide trigger has an adjustable stop
against backlash, easy to get at when the trigger is
hinged down for dismounting the pistol. In General
Hatcher's report in the January, 1958, *American Rifleman,* from which much of the foregoing data were
gratefully taken, he stated that two of the three N.R.A.-
tested guns had good or better trigger pulls; only one
had a slight creep. He has known this model in pilot
form since 1941, a few months before Pearl Harbor.
At that time, C. R. Hellstrom, Smith & Wesson's president, showed him one that had been developed from
an idea that the long-discontinued .35 auto might serve
as a start toward a target .22. In 1950 General Hatcher
and a few others saw another pilot model at the mid-
winter matches at Tampa. By March, 1957, anyone
who wanted to could see the gun at Tampa. Late in
1957, quantity production began.

More or less in European fashion, like the optional
and extra-cost counterweights hung from the barrel,
the stock of this pistol is very much straight-down.
This is a great contrast to the 1958 Hi-Standard ar-
rivals, which were slanted abruptly back, and to earlier
Hi-Standards, too, and Colt Woodsman automatics.
The S.&W. grip is almost a throwback to the old .22
Reising auto, stocked so much like early .38 Auto

Colts. It has a bit more slant-back than that obscure great-uncle had, the .35 S.&W. Auto that lost his shirt in the market and is rarely mentioned at tribal feasts. The rake-back of the modern Smith's handle resembles those of the still well known .32 and .380 Colts. But the feel is entirely different, and for that we can be glad. The .35 S.&W. was superbly made, but its price and its odd caliber crippled its sales appeal.

As an outdoorsman's pistol as well as for target, this gun is inviting to many. They like its grip, weight and balance. Without the muzzle brake, not needed afield, it is convenient in a holster. Extreme rapid fire in hunting can't make up for poor marksmanship, as we all know or learn. Much of the best small game shooting with weak little .22 rimfires, still weaker when fired from pistols, has been done with single-shot Stevens and Smith & Wesson models. Some of these auto Smiths have made ½-inch 50-yard groups from a machine rest, and that's practically rimfire match rifle accuracy. It is not likely that a poor one can leave the factory.

The rifling twist of the six grooves is interesting, one turn in 16⅜ inches. Sixteen is usual match rifle standard, and this slower twist should be right to stabilize standard velocity .22 long-rifle bullets at the reduced handgun speed—so close to the original rifle speed for which the cartridge was designed in the beginning. An unimportant difference might be 30 or 40 f. s. velocity, either way. All this is quite theoretical, and only one accuracy detail among many. This gun can lay 'em in. Incidentally, the precision of high velocity .22 long-rifles has improved greatly in the last few years. Some match rifles, and perhaps others of less expensive grade, can put five and maybe ten consecutive shots in the Standard American rifle target's 2-inch 10-ring at 100 yards. Well made hollow points do about as well as solids; that's important to small game hunters, though 100 yards is well beyond the sportsmanlike range of a match-quality .22 rifle using 1-r cartridges. Seventy-five is more like it, and that only on a day when there is no breeze to pull the tiny bullet off course and change a killing shot to a crippler.

Smith & Wesson .22 Automatic Model 46

Caliber: .22 long-rifle.
Weight: 44 ounces, less 2-ounce counterweight furnished with gun. Set of three adjustable Olympic counterweights at extra cost. Five-inch gun, 38¼ ounces; not adaptable for S&W counterweights.
Barrel: 7 and 5 inches. Interchangeable, at extra cost for added barrel.
Overall: 10 9/16 inches with long barrel. No muzzle brake.
Sights: Similar to those on Model 41, and with same 9⅜-inch long-barrel radius as on Model 41. Barrel is not extended forward for attachment of a muzzle brake.
Stocks: Nylon thumb-rest stocks for right- or left-handed shooter.
Finish: Satin blue, as on S&W Highway Patrolman revolver. Sandblasted around sighting areas to avoid light reflections.
Magazine capacity: 10.

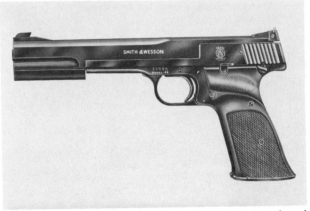

S.&W. Model 46 .22 auto of 1959, with 7-inch barrel, and an interchangeable 5-inch available. A two-ounce detachable counterweight comes for the longer barrel. With the 5-inch barrels you get the sighting radius of a 6-inch target revolver, for the rear sight is back over your hand.

The more expensive 41 sold so well that its retail price was lowered, and 46 is a still less costly arm. It hasn't the 41's bright blue finish, muzzle brake, cocking indicator, and built-in trigger adjustment. Some of these extras, perhaps the bright blue and the brake in particular, wouldn't be missed by a good many competitive target shots. Brakes help in the extreme rapid fire of the Olympic course, but they seldom are downright beautiful, and most of them increase the sound of the report. A .22's blast scarcely matters on an outdoor range, but just give it a chance in a low-ceilinged gallery! Naturally we prefer spacious, luxurious galleries, but many of us are thankful for one where we can stand up without scrooching. The increased sharpness and volume of sound are not much, but the mere fact that they are increased throws some of us.

The 46's broach-rifled barrel is lead-lapped for smoothness, like that of the 41 and many other top-quality target arms, and it's doubtful if any except individual-gun accuracy difference would be noted between these two Smith models. Much depends on the make and lot of ammunition that a particular weapon likes best. This calls for much testing, but it can be worth the time and expense to a shooter who wants the best for important firing. It's true that far more riflemen than pistol-shots can profit by such painstaking effort.

Practically nothing has been skimped to make this gun a good one, from the comfortable, reassuring ⅜-inch-wide trigger to its excellent barrel, sights and grip. Trigger work, if it were called for, shouldn't cost the difference between the 41 and 46 retails, or so I think. At least the first payment, cash or instalment, would be lower on the 46, and if we were budgeted we could be shooting it and getting used to it while paying for it, or buy a bigger slug of ammo to go with it. I should see no reason, even if I weren't hard-shelled and independent, to apologize for this gun as being cheap. It is not cheap in price, looks or behavior.

Smith & Wesson 1953 .22-.32 Target Revolver

Caliber: .22 short, long and long-rifle.
Weight: 25 ounces. Two ounces heavier than earlier model without barrel rib.
Barrel: 6 inches. Longer ones have been made for the old model, on special order.
Overall: 10¼ inches.
Sights: 1/10-inch Patridge-style front; S.&W. micrometer click rear, two-way adjustable. The rear sight is a smaller model than that on the heavier frame Smiths, and some would prefer ⅛-inch sights, partly because they're used to them.
Stocks: Checked walnut, Magna-style.
Finish: Blue.

S.&W. Model 1953 .22-.32 Target Revolver. Individually recessed chambers support case-heads, giving a higher degree of safety in the event of a burst head. Unsupported, burst heads have been known to set off a neighboring cartridge in the cylinder.

Just at present this may be the slowest-selling Smith & Wesson; yet for some purposes it may be "among the best"—to use a deprecating and coldly-comforting phrase. For the beginner who can use the best in factory-issued lockwork and sights, and appreciate the best in obvious quality of finish and inside workmanship, too, and who *must* have a light weapon until he or she is hardened to more weight, it's the gun. That is a flat but considered statement.

In the .22-.32 you get close barrel-and-cylinder jointing, fine trigger pull, and easy opening and closing, or you raise Cain and his puppy-dog with the folks at Springfield. This little squirt of a .22 did a lot to raise their reputation because many people always have had the money and the opportunity to shoot a smallbore, rather than the more expensive larger calibers. It isn't a big seller now, when so many who want a light .22 for plinking prefer a short barrel. To some of them the term "snub-nose" is positively romantic. Then too, a revolver with more of its weight in the hand generally seems much better for hip or point shooting, a trained-instinct kind that's fascinating, and highly practical, too. Target shots generally want at least a two-pound gun to steady-out at arm's length.

For the beginner who wants and can afford it, the .22-.32 is a sensible choice. It is better than it was before the barrel rib added weight out front, though it always was able to stand comparison with any and all others, including the heavier-barreled old Colt Police Positive Target .22, long discontinued. It is built on a generous-sized .32 frame, whereas the Colt .22 went on a light .38 S.&W. short frame. When the Smith became a .38, its cylinder held only five rounds, not six as the Colt did. The actual difference in balance between these two .22s is mostly in the barrel; so it is plain that the S.&W. rib helps.

The Smith is also a useful outdoor gun, perhaps shining most of all in that kind of service. When the shadows are falling, the lunch-hour long past, a half- or three-quarter pound heavier gun sagging and sawing at your empty belly is far more uncomfortable than this little pop. Surely, you can shoot the K-.22 or Officer's Model better, after you are indoctrinated and seasoned, but let's all remember that woodcraft and patience shorten small game ranges, and the .22-.32 seems to be as fond of the woods as you and I are!

Now you may deduct a percentage for long-held enthusiasm, if you like, for this was my first revolver. I had ordered a Colt Woodsman .22 auto from Abercrombie & Fitch, but World War I was on and no Woodsman in stock. So A.&F. sent me the Smith on approval. It stayed with me for years, traveling probably thousands of miles afoot or aboard a canoe, and later I had one or two others of this model. All were fine.

Good shots used the .22-.32 at target, several times winning the U. S. Revolver Association open or "Any Revolver" match, and they toted the gun afield, too. Colonel Townsend Whelen won matches and killed small game with his, which was specially stocked, like many other handguns belonging to experts.

The original grip was, I think, an oversize Target, long, full, and coming well behind the backstrap at its top. Later a pocket gun grip, Regulation Police style, was more or less optional, and that is what the gun has in today's shaping. That means rounded at the bottom and carried up into a top swell, the Magna stock that fills the hand and takes up recoil, when there is any. The rounding and swell are *modern*.

After some years, the original Model 1911—which had been around earlier, by the way—was made in .32 S.&W. long as the Regulation Police Target with small, square-butt grip and adjustable sights. It was perfectly comfortable to fire just about all day long, though it weighed only some 20 ounces. Colt had made the Police Positive Target in .22 long-rifle and .32 long for years, and in .22 Winchester Rim Fire also.

Now the .22-.32, the model of 1953, has its best sights ever, barring custom jobs like the old King; yet in early days people wobbled along with U-notch rear and round bead front, and did fairly well. The general use of square-cut Patridge sights has done a lot for marksmanship. I see, too, that the good S.&W. Call gold bead, red ramp, and red post are available "for S.&W. Target Models having full-length barrel rib only." So this small gun should qualify for them. They show up well even in a cedar swamp, and some use a red post at target also, or the Call bead (a round insert in a square post), blackening that and leaving the red plastics alone.

Colt and S.&W. .22 revolvers have been made as six-shooters in modern times. This wide-spaced cylinder boring leaves plenty of drillable steel going to waste. Complete redesigning could increase the number of shots. It would also increase the time allocated to cleaning! No .22 rimfire is a gun for tight corners; and for woods use, six rounds at a time should be more than plenty, unless we ask too much of a .22. However, this matter can be debated pro and con, and with sense on both sides, too.

Smith & Wesson Masterpiece

Caliber: .22 long-rifle, .22 Winchester Magnum Rimfire, .32 S&W Long, .38 Special. The shorter sizes can be used; this is a sixgun, not an autoloader. The standard .22 is not for conversion to .22 Magnum.
Weight: All calibers, loaded, in 6-inch barrel length, 38½ ounces.
Barrel: 6 inches, also 8⅜ in all except the .32. The .22 Magnum comes in 4-inch, too, and the *Combat Masterpiece* in .22 long-rifle and .38 Special has a 4-inch barrel.
Overall: 11⅛ inches with 6-inch barrel.
Sights: ⅛-inch Patridge front; two-way adjustable S&W micrometer rear.
Stocks: Checked walnut, Magna. Like the large-frame Smiths in .357, .38 and .44 Special, and .45 Auto, the K can be furnished or fitted with oversize target stocks, or with S&W soft rubber adapter (like the Pachmayr but without the inner metal stiffening), and with target hammer spur and trigger, swaged wide for surer contact.
Finish: Blue.

In .22 Magnum caliber the K has probably the fastest rifling twist of all the arms made for that 1959 cartridge, a complete turn in 10 inches. A 16-inch rifle and 14-inch pistol twist are common, the latter made a bit faster to stabilize the 40-grain .22 long-rifle bullet at the considerably lower handgun velocities. Some years ago, General J. S. Hatcher told in a *Rifleman* story of early S.&W. experiments with a .22 long-rifle caliber revolver on a .38 Special frame—a gun that much later became the K-.22. Its 10-inch twist failed to give accuracy, and the conclusion was that the fast spin overstabilized the bullet. Yet the .22-.32 S.&W. sixgun got on well with 10-inch rate,

S.&W. K-.22 Masterpiece as now made with new style hammer and sights, and barrel rib. Some prefer less muzzle-weight, as on old K-.22s, which set the fashion—a most sensible one —for recess cylinders. However, you may find an old cap-and-ball revolver converted to metallic ammunition that had this feature long before our fine modern target revolvers were dreamed of.

though the equally good—wouldn't you agree?—Colts used a 14-inch. On the other end of the line, the S.&W. single-shot target pistols had a leisurely 15-inch twist, and they shot superbly in grueling slow-fire matches. A quick twist in a revolver barrel, however, can have the (dubious?) advantage of grabbing the bullet quickly as it emerges from the long chamber, steadying it, and starting it to take the rifling grooves. A not badly mutilated revolver bullet shows this: the upper part of the rifling engraving is straight, not slanted.

Anyhow, the .22 Magnum S.&W. is an accurate revolver, one of the best in the caliber, and one of the first to come out, too. It's a useful arm. For downright practical purposes it is superior to the .22 long-rifle K because of its greater power and flatter trajectory—for those who can use this trajectory by very fine long-range shooting. The .22 long-rifle ammunition shouldn't be used in the Magnum, but the .22 WRF cartridge, still made at this writing, is a natural subload for it.

The short hammer-fall action K series is one of the best matched sets in the firearms world, including custom-made rifles, shotguns and pistols built as gun families handling different calibers or gauges, yet all feeling much alike. The Ks rank with the .38 or .45 automatics and their .22 long-rifle conversion kits, even though those selfloaders have the advantage of having just one trigger pull to learn. That advantage is partly psychological. Not that psychology can't help. There is no reason why whistling should keep ghosts, jumbies or demons at a distance, but in dark places, some of us think it helps.

The loaded-gun weight equality of these Ks comes mostly from the barrels. The barrel rib of the .38 is much wider and heavier than that of the .22. Thirty-eight rounds are heavier than .32s, and .32s heavier than .22s; so as the larger bores are emptied in firing they become progressively lighter. This effect means little, except something to talk about, and still less because the larger bores have more weight out front in the barrels, and less back in the cylinders. That's enough hair-splitting. The guns make a splendid, practical team.

However, most match shooters now use .22 automatics in smallbore events. In the more or less unrestricted centerfire shoots, a .38 Special revolver remains the usual choice; the two totally different handguns are justified by the scores they turn in. In .45-Government-only matches, the Colt autoloader is the common arm, though Colt and Smith revolvers compete, too, despite the handicap they put on in rapid fire. For the auto, the Colt conversion unit makes a generally good understudy. Some shooters, for economy, because of wisely narrowed familiarity, or just because they like that great old gun, shoot a .45 in all centerfire matches. Some say they'd just as soon throw stones—and incidentally beat the inflated price of metallic ammunition—but that I'd call an unsportsmanlike exaggeration, wouldn't you? The longer .22 revolvers and automatics, with better shaped and/or slanted stocks, are easier to master than a .22 on a .45 auto frame.

All this may be too-too obvious, and perhaps also the thought that using a matched .22 and centerfire revolver twin or triplet set is practical. Learn to shoot the .22, and the bigbore is just that much more familiar when and if serious handgun business comes up. So the specialized target .22 auto may seem "impractical." But isn't almost any kind of shooting good for us, and for our Country's strength? A gun-familiar nation, including both sexes and all sufficiently mature ages, has potential strength. It's an ideal to work toward, and, believe me, a practical one!

It is wise to go easy on shooters' preferences, provided they are safe. We're a brotherhood too small for caste lines of any kind.

Sorry about the moralizing. It seemed necessary, though obvious.

The K is really the old Military & Police Target modernized in materials, weights, sights, stocks, and lockwork. The M.&P.T. used to come in .32-20; the .22 was a late commercial development, the .32 later yet. The grooved tangs and trigger have been around for a long time; and soon after the advent of the K-.22, the rear sight got its first modern improvement. This was a locking screw for the elevation screw. I don't remember my old .38, without it, ever shifting its elevation under recoil, but probably other shooters recall having experienced such a disaster. The old windage screws worked against each other (back out one, turn in the opposite), and they usually stayed put. At least, all of mine did, and it's hard to see why others wouldn't. Now we have a sight that clicks off its changes accurately and is adjusted by a good big screwdriver.

With the coming of the revised K-.22 in 1940, called the Masterpiece but neither sighted nor barreled like the current one, the short hammer-fall "Speed" action, micrometer click rear sight, and built-in anti-backlash trigger improved things for target shooters who preferred a sixgun to an auto in smallbore. After all, the revolver's big competing advantage over the autoloader is its single action trigger pull, which just must be of the best quality. Yes, as Ed McGivern proved in his fast shooting, the double action revolver —and the K-.22 seems to have been his special pet— can beat the auto for making fractional-second hits. He used the double action pull because he had to within his time limits. But in competitive paper-target shooting, it takes a master of double action to use a sixgun for rapid fire events. If this practical way of shooting gets the attention and promotion it deserves, the picture would change. I hope to see it. I can do that, can't I?

The K models have put on weight with the years. Old figures were .22, 35 ounces, .32, 34 ounces, and .38, 32¼, all empty guns. Later the .32 went to 36¾ and the .38 to 36, both loaded, and just noticeably different from the present standard of 38½, loaded,

for all three. They had less heavily ribbed barrels than those we have now. Soon thereafter, the centerfires were brought up to equal the weight of the .22, all with six cartridges in their cylinders.

There is simply no comparison in handling of .38 Specials, as between an early and a late model. The extra quarter-pound or so of steel goes where it helps to dampen recoil and steady our hold. You'd have to look sharply at the cylinder to know that you were shooting the same basic model! For special purposes, some of us would prefer the lighter old unribbed guns. In first-rate condition, they are just becoming scarce, although they are not yet collectors' items in standard issues. For that reason their prices haven't ballooned halfway to the patient moon.

The short modern action is faster than the old long-swing hammer fall. Some people find the hammer easier to cock because of its reduced arc, and perhaps also because of that new, deeply curved hammer spur. Those who aren't used to the new spur may curse it as a steal from a cap-pistol, but with practice they may come to prefer it. Just use the blinkin' tip of your thumb on it, not the full-length pad. And just be patient while you learn. It could pay off. Modern extras for the Ks include a low, broad, deeply checked Target hammer, and a wide-swaged Target trigger.

There are also, as extras, selected walnut stocks, plain or checkered, and the big Target stocks with integral filler for the second finger to rest on. An earlier change than that one was the Magna grip, now long-time standard on about all S.&W. revolvers, and made large at the top to help absorb recoil and give a better feeling hold. Smith stocks had been criticized as more punishing than the Colts, under stiff recoil. The standard stocks can be fitted with a filler or adapter like the Pachmayr. S.&W. used to make one as an extra, but *not* for use with the Magnas because the thick steel side-plates, which made the grip fuller and rounder, left a gap at the top, unfilled by the Magna wood. For most hands, the standard K stock is full enough, though most need an adapter unless the hand is really big. That size could use the Target stocks; they feel too large to a small or medium-sized hand, I believe. We should do well to wrap our fingers around all the gun grips we can find and try them out.

K-.22

This was our first well-distributed heavy-frame .22 revolver, and like the Colt Woodsman .22 automatic enjoyed quick popularity because it was so new and different. Both guns retained their popularity.

For a beginner the K may be a bit heavy—especially in the newer ribbed-barrel models. After he or she has gone through a good bit of training and practice, then improvement comes fast, for there is almost no recoil, and with any standard-velocity .22 cartridge, not much noise. (These guns, like other good ones, do not have a cylinder-barrel gap you could even poke a pipe-cleaner through!) The fact that the revolver is first-quality, like the Colt Officer's Model, may help the novice, too. It should, and to an earnest shooter, such a fine weapon is worth waiting and even sacrificing for. For slow fire work, it's about as accurate as any handgun made, and that too is a psychological help to the beginner. Within the narrow limits of its power, it is a serviceable arm for the outdoorsman. The working parts are so big and strong that breakdowns not due to gross ill-treatment are extremely rare. All three of my variously dated K-.22s stood up well and stayed like new inside.

It is hard to think of a better training handgun than the K-.22, within its weight classification (much lighter than the Colt Officer's .22, for instance), and it should give lifetime satisfaction. You can take it almost anywhere legally, and enjoy it. In extreme cold it's better than an automatic .22, because there's at least some chance of ejecting stuck, greased or waxed empties by a careful push or tap against a small tree or branch. But we must be careful not to risk bending the ejector rod, which in the Smith carries the cylinder-locking pin. At any rate, you are sure of six shots, not just one before the gun is deactivated by the cold. In the Arctic, an inside-lubricated cartridge like the .22 Winchester Rim Fire or Remington Special (they won't enter .22 long-rifle chambers), or almost any centerfire, is obviously the best in pistol or rifle.

Some of us prefer old K-.22s because of their lighter weight or because we dislike a barrel rib for our own sufficient reasons. At first the chambers were bored straight through, all one size. Later they were tapered up front to improve accuracy by a tighter bullet seat. It would take remarkably fine shooting to discern the difference, though the change was a definite improvement.

K-.32

This is the red-headed stepchild of the K family, and as a result gets my sympathy and perhaps yours, too. Judged impartially, the .32 has its points, even though it is now a gun-crank's caliber.

S.&W. K-.32 Heavy Masterpiece that matches the K-.22 and K-.38 in loaded-gun weight. With full-velocity loads this .32 is pleasanter to shoot than a lightly-loaded .38 of similar weight and length. Can its little bullets fight wind as well as .38 Specials just above squib power?

By that I mean its limited usefulness. Today's standards correctly call for nothing under .38 Special or at least .38 S.&W. or Colt New Police, for self-defense. Also, if there's a respectable breeze across the 50-yard target range, we should be better off with the .38 Special, for the little .32 bullets are more wind-sensitive. Not many matched sets of Ks include the .32.

But anyone who's annoyed by muzzle blast and recoil shoots the .32 better than the .38 until he becomes hardened, and perhaps even then. The .32 bullet-hole may miss a high-scoring ring that a .38 would clip, but only in consistently good shooting does this fact matter much. Indoors, the .32 may be shootable when and where the .38 isn't. This statement is based on handloading facts as well as on the use of factory ammunition. The .32 ammo is cheaper to buy, and a little cheaper to handload. Both calibers can be put up at lower costs than store-bought .22 long-rifles come to, if we can get free lead from target backstops and put no dollar value on our reloading time. We shouldn't, for handloading is or ought to be a recreational, relaxing hobby.

Afield, the .32 is deadlier than the .22 long-rifle high-speed, usually. Flat bullet points like that of the Colt New Police should certainly be used, or, even better, semi-wadcutter hand-cast bullets like Ideal 313445, which in my experience did *not* lead the bore in spite of its sharp shoulder. Careful, skilled handloading can send the full weight bullet at about 1,000 f. s. muzzle velocity, which with a well shaped point and lead that is not too hard, increases killing power and flattens trajectory more than usually needed. The instantly vital parts of small game are of about thumbprint size, on an average, wouldn't you say?

For those who want to speed up a pistol load the K-.32 is a fine starter. Cylinder walls and barrel breech are thick, but of course not foolproof. Recoil is always mild, though it can become quick, like the .32-20's, and report goes sharply up in pitch. However, standard .32 speeds with correct bullets—and excellent marksmanship—are pretty deadly on small game, and the report from the 6-inch barrel is too mild to carry far. It is much lighter than the sound of the standard .38.

The .32 is no gun to take woodchucking; it is just for *small* game that is on the regular "edible" menu. For killing chucks we need more gun, and most of us, if we're honest about it, admit that we need a rifle. I know I do and always shall. For eating chucks, we need an open mind and a cook who knows how to prepare them, even that delicate, delicious liver.

It may be unfortunate that the K is the only magnum-sized .32 revolver now made, one that's really suitable for stepped-up loads in the matters of safety and of comfortable and therefore accurate shooting. We can be thankful that we have any at all left in production, for this is one of the few cartridges in the small handgun lineup from .22 to .45 that hasn't been investigated as fully as it deserves.

K-.38

In this caliber, the K could be a fine all-round, one-and-only pistol, unless more power were needed or pocket carry were an essential part of the gun's travel. The .38 is not for the most exacting, or the most probable, defense use, and it isn't for game as heavy as deer. Forget the lucky shots, and forget superb woodcraft and marksmanship. Yes, we all know that in some localities deer are amazingly tame, but they are still deer, still vital, steel-sinewed and gritty. They have the will to live.

S.&W. wisely do not recommend the K-frame Specials for high velocity factory rounds. This applies to heavy handloads, too. The former, and not-too-extreme examples of the latter, could be dropped in and shot out with no particular danger of bursting the cylinder or even of belling or cracking the barrel breech, unless the bullets were oversize. But the frame was worked out originally for black powder ammunition and rather low pressure smokeless stuff. Strong modern steels do not convert the K into a magnum. Long, or perhaps not so long, use of heavy charges will almost certainly loosen the cylinder lineup, and a K is just too good to spoil. We feel the same about even smaller-framed Colt .38 Specials, using a gun-crank's license to be independent.

The Military & Police Target or K-Target was de-

The S.&W. K-.38 Heavy Masterpiece with 6-inch barrel.

K-.38 with target hammer, wide, swaged trigger to give better control and make the pull seem lighter, and oversize target stocks that need no adapter or filler behind the trigger guard. Unaltered, these are stocks for a fairly large hand.

S.&W. .38-.44 Outdoorsman, similar in outline to the 1950 .44 Target and 1950 .45 Target.

signed for a specific purpose, i.e., competitive match shooting. To be sure, it was used at distances over 50 yards, even up to 300, and commonly, by a choice company, but with standard velocity rounds for the most part, because of the accuracy they gave. It is too bad that there is no longer a factory-loaded .38 Special with flat point, in either low or high velocity, like the old .38 Colt Special. But a handloader picks his molds for his purposes.

The current K-38 is at last actually heavier than the current .38 Colt Officer's Model; it wasn't in the past. But they run close together, and we choose for things other than mere weight. Their respective quality is nothing to choose by and seldom has been; they're both so good. I can report only what I believe.

Smith & Wesson .38-.44 Outdoorsman

Caliber: .38 Special, standard or high velocity. Short and long Colt .38s also fit.
Weight: 41¾ ounces.
Barrel: 6½ inches.
Overall: 11¾ inches.
Sights: ⅛-inch Patridge-type front; S.&W. micrometer click rear.
Stocks: Checked walnut, Magna. Oversize Target stocks, broad Target hammer and trigger available as extras, as on the other large and medium frame S.&W. target revolvers.
Finish: Blue. Tangs and trigger are grooved as a matter of course.

Many shooters want reasonable power in a medium-bore pistol but simply don't care for a .357 Magnum. In part this is due to Maggie's rough, loud ways, and in part to a great liking for .38 Special brass for reloading for chambers made for it, not reamed out to greater length. There is much the same reluctance to adopt a .44 Magnum instead of a .44 Special. It isn't hard to see logic on both sides of this question. After all, the .38 and .44 Specials, long familiar, do have definite, proved abilities, which could appeal to an individual.

Now that the heavy-frame Colt double actions are gone, the Outdoorsman and the service-sighted S.&W. Heavy Duty are the only revolvers of the type made *especially* for heavy .38 Special loadings. They are not meant to rival magnums. Besides their ability to take strong stuff in .38 Special brass—which hasn't, let us remember, the capacity of the .357—they offer another advantage to certain shooters. These shooters are husky and usually long-trained handgunners who can profit on the range or afield from the half-pound extra weight. There are perhaps not many of them, especially in long-drawn-out target competitions. Lots of our best shots would hesitate to take up the Outdoorsman as a competition gun, knowing their own endurance limitations, and finding their own medium-, or slightly-over-medium-weight revolvers to be heavy enough—even with the conscientious dry or live practice they take almost every day. They have what they like and what will perform for them. Why change?

But there is another specialized use for this big .38, and that's in the field, where the outcome depends on single-shot, all-out-effort shooting. A heavy handgun hangs steadily. It jumps around less after a bit of mild exertion, and it lies closer to the wind as you hold it, trying to ease off that shot at a propitious moment. A chore to lug? Yes, but the extra weight can seem worth-while to the outdoorsman sooner than it can pay the target shooter. The gun is named exactly right—subject, as always, to the power of its ammunition.

.357 S.&W. Magnum, Original Grade*

Caliber: Takes .38 Short and Long Colt and .38 Special as well as .357 Magnum rounds.
Weight: 41, 42½, 44, 44½, and 47 ounces.
Barrel: 3½, 5, 6, 6½, and 8⅜ inches.
Overall: 11⅜ inches with 6-inch barrel.
Sights: Two-way adjustable micrometer-click rear; choice of any S.&W. target front sights including plain black Patridge, inset Call gold bead, convex McGivern gold bead, and S.&W. red post. The short barrel has the slanted Baughman quick-draw front sight.
Stocks: Checked walnut, Magna. Oversize Target stocks at extra cost, as well as the broad Target hammer or trigger.
Finish: Bright blue or nickel. Top strap over cylinder is checkered to match barrel rib, and front and rear stock straps and trigger are grooved for sure grip and for trigger control.

*The similar but less expensive Highway Patrolman is discussed in the "Work Guns" chapter.

S.&W. 3½-inch barreled .357 Magnum. Recessed chambers enclose case-heads in usual Magnum style. This shorty is a pocket or waistband holster model—though it's good and heavy!—but the 6- or 6½-inch barrel models handle nicely at target, if you like the weight. This short gun has the Baughman front sight for pocket use.

Don't sell this outdoorsman's caliber short because the 1955 .44 Magnum has even higher bullet velocity and much more power. The .357 is still big enough for many of us who want power, extreme range, or—particularly with metal-piercing bullets—deep penetration. Like almost all other calibers, it can be improved to some extent by judicious handloading.

When it came out in 1935 it was terrific enough to frighten some of us a bit by its noise and recoil. Since then it has done much to educate us as to the amount of such ruction that we can stand and still do effective shooting. There are three camps, or more. One maintains that marksmanship can always—or anyway, almost always—do the job of great wallop. Another prefers its power to come from big, well-shaped, comparatively slow pistol bullets. A third likes the Magnums for any sort of carrying where they might be needed, and likes, too, becoming familiar with them from much use. But what used to seem a ferocious gun is accepted in handgun society today, with almost everyone agreeing that it has its points.

Few choose the .357 especially for targets! It is often the choice as a more all-round caliber. Back in 1940, on my way to Camp Perry, I met a young man going there for the pistol competitions. His gun was a .357, a *Colt Shooting Master* target weapon on the big old New Service frame, now, alas! discontinued. With the 6-inch barrel, it weighed 44 ounces. The sights were pretty good at that time, although they did not have the close adjustments demanded now. His burden of handloaded .38 Specials was heavy. The bulletin board later carried some nice scores he'd made, not top, but certainly creditable. Around his home in central New York State he used .357 ammo for short-range hunting.

In 6-inch the S.&W. Magnum and the less finely finished S.&W. Highway Patrolman for the same cartridges also happen to weigh 44 ounces, the same as the young man's Colt. Naturally the grip and hang of the two makes differ, but all .357s shoot smoothly with standard .38 Special rounds, or with equivalent reloads in long Magnum or short Special brass. For long shooting, target or game, Magnum loads may be just what some people want, even though most old target records were set with more nearly standard velocity stuff.

For long-range field shooting, the 8⅜-inch barrel offers higher velocity, great steadiness in two-hand hold, *and* lighter report, which is easy to appreciate if we have to (unwillingly) fire from prone or any other position that brings the gun closer than full-arm's length. The original barrel lengths were what you chose from 3½ to 8¾ inches. The front sight went on the rib as the integral sight base on which Smith & Wesson always insisted. The 8¾-inch barrel gave just the 10-inch maximum inter-sight distance that Standard American rules permit, but barrel and cylinder went to about 10¼ inches, or over the 10 inches allowed. Magnum lengths well under 8 inches always have been popular, certainly for all-round use, and the 3½ was adopted by the F.B.I. With that short length, a good bit of power is sacrificed, but the gun is still a potent .38 caliber. In his book *Sixguns,* Elmer Keith points out that ultra-short barrels often give poor accuracy with soft lead bullets (like practically all factory bullets in that metal or its alloys) when velocities are high. The bullet base is actually distorted by the muzzle blast.

The old S.&W. adapter or filler gave a rest for the the middle finger, much needed with this heavy gun unless your hand is huge; but you couldn't—with factory sanction—use it with the Magna stocks, which are fat up top to cushion recoil against the web of the hand. The gap at the top of the Magnas was unsightly. Modern adapters (the S.&W. is discontinued) take care of all this, and it was logical that the Magnas became standard factory issue. For a big hand, the S.&W. oversize Target stock provides ample filler; it's part of the wood.

The .357 case is 1/10 inch longer than .38 Special brass, giving good powder capacity, although deeply seated factory bullets produce an overall like that of standard Specials. The cylinders were and are recessed to make each chamber enclose its case-head, even though heads that split clear across the rim are rare even in heavily loaded centerfire rifle rounds. But the enclosure helps to block escaping gas from a burst higher up.

In 1926 Smith & Wesson revived the old Triple Lock .44's ejector rod casing under the barrel, but not the third lock itself, up at the front of the frame where the cylinder crane swings in and out. That was a really expensive job and was done, some say, more or less to prove that it could be done. The casing or recess went on the 1930 Heavy Duty sixgun, a medium-bore like the .357 but handling only high velocity .38 Specials as maximum. It adds muzzle weight where it helps most of us in steady holding, it reduces recoil very slightly by its weight, and at least theoretically it stiffens the assembly. It belonged on the .357 S.&W. and has been there from the first.

For some time, many folks thought that the Smith & Wesson Magnum was the only revolver able to stand up to long-continued .357 firing. Slowly this opinion drifted away, with the improved work coming along, and today we have the Great Western and Ruger single actions for this cartridge and the much more rigorous .44 Mag. Their slope-gripped Colt Single Action Army style of stocks does allow the guns to slide back comfortably under almost any recoil—the .357's, at least—but with Magnas and an adapter the Smiths are all right, too. All the good specimens, new or old, shoot well, and the lighter-framed double-action Smiths and Colts made for .357—not rechambered for it—are to be regarded as perfectly safe. But the lighter the frame and the smaller the action parts inside it, the more liability there is that the gun will shoot loose after a steady diet of Magnum rounds.

On page 42 of *Sixguns,* Elmer Keith mentions the fact that the old .38 Service Colts with chambers bored straight through will accept the Magnum cartridge, but with liability of a blow-up. Taking much too long a nap at the switch, I had never thought of this. Some years ago, I remember, I gave a friend some factory loaded .38 Specials, black powder, not smokeless, to use in his Army Colt made for the original outside-lubricated .38 long. With no bullet seat for any cartridge, they of course went in, and were not too long for the cylinder. They did no harm, but the best cartridge, store-bought, for these old guns is the .38 short Colt, which is still made with outside lubricated bullet of full case diameter. Their rifling groove diameter is about .362 inch, much larger than the .357-inch (or even .354 in some old guns) so well standardized in modern. 357 Magnums and .38 Specials. They need the big-bullet short Colt to shoot well, now that black powder .38 longs are no longer manufactured. The long's hollow bullet base was expanded by the quick blow of black powder, filling the bore very well. Few smokeless loadings are as good in that respect. The .38 short Colt is such a light load, and its bullet so soft, that it is safe to fire through .357-inch or even somewhat smaller barrels. As Keith remarked, the overboring of the old Colts helps reduce .357 Magnum pressures when these rounds are fired in them, but it may not help enough! A somewhat similar practice, in minimum style, is the firing of high velocity .22 long-rifles in a dainty little S.&W. Ladysmith made for pressures about half as potent. The difference between .38 long and .357 Mag pressures is even more terrifying.

Such gun and ammo hazards do exist, and all of us who know them owe it to the fraternity to pass the warnings along.

The .357 and .44 Magnums are accurate as guns and as cartridges. Few of us are able to use the best that they offer. The guns do well, also, with shorter brass, .38 and .44 Specials, though the best revolvers made for the Specials only may be just a little bit more accurate. We need not worry too much about fairly short cases in long chambers. Many years ago, one of our biggest cartridge factories ran tests of .44 Russian and .44 Special in the same gun, made for the longer Special. The short ammunition won; it shot more accurately than the stuff that filled the chambers. At that time, the Special was loaded to a bit higher velocity than the Russian. Of course this was a long time ago, before accuracy standards were quite as high as they are now. It was only one instance, too.

The choice between the Model 27 standard S.&W. Magnum and the much less expensive Model 28 Highway Patrolman (4- or 6-inch barrel only) depends on the barrel length we want and how much we care to pay for a truly beautiful finishing job. Both are finely fitted, chambered, bored and rifled. But again, always examine a gun carefully, if it's possible, before buying it. Even in the very best makes and grades, individual specimens do vary a little.

Smith & Wesson 1950 .44 Special Target

Caliber: .44 S.&W. Special. Perhaps some still use the short .44 S.&W. Russian cases for handloading squib-type gallery charges, because the decreased powder space helps to perfect the combustion.
Weight: 39½ ounces.
Barrel: 6½ inches.
Overall: 11¾ inches.
Sights: ⅛-inch Patridge-type front; two-way adjustable micrometer click rear.
Stocks: Checked walnut, Magna. Extra target accessories available as for the .357 Magnum and all the medium- or large-bore S.&W. target revolvers.
Finish: Blue.

This .44, like the other big Smiths of similar kind, has the encased ejector rod that returned in 1926, though the barrel rib and short-action, deeply spurred hammer are 1950 arrivals. Except for boring and a necessarily higher front sight because of its greater recoil, this gun is like the .38-.44 Outdoorsman.

The .44 Target is an old favorite. It was well-liked even in the interim between World War I and 1926, when it had no recessed ejector housing to add weight, as the previous .44 Triple Lock had had. The Triple, made off and on for many years and still around—mostly in hands where it belongs and is appreciated—had its third lock at the front of the frame.

Today this model stands as the only .44 Special (not Magnum) target revolver currently made. For shooters who like a bigbore and can handle its weight on the firing line, and can absorb its heavy recoil, it is a sensible buy. It seems a safe enough statement, from even the most careful, that no other centerfire revolver caliber surpasses it in accuracy. And few equal it. With light handloads, such as we should fire in an indoor gallery unless we hoped to shatter the ceiling, it gives less recoil than a standard .38 Special with standard velocity cartridges. Much less! Usually there is still a fair-sized boom, but not an ear-splitting crack, with those loads. It speaks up rather sharply with the standard velocity factory stuff. Reduced loads have been discontinued so long that they are almost forgotten. High-velocity loads are tailor-made, put up by hand, even though the old introductory Triple Lock was a good, strong gun, almost modern in strength. Some will object to that "almost," and they could be plenty right!

For those who want target sights and a rather long barrel, and who do not object to considerable weight and 'midships bulge of a cylinder, it is a sensible all-round sixgun. Naturally there would be times when a .22 or a pocket gun would be more accommodating, but what times are most important? Probably most of us could worry along with a .44 Target and no other handgun at all. Its loading range of usefulness is tremendous, well below .44 Magnum power, it's true, but capable of beating any other factory cartridge except the .44 Mag in deadliness. With a round ball and, oh! 2 or 2½ grains pistol powder (the caliber deserves careful trial, always) it is as gentle as a pocket .32, and

that is really delicate! With these light bullets the gun needs plenty of elevation, even at 50 feet. So the adjustable sights pay, as they do in practically any other precision use. With standard weight bullets—I like the Ideal wadcutter in spite of its leading my barrel with its big, flat nose—powder charges can be light indeed and still bring the elevation at short range up to about factory-load height of printing the target paper.

Smith & Wesson .44 Magnum

Caliber: .44 Magnum; .44 Special also usable.
Weight: 43, 47 and 51½ ounces.
Barrel: 4 and 6½ inches; 8⅜ added in 1959, as on some other S.&W. target guns. Greater sight radius and muzzle weight help in the field, and some target shooters do better with them. You get more velocity with heavily charged ammunition that can use the extra barrel length.
Overall: 11⅞ inches in 6½-inch style. Oversize stocks add length.
Sights: ⅛-inch red ramp, flat-topped front; micrometer click two-way rear with white outline for the field, but the color contrast aids some target shots, even in bright sunlight.
Stocks: Special oversize target-type Magna, grooved at top, of checked Goncala Alves. Wide hammer spur and trigger. Unchecked stocks available in finely grained wood.
Finish: Bright blue or nickel.

This revolver may seem unsuitable in caliber and weight for target. But power is adjustable through handloading, or much reduced by .44 Special factory rounds, and weight is relative. If you need a 32-ounce revolver for steadiness *and* can handle it through a day's match, wouldn't you be glad to have a gun like this? Recoil too is relative. Few big guns show up on a firing line *except* some of the latest and well liked .22 match autoloaders complete with counterweights. Some of them outweigh this Magnum, don't they? And for some people, they pay off.

Certainly this 1956 model S.&W. has target refinements of a high order, such as lapped bearing surfaces in the lockwork, a grooved and sandblasted sighting line, and a long, full grip for comfort with full or moderate loads. Whether or not one would care for its heft and size, or stop happily at .38 or .44 Special stations, is personal. No experienced shot is likely to buy this gun for its glamor—equal in its intensity to that of the .357 in the late 1930s—but some could

S.&W. .44 Magnum, 6½-inch barrel. Target-style hammer, trigger, and stocks are standard issue.

do excellent competitive work with it, and they realize that fact.

Although it is built on the standard .44 Special frame, it's an extra strong gun. Naturally the most suitable materials go into it. The long cylinder—1¾ inches against just over 1½ for the oldtimer—gives a short barrel breech, not likely to be swollen by heavy loads if bullets of barrel-groove diameter or only .001 inch larger are used. Part of the additional cylinder length, just as with the .357 Smith, comes from the lengthening at the rear to provide recessing for the heads of the cartridge cases.

For 50-yard or shorter ranged target competition, the use of full factory Magnum loads would be insane —hardly a step toward winning a club popularity award. For really long shooting, these rounds would have advantages and would carry quite a bit of smack along with them. But the same flat nose and bore-bearing shoulder that add to killing power do not make a long range, low trajectory contour. For 'way-out target competition or just shooting for fun, not at game or varmints, a round-nosed bullet would be better. Even though the .44 Magnum case is some ⅛ inch longer than the .44 Special, the overall of factory rounds is about the same. So the long cylinder allows us to handload round-nosed bullets farther out, as most such bullet designs call for.

Smooth, uncheckered stocks could be ordered, and they might well pay off. In that fine coverage of the .44 Magnum that General Hatcher wrote for the March, 1956, *American Rifleman,* he recounted the stinging sensation the full loads gave him when they recoiled, and the skin abrasions caused by the sharp edges of the checkered hammer spur and cylinder latch. As you know, he is one of the most experienced pistol users and analysts that our country, or any other, ever has had. He suggested wearing gloves, which was a good idea. Smooth stocks would help in the grip. And is it really necessary to checker the cylinder latch, or even the hammer spur?

Power

No firearm's power means much if we cannot hit with the gun. There is also a human tendency to over-rate anything new and good, which happened with the .357 Magnum when it came out. Even though the .44 Mag is about twice as powerful as the .357 in foot-pounds energy figures, and probably in actual effect, too, by and large it is still only a pistol cartridge. Yes, it's like the .357 in being popular in re-modeled rifles, such as the 1892 or 92 .44-40 Winchesters. But here are some comparisons. Of course you can take a pistol where you can't take a rifle— shower baths, New York City, and some other areas excepted—but can you shoot it as well when you get there?

The no longer manufactured .44-40 High Velocity cartridge (not for pistols) sent its 200 grain full jacketed or soft point bullets at 1569 f.s. velocity.

(Oldtime ballistic figures were not rounded off as such figures, and some others, are today.) The energy was 1095 foot pounds. Remington lists the 240 grain .44 Magnum, from a 6½-inch barrel, at 1470 f.s. and 1275 f.p.; heavy bullets help, though not as much as large velocity increases, in raising energy. *Rifle* handloads for the .44-40 92 and 53 Winchesters, late 1894 Marlins, Model 14½ Remington pumps, a few strongly breeched single shots and some others I don't recall—all of them in sound condition, of course— well, these handload prescriptions go as high as 1890 f.s. velocity with the 200 grain soft point bullet. Another factory cartridge, not a handload for a skilled and sensible user of the tools, is the currently made .351 Winchester for the 1907 or 07 self-loading rifle. Those short, chunky, still useful little autoloaders fire an actual .351-inch diameter bullet, soft or hard point, at 1850 f.s., for 1370 f.p.

These three rifle loads are marginal for deer shooting, good only at short ranges because of their accuracy limitations (from most rifles) and their high trajectories. As for power, they must be placed just about right; but the rifles and even the carbines—some .44s came with barrels as short as 14 inches, before the Federal Firearms Act—were and are much easier for most of us to shoot well than a heavy, steady-holding handgun is. Penetration on deer is adequate, usually, from almost any angle, but the bullets leave small wound-tracks because of their comparatively low velocities. It seems that the design of the .44 Magnum bullet is the best of the lot, by long odds, for deer killing when the speeds are of high pistol or low rifle classification. The big .44 Magnum revolver is over-loaded to supreme handgun power, unless we go to a huge muzzle-loader, an illegal sawed-off shotgun, or something on that order.

"Overloaded?" That was bait you were supposed to rise to. The big Smith, like the .357 before it, fills a definite place in the handgun world. Both were long wanted by folks who knew what was needed for certain jobs. Experimenters had blown up .38 and .44 Special guns while trying for ultimate power, and the wiseacres stood around and laughed. Here and there, one of them still sneers at what happened to good barrel and cylinder and top-strap steel, but the experimenters made these two Magnums possible. They had been limited in sixgun cylinder length, size, and strength, even in Colt New Service production compared to S.&W. designs of the past, and the cylinder is the heart of the revolver's resistance to high pressures. It needs to be wide enough in diameter to afford plenty of wall space for the six holes drilled in it, and the quality of its steel—well, that we can take for granted in our two makes longest respected.

The experimenters did what they could, even making their own long and strong cartridge cases from thick .30-06 rifle brass, reamed up front to take .44 Special bullets. Their need and American inventiveness drove them. May their kind always have those essentials. We don't dare be complacent, as we realize if we stop to think.

The factory .44 Magnum case is strong, sacrificing the extra capacity that a puffed-out, balloon-type primer pocket would give, to get the greater ruggedness of a flat-bottomed solid head or base. The Remington bullet has a copper gas-check cup on its rear to prevent fusion of the lead. The Western lead bullet is coated with Lubaloy. Like British Nobeloy, it's a copper-zinc-tin alloy in about 90-8-2 deal-out and in most guns it does help to reduce leading.

The big revolver is meant to take about 40,000 pounds' pressure, heavy compared to some 25,000 pounds' conservative pressure for early .44 Specials, and around that of a .30-30 or .35 Remington rifle cartridge. One can blow up a Smith or any other .44 Mag by careless or even by too ambitious handloading. As for the latter kind, why? The factory load has close to ultimate power. But there's interesting if non-spectacular work to do in loading it for special purposes, including gallery shooting, just as there still is with the .220 Swift rifle cartridge.

For a practical and interesting revival of 200- and even 300-yard revolver shooting at man-sized targets or just the big head-and-shoulders of the old Army-type rapid fire paper, the .44 Mag would be right—and has already proved itself in long shooting. Very fine oldtime shots did this sort of work with standard-velocity .38 Special rounds, generally using special high rear sights to get on the paper; but there were only a few of them. Improved ballistics should encourage more pistolmen to try it and become good at it. It is a valuable accomplishment that obviously could pay off in defense or offense.

Smith & Wesson 1950 .45 Target

Caliber: .45 Auto Colt, with or without three-cartridge clips, or .45 Auto-Rim.
Weight: 39 ounces.
Barrel: 6½ inches.
Overall: 11¾ inches.
Sights: Same types as on 1950 .44 Special Target.
Stocks: Checked walnut, Magna. Grooved tangs and trigger.
Finish: Blue.

For .45 Government matches in which we aren't restricted to an "as issued" handgun, this refined target model is splendid, provided we choose the thumb-cocked sixgun instead of the autoloader. A master of double-action shooting, capable of scoring at 25 yards, would be likely to call it tops because in slow and timed fire—20 seconds for five shots, in the latter—he would have the advantage of a good revolver's crisp and clean trigger pull. This is hard to get, and to keep under the long hammering of recoil in a bigbore autoloader. Even with this dispensation in an auto, there would still be on the other gun the sixgun grip, which most of us prefer in really big-frame guns. The only .45 Auto-Colt revolver to equal or perhaps beat the 1950 is the 1955, and that is heavier—with all that that means, pro and con. In accurate double-action

S.&W. 1955 .45 Target, heavy-barrel. Target hammer, trigger and stocks are standard. Muzzle brake or recoil compensator is available from the Smith & Wesson factory.

fire it might be better, just because it does weigh more out front; and the muzzle-steadiness could pay in thumb-cocked rapid fire.

The 1950 is also a service gun, perhaps a little long overall for military use, in which a pistol must be quick and handy to draw in sudden danger. But afield, in hunting or in just plain spot shooting at small, perhaps not too distinct, marks at estimated ranges, this gun has the advantages of a bigbore. It is true that its rifling grooves are cut shallow for jacketed bullets, but they handle hardened lead nicely. The bullet's front profile can be as bluff and destructive as you like, because there's no magazine feed problem. The .44 Special, .44 Magnum and .45 Colt calibers are more suitable for the outdoorsman; and some of the 1950s have been made in .45 Colt "long," the old buster, as well as in special barrel lengths.

The Government .45 ammunition with its jacketed bullets, which fail to seal the bore as promptly as even rather hard lead does, shortens barrel life to some extent. In a loosely-chambered gun like a semi-automatic this erosion can progress all the faster. But an N.R.A. member can buy the issue rounds or bullets at low cost, then reload the good brass to his liking. Really high velocities, like those of the .44s, are not to be had from this small-capacity case. The standard jacketed rounds have their uses, and not only in match firing!

Smith & Wesson 1955 .45 Target

Caliber: Same ammunition as for preceding 1950 .45 Target.
Weight: 45 ounces.
Barrel: 6½ inches.
Overall: 11⅞ inches. The ⅛-inch over 1950 .45 length comes from the longer stocks furnished on the '55.
Sights: Same as on preceding 1950 .45 and 1950 .44 Special.
Stocks: Checked walnut, Magna; oversize Target style.
Finish: Blue. Tangs are grooved, even under the stock wood. Trigger also grooved. Wide hammer spur and trigger.

Except for the heavier barrel and rib, and the long, large stocks (which could be replaced with standard size), the 1955 is much like the 1950. Its greater muzzle-steadiness would help some shooters on the firing line, especially in rapid recovery from recoil, but others wouldn't care for the extra weight. Afield, it would be the same, although the extra all-day carrying sag just might cost more than the greater precision would be worth. After all, the 1955 is of magnum weight, though it hasn't magnum power or flat trajectory. Some would say it has no suggestion of those qualities. But there is a lot of respect floating around for .45 Auto Colt killing power.

At reasonable extra cost an S.&W. muzzle brake can be had for this heavy-barreled .45, allowing it to compete with autoloaders so equipped. Certainly it would help—as the heavy barrel helps, to an extent—in reducing the muzzle-climb and thus permitting us to get back sooner on or under the black of the target. In .45 competition most shooters plug their ears against the blast of their own and their neighbors' guns. Muzzle brakes already have such welcome acceptance on .22 pistols that they are almost sure to become common

on bigbore target arms, too. Their added racket is accepted as anything else that's legal is accepted when it makes for better scores or for higher development of our shooting game. Some shooters don't mind noise, so long as it comes from guns and not from traffic, students of music in their first struggles, or other people's children. It seems, too, that some ears really don't lose their acuteness of hearing from long-continued—and dog-goned tiresome—exposure to loud and sharply pitched sounds. We all have our own kinds of good luck, I suppose.

Cartridge clips for the .45 rimless are no problem to find, although once they may have been. A few stores carry them, and Smith & Wesson sells them at a nickel apiece, minimum order a half dollar. With them, two drops and the chamber's reloaded.

Since the above was written there have been important changes in the line of American-made target handguns.

The Colt Python has had an optional barrel length added, 4 inches. Perhaps few will want such a short barrel for target, unless the reduced sight radius lets them see the sights more clearly. But for a heavy business gun, with adjustable sights and other aids to accuracy, the new short barrel will in many cases seem just right.

The Smith & Wesson K-.38 can be had single-action, non-self-cocking, and some target shots will like it so, for there will be no more disturbance from a trigger-return spring—a minor disturbance, I think, unless you look for it. The K-.32 seems to have been dropped: not enough enthusiasts to put up with the

wind deflection and small-caliber scoring holes, and for that I am sorry, even if lonely in feeling so.

The S.&W. Model 41 .22 target auto can be had in .22 short caliber, particularly desirable for Olympic rapid fire, and the five-shot magazine capacity of this gun prevents over-counting of rounds. It comes as a unit, one gun, or as a conversion kit for the .22 long-rifle 41—or the other way around. Very likely the less expensive Model 46 will take on this dual usefulness.

New .44 Magnum soft point factory rounds, of high velocity but building up no barrel leading, may give supreme long-range accuracy in revolvers. Though intended for carbines and rifles, they are safe to use in sound modern revolvers originally made for .44 Magnum.

EVER since World War II, a .22 caliber handgun has been the pride, plaything, tool or defense weapon of more and more of us Americans. Yes, there have been some accidents, but so have there been with cars under poor or no control, with unaccustomed or no hands on the wheel! The number of pistol mishaps may not equal those with that more commonly used weapon, the shotgun, though that comment is no consolation for *any* gun accident.

The .22, even with a fairly short barrel, makes so little noise compared to the bigbores that we can use it in more readily accessible places. So it has become a common weapon in that perhaps most enjoyable of all forms of shooting, the family outing. Compared to factory-loaded centerfires, .22 ammo is cheap. Sure a handloader can fire his bigbore pistol or revolver even more economically if scrap or range backstop lead comes for free. But reloading is still too commonly regarded as a mysterious art, and hard to learn; some people just aren't interested in it.

So, a good many new or revised .22 handgun models have come out, and the crest of that welcome flood hasn't yet passed. It *is* welcome, too, when you consider that each new model stimulates general interest in guns and shooting, which our Country needs. Some of us like almost anything new, and find satisfaction in owning the very latest. I don't know that that is an unhealthy attitude, looked at fairly. At any rate, the manufacturers have profited from it, both U.S. firms and some abroad. A nation with lively arms and ammunition industries seems to have right there one means of maintaining its independence.

Cartridge Lengths

Today, most .22 rimfires are chambered for one, or all, of the three popular sizes, short, long and long-rifle. A .22 short chamber won't accept a long or long-rifle, and even if it did, that would not be of much help. Pistols—good ones, that is—are for accuracy. In rifles, a .22 short cartridge requires a slow rifling twist, from about 20 to 25 inches in a complete turn. A .22 long could use a little slower twist, but long-rifles in slow twists don't shoot particularly well because their heavy bullets need a fast spin to keep point-on to distances greater than, say, 50 yards or so. A 16-inch twist in rifles for this cartridge is accepted commonly and perhaps thoughtlessly. In handguns, that rate is often stepped up to 14-inch to take care of their lower velocities. Comparatively few have the 16-inch rifle twist. Some pistol twists for the *.22 Rimfire Magnum* go as fast as one-in-ten, and do all right, too.

'Way back when rifles using the l.r. cartridge loaded with black powder developed only about 900 f. s. velocity—and considerably less with the smokeless charges employed then—a 16-inch twist for them took firm hold. It is still standard for such rifles. But a fast bullet, within rather narrow limits, can get by with a slower twist to keep it point-on in flight. Prob-

ably an 18-inch twist, for rifles, would help to bring out the really good accuracy built into today's finely made high-velocity long-rifles. A 10-inch twist used to be cut into .22 target revolver barrels, some of them at least; and with modern ammunition, standard or high-velocity, long-rifle bullets would be grossly overstabilized with such a spin. In fact, an early and little-known form of the Smith & Wesson K-.22 target revolver with 10-inch twist failed to shoot well with the ammunition loaded then, and little if any of it reached modern "standard velocity" rate.

The .22 long cartridge, at least from the good production runs so common today with improved machinery all along the line, shoots well up to 50 feet from match rifles. It is possible now and then to keep five consecutive longs in the 10-ring of the standard NRA target. From revolvers it can hardly be expected to shoot that well because many of them are throated out so enthusiastically at the barrel breech that the stubby 29-grain long bullet must wander in a bit uncertainly before it's trued up by the rifling lands. The 40-grain long-rifle bullet is more certain as to where it is going. These coned-out barrel throats have the advantage of accommodating a long-rifle bullet hopping out from a perhaps rather poorly lined-up chamber. Under today's production-cost problems, some of them *are* a bit off the beam

A few .22 auto-pistol models come in .22 short only, for inexpensive practice or for the sharp competition of Olympic rapid fire. A .22 long-rifle auto will take shorts or longs as a single-loader, for economy or to

CHAPTER 6

A WEALTH
OF
TWENTY-TWOS

reduce racket. Few of us choose the longs for these or any other sensible purpose, but longs stay on the market because many people seem never to have heard of the excellent long-rifle—or at least not to be aware of its manifold virtues.

We don't need to worry about a few hundred, or probably a few thousand, modern shorts eroding our long-rifle chamber, or about longs ruining the bullet seat so finely fashioned in the barrel of a long-rifle automatic. But there is some liability of the long, or possibly a high-velocity short, damaging an autoloader made for the .22 long-rifle only. The backthrust of firing pressure may be just enough to extract but not eject the empty, and when the recoil spring slams the partly blown-back slide forward, the empty may be in the line of the extractor. Then that useful little hook may be bent or broken. A reasonably good and well cared for auto seldom fails to eject its own empties clear of the works, and usually far out in the Land of Nod.

Quality

Let's start with a swallow of unpalatable facts. Few guns made now have oldtime, pre-war quality, and we have no right to expect them to. It is not a question of labor's spiking the public, but of costs vs. "sensible" prices. Materials, manufacture and inspection all come high. So do promotion, shipping and inventories. We do have fine precision workmen in our Country, lots of them. But to keep sales prices reasonably low, and dividends high enough to invite investment, something has to give. At pre-war quality our guns would cost still more than they do now. Such quality is, generally, for custom gunsmiths to provide, and darn few of *them* can do it, under modern pressure.

So creepy trigger pulls are common, and tough operation, too. We sweat and struggle to ease off our shots, and after the string is fired we wrench to open a cylinder or remove a magazine. That's something of an exaggeration, but you get the idea! Now I don't mean to say that modern gun parts are soft, for few of them are, compared to many of 40 or 50 years ago, but they often do smooth up. Great skill and a hard Arkansas stone—or sometimes a file!—can do wonders, and so can oils like Anderol or the less expensive Winchester, for example. The latest general production I have seen shows considerable improvement.

Some inexpensive revolvers—and most of those in this chapter are at least fairly so—may have rather roughly bored chambers and/or barrels. These ailments can disqualify them for fine target work, but it is the exceptional .22 handgun that won't tink its bullets into a gallon can right along at 50, 75, or even 100 yards, when the hand that holds it does its part. We are getting serviceable and generally long-lived guns at pretty reasonable prices. I don't say that prices could not be lowered without starving anyone to death, and I don't say that I like an absence of fine workmanship. I think my philosophy is: to do the best I can with what

I have, but meanwhile to try to improve the tools, cautiously, and improve myself, unsparingly, as much as I can. Neither attempt is bringing startling results, but at least I am half a world away from boredom. So are most other shooters, I'm sure.

Oscar Hammond contributed the following comments to this section, and I am glad to have them.

One thing you brought up in your letter I think I can help on. Poor extraction.

Try this—take a good .22 revolver and do a fussy job of cleaning the cylinder, especially the recessed parts. Now slowly load it with grease-free cartridges, like the wax coated kind. Note that they go in easily but for sure are not sloppy. Take a magnifying glass and observe how closely the case-heads fit the recesses. Shoot all these rounds and notice, with your glass, how each one has been dented by the firing pin or hammer nose and thus distorted at that part into the outer edge of the counter-bored recess. Now consider, too, the fact that the usual corruption adds up as you fire, and I think you'll find the poor extraction explained. Remember that a lot of us don't clean our guns often when we use modern cartridges.

Look over the average .22 revolver, even if it's been cleaned and I'll bet you the *recessed* part of the cylinder could stand a *lot* more cleaning. Personally, I just wipe the finger-marks off my guns with an oiled chamois after I shoot 'em, and stick 'em back in the holsters. Of course mine don't lie there to rot for the next year or two.

I'm sure that if you get a small inside caliper and a mike and check carefully the diameter of recess and diameter of cartridge head, both before and after firing the latter, you might find one answer that has not occurred to you.

Some years ago one of the cheaper guns came out without a recessed cylinder—recessed for each separate cartridge, that is—but with an extended rim at the rear of the cylinder, all around it. It didn't bother with poor extraction or with flying metal from burst case-heads.

A long while ago I had a Colt's Police Positive .22, 6-inch barrel, plain cylinder. I fired the regular ammunition and *never* had *any* trouble. I sold it, like a damn fool, because the barrel was slightly pitted. It shot like a million dollars, though.

Sights and Barrel Lengths

Many of the .22s in this chapter have "non-adjustable" sights, in the formal meaning of that word. But more and more, praise be, we are coming to have low-cost handguns that carry at least a drive-in rear sight which can be smacked to port or starboard, carefully and almost microscopically, to give us left or right windage. If there is no elevation adjustment, that's too bad, but most of us seem to need windage much more. A front sight that is too low makes us raise the muzzle to align its top evenly—as we should, according to sound theory and practice, with the top of the rear sight. When it is too low, we shoot high. With .22 shorts the gun may do nicely at 50 feet or so, if we consent to using shorts. Some rear sights can be filed down as a remedy, though a very shallow rear notch is a handicap, not giving us enough light and leeway. If the front sight is too high, go slowly in filing it down. Don't even start before the gun has become familiar in actual shooting, and what's more, before you have developed the method of hold that gives the best grouping on a paper target at 50 feet or even more. A front sight can be built higher by peening it—which is undesirable because it may thin it too much—or by welding on metal, but lowering it is always a lot easier!

You may need to widen the rear sight notch to get good light and quick and sure alignment of the front sight right spang in the middle of that rear sight notch. Perhaps this work is needed more often with short than with long barrels. At least it's usual that the shorty figures more commonly in quick but accurate pistol practice, and we just can't align squinty sights in a hurry.

Nearly all of our modern handgun sights, fixed or adjustable, are of Patridge type, named after a famous shooter who designed them. The front sight is square-cut, not tapered up to a narrow top width or of bead shape, a long fore-and-aft cylinder mounted on a thin stem. This straight up-and-down front sight post fits into a square-cut notch in the rear sight, which is flat-topped, too. There should be more, or less, light, as you need it, showing equally on each side of the front sight. When visibility is poor, just as for quick shooting, the notch in the rear sight should pass plenty of light. To go at this hind-side-before, by narrowing the front sight, is a poor way out.

With practice, a shooter learns to overhold or, much better, raise the front sight above the rear sight level for long shots. Some are really good at it. But to draw the front sight down below the rear sight level for shots at closer range than the gun is aligned for is much harder for most of us, than to hold the sights below the target, lining them up in the usual way.

Our modern .22s come in well assorted barrel lengths. Most of us shoot better with the long ones. They don't require *quite* so perfect sight alignment as guns with barely finger-length sight radius—the distance between the rear faces of both front sight and rear sight. Extra barrel weight out front, unless it is excessive, tends to make the gun hang more steadily.

But these are not universal rules. A short, heavy barrel can be steady enough, like that on the 3-inch Hi-Standard Sentinel revolver. Then too, some eyes can align close-coupled sights more accurately than those with a long stretch between them. They find the focusing easier.

Short barrels are noisier than long ones, and less productive of high velocities, other things being equal. But a revolver with a decided gap between cylinder and barrel can let power go to waste through that space, and in calibers as light as .32, at least, it can be as noisy as all get-out. The short barrels are easier to pack, even in the woods, sometimes. In time we choose our favorites, short or long, or perhaps short *and* long, each for its own duty.

These .22s Are Useful

A fine .22 target pistol—revolver, autoloader or single-shot—is too expensive for many kids to buy, and it *seems* too expensive to the average adult beginner whose interest in pistol shooting is new and uncertain. For these reasons, the guns in this chapter, or at least most of them, are important armament. Thanks to them, a great many Americans are getting more than a nodding acquaintance with handguns. In time of trouble, great or small, how this could pay off! It has, already. Safely and rightly used by those who wear a local, state or federal uniform and by many who don't, the compact, easily carried pistol is a powerful deterrent to crime. It means much in national defense, too.

Probably most of us get our first practice on official pistol target paper with some gun of this sort, and many of them are really fine trainers. They are generally our first handguns for plinking, too, a jolly recreation that can—and must—be safe. That sport can develop us into good, practical pistol shots if we take it seriously, counting the misses as well as the hits!

Small game hunting with a handgun is for the expert only. Otherwise, it is brutal as well as non-productive. In some states it just isn't allowed. But there are two kinds of expertness, marksmanship under ever-varying and tough conditions, and the ability to get within sure killing range. Both take patience, and common decency requires them.

But some people are qualified, and hunting with a handgun is a sure cure for any monotony experienced in hunting with rifle or shotgun! There is an additional use for the reasonably light and compact pistol afield, and that is just to take it along, holstered or pocketed, as the law may require or allow. During an unproductive noon-hour it's there for the fun of plinking. And at non-missable range, whatever that is for us personally, we can finish off downed game with it, quickly and humanely.

Even the confirmed and advanced targeteer should have one or more of these inexpensive pistols, I believe. They serve well afield in rough country—he could lose one overboard in deep water and still not be quite heartbroken—and most of them are light enough to use in training a far from rugged but still interested beginner. He wants more followers of his chosen sport; doesn't he? And who's to start them right if he and his fellows don't do their part?

Sheridan Model D Single-Shot
Weight: 24 ounces.
Barrel: 5 inches, tipping up at the breech to load.
Overall: 6¾ inches.
Sights: Fixed, not adjustable except by filing or buildup. Square notch rear.

Stocks: Checked black plastic.
Finish: Blue.

This seems to be the least expensive American-made .22 handgun, bought new at retail price. A used pistol sometimes can be had for less, but it takes some knowledge of firearms, and perhaps even some familiarity with a particular model, to judge its quality and condition accurately.

Some years ago, Major General J. S. Hatcher, in his book *Pistols and Revolvers and Their Use,* spoke of a 1½-pound weapon as being just about right for a beginner, as far as its heft is concerned. The Sheridan qualifies exactly in this respect; and a good bit of its weight is out front, where it helps a shooter to hold steadily on target.

Not that the Sheridan was designed for target; it's made to carry hunting, fishing or just rambling outdoors. It weighs enough to hold well, even in a breeze; yet it isn't likely to sag the bottom out of your pocket. But the sight radius is rather short, the grip a bit short, too, for a really big hand, and the trigger is so far back that it is practically a part of the grip. To a person who uses "pistol-grip" electrically powered tools, this close-up trigger might feel very good. After all, the Sheridan is designed in every way for compactness. The grip's rearward slant is enough for most shooters, and the curved rear contour accommodates our closed hand's natural curve, somewhat as on the old, discontinued, but still respected Remington .32 and .380 pocket autoloader.

As to safety, the Sheridan has no half-cock notch on its hammer, but it hardly needs one. The rotary bolt-type safety lets the hammer down on the firing pin when its flat side is up; it keeps the hammer away from the firing pin, just like a half-cock notch, when its rounded side is against the hammer. This feature, like the flat stock, helps a beginner to become somewhat familiar with an auto-pistol like our Service .45 before he's even used one!

You can open and unload the Sheridan when its safety is on, and that is a rare advantage. The barrel is spring-loaded, and its opening latch is just ahead of the trigger guard, handy-like. This barrel opening or droop is short; it doesn't remind you of a cat chasing its tail, as some of the old single-shots do. The lockup is strong, like those of the old ones. You can trust the extractor to pull empties reliably. And when you draw the gun from your pocket, its low hammer spur can hardly catch.

Recalling the oldtime kid-priced single-shots, I am about convinced that the Sheridan offers equal or perhaps superior value. My first handgun was a half-pound Stevens .22 short Tip-up, 3½-inch barrel, fixed sights, and a grip about big enough for a gremlin or a swamp elf. It came to me by mail, when I was a struggling senior at Andover—very democratic school always, but tough to get through—and what an antidote it was to Ancient History, French and Latin! I think the cost was about $3.75, but I am not sure. My room-mate and I used it a great deal. Anyway, the 6-inch, 24-ounce Stevens Offhand pistols we both got a year or two later were much better, and the Tip-up went its way, without due appreciation, I'm afraid, of the fun it had given us. The .22 long-rifle Offhand had a crudely elevatable rear sight; but as long as this model was made (up to about 1940), its general quality was maintained.

If the Sheridan's trigger were built out forward—and that seems possible for a tinkerer to do—it would be a little more shootable than the Offhand, for that gun had terrific backlash to its trigger, "giving" what seemed like a full quarter-inch after the hammer had been tripped. But a pencil eraser lashed behind it did help.

Wamo Powermaster Single-Shot

Weight: About 32 ounces.
Barrel: 4¾ inches; ten rifling grooves. Six are about standard, but many more grooves are not at all new. The claim is that many shallow grooves draw back much shorter "fins" on the base of a fired bullet and thus contribute to accuracy and easy cleaning. The claim seems sound, in general.
Overall: About 10 inches.
Sights: Patridge square-cut type. Front sight is fixed, and of ⅛-inch target width. Rear sight has movable blade, can be tapped sidewise for windage, and pried up or pushed down for elevation adjustments.
Stocks: Checked brown plastic with thumb-rest.
Finish: Die-cast Zamak zinc-alloy frame is anodyzed a dull black to prevent light reflection.

This single-shot pistol is entirely different in design, appearance and purpose from the Sheridan. It costs about two dollars more but it still in the lowest price grade of reliable handguns. The Wamo Mfg. Co., 835-R East El Monte Street, San Gabriel, California, is its maker. The Sheridan is part of the line of Sheridan Products, Inc., Racine, Wisconsin, known for medium priced air rifles of good quality.

Sheridan Model D Single-Shot.

The Sheridan "Knocabout" .22 pistol, as its name implies, is short, compact, easily carried. Solid, nonadjustable sights add to its ruggedness, just as they do to a Colt or Smith & Wesson so equipped. The Wamo is for the target range, a well-balanced gun suitable for coaching a beginner, and the single-shot capacity is definitely on the side of safety. Its lack of a positive manual safety lock disqualifies it for field use unless it is carried empty. But loading is simple and rather easy: insert the cartridge (short, long or long-rifle) and push the left-side bolt handle forward. If the trigger is pulled while the bolt is clear back, that bolt will go forward, rather gently, but it just might fire a cartridge with a weak, sensitive rim.

The Wamo is a self-ejecting single-shot. The recoil of the fired cartridge blows the bolt open, as with a .22 autoloading pistol, the brass pops out, and then the bolt goes shut again. To unload without firing, you open the bolt and push a ramrod down the muzzle, or pick out the cartridge with your fingernail. The gun has no extractor and seems not to need one.

It is less simply constructed than the Sheridan, but it certainly isn't complicated. To dismount it for cleaning, removing the top frame, barrel and so forth is easy. But the lower frame, except for the plastic grip sideplates, should be left alone. The washer of the sear pin lock that holds the sear in place can't be removed without breakage, as the good NRA Technical Staff coverage in the July, 1956, *American Rifleman* explained. Since the Wamo is a .22 rimfire blowback, its breech-bolt face, barrel breech and adjacent areas need to have grease and carbon sludge wiped away rather often. The moving parts should be kept clean and lightly oiled, except in extremely cold weather, just as with a semi-automatic that uses outside lubricated ammunition. This is not a big chore, and it's worth doing. Some .22 rimfire bolt action rifles tell you when it is due by spitting gook back into your face.

The Wamo is well stocked and balanced for target or any other precision shooting in slow tempo, and it's capably sighted, too—at least for the long stages of a beginner's progress. The grip slant is right for most hands, and a rather short-fingered hand can reach the trigger, for the grip frame bows inward just behind the trigger. This shows intelligent planning.

No freak, despite its slightly odd appearance, it is a good starter for target ambitions. Also it costs so little that a shooter whose main interest lies in field work could be tempted to buy it just to have a gun handy for straight target work. Let us hope that he will share it with beginners, coaching them into the handgun game. And how we need the beginners!

Savage 101 Single-Shot

Weight: About 20 ounces.
Barrel: 5½ inches, including the fixed, non-revolving "cylinder."
Overall: 9 inches.

Savage 101 single-shot .22.

Sights: Patridge type, clear-cut and square. Front sight is fixed; rear sight is movable for windage, and slanted back.
Stocks: Compressed, impregnated wood, luster finish, with Savage Indian head design. Shaped like those of Colt Single Action Army, but smaller and with decided flare-back at bottom of back-strap.
Finish: Blued, except for bright-finished hammer. Precision die-cast, light-alloy frame of one-piece construction is blued to match steel barrel and cylinder.

As we went to the gun show at the March, 1960, NRA convention, my friend Louis Childress told me there was one new pistol from a source I couldn't guess. As usual, he was right. Savage Arms hadn't made a handgun for so many years that I'd written them off in that line. Their .32 and .380 autoloaders—and the rare .25—had been quality arms, ranking with Colt opposite numbers, and with the Remington .32 and .380. The Rem and Savage were discontinued at about the same time, and some of us disgruntled gun-cranks thought and said that their drop-out was due to their native state's harsh Sullivan anti-pistol law. You could still get a pistol license in New York State, usually, but it took time, and sharpened your virtue of persistence no end! In New York City it was a weary lot harder than upstate.

This 101 single-shot was needed for 20 years or so, since the Stevens Offhand went out. It's one of our least expensive pistols and that means much to kids. Weight and balance are good for nearly all women and children, and for many men, who would like it for fishing trips, hiking, camping and so on, for if it were lost or damaged, few tears would fall. Still, a guy could become right fond of it.

For some kids in our Winchester Junior Rifle Club I have handloaded .32 S&W short and long, and .32 Auto, at a price well below that of .22 long-rifle, just so that they could have some use of a pistol of their own. The other adult coaches and I have supervised this centerfire shooting, and a good bit of .22 rimfire, too, after the regular hours at the range. It might pay off some day, though we hope it never must, in any serious emergency. With a solid background of .22 rifle shooting, and an equal and unremitting dose of gun-safety mindfulness, most kids are safe with a handgun. Some become trustworthy to turn loose afield, alone or with one or two others equally well grounded. The pistol as well as the rifle is a military weapon, and early familiarity with *both* means much if the youngster ever goes into combat.

The Stevens Offhand was a pretty good .22 for kids, and many woodsmen used it, too. It was of better quality and easier to shoot than .22 revolvers at comparable price. With the heavy 6-inch barrel—8s and 10s could be had, also—it weighed about a quarter pound more than the new Savage, and its fairly muzzle-heavy balance helped. It had its faults. The rounded grip, really needing an adapter to fill the space close up behind the trigger guard, was less sure and comfortable than the hard-to-beat Colt S.A.A. type which the Savage grip follows in miniature. Both Stevens sights were dove-tailed into the barrel, making windage adjustment possible, and the rear sight had a stepped slide for elevation, useful when you fired .22 shorts or CB caps. But these sights were out of date and hard to shoot well with, for the front carried a round gold bead and the rear had a stingy "U" notch. The Patridge design is more visible and more accurate, and for woods use a white, gold or red tip can go on, and the rear sight can be outlined in a contrasting color. Here we get out of the Savage 101 price class, naturally. In most uses a black front and rear show up well.

Inexpensive revolvers—and some that cost plenty—often do have a creep in the trigger, and this liability applies to low-cost single-shots like the Offhand and the Savage. A creep can be smooth, without apparent change in pull weight, or it can halt, hitch and give disconcertingly. There can be backlash, too, a decided rearward movement after the sear or the trigger has set the hammer free to fall. In a pistol, backlash is even more annoying than in a rifle, for it is a comparatively light gun and usually held in one hand. Backlash of the Stevens Offhands I had was terrific, like that of many cheap modern .22 rifles. There's little if any of this noticeable in the Colt Single Action Army mechanism, a type that includes the Savage. The 101 pull I tested had a fairly long smooth creep, which might not have bothered some beginners, for it takes time to develop trigger sensitiveness. Sometimes use will smooth out a mild creep, and some triggers are rid of it by occasional doses of gun oil. To apply them it's seldom necessary to dismount the pistol, unless it's an autoloader or an odd sort like the obsolete S&W Straight-line single-shot, and the Savage isn't designed for easy dismounting, by any means. In this respect it somewhat resembles the Hi-Standard Sentinel revolver. Cock the Savage hammer and let two or three drops of oil fall in; then work the trigger and hammer a few times to distribute the oil.

Being a single-shot, the Savage is easy to clean, with no barrel-cylinder joint to leak gas, smoke and grease. Theoretically a single-shot is more accurate than a revolver, for its chamber is of cartridge length. The bullet needn't hop into the rifling. Fine revolvers shoot with more accuracy than most of us can use, but they cost a fine lot of money. Few revolvers have every chamber perfectly aligned with the barrel—few indeed!

Safety

The safety of the 101 is stressed in advertising. No gun, however, is safer than its user.

One good point is the rebounding hammer. After striking the firing pin it goes back to a sort of half-cock position, which it holds when the uncocked arm is loaded or empty. If the gun falls and strikes on its hammer spur, no discharge occurs unless the steel is faulty, and that's most unlikely.

But if the hammer slips from your thumb when you cock it, and an ignorant forefinger is holding back the trigger the loaded gun fires if the hammer falls in a long enough arc to apply the necessary force. This is true of other exposed-hammer weapons. The Savage is no safer for quick-draw than single-action revolvers. One shot in the leg or foot calls a halt, anyway! You don't need six of them.

So keep that forefinger away from the trigger until the gun clears the holster and points well out front, and use only an empty gun until you're well along in mastering the manual handling alone. This may take weeks, or months, but impatience gives us no more in training ourselves than in training a dog or horse. The expert at quick-draw fires as soon as the muzzle snouts out toward the target, but he became expert after long and patient practice.

Since the Savage is loaded with its hammer in safe half-cock position, it avoids another hazard. The Stevens could be opened, with difficulty, with its hammer clear down, the firing pin scraping a loaded round. The scraping didn't help the firing pin, or make for gun-safety! Once we got used to that gun, we set the hammer at half before opening or closing it, and if we'd received no advice we had to learn on our own.

Just being a single-shot makes a gun safer. Complete unloading is simple. And with only one shot available we try harder to hit, instead of pouring them out. We're more cool and careful.

And how single-loading helps in learning to shoot! The reloading slows us down; and we can, if we like, keep the same hold on the Savage stocks through a ten-shot target string. We swing the barrel, and the "cylinder" in which it's mounted, to the right—no gadget to hunt for and push or shove—draw back the ejector rod and let it snap back, reload, and snick the assembly over into place. The swing-out is so short that the ejector fails to scrape our hand.

Wind-Up

The 101 is small, but well balanced out front, and the grip is big enough for most hands. An idea of its size comes from comparison to the S.A.A. Colt with 5½-inch barrel—not including the Colt cylinder length, of course. The Peacemaker is two inches longer overall. Still, I think that many grownups will buy the Savage for their own use. Really expert shots and hunters could use it on very small game, making sure of their work and not needing follow-up rounds. It's a question of whether people with less than their abilities have any right to hunt any game with any pistol. However, this world is still short of the millennium, and .22 and more capable pistols do get used in the game fields. Out there, enough handicaps already exist for most of us, and a one-shot smallbore pistol is a serious one. Best wait till you have something better in both caliber and capacity.

The single-shot .22 pistol was a favorite of some skilled woodsmen before the .22-.32 S.&W. revolver became well known as the Model 1911—though it did come out some years before that date. Stewart Edward White used a 6-inch S.&W. 1891, and on a long—and tragic—exploration in Labrador Dillon Wallace and Leonidas Hubbard—the latter starved to death up there—carried a couple of 10-inch single-shots, Stevens, I think, but I'm not sure. White lived well in the wilderness. Hubbard and Wallace had terribly hard luck, traveling much of the time through country that should have been alive with game, but wasn't. Even so, their pistols proved worth their weight.

If you can find either or both of Wallace's books on that country—he made a second trip for obvious reasons—read them. You can hardly find an equal record of selfless heroism and of the friendship between two gallant men. The accounts are not in sentimental vein. As I implied, theirs is the record of real men, not so-sos. The titles are *The Long Labrador Trail* and *The Lure of the Labrador Wild*.

It took good shooting in those days, with the .22 caliber black powder rounds. The same is true today with much more impressive ammunition, from the modern .22 long-rifle to the .44 Magnum, though the latter cartridge, as bought over the counter, is hardly a small game special!

Cody Thunderbird Revolver

Weight: 22 ounces with 4-inch barrel.
Barrel: 2½, 4 and 6 inches.
Overall: 8¾ inches with 4-inch barrel.
Sights: Front adjustable for elevation, rear for windage. Square-cut.
Stocks: Checked plastic. Square butt with longer barrels; rounded butt with 2½-inch barrel.
Finish: Brylite Black anodyzed, or more polished Hybrite Blue at extra cost.
Capacity: Six shots in cylinder, which is counterbored to receive the case-heads of the cartridges.

Except that it has a top-break, tip-up cylinder frame instead of a solid frame with swing-out cylinder, the Cody revolver has lines that remind you (or me, anyway) of the Colt and S.&W. pocket guns. And just as with them, the space between guard and grip comes too high for a good hold. Your forefinger must slant down a bit unnaturally to pull the trigger. If no adapter or filler is made for the Cody—and so far, I believe none is—a clever amateur gunsmith could make his

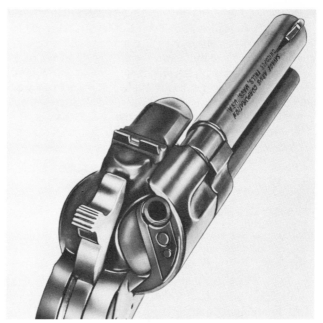
The Savage 101 open for loading.

own and like it, short though the unaltered grip is. Compactness seems to have been one of the chief aims in designing the Cody.

The gun is a double-action, though a far better pull can be had, naturally, when the hammer is thumb-cocked for single-action firing. Automatically, it ejects its empty or loaded rounds when you open it. Choice of barrel lengths is good, from pocket to woods use. This inexpensive revolver has nearly all the desirables of its type, necessarily limited in quality by its production cost. Any roughness or undue heaviness of trigger pull, or any stiffness of opening and closing action, could be made right by a good gunsmith. Whether or not this would be worth-while is for the owner to decide. He can be sure of one thing: it is not the only handgun made that may need refining! Some that cost $60 or more today need it, too. According to my latest observation, this plague seems to be lessening.

Hammer and trigger are made of steel, and the hammer rebounds, as we should expect. It is safe over a loaded round because of a block that holds it in a sort of half-cock position, like those of modern Smiths and Colts. *Any* of them should be tested, of course, even on new guns. With an empty case in line, draw the hammer nearly all the way back and let it drop. Hit the hammer spur rather smartly, too. If this makes no new or deepened mark on the empty, the hammer has passed a practical test. Don't touch the trigger while doing this.

To reduce cost and weight, the Cody cylinder and frame are of aluminum-alloy, and even the barrel is only a steel tube inside that alloy. This construction is strong enough for pressures higher than those a .22 long-rifle cartridge gives.

More serious than a rough trigger pull or stiff action,

are poorly aligned chambers that result in tipped bullets which punch oval or even full-length holes in target paper. The latter grief is common with rust-eaten barrels, but no manufacturer who thinks as far ahead as next payday will ask his customers to put up with serious faults. To get really high precision from a .22 or any other caliber revolver calls for quality work. As an old S.&W. catalogue said of the .22-.32 target arm: "The little 40 grain bullet cannot be deformed at all if accurate results are to be attained."

Colt Huntsman Autoloader

Weight: 30 and 31½ ounces.
Barrel: 4½ and 6 inches.
Overall: 9 inches with 4½-inch barrel.
Sights: Ramp front; rear movable for windage.
Stocks: Checked black Coltwood plastic; small thumb-rest.
Finish: Colt Dualtone blue.
Magazine capacity: 10 .22 long-rifle cartridges.

The Colt Woodsman has been popular for some 40 years; but in the later years, this rather expensive gun felt the competition of less costly grades of automatics by other makers. To meet it, Colt produced the significantly named *Challenger* in the early 1950s.

Both the Challenger, now discontinued, and the present Huntsman are much like the contemporary Woodsman models, except for the lack of easily and precisely adjustable sights and for the little differences in fitting and finish that the price differentials would suggest. But all guns are individuals, and it is possible that a "lower grade" specimen might have as good a trigger pull or as smooth and well-blued a finish as some Woodsmen. Certainly, a happy owner might be convinced that it had. Wouldn't that count in a rather important way?

The most obvious external difference between the Huntsman and the discontinued Challenger is the shape of the trigger. On the Challengers, or at least all that I've seen, triggers are straightened where the forefinger rests, as on Woodsman models of that time. Many marksmen thought that this surface, almost at right angles to barrel and breech-block, made a straight-back pull easier. In appearance it wasn't as attractive as the present-day trigger that curves back close to the rear of the guard, almost following the guard's contour at a barely respectful distance. Most modern auto-pistol triggers do this, except those on double-actions like one form of the 9 mm. Smith & Wesson. In a sense, they are derived from the Luger trigger, which is almost a semi-circle.

The first Woodsman pistols, light-barreled guns that are becoming a bit rare, had curved triggers 'way up front, almost in the middle of the guard. They make shooting difficult for a short-fingered person, but a man with a big hand often finds them just right.

I doubt that any of our .22 autos made now are "cheap" in the sense of being shoddy and unreliable. Properly taken care of and given fresh ammunition, not old stale stuff, they seldom fail. Proper care includes a fond, almost parental, watch over the magazine. Let no one abuse it! The guide lips at the top are critical. Bent out of shape, they hardly feed the ammo surely into the chamber. Good metal goes into the magazines, but even so, it seems poor practice to force the last round down into the magazine through the lips up top. If it can not be slid down under them, why not use that magazine at one round less than the stated capacity? Even a casual or plinking gun deserves care. Sometime in a critical situation it might repay that care.

In this book we quote the magazine capacity as given by the manufacturers. Five-shot mags have been made for Colt .22s, and probably still are. They are for timed and rapid fire runs that call for five shots only in each of the two strings. Using them, we are relieved of having to count the loads as we slide them in.

For field use, an extra cartridge can be preloaded into the chamber before the filled magazine is put in. Let's not forget to put the gun on safe immediately after chambering that extra. Some of us distrust some safeties, and it's true that some of them can be shifted to firing position much too easily in pocket or even holster carrying. If the hammer is at full cock over an empty chamber, it's easy to move the slide back and forth quickly and quietly, thus chambering the first cartridge from the top of the magazine. All this refers to hammerless automatics like the Colt guns. Most of those equipped with visible hammers, like many of the old Hi-Standards, practically require two hands, or at least a hand and a thumb, to cock them smoothly and easily, *and* with the muzzle always pointed in a safe direction. But practice with an empty gun makes a difference, as practice always does.

Like the Huntsman, the Challenger is a good Colt, a safe buy for economy's sake or in order to have a "knockabout" pistol handy. It ranks well with the other autoloaders described in this chapter. One sensible reason for buying it would be that it fits your hand. But there are also sentimental reasons for doing things. The old, historic gun names carry weight; there's no doubt about it. So we choose for this or that reason, but at least let's get a gun that will give us, individually, the hits that mean 99% of "everything."

Choice of barrel length depends on ease of packing and carrying, if that seems important. But sometimes

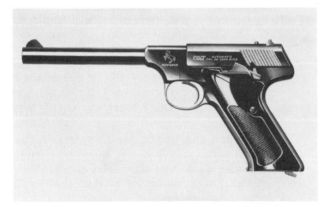

Colt Huntsman .22 Automatic, 6-inch barrel.

it doesn't. There is the significant matter of shootability, too, and in the long run that may mean far more. Usually, barrel weight helps, unless it is excessive. But some eyes align the fairly close-coupled sights of a short barrel best, and some hands actually cannot hold a long-barreled gun as steadily as a short, compact one. Only trial—and as a rule, lots of it—will tell. Long barrels give higher velocities with most loads, and less noise. But these two details do not figure very highly, I think, within the 4½- and 6-inch limits of this Colt. The longer barrels generally permit me to do better shooting, but I'm one person and you are another.

Colt Single Action Frontier Scout Revolver

Weight: 23 ounces; 28½ in Buntline Model.
Barrel: 4¾ inches; 9½ in Buntline. The .22 Winchester Magnum Rimfire caliber is furnished as well as the usual .22 short, long and long-rifle gun.
Overall: 10 and 14¾ inches.
Sights: Fixed, Patridge type.
Stocks: Checked black rubber. Smooth walnut at extra cost.
Finish: Blue barrel and cylinder, bright aluminum-alloy frame and guard. All-blue finish came, optional, in November, 1958, and the 1959 Buntline is all-blue.
Capacity: Six in cylinder.

Much of the great popularity of these little revolvers stems from their bearing the Colt name. Moreover, there is a close general resemblance to the Single Action Army, that Peacemaker so famed in Western history and fiction, in the movies, on the TV screen— and, even yet, in wild places of the earth, and in some not so wild but refreshingly primitive and basic, where a handgun can be worn as casually as a watch, or more so!

Some of us gun-cranks and gun-users would say that the Scout has done the Colt name no good. "A cheap imitation, not worthy of bearing the Rampant Colt trademark." But quality is relative; or rather, times have changed. We are thankful to have now a great upsurge of *general* interest in pistol shooting. And we shooters are proverbially poor. We get that way by

buying guns, ammunition, slews of accessories, and by traveling to places where we can shoot. Even though prosperity has changed that picture materially, some of us can't buy the best and still eat, sleep warm, and keep socks in our shoes. Then there are the tasters, who want to give the shooting game a try. They deserve all the smoothing of the way they can get. A high starting investment discourages a lot of them.

There is also the practical, business-wise side in the ledger of costs, sales and profits. All the other pistol manufacturers except Great Western and Smith & Wesson were making inexpensive guns. The Frontier Scout and the Buntline Scout line up beside the Colt Huntsman autoloader as allies in the competition.

In the good *American Rifleman* coverage of June 1958, the point was made that the Scout is about four-fifths the size of the Peace-maker. Why isn't that right for the hands of most middle-teeners and ladies? And the weight, approximately three-fifths that of the Peace-maker, is easier to hold, and to tote along trails. As for looks, if some objected to the two-tone color of the first Scouts, early in 1958, the later all-blue finish has nothing "odd" about it. Peacemakers could be had as standard in full nickel plate, which some liked, especially in damp countries, better than the more familiar blue barrel and cylinder, and color case-hardened

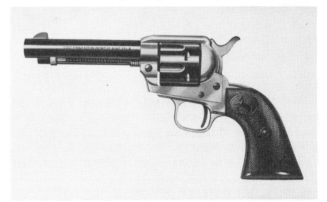

Colt Single-Action Frontier Scout in original two-tone finish

Blued Colt Buntline Scout.

frame. And who knows all the variations in finish that came on special orders?

The introduction of the Buntline was clever, because, right now, variety is the spice of business. Almost anything new will sell; and if it proves to be good, it will keep on selling. That great new host of gun-users has liberal tastes; in fact, they seem to like extremes. In the last ten years, the short-barreled revolver has had enormous popularity, even among those who would be better off with something more conventional. To some of them, I'm sure, the adjective "snub-nosed" has a romantic ring, because they see many of those short-snouted sixguns on the screens, in newsprint, and on slick paper.

Now the extremely long barrel is having its turn. It isn't new, and it has its points. If it has reasonable weight—and for many of us the .22 Buntline has—it can lie steadily in the hold. Even on a revolver, with that gas-escape gap between breech and cylinder, a long barrel reduces noise. With .22 rimfire ammunition, practically all of it made for both rifle and pistol use, there is also some gain in velocity, as there would be with black powder and some smokeless sixgun loadings.

But just as a horrible example there is the H&R Trapper Model, No. 722. With 6-inch barrel this one looked longer than the Colt .22 Buntline, for it was so little with its tiny frame, thin-walled 7-shot cylinder, and total weight of just 12¼ ounces. It's no longer made, but in its day it had some popularity. Though the long, pin-weight barrel magnified every tremor, some of the boys would shoot this gun and similar ones two-handed, holding both grip and barrel. One burning from the hot gases blasting sidewise from the cylinder-barrel joint was lesson enough. After that, they would put the forward hand about midway of the barrel, well away from both muzzle and breech.

Those of us who remember when shoulder-stocks on pistols were legal, naturally think of one on a Buntline. We think, but don't act, because of the Federal law prohibiting them unless . . . . . Well, why not buy a carbine and avoid the trouble and expense?

There are natural shortcuts in manufacture. The loading gate is full and round, not a flat slab, but the ejector tube is a plain round job fastened but not snugly fitted to the barrel. The ejector rod looks thin and may not be centered perfectly to go straight down the chamber mouths, but are .22 cases hard to poke out of a well-cared-for gun, or even one that has been neglected somewhat? Yes, ejecting six to nine cases at once can be difficult.

To remove the cylinder, you turn out the base pin screw, as on early Peacemakers, not just push a plunger and pull. And as Elmer Keith explained in the April, 1958 *Guns,* this inexpensive revolver has no base pin bushing in the cylinder, as the old Colts and the Rugers have. If excessive loosening develops, it could call for a new cylinder, or at least some skilled gun-smithing. As all .22 revolvers probably should have, the Scout has a separate, spring-loaded firing pin, not integral

Cased set of the 1961 heavy-frame Colt Frontier Scout and Buntline .22 revolvers. Though of the same size as the earlier Scout and Buntline, they are six ounces heavier, and some shooters will prefer them for steady holding. This pair has the extras of smooth walnut stocks and nickel finish.

with the hammer or attached to it. Some customized Peacemakers and quite a few modern centerfires in standard production now use this system.

But this Saturday morning, with a range session ahead if the rain hauls off, the thought of the Colt Police Positive Target .22 sixgun of my old friend Francis Clarke comes to me. After some forty-odd years it is still in fine shape. Its record, for out East, is a long and honorable one. Canoe, ski, snowshoe, moccasin and boot travel took it around. It punched countless paper and plinking targets, killed a variety of small game and varmints—including a fox, one shot, fired before the skis had slowed down—and in general traversed a great amount of wild, beautiful, free country. No repairs came up in its long and useful life. Its firing pin was fitted to the hammer nose, solidly; and it did fire some high-speed loads as well as the old low and modern medium velocity .22 long-rifles. No case-heads burst; nothing ever went wrong with that gun—except on one morning. Before we launched the canoe from our night's campsite, Fran cleared the cylinder of the six rounds. All shots struck low, and the reports were awfully subdued, too. Reason? In that damp country we would keep bores and chambers swimming in oil, over-night, and oil has a way of getting under a heel-based bullet like the .22 l.r.

Many would call the Scout's one-piece grip frame an improvement in design, compared to the old Colt. The Nylon washers under the screw-heads are praised because they at least help to eliminate loosening under recoil, a plague with many Peacemakers. Both new and old Colt single actions—great Westerns, too, or at least most of them—use flat hammer mainsprings instead of the coiled-type that Ruger employs. A big double-action gun with coil mainspring may be easier to cock than a similar one of the older type with a flat spring. But the Scout is only a little gun, and to most of us it should give smooth and easy hammer-thumbing unless our thumbs are very short or decidedly unaccustomed.

Since it is a modern .22 revolver, its rear cylinder face is counter sunk for cartridge rims, safety insurance against possible case-head bursts. Well, I haven't had or seen one of those things for several years, but they can happen, even yet. You or I may get a case rupture today, tomorrow or next week. Fired cartridge-brass splinters driven into the thumb can have extremely serious results.

Harrington & Richardson 929 and 930 Side-Kick Revolvers

Weight: 25½, 28 and 31 ounces.
Barrel: 2½, 4 and 6 inches.
Overall: 10¾ inches with 6-inch barrel.
Sights: Fixed ramp front. Early round-barrel model had for a rear sight only a cut in the top-strap. Present flat-barrel model has rear sight dove-tailed into the top strap, thus providing windage adjustment.
Stocks: Checked "Clingfast" plastic.
Finish: Blue. Model 930 costs a little more and is chrome-finished.
Capacity: Nine in cylinder.

The gun is well named. It is sturdy and companionable for day-in, day-out carrying and use. During World War II another H.&R. was made that could have deserved the same name. It was a 2-inch barreled job for .38 S.&W. and .38 New Police rounds, the latter, with its flat-pointed bullet, being a rather effective defense size. (Britain's service .380 had a similar case, interchangeable, but with heavier bullets, at first a 200-grain lead, later a full-jacketed one of about 173 grains.) This H.&R. .38 revolver was a business companion, not for sport. It had two-way adjustable sights, and the overall blueing was dulled along the top rib to give better visibility under light glare. The checked walnut stocks were for fast but reasonably accurate shooting, not for looks. The space behind the trigger guard was filled in high enough to give an easy, straight-back pull on the trigger in either single- or double-action firing. How popular this model would be today, if it were still made!

The present .22 Side-Kick has a swing-out cylinder, unlike the warrior just mentioned; it is a solid frame gun, not a tip-up cylinder arm. The extractor returns automatically into the cylinder breech, unlike that of the Hi-Standard Sentinel .22, which costs less. This feature is not important except perhaps to an absent-minded person! Coil mainspring, countersunk chambering for the cartridges, and grooved trigger for non-slip contact are such common modern advantages that they scarcely rate mention.

The Side-Kick is one of the many revolvers that need a fill-in high up between the trigger guard and the grip's front strap, such as the H.&R. Ultra Side-Kick has. It is also one of those revolvers, like the smallest frame Colts, that are just too pinching narrow up there

Harrington & Richardson Model 929 Side-Kick (Model 930 is chrome finished) with 6-inch barrel and the handy swing-out cylinder.

when no adapter, either integral or applied, is used. With .38 S.&W. or New Police cartridges you get a good sound rap on the joint of the second finger when you use that sort of grip. Heavily loaded .38 Specials are tough indeed to fire under these conditions. A few shots are endurable; but soon, oh-oh! We can shoot the 929 indefinitely, for it's a .22; but we could shoot it better with our second finger nicely bedded, not cramped. Unfortunately, an adapter for it may have to be specially made. The less expensive pistols—and rifles, too—are likely to be treated like red-headed stepchildren, as far as handy little extras are concerned.

The crane—which holds the cylinder and swings out with it—has an adjustment screw which can be eased if the cylinder is stiff to turn out. This tight screw may be one of the causes of such stiffness. Of course, there may be no stubborn performance at all. The crane lock and the cylinder pin, which runs through the ejector rod, make up the two-point cylinder lockup, which is unusual in guns of this class. It is not essential. You and I have heard of, and perhaps proved, the accuracy of Colt revolvers. It seems as though they still win quite a few matches!

Harrington & Richardson 922, 923, 622 and 623 Revolvers

Weight: Nine-shot 922 goes 26 ounces in 6-inch, 25 in 4-inch, and 20 in 2½-inch Bantamweight. The standard-weight 622 6-shot figures are 28, 26 and 25 ounces.
Barrel: 2½, 4 and 6 inches.
Overall: 10½ inches with 6-inch barrel.
Sights: Ramp front. Rear sight can be moved for windage.
Stocks: "Clingfast" checked plastic. Square butt except on 2½-inch, which has a rounded, pocket-type grip.
Finish: 922 and 622 are blued; 923 and 623 are chromed.
Capacity: Nine or six rounds in cylinder, as indicated by first numeral of model numbers.

These inexpensive revolvers are of solid frame construction but not with swing-out cylinders. To load them, you pull out the cylinder pin and roll out the cylinders, either right or left, and pushing back on the pin forces all the empty cartridges out at once. Sometimes it's more fun to use the Colt Single Action

H.&R. 922 with 6-inch barrel. You reload through the gate, Colt-Single-Action fashion, or remove the cylinder pin and roll out the cylinder. If cases stick in a gun of this kind, the cylinder pin will punch them out.

H.&R. starter's revolver, for blanks only. The chisel-shaped "barrel" breech is to break up the blank cartridge's cardboard wad.

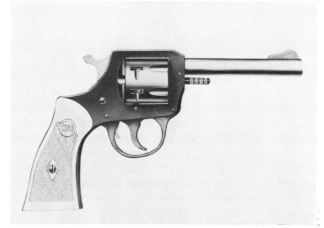

H.&R. six-shot Model 622, 4-inch barrel. A conscientious gun cleaner sometimes goes nuts while swabbing out an eight- or nine-shot cylinder, but counting up to six is easy; so there's still a market for .22 sixguns with cylinders big enough to hold nine chambers. I shudder to think how many .22 holes could be bored through a K-.22 or Officer's Model cylinder blank.

method, leaving the cylinder in place and ejecting and loading through the gate on the right-hand side of the gun. A short, smooth rod of wood or of soft metal like copper cannot harm the chambers, and it will punch out the empties. By doing this when only a few rounds have been fired, you have the gun readier for action than when the cylinder is out. It's the slow way, but anything like precision shooting is not a hurried job.

With little doubt, these revolvers are sturdier than those in a corresponding price range of a generation or so past. The 4- and 6-inch barrels are easier to shoot than the 2½-inch, but decidedly less convenient to pack in the pocket. Most of the real oldtimers in this class were too light, though some had reasonable heft, and good-sized stocks could be had on order, as a rule.

The slight extra weight of the 6-shot cylinders may be worth considering, and it is easier to count to six than to nine when we are cleaning chambers! Those who clean their guns carefully—I am still in that class, and so is a federal agent I talked with last week down at the range—might prefer the six-shooters.

It's a pity that these sound, reasonably-priced re-

volvers are so poorly stocked. By an extension of the trigger guard, as on the H.&R. 999 Sportsman and 939 Ultra Side-Kick, this fault could have been eliminated. Any redesign is expensive, but they have been made on many firearm models, and presumably they have paid off on the long financial haul.

The Harrington & Richardson 970 .22 and 960 .32 centerfire are race starters' revolvers, for blanks only, and will not take standard ball ammunition except possibly the obsolete .22 caliber BB and CB caps. (Yes, both are imported today; keep them away from the 970.) These guns have short cylinders and no barrels. A solid steel rod fills the place of a barrel, and its breech end is chisel-pointed to break a cardboard wad into fragments too small to be able to do *much* harm. But like all other firearms, this type is not for foolishness. On the stage of a theater or while training a dog, blank cartridges serve commendable purposes, as they do at a track meet. It's good that they are still made.

Harrington & Richardson 660 Gunfighter and 949 Forty-Niner

Weight: 29 and 31 ounces.
Barrel: 5½ inches, a popular length in Colt Single Action.
Overall: 10⅜ inches.
Sights: 660, fixed, rear sight a cut in frame; 949, adjustable.
Stocks: Shaped like those of Colt Single Action Army.
Finish: Blue.
Capacity: Six in 660 cylinder, nine in 949.

The 1959 model 660 and 1960 949 are stocked in the manner of Colt Frontier, Peacemaker or Army single-actions—so popular now on medium and light .22s. There is single-stroke rod ejection of empties, the cylinder being free to turn when the hammer is at half-cock. As on the standard Colt, the 660 rear sight is cut into the frame, not a separate piece dovetailed in. So windage adjustment would be made by thinning or bending the front sight, or preferably by filing one side of the rear notch, a job needing some gunsmithing ability—for sure. This system makes the gun smoother to draw, especially from a hunting coat pocket, and it has the romantic appeal of one

H.&R. Model 660 Gunfighter revolver, 5½-inch barrel, six shots. Grips are thick, well rounded, and feel good in most hands.

more resemblance to the Colt. Drawing from an out-side holster cut to leave a dove-tailed sight free would offer no great difficulty.

These guns are all-steel, with no light-alloy parts, and weight and balance are good for the average beginner who's fairly husky and appreciates steady balance out front. To compete against some other .22s built in Peacemaker style, they are double-actions that can be fired single-action, too. Loading is in old Colt fashion, through a gate on the right-hand side, one round at a time. Many shooters find this satisfactory, and have since the early 1870s. Few choose this slow system for actual gunfighting, and fewer still would pick .22 long-rifle ammunition as first choice!

J. C. Higgins Model 80 Autoloader

Weight: 35 and 36 ounces.
Barrel: 4½ and 6½ inches, detachable and interchangeable.
Overall: 10⅞ inches with 6½-inch barrel.
Sights: Fixed, Patridge-type. Rear sight movable for windage.
Stocks: Plastic, checked, with right thumb and forefinger rests.
Finish: Blue.
Magazine capacity: Ten .22 long-rifle cartridges.

The High Standard people make this gun for Sears Roebuck, pretty much on the pattern of the H.-S.

Duramatic, though its barrel and stocks are decidedly different, and it weighs more. Model 80's barrel is rounded at top and bottom, flat on the sides; and the stocks almost suggest those of a free pistol tailored for International competition, the thumb and finger rests are so wide and comfortable. It does lack a cup on the right grip, for the base of the hand, and of course the painstaking fitting to an individual hand! It is really a semi-target gun without the so-important helps of a specially smoothed action and precise two-way sight adjustments.

Interchangeable barrels are offered at extra cost, though even the shorty might prove too bulky for easy pocket carry because of the large thumb-rest and the fact that the center of gravity comes rather far back. But how many automatics do ride comfortably and securely in a hip pocket except those with full-length, Browning-type slide? In a hunting coat pocket the short ones hang quite differently and well. It's a good berth if the law allows it.

The safety is not a lever, but a cross-bolt. It is slower, but probably less likely to be scuffed off when you carry the gun. Some shooters punch it off handily with the first joint of the thumb. The red-dotted tail of the firing pin shows when the gun is cocked. If the safety is inconvenient, the magazine release button certainly is not. It is above the trigger guard, not at the bottom of the stock.

Barrel removal is simple. Take out the magazine, pull back the slide or breech-block and lock it there by pushing the safety button all the way to the left. Unscrew the coin-slotted barrel nut, ahead of the guard, and lift out the barrel. The barrel goes back easily. Align it with the frame, tighten the nut, and push the safety to the right to let the slide go forward.

Removing the slide can get you into trouble. With the barrel off, grip the slide and push the safety to the right, the "off" position, and the slide then goes forward and off the frame under its own power, the trigger with it. Cup your hand over the front of the

J. C. Higgins Model 80 auto-loader with 6½-inch barrel. A nicely hanging gun at a moderate price.

slide and catch the striker, striker spring, and slide (recoil) spring. This is not painful, but an unrestrained pin or spring flying out wildly is obviously dangerous—it might hit a person's eye. At the least, it's usually dog-goned hard to find before a pet kitten, 'coon or puppy does! And they might have been hit, too. In the May, 1958 *American Rifleman* a better restraint was mentioned in the technical staff's writeup. Pull the trigger when the slide is about at its normal firing position. This relieves tension on the striker spring, and it is worth doing.

With the long barrel the 80 hangs well—for a right-hander—and it is one of the best low-priced training automatics to use. If the trigger pull needs smoothing, and if there is too much backlash after the striker has been released, some work would be worth doing or paying for. Too many more expensive auto-pistols also need it. These are common but fortunately not universal faults of the whole class.

J. C. Higgins Model 88 Revolver

Weight: 23 ounces with 4-inch barrel. Barrels are lighter than those on the Hi-Standard Sentinel revolver, and they have no rib on top.
Barrel: 2½, 4 and 6 inches at present.
Overall: 9¼ inches with 4-inch barrel.
Sights: Fixed, Patridge-type. Rear sight is movable.
Stocks: Checked plastic with thumb or finger rests on each side. "Oversize" target stocks on De Luxe grade.
Finish: Blue. Nickel at slightly advanced price. Hand engraving, gilding, and contrasting nickel frame and blue barrel, cylinder, etc., at further advanced prices.
Capacity: Nine shots in cylinder.

Made by High Standard for Sears Roebuck, this gun sells for somewhat less, grade for grade, than the Sentinel. As we should expect, it is still a safe and reliable revolver. Just as with the Sentinel, the light-alloy frame puts the weight so well forward that even with the short barrel the gun hangs steadily in deliberate firing at arm's length. And odd enough to surprise some of us shooters, there is sufficient weight in the hand to adapt the 4-inch barrel—or the 3-inch in H.-S.—for point shooting, with the gun shoved out below eye height and aimed by well-developed co-ordination. Naturally this sort of hitting skill comes

J. C. Higgins Model 88 revolver, 4-inch barrel.

slowly, and it's for short ranges. But these short, big-cylindered guns have what it takes.

Only one screw is used in the 88's construction. It holds the one-piece stock in place. Wire springs are used instead of flat springs. The gun is made as simple and durable as its able designers could manage. But it is not a pistol to be dismounted by anyone without gunsmithing skill. Oh, it's easy enough to dismount, like the alarm clocks we ruined when we were kids, but reassembly is something else! Take off the stock, if you like, and cock the hammer. This is enough for the oiling get-at-ability that is necessary. If the 88 gets a dunking in the creek, take off the stock and toast the gun over moderate heat. Then oil it. The frame is rust-proof because it is made of aluminum-alloy.

J. C. Higgins Ranger Revolver

Weight: 28 ounces.
Barrel: 5½ inches.
Overall: 10¾ inches.
Sights: Fixed, Partridge-type. Rear sight in dovetail can be moved for windage.
Stocks: Plastic, with medallion, in "Western" style similar to those of the old Colt Peacemaker single-action.
Finish: Blued barrel, anodized frame, the remainder chromed.
Capacity: Nine in cylinder.

Resembling a single-action Colt in its general lines, it is still, like the Hi-Standard Double-Nine, a double-action gun which can be thumb-cocked for deliberate firing. Also, the cylinder swings out for ejection and loading.

This gun is so much like the Double-Nine, even in its price-tag, that the choice between them depends on personal preference and availability. One might have a better trigger pull than another of the opposite nominal "make." And so on, in such matters as action smoothness, appearance, and general styling. The guarantee on one should be as good as that on the other. Some people do a great deal of their buying at Sears Roebuck, and some do not. Perhaps that will button up this discussion.

Hi-Standard Sentinel Revolver

Weight: 20, 23½, 24 and 26 ounces.
Barrel: 2⅜, 3, 4 and 6 inches.
Overall: 8¼ inches with 3-inch barrel and long, square butt.
Sights: Fixed, Patridge-type. Ramp front. Rear sight movable for windage.
Stocks: One-piece, plastic. There are two styles: the long, flowing square-butt sort on guns with 3-inch or longer barrels, and the rounded pocket shape on the "Snub Barrel," the 2⅜-inch shorty. White is its usual color, but the square stocks are brown. Stag grips available for square butts.
Finish: Blue is standard on the longer-barrel guns, with nickel at extra cost. The snub-barrels add choice of gold, turquoise and pink "Dura-Tone" colors.
Capacity: Nine in cylinder.

This is Hi-Standard's own gun, generally similar to the Model 88 revolver which that company makes for Sears Roebuck. It has the aluminum-alloy frame, and the steel barrel, cylinder, hammer, trigger, inner working parts, and sights. A heavier barrel and a front sight ramp account for its slightly greater weight. Both seem to be naturals for the .22 Winchester Rimfire Magnum cartridge, having good, long cylinders; but on this particular afternoon of writing they are no more than a gleam in a shooter's eye. Possibly a steel frame would be used for the Magnum, although it wouldn't seem necessary. It seems certain that a great many revolver models will be adapted to the Magnum, and that some new models will be made for it, too, with the cylinders lengthened and perhaps the barrel breeches shortened to take that long cartridge. Its actual effective pressure is not much over that of the .22 long-rifle high speed.

Both the Sentinel and the Model 88 have the right-and-left thumb or finger rests formed in the frame. They feel and handle much the same.

Modern improvements such as counterbored case-head-enclosing cylinder breech, grooved trigger, and optically correct Patridge-style sights of course are present. A particularly smart precaution on the Sentinel is the cut-out at the top of each chamber breech. Few modern firing pins (or hammer noses, as in these guns) are permitted to dull and possibly break themselves against a breech face, which suffers, too, in such malpractice. Such clearance we should expect, but there is more. Rimfire cases, when they burst, often let go just where they are struck by firing pin or hammer nose. The slots in the Sentinel, therefore, are located where they are likely to do the most good.

Most of the snub-barrel Sentinels' rear sights are rounded on the sides, in old S.&W. .22-.32 Kit Gun style, to improve pocket carrying and drawing. One variety of Snub has a dehorned hammer; its spur is ground practically off. That hammer could still be cocked by hand, but the theory is that most people want to use their "fastest gun going" as a double-action.

The ramp front sight of the longer barrel Sentinels is attached by an Allen-type of screw. It stays put under recoil. Those I have heard of, or used, are too low, and the guns "shoot high." They have to, when you align a too-low front sight evenly with the flat top of the rear sight. In *Sixguns*, Elmer Keith described his friend Judge Don Martin's Sentinel as "a good 200-yard gun!" Any such exaggeration is welcome satire, for a low front sight calls for either a buildup or a sometimes impractical filing down of the rear sight. Both are *unwelcome* jobs, compared to gradually filing down a too-high front. It is too common for Sentinels, at least in my experience, to shoot high at 50 and even 75 yards. But in the nature of things, they are not the only over-ambitious handguns you and I have used.

Major Seabright and I shoot together every week at least, in all sorts of weather, unless something serious prevents it. In summer we usually get in two or three trips a week, either to a range or afield. He has had his 3-inch barrel Sentinel for a couple of years or so, and though it is about the least expensive gun in his battery, it does get the use! The little trick goes almost

Hi-Standard Sentinel with the popular 3-inch barrel.

With 6-inch barrel the Sentinel is a holster gun. Weight out front makes most of us prefer it for target, but not for "hip" shooting. For woods use this long-barreled .22 is fine.

everywhere with him in his free hours—perhaps not to movies, concerts or dances—and he can shoot it! He's a good pistol target shot, though not up to his proven high rifle ability. As that wasn't enough, he had to learn point shooting, double-action, and, after the first few weeks, sustained rapid fire by point. The gun proved to be just right for this, on its own merits and not merely because it is a companionable little gat, easy to stuff into or draw out of a high belt holster. We think it will be a good trainer for the 4-inch .44 S.&W. Military he has on order. Neither of us has illusions about the killing power of a .22 rimfire. Still, we have some idea of what it *can* do, too.

Noticeable in at least some Sentinels is the abrupt start of the rifling lands at the breech. They come up square, not eased into a taper, at the end of the wide and fairly long throat or "forcing cone." This would seem to invite heavy leading of the start of the lands, as well as in the cone, where it's so common in a great many revolvers. It can occur, even to the point where bullets are tipping or even keyholing side-on at ranges as short as 50 feet. The remedy is scouring with a soft brass wire brush, or else a change in ammunition. Sometimes a fairly hard .22 bullet, like one plated with copper or copper-alloy, does better than plain lead—all of them lubricated by the factory, of course, with an adequate coating of grease or of hard wax. The .22 long-rifle bullet has a better chance of getting through

Snub-barrel Sentinel with 2⅜-inch barrel and no hammer spur to snag in your pocket.

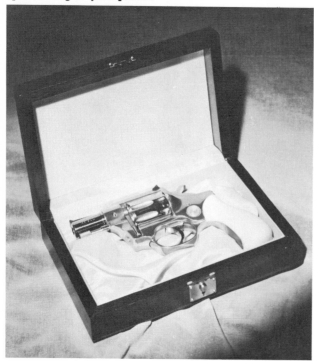

Snub-barrel Hi-Standard Sentinel with white stocks and DuraTone color finish, 2⅜-inch barrel, and hammer spur. Nested in its case. Best protect the royal bedding from gun-oil by means of "oiled" paper or such. Seriously, this neat kit should catch a feminine eye, and some others, too; and we do need more shooters in this country.

the cone and into the bore and rifling without a smearing-off of its metal than the stubby .22 short and long bullets have. But guns vary. My Sentinel did foul, as most revolvers do, but even with shorts and longs it tipped no bullets.

The rounded grip of the Snub Sentinel is a good one for that type of gun, but the square grip of the longer-barrel models is close to, if not right at, perfection. Its size and slant suit most hands, small, medium and large. I have never heard anyone complain about it.

Some of this excellent fit is due to the fact that the space between trigger guard and the grip's front strap is so low that no fill-in adapter is needed. Your trigger finger is positioned for a natural, straight squeeze-back. These comments apply to the J. C. Higgins Model 88 revolver, too, of course.

Hi-Standard Double-Nine Revolver

Weight: 28 ounces.
Barrel: 5½ inches.
Overall: 10⅞ inches.
Sights: Fixed front sight has the forward-sloping curve of the Colt Single Action Army. Rear sight is like that of the long-barreled H.-S. Sentinel, just discussed.
Stocks: White composition, with gilt medallions bearing Hi-Standard trademark. In shape, this grip resembles that of the Colt Single Action Army. Plain wood stocks also furnished.
Finish: Blue barrel and cylinder, dull black light-alloy cast frame. Nickel finish at extra cost.
Capacity: Nine in cylinder.

The Double-Nine's action is similar to the Sentinel's, although trigger and hammer are shaped differently. Some of us might find the Double-Nine trigger not so well suited to double-action firing. I think that the consensus rates the Sentinel's among the very best.

A down-to-earth choice between these two Hi-Standards would depend mostly on which fits the individual hand the better. The Colt Frontier or S.A.A. is hard to beat, but the unique grips of the Sentinel and of the Higgins 88 are certainly splendid, and probably

Hi-Standard Double-Nine in blue-and-black finish, with plain, uncheckered stocks. Combined cylinder latch and ejector rod tip lies just under the barrel legend ".22 cal."

The H.-S. Double-Nine with nickel finish and white stocks.

better for really small hands. It seems likely, that most Double-Nine buyers will select it because it is so obviously "Western" in shape, even though it only *looks* like a single-action "hog-leg."

Actual resemblance is not even skin-deep. There is no loading gate on the right-hand swell of the breech, and none needed, for the cylinder swings out to the left for ejection and recharging. The under-barrel attachment isn't an ejector rod housing of Colt single-action, single-poke ejection style. It houses the Sentinel-type of ejector rod that carries the cylinder pin as a sort of core—Smith & Wesson fashion, really, except that the rod has no spring to make it self-returning. You pull it back into place as you do with the Sentinel. This is no hard luck: returning the rod soon becomes second nature, although you push and pull the rod deliberately enough, it seems to me, to avoid liability

of catching an empty between ejector and cylinder face. Do you remember such embarrassing goofs with the usual spring-returned ejector? I do.

The housing of the Double-Nine's ejector head is neat, but it could be a little hard to operate with cold, stiff fingers. Certainly, the pull-away unlocking of the Sentinel, like that of some models of the old S.&W. Ladysmith .22s, is easier. A great part of the Double-Nine's housing is there just for looks.

Like its older brother the Sentinel, it has a rebounding hammer that comes to a sort of half-cock when the trigger goes forward. A safety block prevents it from striking the cartridge, if the gun falls and alights on its hammer spur. Such blows have set off old Colts accidentally. Now, with modern steels, the danger is lessened, and probably most of today's single-actions can be considered rather safe with the hammer at half-

Popularity of the two original Hi-Standard Double-Nines, blue and nickel, led to the appearance of these 1960 models. 1: Natchez, 4½-inch barrel, rounded grip somewhat in old Colt Lightning double-action style, but without spur at top of back-strap to hold the gun down against recoil. 2: Longhorn 9176, 5½-inch. 3: Posse, 3½-inch, with walnut grip. 4: Longhorn 9177, 9½-inch. 5: Longhorn 9179, 5½-inch, stag grip. 6: Longhorn 9180, 9½-inch, walnut grip. 7: Longhorn 9175, 4½-inch. 8: Longhorn 9178, 4½-inch, simulated pearl grip.

or quarter-cock. Or can they? A safety block that holds the hammer back from the firing pin or cartridge seems more secure than a hammer notch, to most of us. But even apparently definitive break tests might not give a sound answer. Even high-quality steel can have flaws though defects of that sort are rare indeed. However, just one could be a fatal too-much.

Hi-Standard Sport-King and Flite-King Pistols

Calibers: The Sport-King is made for .22 long-rifles, the Flite-King for .22 shorts.

Weight: "All-Steel" Sport-King, 38 and 41 ounces with short and long barrels, respectively. In "Lightweight" model, 27 and 30 ounces. Flite-King, 35 and 37 ounces. In "Lightweight," 24 and 26 ounces.

Barrel: 4½ and 6¾ inches. Interchangeable barrels for the same cartridge are available, and at lower cost when ordered originally than when fitted later.

Overall: 9⅛ and 11⅜ inches.

Sights: Patridge-type. Front, fixed. Rear, movable for windage. A two-way adjustable rear and a higher front to match it could be had at moderate extra cost for early models of the Sport-King.

Stocks: Checked plastic, (different from those on early Sport-Kings).

Finish: Blue. A de-luxe nickel was made available recently, at small extra cost, in at least some models.

Magazine capacity: Ten in either cartridge length, but not interchangeable.

There have been many Hi-Standard models; but when this type was modernized there was no change in name. During World War II the Model C, our first generally available American auto-pistol for .22 shorts, went out of production. It was never restored, although there was demand for it. Finally, the Flite-King came, a gun long needed in its price range.

In a way, the Flite-King, Sport-King, and some other Hi-Standards follow the *general* design of the pioneer Woodsman Colts that were announced, but not always available, back in World War I times. The slanted steel grip frame is part of the receiver; it is not a separate unit, as it is with the good but inexpensive Hi-Standard Duramatic or the J. C. Higgins made by H.-S. for Sears Roebuck. The magazine release is at the bottom of the butt, as in the early and latest Colt fashion. But the modern H.-S. barrel is detachable, not screwed

Light-weight Hi-Standard Sport-King, .22 long-rifle caliber, 4½-inch barrel.

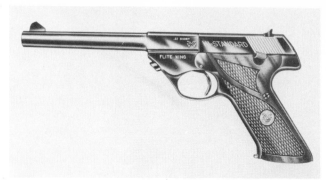

Standard H.-S. Flite-King, .22 short, 6¾-inch barrel. A fine, economical .22 auto. Quiet to shoot, accurate up to 25 yards and who knows how much farther? Fifty, at least, on a calm day.

solidly into the receiver. In disassembling, the breech-block slides off forward, not to the rear. It is true that the earliest Woodsman pistols were considered not quite up to strength standards after high velocity .22 long-rifle ammunition came in, although it is more than doubtful that one ever shed its breech-block to the rear under stress of firing. These Colts could be modernized, and often were, by merely substituting a new model mainspring housing—the rear portion of the grip, which you pressed inward (right at the angle of that backstrap where the web of your hand goes in firing) in the dismounting procedure. Old housings were checkered at that point; later ones were scored only in horizontal lines.

For some time the Colt Woodsman pistols had a magazine disconnector safety that prevented their being fired when the mag was out. It was discontinued about 1955. At this writing the only American pistols with this accident insurance seem to be the Smith & Wesson and the Whitney. It is not an unmixed blessing for the careful shooter (who extends his care to policing others who might get into trouble by assuming a gun is empty because its magazine is out). The medium-priced .22 autos are used more afield than on target ranges, it seems, and sometimes they are carried into real wilderness. If by bad luck (or by carelessness) a fellow loses the magazine, is such a gun a much more effective weapon than a very short club?

Hi-Standard autos long have been popular with shooters who have large or even medium-sized hands. The grips are long. Late model H.-S. stocks, too, are in effect longer at the back than at the front. This is a decided contrast to those of the earliest Woodsmen—pistols which, by the way, are becoming almost collectors' items.

Recent Flite-King and Sport-King have a wider trigger—serrated, of course—that makes the pull seem lighter and gives better control, a less obtrusive magazine catch on the bottom of the butt, and improved firing mechanism. The latter has a chrome-vanadium steel firing pin, which should be nearly 100% break-proof. Most of us like to do a great deal of dry-fire practice with our empty guns. Firing pins have broken under this stress, with no empty case in the chamber to pad the blow. It has happened with both high- and low-priced guns.

When the last cartridge has been fired, the modern Flite or Sport breech stays open to notify you that you are through. That's fine. The only objection I can dredge up is that your mortal enemy might see it happen and pounce on you from some bullet-proof shelter the scoundrel had been hiding behind. (You know how we gun-cranks scrape our brains for every possible argument, pro and con.) A good many auto-pistols do have this hold-back feature, including the Colt .45 and some Lugers. Why shouldn't it be universal? Push down the safety catch on the H.-S. or the .45, and the breech goes shut. It does *not* do that, with these pistols, as soon as you have inserted a filled magazine. That is desirable or not, depending on your opinion. In a gun-fight, it would save a fractional second, and perhaps ensure years of continued living. Elsewhere, it might upset one's peace of mind!

Hi-Standard Dura-Matic Autoloader

Weight: 31 and 34 ounces.
Barrel: 4½ and 6½ inches. Interchangeable.
Overall: 8⅞ and 10⅞ inches.
Sights: Square-cut Patridge-type. Front is fixed; rear, movable.
Stocks: Checked plastic, with thumb-rest.
Finish: Blue.
Magazine capacity: Ten .22 long-rifles.

This least expensive H.-S. automatic costs a bit more than the closely similar J. C. Higgins Model 80 that the company makes for Sears Roebuck. It is somewhat lighter than the 80, and for that reason it just might be better for general non-target use.

Although the cross-bolt safety used on both of these guns appears less handy than the up-and-down lever type—which suits a righthander, at least!—it is positive and reliable. Some find it handy for a thumb-thrust.

Placing the magazine release just above the trigger made it quick and easy to get at, almost as efficient as that on the Colt Government .45.

More weight in the barrel would have pleased the seasoned target shot; but then, it would have made the gun less handy for woods use, more liable to be left at home or at camp than taken along. With the longer barrel, this gun weighs almost exactly the same as the standard 4¾-inch barrel, exposed-hammer P-38 German service pistol of Walther design. But when both had loaded magazines in them, the army handgun would be noticeably heavier. Eight 9 mm. Luger rounds add up to a bigger sinker than ten .22 long-rifles! Even so, the long, thick-walled .22 barrel would put more steadying heft out front. As for *average* quality and downright safety from dangerous malfunctions, there would be simply no comparison. The "cheap" .22 would win in a walk, in an amble. We refer, of course, to some wartime German production, not commercial Walthers. There is a superficial resemblance, I think, to the American gun discussed here; and some Walther P-38s were made with enclosed hammer, "hammerless," as that word is commonly used. (Some Walthers had duraluminum slides and receivers, for lightness.) The Dura-Matic is truly hammerless: no swinging hammer hits the firing pin. That pin is a striker, driven forward by its own mainspring, in bolt-action rifle style. This simplifies production and cuts costs in a thoroughly acceptable manner.

It is perfectly possible that a gun-wise choice between Dura-Matic and Sport-King would depend on which feels better in the hand. They are a little different—some would say quite different. The Dura-Matic stock is not integrated with the receiver. It is placed at the bottom of the receiver and held there by a big, strong bolt. This method is satisfactory.

There are two model numbers, M-100 and M-101.

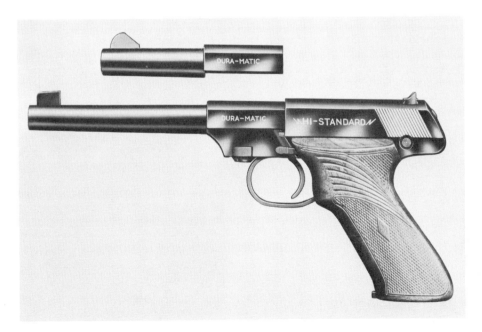

Hi-Standard Dura-Matic with 4½- and 6½-inch interchangeable barrels. Well worth trying for grip fit and balance.

Look for it on the slide, the breech-block. M-100 has a barrel lock plunger that must be pressed in when you unscrew the barrel nut. M-101 hasn't, and the barrel nut is coin-slotted.

With both models, or types, the company advises the use of an empty case or a dummy cartridge (if you can still get one; they're scarce these days) to ease firing pin impact in dry practice. Evidently the Dura-Matic does not have, at least at this writing, a chrome-vanadium steel firing pin. How sad, if true! But should we expect frosting on that good old sticker-to-the-ribs, oatmeal—or all the modern extras on a very inexpensive gun?

Iver Johnson 55 Revolver

Weight: About 27, 29 and 30 ounces.
Barrel: 2½ (the Model 55-S), 4½ and 6 inches.
Overall: 9½ inches with 4½-inch barrel.
Sights: Fixed. Front sight is on a long but atractive-appearing ramp. Rear sight is a notch cut into the top of the frame, integral with it. It would not be surprising if future production brought a rear sight let into a dovetailed slot, so that it could be adjusted for windage. Many other inexpensive revolvers now have this sort of rear sight.
Stocks: Plastic, checked, square butt, and with thumb-rest on 4½- and 6-inch models. Rounded, smooth and smaller on 2½-inch 55-S pocket gun.
Finish: Blue.
Capacity: Eight in cylinder.

These are almost the least costly of all American revolvers. They come from a sound, long-established company that rarely has made even moderately expensive arms, except its double-barrel hammerless skeet shotgun in bores from 12 to 28 and .410. This one costs only a little less than the Fox Sterlingworth, which many of us remember and still can occasionally buy in used condition. Both of these excellent medium-priced shotguns have "gone down the stream of time"; not made for years.

The "non-adjustable fixed sights" help keep Model 55's price down. But you or I could do small wonders with a file. If you are a welder, you could do more, building up the front sight if the gun happened to shoot too high. It isn't easy to file a rear notch, one-sidedly, to get windage, but Necessity had at least two children, Invention and dogged old Patience.

What counts the most is in the 55: a grip not so

I. J. 55-S or Cadet revolver with 2½-inch barrel and rounded stocks without the thumb-rest that goes on the longer Model 55. This barrel length was popular on old small-frame Colt .32 pocket guns, and with good reason.

pinchy-close to the trigger guard, coil springs throughout, a half-cock safety (though with this type I like to let the hammer down on a fired case), recessed cylinder breech to enclose case-heads, and good steel in the works, frame, barrel and cylinder. Up front, that cylinder has a rim around it, the "Flash Control" that I. J. features, to deflect flying particles of lead, grease, powder and fouling out front and down—not to the sides, where they might hit close eager by-standers. It was worth the patenting.

This gun has a steel frame, as noted above. I do not suggest that steel is superior to aluminum-alloy for a frame, for the latter has proved its worth in arms that must be serviceable and still must be light. The rust-proof quality of the alloy is worth consideration, too.

The 55 has a solid frame, like that of the I. J. 57 with adjustable sights, which costs only a little more. But that little can mean the difference between purchase today, and a wait of weeks or possibly months if you are young and/or not heavily subsidized.

Iver Johnson Model 56 is a blank pistol, an 8-shot

Iver Johnson Model 55 revolver with 6-inch barrel, solid frame.

Iver Johnson Model 56 Starter's Revolver, for blank cartridges only. Sharp "barrel" breech breaks up the wads.

.22 on the 55-S frame. Its cylinder will just take the short blanks, and perhaps it should have (and may have, now) the flash control ring. That might help a bit when the cardboard wads break up on the pointed rear tip of the solid 2½-inch "barrel." Doc S., our gym instructor, used to fire his standard-barrel revolver at our bare legs as we were set for the 100-yard dash. He thought it gave us a quicker getaway, and indeed it did. The wads broke up in the bore, or soon after, and did no more than sting us. Still, I suppose that those were unenlightened days. I approve of Doc, now more than ever because the years have given me a little sense to appreciate what's what and who's who, in this mortal life; but approve of his gun and his method in that case, that I cannot!

Ruger Standard Autoloader

Weight: 36 and 38 ounces.
Barrel: 4¾ and 6 inches. Now offered interchangeable, complete with receivers.
Overall: 8¾ and 10 inches.
Sights: Patridge-type, rear movable for windage.
Stocks: Black Butaprene-type hard rubber, shock-resistant and checked.
Finish: Blue.
Magazine capacity: Nine .22 long-rifles.

A surprising thing about this pistol, the first of the Sturm, Ruger & Company line, is that throughout the years of inflation its price has not been raised. At this writing it is the same $37.50 tag as at first. This firm price anchorage goes for later Sturm, Ruger models, but for how many other makes? Just the other day I heard of the opening of the firm's new plant, and unencumbered by mortgage, too.

I can only guess at the Ruger secrets. Economical, efficient engineering designs, which will not be outdated for years, thanks to the foresight of men who themselves are active shooters and outdoorsmen. Few models and few choices in barrel lengths; none at all in

grip shapes. For a long time the company made this .22 auto only, and in just one barrel length, 4¾ inches; yet it kept busy. It satisfied a host of post-war shooters, many of them veterans, who wanted a high-quality .22 automatic at a reasonable price. Glamor helped, too, for everyone familiar with firearms remarked on how much it resembled the German Luger in general appearance, and still more in its grip fit. The first four Ruger sixguns, regardless of caliber and weight, even more plainly suggested the famous Colt Single Action Army, another glamorous gun that fits many hands well—even more than the Luger.

When parts can be used in more than one Ruger model, they naturally are so used. But still there are not many models; there are just enough to answer, deliberately and without hasty production, most of the big, popular demand. It is true that Ruger does special work—engraving, fitted gun-cases, and so on—but more than 90 per cent of production must be of standard jobs, and even then some models are, from time to time, on back order.

The foregoing brace of paragraphs are not plugs, not advertising. It so happens that I am nobody's man but my own. That recital merely shows what American industry can do under progressive management.

There are some disadvantageous features in the Ruger standard grade .22 automatic. Like most others, including some expensive specimens, its trigger pull may have both creep and backlash. The trigger itself is well forward in the guard; it does not hug the rear curve of the guard like that of the German Luger. This characteristic, coupled to the rather husky grip size, makes the gun unsuitable, or at least hard to master, for a shooter with a small hand or short fingers. In trigger location it is somewhat like the earliest Colt Woodsman autoloaders.

Then too, the barrel is light, compared to the weight

Standard Ruger .22 auto with original barrel length of 4¾-inches. Enormously popular since its first appearance.

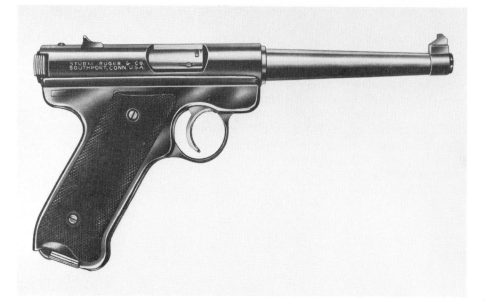

The 6-inch Ruger auto came out much later. Most of us find it easier to shoot well and not troublesome to tote in a belt holster.

of the gun that rests in the hand. With the short barrel, this is especially noticeable. For the same reason this type fails to be a first-class pocket automatic. Few autos are right for such carrying, except those centerfires with long, barrel-enclosing slide of Browning or Colt type. The front sight, too, is cut more for sharp, quick definition on target or game than for drawing from a pocket of soft, thin cloth! But for holster packing and for accurate shooting, which sort of front sight would you choose?

In spite of minor drawbacks, the short Ruger promptly became and consistently stayed popular. It feels good in big or medium-sized hands, it points naturally for most of us, and you can *see* its sights. They are 7½ inches apart. Compare that with the 5½-inch sight radius of the S.&W. .22-.32 Kit Gun with 4-inch barrel. Neither is a target arm, of course. The heavy, ribbed barrel of the 22½-ounce Kit does seem to hang a bit more obligingly on the mark. The Kit should be better for deliberate fire, in spite of its very small stocks, when there is time to align its close-coupled sights; the Ruger is better for quick aim. All this disregards the effects of total gun-weight, grip fit, trigger ease, etc., etc. Quick work—rapid fire, plinking, snap-shooting—is practical defense training. To the majority of us pistoleers, including all ranks from beginner to master, it is certainly the most fascinating kind.

With the 6-inch Ruger, 1¼ inches more barrel and two ounces more weight, you get into a quite different class of handgun. For me it is definitely steadier, and its sights are easier to align truly. Even if the rear sight were farther back, *and barrel weight the same,* the long-Luger complex probably would not come up. With a 6- or 7-inch Luger having its solid, or sometimes stingily-adjustable rear sight at the extreme rear of the toggle-type breech, there is a criss-cross of wobble in aiming.

Incidentally, the cross-pin that keeps the Ruger breech-block where it belongs in firing—not shooting out at your face—is of chrome-molybdenum steel, and 5/16 inch in diameter. Hence, there's no cause for worry.

It would be interesting, if federal law allowed it*, to fit the 6-inch Ruger with a shoulder stock. That barrel length does not wring out all the inherent velocity of the .22 long-rifle cartridge, but it helps, and of course almost any length gives good accuracy if other things, including the ammunition, are right.

The Ruger's cylindrical breech-block, sliding in and out of the receiver tube, has been publicized widely. The rear sight isn't shucked back and forth in recoil. There is little, if any, tendency for it too loosen or shift adjustment, if it *is* adjustable like the one on the more expensive Mark I target Ruger. And when the breech-block goes shut, the sight doesn't have to return precisely to battery, because it's always there. The assembly is simple and, when you think of it, perfectly natural. It helps in easy dismounting for the cleaning and lubrication that a .22 semi-automatic pistol (or rifle) that fires greased cartridges ought to get frequently, in order to stay in absolutely reliable shape. Yes, practically all of the self-feeders do continue to operate long past the plain dirty stage; but any one of them, in the end, is likely to quit in disgust. Then who's to blame, and who's perhaps more than mildly "shook up" or frustrated?

The Ruger safety locks the sear and the breech-bolt. When the latter is drawn back, the safety can be pushed up to hold the breech open. It won't go on safe unless the gun is cocked. All these kind services are very common with autoloading pistols. Although the Ruger's

---

*The 1960 revision of the National Firearms Act does not forbid pistols with shoulder stocks. It does impose a $200 tax on making or transfer of such a gun.

small safety button is less handy than the German Luger's big, swinging lever it still is a good one.

Ruger Single-Six Revolver

Weight: 35 ounces with 5½-inch barrel. In 6½-inch .22 Magnum, 38 ounces.

Barrel: 5½ inches. 4⅝ and 9½-inch lengths announced in May, 1959, widening the selection. In .22 Magnum, 6½ and 9½ inches, also 4⅝ (in 1961).

Overall: 10⅞ inches with 5½-inch barrel.

Sights: Fixed front; rear movable for windage. Some fronts have the Colt forward slant; some are semi-circular.

Stocks: Hard black rubber, checked. Stag or ivory at extra cost.

Finish: Blue. Engraving, burnished aluminum-alloy grip frame, etc., also cased singles and pairs at advanced prices.

Capacity: Six in cylinder.

Human nature so arranged it that when the Colt Single Action Army went out of production for many post-war years, the dear old hog-leg became more desirable than ever, and not only to beginning shooters. "Just got to have one," was the driving thought, and prices of used S.A.A.s in almost any condition kited high, sometimes out of reach of folks who could have used them to best advantage.

So the Ruger Single-Six, resembling the Colt and using the economical .22 short, long and long-rifle cartridges, sold faster than it could be made. The fact that it is a little smaller and lighter than the Peacemaker did not hurt its general appeal much, if any. It holds its popularity even though Ruger followed it

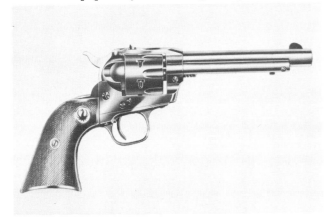

Ruger Single-Six in original barrel length of 5½-inches.

In 1959 the Single-Six was chambered, bored and rifled for the .22 Winchester Magnum Rim Fire cartridge. This one has a 6½-inch barrel.

with two other, lighter .22 caliber models, and Colt made one, too.

Since it is in the medium-price class, it costs considerably more than the standard Ruger .22 automatic. There are short-cuts in its manufacture, but there are also modernizing improvements. The grip frame is cast of very strong aluminum-alloy, not machined out of steel, and it is in one piece, not two as with the old Colt. This material lightens the gun and helps to put weight out front. In its price class, or in almost any at present, we can hardly expect perfection in every specimen. Some Single-Sixes I heard of came out with sticking cylinder bolts—that part in the lower cylinder frame that rises into the cylinder notches to lock each chamber, in turn, in alignment with the bore. The bolts in these guns had not been polished on both sides, and at times they would fail to rise.

Some of us wondered, right from the first, why the rear sight had been inletted so far forward on the top strap. It could have been set helpfully farther back, for this sixgun was built for .22 rimfire ammunition. It was so strongly built that we began at once to hope that it or a similar Ruger would be made for husky centerfire cartridges. They came later, the .357 and .44 Magnum Blackhawk models. We should still like to have two-way adjustable sights on the .22, though we know they would boost the price.

The first .22 Ruger loading gates were flat, not thick and rounded to match the breech contour. They didn't look "right," and they weren't as easy to flip open as those of the Colts, especially in cold weather. So now the current ones *are* right. Ejector rod heads are made longer, too, and more or less by demand. When only a few changes are called for, *and are made,* it is plain that a gun was designed well, and that its maker was cooperative.

Modernizations of the old sixgun patterns do help. Chrome-moly steel frame, instead of case-hardened; strong, almost 100% snapping-resistant firing pin, housed in the breech, not out on the hammer nose; cylinder recessed to enclose case-heads; music wire springs, not flat ones; strongly designed working parts replacing the oldtime vulnerable cylinder hand, cylinder bolt and hammer notches—all these are in line with progress. A good rule is never to carry a single-action revolver with a loaded round under the hammer. Perhaps it might not apply to one with modern steel working parts. Thus, if you and I prefer to stick to the rule, we may be over-cautious. Personally I like to be over-cautious with firearms. I hope that the difference between five and six instantly available rounds never means anything to me.

The Ruger's trigger sits a bit farther forward than that of the big Colt, and it is slightly more curved. The spring-actuated stop behind it, to eliminate backlash, is a fine thing. On the target range, or anywhere else, a side-fed cylinder is slow to eject from and reload. In some timed and rapid fire the long cocking arc would bother a few shooters who are used to modern short-action guns—or who shoot double-action, as more and more seem to do. The coil mainspring does ease the Ruger's cocking to some extent. Even the big .44 Ruger's hammer is a cinch to thumb back if you are used to single-actions and have a fair-sized hand. If this .22 Ruger fits your hand as perfectly as no-never-mind, it could be worth-while to have custom-built two-way adjustable sights fitted, provided they could be kept low, unobtrusive and easy to catch with the eye. Then they would pay off in field use as well as on the range. We could sight the gun in to suit us, at different ranges and with different cartridges, and for a low or a dead-center hold. For really long .22 range, two-hand holding, such a revolver would be a "sweet cake" to project around with, wherever it was safe to do so.

In thinking this over, I have to weaken. Two-way crankable sights help so much that they are almost indispensable. Even if they stand so high that the gun seems like a stranger, we can get acquainted. This may take two or three careful range sessions, including rapid fire, or twenty or thirty. Up to thirty, a glum guess at a maximum, they would still be worth the fraternization necessary.

Ruger Single-Six Lightweight Revolver

Weight: 23 ounces with aluminum-alloy cylinder, 27 ounces with steel cylinder.
Barrel: 4⅝ inches.
Overall: Ten inches.
Sights: Front, fixed; rear, movable for windage.
Stocks: Hard black rubber, same as on standard Single-Six, with same special extra-price choices.
Finish: Blue. The blue on the aluminum parts is described as wearing as well as that on the steel.
Capacity: Six in cylinder.

Like the old 4¾-inch Colt, this 4⅝-incher has its muzzle flush with the end of the ejector rod housing. Otherwise, it resembles a standard Ruger Single-Six in appearance. But on picking it up you at once notice a difference in weight and balance. Even with the aluminum-alloy cylinder, it has good practical heft because the weight is well out ahead of your hand. Still, in 23-ounce alloy version it is light enough not to burden the average beginner, though it is decidedly more muzzle-heavy than the old model .22-.32 S.&W. Target of equal weight. This latter gun started many a young or inexperienced shooter, and started him right. Often he kept on using it for years, or a lifetime, of good target and field shooting.

However, I do think that the standard 35-ounce Ruger performs better for most of us past the early stages, simply because it's heavier. The two models are priced the same.

But for real wilderness travel—and these well-stocked, nicely balanced .22s might pay their way there—the Lightweight could be preferable if we shot it as well, or nearly as well. On such trips a smallbore pistol using light ammunition, certainly not above .32 caliber, can do a surprising percentage of the necessary shooting. When it is shot capably, it can kill small game, and finish off much big game, close-up, with a brain shot. This cuts down the amount of heavy, bulky high-power rifle loads we need to pack along. And if one firearm breaks down, or is lost in a canoe wreck, there's probably still the other. A handgun in a snapped-shut holster seldom gets lost.

Let us not underestimate this liability. One of the justly famous and respected outdoor Roosevelts did lose his .30-06 Model 1895 Winchester—and a grand old rifle that was, like all the others of that pattern! —in rapids on the South American River of Doubt expedition. These men were seasoned outdoorsmen, careful of themselves and their equipment. But any of us can slip at times. Perhaps you too have seen and shot rapids that proved much less demure than you thought they were when your keel slid over their smooth lip. Did you always lash your rifle to a thwart, just in case?

Sturm, Ruger and Company report that their anodyzed aluminum frames stand up to motor-driven dry-fire tests as well as their steel frames do. To me this sounds like a confident guarantee. The Martin Hard Coat skin of the cylinder, they say, wears like that of hardened steel, and of course it doesn't rust. That feature can be pretty nice in outdoor service.

Ruger 1958 Bearcat Single-Action Revolver

Weight: 17 ounces.
Barrel: 4 inches.
Overall: 8⅞ inches—just about the length of an average hand-span.
Sights: Fixed, Patridge-type.
Stocks: Walnut colored wood, not checked, impregnated with scratch-resistant plastic.
Finish: Blue. Aluminum trigger guard anodyzed to a dull brass color like that on some old cap-and-ball revolvers. Cylinder is smooth and not fluted between chambers, in the same old frontloader fashion, and decorated with rolled-in engraving.
Capacity: Six in cylinder.

This gun is in a lower price class than the standard Ruger Single-Sixes. In shape and finish, it is meant to resemble old Remington cap-and-ball revolvers, not Colt Single Actions for metallic cartridges. Besides being smaller than the Single-Six Rugers, it feels different because of its light weight and the old Remington design of stock. The fit and weight of this little Bearcat are for a small and perhaps not very strong hand. But the gun is so neat and compact that it is sure to see a great deal of woods use as well as plinking. Barrel and cylinder length are enough to develop rather good velocities.

The sight radius of 5⅛ inches is some ⅜ inch less than that of the 4-inch barreled S.&W. .22 caliber Kit Gun, although this Ruger's overall length is about ¾ inch greater than that of the little 22½-ounce Smith in the popular rounded-butt pocket type. These comparisons are not odious. They only illustrate the different shapes of the two guns, between which we should choose, if price meant nothing, according to which

Four-inch barrel, small frame, and small stocks make up into a nicely proportioned little .22 revolver, the Ruger Bearcat.

Smith & Wesson .22-32 Kit Gun

Weight: 22½ ounces with 4-inch barrel and round butt; 14¼ ounces Airweight style with 3½-inch barrel and square butt.

Barrel: 2 and 4 inches; 3½ inches in Airweight.

Overall: 8 inches with 4-inch barrel and round butt; the same with 3½-inch barrel and square butt.

Sights: 1/10-inch serrated ramp front; two-way adjustable S.&W. Micrometer Click rear sight. Both are of square-cut Patridge-type.

Stocks: Checked walnut, round or square butt. Only square butt listed at present for Airweight.

Finish: Blue. Nickel at extra cost.

Capacity: Six in cylinder.

felt better in the hand and thus promised us superior shooting.

Bearcat's sights are "fixed," but good! There is no adjustment except by a file, for the rear sight notch is cut into the top strap. It is not a separate piece dovetailed in and adjustable for windage. However, this characteristic makes the gun much smoother for out-of-pocket draw.

For light weight, and economical yet exact manufacture, the frame is one-piece, cast aluminum-alloy, anodyzed to blend with the barrel and cylinder finish. Coil springs serve throughout. The firing pin is mounted in the frame, as we should expect.

Pushing in the base-pin (the cylinder pin) latch allows us withdraw the base pin and turn out the cylinder to the right, after we have opened the loading gate on the right side of the gun. Then we notice that the cartridge heads are not enclosed fully. However, a substantial shiield runs around the outer edge of the cylinder breech. Thus, a burst case-head should not burn the thumb even if its is held high up on the breech swell.

In usual single-action fashion, there are quarter- and half-cock clicking notches on the hammer. The second or half-cock position is to give the cylinder free roll-way while we punch out empties and reload with fresh rounds. Since the Bearcat is so small, almost tiny by today's standards, it is inevitable that big fingers may be a bit unhandy in thrusting the cartridges home. If the load-way were made much bigger, the gun might not be as attractive and well-proportioned as it is now. A single-action revolver is not for quick reloading, anyway, and getting used to a good gun pays off. Any slight difficulty in reloading, if it exists at all for a particular owner, should not amount to much except when his fingers are stiff with cold.

Whether it is ultra-conservatism or common sense to carry this single-action with an empty chamber under the hammer I cannot say. Strong steel goes into it, but even so, I would make it in effect a five-gun rather than a six-gun, and still be happy.

This particular afternoon, Kit prices run from $70 to $84. Nickel costs extra, and so does the light-alloy Airweight construction. All three models do look good. The all-steel gun is Model 34 of 1953 and the Airweight is Model 43 of 1955.

In general, all of them are special-purpose guns, for plinking or for the field, the latter more as a supplement to a rifle or shotgun, than solely for serious outdoor use. But the June, 1956 *Guns* carried a picture of a high school girl who could score in the 90s with a 4-inch, round-butt Kit. She had what it takes, and the gun fitted her.

Those of us who haven't used a round-butt sixgun —and a light one at that—for some years, may experience deep dismay when we grasp one prior to loosing off carefully held and aimed shots! The small, short, round grip of the Kit feels more like a rope than a sixgun stock. If we fit an adapter like the Pachmayr into that too-high space behind the guard, the little finger is likely to float on air. The base of the hand feels unnatural, too, as there is no backward-curving grip heel to support it. Friends, this ain't funny!

It is funny, though—or let's say "odd,"—how continued practice with the little dwarf, as with any good suitable pistol, shrinks the target groups and sometimes results in chest-inflating scores. Since the Kit is companionable and easy to pack, it is decidedly worth mastering. It can give practical service as well as great pleasure. Perhaps it is one of the very best handguns

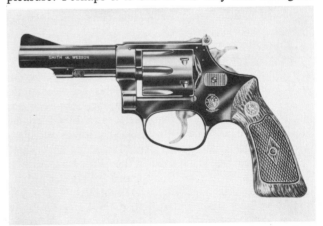

The .22 Magnum S.&W. Kit Gun, pilot model, 3½-inch barrel, as shown at March, 1960, N.R.A. convention's gun exhibit.

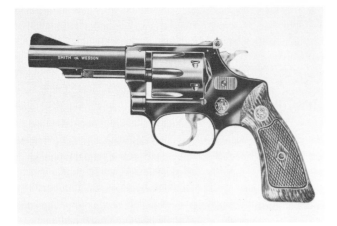

Airweight .22-.32 Smith & Wesson Kit Gun has excellent sights and good balance in spite of its lightness. This 1955 Model Smith has a 3½-inch barrel and weighs 14¼ ounces, empty. It should suit a youngster getting his first lessons (not with high-velocity ammunition, please!) or an oldtimer carrying a heavy pack into the wilderness but still wanting some kind of handy, reasonably effective little gat on his person. This one has the new-style long trigger guard.

ever made for introducing your wife to informal pistol shooting. There is the risk, however, that she might insist on toting it when you yourself would want to belt it on or pocket it!

In 4-inch, the 1953 model weighs 1½ ounces more than the earlier Kit, thanks to its heavy, ribbed barrel. This adds noticeable steadiness, it seems to me.

The front sight is driven into the rib groove; it is not pinned in place as on some of the heavier S.&W. target revolvers. An insecure front sight can fly off a pistol and be lost forever, but with the Kit, I don't believe this would happen.

Its rear sight is a small edition of the Micrometer Click used on the big Smiths, easy to adjust with a screwdriver—or with a knife blade, if we care nothing about the gun's good looks. One Kit specimen I saw had its rear sight blade or leaf loosened by only a few hundred rounds of firing. Well, lemons come in any model, it seems. But this one must have been unusual. Even with it there was no lateral shucking-about to make windage adjustments meaningless; the motion was only fore-and-aft.

It might be well, though, to limit the use of high velocity .22 long-rifles in these guns. No danger of bursting a chamber or swelling the sturdy, square barrel breech, but cylinder alignments do wear under heavy shooting, even though chambers may still turn up accurately when the hammer goes back. Of course, the light-framed Smiths are made in calibers including the .38 Special, and though high velocity .38 Specials are supposed not to be used in them, they are so used by some of us. In the light-framed, short-cylindered Smiths like this one, originally made for .32 S.&W. longs, calibers went and still go as high as .38 S.&W. —the short cartridge which in the past was loaded with bullets as heavy as 200-grain Super-Police. These guns held their cylinder alignment pretty well for thou-

sands of rounds, as I know from my shooting with a Smith .38 Regulation Police. So the foregoing comment on hot .22 long-rifles in the .22-.32 may sound stupid, and may be stupid. Yet when I can favor a pet gun, I do. Many good fellows would say, "Well, I don't expect a lifetime's service from the thing." But can I help having "great expectations"?

A 4-inch Kit should be made in .32 S.&W. Long, a much more effective caliber when properly handloaded with a wadcutter or semi-wadcutter bullet than ordinary .22 rimfires. Both Hand Ejector and Regulation Police are fine .32 woods guns, but they have solid, non-adjustable sights. The 6-inch .32 Regulation Police Target, with finely adjustable sights, was discontinued long before the newer ribbed-barrel .22 Smiths came, and it is almost forgotten. That long-barreled .32 was light for target; but in wilderness where a good hunter can get close to some small game, the caliber does pay off in killing power. A 4-inch, well-sighted .32 would be easy to carry and nearly as easy to shoot. The .32 Long is really too good to be forgotten. Unfortunately, it has such narrow usefulness that it is not popular now. Only one top-quality, well-sighted revolver is made for it, the rather heavy and bulky S.&W. K-.32. That one is hardly made for go-light trips.

.22 Magnum Kit Gun

A long letter of March 28, 1960, from Mr. F. H. Miller, sales manager at S.&W. recounts with his usual care the company's plans for this little gun. It seems likely to be produced, and perhaps within three months of the letter date. There are both demand and uses for it.

Probably it will be of all-steel build, with no aluminum alloy for lightness, have a 3½- or 4-inch barrel, square butt, and about 23-ounce weight. As the illustration shows, the frame and cylinder are longer than those of the standard Kit, which is built on .32 S.&W. Long housing accommodations. It seems that the standard Kit frame could be used, with lengthened cylinder, and a shortened barrel breech coming out to it, in the general style of the Chief's Special, Bodyguard, and hammerless Centennial for .38 Special ammunition, which of course have to be long-framed as well as long-cylindered. But just as it is, in the pilot model .22 Mag shown in the picture, this young candidate looks good.

In any kind of pistol-length arm the .22 Magnum is a loud-cracking cartridge. To get high velocity in pistol or rifle, the bullet is light and the powder charge heavy. The .22 W.R.F. round can be chambered in a .22 Mag, but in modern loading it makes a sharp report from even a 6-inch barreled revolver. The old low or "standard" velocity rounds are made no more in the U.S.A.

But people vary in the amount or pitch of noise they can take from a firearm and still shoot up to their par. Racket goes with high velocities just as it goes with having most children, puppies, and even some just decently spoiled cats in your house; and we put up with one or maybe all. Not that a 4-inch .22 Mag develops full pistol velocity for its cartridge. Still, it's effective on small game when the bullet is placed well, and for defence it should equal or beat the .32 S.&W. Long or the flat-nosed .32 New Police, Colt's improvement in killing power.

This light, small .22 Mag sixgun has practical purposes that may make it outsell the K-Target Smith in the same caliber, which came out much earlier. It is carried easily in pocket or holster, it is impressive as such a little gun, and for the handgun-loving outdoorsman who must go light in big or small wilderness it's an inviting choice. Here its sharp report might come in handy, for signalling.

More Kit Comment

The two-inch barreled Kit for .22 long-rifle ammo hasn't the power to rely on for self-defence, unless we desperately have to! And the .32 is little better for shooting as serious as that. Even with long pistol barrels such calibers are weak. But many good people like to carry a snub-nosed little revolver just for fun. For them the shortest Kit .22 with its excellent sights is a de-luxe and extremely practical gun. That is why it sells.

Later 1953 and 1955 Kits, and other small Smiths, now have a larger, more oval trigger guard with added finger space when the trigger is in the forward position. The general effect is somewhat rakish, or possibly unsymmetrical; but for quick double-action shooting it is practical. On my wife's Kit Gun, this space is actually over ⅛ inch longer than it is on my old .44 S.&W. Military.

Such little changes come and go. Some are for good reasons and some just for newness.

The action of the modern .22-.32 is different in design from that of the older gun without the barrel rib. Its mainspring is coiled, not flat, and it seems very slightly easier to cock the gun with the thumb or to fire it double-action. It does not have "short action," at least not to the extent that modern K models have, for instance. Yet the .22-.32 always was easy to handle, and the arc of the hammer fall was short enough for quick ignition. The present hammer spur is wider and more deeply checkered. Anyone used to the old Smiths and Colts might not find that any great advantage, although it should help a beginner to thumb the hammer back.

Not all of the factory personnel, I hear, approve of the new thumb-piece on small Smiths—the latch you thrust forward to free the cylinder. It's flat and more compact than the old type was. Under heavy recoil, like that of a .38 Special in a gun weighing a pound, more or less, it is certainly more considerate toward a thumb that rides it. But the old, higher, hollowed-out thumb-piece is much better suited to a thumb-piece's job!

The serious faults of too many Kit Guns are a heavy trigger pull or sometimes a creepy pull. It is hard to hold a light gun on the mark while wrestling with a single-action pull that is three to five times heavier than the gun itself. Pulls can be reduced and creeps hexed away, but when the moving parts are of case-hardened steel, there is danger of filing through the hard skin, with the result that the pull can wear lighter and lighter until it is no longer serviceable. Rehardening is a job that some gunsmiths prefer to pass on to the factory, where, if rehardening is impossible, new parts can be installed. Sometimes a creepy pull on a new gun will smooth up after a comparatively small amount of use.

A generation ago, a Smith, Colt or any other good revolver almost never showed up with a poor pull. Many old specimens are still perfect in that respect. Now the manufacturers' problems are entirely different. I don't want to exaggerate the defects in workmanship, but they are all too apparent in some new guns. We can understand why they are there. Rifles and shotguns also get through inspections with faults that would not have passed in earlier days.

Whitney Wolvering Autoloader

Weight: 23 ounces.
Barrel: 4⅝ inches.
Overall: 9 inches.
Sights: Patridge-type ⅛-inch front; rear sight movable for windage. Low-lying for pocket use, but clean-cut. Frame top is serrated to eliminate reflection of light. Since the breech-block slides back out of the frame or receiver in recoil, and the sights are attached to the frame, the rear sight, like the front sight, stays put during the reloading process and is always in battery; it does not depend on the fit of the breech-block for its alignment. In this respect, the Whitney resembles the Ruger autoloader.
Stocks: Checked plastic.
Finish: Blue. Nickel at extra cost.
Magazine capacity: Ten .22 long-rifles.

The Whitney at first, second and later glances looks neat, racy, and "modern," yet a thing of earth, not a parachute delivery from Mars! It points about as naturally as a handgun can, provided, of course, that it fits you, personally. At first, the barrel nut at the muzzle looks odd, but it may improve the contour, at that, by making the muzzle seem less blunt and stubby.

Whitney .22 Autoloading Pistol.

Many shooters have admired the Whitney's flowing lines.

This pistol looks heavier than it is, because the frame and some other parts are of dural, not steel. Weight and balance are good for a pocket pistol, or one used afield for all but the most exacting .22 work. The rail extending back above the web of your grip-grasping hand is more than sufficient insurance against having your skin bitten by the recoiling breech-block, and it is long enough not to catch in an average-sized hip pocket. (The Whitney is actually longer than the .45 Government Model automatic.) This rail or spur would help many of us get back on the target quickly in rapid fire, for it tends to reduce the muzzle up-chuck of recoil. The high grip and the low barrel make for fast pointing. Bill Edwards, technical editor of *Guns* magazine, once suggested that the Whitney might come out in target form. If so, it almost certainly would have a longer barrel, higher and more closely adjustable sights, possibly a larger grip, and at least an extra half pound of weight. Edwards and others have thought of the general design as being adapted to more powerful cartridges, for the magazine is tapered from front to back and therefore seems a natural for rimmed cases. Taking .38 Specials, for instance, it could be extremely popular in the "center-fire" target class, below .45 Auto in blast and recoil, like those Super-.38 Auto Colts that have been gunsmithed to handle the short wadcutter .38 Special loads. There is so much slant to the Whitney design for grip and magazine that perhaps such a gun could handle the full-length, full-power .38 Specials with the long, rounded bullet nose protruding beyond the brass. Some target shooters prefer the full load for 50-yard work, particularly in a strong cross-wind. If this could be engineered without making the grip too large, fore-and-aft, for, say, 25% of targeteers, we might have something very good indeed. For reliable service work, most of us would prefer a round-nosed bullet in an automatic to one as uncompromisingly bluff as a square-cut wadcutter, even though some customed .38 Special auto Colts have performed splendidly. The round-point *looks* more certain to feed, and that would help morale!

The .22 Whitney magazine is something of a wonder, so strongly built. It nevertheless needs care: keep it clean, and make sure that its lips are not damaged. The bullet guide, which noses cartridges into the barrel chamber, is a part of the Whitney magazine. Most guns have a ramp built into the frame. The reliability of Whitney feeding has received much praise. It's evidently one of the best, although with today's excellent runs of .22 ammunition we get fine performance from other auto-pistols, too—not to be compared with the halting uncertainties of forty years ago! It seems more than just likely that the general Whitney system could be applied to centerfires, with a locked, not a straight, blow-back action.

The thumb safety on the Whitney is unusual: you push it up, not down, to ready the gun for firing. This may seem slow and awkward. Some German Lugers did have this unusual safety throw; and of course, the Luger was meant for quick offensive work, fast-pointing, too. It was not for target, though target models, of a sort, were made. Ordinarily you draw a pistol's safety *down*. The Whitney safe blocks the sear and disconnects the trigger. It can be operated only when the hammer is cocked, as is usual with most hammerless pistols and rifles. Thus you know whether or not the hammer is cocked; but to unload the arm, you must throw off the safe.

The Whitney is an exposed-hammer gun. The small hammer spur is exposed to plain view, or easy to feel in the dark. It is not meant to be used as a safety device when it is down on the half-cock notch. This notch is a "slip safety" to prevent discharge if the full-cocked hammer falls as a result of misuse or a (very unlikely) failure of the mechanism. A pull on the trigger will drop the Whitney hammer down from the slip notch, though it will fall so lightly that it will hardly cause the gun to fire unless this tap-tap is repeated indefinitely—and stupidly. Always carry the hammer fully cocked, therefore, and the thumb safety down in its "on" or locked position, when there is a loaded round in the chamber. Or leave the chamber empty and the magazine loaded—or both of them empty when the gun is put away, even though this gun won't fire when its magazine is out.

Most .22 auto-pistol magazines copy the old center-fire 7.65 and 9 mm. Lugers, in having a button on the side to depress the follower as we slide the cartridges one by one into the magazine. For compactness, the Whitney does not have the button. Instead there is a hole in the magazine follower that takes an empty .22 long-rifle (or .22 long) case to serve as a thumb button in loading.

An empty is recommended, too, for snapping practice, to avoid possible damage to the firing pin or the barrel breech. Most rimfire pins are now made so short that they can't reach barrel steel, but the bitter days when a snapped-off firing pin can go whizzing down a barrel aren't yet over. It's an uncommon breakage, but quite commonly we outdoorsmen are a long way from gunsmiths or spare parts. The easy disassembly of this gun makes it no great trouble to replace a firing pin—if there is one in the kit. When assembling or merely cleaning this pistol, go easy on the oil. The makers explain that it doesn't need much, and that it should be light oil—the kind that's right for almost any firearm's working parts. In extreme cold we ordinarily use no oil, just powdered graphite, or an anti-freeze oil we can trust.

Although the Whitney is light for its size, it is strongly made. Its mono-bloc cast-aluminum frame is credited with the strength of 44,000 pounds per square inch, for instance. (The pressure of a .30-30 rifle cartridge amounts to some 40,000 p.s.i., under normal conditions.) Precision light-alloy casting permits needed size and bulk with little weight, and intricate inside shaping (for working parts) which would be too costly, or even almost impossible, with steel.

The care of this gun's extractor needs some comment, and some commendation, too, for it is not difficult to remove and replace. But cover it to prevent it from jumping out of the breech-block in disassembling. A .22 auto-pistol's extractor does need cleaning rather often, and it's a help when you can take it right out, easily, to do that job. A dirty extractor can be gummed into uselessness with bullet lubricant and fouling. Then sometime when you think you've pulled a loaded round from the chamber, maybe you haven't, and that means danger. Naturally, it is sensible to *look* into both chamber and magazine to be sure they are empty, but it is also natural to forget, once in a while, until the habit has been ironed into the brain.

The forward-flowing of the Whitney's trigger guard, in Mauser H SC .32 auto style, is more for looks than for utility, but it might help in holstering the gun. We see this on modern Remington pump and autoloading shotguns and rifles, and on some other arms. Whitney dural construction is too light for this extension to add much steadying weight out front, but this pistol is balanced nicely for quick shooting, anyway.

It's possible that all or nearly all of the handguns described in this chapter are built a little too much around the idea of fast shooting. Obviously, the single-shots are not, and many of the autoloaders or revolvers can be had with enough barrel length and weight for good slow-fire work.

Among rather occasional and beginning shooters there is certainly considerable accent on rapid fire. Television and movie westerns and crime stories feature it, and most of us do some screen-scanning. With some background of powder-burning experience most of us are amused, rather than amazed, at the high precision of screen shooting, not that some of the actors are not really good shots in either fast or slow tempo. A guy pops up, flips his handgun muzzle in the general direction of the hero or the villian, cuts loose, and drops back behind cover. Yet the hits come, or at least the terrifying near-misses—and ain't good shooting nothing at all when you're dressed and play-cast for it!

This phooey misleads the younger generation, the teeners; and I, for one, do not like it. When they make their first visit to a junior club rifle range, they are confident of kocking the black out of the target. Well, at first they rarely hit it, and in fact they do rather well to punch the 50-foot junior two-point-scoring square that is some 6¼ inches on a side. The tiny 10-ring, smaller than a .22 bullet, is just for happy chance. Some kids take disillusionment well, and continue to try. But some don't.

Another screen-shooting fact burns me. Why don't the directors teach the supporting characters, and some of the heroes, too, that a lever action rifle is reloaded from the shoulder by men and women who understand it? These folks don't take the rifle down, heave and pull at the lever, and bring it up again to shoulder and face. The *back* of their fingers throws the lever down; they don't use the lever as a sort of pistol grip, except of course to haul the buttplate snugly back into the shoulder hollow where it belongs.

But even if our beginning pistol shooter hasn't realized that accurate rapid fire comes a long, long time after accurate slow fire, he can still have a great deal of fun in fast shooting. He's bound to learn hitting if he keeps at it. Any shooting, that is careful and safe, is a lot better than no shooting at all. And these handy, relatively inexpensive .22 pistols are fascinating to own, gloat over, and use. Most of them are light enough for any beginner, and unless barrels are very short, or the gap between the revolver's barrel and cylinder excessive in tolerance, they are not really noisy. They can see a lot of rather close-to-home use. Unlike most initial investments in equipment, they are, almost without exception, of good enough quality and durability to be worth keeping for a lifetime. There always will be some uses for them.

And just in themselves, they are worthy possessions. However, most of us who start with one of them will later consider buying and learning to shoot another pistol, of better quality, perhaps, in the same useful little .22 caliber, or of heavier caliber. Even so, don't you suppose that more lives have been saved by the .22 than have been lost because that smallbore was too weak to do the business?

———————

Since the above was written, important new .22 revolvers have appeared. One is the Ruger Convertible Single-Six, in two calibers and with two interchangeable cylinders. One takes .22 long-rifle and shorter rounds; the other cylinder takes .22 Rimfire Magnum, and .22 WRF as a subload.

High-Standard's Imperial is a Sentinel in practical, work-day full-dress. It has two-piece walnut, checked stocks, a spring-returned ejector, and either black or nickel finish. There is less flare-back at the bottom of its stocks than the original and standard Sentinel has. For some hands this will be an improvement. For use by a number of shooters, such as a family of them, the old grip fitted pretty small hands; yet the flare at the bottom, which little hands hardly felt, was a help to he-man mitts, which in fact might have been lost without it.

CHAPTER 7

HOME GUNS

BY OSCAR R. HAMMOND

A WELL-MADE home defense gun, always loaded and instantly available, gives us a sense of security that we can get from nothing else. A deposit box containing the best insurance policies, or the thought of our wonderful police system, is small consolation if we stand helpless before one or more drunken, doped, crazed or just plain ignorant marauders bent on robbery or even worse hellishness. By comparison, robbery can be trivial indeed!

We should be thankful that we live in a country that permits every law-abiding citizen to have a defense gun. Although in some states there is a certain amount of red tape to be cut—and perhaps very tough tape, too—it is worth the trouble to be armed, and to know how to use arms.

Generally speaking, the home protection handgun should be one of the larger calibers that deliver plenty of stopping power and nerve shock. The desire for wallop can be overdone, however, as many of the big-bores are too heavy for women to manipulate, or just too much for them to shoot well without more practice than they may be able or willing to give to this detail. Since most of them spend more time at home than the men do, any compromise on a house pistol should lean to their side. The .38 S.&W. cartridge—or the .38 S.&W. Special, mid-range loaded with keg-shaped, wad-cutter bullets—has good shocking power and is not too unpleasant for ladies' use, considering both recoil and weight.

Calibers smaller than the .38 S.&W. or the flat-pointed .38 Colt New Police are serviceable for home protection only if the family is well trained in using them. Small diameter, lightweight bullets do not strike the immediate knock-down blow so necessary in defense shooting. Yet these lighter bullets kill quickly and easily when properly placed; ask any farmer who uses the lowly .22 short rather than the sticking-knife at butchering time.

I know of one couple who are both gun-bugs. They have excellent and identical guns in .22 caliber, take perfect care of them, and use them a great deal on the target range and at plinking. They both keep their guns loaded and available. I consider their home adequately protected.

Guns using cartridges whose bullets have long range and deep penetration should be avoided, particularly in the more thickly settled areas. The bullets can easily go right through our robber and continue into the next apartment or the upstairs bedroom where the twins sleep, or wander across the street to invade other innocent slumbers. Unless a vital place is hit, many of these slugs would leave our prowler feeling as though he had been stabbed with only a hatpin, and consequently madder than a wet hen. But the blunt, large diameter bullet with plenty of weight leaves him flat on the floor, feeling as though he had been hit with a sledge-hammer.

Barrel length is not too important, for the home gun is for immediate availability more than for carrying.

We must remember that ultra-short barrels, popular though they are, give a terrific muzzle blast, especially indoors. Largely for this reason, their recoil is much more pronounced. Grip style need not be stressed, either, as long as the grip is small enough for a comfortable hold by every adult member of the family. Some are better than others for instinctive pointing; they make the gun feel almost like an extension of your hand. In the dark, or perhaps with the light in *your* face, an easy pointing gun may mean quite a bit!

Target sights on home protection guns are just a waste of money unless the family goes in for real handgun expertness; and even then there will be an endless readjustment of the sights, for nearly all of us hold and perhaps aim differently. Our hands and perhaps our vision, too, vary. When we *have* to shoot a defense gun, we rarely get time to use the sights at all.

We might better spend the target sight money on cartridges and take the family out in the country for some plinking. After becoming familiar with the gun by snapping it for a time with no cartridges, except perhaps empties for the firing pin's sake, most people find it surprisingly easy to extend the gat naturally, "touch her off," and hit a man-sized target at short range. This builds up confidence, and it is really practical.

The finish of the house gun is not important, but the nod seems to go to nickel or chrome plating rather than to blue. Many home guns are neglected for months on end, and plating, or an aluminum-alloy frame, resists

One of the fine, old, five-shot, double-action revolvers once made by Smith & Wesson for the short .38 S.&W. or Colt New Police cartridges—the latter with flat-point bullet. Fifty years ago this type would have been considered one of the best home guns available, and it would have doubled easily as a pocket gun.

rust caused by perspiring hands or damp weather much better than blueing does. Although the target fan doesn't care for the sun-glare on a brightly finished gun, the householder doesn't give a hoot about it; neither does he mind if his gun shows up like a bomb-blast in the night. It shows he's armed.

In purchasing our home gun it is wise to spend a few extra dollars and get one made by a reliable manufacturer. When we need this type of firearm we want all the confidence we can have, not the feeling of holding a cheap piece of junk in our hands. A second-hand pistol can be a great bargain if the buyer knows what he is getting, and is satisfied with it. But to judge correctly the general condition and in particular the absolute reliability calls for considerable gun knowledge.

The question of revolver vs. automatic also should be discussed before deciding on a house gun. In some instances the revolver gets first place. Poor cartridges may cause a disastrous misfire in the auto, and the intruder might not wait for the bad round to be ejected and a good one thrown into the barrel. The double-action revolver needs only to have its trigger pulled again to bring up a new cartridge. Many home guns lie untouched in the bureau drawer for years, and the best of ammunition "surrenders" if given time enough. Springs have a habit of staying in the same position if left contracted for a long time. This applies to the auto-loader's magazine spring, as well as to the striker or hammer spring. I have seen these springs snapped completely in two, and then they are naturally worthless. I have also seen magazines so full of gummy oil, grease and dirt that the spring could not function, anyway.

The larger and more adequate automatics are rather tough for some of the weaker sex to make ready, if they are left with only the magazine loaded and no cartridge in the chamber. Their grips are big and cumbersome for small hands. The auto is rather a misfit for the left-handed person, as the thumb safety is on the left. Picture the southpaw doing a sleight of hand on one of them in a hurry! And don't try to shoot them

from the pocket, because they will almost certainly jam after the very first shot.

But if, for reasons best known to the home owner, an automatic is chosen to be the "defender," may we suggest the purchase of two magazines? One is to rest empty for a period of time while the other sits loaded in the butt of the gun. Then, rather than unload the "tired" magazine, take the gun out and use it for plinking practice. In that way we rid ourselves of old cartridges and also renew our friendship with the gun. After cleaning and oiling the weapon—which will be so faithful if it is encouraged to be—put in the other clip full of fresh cartridges. The mainspring may also be coddled by snapping the hammer of the positively unloaded gun before inserting the loaded magazine. This necessitates a pull-back of the slide before the gun is loaded, cocked, and ready to shoot. Make sure the adults are able to do this and that they know it has to be done! They must realize, too, that withdrawing the magazine does not eject the cartridge which may be in the chamber. Few automatics have a "magazine safety," that device that makes it impossible to fire the arm when the magazine has been removed. The operation of the safeties, and what they do, should be explained thoroughly, especially to those who are used to "pointing and pulling," as with a double-action revolver. To most people with only a general knowledge of firearms, the auto is still an enigma. It *seems* untrustworthy, vicious.

Remember that the common outside-lubricated .22 rimfire cartridges are unreliable after even a comparatively short residence in a heavily oiled chamber—rifle, revolver or auto-pistol. If the crimp of the brass case is too light, oil gets in and destroys the usefulness of powder and priming. For this reason a .22 caliber home gun, if that size is chosen, just might best be an automatic. The magazine could be kept fully or partly loaded, the chamber empty. The recoil spring that holds the bolt shut is much lighter than those on .32, .38 and .45 auto-pistols, and to draw the .22's bolt back fully is not so hard when a person has been taught that it is not really a drawing motion, but a quick thrust forward of the hand-gripped gun while the spare hand clamps tightly down on the bolt or the slide. Yes, it does take two hands to make ready, not just one as with a revolver, loaded, but with its cylinder swung out, if you like, for safety.

In spite of all drawbacks, the autoloader is still the choice defense gun of many who understand it. The reasons can be weighty, too. The auto fits their hands; it holds a lot of cartridges; it is easy to shoot fast and with good accuracy, if it needs to be. For carrying, it is flat and short, but perhaps a home gun should not be asked to do double duty. Instead, it should stay put on its primary job, except when it is taken out for practice shooting.

The proper place to keep it is a poser that will have to be worked out by each family. Probably the most popular hideouts are under a pillow or on the top of a bedside stand at night, and in an unlocked drawer near the entrance during the day. If the family works during the day, the gun should be locked in some safe place, but to keep it so when the family is at home is foolhardy. The noise of unlocking and opening a drawer is all the average intruder would ask for! He would be on his way or giving us trouble before we could do anything about it. In short, leave the pistol where you can grab it at a moment's warning, but also where a stranger wouldn't notice it.

There are no hard and fast rules to tell us when to shoot, when to just show our gun, or when to leave it concealed. Almost every intruder calls for a different technique. If we know our lives are in immediate peril we can shoot quick as hell for the upper middle, and more than once! It's a case of our lives against his, and he is "in wrong," anyway. If he just looks tough but is obviously unarmed we can show our gun. If that isn't enough we can always loose off a shot near his feet for a starter. Naturally, he never must be allowed to get close to us! A questionable character might be greeted with the gun in our pocket, just to bolster our confidence if he looks larger than we feel at the moment. And remember that previous caution: don't let any of them get too close! A handgun is one of the easiest things in the world to take away from another person, especially at night when his reflexes may be slowed down considerably if he's just been awakened.

The other fellow, however, is quite sure to be highly strung, if only from a guilty conscience or a feeling of unsureness.

One evening a farmer noted a light truck stopping near his orchard. He took his gun and a roundabout route to investigate. Sure enough, one man was on a ladder picking apples and handing the pailfuls down to an accomplice on the ground, who was dumping them into potato crates. After watching for a few moments, the farmer, who was a good shot, put a hole through the empty pail as it was being passed up to the man on the ladder. Seconds later he was richer by a good ladder, six new potato crates, a bushel of his own apples, ready-picked, and a worthless pail.

Another evening a city dweller heard someone sneaking up on his porch and quietly trying a key in his front door. Taking his Colt .38 Detective Special with him, he went to the door, which had a night-latch, turned the knob, jerked the door open and quickly stepped back, ready to clout his visitor on the head or shoot him, whichever the situation demanded. The intruder pitched headlong onto the floor and stayed there. He turned out to be a near neighbor who had imbibed too freely and had picked the wrong home. His stealth was naturally due to his consideration for his family; he wouldn't want to disturb their sleep at that time of night.

Both of these home defenders used good judgment. Let's hope that if occasion arises we can do as well.

WAITING between trains, humoring an attack of spring fever, or simply passing time in one of the pleasantest fashions, the gun-crank does a good-sized spot of haunting the stores that carry second-hand as well as brand-new shooting-irons. Often and obviously he has no money to spend; it has gone for ammunition or a still "new" gun.

Then his visit is no pleasure to a certain sort of salesman, who straightway assumes a lofty and distinguished air. This fellow cannot see beyond an immediate sale, or at most beyond the thousand-yard sight elevation of his nose.

Most certainly, he's wrong. I have bought many a gun only after several look-sees and thoughtful fondlings, and I have sold a few good ones to other customers in a store by a word or two given at the right time. So this showcase-shopping is justifiable, and the disapproval of the bored beauty behind that case needn't raise our breech pressure a particle. We can remember Walt Whitman's good-natured sarcasm:
"The little plentiful mannikins, skipping around in collars and tail'd coats,
I am aware who they are—(they are positively not worms or fleas)."
But there are wise and friendly dealers, and probably they are in the majority. They are helpful because they know that our tribe buys second-, third- or fourth-hand merchandise for sound reasons. Some guns are unfamiliar, whetting the desire of the collector or the shooter who loves to investigate, and some are cleverly altered, gunsmithed into finer appearance or more efficient form. And there are rare bargains, explainable only on the assumption that the dealer doesn't always know value.

Ammunition Supply

Most collectors, shooters and just plain gun-lovers would agree that there have been far more metallic rifle than pistol cartridge sizes. For the last half-century or so, it has been common knowledge that the casualties in rifle sizes have been tremendous—and that they had to be. New sizes caused the discontinuance of old ones, not quite immediately, of course; but the demand for early sizes dropped until it was no longer profitable to make them. We don't like this, but we see why it must happen.

Several pistol-caliber cartridges still come out of the loading plants, at this writing, with no currently made American handguns to shoot them. In rimfire there are the .22 Winchester (or Remington Special) and the .32 short and long. Centerfires are the .32 short and long Colt, the .32-20, .38-40 and .44-40 Winchester, and the .41 Long Colt. Then there are the familiar Browning-designed, Colt-adopted .25, .32 and .380 Auto, and they seem sure of long survival because a great many old American pistols as well as old and new imports are still here to use them. The typically foreign-made sizes, long popular here although few if any U. S. handguns have ever been made for them, are the .30 Mauser and .30 Luger. They are still fur-

CHAPTER 8

USED
GUNS

nished by our loading companies, but in the modern concept of mass sales they are not as popular as they used to be.

Every one of the cartridges listed in the foregoing paragraph has its own peculiar usefulness, and it is safe to say that every one still has its admirers. How many of those people will continue to buy the domestic rounds and thus keep them in American production, calls for some mighty sharp forecasting. I should be personally sorry to see any of them go, but that cuts no mustard.

Some of the discontinued sizes, none of them really ancient, are the .25, .30, .38, .41 and .44 rimfires, though the .41 short is still available from some sources, and freshly loaded. In centerfires, there are the .35 S.&W. Auto, .41 short, .44 Bull Dog, .44 Webley, .44 Colt (as used in converted cap-and-ball guns), .44 S.&W. American, .44 Russian, .44 Merwin & Hulbert 1876 model, .45 Webley, .45 S.&W. Schofield, the old .45 Colt Auto with 200 grain jacketed bullet, and the .50 U. S. Government Pistol—which at first was a rimfire of 1866 but soon appeared with centerfire priming and in that form hung on until 1920 or so.

But there are ways to feed some old handguns. A rimfire .32 or .38 could be converted to fire the .32 or .38 short Colt safely, subject to a good gunsmith's approval. Two popular and capable old sixgun loads are simply shortened forms of others—the .44 Russian from .44 Special, and the .45 Schofield from .45 Colt. Yes, the Russian is thirty-odd years older than the Special, but only their case lengths and powder charges differ. Sometimes rifle cases can be cut down to fit revolver chambers, like the obsolete but not yet terribly scarce .32 Winchester Self-loading for the fine old

.32-.44 S.&W. Or, to keep an excellent oldtimer shooting, it may be necessary to use brass that is somewhat too short, like .351 Winchester Self-loading in a .38-.44 S.&W. target gun. That is the old one, for which the factory cases ran the full length of the chambers, putting the flush-seated bullet noses about as close to the rifling as any practical system could manage. These guns really shot. Their accuracy should not be deprecated by comparison with that of the old Russian Nagant revolvers that hitched the cylinder forward, cupping against the barrel breech when the hammer was cocked.

It is seldom that a sufficient supply of obsolete ammunition comes with an old gun. But if this "Ancient Pistol" is so tempting that we just must have it, we needn't give up. Want ads in columns such as those of *The American Rifleman,* 1600 Rhode Island Avenue, N. W., Washington 6, D. C., or of *Shotgun News,* Columbus, Nebraska, may bring us what we need, thus eliminating the job of adapting other cartridge cases, or the gun itself. Bullet molds for almost any American handgun, and a good many foreigners, can be had; also obsolete or specially made loading tools or loading dies for a modern tool.

Frank Miles, The Gunsmith, Bedford, Virginia, has been making good cartridge cases to order for a long time. Naturally such hand-made cases are not cheap. He has, or did have, two ways of making the primer pockets, at least for more or less high-power rifle cases. One method is to cut them a bit undersize, and in these it is a bit difficult to insert primers without distorting them somewhat. But firing gradually forms them to size, for large rifle primers are potent things. The other method is to cut them of factory standard size. I chose the latter. These cases are standing up finely with the loads I had them made for—reduced-charge .220 Swift that give about "average" (if we can use that word) handgun pressures in my rifle. So I should expect that pistol cases made by him, for an oldtime handgun, would be long-lived.

In handloading, consider the age of the gun. Most of us buying used arms for our shooting purchase moderns. It is true; but many practical shooters have a yearning for oldtimers, or else are tempted by a particularly beautiful or fine-fitting pistol made long ago. Many of these are not for modern loads. A rather common one is a Colt Single Action Army or Bisley with serial number under 160,000. It would be for black powder only—now that the semi-smokeless powders like King's, and Du Pont's Lesmok, are gone.

It was and is quite all right to handload many old centerfire black powder *rifles* with a pinch of smokeless powder under the black. About as much as 25%, by measure, *not* by weight, of smokeless could be used in cases up to the .32-20 (nominally a 20-grain black powder capacity hull), and much less, progressively down to 10%, in big cartridges up to the .50-100 and .50-110 Winchesters. The best powders to use now seem to be Du Pont 4759 Rifle or Du Pont *Bulk* Shot-

gun. The latter is soft. It can be powdered to dust under close compression and long storage, and then pressures go up. But I have never used this duplex loading system for an old handgun, and I don't intend to! I think straight black powder should be used, the FFG granulation for almost all case sizes. The finer FFFG is right for the 9-grain .32 S.&W. short and .32 Short Colt loads. Since the coarser powders burn more slowly, I think that FG, though it is really meant for rifle cartridges above 40-grain capacity, is a good choice for the full 40-grain charge for one of the old .45 Colt S.As. Its cylinder walls are thinner than those of most smaller calibers, though the old gun actually was made in the British .476 Eley!

I think, too, it pays to be cautious with the oldtimers—or with any gun. A burst cylinder isn't pretty, and it can happen so suddenly! An old black-powder Bisley Colt .45 was doing all right with moderate charges of smokeless and a 250 grain lead bullet. Then one of the slugs jumped its crimp. Its nose stuck out of the front of the cylinder and locked the gun. Whereupon the shooter shoved it back with his forefinger, and fired. Since he had poked it back beyond the normal seating, the nitro powder was—not compressed, but given less air-space than it wanted. Excessive pressure blew three chambers out of the cylinder and bent the gun's top-strap. The flying steel went out to the sides, naturally, but no one was hurt. The late Alan MacDonald, then at Shenandoah Guns, Berryville, Virginia, fitted a new cylinder, which was comparatively easy, and bent the top-strap back to perfect alignment, which was not easy at all. What is more, it *stayed* in alignment.

Bullets and primer types must be right, too, in handloading for old guns, as much as or possibly more than for modern, strong ones. Oversize or too hard bullets raise pressures; and superweights are not right, either, unless we make intelligent allowances for them. Some chamber mouths are much larger than barrel breeches ahead of them. They allow a soft bullet, which we would use instead of very hard ones in the hope of keeping pressures down, to expand in the chamber mouth and then abruptly hit the much smaller barrel throat. Obviously that makes rough going.

Heavy-hammered revolvers can fire tough rifle primers satisfactorily. But the heavier priming charge raises pressure, and it is not needed for good ignition. Even with much reduced powder loads, there is danger of these strong primers backing up so violently that they batter the recoil plate in the breech. Sometimes, under shortages, we have to use rifle primers in a handgun. Let's plan ahead and make the shortages as short as possible. This goes for modern handguns, too.

There are many old, small caliber handguns, really collectors' items, that need just as careful loading as the big veterans of half-century or greater age. Black powder is the thing for them, I'm convinced, even though most factory loads—smokeless today, of course—are held down in power to humor them.

Before wartime shortages cleaned out most of it, we

shooters often bought bargain-basement ammunition that served many purposes, as purchased or broken down for its components. There is still some in stores, attics, and barns. "Nobody" wants old corrosive-primed cartridges or long-obsolete sizes—but *we* do! We can get the brass by firing them and cleaning the gun, or do it the hard way by extracting the bullets. Patient squeezing with pliers loosens most crimps, though jacketed bullets are hard to get out unless the brass is "season cracked" from long tension. Another method, *not* recommended, is to tap the junction of case and bullet lightly with a hammer. Either way, most bullets become so distorted that they are fit only for the melting pot—after clinging kernels of black powder have been scraped off. For quantity disassembly, we should need a commercial bullet-puller or a rig such as Bert Shay describes in his chapter on handloading. For occasional jobs, the Inertia Bullet Puller does well. It does mar some rims, and it is decidedly not for rimfires. The ordering address is Guns, Box 8333, Houston, Texas. It's a hollow plastic mallet, and the cartridge is locked inside it.

Wearing gloves for protection in case of a premature explosion, we can punch out some primers for use, and even the mercuric type seldom if ever gives trouble in straight black powder loads. The fouling of the black coats the inside of the case and, usually, prevents the mercury from getting into the brass and making it dangerously brittle. Salvage the powder unless it has crumbled into dust or gone sour chemically, but never try to identify smokeless types, as factories have their own special formulas, in most modern loadings at least. Use the powder in charges that start low and rarely if ever reach full power.

Such disassembly is necessary if the cartridges are too old to go off with one or two taps of the firing pin, for no one likes to work with rounds that might decide to let go under further stress. It is necessary, too, if there is the least suspicion that the priming is mercuric. Few of the old copper, corrosive primers contained a serious percentage of that poison, if any at all. "White" nickeled primers may be either mercuric or of the bore-corroding potassium chlorate type, or neither, or both. Practically all modern primers, fresh stuff, that is, are free from both undesirables. Sometimes a lot number stamped on the cartridge box gives a reference which the factory can translate into the information we want. Season-cracked brass is worthless unless it can be cut back for short cases to feed the original gun or one requiring shorter hulls. Such split-mouthed stuff is rare in handgun cartridges, even the auto-pistol sizes or others with jacketed bullets.

"White" jacketed bullets are usually plated or washed with tin. This helps fight off verdigris and does no harm at all. A magnet latches on to steel jackets, which probably give a little more barrel wear than copper does. Badly corroded jackets can be polished bright.

Practically any American rounds are safe for arms entitled to take them, except those poorly stored, like old-type smokeless shot-shells parked for years near the kitchen stove, with the original dampness cooked out of their powder. *They* can be rough. Old black powder rounds may contain "coal dust" so pulverized from tight packing that pressures would be serious if they were fired. Best open a sample and see. Some 9 mm. Luger loads, and perhaps others, were made for sub-machine guns and are unsafe in almost any pistol, no matter how proud we may be of our specimen! Some pretty poor stuff has been made for export, like certain Geco offerings of long ago. On the other hand, D.W.M., R.W.S., Eley, Kynoch and, of course, Dominion from over beyond Niagara Falls are usually fine fodder.

Many foreign cartridges use Berdan primers with no anvil in their cups, that part being formed in the case itself. The fired cups can be pried out with a sharp pick driven into them at a 45 degree angle. Sometimes it is difficult to find primers for reloading them, but Stoeger Arms Corp., 45-18 Court Square, Long Island City 1, N. Y., imports the Sinoxid brand in various sizes. They are non-corrosive and non-mercuric. It used to be fairly common to alter Berdan-type rifle cases to take our own Boxer-type primers; but in pistol ammunition problems, this need seems seldom to have come up. One way of working it was to reform the brass itself; another was to use an insert containing the Boxer primer pocket.

There is no handloading of rimfire cartridges for us now, although factories offered the empty, primed cases, not the bullets, at least as late as 1919. Old light, .22 revolvers and pistols should be used, if at all, with the "Standard Velocity" or low pressure rounds, and probably shorts, at that. Our tiny BB and CB .22 "bullet-breech" and "conical bullet" cartridges are no longer made here, though Stoeger imports BBs. The BB gives the lowest pressure of all, and is safest, therefore, in very small, black powder type pistols, the collectors' items that some collectors want to shoot. No one can guarantee the safety of such practice unless he has examined the gun in question. Most of the old Iver Johnson, Harrington & Richardson, Hopkins and Allen and similar .22 revolvers of some 12 to 18 ounces' weight should handle low pressure shorts safely if they are in sound condition. Remembering that the real oldies were made for black powder, we should hesitate to use long-rifle rounds in them. On the other hand, husky single shots like the Smith & Wesson target guns, and the heavy-frame Stevens, too, should certainly be safe with .22 long-rifle ammo. The low pressure stuff should give the best accuracy, though when these guns are in very good shape, many of them take the high velocity ammo without a bobble. The very small-framed, pipestem-barreled *Stevens Diamond Model single shot* .22 is not, to my mind, suitable for anything above low pressure shorts. Early Colt .22 Woodsman automatics, still fitted with the original mainspring housing at the back of the grip, and checkered, not cross-barred at its angle, were made for black and semi-smokeless long-rifles. So were the fine and interesting Reising autoloaders. It would be foolish to shoot hot stuff in them, though it has been done through ignorance or bull-headedness. Late imports are the Eley CB caps, a size generally much more accurate than the BB, and still of low pressure.

Most of the larger rimfire pistol calibers are practically unavailable, even the lately discontinued .25 Stevens short and long. The .32 short and long are still with us, at this writing. Although they are loaded with smokeless, the charges are so light that these rounds are still almost in black powder pressure ratings. The .41 rimfire can be had on special order, and it is made for the old light derringers and revolvers—but I should not expect anyone to guarantee an ancient untested firearm of any sort, would you? An old, tip-up barrel, S.&W. five-shot revolver that I used a great deal with modern smokeless .32 shorts and longs, stood up perfectly; but then, it was of a good make and in sound shape. The chamber walls were not paper-thin, and the hinge that held the barrel to the frame was not weakened by ancient rust.

Sometimes a handgun is altered to take different ammunition. A few long-cylindered old Colts were chambered for the short .44 Russian because that was such a famous target cartridge. Our factories have dropped it from their loading lists, and though the brass could be made from the still popular and easily available .44 Special, a shooter might want his old Russian chambered out longer for store-bought Specials. Or he might have a new cylinder fitted. That would be the way to have a .32 Long Colt gun altered to handle the more efficient and more easily reloadable .32 New Police or S.&W. Long. The .41 Long Colt and the .38-40 Colt have similar barrels; so here, too, a change could be made. Such changes always depend on two factors: are all the necessary parts available, and are gun strength and barrel bore and groove diameters suitable for a 100% safe alteration?

Then too, there is the accuracy problem. Changing from .32 S.&W. Long to .32-20 Winchester and leaving the original barrel attached means that we should have an over-bored gun. We should need special over-sized .32-20 bullets for it. This matter did not come up when I had a .22 W.R.F. caliber Colt Police Positive Target fitted with an extra cylinder for practice with economical .22 long-rifle ammo. Some companies, Colt among them, bored and rifled to the same diameters for both cartridges.

There are almost endless combinations of changes. Some work well, and some not so well. When the change is to a more powerful cartridge (or a modernized loading), we need to be careful. With strictly modern well-made handguns, the safety margin may be ample. A common example is the S.&W. Military & Police model made for British use in World War II. Chambered and bored for .38 S.&W., the short cartridge called the .380 over there, this gun can be chambered out for .38 Special. But S.&W. groove diameters for the two loads

are different, .360-.361 inch for the short, .356-.357 for the Special. Colt figures normally run .353-.354 inch for both. For the altered British Smith, we should need oversize bullets. A higher front sight for the more powerful .38 Special loads would be necessary, too, in all likelihood, unless we handloaded with bullets lighter than Special standard.

Contacting the Seller

Perhaps we've spent far too much time on ammunition, but then, who wants an unsuitable or an unsafe gun-and-cartridge combination? We want to use our guns as firearms, not as grenades!

We may encounter the would-be seller hand-to-hand in a store, or a home, or down at the club range. Let's go to the meeting as well prepared as we can. Ask around; find out about the fellow's reputation. Then, upon meeting him, size up his manner, his look, and what he says. If he has no good word for others in the business, or for their wares, if he tries to impress on you the rare value of his stuff, its almost complete unavailability elsewhere, either go your way or peel your eyes. His goods are likely to need sharp inspection.

I have had both handsome and thoroughly bad luck in long-distance encounters, buying from those who advertise on paper, as in *The American Rifleman* or *Shotgun News*. Publishers can't absolutely control their patrons! Two or three lifelong friendships have resulted, and several disappointments, though in time I "got well" and forgot the latter.

Personal ads in print cost money, from five to thirty cents or more a word, and even an honest shooter seldom tells the story in detail. If he has a piece you've sought for years, you may fear to delay. Instead ask him to ship it at once, express collect with examination privilege. Then take your rod, cleaning patches, and—to be considerate—your preservative oil to the express office and give the gun as thorough a once-over there as you can, rejecting it if you must.

But if there is no rush, even though the price seems reasonable, it is more satisfactory to exchange letters with the seller, find out the details that interest you, and size him up as well as you can. If he's straight he'll give straight, complete answers. Unfortunately, some who are as crooked as the usual old slotted wire .22 cleaning rod will give definite answers, too, but quite false. If you must really challenge him, ask if he will pay the return charges if the gun does not come up to his claims. This is a kill-or-cure resort, but so what? Sometimes—particularly in home-town dealings—we are given the opportunity of making a range test before deciding, if the seller knows us to be responsible—or if his gun is beyond damage by any minor neglect or abuse. A box or two of cartridges, and sometimes fewer, should show up any tendency toward malfunction or any serious inaccuracy.

But as long as we can, let's assume that the seller is a decent member of the brotherhood of shooters. And let's make sure from the start that he understands exactly what we want.

Bore and Chamber

Since we want good shooting, the bore and chamber, or chambers, get our first critical look. This can be revealing if we scrub out all oil, grease or old fouling, and move to a well lighted spot. Take the barrel out of an automatic or remove its breech-block so that you can examine both ends. A squint down a solid frame revolver's bore, with a white card held below the breech, tells us precisely nothing about the breech end of that bore; but a little piece of mirror, an old Winchester barrel reflector, or a Boreskope from J. G. Mundy, Collingdale, Penna., gives a good look. You hold the mirror type at a 45 degree angle and peek in so that your gaze is perpendicular to the bore's axis. You look straight down into the Boreskope, held at a 90 degree angle. Lacking these, you may be able to get a fairly good view of the barrel breech through the firing pin hole, if that pin is attached to the hammer.

Sometimes the news is not as bad as it appears to be. Many revolvers are plated with lead at the tapered start of the rifling but shoot rather well in this condition and would show no pitting of steel if the lead were brushed out. Likewise, auto-pistol barrels often look like a chimney because the previous owner never bothered to remove the tenacious fouling of jacketed bullets. If he has used only non-corrosive ammunition, and not too many rounds, a perfect bore may lie beneath.

To a trained eye, erosion, the burning of steel from long use, and corrosion, the result of rust's evil feasts, are at once recognizable and more or less distinguishable. Burning starts at the breech and walks up. First, it's a mere darkening, then roughness, and finally deep pits. A rusted barrel can be pitted anywhere and, in the nature of things, rust generally shows elsewhere on the gun. Hard lead or jacketed bullets frequently shoot well in a pretty rough barrel, but it is pleasanter to start with a good one, its rifling lands clean and sharp, and keep it so. Few well cared for handgun barrels wear out from use, unless they have spun out a good many jacketed bullets, which do not dam back eroding powder gas as well as properly fitting, rather soft lead bullets do.

A bulged barrel shows that someone has shot an obstruction out of it, such as snow, mud, excessive grease, or a stuck bullet. The latter, if it was near the muzzle, may have been shot out, and then the bulge up front is easy to see. A bulge farther down may be more difficult to find, but if you shove a tight cloth patch through the barrel you will feel a jump when it hits the swollen place.

Some old revolver barrels, thin at the breech, have been belled out there by heavy loads carrying too-hard or oversize bullets. But a barrel may give fair accuracy for a long time when it's bulged almost anywhere, except perhaps at the muzzle.

And some barrels, fifty years old or more, may be in magnificent shape because they obviously deserved the best of care. Most people who had a .32-.44 or .38-.44 S.&W. looked after it. Many later handguns, like the Smith and Colt target revolvers, or single shots, or pistols with custom barrels like those from the old Niedner firm, were cherished until advancing years or the last chapter of all made shooting impossible.

As the barrel goes, so goes the cylinder, usually, though its chambers number five and up and thus divide the wear of erosion that is passed on to the one lone barrel. Many revolver chambers that look badly eroded are only lead-fouled where the taper starts at the end of the case-mouth. Some guns that are warranted "factory new" are not quite that. Lead smears on the front of the cylinder suggest that little Junior, the dealer's son, has fired them since they left the factory. This can mean nothing.

Although it takes a really fine shot to test a handgun's accuracy, almost any of us can hit a three-foot square of paper at 50 yards, two-handed or with a rest. If the pistol keyholes its bullets or even tips them badly at this range, making oval holes, we know that the gun-and-ammunition combination isn't up to par. It could do for a short-range defense, but not for precision work. As Elmer Keith points out in *Sixguns,* long range—well beyond 50 yards—really tests a handgun's accuracy. Two-handed, down close to the ground, the body as firmly planted as possible, yet relaxed, we might surprise ourselves, if we had never tried those legitimate field aids to making hits and what's much more, making close, consistent bullet groups.

The junction of barrel and cylinder needs examination. On a very old and much used revolver the top strap above this junction may be eroded deeply enough to mean serious weakness. Some guns have an oval section neatly milled out, just behind the barrel breech, to help carry away the hot gases of firing; some are left flat here. With either system, a serious burning-out is uncommon.

But another fault to look for at the barrel-cylinder joint is an excessive gap, and that is rather common in new or old revolvers. Close even fitting is such a precise job that it costs plenty. Usually a definite factory maximum is allowed. A modern .22 revolver I had—not one of the "old-line" and more expensive makes, but serviceable and accurate—gapped about .010 inch; its maximum factory tolerance is .013, I believe. Three revolvers on the table this morning go .004, .007 and .008, approximately. When the figure reaches .020 inch or more—and it can—we get an unpleasantly sharp report, even with loads as light as the .32 S.&W. Long, and we lose bullet velocity. This loss may be as much as fifteen or twenty per cent, other things being equal.

It is true that old guns, and some not so old, may have a back-and-forth cylinder play. Except with the weakest of squib loads—the kind that lets soft brass centerfire primers occasionally back up into the firing pin hole and lock the gun temporarily—that cylinder must go back, enlarging the gap, when the charge is fired and the brass case expands momentarily and grips the chamber wall. Unless this playback is extreme, I, for one, wouldn't let it keep me from buying a revolver I wanted very badly. It is much less serious than an uneven cylinder face, which shows more of a gap with some chambers than with others, for at least an evenly faced cylinder is a consistent factor, and consistency— *all* through the gun and its ammo, we admit—makes for accuracy.

Revolver Actions and Frames

One of the first questions, when we consider buying an old model, concerns the availability of spare parts to replace broken ones. Early this week I had a letter from one of our big rifle manufacturers about one that was made from 1909-1936, when a new model replaced it, with some different component parts.

"This model was discontinued quite some time ago. Our supply of parts is depleted and we no longer manufacture them, or make repairs to this arm."

Sometimes a gunsmith can supply a part from a "junker,' 'an old, scarcely serviceable gun that he has latched on to for its parts. If he's capable, he can make almost any part. It's true that many 50- or 75-year-old arms are still giving splendid service with all original parts, but then, some much newer guns are not.

Sometimes parts have been put in before we ever see the used gun. How sound and reliable they are may be questionable, and how well fitted, too. I remember a .32-20 Smith & Wesson with a hammer nose replacement. This firing pin was needle-pointed—almost certain to puncture every primer—and so long that it protruded from the face of the recoil plate when the hammer was back in the safety position. An extreme and horrible example, and perhaps so uncommonly stupid that it should not have been mentioned. But if a used revolver works smoothly—and it should, from long service—and it isn't really loose in its cylinder fitting, we can go on and consider it.

A replacement barrel may be much too tightly bored for the chamber mouths that lie behind it. Soft lead expands under the blow of the powder, and it doesn't do to have an oversize bullet rip into the barrel's rifling throat at high or maybe even standard velocities. This raises pressure and may bulge or crack the barrel breech. A difference of .003, .004 or .005 inch between chamber mouth and barrel diameters is too much. Smith & Wesson, it's true, have commonly bored taper barrels, tighter at the muzzle than at the breech, just above the rifling throat. This is OK. Some rifle barrels are cut that way.

It is not only replacement barrels that may be too tight, compared to cylinder mouths. Revolvers have left factory warehouses in such condition.

Best see that the play of the cylinder is reasonably small, that it is tight when you snap the hammer and hold back on the trigger. The cylinder should revolve and be ratcheted fully into place when you cock the hammer, grasping the cylinder and forcing the mechanism to work against fair resistance. It should click into place when you release your hold, or at least when you pull the trigger. Most old Colts, except those badly worn, will do that, for the hand that turns the cylinder rises still a little higher when the trigger is pulled far enough back to drop the hammer. By comparison, the play of the cylinder when the trigger is pulled *and held back* is greater on the Smith & Wesson than on the Colt. Nearly all Smiths do show some right to left to right turning in this test, but it is seldom enough to worry about. Both Smiths and Colt have shot target records!

Perfectly accurate chamber lineup, for each one of the five, six or more shots that the gun holds, is perhaps an ideal—as perfection usually is! But a gun that shaves lead because one or more of its chambers are out of line is a pest. It can't be accurate with the misaligned chambers, for accuracy requires that bullets be delivered straight and undistorted into the rifling. By looking through the firing pin hole—on some models you must remove the firing pin, not just cock the gun, to do this—you can get a fairly good impression of alignment quality, at least with medium or big caliber revolvers. You can hold back on the cylinder as you cock the gun, and if it is one of those that lack sufficient hand strength to overcome your resistance, you can easily see the difference when you ease off and then push the cylinder into line! This and other visual tests are described by Elmer Keith on page 84 of his *Sixguns*.

A firing test can surely show if the gun shaves lead. The ammo cost is two cylinderfuls, not one, if you are like me in wishing to conduct your gun tests as safely as possible. A piece of fairly stiff white writing paper long enough to be held close beside the barrel-cylinder gap, with your hand well below that space, takes the imprint or puncture of any flying lead particle. A beautifully aligned and tighty fitted gun will only smoke up the paper, and not much at that. It would be possible, with such a gun, to fold a long piece of paper so as to cover each side when you fire; but a leaky gun could make the test extremely uncomfortable!

Examine hammer notches. They should hold at full cock so that you can't press the hammer forward with your thumb, as you could with an almost new postwar gun I looked over. Quarter- and half-cock notches on old Colt Single Actions frequently have been broken, and filed or built-up repairs may not be sound. An old Bisley Model Colt that I remember with affection would drop its hammer from the quarter or safety notch at a gentle nudge of the thumb. This didn't matter much, because its owner always carried or stored it, when loaded, with no more than five cartridges. Nothing lay under the hammer nose except air, for we found that a fired case wouldn't do: the fully-down hammer nose could be worked off it, or rather, the brass worked off the hammer nose. The primer of the neighboring cartridge, loaded of course, could also get under that hammer. But when the hammer was clear down on an empty chamber the Bisley was safe. However, every gun is a law unto itself; it isn't a robot. We must know them as individuals.

The hammer nose or the separate firing pin, whichever the revolver has, should be rounded smoothly, not burred or pitted, or filed sharp by a nitwit. The hole in the recoil plate—a separate part or one with the breech—should not be beveled out by wear. If it is, primer metal can flow back into it and lock the cylinder. Then, to get it out, we must either remove the cylinder—and there may be no screwdriver along —or whack it with the hand, which is a shameful way to treat a gun. A lop-sided hammer nose may have worn that firing pin hole, though gas escaping from lots of pierced primers can do it, and pit the firing pin, too. Fired cases, if there are any, enable you to judge the firing pin's centering and force. Some recoil plates have been cracked by the abuse of heavy loads. They are uncommon in well-made guns, but they exist.

Look at the fired cases, too, for signs of chambers that have been bulged in the middle from taking over-high pressures. The really weak spots are the bolt cuts at the rear of the cylinder—put there for the bolt on the bottom of the cylinder frame to lock into and align each chamber. With heavy brass cases, especially the solid head ones we are getting now in some revolver sizes as small as even the .32 S.&W. Short, there is a little more protection for bolt cuts, but not much.

The crane, which goes out with the cylinder of a side-swing revolver, should fit the frame snugly up front. Ideally, it shouldn't wobble when we try to work the cylinder from side to side. Many old Colts have this wobble because previous owners would not hold the latch back when they closed the cylinder. Doing that soon becomes second nature, and it pays! Slamming can bend the crane. It may look smart, but closing the cylinder with a snap is inexcusable.

You will find that some old Colts that show considerable crane wobble are very good, after all, when the hammer is down and the trigger held back, in either dry or live firing. That faithful old hand, unless it's almost worn out, pushes against a cylinder ratchet. As the Colt cylinder turns to the right, and the crane swings out to the left, this shove tends to force the crane home, where it should be when the gun is closed.

Test the trigger pull's weight and smoothness. Few prewar revolvers of good quality had or have a rough, creepy pull. This fault can be smoothed out, and the pull lightened, too. But take warning that case-hardened parts, like those used in S.&W.s, have a certain amount of tough skin, which if penetrated allows the softer underlying steel to wear into a pull that is entirely too light. In time it won't even hold the hammer back. So an extremely light pull on a used gun may give grounds for suspicion.

Flat main or hammer springs may have been filed thin, and coil springs shortened, to make cocking easier. The first kind may finally break, and either kind may give misfires and hangfires, or at best uncertain ignition that is detrimental to accuracy.

If the Colt cylinder latch is worn on the left side, the gun has been forced shut, with the latch not held back. Marred screwheads on a revolver frame indicate someone's carelessness, though no real harm may have been done. But careless people sometimes pry a Colt or Smith sideplate free instead of tapping the frame to get it out, and that may have bent the plate. Run a fingernail along the junction of plate and frame to find out.

We cannot always get firing tests on a used gun, but they are certainly desirable. If a single-action tends to shed its base pin, or cylinder pin, with recoil, a reasonable slug of full charged ammunition fired in testing will reveal that habit. But do not ask any old handgun to digest ammo that is fifty years ahead of the gun in "improvements." Most revolvers that function well in dry firing will do all right with live rounds that are correct for them, though accuracy is a different matter. It is the autoloaders that most need test firing to see whether they will handle their cartridges reliably.

Auto-Pistol Actions and Frames

Examine an automatic pistol first of all for follow-through. Draw back and lock its slide, then snap it free and see if the hammer falls. If it does, you have a full-automatic, not a semi-, and it must be repaired. An actual firing test, with no more than two or three rounds in the gun, may be better. Hang on for all you're worth, and even then it's better to make this test in real wilderness, or at least in front of a very high gravel bank or a cliff, because the muzzle climbs as each full-automatically fired round goes off. A magazineful can leave you apparently trying hard to shoot the midday sun.

Some years ago, I was going to buy another Savage automatic—.32 or .380, I don't remember which. After I got home with it I did what I should have done in the store—let the slide snap forward on an empty chamber. The hammer followed through, every time. If the old W. S. Brown Company in Pittsburgh hadn't been a thoroughly honest one I should have been left holding the gun. They took it back, and not just because I was an old customer, I believe. A new disconnector should end follow-through.

Check an exposed hammer's full and half-cock notches (if it has a half; the Savage sometimes didn't) as with a revolver. Be sure that there is a complete firing pin, that its point or its mid-section has not been broken. To make fully sure, you will need to disassemble some guns. You'll want to, anyway, to get a look inside.

With the gun assembled and closed, remove the magazine and grasp the top of the slide. (Some autos, like Ruger and Whitney .22s, and centerfires such as the Luger, do not have moving slides that are integrated with the breech-block; their breech-blocks move within the fixed frame, or within a part of the frame.) See how much wiggle or looseness there is to defeat your efforts to shoot a good score. The Colt or Hi-Standard .22s' short breech-blocks can be fairly loose and still not destroy accuracy. But a really sloppy breech-block may not return to the same alignment every time after the gun has been fired, and then we get free and unwanted change in sight adjustment. The long slide of a Browning-type centerfire, like the Colt's, houses the barrel. If it is too loose—of course there must be some freedom for certain functioning—even 50-foot accuracy may be impossible. The muzzle housing or bushing of a Colt .45 or similar gun—early Colt .32s had one, too—must be snug on the barrel and snug in the slide in order to contribute its part towards accuracy. Part of the "accurizing" of customed .45s is a sharp attention to this matter. Well worked over, such bigbore autoloaders give spendid accuracy.

An automatic slide stop, like those on big Colts and many other self-loaders, holds the slide open after the last shot has been fired, an obvious advantage in reloading and in knowing when to reload. It should go into action in dry firing, too, holding the slide back when the empty magazine is in place. In a used gun we plan to buy, it is one of the things to be checked for wear.

So is the extractor. Is this hook badly worn, or has it started to crack away? After all, it gets a lot of use. Check the ejector blade, too. It kicks the rim of the fired case and throws it out. This may not seem like a lot of work, but a semi-automatic's breech-block comes back pretty fast. When it's feeling good it's a willing worker. After the extractor of a Colt .32 auto I once had was broken, the little gun continued to function with fair reliability until I could have it replaced. The straight blowback action of this pistol blew the empties out of the chamber, and the ejector hurled them out.

All safety devices on a semi-automatic should work. These include the disconnector, mentioned before, that prevents follow-through of the hammer or striker in full-automatic style. Try the thumb safety, and the half-cock hammer notch, if there is one. A revolver can be carried with an empty chamber under the hammer and still be ready for instant action, but an autoloader can't! Some autos have magazine safeties, so called. They make discharge impossible when the magazine is out of the gun. The Whitney and the Smith & Wesson .22 autos have mag safes, and so did the last issues of Colt pocket autos, the .25 from serial number 141,000, the .32 from 468,097, and the .380 from 98,894. For a while after 1946, Colt Woodsman .22 autos had it. It's not necessary to have a cartridge in the chamber when testing a magazine safety on any of these guns.

Testing the magazine feeding by running cartridges through the gun and not firing them is not enough. At least a boxful of cartridges should be fired, and a few more, or others of different makes would help. Most feeding failures come from bent or otherwise distorted magazine lips, if the ammo is up to par. The surest remedy is a new magazine.

According to the type and condition of the used autoloader, we may or may not have a right to be fussy about its trigger pull! We can just about demand a good one on a revolver, clean and sharp in release, and with no disconcerting "give" or backlash after it has released the hammer. But truly, few automatics except the best have these qualities. At least, the auto trigger, or any other, should not vary in resistance from pull to pull, and a too-light release is dangerous and usually shows excessive wear. This over-soft touch is much more common in revolvers and single shot pistols, by far, than in autoloaders. Some handguns have efficient trigger stops in them, either factory or custom jobs—or home-installed, for that matter. Considering how many of us demand an excellent pull on an auto, it is rather pitiful to see how much disappointment there is in our shooters' world! This doesn't mean that a good gunsmith can't improve almost any pull, some vastly if not to perfection. Even the Luger has been refined to a point where there was a clean release after a spongy preliminary takeup, and that German gun is a toughy to work over for pull.

Look at the auto's firing pin hole, just as with a revolver's. An off-center firing pin may have worn it lop-sided, or the rust of neglect may have got at it. An over-large hole in the Colt .45, for instance, may allow primer cup metal be driven back into it, and then when the barrel drops down the face of the breech-block in unlocking, some of that metal may be sheared off. Metal particles flying back into your face aren't "healthy." You may have experienced them with the .45, as I have, though rarely. But once I stopped one from a Luger, too, and its barrel doesn't drop. Most sophisticated riflemen wear glasses of some sort, at least when shooting a bolt action or hammer gun with breech not sealed in hammerless fashion. Perhaps more pistol shooters should, too.

Look at the breech face of a .22 autoloader. Is it marked by the firing pin from dry snapping? Most modern .22 rimfires, pistol or rifle, are engineered to make this impossible, and many old ones were, too. But it takes only a moment to check this detail.

Both slide and receiver should be examined for signs of abuse or of long wear. Someone may have used the pistol for a club or a hammer. Take the gun down for a good look-over.

In *The Pistol Shooter's Book* Charles Askins calls attention to a too often overlooked detail, i.e., cracks or flaws in the receiver or in the slide. They need close inspection if the gun appears to have been used a great deal. All of his chapter on used handguns is well worth study.

An old model may tempt us because of its reputation or because we once had one and foolishly let it go. Take an early .38 Colt Auto. Loads like the factories' Super-.38 may have started to crack the slide near the ejection slot. Most of us are mighty sudden in quitting the use of these hot potatoes in oldtimers. But other Browning-type autos run the risk of this sort of damage: their slides take rough and sudden strain in normal firing. However, most of them hold up splendidly, and for many thousands of rounds.

While on this subject of autoloaders, centerfires at least, it seems well to speak particularly of barrel throat condition. Autos are chambered rather loosely, almost without exception, to make cartridge handling more nearly certain. They shoot jacketed bullets most of the time, in centerfire calibers. Loose chambers and hard jacketed bullets are part of the buildup for throat erosion; so we find a good many old .45s burned out at the barrel breech. A new .45 barrel doesn't cost very much, and on a special job it could be fitted carefully to the individual gun, which then might do the best shooting it ever had done. But sometimes a barrel that looks like an incinerator is only fouled; it may not have been used much. Cleaning it with ammonia, and a brass brush if you need it, can dissolve the copper fouling, and the result may be a mirrorlike perfection to delight you. This sounds like exaggeration, but it can happen.

Very few rimfires that have been treated right have barrels worn out by shooting. But some have been unfortunate in the people who owned them, and the rust of neglect has got in. Not all corrosively primed .22s, even, have been shot up, and some folks don't know the difference! Others tote greased ammunition loose in their pockets, and the lubricant can pick up gritty particles and drag them through a barrel when the dirty cartridges are fired.

Sights

Sights should get a brief look. Fortunately, the square-cut Patridge-type is now standard on both duty and target arms, and it is the best. For use in poor light, as in the woods, the square rear notch should be wide enough to show a good slice of light on each side of the front sight that is centered in it. Few of them are cut that wide. The front sight, still of square Patridge shape, may need a red, gold or white facing to show up in dim light, and a contrasting color outlining the cut in the rear sight certainly does help.

Old arms with fixed sights commonly had a round-topped front and a U-notched rear. They are harder to shoot with, but sometimes they can be altered. Old target arms, even the first of the Colt Woodsman automatics, generally wore an adjustable U-notched rear and a round bead front sight, this bead mounted on a thin stem—like the general issue sporting-rifle sights of today. Sometimes the elevation is in the front sight, and only the windage in the rear, as on Colts up to rather recent times. For some models the factories supply Patridge replacements, but occasionally the making and fitting of modern target sights is a gunsmith job.

Adjustable sights must be rigid, and lost motion in a screw-adjustable rear sight is just too bad. We are probably as liable to find it in a click-adjustable sight as in an old one where we back off one screw and turn up its opposite number to get windage. Some of the old screw-adjustable, non-click S.&W. rear sights did not hold elevation adjustments under heavy recoil, but after the K-.22 sixgun was well established, along came an improved rear sight that had a screw to lock elevation. This worked well, at least on guns of moderate power. What we should get in a shop or a swap is sights that are rigid at that time, and that look as though they would stay so.

Outside Finish

The exterior finish of many fine old guns and of some new ones is a dark, rich blue or black, or smoothly laid-on nickel. Both Colts and Smiths have varied a good deal throughout the years. It would be hard to say which make has been more consistent in keeping up its quality. But a beautiful oldtimer that is slick inside and out has its charms, as most shooters admit, even if it's not a gun that they, personally, would have use for. Most of them are "efficient," if you insist on that detail, although pistol ammunition hasn't kept up with rifle rounds in ballistic advances, by any means. At this writing, exclusive of the .22 rimfires, there are few fairly new and definitely more powerful handgun cartridges. These are the .38 Special high velocity, the .357 and .44 magnums, and the .38 Special, .357 and .45 Auto with metal-penetrating bullets. Most of the other revolver loads are no more powerful than handloading with black powder can make them, with entire safety. In fact, black sometimes gives higher velocity stuff than we can buy from the dealer's shelves. Add the new .22 and .25 Magnums.

But this is a long way from "Outside Finish."

To some of us, the appearance of a gun means little, provided it will perform. There is this thought, however: a badly marred or deeply rust-coated weapon may have interior ailments that are less obvious.

How Old Is This Gun?

The age may matter, if replacement parts must be had. An old Forehand & Wadsworth pocket revolver or a Merwin & Hulbert army revolver may be enticing; they were well made. Real quality always is tempting, isn't it? These revolvers had it, along with some from other makers, still active or long out of business. A skillful gunsmith can make almost any part; and if disinterested, he can name the approximate life expectancy of the innards of both old and new guns.

The age of a handgun can be important to a buyer if you ever want to sell one. Some models, makes and calibers have more resale value than others. Try to figure out what will become "obsolete" and no longer made, or what is extreme in style, like an excessively long or short barrel. However, there certainly is, at present, some demand for out of the ordinary handguns. Let's hope it persists. They can be as fascinating as "different," highly individual people. Who but a dolt goes through life without appreciating that kind, and liking them when he can?

Never buy an impractical caliber because the gun looks like a bargain. A dealer who tries to palm off a .35 S.&W. automatic should have his license revoked in the interest of the general public! At least he should if he's selling that gun for shooting, because the ammo is for collectors. It hasn't been available in quantity for about 30 years, more or less. Oh yes, cases could be made, but if you want an S.&W. pocket auto in small caliber, why not get the .32 caliber model that followed the .35, if you can find one? So if you intend to use a pistol, be sure its caliber suits you in every way possible.

Foreign pistols, of which there are many obsoletes, vary more widely in quality than our standard makes do. Sometimes we can spot a potentially good one by its fine finish, like that on most pre-1914 Lugers, and some later ones. Other things to look for are parts bearing the same serial numbers (if any), and the design, which may be both startling and sound, and the usual good or bad condition qualities which we should investigate in an American-made arm. But there have been poor and even dangerous Lugers, many P-38 German service Walthers of that kind, and a great many Spanish arms made in the 1920s and thereabout. An odd caliber like the 8 mm. Japanese auto almost always incurs both uncertainty and high cost for its ammunition supply, though this particular one may have been made available to some extent.

Some guns are dated, like so many war-relic Lugers, and a good many others are so well-known that their approximate dates can be guessed. Just as an example, the Colt line of New Service, Army Special, Police Positive and Pocket Positive is recent enough to be entirely safe with modern smokeless ammunition if the individual specimen is in good shape. The Army Special was made for years. Those with hard black rubber grips came before the regular production of those with checked walnut grips. But we can generally check age by telling the factory the gun's serial number, although records *have* been lost, or destroyed by accident. Probably an old Army Special would stand the pressure of high velocity .38s, but why find out? Since this form of .38 Special is no longer made with a flat-nosed lead bullet, there would be little to gain. Metal-pointed bullets or the fast Remington zinc-alloy slugs give a great deal of penetration, but a policeman who needs that to stop a bandit car should have a modern arm. He usually does, too!

Oldtimers Can Tempt You

Many post-war arms have been called "guns for the sucker market," and sometimes the expression is justified. Blueing may be dull and lifeless over poorly polished steel, the action may grate, the trigger pull may be hard or creepy, and the grip checkering may have been clawed on casually over wood that has no

right to the honor of serving as a handgun's stock. Then you see a fiinely kept oldtimer, perhaps late enough to have a heat-treated cylinder and digest loads of considerable power—and you note the differences. The oldie may be well worth the 75% or so of retail that is marked on its price tag.

Or it may be a really old handgun, still safe with at least certain types of modern factory loads, or with handloads lower in power; and you want it for practical use because it fits you and it is interesting. We do not here discusss these guns from the collector's standpoint, or their rarity and their consequent value in trade or sale, but simply as shooting guns.

As the really old arms become scarcer, both new and experienced collectors go to later guns. Last night a man called me up about Winchester Model 70 rifles, which came out in their fist commercial form in 1937. He was interested in 20-inch barrel versions, and particularly the 70s for the 7.65 mm Mauser cartridge, for some had been made up with left-over Model 54 Winchester barrels. I couldn't help him, and I was sorry. I like gun collectors although I'm not one of them; I'm just a shooter. Of course some collectors do fire their specimens, some of them at least, but the point is that anyone interested in guns belongs to the brotherhood. They are not anti-gun; they believe in "the right of the people to keep and bear arms."

Old, discontinued handgun models, long wanted, show up in all sorts of condition, from truly hopeless and perhaps dangerous to downright mint shape, satisfactory to use if they get the right ammunition. A listing could go on from here to tomorrow's breakfast, but here we'll drool over only a few more or less representative specimens. If there's too much personal preference, please forgive it.

The Smith & Wesson Triple Lock or New Century came out in 1907 and did not have the strong, heat-treated alloy steel cylinder of the later Military Models beginning with serial 16,600. Its barrel breech is obviously thinner than that of the latest Military built for heavy loads, for people will use them as the factory .44 Special cartridge isn't loaded nearly up to par. Barrel lengths were 4, 5 and 6½ inches regularly, though some target models went to 7½. Special lengths have been furnished on a good many Smith and Colt guns.

The standard caliber was the then new .44 Special, but some Triples came in .45 Colt, and probably in .38-40 and .44-40, too. What really makes your tongue hang out when you first (or any time) see this gun is the beautiful, almost intricate fitting of its special, third lock at the front of the frame, where the cylinder-carrying crane swings in. When you push in the cylinder thumb-piece it is rather wonderful to see the lock at the breech and the one up front disengage, perfectly timed, and to feel how easily the cylinder swings out. The heavy, under-barrel recessed extractor lug, which modern heavy-frame S.&Ws. have, started with this 1907 model. When the war of 1914 came, the British wanted it removed, fearing it would collect mud and dirt and thus prevent the gun's being closed; so off it came. Their guns took the .455 Mark II cartridge. In the 1926 Model Smith, the lug was restored. All of these guns are good, but most people prefer those with the recessed lug.

The Colt Single Action Army is an 1873 model, and the saw-handled Bisley an 1896. The difference is in the grips, the S.A.A. easy to point, fitting almost any hand, the Bisley pointing too low, but so wide at the top that it is comfortable with heavy loads. I don't mean that good hip or point shooting can't be done with the Bisley, but it would take much doing to "learn" the gun well enough to use it effectively that way. I think that for woods use I should prefer the Bisley, but it might be a more personal than sensible choice. Both models came in Target style, usually with 7½-inch barrel, and a windage-adjustable rear sight rode on a flat-top frame.

Barrels came as short as 3 and 4 inches without ejector rod, the standard lengths were 4¾, 5½ and 7½ inches, and Buntlines went as long as 18. In March 1959, Colt announced a long-barreled .22 Buntline in the little Scout model. There were factory-fitted skeleton stocks on some of the old guns. They would be illegal now except on payment of the high federal registration fee. So would the holster-stock that some 1905 model .45 Colt automatics had, and some Stevens single shot pistols, and so on. Many single action Colts have been much altered by gunsmiths and others, as collectors know so well. Late in 1960 some .45 Colt 3-inch barrel guns came out, the Sheriff's Model.

The factory variations were nearly endless, and probably not completely recorded anywhere. Even the calibers are hard to list with surety. Here are some: .22 rimfire, .32 and perhaps .38 rimfire, .44 Henry and Winchester rifle rimfire; and the centerfires, .32 Long Colt, .32 S.&W. short, .32-20, .32-.44 S.&W. and perhaps .38-.44 S.&W. target sizes with standard weight bullets set flush with the case-mouths, the S.&W., .357 Magnum, .38 Special and almost certainly the .38 Long Colt not chambered out for the longer Special round, .38-.40, .41 Colt, including a special wide-rimmed variant that would not fill an Army Special double-action cylinder as only three non-neighboring rounds could be slid in, .44-40, .44 Russian, .44 Special, perhaps the .44 S.&W. American and the old .44 Colt made for guns altered from cap-and-ball to metallic cartridge, .45 Colt, .45 Colt Auto, and the .450, .455 and .476 Eley, the British loads not used much here. That .476 left the chambers pretty thin, for the Single Action cylinder isn't quite as large as that of the Colt New Service double action. However, it was a black powder load, at least in regular manufacture. The British haven't gone in for heavy pistol powder charges to boost velocities—they like big bullets.

The Colt Lightning of 1877-1910 seems to have been that factory's first double action. It is possible to find one in good, tight shape, turning and locking its cylinder properly, though Colt systems that were engineered much later are likely to do those jobs better. Calibers were .32, .38 and .41 Long Colt, good in their day and certainly not too bad now, especially with careful handloading. Elmer Keith, in *Sixguns,* speaks of a rare 7-inch barreled target model. Rod ejection was standard except on Lightnings too short-barreled for it, and the loading gate was rounded, as on the Single Action Army and Bisley.

The Colt Birdshead of 1878 had a flat loading gate more or less like that of the first—and very much later!—Ruger .22 revolvers. A pin stuck out to give your thumb-nail a purchase in opening it. The standard caliber was .45 Colt, and a special Alaskan model had a huge trigger guard bow that a gloved finger had some chance of getting into. Some of the Model 14 Japanese automatic pistols apparently copied this idea. The frame and grip straps of this Colt were all in one piece, unlike those of the Lightning. Birdshead and Lightning both have round-bottomed, hump-topped grips, the hump sometimes copied in light, inexpensive .22 revolvers because it helps to hold the gun down in recoil. It is possible to alter these stocks to a very fine fit indeed, and it is possible, but not easy, to learn to use them well as they are—as many an old woods, mountain or plains man could demonstrate.

The Birdshead, also called Army or Frontier Double Action, was made for other cartridges in addition to the .45. Keith lists the .32-20, .38-40, .44-40, .450, .455 and .476. They are about as fascinating as any other oldtime guns that have made history, and they could do it again if the need arose.

The Smith & Wesson .38 Perfected is almost surely the finest of its type, the tip-up cylinder, jointed frame, pocket gun. No longer made, it is a prize for a shooter who needs such a revolver. There is the usual lock at the rear of the top strap, and another at the side, the familiar S.&W. thumb-latch. The gun should have taken the old 200 grain factory loads, which were considered too rough for the usual top-break .38.

In this general class were others less desirable, but still good, earlier S.&Ws., Iver Johnsons, and Harrington and Richardsons. No doubt some replacement parts are available for many of them, but they would hardly be for long-discontinued Hopkins & Allen, Forehand & Wadsworth, or even perhaps the "U. S." brand. Unless they are in perfect working order, they could be a liability to buy, and it is possible that some of the oldest ones would not be safe with modern ammunition. There were hammer and hammerless models, and .22s and .32s as well as the much more serviceable .38s.

The Colt Border Patrol .38 Special has aroused much attention because it is so very scarce. It has its own peculiar merit, a .770-inch non-tapered 4-inch barrel that adds steadying weight to this short gun. Weight was about 35 ounces, and sights fixed. It is described by M. D. Waite, N.R.A. staffman, in the

September, 1958 *American Rifleman's* "Dope Bag" section. Only a few were made, from 1952-53, on U. S. Border Patrol specifications, and "Border Patrol" and "Heavy Duty" are stamped on the barrel.

Among the old target single shots were the *Colt Camp Perry, S.&W. Perfected* or *Olympic* and *Straight-line,* the *Hopkins & Allen,* and the *Harrington & Richardson USRA,* named for the U. S. Revolver Association, which did so well in keeping the slow-fire target game alive. They all have possibilities as woods or training pistols. Some of the *Stevens single shots* and early S.&Ws. were made in larger caliber than .22 long-rifle, the Stevens in .25 and perhaps .32 rimfire (as the pocket rifle was, with its detachable skeleton stock), and the S.&W. targets in centerfire sizes. But the .22 long-rifle is probably for 99% of us the most practical, except maybe for Stevens .22 shorts, if any remain in shape for good shooting.

All of them had tip-up breech actions (including a special Stevens that had a thumb-cocked straightline striker instead of a hammer) except the Colt and the Straightline Smith. The Colt barrel swung down to the side on its crane, just like the Officer's Model revolver's cylinder, and the Straightline's barrel turned to the side for loading. It had straightline ignition, not a swinging hammer; but the ignition wasn't particularly snappy. Like that odd Stevens, it had an auto-pistol style of grip, not one of the rounded revolver shape. Most of these old target arms had light barrels, by today's standards—especially the old Hopkins & Allen —but shooters often used to tape on weights such as steel or lead rods, and profit thereby. Some revised versions got away from the overlight, too-long barrel misery. The Colt barrel went from 10-inch to 8-inch, and its hammer fall was shortened to an arc like that of today's S.&W. K-Target guns. Heavier H.&R. barrels came, even the 7-inch having quite a bit of weight in it. Shortening that barrel from the original 10 inches made a sighting radius that helped a good many shooters. This gun had a fast hammer, seven different stock styles, and an ejector so strong that it could almost remind you of a bazooka's back-blast. Empty cases achieved a respectable velocity from that pistol, just as some did from the old single-shot Winchester lever action .22 rifles.

Our little American-made pocket automatics are off the market except as used guns. Many of us miss the Colts, Savages and Remingtons. The H.&R. is pretty well forgotten, and probably it would be a collector's piece now. The other three are met fairly often, except the Savage .25. In .32 and .380 it can be an excellent buy if it's in good shape and you like it. Two main models were made, the second with a larger grip because considerable slant-back was given the back-strap. The small original Savage could be better for small hands, or for a medium-sized hand with a glove on. Magazine capacity was high, ten .32s or nine .380s, and barrels were usually a bit longer than the Colts' were. It was a locked-breech gun, not a straight blow-

back, and this delayed action was achieved by the torque of the bullet against the barrel's rifling. That twist held the breech-block until the bullet had gone out. Most Savages had a tough trigger pull, but the safety lock was absolutely positive. There were hammerless and exposed-hammer models; the latter didn't as I recall, usually have a half-cock notch. When the hammer was down, the firing pin was not in contact with the cartridge primer because the pin was short, like those on hammer-model Colt autos, and it depended on a swat from the hammer to send it forward. The design was different from the Colt's because hammer and firing pin were hitched together, though not tightly. There was considerable leeway, to allow the pin to go forward by inertia and do its job.

The Remington 51 was famous, too, for its pointing qualities, even more so than the Savage, but it was of course a much later model. It came in .32 and .380— and a few big .45s were made for Service trials, I believe. Both of these brands were made in New York State, and it was commonly said that the Sullivan anti-pistol law was in part responsible for their discontinuance. This is hard to believe because there were about 47 other states where you had little, if any, difficulty in getting a pistol license, and both makes were popular. As a matter of fact, you can get licensed almost anywhere, though in some places it is a full day's job!

The earliest of our three most common makes was the Browning-designed Colt hammerless. Probably more people have regretted its discontinuance than that of the others. Colts came in the 12- or 13-ounce .25 and the 24-ounce .32 and .380. All needed a certain knack to shoot well, for their grips had little slant-back, and the grip of the .25, like that of the Savage in that caliber, accommodated only about 1½ fingers. In reliability they were up to par with the Savage and Remington. Almost all of them handled their ammunition well if they were taken care of and fed reliable stuff. Unaccountable jams were so few that in the past the light auto-pistols saw a good deal of police service, though now the revolver has almost completely ousted them, at least in America.

Imported Browning duplicates of the Colts were seen here rather seldom, though even then the difference in foreign labor costs did permit mighty good workmanship for the prices asked. Against the equally good Savages and Remingtons, the Colts marshaled the power of a name long famous in handguns. The old Browning-type slide, encasing the recoil spring under the barrel, not wrapped around it, gave the .32s and .380s good weight out front. Since all three of these American makes still have plenty of admirers, there are not too many second-hand specimens to be found in good condition. Someone who is familiar with their virtues comes along and pulls out his wallet.

Relic guns are more for the collector than for the practical shooter. We could define them as arms that are a little questionable about firing with modern ammunition, or that offer no particular advantage over today's current products. The little *.22 S.&W. Lady-smith* seven-shooter is certainly attractive, but the gun could hardly be recommended for any loads more powerful than modern low-speed shorts, if even for those; and it was much too light for good holding. It came with 2- and 3½-inch barrels, and perhaps other lengths up to the 6-inch target-sighted model. We can get similar lengths, adequate strength, and more weight in the modern .22-.32 S.&W. line.

Tip-up barrel S.&Ws. in .22 short came in several pioneer models and are fine for a collection. They are definitely out for shooting except possibly with BB caps. But the almost contemporary .32 rimfires on the same type of action—tip up the barrel and slide the cylinder off front—were much heavier-made revolvers. Some are still in use with modern smokeless, non-corrosive cartridges. Pressures of this .32 ammo are kept down, and a still sound old Smith should corral them. I had no trouble with this gun and ammunition, but I can't recommend such shooting. A rusted, weakened barrel hinge might allow the barrel to be torn off and go flying end-over-end—who knows where? Some of these .32s were beautifully stocked for holding, but shooting them is a person's own responsibility.

These are just general examples of ancient solid-frame side-swing and tip-up revolvers. The comments made on them could apply as well to tip-up cylinder guns of uncertain age and condition. There is one advantage to a centerfire specimen: you can handload it lightly with black powder. All our American-made .22 rimfires now come in smokeless, except for some blanks, and pressures have gone up. But we remember that modern guns—though very few pistols—have blown up because of defective materials, as well as from abuse. An oldtimer may have been well proved by firing cartridges that are correct for it, but to abuse it is too easy!

Cap-and-ball revolvers and muzzle-loading pistols are different from early metallic-cartridge handguns. A good many of the fellows and girls shoot them, with black powder only, and get by safely because they know their guns' condition. There were various calibers, such as .28, .31, .34, .36 and .44. Almost all of the big-frame revolvers—except the earliest, which are priceless—are beautifully stocked for shooting. For most calibers a comfortable-handled modern mold can be had, round or conical ball. Early molds were for salamanders, mostly, with integral metal handles so short that by the time the mold was warmed up to cast good bullets it was unbearable to hold. Wrapping the handles would help, and extending them would do better. There is a lot of fun in shooting these guns; and in the large calibers, especially with blunt bullets, they are killers.

It used to be said that a round ball was the most effective lead bullet, weight for weight, that could be cast. When you think of its size and bluntness and the black-powder velocity its small bore-bearing surface made possible with low pressure, you can see sense in that statement. Its velocity soon fades away, but not so fast within pistol ranges that most of us find sure and effective.

The Ideal-Lyman *Handbook* contains some helpful print on muzzle-loading arms, and in *Sixguns* Elmer Keith offers a short but informative chapter on "Loading and Management of Cap and Ball Sixguns." Since shooting the front-loaders has become a popular revival, there is a good deal of literature on the subject; and it seems likely that within half a day's drive there's a practicing enthusiast who can give you first-hand pointers, if you can find him. I was once run to earth by a couple of friendly and much interested woods-wanderers who saw the smoke of my .40-50. It's a breech-loader and uses brass cases, but black powder goes into it.

Tuning-Up

After the gun is ours we should turn to its tuning-up, if that is needed. New or old, a handgun is such a personal weapon that a rather experienced shooter must adapt it to his way of use as well as adapt himself to it.

But there may be more immediate details that need his attention. The gun may have been a good bargain even though it required a new barrel, cylinder or magazine. Perhaps the action was rough or the trigger pull hopeless, or the sights loose. Some mechanical parts may have been missing or in need of repair or replacement. Such things may have shown up in his pre-purchase examination—and let's hope that they did! Even a new arm can have its faults, pretty much regardless of the name branded into its steel.

Most double-action revolvers except those stocked in Colt Frontier fashion, and the Hi-Standard Sentinel and the similar J. C. Higgins, need a grip adapter, a filler for that too-high space between trigger guard and grip. Some of us do all right without one. Of course they are fairly new and it is certain that many nineteenth and early twentieth century top shots used their guns as issued but a bent-down position of the trigger finger handicaps the majority of shooters. To bring out the best of which the gun is capable, to flip it a fair deal, we need a more nearly straight-back pull such as the autoloaders give. An adapter can make a great deal of difference in most revolvers.

So can a grip of size and shape to fit our hand, as target experts and some others well know. Mrs. Gertrude Backstrom, longtime holder of National Woman's Indoor and Outdoor Championships, got where she stands *partly* by having grips made to fit her small hand. Her guns have other alterations and refinements, and above all she had the determination that drove her through years of conscientious practice, even though her rise was unusually fast.

A special grip, home-made or custom-made, had best come after we know the gun rather well, unless we're sure at the start that the as-is handle won't do.

But the inexpensive adapter should be an early purchase if we think we need it. Then the pleasurable process of getting acquainted with the weapon can start with one handicap out of the way.

Of course we want the sights to be visible—"sight" and "vision" are synonymous, aren't they?—and some rear sight notches are so narrow that it's almost impossible to center the front blade truly and confidently in them, even in good light. They should be widened at once, and by degrees, not by a rash guess. Don't take the easy way and narrow the front sight: it needs to be wide. One-eighth inch is now the accepted target standard for most shooters, though some like them even thicker, and have their sound and personal reasons. All this pays off afield as well as against target paper.

Adjustable sights are easy—or they should be—to set for elevation and windage. But it is wise to get used to the gun, find what method of holding it is best for us, individually, before becoming too active with the screwdriver. This chumming up with the handgun under treatment is far more important, of course, if it has fixed sights. Square-notched rear sights cut into the topstrap are fairly easy to adjust for windage by widening the notch on the side toward which we wish to lay our bullets. An old-fashioned "U" notch is harder, by a great deal, but some can be filed square and wide without weakening the frame into which they are cut. We can add elevation by filing down the front sight, and here a little does a lot, especially on short-barreled arms. We can reduce the elevation by building up the front sight or—if we simply must—by peening it up and thus thinning it. Sometimes a rear sight dovetailed into the frame can be filed down and still have enough stock left for deepening the notch an equal amount. A rear notch can be too shallow for good definition in all sorts of shooting lights, as a look at some of the oldtimers will prove. Sometimes it is practical to get windage by bending the front sight in the direction opposite to that in which we want the shots to go.

In all this sight-zeroing we need plenty of shooting with the load we shall use mostly, before we make liberal changes. Some of the old adjustable target sights, and some of the more recent ones, too, are so hard to move *and lock* for close adjustment that it pays to shoot enough to make sure just how much change is wanted.

It may be a home-cast bullet, much different from a factory standard, that we'll choose for more than ninety per cent of our shooting. Final sighting-in obviously should be for that bullet and its favored powder charge. Some cartridge sizes and some pistols handle a given bullet with considerable latitude in kind and amount of powder used, and show little change in elevation at short ranges like 50 or even 75 feet. But not all of them are as obliging as that!

FOR over a half-century these immigrants have played their part in the American scene. Some have served in serious business, and some have given fun to shooters or satisfaction to collectors. A few have been good enough, in one way or another, to stimulate U. S. production.

The words *Luger* and *Mauser* pass as legal tender in our fiction and newspaper stories. Many old Remington rifle and shotgun models were Browning-designed, and some were made under his name in Belgium—and still are. As battle booty and as made for export to us, foreign handguns of almost countless sorts have flooded in.

Imported pistols interest the gun-crank, now perhaps more than ever, and often their special features please him and are not duplicated for some time by our guns. Examples are the high velocities of even the earliest Mausers and Lugers, and modern semi-automatics like the Walthers, with double-action triggers that cock and release the hammer, so vital in getting off the first shot fast. A misguided patriotism needn't condemn them as "foreign." Any serviceable weapon is proper in the grasp of a good American defending himself, his home, or his Country.

But quality of materials and manufacture has varied more than in our standard products. Ammunition or spare parts can be hard to get, of doubtful quality, or even unsafe. The resale value of imported arms fluctuates, for tastes change. Glamorous though they are to some of us, their fit, hang, reliability and downright safety should be considered as impartially as when we select an American gun. Not all of them are guaranteed as unequivocally as ours, and that might be the understatement of the month!

Like some of our older guns, some of their elders, too, need special consideration. Early Lugers, for instance—and many wartime made or post-war assembled jobs—may be too weak for stiff loads, even positively dangerous. Our .30 or 7.65 and 9 mm. Luger cartridges, and our .32 and .380 Colt Auto, all have been speeded up since early days, some much, some only a little. They should be safe in sound arms, but some of the earliest .32 and .380 (7.65 mm. Browning and 9 mm. Browning Short) foreign autoloaders just might be unsafe with them. Then there are the later special high-velocity loadings, such as the 9 mm., for sub-machine guns—and our own Super .38 for the modern, never the early, Colt auto-pistols. With that last one as an exception, we can be pretty sure that American handgun ammunition is satisfactory, even in old *American* semi-automatics that were well made to start with and are still in sound condition. There are of course the high-velocity .38 Special rounds for modern American arms (though not advised by Smith & Wesson for their Military & Police, K-.38, and lighter S.&Ws.). So with revolvers too we must be careful. Our very old service-model .38s originally made for the ancient, outside-lubricated Long Colt cartridge, have chambers bored right through, with no stepdown or shoulder for the

CHAPTER 9

SOME FOREIGN PISTOLS

bullet seat. They will take Specials and even .357 Magnums—but they shouldn't be asked to. Even factory proof-loads do not commonly go to a 100% increase in pressure!

Just as with our handguns, there are variations in detail among the foreigners. From time to time, models are changed slightly, or considerably. Some of us think there is too much of that. However, changes stimulate business, and some foreign makers who ship their goods to us have been quick to find out how well that principle works with a big percentage of us.

In this chapter we deal with only a few of the great variety of foreign pistols, but we have tried to touch on those that are either most useful or most interesting. The majority of them are semi-automatic pocket arms. This kind has been popular abroad for a good fifty years, among those who were able to possess handguns. Since our own good old pistols of this type—Colt, Remington and Savage—have been out of production since Hector's grandfather was a little bit of a puppy, the Europeans have had a field day in making them. There's more demand here for such guns than ever before; but then, there are many more Americans who have an interest in firearms. That's to the good, when they use them safely.

In the long period of European industrial history there have been simply countless models of handguns. We are, probably, the most pistol-conscious nation in the world, but over there all the common varieties of our new and old pistols have been made: the single-shots, the double- and four-barreled arms, the revolvers (even some in hammerless, so long popular with U. S.

makers), and the autoloaders. These Europeans have been plagued, like us, with imitators. A good many have been made in Spain, and in Asia, too. Sometimes an imitation is a copy straight through; sometimes there are internal differences, though on the outside the gun may look the same, except perhaps for obviously poor finish. Imitations may be of first-class quality, or pretty sad, or even positively unsafe to fire.

ARMINIUS

These are oldtime German revolvers, and not at all common here now. The quality was just about fair. Some of them safely take the .32 Short Colt cartridge, a centerfire, but outside lubricated like the .22 short. Originally this contained a light, 9-grain charge of FFG or FFFG black powder behind a light, 80-grain bullet. Now the powder is smokeless, but even so, the pressure is kept down in factory loading; and the old guns made for it, American and foreign, are not candidates for the Magnum class of pistol by way of handloading!

Only a "heel" or narrowed section on the base of the bullet enters the brass case, which must be crimped into it to hold the lead in place when another round in the cylinder kicks back in recoil. To do this uniformly and well, cases must be trimmed to equal length, and that length must suit the chamber of the loading tool. Still, every new thing we do, safely, in gun-tinkering teaches us something; and the old, old methods are just about as interesting as the modern.

The British .320 is almost identical to the .32 Short Colt, but not quite as long overall. It too is essentially a black powder load, and black powder and old guns go together well. But do not use too fine-grained "soft coal" in handloading. It burns too fast and thus raises pressure. It is not advisable, either, to try to cram the full factory-advertised black powder load into a cartridge.

ASTRA

Made by the Unceta firm in Guernica, Spain, Astras are one of the good, modern lines of Spanish pistols. We must not confuse this sort of production with some of the stuff that was exported from Spain in the 1920s. Those who knew the worst of those dogs would have hesitated to fire a midrange .32 S.&W. Long in a copy of the good old Smith hand ejector, for an example. Thing might blow up. But Astras have been good right along.

As you probably know, the unsafe Spanish revolvers carried, often, a big bold *SMITH & WESSON* marking on the barrel. The words *For* and *ctg.* preceding and following were purposely faint and fuzzy. Some people may have been fooled.

The Astra 400 semi-automatic is unusual in two ways: it handles rather heavy ammunition for a blowback action self-loader, and it operates with cartridges of different lengths. The 8-shot magazine takes 9 mm. Luger, the longer 9 mm. Steyr and the still longer 9 mm. Bayard Long, also our .38 Auto Colt with either

Astra Cub .22 short auto weighs 12 ounces and carries six rounds in its magazine. Compare it to the Colt Junior .22 and .25.

The Astra Camper .22 short is fitted with a longer barrel—4 inches as compared to the Cub's 2 3/16—and weighs 13 ounces.

the old standard or the present Super loading. A 5½- or 6-inch barrel gives good velocities with any of these charges, but some Luger rounds may not chamber snugly enough to insure firing; some are fatter than others just above the extracting groove or cannelure.

It seems that this gun, once an official arm of Spain, is out of production. In a practical way it would be of little interest to our shooters, for we have the Super .38 Auto Colt, which is only a little heavier, and the Colt Commander, which is lighter, as well as the fine S.&W. 9 mm. automatic. The Astra 400 is hammerless, which may be desirable; but its straight-pitched grip is no help in quick, natural pointing, or in slow fire. But for a personal gat to be carried all over the world, as some are, the 400's acceptance of various .38-caliber rounds just could be a decisive point in choosing. However, each year, it seems, the 9 mm. Luger cartridge is more widely distributed.

There are smaller Astras in calibers .32 and .380 Colt, and 9 mm. Luger or Parabellum. Also there were copies of our 1911 Colt, in 9 mm. Luger, 9 mm. Bergmann, and .45 Colt Auto. In pocket pistols the Unceta

The Astra Firecat .25 is hammerless. Weight is 13 ounces, barrel length 2 3/16 inches.

A chrome plated and engraved Firecat .25.

200 Astra is a .25 of about old standard 12-ounce weight, and the 300 Astra is a 22½-ounce .32 or .380. The latter has too small and straight a grip to suit most informed people, and of course the handle on the little .25 isn't for precision shooting, but for such reassurance as a tiny pistol can give the grasping hand in a tight corner. The .22 short Astra auto is really small, but it has its points and purposes. Astra quality is high, at least under normal conditions. Firearms International, 4837 Kerby Hill Road, Washington 22, D. C., handles the modern Astra line.

BAYARD

Good Bayard imitations of Smith & Wesson revolvers have been made. These are not to be confused with the poor Spanish imitations of the 1920s. The Bayard name has gone on Belgian-made .25, .32 and .380 auto-pistols, and they too were all right.

Bergmann's design went into the Bergmann-Bayard (later just Bayard) locked-breech military automatic.

It took the 9 mm. Bayard ammunition, and like the military Mauser it carried its box magazine ahead of the trigger guard. The mag could be clip-loaded. Some held six rounds; some held eight. In Belgian make, the grip is thick and rounded, with fair back-slant for good pointing. There were modifications when the Germans took over the manufacture.

This Bayard auto is really a sort of pioneer model of the self-loading type, and some would call it long and clumsy. It is probably not worth converting to accept an American cartridge, though evidently it is a shootable gun—amazingly so, perhaps, compared to a few older and a few much newer models about which we hear a good deal. But we have plenty of other shootable pistols, of various vintages, and chambered for some size of American-made cartridge, too. The 9 mm Bayard is longer than our .38 Auto Colt, but perhaps .351 Winchester brass could be shortened and used in handloading a Bayard.

BERETTA

The firm of Pietro Beretta in Brescia is one of the best in Italy, and good by any standard, anywhere—or

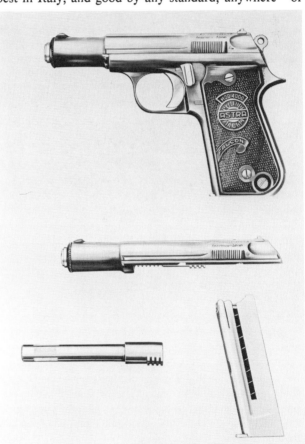

Astra Falcon weighs about 24 ounces and mounts a 3⅞-inch barrel. Calibers are .22 long-rifle, .32 and .380 Colt Auto. With an extra barrel you can have a .32-.380 combination; and with slide and barrel assembly, and an extra magazine, you get a three-caliber outfit. There is also an Astra Cadix 9-shot .22 revolver with an action somewhat resembling the Smith & Wesson's. This one has a barrel length of 4 inches and a weight of 25 ounces.

so a great many Americans are beginning to think. Commercially, in designs and promotion, it is right on the job. J. L. Galef & Son, 85-R Chambers Street, New York 7, N. Y., represent it.

The simple 1934 design of .32 or .380 auto-pistol worked out well, and many Berettas in .380 (9 mm. *Corto,* or Short) were carried by Italian forces in World War II. Since then, a wide variety of Berettas has come over as import goods. Calibers chosen are popular, naturally, the .25, .32 and .380 Auto, and the .22 short rimfire for plinking. There are hammer and hammerless (with grip safety) models. The name "Beretta" is becoming extremely well-known among users of small handguns—some of whom perhaps have never heard that our own companies once made a fine line of such automatic pistols.

The old military .380 may need some working over, for a trigger pull too heavy by several pounds, perhaps. A butt spur on its magazine can help greatly in holding, for these guns tend a bit to squattiness, being designed particularly for easy transport, and all-time faithful companion use. The empty magazine holds the slide open after the last shot, and some have held on so miserly hard that it is almost impossible to haul out the mag. Such things need smoothing up. They are more or less common under military production. They shouldn't—repeat, shouldn't—appear under peacetime manufacture; but you weren't born yesterday, neither was I, and together we know that it's best to personally inspect *any* gun before we buy it.

There was also the much heavier 9 mm. service pistol for a special light loading as used also in the Model 1910 Glisenti service pistol. It fired the standard 124 or 125 grain bullet at about 960 f. s. velocity, and the case was some .02 inch shorter than Luger brass.

Some of the modern pocket Berettas have the barrel hinged to make loading the chamber much easier than by opening the breech with a stout haul on the sliding breech-block. For people with small, not very strong hands, this could pay off well in time of emergency. One of the lightest of all defense pistols must be the Panther .25, a 10-ounce Beretta with the good barrel-length of 2.7 inches (about 2 inches is standard). A dural frame does it, as we should expect.

With .22 plinking so popular among some of us shooters, the pause for reloading is not considered as refreshing as it might be. People want to get on with the shooting. Is that strange if they live in a city and have perhaps not more than three or four hours a week outdoors with no concrete under their shoes? Long ago, Winchester made a "gravity charger" for their Model 1903 .22 auto-rifle taking its special cartridge in a 10-shot buttstock magazine. Without the charger, loading was like dropping beans into granpappy's cigar holder, one at a time, and careful. With it, there were two quick twirks and the cattidges went in, five rounds, then five more. So it was timely and natural for Beretta to bring out their 20-shot .22 magazine, a horrendous

long adjunct, of course, but equally a plinker's delight. It is for the Silver Gerfalcon type of Beretta rifle, but it can be altered to fit the Walther PP and PPK .22s.

Don't laugh. Sustained accurate fire is practical. Why limit ourselves to the usual small magazine capacity of pistols, when some day we might have much more fire-power in our hands, and need it?

Beretta succeeds Walther, right now, as manufacturer of the Walther pre-war design of Olympic .22 auto-pistol, much the same but with an exposed hammer. It can be had for .22 short or .22 long-rifle, and it has the usual Olympic rapid-fire equipment of recoil-frustrating compensator at the muzzle, detachable barrel weights, and rather fat, straight grip with thumb and finger rests. With the muzzle brake or compensator attached, the barrel goes to 8¾ inches. The gun weighs some 38 ounces and costs about five dollars an ounce. But what competitive shooting means more to our Country than the Olympics do?

The Beretta is well established, but comparatively new at this writing is the Jaguar Plinker. In .22 short it has dural slide, and in .22 long-rifle, steel. Interchanging slide, barrel, recoil spring and magazine means interchanging ammunition, shorts to long-rifles, or the other way if you are shooting indoors, let's say. The cross-bolt safety is smoothed up to go to the right and off at a nudge from the thumb. A spur or butt extension helps in holding. If you need a light .22 automatic with a barrel up to six inches long, this is one to consider.

The Model 1951 or 951 Brigadier is a business Beretta: 9 mm. Luger caliber, 4½-inch barrel (not bad for this caliber), locked-breech action, exposed hammer. There is a cross-bolt safety at the top rear of the frame, a poor location; but the gun has a hammer, too, which most servicemen in any country, right now, probably would say is a good thing on a pistol. Eight- or ten-shot mags are available, and a butt spur for the shooter's little finger. After the last shot the slide stays open as we should expect with a military handgun. Perhaps the Brigadier has the ambition to become just that: a military sidearm officially adopted by one, two, or how many countries? A lot of them once used the Luger, but now it costs too much to make Lugers, at least as standard items.

BERGMANN

These German designs go back to 1893. There have been many calibers and models—hammer, hammerless; locked breech, blow-back; detachable and built-in magazines. An 8 mm. Simplex autoloader made in Belgium took a short cartridge case much like the later 7.65 Browning or .32 Colt. There were also Bergmann machine guns, and in 1934 a nine-pound machine pistol for 9 mm. Luger or Parabellum.

A double-action Bergmann autoloading pistol for the .32 Colt marked a step toward what we expect in a d.a. auto today. A pull on the trigger cocked the hammer, all right; *but* to fire the rather complicated arm, it was necessary to release the trigger and pull it again.

BERNARDELLI

This Italian firm was organized in 1865 and made its reputation on shotguns. Since the war it has become quite prominent in the auto-pistol line, in calibers .22 short, .22 long, .22 long-rifle, and .25, .32 and .380 Colt.

The .22 shorts and .22 longs are for a tiny 9-ounce pistol, which has its counterpart in .25. These three rounds are a bit shorter overall than the .22 long-rifle. Almost every vocal shooter has taken his turn at cussing out the .22 long as a no-good; yet here is one gun still made for it, and a new model at that. Still, these barely half-pound .22s are more for sub-caliber practice in order to become good with the .25 than for defense arms in their own right. Or so you could say, if you have any respect for the .25 as a stopper; and some probably have, including a few that have been punctured by a .25. These midgets have 2⅛-inch barrels, and their complete overall is only two inches more. In .25 at least there is an extension magazine as an extra. It takes the grip out of the 1½ finger size and holds two or three more cartridges than the standard magazine.

A good-sized, 25-ounce Bernardelli in .22 long-rifle, .32 and .380 calibers has checked walnut stocks with a small thumb-rest on the left-hand side; and this, with the rigid mounting of the barrel in the receiver, should help make good shooting easier. It is certainly not a pin-weight for a pocket gun. The sights on the .22 stand up clean and sharp, but on the .32 and .380 they are streamlined into the slide contour because in these calibers the gun is more than likely to do duty as a defense arm.

BROWNING

Various Colt, Remington, Stevens and Winchester arms have been designed by John Moses Browning. Many of these guns have been manufactured under Browning's name in the Fabrique Nationale d' Armes de Guerre at Herstal, Liege, Belgium. Some were commercial; some were military. The reputation of Browning development and manufacture is still high.

The "FN" is called so from those letters molded on its hard rubber grips. It is one of the earliest Browning pistols well-known overseas, a 1901 invention. Your first look at this autoloader, if you are familiar with the Colt .32, brings the reaction, "What a beauty!" It is a big gun, weighing two pounds, some ten ounces heavier than the .32 pocket gun. If you have learned to shoot the Colt in spite of its rather straight-pitched grip, you feel sure you can do much better with this man-sized job, and that it will do better for you, with its larger, more powerful cartridge.

But there is the trouble. Apparently the 9 mm. Browning Long never has been made here, and if so, it certainly isn't now. This .38 sent a 110 grain bullet

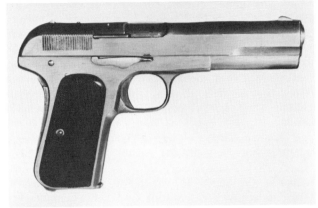

The inventor's original model of the 9mm. Browning Long semi-automatic, hammerless pistol. Note the slide lock on the right-hand side of the gun, just above the trigger. Courtesy Browning Arms Company, St. Louis, Mo., and Ogden, Utah.

at 1110 f. s., just a little below the power of the old standard .38 Auto Colt. Both rounds use semi-rimless cases, and possibly .38 ACP brass could be reworked for the FN. It would be a handloading proposition. You can tell from my having spent this much time on the gun that it is a rather fascinating job.

Well, it is, and rightly so. It's a smooth-lined hammerless, eight inches overall, and five of those inches in barrel length. The long Browning slide, enclosing barrel and recoil spring, gives you steadying weight out front. The thumb safety is handy, and there is a grip safety, too. After the last shot, the slide stays open. The gun is so flat and comparatively thin that it is much more easily carried concealed than a .38 Special revolver of equal weight. All in all, it is one of those obsolete, scarcely obtainable guns whose departure we can regret.

Browning M 35 High-Power

By contrast this 1935 model, the last of the Browning-designed semi-automatic pistols, is readily available, and one of the most popular service-type handguns imported. Its design goes back to 1927; yet it is commonly called the Model 1935, dating its manufacture at Fabrique Nationale in Belgium. During the war it

Standard Browning 9mm. Parabellum autoloading pistol, a splendid military handgun in this Luger caliber.

was made under German occupation, also by John Inglis & Co., Ltd., Toronto, for Canada, England, Greece, and the Chinese Nationalists. It seems to have almost everything a modern military auto-pistol needs, except for its medium-powered 9 mm. Luger caliber, and the lack of a double-action trigger. It does have a handy thumb-safety, though, and many authorities, including a big share of combatants, think the 9 mm. is enough.

The story is that Colt had a chance to make it, back in 1935, but declined. The reason is not hard to discover. They already had a good medium-power autoloader in the Super-.38, which was furnished then in target style, too; and that took care of the demand. We must remember that the .38 Automatic never had been a popular size, compared to the big .45 or the little .25 and .32. The 9 mm. Luger cartridge, at that time, had not earned popularity in this country. No generally available American pistols had been made for it. Of course the picture is much different now. If you wanted either 7.65 or 9 mm. Luger ammo in the 1920s or '30s, you generally had to go to a big-city store or order the stuff from your home-town man.

The M 35 holds a lot of cartridges without being a freak, although it is really a gun for a fairly large or downright big hand. The double-column magazine takes 13 rounds, and the empty mag is ejected by a thumb-nudge on the button at the left rear of the trigger. Meanwhile, the slide is held open, and late models cannot be fired when the magazine is out. (This last detail is not a part of Colt .45 functioning, but otherwise these two guns are similar in their handy action.) Shove in a fresh magazine and close the breech on it.

The grip, though rather big, is curved at the back to fit the hand. Some military models have had detachable shoulder stocks, hollowed to act as holsters, too, and rear sights adjustable for elevation. Barrel length is given as 4 21/32 inches, and weight as 32 ounces. Both are well adapted for the standard 9 mm. Luger cartridge as made here for pistols. Heavy sub-machine gun rounds giving up to about 1450 f. s. velocity and almost 40,000 pounds per square inch pressure (approximately .30-30 rifle equivalent) have been fired in Browning M 35s, and apparently with safety; but why use such stuff with full-jacketed bullets? The only real gain would be increased penetration. But for most purposes the standard Luger loads have quite enough, at least in the sporting field. Muzzle blast and recoil make a pistol harder to shoot.

This Browning has accuracy built into it, worthy of finely adjustable target sights. There is no readily detachable, loose muzzle bushing as on standard .45s or .38 Supers. Extra grooves in the forward end of the frame help to reduce play, and the trigger action is simpler than that of the 1911 Colt. The exposed hammer does bite some hands when it recoils. The Colt has a bad reputation for that. Generally you can find a change of grip that will prevent that and still allow you to do good work. Many of us like a visible hammer on

any pistol, even one like this, with a good thumb safety. On this one it locks the sear, and it can be put on whether the hammer is at full- or half-cock. The spur is small and rounded, old Mauser military style, or like that of the Colt Commander. It's also pierced, and you can get dry-fire practice by tying a cord to it and yanking back to simulate recoil—and recock the gun.

Like the Colt, it has what is called an "inertia" firing pin, one that is too short to contact the cartridge primer when the hammer is fully down on it. So the gun is safe to carry with the hammer down. When the hammer falls through its arc, it strikes the firing pin such a heavy swat that the latter flies forward against the restraint of its coiled retaining spring and arrives at primer metal with all the transmitted energy that is needed.

Present-day commercial M 35s are finished in a good blue and carry checked walnut stocks. Artificial pearl grips and engraving of the steel come as extras. Under all this there's still the sturdy, reliable action, even to the rugged lips at the mouth of the magazine. The real and hopeless gun-lover will like the detachable magazine bottom or floor-plate. Most magazines do collect a shocking amount of dirt in the course of long service.

There have been French modifications, made at the St. Etienne establishment. Since they chambered the weak and scarcely available long .30 cartridge like that used in the Pedersen-Springfield device, they would not interest us in a practical way.

Pocket Brownings

There have been various forms of these, including the present models. Early ones resembled the Colts, though Browning fans would tell you they were finished better, by far. They may be right, or they may have forgotten some of the really fine Colts. The earliest of all small Brownings, the 1900 models, were no beauties, but they worked well enough to start a great line of semi-automatic pistols. Their cartridge was the 7.65 mm. or .32-inch, our .32 Auto Colt.

The current .25 caliber "vest pocket" auto-pistol resembles the old hammerless Colt, though its trigger guard gives more finger room and its sights stand up where you can easily see them.

Shielded sights and less depth of the slide up front make the modern .380 Browning more streamlined than the discontinued .32 and .380 Colts.

The present .25s and .380s—the .32 has been dropped, though for years it was by far the most popular of all pocket auto-pistol sizes—are streamlined affairs, light and compact. The .25 has raised sights, the .32 shielded sights, hidden in the groove on top of the slide and therefore unable to snag in the pocket— just the opposite of some of the old models. But the .380 is going pretty big as a pocket caliber, now. Both .25 and .380 models have magazine safeties, and the .380 has a grip safety.

Grips are a bit straight on both these pocket Brownings, a good deal like those of old Brownings and Colts. Still, for their class, they have a good reputation for *working*. That means much in small-caliber auto-pistols of the pocket class. The .380 has a rounded slide, not quite so flat as on the old, familiar Colts, for the recoil spring is coiled around the barrel, not tucked away under it. Its barrel is fixed rigidly to the frame, not a more or less loose assembly, as in center-fire Colts to this day. This should ensure its accuracy, especially through long years of service and much more shooting than most pocket pistols are lucky enough to get—lucky so that they can serve their owners better.

CLEMENT

This is one of the old names in semi-automatic pistol history. Back before World War I broke out in 1914 it was known and used over here, to some extent, along with a few other imports such as Browning, Mauser, and the British Webley & Scott.

The first design of Smith & Wesson auto, the one chambered for its special .35 S.&W. cartridge, was derived from the Clement, with recoiling breech-block instead of a recoiling slide in the Browning fashion.

Clement calibers were the .25, .32 and .380 Colt. The latter two are factory-loaded now to higher than 1914 standard velocity. Perhaps we should consider that if and when we get one of these now uncommon Clements to try. They were well made, and of good materials for their time. But time does march on. This

warning could be applied to other very old makes of foreign autoloaders. It may be over-cautious, it may be completely unjustified, but I'll take that risk. A risk that I refuse to take is responsibility for any gun-accidents except my own, and I don't plan to have any.

CZECH HANDGUNS

These are not particularly popular arms in our country, but some have got here by one way or another. The Czechs have made good, serviceable weapons.

A 1910 model .32 auto, a little like Mausers of the time, had one or two advantages. Its trigger was hinged better, could hardly pinch your forefinger as some Mauser trigs did, and instead of being hammerless it had a small outside hammer. Some people prefer this by far, feeling that it's safer, especially for those not much used to firearms.

Other Czech pocket autos followed, such as the 1924 and 1926 in 9 mm. Browning Short (our .380) or in a 9 mm. Czech Short. These guns have long, almost perfectly straight-down grips, and almost no bulge to the rear, just above the point where the web of your hand comes in firing. Consequently they look queer, and less desirable than they really are. They are not bad at all. Making them of locked-breech type was a mistake, for their loads aren't powerful enough to demand it. A Czech 9 mm. Short chamber can be altered to take .380 Colt cartridges, which are a bit bigger at the head.

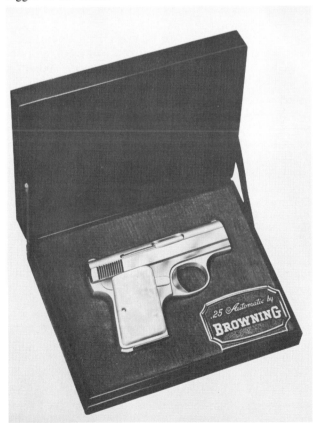

Cased light-weight Browning .25 as made for presentation or for a buyer's own pleasure.

Cased sets of Brownings in threes, both plain and highly decorated guns.

The grip of the CZ-47 is much improved. This 32-ounce gun for the 9 mm. Luger cartridge is in the military class. It has the short-recoil Browning locking system, with its barrel, fitted with locking lugs at the top, swinging down to unlatch itself from grooves cut in the top of the slide. There's no manual safety. But since it's a military gun with double-action pull for *every* shot, not just for the first round, perhaps a safety catch is unnecessary. It is meant for close-up fighting, and in a sense it's a double-action revolver holding eight rounds, not six, and reloaded fast if extra, fully charged magazines are handy. But half-moon revolver clips, U. S. 1917 fashion, are just as quick. Which in general is more reliable, a revolver or a semi-automatic?

Page 6 of the April, 1959 *American Rifleman* pictures a ZKR 551 Czech target revolver in .38 Special, as used by the Czech team during the International Shooting Union's 37th World Championships at Moscow, 1958. It is interesting but not mouth-watering. The gun is a six-shot single-action of about 2¼ pounds, with two-way adjustable rear sight, an adjustable trigger, and a short, fast hammer fall. A heavy barrel adds to steadiness, and the grip appears low enough not to need an adapter or filler. Its backstrap is somewhat like those on Colts and Smiths, except that it has hardly any hump at the top, just above the web of your firing hand. With the unusually heavy barrel fitted to this target sixgun, there should be little tendency for the grip to work down in your hand during rapid fire.

There are other Czech pistols, of course, including a .25 with a perhaps unique double-action trigger mechanism. On a little vest-pocket gun the comparative safety of double-action does seem good, for these weapons are not for accuracy. In general, Czech autoloaders are rather notable for simple design and easy dismounting. And when they could, it seems, the Czechs used good materials and real workmanship in their output.

DREYSE

The Dreyse family has been important in the history of military arms, but their pistols are not common sights here. Long ago, a good many 1907 .32 autos were imported, but they are about in the collectors' class today. Old Dreyses for 9 mm. Luger ammo probably should be considered a bit too weak for those cartridges in full modern loadings.

ENFIELD

Britain's commonly used .380 service revolvers of World War II are known as Enfields, although they are a sort of variation of the Webley .455 Mark VI Pistol No. 1, a revolver made at the commercial Webley & Scott plant at Birmingham, not at the Government arsenal at Enfield.

The Enfields use the .380 British or Webley & Scott Special, which has a case similar to our .38 S.&W.— the short S.&W., not the .38 Special—with 145 or 146 grain bullet. But the British load took, at first, a 200 grain lead bullet, blunt, slow, heavy, and quite a stopper for its caliber—similar to our discontinued .38 S.&W. Super Police 200-grain. In World War II the 178 grain full-metal cased service bullet came in, for plain lead slugs had been bitterly and viciously outlawed even in pistol ammunition (men could have been executed for having them in their possession in combat).

At short ranges heavy bullets throw high when fired from handguns. So for awhile, at least, a special low front sight blade was available to bring the standard S.&W. bullets up to zero by interchanging it with the issue front. Few of us here would use super-heavy bullets in the short .38 S.&W. cartridge; and it is simple to file down a front sight to get the elevation needed for lighter slugs. The chief difficulty lies in not taking too much at a time!

The Enfield No. 2 .380 came in two forms, Mark I and Mark I*, the latter being double-action *only,* with no hammer spur for cocking. That sounds ridiculous—a well-made, nicely balanced revolver that can't be cocked for a short, clean trigger pull of reasonably light weight. But for close in-fighting who'd use it single action, and who wants a hammer spur sticking out from a concealed gun, ready and willing to catch in his pocket lining?

Like the Webley service sixguns, these Enfields have comfortable, well-shaped, extremely shootable grips that need no adapter. The guns hang well, and the sights are square-cut Patridge type. They are of jointed-frame construction, with tip-down muzzle, tip-up cylinder opening, and of course automatic ejection of empties when you do your part—roll the butt forward and down, and the muzzle back and up, after you've pressed the left-hand thumb-latch and unlocked the action. They are just a little quicker to open and empty than a side-swing cylinder Smith or Colt. But practice with them so that no empty can possibly drop back into a chamber and block the extractor from going home where it beyongs. This applies to our own old U. S.-made tip-ups with auto-ejection, and to our side-swings.

With 5-inch barrels these revolvers weigh about 28 ounces empty, a shade lighter than Smith & Wesson Military & Police guns made for the .380 British cartridge and much used alongside the Enfields—for, after all, handguns did play a pretty active part in World War II. To choose between these two, for a personal gun, might not be easy, for each has its points. It seems that most people who buy a .380 British S.&W. start at once to figure on having it altered to take .38 Special rounds. For them, the .380 barrel is normally oversized, and of course the chambers are too short.* Chambers could be bored out for the long Special brass, and such work has been done wisely (though rarely so) for people who needed a revolver that would take almost anything made anywhere in centerfire ".38," actually .357 inch or maybe a full .360. These folks got around to remote and sometimes primitive countries, where they needed ammunition even if it was far indeed from being ballistically right.

The best way to convert a .380 Smith to .38 Special is to have a new cylinder and a new barrel fitted. A sensible way out is to leave the gun as-is, for the .38 S.&W. load is accurate, being well designed. Unless you need considerable penetration—of hide, flesh, bone, clothing or what-not—it's about as deadly as the conventional round-nosed .38 Special bullet. Naturally it's much easier for a beginner to shoot well, comfortably and quietly with a 5-inch revolver weighing some 31 ounces. Most of the S.&W. .380s I've seen happened to be in excellent shape. I thought and still think they would be competent house guns, family guns. The Ideal 360271 bullet of about 150 grains shot finely in an S.&W. Regulation Police we had, and it was a semi-wadcutter, no round-point. The square shoulder punched out clean-cut holes in target paper, and the wide, flat nose would have had a sickening effect—it seems—if it had been obliged to protect any of us.

French Handguns

The 1873 and 1874 six-shot, double-action service revolvers are of 11 mm. caliber, about a ".44" or an actual .429 inch. So they might intrigue a handloader with a variety of .44 S.&W. Special molds. Rod ejection makes these guns slow to operate, but somehow the single-action Colts, Rugers and Great Westerns which seem fairly well liked, are equally deliberate about getting rid of their fired brass!

The top-strap of these guns is not very rugged-looking, and the metal in them was cooked up a long time ago. They belong to the black powder era, and it would seem smart to use black powder in loading for them, or for the old German opposite numbers, which as I recall used about an 11.2 mm. bullet.

The 8 mm. Lebel 1892 service revolver was much used in World War I, and some got here with returning troops. They are well made, if odd. The swing-out cylinder, six-shot, turns out to the right, not to the left. Swing the cylinder catch back and then down on its pivot to open the gun.

The usual barrel length is 4¼ inches, and gun weight 28 ounces. These make soft, pleasant shooting with the service charge, about a 100-grain flat-nosed bullet, lead or full jacketed, at about 625 f. s. velocity, well below our .32 S.&W. Long and Colt New Police. I think heavier loads have been put up for the Lebel, not as heavy as .32-20, by any means, but pretty fair. Black powder was the service propellant for most if not all of this cartridge's useful life, and very fine-grained it was, quick-burning.

Handloading it today, we should be satisfied with FFG black, moderately fine. (The gun is not a kluck, you know; it has quality.) It would be interesting to feed a Lebel revolver of this caliber. Probably old .32 Winchester Self-Loading Rifle brass could be had and worked down; it has been off the open market only about 20 years, and boxes of it can be had here and there, or at least a few rounds at a time. It's thick and almost everlasting if you wash the black-powder sludge out of it after each firing.

Sure, sure; I know. "Is it practical? What a bore, all this bother!" But some of us *are* fussy gun-cranks, and do we enjoy it! We might help *you* out, some time, if standard supplies ever become short—as they have in the past.

Bullets? Cast, of course, and about .315-inch diameter. A .32 Ideal rifle or .32-.44 S.&W. revolver mold would drop oversize lead, and probably of about the right weight. We could size it down. Use .32-20

---

*Bored out, they'd take the popular .38 Special wadcutter load with its bullet flush with the case-mouth, and the .38 Short Colt also could be used. Even the .38 Long Colt would fit, with bullet nose cut or filed back.

or .32 S.&W. Long or Colt? Much too small, unless your Lebel is off-standard.

The whole thing would be a nice problem for a ballistic dietitian, and he would love it.

Spanish-made Ruby auto-pistols used by the French Government go to about two pounds and carry nine .32 Auto Colt or 7.65 Browning rounds in their magazines. The grip is terrifically straight up-and-down, but liberally long. The action is straight blow-back, satisfactory for the cartridge. But the gun is not quite of first-line quality, though it could serve for purposes that weren't too exacting.

The 1935-A 7.65 mm. Long is a locked-breech auto, somewhat like our Colt .45 in its short-recoil unlocking action. This gun is normally rather well made, and possibly its recoil mechanism could be altered to use .32 Auto Colt cartridges, with their casehead semi-rims or flanges worked down to function. The 7.65 mm. Long is an odd size, like the Pedersen round for the sub-machine gun device once made for specially prepared 1903 .30-06 Service Springfields. It gives a good pistol velocity of about 1100 f. s., but is well below the 7.63 Mauser and 7.62 Russian in power. Outside of France, it is not particularly easy to acquire.

Magazine capacity of the 1935-A is eight of these rounds, gun weight is some 25 ounces, and barrel length just over 4½ inches. You can see it's small; thus, if you want a practical handgun and a collector wants this one, it might be well to trade.

The French Star 7.65 uses our .32 Auto cartridges, weighs about 30 ounces, and has a long barrel for the caliber, 5¼ inches. Eight cartridges go into the magazine, and the grip is fair-sized, though rather straight. The Spanish manufacture of this model is good. If an 8-inch overall length is not too much for your needs, it would be worth thinking about. There's an exposed hammer, and on the *right*-hand side of the slide, ahead of the hammer, there's a thumb safety.

Action is blow-back, barrel is rigid on the frame, and the top of the slide is cut away in rather common Spanish fashion. In dismounting, the breech-block goes back, then forward, up and off. The takedown catch is ahead of the trigger; it is a simple and good device. In this gun the accuracy and power of the .32 Auto cartridge should be a bit unusual. Light muzzle weight and considerable breech weight make this Star somewhat unhandy for hip-pocket carry; it's eight inches overall. For a light holster pistol it should qualify well, subject to the power of the light, hard-jacketed .32 bullet.

Modern French Imports

Winfield Arms, 1006 South Olive Street, Los Angeles 1, are agents for the M.A.B. and W.A.C. pistols. Few French handguns have been imported on a real commercial scale in the past, but Free Europe is well aware, today, of the American demand for firearms.

There is nothing about the French people to prohibit their production of good weapons.

The M.A.B. Le Militaire is a rather heavy, 37-ounce auto for the 9 mm. Luger round. It has a 4¾-inch barrel and eight-shot magazine. It is not cheap. The slide is of the long Browning type, and the large grip has good slant. It is more for a holster than for a pocket; so the fact that the sights stand up high and clear is to the good.

The Wac Le Chasseur (The Hunter, though it is advertised as a target pistol) is a moderate priced .22 auto holding nine long-rifle rounds in its magazine—which must be in the gun if you want to fire it. The grip is a bit straight, but the curved back and the thumb-rest on the side help in holding. Like the M.A.B. Militaire, it has an exposed hammer. A 4½-inch barrel is standard, making the gun compact but rather muzzle-light. The 7½-inch model costs a little more and is three ounces heavier, or 31 ounces—a nice weight for a great many shooters who haven't taken special pains to train themselves to handle heavier arms.

On some of these Wacs, the trigger pull varies in weight from shot to shot, not at all an unusual fault with medium-priced pistols. But is it, in its essence, really a fault? If you don't know when the gun is going to fire, how can you flinch? Some of us have been surprised at our good shooting with such a temperamental trigger pull, and some have had such pulls built into their target guns purposely. It is quite possible to flinch with a .22, either rifle or pistol. (Watch for this when you coach a beginner. Sometimes you find it and then know what you must do to help him, for often he doesn't know that he flinches.) A soft, not crisp and brittle pull is in favor with many European shooters. This does not mean a creepy pull, or one with a lot of rear movement after the trigger's job is done. Those two are abominations.

The W.A.C. Chasseur looks a little like the 7.65

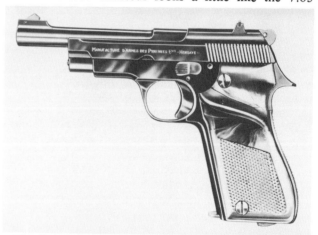

The Corsair Unique .22 long-rifle auto (the Escort Unique is a .22-short gun) from Firearms International, 4837 Kerby Hill Road, Washington 22, D. C., is made by Manufacture d'Armes des Pyrenees Francoises, Hendaye, France. It has a 4 5/16-inch barrel, weighs 24 ounces, and has adjustable sights.

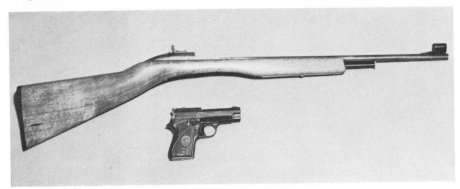

Model L Unique pistol and its interchangeable rifle stock and barrel, The "Combo."

mm. centerfire French service Star, having its slide cut away on top instead of running full-length or nearly so, as in Browning fashion.

The W.A.C. Gendarme hammerless auto comes in .32 and .380 calibers, has a 4-inch barrel and weighs about 25 ounces. In 3½-inch-barrel style and a little lighter, this general design is called the Cavalier. The smooth-lined little Defendeur is a .25 of average old-time size and weight, 2-inch barrel, 12¾ ounces, and six-round magazine in a short, finger-and-a-half stock.

The Combo Unique

The French Unique make of auto-pistol is imported by Firearms International, Washington 22, D.C., which has handled the Spanish Stars for a long time. Perhaps the most interesting Unique is the Combo, which was featured at the F. I. booth at the 1960 N.R.A. gun show.

The Combo is the Model L Unique ten-shot .22 pistol with rifle stock and barrel assembly completing the kit. As far as I know, this is something new, though single-shot and auto pistols with detachable stocks are old stuff, and useful, too, when the stock is long enough to keep muzzle blast comfortably distant and to give good focus on the sights. Some single-shots, revolvers, and modern auto-pistols like Hi-Standard and Smith & Wesson, used or use interchangeable barrels of different lengths. Takedown single-shot rifles, and the Model 99 Savage takedown lever action repeater as once made, took interchangeable shotgun barrels, though the .410 bore 99 functioned as a single-loader with shot-shells. And so on: the permutations and combinations of firearms curiosities are nearly endless. All are interesting; some are useful.

The Model L .22 auto is a compact little pistol, easily taken down, and with magazine safety, thumb safety, and weight of 21½ ounces in black steel, or 15¼ in colored aluminum-alloy. Barrel is 3 inches long, overall 6. In steel construction the weight is not bad for such a short pocket pistol, but in alloy the Model L isn't much heavier than the old Colt .25 of 13 ounces. However, this featherweight is longer, better stocked, and better sighted than the Colt, and smaller and lighter foreign .22 autos have been made.

They are toylike in feel, these dwarfs, but can be deadly, particularly, it seems to me, by accident!

If the 3-inch barrel of the Unique Model L seems too short, the 18-inch rifle tube in the Combo is about right to develop full .22 long-rifle velocities, at least on the average, though I've clocked 27 and 28-inch .22 rim-fire rifle barrels that developed more speed than a 20-inch. Much depends on the snugness of chambering and on the shortness of the rifling throat ahead of, or biting into, the bullet. A 16-inch rifle barrel is legal on rimfire .22s, but the overall of the Combo as a rifle is only 34 inches, and the weight is about 2¾ pounds —less than that of today's Smith & Wesson 6½-inch .44 Magnum.

The walnut rifle stock is, in appearance, without any comb, like the Model 1917 .30-06 Enfield's wood, and that of the 1913 .276 and 1914 .303 that the '17 came from. That could have been for bayonet fighting, and probably was. Unlike the Enfields, the Combo comes up pretty snugly to your cheek, and offers some support in steady holding, as it certainly needs to, with this pinweight arm.

Combo rifle sights are a peep rear and a ramped front, without much latitude for adjustment, which is regrettable, though after we've zeroed in at 50 feet it ought to be good up to 50 yards or so, with the high-velocity stuff we'd use for hunting. To get the first load into the barrel, or to unload *after* we've removed the magazine, we'd push back the operating rod, which is located, in the handy Winchester Model 63 fashion, ahead of the forearm.

Now then, what is this odd firearm good for? I think of it as a wilderness gun, for I could have used it thankfully on some trips I've taken, and it could come in just as handily on some I hope to take. More on that later, but first let's consider its appeal as a close-to-home plinker. With either rifle or pistol barrel it's fairly noisy, for both are short, in their class. But this means going only a little farther from home, at the worst. The lightness of the rifle, which could be fitted with a gun-sling for steadier holding, would help in teaching seven or eight year olds to shoot, though they'd need a stock from 1½ to maybe 2½ inches shorter to have a fair chance. OK, cut off a hunk, but save it to screw or dowel on later. And of course let

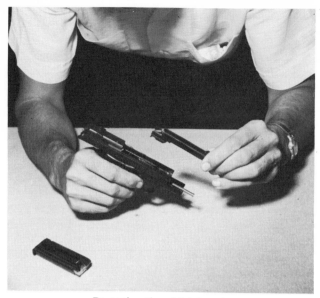

Removing the pistol barrel.

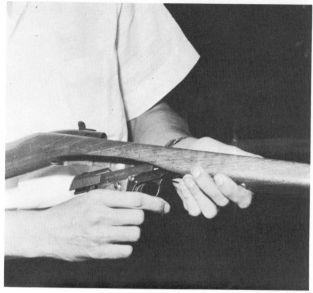

Converting the pistol into a rifle.

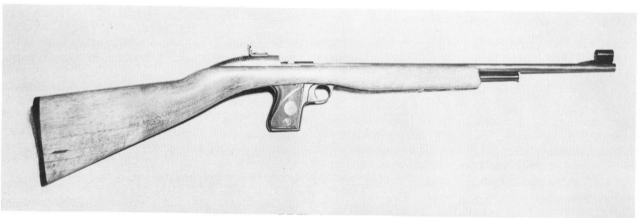

The Combo as a rifle.

Junior use the rifle, or the pistol, only as a single-loader—for safety.

This lightness will appeal to older beginners, even some adults, for it doesn't take much imagination to see how unwieldy a firearm feels to totally unfamiliar hands. Being in a sense two guns in one, the Combo appeals to a good many plinkers. Never mind about the true pistol grip on the rifle. The Marble Game-Getter .22-.44 and .22-.410 combinations had it, and so did the No. 7 Remington rifle—see page 135 of James Grant's *Single-Shot Rifles,* if you don't know the No. 7. These guns were not disqualified as good shooters because of their grips. Some top-ranking smallbore competition riflemen have similar custom grips on their old reliables.

Sure, the Combo should sell if its quality is kept up, just as many others do.

And now I leave, in spirit, this scene of pleasant toil and take to the wilderness. Come along if you like. On a canoe portage, for instance, we need two hands and maybe an extra pair. We pocket the pistol assembly and roll stock and rifle barrel in bedding. We're still armed, though to kill small game cleanly with a short, light handgun we need to have developed a whole lot of skill. However, a snake is usually close-up. At night we garage the pistol within easy reach. It's quick to get out and aim. On horseback, if we travel that way, this pistol needs no holster. Best carry it with an empty chamber, for safety aboard the mount.

But as a rifle the Combo isn't too bad on a go-light trip. We can shoot it about four times more accurately than as a pistol, or even better; and we need to. We know the .22 long-rifle cartridge's steep limitations as a killer. Its small and relatively slow bullet must be placed right for sure, humane work. In real wilderness our chances often come at well under 50 feet. That helps, but still we must place our shots. Often we'd have time to use the hasty sling, the arm thrust through and back over the leather, and believe me, that helps, too. This motion can be made smoothly and slowly so as not to alarm the game.

FROMMER

Frommer is an old Hungarian name, and some of these handguns were imported years ago. A Model 1912 had an unnecessarily locked breech action for so small an autoloader—.32 and .380 caliber. The Lilliput blowback-action .25 had an almost incredibly short, ungraspable stock, and an exposed hammer that was rather uncommon on .25s.

For those who needed extra-small automatics there were the 1937 Baby Frommers in .32 and .380, so little and light that a locked-breech action was sensible in them. They are of about usual .25-caliber size, and are a common Frommer type in having the barrel mounted below, under the recoil spring, instead of above it in the enclosing slide.

Of this make it can be said, in general, that these auto-pistols are well and ingeniously made, but perhaps a little over-complicated. However, they do get a lot of use in their part of the world, if little here.

GABILONDO

The Gabilondo firm of Elgoibar, Spain, was organized in 1904. It has made a considerable variety of arms, and at present some pistol models are imported regularly by Stoeger Arms Corporation of New York, and well distributed throughout this country.

The "Llama" trademarked .38 and .45 autos look much like the Colts except for the barrel rib added, and the checked walnut, not plastic stocks. They sell for a little less than Colts of standard grade. Probably the scaled-down Llama .22, .32 and .380 automatics are more familiar to most of us, and when they first appeared here—then in the centerfire calibers only—they created quite a stir. They were certainly attractive, these miniature .45s. Inside, they were different, as we should expect. Those who wanted a smooth-lined, hammerless pocket pistol weren't interested, for these guns have external hammers and long-horned grip safeties, just like the U. S. Government .45. Even the slide stop ahead of the left grip, and the thumb safety behind it, looked the same. However, a good many shooters prefer a hammer gun. Probably most of the buyers gave little attention to these details. The Llamas looked like baby .45s and for all their small size they felt good in the hand. Despite the arrival of later and different foreign pocket persuaders, they seem to retain their popularity.

Although these Llamas are not by any means exact internal copies of the Colts, the Gabilondo-made Ruby revolvers resemble Smith & Wesson sixguns closely. Do not confuse them with S.&W. Spanish copies of the 1920s and '30s, those cheap, even dangerous "pot-metal" arms. These modern ones are good. In Central and South America they are very well liked, for a

Llama .380 and .32 semi-automatic pistols quickly became popular because they looked so much like baby .45 Colts. This one is a .380. Photo courtesy Stoeger Arms Corporation.

Smith & Wesson or anything close to it is regarded highly there.

Some are sold here, too, by or through Stoeger's. They include .22 rimfire (note that) and .32 S.&W. Long caliber copies of recent, not the very latest styling, Regulation Police Smiths, copies of the .38 Special Military & Police, and variety of highly engraved and plated specials that go up to $400 in price. The K-Target S.&W.s have been copied, too; but they may not have reached this country in any great quantity. After all, these target Smiths are easy to find in first-class second-hand condition.

It seems that the pocket autos, the little Llamas, are the most likely of all Gabilondo pistols to hold their popularity here. They are of just about average pocket-auto size and weight, having 3 11/16-inch barrels in their short 6¼-inch overall, and weighing about 20 ounces in steel. The .22 can be had in a 17-ounce "Airlite" model. These guns, except the .380s, have a blowback action, but the big models for .38 and .45 Colt (also 9 mm. Luger and 9 mm. Bergmann) have the Colt or Browning type short-recoil locked action.

Another Ruby pistol that we still hear of shouldn't be confused with the Gabilondo revolvers handled by Stoeger Arms. Made by S. A. Alkatosuna at Guernica, Spain, it is a .32 auto taking our Colt cartridges, of which it holds nine in its magazine. Gun weight is heavy for its caliber, 34 ounces, though the barrel measures only 3 5/8 inches. Its grip is long, but almost perpendicular to the slide and receiver. For quick pointing it couldn't be much worse, but the French Government used it in large numbers and a great many gendarmes carried one of these odd-looking gats at their sides. This pistol, and others like it, should not be hastily condemned because of poor balance and stock hang. Most of us rely on aimed fire, not instinctively thrown shots, and we can learn to shoot effectively at short ranges with ill-fitting weapons, if we have to. It's simply doing it the hard way.

GALESI

Galesi autoloaders have been imported from Italy by Sloan's Sporting Goods Company, 88-R Chambers Street, New York 7, and later by The Omega Import Company, 307 Fifth Avenue, New York 16, among other distributors.

The .32 is about standard-sized for its caliber, and it has a handy safety just behind the left grip. The slide is rounded, since the recoil spring encircles the barrel instead of being stashed away under it. This is the popular sort of pocket-auto design today. It can save a little weight out front—where some of us like to have it, as on the late lamented pocket Colts.

Galesi guns have a good reputation; they aren't junk. There are blue and chrome finishes, white and dark stocks, and of course engraving at extra cost. Various models, styles and calibers of Galesi auto-loaders include beside the .32 caliber the .25 Auto, the .22 short, and the .22 long—the latter in guns specially made for it and not functioning with the .22 long-rifle.

GERMAN

Germans have designed and made any amount of firearms, but right here we give our attention to the .22 double derringers that have been coming over recently. In general outline and pretty much in action, they resemble the once-familiar Remington double der-ringer, Model 95, made from 1888 to 1935. This little 11-ounce pistol, with 3-inch barrels mounted one over the other, fired .41 rimfire loads—the short with a pointed bullet, the little-known Winchester long with more powder and an equal-weight bullet (130 grains of dead-soft lead) that had as bluff a rounded point as that of the still made .41 Long Colt centerfire. It looked tremendous, but the low velocity made it, really, not much of a stopper compared to big sixgun cartridges, and penetration was very low. However, it was enough to be fatal, most certainly, when the lead struck a vital part and the germs riding along on its exposed lubricant got in their dirty work.

The change, in this German derringer, to .22 long-rifle ammunition wouldn't help much, if any, in spite of occasional wild enthusiasm for .22 rimfire killing power. But these .22 imports cost less than $30 right now, they are cheap to shoot for practice (which doesn't help much with a derringer!), and the reli-ability of a double-barreled pistol is greater than that of most muffin-sized automatics.

Since the old Remington system was good for the purpose, this two-shot .22 has a swinging lever to unlock the barrels and let their muzzles turn upward, and a manually operated extractor—slide a button back. The mainspring is modern, coiled, not flat, and the barrels are also modern, just steel liners in a light-metal enclosure, to keep weight down. Chrome and blue finishes are offered. These guns are supposed to be, and appear to be, entirely safe for use with high-velocity .22 long-rifle ammo.

The grip is typically small, curved, and durn near useless, and trigger pulls I have tried and heard of are really tough and hard. But the guns are portable: one of two of them can be with you—if laws permit—wherever you go except under a shower-bath or into a tub. The hammers are not hard to cock for a second shot. With a little practice a shooter can become deadly—or at least sure to hit vital spots, even if the effect of a .22 isn't instantly apparent—at 10, 15 and probably 20 foot ranges. Those ranges are among the most common danger zones; aren't they? I think that these derringers should be bought and carried in pairs, as derringers used to be, out west, down south, and in other parts of our nation.

A practical use for this German .22 over-and-under is as an understudy to derringers of reasonable power, such as the Great Western .38 Special. But in some places haven't you longed for even a .22 and felt you could do all right with it if you had to? If you had one, you probably wouldn't have to use it.

GLISENTI

In World War II the Glisenti 9 mm. automatic pistol was one of the official Italian arms, and there should be many of them here, brought back by servicemen. It is a 1906 design, army-adopted in 1910, and its standard rations are cartridges that look like 9 mm. Luger but are about .02 inch shorter, and very much more lightly loaded. If I had one, I should want to shoot it, for the grip and general outline, if you don't look too hard, resemble Luger architecture. I'd order empty Luger cases, trim them as needed, get an Ideal 356402 mold like the one I had for my first Luger, buy or adapt loading tools, and start with low powder charges, stopping when my handloads would work the locked-breech action. W. H. B. Smith, in his *Small Arms of the World,* lists bullet weight at the standard 125 grains, and velocity at an extremely modest 960 f. s. Evidently the Glisenti is designed for hog-nosed bullets of the old Luger type—a cone with its point cut off square. In soft lead at over 900 f. s. this shape spells fair stopping power and fine small game killing ability, if you place your bullets right. That you cer-tainly have to do with almost any bullets except those with bomb effect.

The gun weighs about 34 ounces and has a 3¾ to 4 inch barrel. It was hardly brilliant to locate the safety lever at the rear of the bolt, though there's also a grip safety under the trigger guard, something like that of the beautifully made, but odd, old Smith & Wesson .35. Ignition should be good, and prompt, for the striker operates in a straight line, Luger style. After the last shot, the bolt stays open.

Glisenti Revolver

Also made in Brescia by Glisenti is a large-caliber service revolver. It takes the 10.35 mm. Italian, about .40 caliber, and is a solid frame sixshooter, double-action, with the usual rebounding hammer. Ejecting and loading are done as with the Colt Single Actions, except that the loading gate rolls back instead of swinging out to the right.

This Glisenti's grip is round and small, but it has plenty of rearward slant. The gun could be shot rather well, though it might need considerable tuning-up first. Naturally we should have to handload for it to get the amount of practice we should want. The powder ought to be FFG black, at least at first, though later we could try smokeless formulas in bashful, even timid amounts. Brass cases might come from .30-30, worked down, and for black powder that is strong brass indeed, which we should want. The bullet might be a .38-40, .41 Long Colt, or possibly a .40-60-210 Winchester, cast soft. We could get samples to try on for size.

Few would call the resulting gun-and-ammo combination practical, but it could be so if it were properly and safely assembled. It would show more common-sense, but give less entertainment and grass-roots ballistic instruction, to buy a good, used U. S. gun of a currently made caliber and let the fun of such involved tinkering go downstream disregarded.

HAEMMERLI

These expensive, top-grade .22 rimfire target pistols for International slow-fire or rapid-fire events are imported by H. F. Grieder, Box 487, Knoxville, Illinois. They are made in Lenzburg, Switzerland. At this writing the single-shot, slow-fire "free" pistol (free from barrel length, sight radius and trigger pull restrictions applied to handguns for Standard American courses) costs $215, or $275 for the highly decorated job.

Prices for the Haemmerli Walther-model autoloader, for rapid-fire Olympic bursts of fire range from $177.50 to $225. Also for this class of shooting, there are the Beretta Olympic at $187.50, the Star Olympia at $108.20, and American self-loaders at standard U. S. prices plus what you have added to them in the way of custom, hand-fitting stocks, refined trigger pulls, and so on. Right now there are Hi-Standard pistols for the .22 short cartridge, the Olympic rapid-fire favorite —but not always the winner—because its light recoil allows you to get back on target quickly.

Haemmerli Free Pistol

It is almost surely the best for International slow-fire. There have been and are others, of course, such as the Tell, briefly described later.

The Haemmerli has the Martini-type, falling breech-block action with very fast lock-time cut loose by a five-lever set trigger. You may remember when the rather well-known British Birmingham Small Arms .22 single-shot match rifle was astonishing some of us Americans by its superb, snappy ignition of the Du Pont Lesmok and King's Semi-smokeless long-rifle cartridges we used then. That striker didn't waste any time in getting to the cartridge's hollow copper rim.

These B.S.As. were not set-trigger rifles, in our competition, for we had and still have a rather sensible and practical three-pound pull limit of lightness to the touch-off. But they certainly did have that sharp, quick ignition that helps to get a shot off right away, not just after the sights have wobbled off the mark.

The caliber is of course .22 long-rifle, for Olympic slow-fire pistol is at 50 meters, and that's quite a stretch for a .22 short to travel straight through with little deviation from even a mild cross-wind. The course is long and grilling, but leisurely as to time limit, and muzzle blast and recoil don't figure a bit— at least, in a .22 like this, with 11½-inch barrel and about 45-ounce weight!

Sight radius of the present standard model is 14 1/3 inches, and the rear sight has micrometer click adjustments for windage and elevation. The front sight has interchangeable bead or flat-topped posts. To get this long sight radius with a barrel so much shorter, the rear sight rides back on an extension and perches above your hand. The front sight is fairly close to the center of the bore, and located in what we should call a normal muzzle position.

Some of the latest imported specimens have a heavy round barrel, more in the American fashion than of the flat-sided European type, so long popular over there. There's a forestock under the barrel, uncommon in American pistols except the old Remington single-shot with rolling breech-block rifle action. The Haemmerli forestock has a lip or swell at the front, hardly standard on the purely functional Remington service or target model pistols. It is hard to keep up with the currently correct, acceptable spelling of this lip's name: snobble, schnabel, schnaubel—let's give up. You see them on old and new rifles; and some of the late rifles with full-length, muzzle-kissing forestocks, have the snob more than halfway back, about where your hand-reach would come in prone or sitting position. But enough of that. This grip is for business, and the Haemmerli's free-pistol handle can be made to the customer's measurements. When perfectly or nearly perfectly fitted, the gun seems to go to sleep in the hand. And it certainly should, for this type of shooting, precision slow-fire.

Haemmerli Olympia Autoloader

It is a close copy of the 1936 German-made Walther International, which World War II and some of its aftermath put a stop to. Perhaps it is the best of all regularly made Olympic rapid-fire pistols.

The stock is about as obliging as that of a single-shot free pistol. An adjustable base positions the bottom of the hand, and a wide but thin shelf above it positions the top of the hand. Atop this shelf rides the bottom of the trigger finger. All this fitting should be individual so that the gun comes up naturally.

Weights and barrel lengths have varied. Present U.S.-imported models are standardized in reasonably wide choice. Model 200 has a 7½-inch barrel, thumb-rest grip, and 33-ounce trigger pull—just an ounce over the two-pound minimum for Standard American .22 rimfire pistol competition. Model 202 comes in an optional caliber, .22 short as well as long-rifle, has a 9½-inch barrel, custom grips, and 24-ounce pull— which is pleasantly light for an autoloader. Model 203, which can be had with adjustable custom-made grips at extra cost, has 7½-inch barrel, .22 long-rifle only, and 33-ounce trigger pull. Thumb-rest grips are standard all through, as on the Haemmerli single-shot.

Muzzle brakes or compensators, to fight the up-chuck of recoil, are of course standard, too; and there are also the adjustable weights for those who need any or all of them. These are becoming general issue on Olympic rapid-firers, including the Beretta, Star, Smith & Wesson, and Hi-Standard. Some shooters, including a number at the top, do better without the weights. It is good to have them to experiment with, not to pass the time, but to see if they will help to keep you within the exacting Olympic time limits of silhouette firing. Gun weights have run from about 26 to 57 ounces, complete.

Early Haemmerlis had elevation in the front sight, but now it's in the rear sight, along with windage, and finely adjustable. These changes are welcome, but some of our shooters may have to *learn* to like the European ideal trigger pull. It has been well described as "soft," not brittle like our good ones. There is no such abrupt break as ours have, but there is also no backlash, movement after the striker or hammer has been tripped—a motion that is thoroughly unpopular both here and over there.

Haemmerli .177 Match

This is a practice pistol that uses CO_2 gas for propellant. It is not as expensive as a fine target arm, which it really is within its limits, but it is rather expensive as a gas pistol. One Haemmerli model takes round lead balls; another takes balls or the waisted pellets of hour-glass shape.

Sights are click-adjustable; the gun has quality throughout, and it deserves good sights. It's intended for 10-meter indoor ranges (about 32.8 feet), at which it should poke 'em into a half-inch group or thereabout. That's shooting! Also to the good is the feel of the gun, so much like that of the Olympic rapid-fire Haemmerli.

JAPANESE HANDGUNS

A good many were brought here after World War II, but few of them seem to get any use, at least as compared to the 6.5 and 7.7 mm. rifles. Both of these, especially the better made 6.5, have served as-issued, or as gunsmith-altered, in hunting field and on target range. Sound, safe specimens are no longer hard to recognize, although they were until the various types had been sorted out. Since they are inexpensive they have provided many an amateur or skilled gunsmith with material to work on. As a result of this popu-

larity, imported Scandinavian-made cases and cartridges are easy to come by, and domestic jacketed .263 and .312 inch bullets as well as molds and loading tools.

Foreign military rifles naturally would be popular because of their cheapness on the used-gun market; but this doesn't apply to the handguns, unless they take American-made ammunition. Otherwise, they just don't seem worth the trouble, to the average shooter. These Japanese service pistols need special fodder.

The 1893 9 mm. revolver, Model 26, is a hard-pulling double-action sixshooter, usually, if not always made to fire with the long d. a. pull only, not thumb-cocked. For its power, that of a short .38, it's a heavy gun, over two pounds; it isn't what we'd call companionable. Except when a collector's piece it should sell for less than a good, used American gun.

It might be possible to handload ammo for this gun by working on .38 Short Colt or the larger-diameter .38 S.&W. brass. To accept it, the breech-face of the cylinder probably would need either filing-away or counterboring. A soft lead slug driven through the bore could report what bullet diameter would be needed for loading, and to be on the safe side, that loading ought to be with FFG black powder, I believe. Remember that old factory black powder loads in revolver sizes usually gave higher velocities to standard bullets than the smokeless charges did; but with stiff, experimental handloads of smokeless, very fine handguns have blown up. That was the price to pay for progress. In this research, low-grade arms just aren't worth monkeying with.

The Nambu 8 mm. 1914 semi-automatic, succeeded by the *Model 14* of 1925 as a simplified production model, shows the influence of the German Luger in shape and in caliber. The grip-slant makes for natural pointing, and the light barrel, usually about 4½ inches, is for quick shooting at close ranges, certainly not for deliberate fire. The gun is exceedingly muzzle-light. The caliber is small, about .32-inch, bullet weight around 100 grains, and muzzle velocity only about 860 f. s., low compared to the 1250 of the 7.65 and the 1120 of the 9 mm. Luger rounds our factories put up. The original Japanese bullet seems to have been standard in hard lead, usually more reliable in feeding an autopistol than soft lead. After Pearl Harbor, the change was made to jacketed lead.

On firing, the empties spin out from the top, as from Lugers and 1911 model Colts. This makes it a little easier to find them for reloading and is generally fine unless you fire from the hip and catch one in the face. This *sometimes* happens with the Colt when you shoot with extended arm, but so seldom that it hardly builds up into a mental hazard.

Cases and complete cartridges have been made here, and may be still available. The B. & E. Cartridge Company of Minneapolis turned cases out of brass and loaded them with bullets of solid copper (like old French 8 mm. Lebel rifle slugs). Using American small-size pistol primers, these hulls are reloadable. Osborne Klavestad, Highway 101-R, Shakopee, Minnesota is the distributor. Frank Miles of Bedford, Virginia, makes turned brass cases of almost any type.

The Nambu locking system is good in itself, but the gun *can* be assembled minus the lock! Like the Ross high-power rifles of some models, it is not for an unfamiliar operator.

Model 1914 rear sights have been supplied with elevation adjustments, which could mean something even on this muzzle-light gun when a shoulder stock was used. A grip safety lies just below the rear of the trigger guard.

Model 14 or 1925 has no grip safety, but a magazine safety prevents firing when that "clip" is out. Its manual safety is above the left-hand stock. In general, it isn't as good a job as the 1914 gun.

Model 94 of 1934 looks like little Philbert's water pistol that Teacher done took and locked in her desk. But it's a killer. The sear is exposed on the left side of the receiver. Press on the front end and the gun, if loaded, fires. The manual safety lies at the rear, above the left grip.

It seems to have been designed as a cheap export item, and an odd number it surely is. The grip is very short, though well slanted, and the recoil spring encircles the barrel. Result, an ungainly bulk above the shooter's hand. Its cartridge is the Japanese service 8 mm. With the short 3 1/8-inch M94 barrel, the velocity, never really high, is reduced below that of the Nambu gun.

Officer's Model Nambu 7 mm. pocket autos resemble the Model 1914, not the Model 14, 8 mm. arms, with grip safety and good workmanship. They were for the top brass, but some were exported. Barrel length is 3¼ inches, and weight 20 ounces, with practically all of that weight in the firing hand—muzzle-light indeed.

The 7 mm. cartridge is a curiosity. Bottle-necked like the 8 mm., it shoots a 56 grain bullet and has actual killing power somewhere between the .25 and .32 Colt Auto. By comparison the 8 mm. falls between the .32 S.&W. Long and the .32-20. Please see the cartridge index in the back of this book for reference to the 7 mm. Japanese. Bert Shay has made it in limited numbers. He tells how to do it, and the text is illustrated.

LAHTI

This Finnish-designed gun, used in Finland and Sweden, resembles in outline the much lighter Luger. It weighs 43 ounces. The 4⅝-inch barrel is screwed rigidly into the slide, Luger fashion. Its short-recoil locking system is entirely different.

Its caliber is 9 mm. Luger, and it will take heavy loads—though that's no guarantee against the results of abuse. It's a fine, strong, expensively made autoloader, and few of them have reached here. In its weight class, a much more powerful American handgun could be carried, of bigger bore and more deadly.

LEBEL

See "French Handguns."

LILLIPUT

This midget has blow-back action, not locked or needing to be locked. Its parts are relatively simple and not hard for a good gunsmith to copy. The barrel is integral to the frame.

It's really tiny, about 3½ inches overall and weighing some six ounces, approximate heft of some of the fine, century-old pocket watches with snap-shut "hunting" cases. The 14-grain 4.25 mm. bullet is credited with 800 f.s. velocity—50-grain Colt .25 has 820—and the report is practically as noisy. From such a short barrel we should expect it to be.

LLAMA

See "Gabilondo."

LUGER

A good gun if you understand it.

There has been tremendous variety in styles, and in quality. Collectors search for unusual, rare, or possibly even unique Lugers, and such prizes are to be found. Many a practical pistol shooter is tempted by the name and reputation of the world-distributed Luger, which has been used in the past by more governments than any other handgun. If he buys one, it will almost certainly be in used-gun condition, for almost none are being made now except a special job occasionally put together in some part of its German homeland. The best Lugers are splendid, regardless of whether or not an individual shooter likes the type; the poorest, assembled most likely from junk parts, are not safe to fire.

Varieties

The common calibers are the .30 or 7.65 mm. and the 9 mm., which is closely similar to our .38 Special in bullet diameter. Just as with the Special, barrel bore and rifling groove diameters vary a good bit. It pays the handloader to measure his Luger barrel with a lead slug driven through it, then get a mold and sizing die that help him approach the correct barrel groove diameter. For a Luger can really shoot! Its barrel is screwed into the slide, and that slide is fitted closely to the receiver runways. A Luger sloppily made in this respect is uncommon.

Lugers made in .45 Auto Colt caliber for our early Government tests, before the 1911 Colt had won the competition, are rare—definitely collectors' items. Standard caliber Lugers, 7.65 and 9, have been made in Germany, Switzerland and England, at least. Now the Swiss have their own SP 47-8 pistol, a modified Browning with barrel enclosed in the slide. Britain likes the Model 35 Browning, another good choice. German manufacturers of the Luger included the famous and often preferred D.W.M. (Deutsche Waffen und Munitionen—German Arms and Ammo), the Erfurt royal arsenal, Krieghoff, Mauser and Simmons.

The D.W.M. monogram is as hard to decipher as any other stacked-up and hammered-down initials I know of, until you become familiar with it. Then it's hailed as a sign, but not a sure sign, of quality. Many old Lugers made for export here bore the American Eagle stamp on the breech, and some later good jobs were marked "A. F. Stoeger" on the side.

Some Lugers, especially early ones, had a grip safety, easy and soft to compress as you held the gun, but still a hazard of a sort. It was possible for some little thing like a twig or bit of shale to get under this grip safety and prevent its being squeezed in. On some guns there is a lug near the bottom rear of the butt, meant for the attachment of a shoulder stock. Until recently, it was necessary to grind this off if you wanted your handgun to be legal—free of the $200 tax that was imposed on a "firearm." This lug did no practical harm; it didn't affect the good fit of the Luger grip.

The operation of the manual safety, the lever at the left rear of the breech, is important indeed. Some go up for safe; some go down. The former is better—to throw the safe you simply snap the lever down, 1911 .45 Colt fashion; but it's not quite as handy. The receiver may be stamped "Safe" or Gesichert," which translate to *real* safety, in the Luger. Notice how that flat bar of steel rises and blocks the sear from moving to the left, as you squeeze the trigger, and thus releasing the striker.

Notice too the loaded-chamber indicator, the extractor blade at the front of the breech-block. When cartridge-case metal is under it, it rises into plain view or easy feeling. Is it marked "Geladen" or is it the "Loaded" translation? English markings on the side of the extractor or under the safety lever ordinarily mean that the gun bearing them was for shipment to countries where people speak English, but the history of the Luger is so checkered, so varied and mystifying that you seldom can be sure of anything.

Quality

Some Lugers are dated, stamped with the year, and that may give us at least fairly reliable information. I never heard of a poor pre-1914 one, and those from 1914-16 are usually good—from Mons and Ypres to the Somme, we might say, and Germany was winning then. So too, as nearly all of us recall, she was winning in the first years of the 1939-45 war. Bombing had hardly hit her arms production.

But mostly you study the gun's condition. Fine finish, a deep and glossy blue, almost implies a good Luger. What an understatement! Most of us do well to see one or two like that in a lifetime. But plenty of safe and reliable Lugers had a finish not quite silky even when new, and most of the other kind, the undesirable or the downright dangerous one, seem to have been pretty gray and sad in their outside appearance. Most of the good stocks were dark-brown walnut, though other materials were used, and need not condemn the gun. The magazine butt or floorplate was walnut, too, hollowed for thumb and finger grasp. As time went on and fine wood became scarce, the plastic butts appeared. They too need not mean a poor gun.

Don't expect a light, clean trigger pull, for the Luger firing mechanism is complicated. A really good gunsmith can reduce most of the long, creepy Luger trigger's takeup, and make the final stage short and almost clean. Probably that's about the best that can be done, and it's enough to permit fine shooting.

We judge bore condition, smoothness of action, and so on, just as in any other automatic pistol. But about the fit of the slide in the frame. I think, we should be unusually critical. The Luger has its faults and limitations; but one thing just as important and unusual as its easy natural pointing for quick short-range work, is its ability to perform at long range. This comes not only from flat-shooting ammunition with very light recoil; it is also due to the tight assembly of the moving parts, which we should insist upon getting if we want the full value of usefulness from our Luger. With the action closed, the breech-block forward and down—not back and arched up like a cat's back—grasp the barrel and check it for wiggle, or rather; check the slide for that, since the barrel's firmly screwed into it. That tuning-fork slide—yes, it can almost double for that instrument—must fit the receiver with the least allowable play. Some is necessary, of course, for sure functioning. By the way, these grooves should be oiled or else cold-weather lubricated.

If your Luger bore and chamber are good, and the slide fit as snug as it should be, that pistol will really reach out and make hits if you hold it right. Time and again, this has been done in the hunting field, in law-enforcement jobs, and probably in war. Use both hands, one steadying the other, not both trying to clasp the gun, and get the sights as far from your eye as possible so that they will show up clearly.

Along this line is the use of a Luger sling or thong, if you like it, and many do. The anchorage is that little crosswise bar at the breech, facing your eye as you line up the gun on a target. A rawhide sling run through it could ensure possession of the Luger when you ride a horse, or when you bullet a canoe through white water. It's also used in shooting. Pass it around the back of your neck and hold it hard with the nonfiring hand. Or, as Elmer Keith instructs on page 98 of his *Sixguns,* make a loop of the sling; pass it behind your neck; and with *both hands* extended and holding the Luger, push forward against the tension of the loop.

For me, the breech location of the Luger's thong bar or swivel seems just right for use with a shooting sling. It is closer to the gun's center of gravity than a ring or swivel down near the bottom of the butt. Down there, it's fine for a retaining sling. If the gun flies out of the holster or pocket, you slide your hand down the leather and there at the end is the grip of the pistol, which you may be rather anxious to get at.

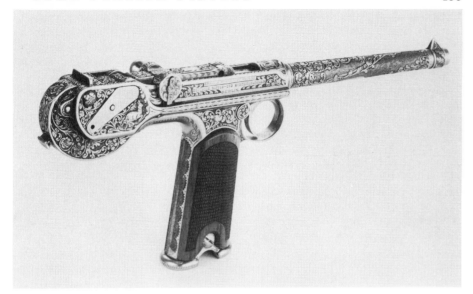

A DWM, Berlin manufactured Borchardt pistol bearing the superb engraving of E. C. Prudhomme, 305 Ward Bldg., Shreveport, La. Photo courtesy of Mr. Prudhomme.

If your interest in the Luger pistol is more scholarly than practical, or if you are at all interested in it, Fred A. Datig's book, *The Luger Pistol, Its History and Development from 1893 to 1945,* should be your reading. It starts with the Borchardt, that pioneer autoloader that used its long, special .30 caliber cartridge much like the .30 Mauser, and goes on down through Luger variants. But your interest in the Luger should not be purely investigative, if I may say so, because it is extremely interesting to shoot. Almost everyone's first reaction, even with one of those stubby 3⅝-inch barrel specimens, seems to be "It shoots like a .32-20 rifle." That's nearly true, but it does other intriguing things, too.

A Luger Is for Shooting

We don't allude to the "snail" or drum magazines of 32-shot nominal capacity—better to put in fewer rounds for sure feeding—that made Lugers some of the earliest of all sub-machine guns. (They figured in World War I, but we'd not want one if we could legally have one.) What we do mean is practical shooting such as you and I do on occasion.

The Luger has gone to far parts of the earth with hunters and explorers. It is light and compact, and so is its ammunition. The killing power on body shots is poor unless vital spots are hit, for its bullets make a long, narrow wound. Bones are more likely to be drilled than broken by them. But since they reach deep, they have been used a good deal to finish heavy game downed with a rifle, head shots of course, and to save excess mutilation or just to save the rifle ammunition. Its bullets are not good small game killers unless they are placed right; they slip through, doing little immediate damage, allowing the bird or animal to escape and die miserably much later.

Since the Luger is a rater delicate arm in some ways, with small, finely made parts, we need to study our specimens as individuals. Be quick to favor a good one, old or modern.

In the 1930s, when the Remington 124 grain 9 mm. bullet went to about 1150 f. s. velocity, some dealers warned us that it was too strong for the breech-block—and that part, with its attachments, really is a more elaborately machined than rugged job. Now the same bullet is catalogued at 1120 f. s. from a 4-inch barrel, hardly any real difference. We realize that those dealers had been protecting themselves, sensibly, for some of the Lugers that came here after World War I were pretty shoddy.

Our present U. S.-made ammo should be safe in sound Lugers, although even the good guns have had minor injuries from too hot handloads. Foreign sub-machine stuff may go to about 1500 f. s. velocity, and only a few late-model pistols are strong enough to take it with absolute safety. On the other hand, weak loads can jam strong-springed guns, though coils of a modern Luger recoil spring can be cut off—not just like that, snip-snip, but by small degrees and cautiously—if the gun won't perk with U. S. ammunition (which some Luger fans call almost ultra-conservative loading). New, strong, high-quality springs can be installed in old guns so well made that they deserve the updating.

However, there's a better way, I believe. It certainly should apply to the Lugers with flat recoil spring, made until about 1906. You recognize these guns, usually, though Lugers are of an interestingly individualized breed, by the shape of the knurled grasping studs at the hump-up joint of the toggle-locking breech-block. Instead of being round as on the modern and most commonly seen Lugers, these studs—rather, the milled faces of them—are less than half-round on the old-timers. Only the front part is knurled.

The way to feed any good but early-vintage firearm that may be of even slightly doubtful strength for modern ammo is to handload for it. It is possible to buy empty cases, primed, or unprimed if you want them to come by mail. Then you have the basic stuff. The primers, powders and bullets are comparatively easy.

My 9 mm. Luger, a war relic I bought in 1927, digested even soft lead bullets. They shot cleanly, and being of the Ideal flat-point or original Luger contour, they expanded to a very considerable degree. If such soft, uncrimped bullets are driven back into the cases when they strike the top of the chamber, as some do on their trip into the barrel, an Ideal shell indentor might hold them in place, even though the brass is thick. However, I had no such trouble, those bullets held well in neck-sized brass. You can crimp the .30 Luger brass on lead bullets because that cartridge case is bottle-necked. The 9 mm. Luger is straight; it has to get its positioning or headspacing in the chamber by the bluff squareness of its thick, uncrimped mouth. A bottle-neck does the same thing, and reliably, as long as the shoulder below the neck doesn't shift.

I like lead bullets in an auto-pistol that has rifling lands deep enough to take a deep bite into them, and Lugers usually do have such lands. It is particularly easy to fit the handload to the gun when you cast and size your own bullets. But at the other end of the dog-run is the practice of using whatever loads you latch on to.

Military 9 mm. burp-gun cartridges may (or may not) have black cases and sintered (compressed dust) iron bullets of about 100 grains' weight. There's no special need to pull this slug and weigh it: just weigh a standard 115 or 125 grain bullet load against it, or use a magnet. Foreign Luger rounds marked "Beschuss" are for proof-firing, and powerful indeed. There are not many ammunition booby-traps in .30 Luger caliber. Probably all the husky carbine loads, some of which came close to 2,000 f. s. speed from the longer barrels, had blackened cases. They used to be available here, but they aren't now, as far as I know. The carbine really was a pistol with a shoulder stock and a wooden forearm.

Sub-Caliber Adapters

The Erma insert barrel for the tiny 4 mm. round-ball cartridge was a single-shot affair for the front parlor—blinds drawn in states with virulent anti-pistol laws—was made before World War II. It's scarce and not particularly practical now. That cartridge, by the way, was like the .30 Luger in getting its headspace from a sharp bottle-neck; it had no rim at all, and you punched out the empty with a rod.

Later came the Erma .22 adapter, carrying ten long-rifle rounds in its magazine. There is a special magazine for them, and the semi-automatic action comes from a special breech-block with recoil mechanism. What's more, this adapter has a hold-open device that leaves the breech open after the last shot has gone. Some of the standard Lugers have this device.

What Makes Lugers Popular?

They are *still* popular, and for use as well as to round out a collection. For one thing, they have a romantic appeal. Some of us, including this one, think there is nothing very romantic about war, but there's the other side of Luger service, the wilderness these guns saw and continue to see.

OK. Unless your hand is on the small side, they feel good and point naturally. When they are up to normal they shoot accurately—and very flat, of course. With a two-hand hold and a good sit you can really lay them in from a Luger, if ever you have to. As you fire, the empties whirl madly out the top of the receiver, glinting in the sunlight, if there is any, and they land a fairly even two feet behind you, not all over the proverbial half-acre.

So generally you can pick up the brass, and you will want to. It's strong and good to reload, and the straight-case 9 is seldom much, if any, off standard length. I for one never had to trim a Luger case. They are very good cartridges still; they must be. The .30 dates to about 1900, the 9 to 1902, pretty close to the time of the .38 Colt Automatic, another light, compact woods load that serves when a small or medium bore can.

We have mentioned the Luger's poor trigger pull, badly muzzle-light balance for precision one-hand shooting, and small, delicate working parts—though very few break down in service if they were good to start with. Yes, the grip is too big for small hands—at least in one-hand shooting—and the huge bulge at the breech disqualifies this gun for pocket use.

It has a bad reputation for jamming, which is strange for so popular a military pistol; still, it can do it. When your .45 Colt fails, you generally know why, if you live to find out. But I think that Lugers are a little less predictable, less understandable. It is not their light ammunition that makes them—most of them, at least—a bit uncertain, for the .38 Auto Colt is but a little heavier, and those guns, old or modern, do right by you, each with its moderate or souped-up factory ammo.

"Would you trust your life to it?" is a question that makes a Luger owner and admirer squirm, or so it affects me. To say, "Well, I'd rather not." Is hardly a flat-out answer!

MANURHIN

These French pistols are made by the Manufacture de Machines du Haut-Rhin as legitimate copies of pre-World War II German Walther autoloaders, the pocket model PP or police pistol. The caliber of 7.65 Browning or .32 Colt, and the small size of the PP, seem acceptable to French military thinking, at least for not too exacting service. The bigger, heavier Star and Ruby, both Spanish-made, use this light ammunition, too. After all, the 1892 8 mm. Lebel revolver is practically a .32. It succeeded, more or less, the models 73 and 74 sixguns in 11 mm., which fired a bullet of about the same diameter as our .44 Special

The Manurhin Walther copy has, of course, the double-action feature that makes geeting off the first shot so quick and easy. It's safe to carry the gun with hammer down and safety off, but still ready to fire by a long pull on the trigger. A magazine extension for the little finger, Walther fashion, makes the little pistol a fair handful in spite of its small size. These Manurhins may not, all of them, equal the best pre-war Walther jobs, but they are sound—and they are being made. Streamlined like the Walther, they are good for pocket or small holster carry, and they point well.

MAUSER

Possibly the Mauser name is almost as famous in connection with pistols as with rifles, at least in military if not in sporting circles. Sometimes we forget how great the Mauser influence is. For instance, the 1888 8x57 mm. (caliber and case length in millimeters) German Army cartridge fathered a long line of military and hunting rounds, including our fairly recent .243, .244, .308 and .358 hunting sizes. The casehead of the old 1888 is rimless, grooved, and giving the jaws of the *1898* Mauser-and-descendants charger clips a good bite, and the claw of the extractor a good purchase in hauling out the fired, empty brass. This case-head size, with some changes in the width and/or depth of the extractor groove or cannelure, has persisted for good reason or no reason in a long array of hunting and military sizes.

Mauser Military 1896

This big old gun, clumsy to carry and to hold though it may be, was one of the first really good, proved, not merely experimental or hopeful semi-auto pistol designs. Now, after more than a half century or so, it is like the Luger in being too expensive to make for reasonable profit. Excellent design and equally good machining got around the need for screws or even drive-in pins, although there is one screw, to hold the stock on.

It's well-known that Winston Churchill as a young man carried one of these then-new Mausers into the battle of Omdurman against savage and determined tribesmen; and with it, he shot his way out of a pocket. Let's remember that the small-caliber, deeply-penetrating Mauser pistol bullets do not kill quickly unless they are placed right. The future Sir Winston must have been reasonably expert and fast with that handgun, and as for his coolness and courage—well, the world was to know of those attributes later, for unquestionably they helped to mold history's course.

In his five-volume history of World War II, Churchill told of England's meeting the 1940 fall of France and the real and present threat of invasion. You recall "We will fight on the beaches, we will fight in the streets . . .," and that war-cry directed to his people, "Each one kill one." Look in the book and read and admire his comment on having examined his own firearms, which, incidentally, he found in good condition. I've often wondered whether or not the Mauser pistol was still among them. How would you bet?

The big, outlandish Mauser Military was used—not officially, but used—in First and Second World Wars,

where it was common in 9mm. Luger caliber, to ease ammunition supply. A red "9" carved into its stock identifies this soldier. The Mauser's own calibers were the still fairly common .30 or 7.63, catalogued 403, and the long 9 mm., No. 487. That Mauser 9 is longer than the powerful 9 mm. Steyr, No. 577, which fires a 116-grain bullet at about 1200 f. s., rather close to the old, light factory loading of the 130-grain .38 Colt. The 7.63 Mauser and 9 mm. Luger are made here, with the latter common on store shelves since the War, and the Borchardt .30 or 7.65 isn't much different from the .30 Mauser.

Standard Mauser Military magazines hold ten rounds, though less and greater capacity mags were made. Some tens were detachable, some built-in as on the early models; but all can be loaded fast with 10-shot stripper clips like those five-shotters you use for your Springfield in rapid or "sustained" fire (a better name, that one) if you use that bolt action rifle instead of an M1 Garand. The Enfield .30-06 also takes our 5-shot clips, though its mag holds an extra round if you want it. (Sometime you might want it!) The Mauser magazine, ahead of the trigger guard, in effect lengthens the gun's overall; but so what?

The usual Mauser with 5½-inch barrel is a foot long and weighs about 45 ounces. Barrels have been made up to 12 inches, at least, and shoulder stocks, such as hollowed-out wooden holsters, were and are used often. With these, a 12-inch barrel would be a comforting proboscis indeed, for the .30 Mauser is a barker. Naturally we should not want a burp-gun Mauser pistol, with that selector switch to convert it to full-automatic fire; and the shoulder stock would make the gun taxable, too.

There have been many copies. Spain and China turned out a good many, including the Chinese-made monster for the .45 Auto Colt cartridge. Some copies are good, some bad. The exact Mauser system isn't always copied.

A good Mauser in 7.63 or in 9 mm. Luger caliber is quite a gun. The long 9 mm. Mauser cartridge has been well liked in South America, though it is hardly ever seen up here. Certainly the pistol is heavy and awkward, and the round grip can cause it to twist in your hand, even though the recoil of its light-bullet rounds is naturally slight, in such a heavy weapon. But sometimes a high-velocity handgun has its uses. Some foreign .30 Mauser loadings have reached about 1600 f.s., though ours are 1410 with the 85 or 86 grain metal cased, "hard-point" bullets. It may be and probably is a decidedly poor one-hand pistol for most of us, but fired two-handed it is something almost unique. (Except in serious business, you'd want ear-plugs when firing it so.) The old Militaries were sighted from 50 to *1,000* meters. Anything smaller than a phone booth, at any range over 300 yards, would be highly optimistic for most shooters; but in go-light wilderness travel, this gun with its compact ammunition just could be mighty obliging to a far-wanderer. Many Mausers—like

Lugers, Colts, Smiths and Webleys—have been to wild places, and still go.

Although the hammer fall is long and heavy, it shouldn't disturb a sitting, prone or slouched-down shooter, as it does a one-hander also bent on accuracy. As a long-shooting handgun it is much, much more for defense than for game-getting, for its small-caliber bullets do not have the instant killing power we need even for light, skillet-size game. The little, needley pellets must be placed just right to anchor what we hit.

Mauser H SC

By contrast to the Mauser Military, the H SC is a late, streamlined pocket auto, caliber 7.65 or .32, weighing about 21 ounces, near-average for its type. It is double-action, like the Walther, and has a small-spurred hammer in plain view. The frame ahead of the guard flows forward almost to the muzzle in an unbroken line, for looks and possibly also for easy pocketing or holstering. Its thumb safety is on the left side of the breech, not low down on the receiver. This safe pushes the firing pin out of the hammer's path and disconnects the sear and hammer engagement.

Like the Walther, it does not have 100% machined parts, but for the amount of firing a pocket gun usually gets this implies no serious weakness. It's a common form of construction today, even in some heavy-duty firearms.

The slide stays back after the last round has been fired, but goes forward as quick as a wink when the magazine is returned. A magazine safety prevents firing when the mag is out; not an unmixed blessing, but popular because it can help prevent accidents when people unfamiliar with guns get hold of them. It is so easy to pull out a magazine and forget the round in the chamber.

Some of us would vote for a slimmer and more raked-back grip, but all in all this pocket Mauser is a good, shootable pistol in its class. It is of course a straight blow-back, not a locked-breech auto, and that is as it should be in .25, .32 or .380 calibers unless a pin-weight gun handles them. With some weight in the slide or breech-block the springs don't have to do it all.

Earlier Mauser Pocket Guns

These come in a variety of models, not so often seen here now as autoloaders of the later crops. The 1910, its slide cut away at top and showing a good bit of barrel, lean and hungry-looking, was made in .25 and .32 caliber, and some .25s were at least as late as a Model 1919. One Mauser .25 was about the only pistol of that caliber that was big enough to permit good shooting. As far as accuracy goes, there's nothing natively wrong with that little cartridge. Put it in a handgun larger than palm-size and it does all right. There were standard dwarf-sized Mauser .25s, too; and they are long-established and sell well enough. Between having one of those and no gun at all, an instant and easy choice is made, and there's no excuse for leaving it at home because it's too heavy to lug!

Some of these early Mausers were made to close— let the breech-block slide run home—as soon as an empty or loaded mag was put in. Anyone careless enough to be holding back on the trigger thereupon fired the gun if even one round had been slid into the magazine. This was bad, and it could be tragic. Some did have a safety that prevented firing when no magazine was in the gun, and that helped in another form of semi-consciousness on the user's part.

A 1934 model of .32 had, like some earlier ones, a one-piece wooden stock, not split in half in the usual fashion, but the shape was changed, fortunately, to give a more hand-fitting grip. Some of these arms have springs that break rather easily, or at least won't stand much abuse.

The button-and-latch safety is ingenious. Pushing down the latch depresses the button below it and makes the gun safe. To get ready instantly, just press the button. There have been quieter safety catches, but few quicker ones. Two-handed, you can ease that one off silently. The pin or striker end protruding at the breech when the gun is cocked is easy to see or feel. Some indicators of this type are dangerous, if only remotely so. If the weapon fell and the pin struck precisely on a rock or a hard, flat surface, the striker could let go all holds and fire the weapon. I have read of this happening with an exposed-hammer Colt .38 auto, but how, I just can't figure out, for the gun was said to be on half-cock. In that position, the hammer is close to the firing pin—which is of the floating or inertia variety, so short that when the hammer is down the pin doesn't touch the primer—and the hammer needs nearly all its full arc of fall to deliver the necessary blow. After all these years I'm still wondering. Could it be that you needn't believe all you see in print?

MELIOR

A description in the April, 1956, *American Rifleman* gave these Belgian-proofed pre-war and post-war pistols small praise. They were classed as roughly made and finished, stiff in operation, and downright unreliable except in the .380 sample. Other calibers are .25 and .32, the former with a long barrel for its class, 2⁷⁄₁₆ inches. The 3⅝-inch barreled .32 and .380 go about 21 ounces in weight, the .25 about 14—all close to normal.

They came from the Manufacturers' Import Company, 409-R East 12th Street, Los Angeles 15. If they are still being brought in we might find them considerably improved, for the *Rifleman* is widely read and exerts a good deal of influence on both suppliers and consumers of arms and ammunition of sporting variety.

The Melior design has a rather straight grip, not slanted much, and magazine capacity isn't exceptional, six rounds in .25 and .380, seven in .32. The recoil spring goes around the barrel, and this barrel-enclosing part of the slide appears rather large and stubby. The prices were moderate.

NAGANT

The Russian 1895 service revolver is patterned more or less after an 1890 Belgian Pieper. The cylinder, holding seven special 7.62 mm. cartridges, hitches forward, the breech or recoil plate backing it, as the hammer goes back. Each chamber is recessed up front, and this recess fits around the barrel breech, thus more or less sealing off gas escape at what in a normal revolver is the barrel-cylinder gap. As further help, the front of the long cartridge case protrudes from the cylinder face, and when the cylinder is shucked forward for firing, the case brass is inside the barrel's throat.

To add to the freakishness of this 7.62 or .30 revolver cartridge, the bullet doesn't stick out of the case mouth, or even lie flush with it. It's denned up behind the opening. In the old .38-.44 and .32-.44 Smith & Wessons the lead bullets of full-power black powder loads were even with the case-mouths. This did make sense with the .38, for its case was full cylinder length, and the lead had only a short hop from brass into rifling throat. The .32-.44—well, it was built just like its bigger and taller brother; and in single shot target pistols this made sense. It did not in the revolvers, of which Colt's made some, too, for their cylinders were too long, and the lead had to travel that extra distance before it hit the rifling.

In accuracy, reliability and power the 7.62 Nagants fell far below the breakdown Smiths in .44 Russian caliber, sold to the Tsar in the 1870s and along after. However, some people, perhaps the politicos, must have liked the klucks, for they were made in both single and double action, and some of them as late as the early part of World War II. Belgian Piepers, too, were made in the same caliber for Russia's armies. They are a little lighter, and they lack—which is just as well—the cylinder-shrug feature that is supposed to seal in power and make the gun a killer.

This cartridge sends a 108 grain bullet, lead or jacketed, at about 725 f. s. velocity. A standard rating of the .32 Colt New Police is 785 f. s. for a 98 grain bullet. That is no military round, and very few informed policemen would restrict themselves to such low handgun power. Both Nagant and Pieper 7.62 revolvers have the slow rod-ejection of empties, one at a time.

NAMBU

See "Japanese Handguns."

NEUHAUSEN

See "SIG."

OBREGON

This is the official Mexican pistol, 11.43 mm., the .45 Colt Auto caliber, and a well-made arm. It's a bit simpler than the Colt 1911, with fewer parts and a different locking system. The barrel breech doesn't swing down as in the Colt, but rotates after the first opening movement, when locked to the slide, so that its two big lugs on top swing out of alignment with the cuts in the top of the slide. This does necessitate an unlocking cam on the bottom of the barrel, which hardly simplifies barrel manufacture.

The slide is smooth and flat, as on the Colt, but abruptly tapered on the sides, not the same width full-length. After the last shot the slide stays open.

The Steyr-Hahn 9 mm. auto of 1911 (same year as our Government Colt .45) had a somewhat similar rotating-barrel design. However, it was loaded from the top, with a clip, instead of using detachable magazines. The Savage 1906 .45 candidate for U. S. adoption also had a rotating-barrel lock, sometimes called a "hesitation lock," in classifying it, and so did the once popular .32 and .380 Savages.

ORIENTAL COPIES

At this date the Asiatics, in general, are handicapped in mass-production machining of fine precision. But there are a lot of them, and in the East time means less than it does here. They have made many copies of the old German Mauser Military 7.63 mm., and some in .45 Auto Colt caliber, too.

In some cases the Chinese, like the Russians, have been clever by skipping some milling jobs through making slight changes in the original assemblies. For instance, in the Russian Tokarev autoloader 7.62, using a cartridge much like that of the 7.63 Mauser pistol, the barrel ribs that engage cuts in the top of the slide are not milled off at sides and bottom, as on the Colt. This saves time. The fact that ribs are needed only at the top of the barrel doesn't mean a thing.

Copies extend to bigger arms, too, such as machine guns. Few of us would want an Oriental copy of any weapon except as a curiosity. This is the general situation at this writing.

ORTGIES

Rather fine German-made pocket autos under this name were popular during the first half or more of the 1920s, but are seldom seen now. Other makes have crowded them out.

Like the American Savages, they had no screws staring at you—none at all, really, for the Ortgies stocks were held on by snaps concealed in the magazine well. The stocks were of smooth, well polished wood, and the general finish was excellent. These little pistols compared well with the best standard-grade American opposite numbers of that time.

Both the .32 and the scaled-down .25 were easy to shoot, in their class, having a grip-slant that was correct for most of us. The .380s came last and were slightly different internally. Some of them had a thumb safety in addition to the squeezer grip safety, which alone the others had.

For those days, the Ortgies design was simple. For example, the firing pin served as the ejector, which it does on comparatively few arms. Another that does make its firing pin do double duty is the 1909 Remington .22 pump gun, Model 12. But when the Model 121 revision came along in 1936, a change was made, even though the Model 12 had hung up a somewhat better than average durability record.

PICKERT

In general, these old German revolvers are similar to the Arminius, described before. They are of only fair quality—even for their times—and today they would be of value only to a collector of European arms, not to a practical shooter.

That last is a casual statement, not quite correct. Some of us who love pistols and want to shoot them either for fun or for practical purposes simply do not have unlimited funds with which to arm ourselves. Some of us, though young, have to earn our spending money, not just ask for it. Old cartridges like the .32 and .38 Short Colt with outside lubricated lead bullets are still made, at this writing. Even though they are factory loaded with smokeless powder, black powder having almost disappeared from factory listings, they are charged so moderately that they should be safe to fire in reasonably sound old arms which they fit correctly. These loads correspond closely to the .320 and .380 British pocket-gun cartridges.

Naturally, this writer and the publishing company cannot accept responsibility for any trouble resulting from any practices that are hinted at here. *The individual gun* needs close, skilled examination of its condition, quality, and adaptation to any ammunition that may be fired in it.

PIEPER

A very early development of a solid frame revolver was Pieper made in large quantities for Russia. Later the Russians made many of their own, the Nagants, with some changes from the Pieper design. These used the 7.62 mm. or .30-inch cartridge, but Pieper revolvers made for Norway took a different round, a 7.5 mm. Although the Nagant shoves its cylinder forward as the hammer is cocked, cupping the front of the cylinder around the barrel breech, the Pieper is a conventional revolver that simply turns its cylinder.

This make is seldom seen now, though it once was fairly well known. An interesting form of Pieper .22 single-shot training pistol was a blow-back auto-ejector. On firing, the breech-block went back, extracting the empty case and throwing it out. The same idea was developed by Webley & Scott in England. W. & S. made conventional .22 rimfire single-shot .22 pistols, too, and both firms put out a variety of handguns. Those mentioned in this chapter section have little practical use for most of us.

RADOM

Radom 9 mm. Luger caliber automatics were brought back and exhibited with great pride by some of our G.I.s, and no wonder. The gun is named after the Radom arsenal in Poland, or called VIS, or P-35 by the Germans, who made it with some changes, after occupying Poland.

The hammer spur is small and rounded, in European fashion, and there is no thumb safety. However, there is a grip safety, and a thumb-operated release drops the cocked hammer into the half-cock or safety notch, at least on early models. During the latter part of World War II the general quality went down under the stresses that many German factories suffered. Some late Radoms have neither a grip safe nor a hammer-dropping device. Some have, and some haven't, a thumb-piece at the left rear of the frame, to press to send the slide forward after it has stayed open from the recoil of the last cartridge fired.

Weight of 30 ounces, barrel length of 4⅝ inches, and magazine capacity of eight rounds are close to old Luger vital statistics, though the gun itself is entirely different. Its grip is larger at bottom than up high and it does not have quite the rearward slant of the Luger. Both are guns for fairly large hands. pointing well and naturally when held in such hands. The Radom is better hung for deliberate, aimed fire, because its long, heavy Browning-type slide puts weight at the muzzle.

The Radom has more than accidental resemblance to the 1935 Browning, but its magazine is single-column, not double-ranked. This makes for a normal rather than a too-fat grip for folks with average-sized hands. There is certainly nothing freakish about its appearance, or the Browning's either.

A good specimen is a fine gun, especially a well-preserved pre-war job. Design and materials chum-up, in almost if not quite all instances, to produce a strong weapon that should handle any sensible 9 mm. Luger loading. There's no sense in buying or handloading little bombs to stuff into it to see what it will take! Gun strength is for reassurance and long service, whether the arm be a military pistol, a big game rifle, a beautifully balanced double-barrel shotgun, or anything else.

RUBY

See "French Handguns," also "Gabilondo," for there are two sorts of handguns carrying the Ruby name.

SAUER

The Sauer firm has been famous for generations. Up to about 1915 or so, Schoverling, Daly & Gales of New York featured the Sauer-Mauser sporting rifles as being among the first long-range, bolt-action, high-intensity arms commercially available here. The calibers listed could almost have come from a modern cataloguing: 7, 8, and 9 mm. Mauser with 57-millimeter case length, and the .30-06 Springfield.

The rifles were beautiful in workmanship and finish. Except for stock combs and forearms on the thin side, they are shootable under even today's marksmanship standards. But then, you can find such stocks today, whittled down to starvation lines to save a few ounces.

Sauer has long been famous for auto-pistols, too. *The Roth-Sauer* fired a special 7.65 mm. cartridge, similar to the .32 Colt, but shorter. Winchester loaded it with a 71-grain full-metal-patched bullet as compared to the .32 with 74-grain full-patch or soft-nosed, as late as 1914, although the gun had gone out of production about 1910. This Hungarian patented job was a locked-breech, not a blow-back semi-automatic, but the recoiling slide did not cock the striker. The double-action trigger did that. It was a long-recoil action, the barrel going back with the breech-block, much as with the still fairly well-known Remington high-power auto-loading rifle of 8 or 81 models, 1906 or 1937 models. The Roth-Sauer now would be called an odd-looking little pistol, with its curved, flat grip, hardly suitable for easy, sure pointing. Cases for it could be made from .32 A.C.P.—Auto Colt Pistol—except for the oddity of the primer pocket. This was deep, the primer seated well below flush with the case-head surface. On firing, the primer was supposed to bounce back in the brass pocket and actuate the return of the barrel.

Obviously that gun would be of little use to any of us, perhaps excepting the experimenter, but other, later Sauers might be. Sauer & Sohn .25s or 6.35 mms. came in various types, usually with 6-shot magazine, though one model held seven. Some had a removable breech-block in the slide. This made for simpler machining, more or less typical of Sauers, but for an essentially complicated design, too. Except for the lack of grip safeties, these little pistols are close to the Browning-Colt in form.

The 7.65s or .32s are blow-backs like the .25s and with rounded, not flat, slides. Model 1913 is unusual in the method of breech-block removal: i.e., push down on the rear sight and unscrew the block! A later model, much used by police, had a rounded grip, not so square at the butt, and some had dural slides and receivers for lightness. Sauers made in peacetime, at any rate, are almost sure to be good.

However, a *World War II designed and made* Sauer .32 is usually well made, and it has attractive features: double-action trigger, hold-open slide, magazine release button on frame behind trigger, the barrel fixed solidly into receiver for accuracy, good balance and grip. Add the ribbed sighting plane, a magazine safety, and thumb safety high on the left rear of the slide, to block the hammer and, for good measure, disconnect it from the sear. A cocking lever behind the trigger but above the magazine button will, when it is pressed down, lower the cocked hammer safely. But, unless the thumb safety is on, the gun can still be fired double-action. To get a shorter, lighter pull, single-action, push up the cocking lever.

Sauers are not commonly met here now, compared to some other makes. The Sauer shotguns are still imported regularly by Stoeger—expensive and medium-priced shotguns—and the *drillings*—the three-barrel rifle and shotgun combinations that just won't die out—for there are always hunters who appreciate them.

SCHWARZLOSE

There was an Austrian Schwarzlose Model 1898 autoloader for 7.63 or .30 Mauser pistol cartridges—now very uncommon. It had only about a half inch of locked, short recoil before the four lugs unlocked and let the breech-bolt go straight back. It was a successful, finely made arm, but it never had wide popularity. W. H. B. Smith, in *Small Arms of the World,* said it was the first to have a hold-open breech device, operating when the magazine is empty.

With no great difficulty as to cartridge-case supply, this pioneer semi-automatic pistol might be a good one for an experimenter to acquire and use, handloading for it carefully. The brand name is respected, although it is really a designer's name.

SIG

Schweizerische Industrie Gesellschaft at Neuhausen, Switzerland, makes an M47/8 auto-pistol—1947 model, 8-shot—that is good enough for the Swiss Army. In fact it is so closely fitted that something sloppier might be better for rough service in either muddy or sandy country. This gun is costly to make.

Calibers are the time-proved .30 and 9 mm. Luger, and there is a conversion to .22 long-rifle by changing barrel, recoil spring, magazine, and slide. A change of barrel and recoil spring makes a .30 into a 9 mm. or vice versa. There is also a 4 mm. barrel for indoor use, single-shot—or there has been. With .22 long-rifle ammo, you get into a practical caliber, one that *can* be used afield when nothing better is needed, and still it is bearable to shoot down a 50- or 25-foot stretch of gallery range. It's not really noisy.

With 4¾-inch barrel the service pistol weighs about two pounds, empty, and as SP47/8 it replaces the Swiss-made Luger. The action is short-recoil locked breech, with ribs on top of the barrel (centerfire) engaging cuts in the undersurface of the slide top, just as in locked Brownings and Colts. A cam on the underside of the barrel unlocks the action after about ¼ inch of rearward travel, slide and barrel hitched temporarily together.

The magazine catch on the bottom of the butt is unhandy, although some very practical shooters like one there, since a button behind the trigger may be pushed accidentally and thus kick out a loaded magazine, perhaps without the user's knowledge of it until he starts shooting. The thumb safe on the left goes *down* for "Off," and that's fine and natural. It's not as fast as a double action, but it's fairly fast in the hands of a trained shooter. The gun has a rather simple takedown, which shows cleverness of design. Since the barrel is snugly fitted and the grip lines accommodating to most shooters' hands, it is made for accurate shooting.

This pistol replaces the *Neuhausen 1944/16,* which with 16 shots in its magazine was bulky to pack and much too big for moderate-sized hands to grasp. It weighed 39 ounces, a lot for a 9 mm. However, it was made also with 8-shot mag, and known as M44/8.

The M47/8 SIG can be had from H. F. Grieder, Box 487, Knoxville, Ill., who also imports the Haemmerli target pistols. He has, too, the target model SIG autos in .30 and 9 mm. calibers, with matted frame and slide, and rear sight adjustable for elevation and windage. Gun weight is 37 ounces, overall length 9½ inches, with 6-inch barrel—or 1¼ inches beyond the 4¾-inch model. The extra reach of barrel protrudes from the front of the slide. A spanner wrench comes in the kit to remove the front sight collar in disassembling. With the 6-inch barrel the sight radius is eight inches. None of these SIG pistols are cheap, but they have quality. Sometimes they go under the name of Neuhausen, like the earlier models.

The SIG stands out as one of the finest semi-automatic service or target pistols made, and the 9 mm. caliber is growing ever more popular here. Abroad, it is long established. The 7.65 or .30 Luger is famous for accuracy, too, and it shoots flatter than the 9. Of course it is of small caliber for killing power except when deep penetration is a must.

There is no need to go overboard on this or any other pistol, as there are many good ones. A Colt National Match Gold Cup for the .45 Auto is a fine gun, too; and if we ever use our target handguns for serious business, the big, blunt .45 bullets in our fists—and the chambered round above—have a way of being reassuring! It would be pleasant to lounge in my old-fashioned rocker, gaze through my bedroom windows at the Blue Ridge Mountains to the east, and dream about how enthusiastic I might-could get with a neat little .38 or 9 mm., but facts are facts. For preparedness, I like chunky bullets in a pistol, just in case I have to fire one or more in dead earnest. Pardon the digression, if you please.

STAR

These popular handguns are made by Star Bonifacio Echeverria, Eibar, Spain, and imported by Firearms International, 4837 Kerby Hill Road, Washington 22, D. C. There are many models; and new ones, or at least new stylings, are rather frequent. For example: the late 1958 announcement of pocket .25s and .380s in colors—black, blue, green, gold, and steel-gray frames, with chromed slides for contrast. Colored guns are blossoming out, and U. S. makers have produced them, too. I can't see that they hurt the gun business. In fact, they may help it, if buyers learn gun-safety and avoid witless and tragic accidents.

Star Olympia

Compared to almost all other rapid-fire International .22 autos, the Star is moderately priced. It takes the .22 short cartridge, is far more accurate than needful at 25 meters, and with 7-inch barrel goes to 52 ounces. It has a compensator or muzzle brake to cut the upchuck of recoil, and three adjustable weights to hang on to get the full 3¼-pound heft.

The exposed hammer is well spurred, as much as or more so than those on other Stars, and the grip is of flat "automatic" type, less rounded than on the Beretta or Haemmerli-Walther Olympic rapid-firers. There is a thumb-rest, of course. By our target and

work-gun standards, the grip seems excessively straight, but this helps to prevent overshooting in the really fast Olympic course, five-shot strings on five silhouettes, timed first at eight seconds, then six, then four. Overshooting is a real hazard with a steeply sloped-back grip like that of the usual Colt or Hi-Standard .22 match gun—but notice how comparatively straight the S.&W. .22 auto's handle is. Let's not forget, however, what good work our American-made guns have done in this course of fire.

Some of our very best shots seem to like much less weight on the front of their Olympic fast-fire guns than the Europeans do. Some, in fact, don't want any such attachments, and we can be sure that they have given these and other available "aids" a fair trial.

The French Star

This low-powered military arm takes our .32 Auto Colt, the 7.65 Browning. It carries eight rounds in its magazine and has the unusual barrel length of 5¼ inches. Four inches is long for the .32 Auto barrel. That was what the earliest Colts and most Savages had.

It is a heavy gun for the caliber, too, about 30 ounces. So it does well for holster carry and for better-than-average shooting in its class. It is used much in Spain as well as by French military personnel.

There is an exposed, nicely spurred hammer, also a reliable thumb safety on the *right-hand* side of the slide, ahead of the hammer. To do away with unnecessary weight, the top of the slide is cut away in the fashion so common with Star commercial pistols—and with early Mauser pocket automatics, too.

The barrel is fixed on solidly, for durability and accuracy, but dismounting is not difficult. Draw back and lift up the slide; then slide it forward off the barrel. It's a simple and entirely sensible takedown.

You may not like the rather straight grip, though it has good size and length for holding. It is not too hard to learn to do good, aimed, slow-fire shooting with a pretty straight grip —after all, our .45 Government pistol does not have much more back-slant—but it definitely is not for instinctive pointing, as in the dark. A great many woodsmen liked the .38 Colt Military and the much later .22 Reising semi-automatics, which were stocked very much like this Star. These fellows generally figured on having a pretty clear, steady sight picture before they cut loose, and the fact that their guns were all wrong in design may never have been known by them. But if so, could they have cared less? The automatics were flat and compact to carry, had good barrel length and sight radius; so they liked them.

The French Star is not a common .32 auto here, but the somewhat similar Star .22 autos have earned a good slice of popularity.

Star Pocket Autoloaders

With 3¾-inch .32 or .380 barrel, Colt-Browning-type slide and muzzle bushing, these exposed-hammer Stars look much like the Gabilondo Llama miniatures.

But the grip is curved at the rear, like that of the old Remington Model 51 .32 and .380, that short-lived gun that could not buck the impact of anti-pistol laws. So the pointing and holding are improved, and there is always some call for a flat-packing, compact gun with exposed, spurred hammer and a convenient safety at the top rear of the frame. These Stars have all that, and a thumb-rest thrown in as extra.

There is also a 13-ounce .25 Star with 2¾-inch barrel, a rather compact job for that comparatively long barrel.

Star .22 Plinkers

These have the easy takedown of the other Stars, also thumb-rest stocks and checkered backstraps, which are curved in Rem. 51 manner. Slides are cut away at the top, and hammers are nicely spurred. With 10-shot .22 long-rifle magazine capacity, these little arms are useful to the plinker. Also, a home-owner who depends on one for protection can pack five or six rounds into the magazine, leaving the spring under no great strain, and still be well prepared in case of need. Fill a magazine to the brim, let it sit around for months, and it may not be able to do its part when emergency calls.

The smallest model, practically a pocket gun, has a 4½-inch barrel and weighs 24-plus ounces. The sights are fixed. But on the more costly 6- and 7-inch guns weighing 27 and 29 ounces, the sights are adjustable. Safety lock and magazine release button are in .45 Colt locations, excellent for most of us who are not left-handers.

About the only possible criticism of the gun's design is that the front strap of the grip is almost straight up and down. Still, not everyone, by any means, would find a thing wrong with that.

The Military Star

You can save only a few dollars by buying this gun instead of a Colt .45 or Super-.38, after which it is obviously patterned in appearance. But the works inside are different. Further, in this model itself, different designs have been used by Star. The gun comes in 9 mm. Luger, .38 and .45 Colt Auto, and it has been made for the 9 mm. Bergmann cartridge, too.

Unlike the Colt and the rather similar Llama, it has no grip safety. As made for the Spanish Army, some at least have a full-auto switch on the right side. That would be nightmarish in a .45 pistol, which kicks enough in semi-auto fire. Cut loose full-auto, it could, with those .45 bullets blaze a trail right up a steep mountainside, though the blazes would be too far apart to help anyone who wasn't familiar with that country. The last round or so would be moon-directed.

But as for grip safeties, are they so important? Few would carry a cocked and ready gun off safe, depending only on the grip, though the Clement-copy first model S.&W. auto, the .35, had only that type. It was located up front, right under the rear of the guard. You did have to shift it to the left before

The Star .32 and .380 Model S weighs 22 ounces and has a 3¾-inch barrel, suggestive of the differently designed and stocked hammerless Colt. Light-weight Star .380s go 14½ ounces, and .25s, 10½.

Star Model F .22 long-rifle caliber auto with 4¼-inch barrel goes 26 ounces and is handier than some other shorties for pocket carry. It has fixed sights, but those on the 6- and 7-inch models are adjustable, and their weights are 28 and 30 ounces. All have 10-shot magazines.

squeezing it back, but not much: the two-stage movement soon flowed imperceptibly into one. Some grip safes, like those on a number of Lugers, can be blocked, and thus prevented from firing, if a twig or some such thing gets under them. And the really stiff grip safeties—for a horrible example the Colt hammerless, pocket-gun sort—are so hard to squeeze that a shooter devoted to a light, easy hand-hold just can't shoot decently with a gun so equipped.

Ordinarily, though, pistols are fired only when gripped in a natural firing position, and what good is a squeezer safety then? Yes, the old S.&W. hammerless, like the present Centennial model, used a grip safe to great advantage, in one way. A small, weak hand, like that of a young child, could hardly depress the light spring and at the same time pull back the long, heavy, double-action trigger of that revolver.

"High-Power" Star auto-pistols weigh 38 ounces in .38 Colt and 9mm. Luger calibers, 40 ounces in .45. All have 5-inch barrels. Magazine capacity of the first two is eight rounds, of the .45, the usual seven. Colt barrel length of five inches is used. Note the long hammer spur and the long "horn" of the frame beneath it to keep the spur from biting the web of your hand when the hammer goes back in recoil. Stocks come up high on the frame, and the forward flare at the bottom of the butt may help some shooters to get a uniform hand position.

STEYR

This is an old Austrian firm that goes back to pretty early times. Right now a hammerless .32 auto pistol of that make is being imported by Stoeger Arms, as well as a rather expensive bolt action .22 rimfire carbine.

It is double-action *only,* for no hammer is cocked as the slide recoils. This makes for a long, heavy pull each time we fire, but for safe pocket carry, too. The gun is never cocked except just before firing. If you change your mind about firing, you ease forward on the trigger and the pistol changes its mind, too. It's hard to think of a safer pocket arm. The trigger itself can be locked by a cross-button safety built into it. Pushed to the right, it locks the trigger, but in normal carrying you would have it protruding to the left so that the gun would be as ready as a double-action revolver.

It is a pocket gun, and the grip is rather small, but an extension spur on the magazine gives some help to the little finger. There is reasonable pitch to the grip. After all, this Steyr is for quick, close-up shooting, not for precision work. It's more flat and compact than hammerless revolvers, and in actual killing power its full-jacketed bullet is about equal to the heavier, slower lead slug of the short .32 S.&W. cartridge. The 7.65 or .32 Auto Colt gives much better penetration than the .32 Smith, of course—at least it is sure to get through a heavy overcoat, jacket, shirt, and even long Johns to boot!

Seven rounds go into the Steyr magazine, and most centerfire hammerless revolvers carry only five in their cylinders. As we all know, a well-cared-for revolver seldom fails to work. Autoloaders, except the very best, do not have quite so good a record for infalli-

bility. If you get a misfire with this or any other double-action auto-pistol you can pull the trigger and try that round again. With the double-action revolver your trigger pull brings a fresh cartridge under the firing pin.

Military Steyrs commonly took their own cartridge, the 9 mm. Steyr, but some were made for the shorter 9 mm. Luger rounds and stamped "P-08"—1908 German Army adoption of the Luger pistol.* The Steyr is an old-fashioned automatic, its butt magazine fixed, loaded with eight rounds from a stripper clip (not a bad idea, at that). After the last shot has gone, the slide stays open. It must be pulled back more, and locked so, to take the clipful of cartridges through the slot cut in its top. The gun is locked-breech in design, and needs to be, for its 28½-ounce weight is light for such powerful loads. It depends partly on barrel torque—to the right, in the direction of the rifling—to lock it shut until the bullet has gone out and lowered the pressure.

The stock is almost straight up and down, and in general this arm just is not for accurate shooting, except perhaps when held in both hands. Its own cartridge is long-ranged, firing a rather sharp steel-jacketed 116-grain bullet at some 1200 f. s., about midway between old and modern .38 Auto Colt loadings.

An early Austrian Roth-Steyr takes a special 8 mm. round, clip-loaded ten at a time. It has a long, curved grip with pretty good pitch-back. The trigger pull is double-action. It is seldom seen here and is of small practical use to us. The old pocket auto Steyrs in .32 and .380 were built to about average weights and barrel lengths, and for guns of this class they were not stocked badly. Odd-looking they may be, but a fine old company built them. Recoil springs lie above the barrels as on old .35 Smith & Wessons and others, and they may be disconnected for easy loading, again like the old Smiths. They had no squeezer grip safeties. Excellent but over-complicated machining puts them in an earlier era than ours, but when they are in good condition they can still serve well.

TELL

A. F. Stoeger of New York used to import these Olympic free pistols, single-shots for the .22 long-rifle cartridge. The Buchel-Tell was made by Ernst Friedrich Buchel at Zella-Mehlis, Germany, with pivoted breech-block that swings down for loading. The set trigger, hand-fitting stock, finely adjustable sights, long octagon barrel—commonly over the ten inches allowed in Standard American slow-fire—and wood forestock are in typical European free-pistol styling. It was an expensive gun, naturally, and it is still good for Olympic, although models improved by *Udo Anschuetz,* also at Zella-Mehlis, succeeded it. We now have the Haemmerli, which resembles both Tell and Anschuetz. Some say that the Anschuetz was an even smoother,

---

*The German Navy was quicker to recognize the Luger's value. It adopted this pistol in 1904.

finer job than the Haemmerli, and in some specimens this may be true, although we should remember that fine old guns have their following, people who believe and insist that nothing later ever equaled them. Another free pistol of the past—though that doesn't mean that it couldn't compete, and win, too, today—was the Luna with falling-block action similar to the Tell's.

Most free pistols do use a falling-block action, the breech-block hinged at the rear as in the world-famous old Martini single-shot sporting and military rifles. But there is at least one simple and not at all bad-looking bolt action, the Danish *Schultz & Larsen*. The S.&L. 7x61 mm. high power rifle is very well-known here, for its quality and its unusual design. The S.&L. pistol has as its bolt handle—we could call it that, because such it is in its function—a rectangular knob (with nicely smoothed edges) at the end of the bolt, not a long lever sprouting out from the side. It is easy to grasp, turn, pull out and push in, and the lines of the pistol are not spoiled. The gun is stocked in the usual free-pistol fashion, that is, not usual at all, for thumb and finger grooves and a lip for the heel of the hand practically support it without effort on the shooter's part.

Probably the nearest we have come to an American-made free pistol were some of the last issues of *Harrington & Richardson* single-shots equipped with triggers that could be used set or unset, rifle-fashion, as described by Bill Toney in the lead article of the 1959 *Gun Digest*. These are long gone, and the expensive *Tompkins* of post-World War II times seems not to be made now, either. Its trigger was of standard U. S. target weight, just over two pounds for a .22, and it could not be set to a few ounces or to a somewhat delayed, long pull that is well liked in Europe. Its trigger did have practically no rearward movement, like that on a Model 52-C Winchester .22 target rifle and some others.*

Our International shooters, many too few, found that for most of them, at least, a true free pistol gave just the edge in scoring that they needed to approach or achieve victory. The reworked American single-shots and semi-automatics would not, as a rule, give them their best, not withstanding the fact that the free pistol is itself a new class of handgun to master, and thus requires special effort. Its long accurate barrel, more tightly chambered than an autoloader can generally be and still be reliable in functioning, helped hit that 3.39-inch ten-ring 50 meters away, and so did the long sight radius and the relaxing grip. Relaxation was needed, for those 60 shots for record sure aren't plinking! There are 18 sighting shots allowed, and they could be needed.

These works of art, these highly individualized arms, probably average some 2½ pounds or more, depending on what the shooter happens to need for the ex-

tremely steady holding he must do. In the really generous time limit given, you can use a heavier, more tiring gun, if it helps you toward steadiness, than you could for Standard American slow-fire strings of five shots in five minutes, or ten in ten minutes. Olympic target rings are so small that this game demands practically rifle-like precision. It is not a practical form of shooting, and Standard American slow-fire isn't much more so; but we want to win in it. For the individual who doesn't need to win, it can be as fascinating and relaxing as any other form of pistol shooting, and that's saying a lot.

The stocks must fit the hand so well that it lies over them always in the same position and feels almost a part of them. Consistent hand-hold is one of the absolutely compulsory requirements for good pistol shooting. This type of slow-fire not only is "good"— it's the best that's done on target paper.

If the question comes up as to using a free pistol for small game shooting because of the accuracy which long training has developed, the answer is "No." For Olympic slow-fire the trigger pull is weighed in ounces, not pounds, and everything, including you, must be right to permit effective use of such a pull. The shot must be touched off at just the right instant. Can you do that in a cross-wind, or with an even slightly cold, stiff forefinger, or when you are breathing rapidly after sidehill gouging or straight-up climbing? And who wants to hunt with a set trigger, set and ready to fire almost from a puff of wind, even if the hunting is done sitting down on the watch for game? However, a two-pound pull, permitted on .22 pistols for Standard American shooting, and a grip that fits your hand, your individual hand, will help a lot in the woods—provided you shoot well enough to use the weak .22 long-rifle for any sort of small game hunting.

I don't mean that a free pistol would be hopeless in the woods. Its value would depend on the ability of the person who used it, and on weather conditions, too. But most of us had best think of these arms as tools for the competition they were built for. In that they are supreme—probably. Some of our best Olympic competitors have used American guns even in the slow-fire events.

We should think deeply about these guns, too, for we want our Country to rank high in that field of competition, even though it is about as far from our own American style of pistol shooting as anything could be. It is so different, in fact, that only a few of our best pistolmen can do well at both games.

TOKAREV

The Tokarev semi-automatic, adopted by Russia in 1930, is a simplified Browning design. As on the earliest Colt .38s, its hammer has a rounded spur, not easy to raise or lower when your hand is cold; and there is no safety except the half-cock notch on that hammer. Grip safety and thumb safety just aren't there.

---

*Since the manuscript was completed, Hi-Standard has come out with the 1960 announcement of its fine single-shot free pistol, described in the chapter on target arms.

Gun weight is about two pounds, cut by some three ounces in some models. As far as taking up recoil goes, that is sufficient, for its cartridge is a nearly identical twin to the .30 Mauser, a high-velocity, light-bullet round with lots of noise and penetration and not much recoil or smash. The 7.62 mm. Russian is commonly loaded to lower speeds than the 7.63 Mauser, and that would reduce recoil a little, both the recoil due to muzzle-blast and the actual shove-back that we feel. Sometimes the Mauser case has a thicker rim behind the extracting groove, but differences aren't great. The Tokarev should have more than adequate strength to handle Mauser pistol ammunition in 7.63 caliber.

Barrel length is 4½ inches, resulting in a sharp report from 1100-1400 f. s. Russian loads. Mauser loadings have reached about 1600 f. s. in the 5¼ or 5½ inch German barrels, with bullets of about 85 or 86 grains' weight. Differences in killing power of full-metal jacketed military .30 caliber pistol bullets at these various velocities would be small, though penetration could be a different story. Russian sub-machine guns took the 7.62 pistol cartridge, and they, not pistols, nor even rifles for the big 7.62 so similar to our T-65 (.308) in power, seem to be the favored infantry arms. They throw a lot of lead.

Inside and out, the Tokarev is a plain and simple job, purely functional, not to be admired by anyone for its looks, as a Colt, Smith & Wesson, or Luger war pistol can be. The black plastic stocks are ribbed vertically for better hold; in general the gun is easily and cheaply manufactured, easily dismounted, too, even its eight-shot magazine. The latter has no feed lips built into it, these being part of the gun itself. Pressed-steel magazine lips, such as most pistols have, are bent all too easily in rough service, and in that condition are probably the most frequent cause of jams.

The short-recoil, locked-breech action is much like those of the Colt 1911 or the Browning 1935. A push on the button behind the trigger ejects a properly fitting magazine, Colt fashion, and makes continuous fire practical; there should be no tugging and hard shoving to change magazines, as with some military autoloaders. The low recoil of the light-bullet cartridge makes recovery of aim faster than with a .45.

But we prefer the .45 for military use and, let's hope, we shall stick with it. Foot pounds of pistol energy from high-speed loads don't spell knockout hitting power if the bullet is light, small, and hardjacketed as the "rules" of war require. A lot of lightweight ammunition can be carried to the place where it will be used. But with a hit placed fast and almost instinctively, just about anywhere in an enemy's body, which caliber, .30 or .45, is the better life-saver for the fighter? Simply stated, the .45 gives more and bigger bull's-eyes of vital scoring values. The lives of *our* servicemen are precious, and in combat a pistol can help to insure them at short ranges, sometimes at only a few inches, as at night, when a bullet must beat a knife. It takes only a little training to teach a man—or a woman, for that matter—to hit a body-sized mark every time at 10 feet, or 20, or even 30. This isn't target accuracy, but that isn't needed at these combat ranges when you throw a big bullet.

Hits are what count, especially when they are hard and instantly disabling.

Or, in imagination, put yourself in the wilderness and under the necessity of killing a deer in order to eat or a black bear in order to live—or the reverse, for even a deer can turn ugly. Would you choose a marble or a navy bean for your bullet?

WALTHER

Modern Walther pistols are imported by Interarmco, 10 Prince Street, Alexandria, Virginia. The military P-38 (Pistole, 1938) has been much discussed, pro and con, and the pocket automatics, also with double-action trigger, have fast earned popularity in America.

Walther models go fairly far back, at least to a 1908 .25 and a 1909 .32. An early blow-back Walther in the powerful 9 mm. Luger caliber was made, but little known here, until about 1917. Nearly all other pistols, except the clumsy Astra Model 400, that fire full-power loadings of this cartridge are of locked-breech type.

The P-38

These service pistols vary a great deal in quality, for many were made in wartime under different degrees of stress! Before the outbreak of war in 1939 the commercial model was listed as made in .30 and 9 mm. Luger, .38 and .45 Colt Automatic—expensive, finely made jobs.

For Hitler's armed forces the P-38 usually had a 4¾-inch barrel and total weight of about 34 ounces. It was as muzzle-light in feel as a 4⅝-inch Luger; and its grip was fully as large (or over-large), and with much less rearward slant. If it was cheaper to make and more rugged than the Luger, those qualities came, I think, at a high price, natural pointing qualities, ideal for a medium sized or big hand, and usable two-handed by almost anyone over ten years old. Any oversize pistol is liable to twist in the hand when fired, and the P-38 is fairly liable to do this in spite of that really nice curve at the rear of the butt.

A very few hammerless models were made, just as with our American Savage .32 and .380 automatic, but most of the wartime jobs brought here have a well-spurred, exposed hammer. The double-action trigger created, really, a new classification of war weapon, combining the advantages of sustained auto-pistol fire and the revolver's prompt delivery of that sometimes vital Shot No. 1.

Poor-quality P-38s earned a still-remembered reputation for being unsafe. Sometimes they were discharged accidentally when the hammer was lowered—as it was meant to be, and what a sales feature that

Post-war commercial Walther P-38 auto for 9mm. Luger cartridge, imported by Interarmco, 10 Prince St., Alexandria, Va. A quality job done under peacetime conditions.

was!—by pressing down the thumb safety, for the part that barred the hammer nose from the firing pin could break. Some certainly did just that. Full-automatic fire was possible, too, when the trigger connecting bar was too worn to operate, or broken. Then allowing the hammer to slam down set the P-38 to firing machine-gun fashion. It was also possible to assemble and fire the pistol without the locking block; not likely to happen, but possible.

After these hazards became known, the going price of about $80 for a captured P-38 jolted down to about $40.

A well-made military specimen is all right for any-one who understands it and watches its parts for wear or the start of fracturing. Probably he would not take it hundreds of miles from a gunsmith, although it is a reasonably compact sidearm, and its ammunition is very compact indeed.

Some wartime specimens have pressed-steel parts, but so do perhaps the majority of all classes of com-mercial arms made today. We accept such parts when they are of good quality, because not to do so would be insisting on something very special indeed!

Like the Luger, the Walther has a cartridge in-dicator. In the Luger this is the extractor at the front of the breech-block, but on this service pistol which replaced it, a pin at the top rear of the breech sticks out and shows that there's a round in the chamber. The sights are like the Luger's in outline, a V rear and an inverted V or barleycorn front, the same picture that a typical Mauser military rifle's sights give to the eye. They are not the best, we folks here think, but they are not useless. Friends of mine who have good eyesight can fire about 2- or 3-inch 100-yard groups from rifles so sighted—or perhaps better. They cer-tainly made the best of bad jobs! At least such sights are quick to catch.

Many companies made P-38s, and there were varia-tions in even military stylings. A few had super-long barrels and detachable shoulder stocks which made

them into featherweight burp guns, we could say. But with standard magazines, such a burp could be no long and guttural drag, but just a quickie. There were also duraluminum slides and frames for lightness, probably to pamper top brass. A practical, effective shooter finds the standard weight just right for the cartridge. Heavy machine gun type rounds have been fired in P-38s, and at first it was customary to brag of it. There was no sensible advantage in it.

If by chance you have one of the early commercial guns, the Heeres Pistole or Army Pistol, there is a real advantage beyond quality of finish and tuning up. With them, putting the safety to "On" and thus dropping the cocked hammer is safe, because this act withdraws the firing pin into the slide before the hammer can touch it. The rear face of the Heeres' firing pin is square, not round like that of the P-38.

Late Model P-38s imported commercially since the war do not have all parts fully interchangeable with World War II guns. And some P-38s made for the post-war West German Army have light-alloy frames that are not smoothly finished on the outside, and barrels not tightly fitted for accuracy. But the imports we get are well-made and well-finished. The safety is stronger, not so much cut away, and these arms are not at all in the hazardous class. Closer tolerances improve accuracy, and light-weight jobs come as low as 27 ounces in weight. Some of the commercial pre-war Heeres guns were polished even inside, in the good commercial Luger fashion, but such refinement almost belongs to an age that is past—except for the most expensive products.

Pocket Walthers

Like the military Walthers, these arms have double-action triggers and exposed hammers. The d.-a. trig-ger goes back to about 1929, but it didn't become really familiar here until years later.

Turkey has made small Walthers for her own govern-ment's use; and in France, the Manurhin factory pro-duces these guns for export. The present Mark II PP

Walther PP model .22 long-rifle caliber auto-pistol with 3⅞-inch barrel and ten-shot extension magazine, imported by Interarmco.

Walther PPK .32 auto from Interarmco; seven-shot magazine.

or "Police Pistol" comes in .22 long-rifle, .32 and .380 Auto Colt, with 3⅞-inch barrel and gun weight of about 23 ounces. This is a good normal for the type, heavy enough for complete comfort even with .380 rounds, as far as recoil goes. It's true that the .380 cartridge is a sharp barker. The PPK (K for "Krimi-nal," though this is a detective model, and the game, not the hunter, gives name to the gun) has shorter grip, barrel and slide. In the .22 and .32 calibers, the PPK can be had with dural frame at extra cost, and so made the weight drops to about 15 ounces. They are imported by Interarmco, 10 Prince Street, Arling-ton, Virginia.

To help compensate for the short grip, a butt-ex-tension magazine can be had. These modern Walthers have grooved trigger faces and square-cut sights in our accepted American fashion. We learned to value them because they make trigger control and sighting so much easier and surer. A good many experienced German workers and overseers are busy in the French plant, and that fact helps. Not that the French cannot do precision work when they set their sights on it: they certainly can! Firearms are simple compared to some of the stuff they turn out. Never sell those in-dividualists short.

The little Walthers have the hammer-dropping feature. When the manual safety is put on, it causes the hammer to fall safely, for the firing pin is locked to the sear, and a block rises and prevents the hammer from falling far enough to hit the firing pin. The owner should watch the safety for wear, especially a flattening that could allow the hammer to contact the firing pin. There is no squeezer safety, but in addi-tion to the thumb safety there is the exposed hammer, in plain sight, and the cartridge-in-chamber indicator pin that also is easy to see or to feel. This pin is not used on the .22 rimfire.

Some stamped parts go into these pocket guns, as we should expect, but they should stand up well under the amount of use such a weapon gets, except perhaps

in the gentle little .22 caliber. The gun is standardized, established, and made by a reliable firm.

Barrels are mounted solidly, for good accuracy. Once on a time, practice barrels were made to slip in-side the standard tubes and convert the arm into a single-shot, parlor-practice thing—not quite a toy, though, in either accuracy or power. The pellet fired was a 4 mm. ball, about the size of an American No. 2 shot.

An interesting old-time Walther pistol was the *1920 Model 8 .25*, which had a grip you could take hold of—long enough to give a purchase. There was too little slant to this grip, but it raised the gun's capacity to nine rounds instead of seven. That too was a worthy feature. The arm was hammerless, but a thumb safety just ahead of the left-hand stock went down for "Fire," as it should, not up or across.

Walther .22 Target Pistols

The old Olympic Walther .22 automatics made world's-record rapid-fire scores, and now we have the Haemmerli-made Walther, discussed under "Haem-merli" in this chapter. Right here we are concerned with the contemporary .22 Walthers above the size of the pocket .22s.

They are double-action-trigger autoloaders with ac-tion and grip similar to those of the PP .22, except that the magazine extension is longer and fuller. Bar-rels come in 6- and 7⅝-inch length, and as extras there are or have been detachable weights, recoil com-pensators, and red-outlined rear and luminous front sights. Click-adjustable, two-way rear sights are stand-ard, and high post front sights. Grips are of the inex-pensive molded sort, but thumb-rests have not been forgotten.

These long-nosed smallbores are unlike anything in our standard American production, a little suggestive, in their lines, of the old Reising that once rivaled the Colt Woodsman. The outdoor man, woman or young-ster might be very thankful indeed to examine them. By examining, I mean: give one or more of them

Another Interarmco import, a Walther PPK .32 auto with relief engraving and extension magazine holding nine cartridges.

Walther .22 long-rifle caliber Sporter auto-pistol from Interarmco. It has a 6-inch barrel and ten-shot magazine. Also available are 7⅝-inch barrels and .22 short chambering. See the convenient cocking spur on the hammer.

a good look-over in a store, get the feel of the grip and the balnce, try the trigger pull, and see whether the rather straight grip suits or is a handicap. The unweighted barrels aren't heavy. Should they be, for you individually? Does the muzzle tend to weave in the holding, and to dodge when the hammer falls? If the answer to such questions is a "Suits me," then these decidedly "different" plinking pistols deserve a chance to go to the woods, streams, mountains or prairies with you.

WEBLEY

Webley and Webley & Scott are names familiar to the British, and in fact to most handgunners throughout the world. They connote quality and reliability from 'way back, just as our Colt and Smith & Wesson names do. For generations it was customary to say that Lugers and Mausers were clumsy and unreliable, but that you could trust a Smith, Colt or Webley. Those acquainted with handguns and with human nature will know about how much sense and how much stupidity give rise to such remarks now.

Many small Webley pocket revolvers came in .320 and .380 calibers, and a few reached here long ago. They took the near-equivalent of our .32 Short and Long Colts, or those actual rounds, and .380s a bit shorter than our .38 Short Colt. There were, too, the Bulldog-type loads for heavier pocket or holster revolvers: the .44-15-168 (black powder and soft lead in grains' weight) Bull Dog, the .44-18-200 and .44-19-200 Webley, and the .45-20-230 Webley. There was an even shorter .450. Some of these bigbore revolvers were good-sized military models. It is interesting to recall that the .45-20-230 prescription was used in the .45-70 Winchester "Short Range" rifle loading. Other factory black powder small game rounds for fairly big rifles followed pistol formulas, the 13 grains powder, 98 grains lead for the .32-40 duplicating the .32 S.&W. Long, and the 20-155 for the .38-55 coming close to the 21-158 of the .38 Special, or the 19-150 of the old .38 Long Colt.

Early Autoloaders

Webley & Scott pocket semi-automatics appeared about 1906. Some had exposed hammers; some were hammerless. They were well and honestly made, but their straight-pitched stocks didn't help in the shooting. Still, their quality was inviting; and for a good many years before World War II Stoeger carried them as standard items. Calibers were .25 and .32 Colt Auto, and back then a Webley was about the only .25 you could get with a hammer in plain view. This reassured people who were a bit leery of automatics and of hammerless guns, too.

A 1908 blow-back auto for the 9 mm. Browning Long (about midway between .380 and .38 Colt in power) never became popular here because of its oddball ammunition. This was probably never made in the United States, although I have a faint recollection carried up from childhood that Remington once catalogued it. Perhaps I'm wrong and then this impression should be junked along with those of ghosts behind the bedroom window curtains and green monsters in the dark upstairs hall. Anyway, in 1910 came a locked-breech Webley for our good .38 Auto cartridge. This was a well-designed if not esthetically delightful weapon, somewhat like the .455 Mark I that the British Navy adopted, and not really a pocket gun at all. It should be a collector's find today.

.455 Service Revolver

The Mark VI Pistol No. 1, a double-action Webley, was replaced almost completely by the double-action .380 Pistol No. 2 Mark I (hammer) and Mark I* (without hammer spur). And now that .38 caliber six-shooter is giving way to the 1935 pattern Browning autoloader for the 9 mm. Luger and Parabellum cartridge.

The old .455 revolver is more complicated and harder to get at for complete cleaning and lubrication, or repairs, than the .380 revolver; yet it gave a great deal of faithful wartime service. With 6-inch service barrel, it weighs 38 ounces, about the same as 6½-inch Smith & Wesson Militaries made for Britain after 1914's Mons and Ypres battles had caught her so tragically unprepared. It seems incredible now, but it's a fact that few civilized, intelligent people had given credence the possibility of an all-out world war.

A 7½-inch barreled target Webley .455 was popular for paper-punching, in spite of the action's typically heavy hammer fall. People could shoot it as-issued, however. In 1914 and later still, the general impression here was that the big Webleys were clumsy guns. They certainly didn't have the fine lines of our Colt Officer's Model and New Service Target or Smith & Wesson Military and Police Target and .44 Military Target. Few of our shots had been educated to what we might call the adapter habit, caused by the fact that the usual American sixgun badly needs *something* to fill in that high space behind the trigger guard—a rubber adapter or filler, or a built-up stock. But now we know. Consequently, the low-slung Webley grip is likely to feel good. Yes, it's true that some of us do our best work with no adapter, and forefinger bent down to contact the curve of the trigger. But notice how popular the Colt Single Action Army style of grip is now, no matter what company makes the gun, with that low, natural hand-hold.

This British service revolver's action is of the break-down, tip-up breech type, not solid-frame, swing-out cylinder. It's essentially like our almost completely discontinued break-down revolvers. To un-latch it for opening you push down a lever at the left of the hammer instead of hauling up a cylinder catch at the rear of the top-strap. (Either type can be unlatched by thumb pressure, but the Webley type is easier.) Then scuff the gun's muzzle against your ribs, your leg, a tree or whatever, and as the weapon yawns open the empties come out. Doing this takes just a bit less time than opening and emptying a solid-frame, swing-cylinder sixgun, and your free hand might need that extra time to grab for and line up a refill of cartridges. It would be possible to open either a Webley or a Smith & Wesson inadevertently by thumb pressure, the former much more likely but still not highly probable, or so it seems to me.

Our companies no longer load .455s, though up in Canada the Dominion people do. The standard car-tridge sent a 265 grain (275 in old Remington lots) hollow-based, taper-pointed lead bullet at about 600 f. s., and it was a famous tipper on impact, like the British Mark VII 174 grain .303 rifle bullet. For World War II use, a 255 grain Mark VI full-metal patched .455 was produced, plain lead having been ruled out even for handgun bullets.

The .455 revolver can be adapted to .45 Colt Auto ammunition, a size for which it is usually much over-bored, or its chambers could be counterbored if neces-sary to take the thick rims of shortened .45 Colt brass, for handloading. The S.&W. .455's chambers can be bored out for .45 Colt, which they are long enough to take, or the cylinders counterbored or cut down for the very thick rims of .45 Auto-Rim ammunition, or for rimless .45 A.C.P. service rounds held in the three-shot, half-moon clips. The best way to handload for this Webley is to leave the gun as-is and get empty brass to fit it, a mold such as a Lyman casting a correct-sized bullet, the loading tools, and the lead, primers and powder.

Don't be afraid that the gun will fly open and shoot the empty case into your head if you press too hard on the unlocking lever when you fire! This is a per-fectly natural misgiving, but it has no justification. The hammer can't strike the cartridge under it unless the gun is locked shut.

Webley & Scott .455 Auto

It fires its own rimless case loaded with a 220 grain jacketed bullet that takes off at about 750 f. s. Its bal-listics fall below those of the .45 Colt Auto, but the blunt nose of the .455 slug makes it pretty deadly.

Colt Model 1911 pattern pistols were made to take this Webley load, and marked on the right side of the slide "Colt Automatic, Caliber .455." They were for the British to use; for us they would be to collect.

A 1904 Webley .455 auto-pistol was not very suc-cessful. In 1913 the Royal Navy adopted the improved model, and it served faithfully according to its lights. It isn't easy to shoot because of its straight-set stock and somewhat butt-heavy feel; the 5-inch barrel pro-trudes for some distance beyond the short, square re-ceiver. The gun was about as graceful as an early-made Alfred Dunhill pocket lighter—that was a chunky thing with a gallows-like spark-snapper on top—but it certainly had the wallop and was safe to handle if you knew guns and used both hands to cock or lower the hammer. The grip safety was enormous, but it worked. About this gun and about the little lighter there was some of the forthrightness that helped make the British Empire great. They had no frills.

This auto has the short-recoil locked breech, and after the last shot the slide stays open. It stays open too, when you fire single rounds, keeping the seven-shot magazine in reserve by pushing it in only until it catches in an upper notch, not the lower one that brings it high enough to feed cartridges into the barrel.

Webley-Fosbery Automatic Revolver

This is not the "automatic revolver" of ill-advised fiction or (possibly) news writers, but the real thing. Zig-zag cuts in the cylinder engage a stud in the frame; and on firing, the barrel, cylinder and upper frame go back in recoil against a spring-returning action. For the first shot, you thumb-cock the hammer or push back the barrel. After that, you just pull the trigger and the cylinder revolves automatically from recoil. So the name is fully earned.

To make the gun work you must hold it rather firmly, and the jump-back and slam-forward effect may be distressing. However, the Fosbery has been pop-ular in Britain for target work that includes rapid fire because it has the advantage (some would say) of a revolver grip without the need of cocking the hammer for each round fired single-action. If you keep this gun cleaned and well oiled and use no squib loads in it, it should operate reliably with its standard rimmed .455 revolver ammunition, the Mark II lead-bullet round.

Some Webley-Fosberys were made for .38 Colt Automatic cartridges. They are semi-rimless and have enough flange coming out behind the nearly parallel sides to give the revolver's extractor a grip on them. There were other automatic revolvers, one by a Union Arms Company in our country, and a foreign Zulaicai. They didn't catch on, and today they would be great finds for collectors.

The Fosbery grip is rather round and straight, but it is long; and at the top of the back-strap a decided hump helps the shooter to keep the gun from climbing in recoil. Even though the recoil of the .455 cartridge is mild for a bigbore—its powder charge is so small—

the heavy slam-back of the barrel, cylinder and a fair share of the frame magnifies what kick there is. Much the same effect comes from the recoiling barrel of the Remington Models 8 and 81 high-power auto-rifles. The later Remington 740 auto is a lighter gun with more powerful cartridges, but its autoloading system is gas-operated, not the long-recoil system of the earlier Rems. It seemed to me that the recoils of the 7½-pound 740 in .30-06 and of the 8½-pound 81 in .35 Rem were just about the same. Other things being equal, a heavy rifle with a moderate charge (like the .35) is the one that's easy on the shoulder.

So we see why the Fosbery was purposely designed, in its grip shape, to help us take the recoil and keep on delivering creditable rapid fire. Almost obviously, this pistol was not born to be popular. It is a bit complicated, it isn't easy to keep clean and ready to function under rough service conditions, and—it's different! A few people must have liked it very much, and it's not hard to imagine that under some circumstances a well-cared-for automatic revolver of good stopping power must have been a real life-saver.

Since the British seem to care little for solid-frame revolvers, this gun, like Webley and Enfield double-actions, has a hinged, not solid, frame. The barrel goes down and the cylinder tips up for ejection of the empties and for reloading. Such a tip-up frame is satifactory for short cartridges, and you notice that practically all British handgun rounds are short. Even the big .476 Eley, used in some Colts as well as in British arms, isn't really long. It follows the usual British pattern of a man-stopping handgun load, short but wide, a big bullet sent by a moderate powder charge. Unquestionably conditions of a century ago in our West influenced our handgun ammunition designs. Buffalo, or more properly bison, took a lot of penetration, and that called for a good scoop of black powder.

In the nineteenth century, Colt revolvers were popular in England, even for such typically American cartridges as .44-40 Winchester and .45 Colt. But these English Colts were chambered for English cartridges, too.

Training Pistols

Webley & Scott made various .22 rimfire single-shot training pistols, some of good target grade. But then, the name has stood for quality for generations even though few Webleys were at all popular here. We are, as a nation, more pistol-interested than almost any others, and we had and still have our own good makes and patterns, as well as safe, serviceable handguns in low-price brackets.

One of these Webley & Scott trainers was single-shot with automatic, blow-back ejection of the fired case. It was meant to accustom new shooters to the behavior of semi-automatic, self-loading pistols.

Webleys were among the first widely known and respected makes of air-pistols with barrels rifled to spin the hour-glass-shaped or "skirted" lead slugs with deep hollow base and blunt, almost wadcutter type nose. How these little coughing guns will shoot! Not powerfully, of course, in this make and design, but accurately. Continental Europeans have used air-powered guns for many years, and some of these arms have real power. But over here the Birmingham Small Arms rifles and Webley pistols were among the first of the fine imported jobs to make a deep impression. The Webley is still sold, at this writing, by Griffin & Howe (a branch of Abercrombie & Fitch) at 114 East 13th Street, New York City. Some of us recall G.&H. as one of the oldest good-sized custom gunsmithing firms in our country.

ODD-SIZE AMMUNITION

What about ammunition, in odd centerfire foreign sizes? You adapt American brass, if you can, for handloading, or you try firms like these:

Continental Arms Co., 697 Fifth Avenue, New York.

Male-Town, Inc., White Plains, New York.

Abercrombie & Fitch, Madison Avenue and 45th Street, New York.

A. F. Stoeger, 45-18 Court Square, Long Island City 1, N. Y.

Frank Miles, The Gunsmith, Bedford, Virginia.

Francis Bannerman Sons, 501 Broadway, New York 12.

Martin B. Retting, West Hurley, N. Y.

Slezak Arms Company, 7712 Holton Avenue, Cleveland 4, Ohio.

Warshal's, First and Madison, Seattle 4, Washington.

Osborne Klavestad (8 mm. Nambu), Highway 101-R, Shakopee, Minnesota.

It seems that every new foreign pistol being imported now takes some kind of American-made cartridge, except perhaps for toy blank popguns. But many interesting and a few very fine and serviceable handguns from abroad require special rations. A shooter has great satisfaction in seeing that they get them. The best of them will repay his efforts bountifully.

ALMOST any gun firing a bullet or a shot charge can kill a person. Even blank cartridges can do tragic harm at close range, for the stiff cardboard wad or hollow paper or wooden bullet leaves the muzzle fast. Safety in handling or firing guns costs unceasing vigilance; it doesn't come any cheaper.

In accidents, any bulleted pistol cartridge has killed or can kill people, nearby, or clear out of sight in wooded or rolling country. We must not be deceived by the comparatively short range of hand-gun bullets as compared with those sent from rifles. It is true that most high-speed revolver bullets, factory- or hand-loaded, have blunt noses to make bigger wounds than rounded or almost sharp bullets do, and that this stubbiness cuts down their ranging power. Still, a distance of over a mile is not too much for most of them, and close to the extreme limit they arrive with killing effect if they strike a vital but easily penetrated part of the human body.

Yet when we need and want killing power against a human enemy, or on game, it may be woefully lacking. The penalty can be the loss of our own lives, or the lives of those we are trying to protect—or the wounding and loss of game. In the latter instance, the game pays the price. There are no veterinarians' hospitals in the big or little wildernesses, ready and anxious to ease pain and promote recovery. The wounded and lost animal or bird pays in long-drawn-out suffering, compared to which the decent regrets that twinge our conscience are trivial.

In this chapter we try to analyze, in a general way, the factors of killing power. Not all of them have to do with either ammunition or handguns.

Human Factors

First and naturally we think of our personal skill. From man to man we vary widely. Each of us has, too, his varying ability under different conditions. On the target range—which we're smart to visit on rough, cold, wet, windy days as well as when the weather can't raise a single grouch from anyone—we almost always get at least good aiming light. This we may not find in the dim, windless quiet of a cedar swamp, or when gazing upward through brown oak leaves that screen a gray squirrel! And on a mountainside, our heart beating above its normal tempo, we may and probably do have unsure footing. There is no hurry in moving to a target range's firing point, and whoever found poor footing when he got there? If he did, a few scuffs with his feet made it secure.

But on the range, a formal or an informal one, we develop first accuracy and then a reasonable degree of speed. These give us confidence before we hunt with a handgun, and confidence, too, of being able to defend ourselves with it if ever we need to.

Just as with rifle or shotgun, a good marksman can carry a lighter pistol afield, or in places where danger may strike, than an indifferent or downright poor shot can. But you notice that those with real skill generally

CHAPTER 10

HANDGUN CARTRIDGE DEADLINESS

favor the surely adequate, not necessarily the extremely powerful, handgun charges. They are likely to know from experience, first-hand or wisely accepted second-hand, that matters don't always go according to plan. (They seldom do!) When one heavy bullet, just reasonably well placed, can do the work of two or three lighter ones with equal placement, they tend to favor the heavy job. There may be no chance for a second shot, no matter how desperately it's needed. Usually the limiting factors are the bulk and weight of the pistol they're willing to carry in confidence of their ability to shoot accurately, and if necessary, fast, for the first shot and perhaps for succeeding shots. Recoil figures here, especially in what the Army calls "sustained fire," and an excellent definition that is, in just two words.

Unless it is exaggerated or false, confidence can bolster courage—when it is needed—or improve performance—which is desirable perhaps 90% of the time. That 90 is a mean low percentage in hunting; and how would you like it in self-defense?

But best of all, no doubt, well-grounded confidence brings coolness, the ability to function well under stress and to be alert to adjust for changing conditions. A cool person seldom is disconcerted when situations change fast and tend to approach the hopeless. He adjusts fast.

The Critical Bullet

Deadliness depends on its caliber, shape, weight, construction, and the velocity remaining when it arrives at the target. The caliber, shape, weight and initial velocity have much to do with a rifle bullet's ranging ability, its progress through the air without losing an unreasonable percentage of speed and consequent striking energy over its practical, useful course; and this, too, without being deflected seriously off-course by wind. A few of us, only a few, are good enough handgun shots to be concerned very deeply about these matters. Most of us think of a pistol as a short-range arm, and, frankly, haven't the ability to use it well at anything like rifle distances. You'll find, I'm afraid, that most long-range game killing by pistol has been messy, nothing like the humane, instant, one-shot kills that your competent rifle-and-scope armed varmint hunter naturally expects, or the same sort of bang-and-be-done-with-it shot that a skilled still-hunter of woods deer expects, too. However, pistols have been used on big and medium-sized game at long ranges, over 100 yards, to put it mildly; and sometimes there was good excuse for the shooting, as under wilderness necessity when the grub had run low.

But with today's material to use, a pistol bullet can hardly be effective on long-range big game except when it is directed by one of a really small band—perhaps much smaller than we think—of excellent shots. This means two-handed shooting and every other possible advantage, all being sportsmanlike in the attempt to kill cleanly.

To kill big game well, the bigbore slug must be blunt-nosed, and that shape limits its trajectory and its grip on velocity. If we lighten it to impart more initial speed with practical, safe pressures, that lowered weight will cut its retention of velocity, and its deep, straight-line penetration, too, other things being unchanged.

There is another sort of long-range pistol bullet for small, but not too small, game—for vital parts must be big enough to offer a reasonable target, shots out of the "ten-ring" being penalized, for they wound or miss, both bad. This is a small-caliber, fast bullet like the .22 Hornet, or rather a sub-weight Hornet, that *can* start at about 2,000 f. s. velocity and hold enough of it to expand, in spite of the more or less stiff copper or gilding metal jacket, at maybe 100 yards or more on the bodies of, say, 10 to 20 pound varmints. Even so, such pistols can't equal Hornet rifles, with similar bullets at much higher speeds. These fine little rifles, we all know, have lost their popularity to more powerful .22 and larger caliber varmint rifles. There is reason for this. The Hornet rifle is not very effective beyond 150 yards—even discounting wind—or at most beyond 200, regularly and reliably. With almost all calibers there have been freak successes and freak failures, which too seldom tell us much, although the failures are the ones to which to pay most attention in our arms and ammunition study.

For this sort of medium game the bigbore bullet, lightened, speeded-up, cast or swaged of soft lead, and of course hollow-pointed, *may* be considerably more effective than the smallbore. It is sure to make a big wound. The smallbore is attractive. It has been since or perhaps before the .25-20 Single Shot rifle cartridge came out in 1889, a slimmer, longer, less sharply bottle-necked round than the .25-20 Repeater that merchants still stock. But for hunting we want sure killing power. Is the added recoil of a bigbore too much to put up with? With both types of these hand-loaded and more or less special sixgun rounds, we get what some would call an unearthly sharp report. That is punishment to some shooters, but not to all. It goes with high velocity, and if we must have that, we must learn to endure the ear-ringing or wear ear-plugs even when we hunt. I for one don't like to, but since I shoot right-handed, a plug in the left ear for rifle and in the right for pistol does help a great deal.

Most auto-pistol bullets, and a few revolver slugs like the .32 S.&W. Long, the .38 and .44 Special, are streamlined enough up front to shoot flat when started at high velocity. But they slip through flesh without much if any tearing, just because they *are* streamlined, and they are more likely to drill a bone than, perhaps, break it.

Once I was told a story of a criminal escaping justice, 'way out across a big field. He was carrying a business ledger, though why, I do not know. Most crooks prefer rustling or clinking cash to cold figures, don't they? Anyway, two of the good guys went to work on him at 150 yards or so, one with a .44 Special, the other with a .30 Luger. Why say more? The fat ledger stopped the slow .44; the .30 went through it like an electric drill, spoiling the accounts but saving the cash.

Personally: I think this story is as apocryphal as Uncle Punk's saga of the sea-serpent he nearly caught in Mud Pond on the day the rest of the boys had gone to the circus.

But sometimes we need penetration, above all, from a pistol bullet, as in reaching deep into the life of some large animal, on its feet or downed by a rifle bullet, or against a get-away bandit car. That means high velocity and hard construction as against big diameter and the speed, shape and soft construction that conspire to increase that diameter considerably as the slug plows its way through live tissue.

Bullet Success Story

Just as with people, not all bullets succeed because they deserve to. But here are some of the things that make for handgun bullet deadliness under the usual conditions.

Caliber. A big one punches big holes. To kill promptly, a pistol slug more often than not must do this. It must destroy either a good-sized section of rather vital tissue or a key spot of absolutely vital tissue like the brain or spinal cord. Since few pistol bullets have anything like the, say, 1600 f.s. impact velocity minimum that gives violently disruptive effect, they need size and smash-through shape to kill.

Shape is about as important as caliber, within reasonable limits. Bullets may or may not expand as they penetrate game or a human enemy, but even with little or no expansion their deadliness can be increased by shape. A blunt bullet pushes tissue aside violently as it penetrates; it does not ease its way through like a round-nose or sharp-nosed projectile at moderate speed, the 1,000 f.s. or so that is somewhere near average for medium or large caliber handgun slugs. The bluffest form of all is the keg-shaped wadcutter, flat and at least bore if not groove diameter up front. Generally its accuracy and well sustained velocity end at about 50 yards, or not much more.

Cutting a square shelf into this bullet, a little behind its flat front, then tapering from this shelf to a still wide, square-cut flat at the nose increases range and penetration without seriously detracting from the full wadcutter-type's flat-out slap and smash. This is the design of Keith-Lyman bullets, so well known and widely used by handloaders, and of a few earlier Lyman or Ideal Mfg. Co. forms like the 150 (or 130) grain 360271 B. F. Wilder type of .38 Special, useful in .38 Auto as a 130 grain, and the 250 grain 429336 C. E. Heath pattern of .44 Special. It is possible to load these old timers like the Keith 358429, -431 and -432 .38s, 429421 .44 Special, 452423 .45 Auto-Rim, and 454424 .45 Colt, to name a few. This loading sets a rifling groove diameter (or near it) bearing band out ahead of the brass case, to true up the bullet in the chamber throat and (in the case of the slightly beveled front band of Keith design) to ease the bullet into the barrel's rifling throat, leade or forcing cone—call it what you like. An abruptly square-shoulder bullet entering the throat can lead that part of a barrel miserably, though some throats foul up with a lead bullet of almost any shape. The square band also adds to clean-cut, not eased-through, penetration. We want that for killing power that doesn't require the utmost penetration. On target paper these flat shelves, like the keg-head fronts of true wadcutter bullets, punch clean-cut holes, much more easily scored than those made by tapered-front lead.

Next in shape deadliness come bullets with good, flat points, not as wide flats as those just discussed, and with sloping sides leading to the flat. Standard .32-20, .38-40 and 44-40 bullets are typical, and so are the .32 and .38 Colt New Police and the .38 Colt Special. The .45 Colt almost always has had only a narrow little flat up front. It is really a semi-pointed bullet.

Very similar to these old Colt and Winchester designs, and perhaps even more effective, is the much blunter hemispherical rounded nose, still factory-produced up to this writing, at least, in .41 Long Colt form. Actually this .41 is blunter than the hemispherical shape. Some special, practically custom-designed bullets, available only from molds, not from the huge factory machines, got good killing power from a flat point rounded off rather abruptly. They do not have the cutting edges of Keith and other square-cut noses and shoulders, but they are at least in the .41 class of deadly shape. In Belding & Mull design they fed reliably through the action of a .45 Auto I had for a woods gun.

All these shapes, even the full wadcutter, can be hollow-pointed to hasten and increase their expansion—and to reduce their penetration, too, of course. When impact velocity is still fairly high, maybe 700 f.s. or so, soft lead hollow points can mushroom. They are a bit less likely to glance from rock or shale than solid are, too.

But the shape of the cave in them is important. A straight-sided cavity, in the old express-rifle style, probably averages wider mushrooming than a conical cavity does, though a wide cone, extending almost across the bullet's flat point, can do business at pretty low velocities. The conical is the easier form to cast.

Handloaders often used to split their cast bullet points, either in halves or in quarters, with a knife or a little saw. They found it easy to make one wide, deep cut, down to the bearing surface of the bullet, by putting a slip of paper between the jaws of the mold. The paper does not burn up. It stays there practically unharmed, and you pry open the bullet nose to remove it, after you've loaded that bullet into its case, for the loading die would force the split front halves shut again, of course. The splitting does help expansion to some extent; and so does cutting or filing off the nose of a tapered, rounded bullet like those of the .22 long-rifle or the standard .38 Special.

Contrariwise, the expansion of hollow-point bullets has been reduced, with more or less success, by filling their cavities with firm and hard-packed grease or wax. There would seldom be any reason to do this with pistol ammunition.

Weight is important. It not only adds to shocking effect, the paralyzing blow we at least hope to deliver, but it also helps in assuring deep, straight-line penetration in the direction of aim, not off at a tangent. The rifleman values bullet weight also because it helps to overcome the frustrating effects of cross-winds that push a bullet off course. The pistoleer, even at 50 yards on the target range, knows what wind is, too!

Of course handgun bullet weight can increase recoil noticeably, make the gun shoot much higher at short ranges, and slow the accurate delivery of follow-up shots. But most of the time these costs are not too much to pay to buy what weight can bring in reliability, in follow-through punch, and so on.

The *construction* of the pistol's bullet is nearly as important in connection with killing power as that of the rifle's missile. Some would say that it is more important. Hard jackets give penetration, and once they were considered almost necessary to the sure feeding of a semi-automatic. You recall that our first commercial American auto-rifle—or at least the first in general use—was the Winchester Model 1903, a

.22 rim-fire using its special cartridge—which is still made, glory be! The modern .22 Auto bullet is of soft, inside lubricated lead. Not so the original. That was tough, as hard as chilled shot, so that it wouldn't be battered in the tubular magazine and fail to find its way up into the chamber. Now we know more about semi-automatic arms and their ideal diet.

But some guns do need specially tempered cast bullets. The rifling grooves of some .45 Auto Colt caliber handguns are purposely made shallow to make it easier for jacketed bullets to seal the bore. In handloading for them with cast alloyed lead, we may have to go to hard mixtures to get sustained accuracy and prevent leading the bore. A soft- or hollow-point jacketed bullet seldom means much with muzzle velocities under 1200 f.s., we might say, although long-exposed soft points, as on the .32-20, have mushroomed well in game. Jackets vary both in thickness and toughness; and some, like those of the late unlamented .38 Auto Colt and .30 and 9 mm. Luger hollow points, have been entirely too thick up front where those of modern, well-designed, high-power rifle bullets are thinned considerably. But again, the shape and depth of the hollow in a lead-alloy bullet are important, and so is the hardness of the alloy.

Velocity gets steadily more attention, with our strong new guns and long Magnum cartridge cases. The 1959 .22 Winchester Rimfire Magnum, a 2,000 f.s. velocity rifle load, has a rather high-proportioned, 75%-plus speed of 1550 f.s. from a 6½-inch barreled sixgun. With its light 40 grain jacketed bullet, it considerably exceeds the 1430 and 1470 rates of .357 and .44 Magnum revolver rounds. This sacrifice of bullet weight to gain velocity is a rather common tendency in speed enthusiasts' handloads of our commercial and wildcat centerfire pistol and rifle cases. Some think it is overdone. For ranging power, long-sustained energy at a distance, and penetration of tough muscle and bone, it isn't the answer when other details, like bullet shape and construction, are similar. But at ranges that are practical for the average good shot, it helps by flattening trajectory, sometimes by resulting in blow-up effect on game, and almost always by boosting the close-up and not so close-up foot-pounds energy of impact. It's well-known that foot-pounds mean little in calculating a bullet's killing power if they come at the cost of needed penetration that a heavier and apparently more sluggish bullet gives.

Along this line, a bulldog cartridge admirer—and there were many in days of the old British Empire, when the Tommies and their officers fought savage, fanatical tribesmen frequently and pretty much all over the map—such a heavy-bullet convert might say that foot-pounds generated by high velocity bought with bullet weight are the least important of all factors. The slow, bigbore hand-gun cartridges reflected experience and consequent philosophy. So did the long line of British express rifle rounds for the biggest African and Indian game. Men like Bell, who used small-caliber rifles with hard, full-jacketed bullets for well-earned set-up shots at an elephant, they were dissenters, pioneers in thinking. But to get a fairer picture, let's remember that really light, really high-velocity bullets, such as the 70 grain .22 Savage ·Hi-Power at 2700 to 2800 f.s. and the almost quarter-century later .220 Swift, with a 48 grain pellet at 4140, caught on promptly, all in their turn, for use against the big, heavy stags of the Scottish highlands. That shooting is extremely careful and precise, with no element of danger. It is practically executions carried out for the best interests of the herd, like scientific timber harvesting.

Today we are only on the edge of high pistol and high rifle velocities. But we are on the edge. The 1961 .256 Winchester Magnum, starting a 60 grain bullet at 2,200 f.s., seems a great stride forward. It may be only a start.

Placement of the bullet means, literally, almost everything. At least, a fellow is tempted to say so after witnessing the ghastly inhumane results of sloppy shooting at game. With correct placement, .22 shorts kill trapped bear when they are skillfully directed into the brain. All a bullet needs to do is to get in and do its work. But since the shooter, no matter how skilled a woodsman and pistol-shot he may be, can't always set up for himself the ideal situation—compared to what the portrait photographer can do for himself and his camera—all of us need reserve power to back up our placement of a bullet.

A bullet isn't always intended to kill if it can. Often disabling shots at a man target are so much better that an unintentional kill would be downright tragic. All our good law officers know this. One I remember risked his life by making it a habit to carry tear-gas cartridges in his .38 Special instead of ball ammunition. But again, bullet placement backed by adequate power can be the answer. A .45 through the upper arm or shoulder might tame a hoodlum immediately, whereas a .38 in either place might fail.

The Target

The distance of the game or human target is important. As bullet power declines, we need to place the slug better. Thus we have not one but two strikes against us in long-range pistol shooting. So have we with rifle or carbine, but these arms are easier to hit with except in split-second or enforced one-hand work, and even then it's partly a question as to which type you are more familiar with. Usually the long-guns' bullets are built to do well for beyond the effective handgun range of the average good pistol shot—whatever that range may be. Yes, "whatever." Simple proof lies in the fact that pistol targets are printed to be about three or four times as easy as rifle paper, at the same distance.

The vitality of the living target varies a good deal in

most species, no doubt more in man than in animals. Perhaps this shows up, among game animals, mostly in white-tailed deer. You so often hear hunters remark upon it. Part of what we call vitality is mere physical build, the size and strength, which can be either pathetic or prodigious. Then too there is the physical condition, or state of health, and the still more significant will-to-live. Some have that last, whereas others give up easily.

Mood, too, plays a mighty part in the temporary resistance to injury, during which time the victim may be "going to do something about it," either run away or attack the aggressor. There is also the unconcerned, unaware mood. Then, as a rule, the reaction of fighting, or of fleeing, builds up slowly. Most experienced hunters know this, and the skilled and humane ones try to profit by it. "He never knew what hit him," they say with satisfaction deeper than the hearer may realize.

Here too we might recall the ever-useful knowledge that the first rather well-placed bullet gives the animal about all the shock effect he's going to absorb for some time. When an old hunter urges a beginner to "try to make that first shot count," his earnestness is understandable. Also, in either offense or defense, there may be no chance for a second try.

The position of the living target can mean a lot. What way is he facing? How much penetration must the bullet give to get into a vital part?

Now, a man is upright, normally, except for the small percentage of hours when he sleeps—small compared to that of most quadrupeds, at least those which make their living by violent exercise. But the four-footer is different from man in another way. To get into the "boiler room" of heart and lungs, you may need to shoot from and into his rear. Will your pistol bullet do this, or your rifle bullet, if the animal is big? There have been far too many hunting-field failures in penetration. A standing man has all his vital parts exposed.

Break a man's leg, and he won't go far afoot. But the animal has four legs. He's like a cart compared to a bicycle.

What Are Game Loads?

In the early 1920s, Remington put out a series of shotgun "Game Loads" in boxes specifically marked, and illustrated, for use on snipe, quail, rabbit, squirrel, grouse, duck, heavy duck, and the like. With thousands of special-prescription loads in the catalogues, the purpose and fond hope were simplification. For perhaps a year or two the idea caught and held; then it gave way to the old system under which you ordered and eventually got the exact dose and make of powder, along with the size and weight of shot, soft or "chilled" with the hardening of tin or antimony, that your experience afield or your daydreams in the living room (no TV then) had taught you were the best for your kind of country.

Well, people know what they want, or at least prefer to have others think they do. This chapter has tried to say why they may have good reasons for apparently zany choices. What a maze of variables there is, afield, or wherever we might use a pistol for serious purposes! Still, here is a sort of classification of some of our common handgun loads, a general survey of them.

To defend our lives against enemies we use what we've got, what we find within reach when danger turns into a struggle for survival. In the near face of danger, no weapon we can handle seems too big. I do think we should always remember that before it's too late and we are caught short. We must, naturally, handle it well, for skill, the ability to direct adequate force where it's needed, plainly counts most of all.

It is admitted rather generally that the .38 Special is the lightest satisfactory handgun cartridge for defense, even though the flat-nosed .38 Colt Special and the wadcutter at full standard velocity have been gone for years. There's a world of .38 Special variants, and loads much heavier and lighter than any within its wide reach are used effectively right along. The sensible choice is the most deadly cartridge that fits (and is safe to use in) a gun that we can pack, have ready with us, and shoot well enough.

For small, easily killed animals like North American snakes, bullfrogs and cottontail rabbits, the .22 long-rifle high velocity with hollow point bullet does well if the shooter does well. But there are certainly some important differences in the depth and shape of the hollows and in bullet hardness, which we can find for ourselves with no more elaborate tool than a common pin. Fired from a reasonably long-barreled handgun, this .22 has almost exactly the same power and effect as that of the old, discontinued, low velocity hollow point fired from a rifle. Time and again it has proved unsatisfactory on gray and fox squirrels—and so, occasionally, does the modern load, shot from a rifle— although with good shooting it was enough, and with raking hits it was often a great deal too much.

Those squirrels are tough and gritty little fellows. They deserve adequate ballistics and marksmanship. So do all other creatures we hunt, including rats. It is a part of rat nature and habit, not a moral lack, that earns man's hatred for the tribe! Seriously, no living thing deserves to be tortured to death; does it?

Grouse, some varieties of course more than others, and crows and hawks also take a good deal of killing by a pistol bullet. For all these, including squirrels, even the red ones, we could recommend no killing power under that of the .32 S.&W. Long with wadcutter or semi-wadcutter bullet, the flat-nosed, reliable .32-20 with 100 grain bullet, or even the .38 Special, flat-pointed too—or at least not too gently tapered into roundness, as some shapes of its "standard" bullet are. The full-jacketed .32 Auto, .30 Luger and .30 Mauser just haven't what it takes. A red squirrel hit just behind the shoulder had to be finished with a head shot; and I, too stupid then to be skeptical of over-enthusiastic reports, had to take this way of learning. Time and again such jacketed, round-nosed bullets fail miserably on really small game; and the hard .38s and 9 mms. are little better. They simply are not made for small game, although the really high-velocity types —which the .32 and .380 Auto are not—spear deeply into big game and *can* reach vital parts.

Some of the loads mentioned in the preceding paragraph will destroy a good deal of not only edible but downright luscious meat, at times. Such times are better than those when game escapes, wounded.

For porcupines, woodchucks, foxes, coyotes and similar tough, often almost unbelievably hard-to-kill varmints, the best in hand-loaded hollow-point lead bullets are seldom a bit too much. For the sake of decency and sportsmanship we should make the ranges short, or else restrain ourselves and not shoot until we've learned to stalk closer. Bullets just must be placed well. Handgun calibers well suited for the special hollow-point loading for such work could start with the .38 Auto as a minimum—it holds more powder than the 9 mm. Luger does, and modern American guns using it are strongly built—and go on through the .357 Magnum and .38-40 to the .44s and .45s, including the .44 Magnum as an excellent choice. That one has the powder capacity and the super-strong guns to burn the powder. If full loads seem to much at first—and they are likely to!—it makes a good hand-loaded .44 Special, not recoiling much in the heavy sixguns using it. You can go on and use its ample powder room as you become familiar with heavy charges. A .44 or .45 makes a good choice in this class because big bullets can kill well without having to reach the extremes of velocity that are accompanied by ear-splitting muzzle blast. This racket doesn't bother some shooters much, if any at all; but some of us feel it, and our skill may suffer thereby, whether or not we are aware of the fact.

Handgun hunting of deer—and a considerable number of still larger animals fall to pistol bullets, too— is right only for experienced outdoorsmen, those who are lucky enough to spend weeks or months, not merely hours or days, afield; and they must be good cool shots. Many who qualify best would enter a prompt and decided "No!" to any suggestion of such hunting, except under hardpan necessity. Also, since dimly qualified people have gone deer-hunting with handguns, the use of these arms for this truly noble and obviously hardy game is illegal in some areas. At least one state forbids any game hunting with pistols, and here the plain, inescapable reason behind the legislation is common humanity: it is not right to subject game to the likelihood of being only wounded.

But for deer, when for the individual it is right and proper to use a pistol on them, nothing much smaller than the .38-40 seems correct. It is actually a .40-caliber, and with much more powder space—and room, too, for a heavier than standard bullet—than

the old .41 Long Colt of similar bullet diameter. The .357 Magnum has been used a great deal, with and without good success. Here it is really a smallbore, with only high pistol velocity and well-shaped bullets to help it, compared to the heavy .44s and .45s, those now manufactured by American factories, and in some instances underloaded.

The .44 Magnum is first choice for killing power, and good as it comes from the factory box. Light fast bullets, solid or hollow pointed, and of big .44 or .45 caliber, too, may lack the needed penetration unless one picks his shots rather carefully—which he should do, anyway. With any pistol load we can hardly expect full-length, stem-to-stern penetration combined with a big, wide wound path. Short, fast, and fairly soft bullets tend to make wide but not deep wounds. This rule goes for some so-called "deer rifle" loads as well as for handgun rounds. Another fault of some rifle rounds is the exact opposite: the customer asks for deer cartridges and gets moose cartridges. Their excessively tough expanding bullets don't mushroom on deer, at least on broadside hits behind the shoulder, or maybe even through both shoulders of a small deer.

The experience of wounding and losing game can be hard to forget, and let us swear by the "Red Gods" of mountain and forest, plain and river, that it damn well ought to be hard to forget. Try instead to avoid these tragedies, for such they are to the beasts!

Pistols and bows could well be bracketed together as deer-hunting weapons. Both nearly-marginal bullets and sharply limited arrows need the best skill to direct them, and the judgment as to when not to fire them, too. Probably the heavy, large-diameter, reasonably high-velocity handgun bullet is the better killer. It has reliable penetration, much better ranging power (though this can be a delusion, making too-long shots tempting), and if it goes clean through and on out, it can make a fair blood trail to be followed if that is unfortunately necessary. A hunting-type arrow in the chest cavity can let air into the lungs and cause them to collapse rather promptly. For most other shots, it isn't so good. An arrow sticking out of an escaping deer is fairly easy, and infallibly disgusting, to see; a little chunk of lead is hidden. Consequently, the bow-and-arrow has been condemned roundly by many sportsmen who have observed its failures.

Personally, I think that both archer and pistoleer should be made to pass a stiff marksmanship examination before they can legally hunt deer or any other game with their own peculiar weapons. Both bow and handgun are so fascinatingly "different" to use that beginners are likely to feel they are rather proficient with them before they have any real skill at all. The comparatively difficult mastering of them might well depend on the individual human, on his aptitude, enthusiasm and, above all, his willingness to stick with it like a puppy to a boot. And don't forget that the pistolman afield is going to use both hands for steady holding, and he hopes to get down off his feet, as well, into a sit or kneel or squat or slump, to make him still steadier.

There are still, you rightly say, the matters of woodcraft and of shooting well under stress and in rough weather. These would be difficult to test, short of businesslike military training methods.

And hunting accuracy must be deadly, not half-good. It must be ten-ring accuracy. The nines, eights, sevens and so on down not only don't count for you; they count against you, for they either scare game off, which is bad, or wound it, which is worse. With reasonable pistol marksmanship, successful hunting with the handgun is largely a matter of getting close to the game. Close up, the bull's-eye looks bigger; and in good truth, it is. Your bullet has more power, too, significantly more power, sometimes, for our modern game-killing handgun slugs certainly aren't streamlined to split the air. And the more power the bullet has, the bigger the vital "bull's-eye" in the game becomes: the lead doesn't have to strike *quite* so close to the ideal quick-killing location. Sometimes it needn't strike nearly as close, though obviously there's much more variation here when we shoot a rifle than when we shoot a pistol. Really high velocity fans out its energy widely.

The confidence based on mastered marksmanship is pretty fair assurance of creditable performance, incomparably more than the ability to pay for a license and the eagerness to go out and get game! That rather sarcastic contrast may sound like ridiculous exaggeration unless you are a hunter. Then, perhaps, you would call it just a weak whisper.

We do need tests for pistol and bow hunters, and for rifle and shotgun hunters, too. We may come to them. Only a few years ago, required Hunter Safety instruction and exams for first-license buyers were unheard of. Now, several states require them—New York, I understand, even for adults—and some others at least encourage the program, which was inspired by the National Rifle Association.

Of course progress is slow—it usually is in such imponderable matters—but when progress is sure, we can be thankful. What a relief, and what a wonderful, startling surprise! Human safety naturally comes first, conservation and decent treatment of game second, but we need them both.

Speed Shooting

This gets more attention and more ammunition today than ever before, and it is perfectly natural that it should. Does it really contribute to deadliness? And if so, how?

Speed of delivery of the first shot in defense shooting can actually take the place, to some extent, of bullet power. If the lead is only reasonably well placed, it *may* deliver enough shock, or enough of the feeling of being defeated, to tip the win to our side. If there are more than one antagonist, and you stand alone, the

" 'Speed' holster and 1½-inch belt, plain." Notice how easily the 4-inch barreled Smith & Wesson .357 Combat Magnum slips *forward* out of this Berns-Martin holster, an excellent rig for fast side-draw shooting. Photo courtesy J. H. Martin of Berns-Martin, Calhoun City, Mississippi.

value of fast and sufficiently accurate sustained firing is plainly supreme. It could put you through.

Often there is no time for aiming. Instead, the gun or the pair of guns must be pointed. Since most defense shooting is at rather close or very close range, good "point" shooting can be good enough. With a single-action like the Colt, Ruger or Great Western, the common fast methods are fanning, slip shooting and the so-called "hip shooting." The latter includes the use of a double-action revolver—which most of us are likely to use as a defense gun, if we are civilians—and of some models of autoloaders, with side, not top, ejection.

Fanning

As Elmer Keith points out in his book on *Sixguns*, fanning is particularly adapted to dealing with "two or three widely spaced targets." Its delivery of fire can resemble, somewhat, the swift sidewise sweep of a submachine gun, though any such fanning takes almost incomparably more practice if it is good—and in business shooting it has to be.

Fanning isn't outmoded: a few modern shooters find it worth learning for more than personal satisfaction. The gun is carried with its hammer clear down—standard single-action practice—and on "Commence firing!" the first thing to do is to grip the gun, with the forefinger holding the trigger back. The pistol is fired by sweeping the palm, or the heel of the palm, of the free hand back across the hammer spur so as to draw the hammer far enough back to surely revolve the cylinder and fire the turned-up cartridge as the hand passes on through the motion rearward. Obviously this sweep of the hand can be repeated fast. Up to some 40 or 50 feet a long-practiced, highly skilled fanner can be deadly accurate.

The question might arise: Isn't it easier to use one well-trained hand than two, which must be coordinated? The answer is a "Yes, but . . ." It is easier, perhaps, but fanning is the quickest method of firing the single-action. In aiming, or rather pointing, the whole body is turned to align the gun. To correct for an offside miss, or to send follow-up shots into second, third, or more offside targets, the body is turned, not just the hands and arms, to combine speed and accuracy.

Fanning, if carried to any extent, is hard on a revolver. As Keith explains, the parts that turn and lock the cylinder, even the notches, the bolt cuts, in the cylinder, all take a beating. The cylinder is being whirled around fast, and being stopped fast.

Few shooters, probably, would have the trigger removed or even tied back to fit a gun for fanning or slip shooting only, for that would limit its all-round usefulness. The more practice we get with any *one* useful gun, the better we become with it. However, those who have the opportunity to do a great amount of shooting—every day, or near it—might elect to have a single-action altered for limited service like this. Yes, some people have done their shooting for long periods of time with a triggerless single-action, and wonderfully fine shooting it was. But part of it was slip-shooting, too.

It is a matter of satisfaction that the art of fanning hasn't been entirely lost. A person decides for himself whether to leave it alone, give it a fair try, or really go into it.

Slip Shooting

This can be done with one hand, but two hands make for better accuracy, really fine shooting indeed, at long range. If the gun is long-barreled enough, the forward hand can go out on that barrel without danger of being burned by the flash from the barrel-cylinder joint. But watch the muzzle, too! And above all, watch any beginner shooting this way.

John Newman, who was a friend of Elmer Keith and is mentioned appreciatively and interestingly in *Sixguns,* was outstanding in slip shooting. He favored an altered Colt Single Action hammer spur, smooth and low, almost a sort of peg. All this is described in Chapter XIII of *Sixguns.*

Briefly, the hammer spur can be cocked and slipped off from under the thumb of the firing hand, to discharge the piece when the trigger is held back or removed entirely. Or the thumb of the other hand can do this work. There are various methods of slip shooting, and of altering guns for this purpose.

As Keith remarks, it is entirely different from shooting with a triggered revolver, and to be good at either, you—unless you are exceptional—must choose between them. There's no doubt that slip makes for fast shooting, and for deliberate, highly accurate long-range work, too. For most of us, it would be more generally useful than fanning. For one thing, we would use the sights! Or, if we couldn't, it seems more natural to aim the extended hand than the whole body; doesn't it? But fanning is still the fastest way of firing a single-action; and within a shooter's short effective range, it has paid off.

Hip Shooting

This delivery of fire, along with quick draw and the guns best suited to this kind of service, is covered well in Chapter IX of *Sixguns.* No specially altered handgun is required, although some shooters like to have the front of the trigger guard cut away, lest the forefinger strike it in a hurried reach, and hammer spurs have been ground off, too, so that they couldn't catch in a pocket during a fast draw. Top-ejecting automatics, like the Luger, the modern Colt .45, .38 and 9 mm., and many other makes and sizes, won't do. They throw empty cases upward and more or less back, not to the side, and stopping one of those with your eye or even with your front teeth would be tough fielding, and no applause from the bleachers.

This is very practical defense shooting at close range, when a fraction of a second on the right side could save your life. It's called "hip shooting," although some of us never use this method of bracing or steadying the arm or elbow against hip or side. It could help under the recoil of heavily loaded sixguns, and employing the body, not the arm, as a pivot has its advantages. That is literally interpreted hip shooting, but there's a tendency to apply the term to the method in which no part of the arm touches or even is near the body—comparatively speaking.

This latter style is a sort of point or thrust shooting. The arm is poked forward, not to its fullest extent, but enough to take muzzle blast and noise noticeably and comfortably farther away. In either style of shooting, you may or may not go into a crouch, which of course should not be exaggerated, or time-consuming. If it is used, it must blend with the drawing and extending of the pistol.

The sights on the gun don't count. Its feel and balance do, and being absolutely familiar with the weapon, most of all. Practice, which should go on for years, should be done on a safe range, a lonely sort of range, one where there is dry ground, preferably in a steep bank, on which the splashes of the bullets will show plainly. It becomes a fascinating sort of shooting whenever we are in the mood for the action it gives in a minimum of time and with a maximum expenditure of ammunition.

J. H. Martin, of Berns-Martin, using S.&W. Combat Magnum on a fast-draw target. Mr. Martin has made a study, and practice, of quick-draw shooting for a good many years.

A western friend, who had been a professional hunter, law-enforcement man, guide, and marksmanship instructor overseas—really the most experienced big game hunter I ever knew—would take a strange gun, loose off a shot to get the range, and almost instantly follow with a second bullet. The target was a bit smaller than your fist, down on the ground some 10 or 15 feet from where he stood. I can't recall a second bullet ever missing it. With his own, familiar guns he could do much better. The point is that he could hit that target with practically any revolver a person handed him, and before firing he would take no more than ten seconds or so to get the feel of it.

As Keith says, you don't need good eyesight to shoot well in quick draw. I once read of a totally blind man who hunted rabbits successfully. As I remember, he used some sort of shotgun, and he would fire at the sound when they broke cover nearby. In most of our small game countries today, with the woods as full of eager hunters as a mince pie is of raisins, he would have been restrained, no doubt!

Another sort of restraint is needed. All our writers on guns, it seems, are aware of the need and have expressed themselves about it. But here goes: practice quick draw from holster or pocket a long, long time before you crack a single primer in learning this art. The gun muzzle must be clear of your anatomy before you go to work on single-action hammer or double-action trigger. There is time to do this. There is also time—quite a slice of it, in fact—to wish you had, if you are in the hospital with a gunshot wound anywhere from thigh to toes. This sort of quick draw accident *has occurred many times recently*. Movies, TV and some rather irresponsible publicity on the subject have made quick draw more popular than ever before.

Why, one of my friends, an experienced and nation-

ally decorated rifle-shot, and not bad at all with the handgun, was deeply thankful he *hadn't* loaded his Colt .45 for the start or near-start of this practice. If he had, he'd have shot himself in the leg. Not all are men enough to admit such close calls.

For point or hip or quick draw, most folks with experience seem to shuck down to short, heavy revolvers. A pair of 4-inch S.&W. Combat Masterpieces, .22 or .38 Special, or the slightly heavier Colt Troopers, or the non-target-sighted Colt Official Police 4-inchers make a good team. The three ounces or so of weight difference between the calibers is partly erased by the heavier .38 cartridges; and having a .22 so similar to the .38 in balance makes for more practice rounds fired, and sometimes fired in places where the noise of the centerfire would be prohibitive. Some prefer much heavier but still short guns.

The 3-inch Hi-Standard Sentinel .22 is relatively inexpensive, but it has an excellent double-action trigger pull, the kind of pull that so many of us prefer to use in hip shooting, when it *is* good. (Still, straight single-action revolvers and thumb-cocking of double-action guns have their devotees, too.) Although it's a light gun, when you weigh it, it has much the feel of a medium-heavy revolver, because the steel cylinder and barrel are well forward of your hand, and the alloy frame and grip don't make up a high percentage of the total heft. As a result, it is a really good understudy for 4-inch or shorter, medium-weight .38 Specials.

What we need most of all is a gun that points well when it's poked out at about hip level, or for that matter, when it's extended at shoulder level. It is balance that is needed, a quality hard to define. For you individually, a pistol has it or hasn't it, just as a brush shotgun or a woods snapshooting rifle has it or hasn't it. All of them must be, after a reasonable stint of dry and live-rounds practice, as responsive as it is possible for a gun to be, to you individually. Then you have a fair chance of getting to be good with your weapon.

Some pistols just won't do for quick work, except at the cost of an enormous amount of practice. The Bisley Colt—I like the old gun—is stocked so that the muzzle tends to hang down. Many old automatics, like the early Colt .38s—also personal pets—the 1905 .45, and a slew of old and not-so-old foreign military and pocket automatics are also too straight-stocked. They too point, or would point, at an enemy's toes, not at his life. Even our 1911 Colt .45 auto, with much more rake-back of grip than the seldom-seen 1905, has been criticized by many, perhaps the majority, of the experienced, for its tendency to point low. The 1911-A, with arched housing at the lower rear of the grip, was an improvement in this respect, for most people. But it does make the grip feel still larger to a very small hand. The early, not the later, Savage auto-pistols were too straight-stocked, and so were the .32 and .380 Colts. These are old guns, only occasionally seen now, since our manufacturers have given this market to European arms makers.

But for more or less deliberate, extended-arm firing, most if not all of these low-hanging guns would do, and that's an understatement, for they have done remarkably well in skilled and accustomed hands. As we noticed before, a straight-stocked .22 target automatic like the Smith & Wesson is close to, if not at, the general ideal for Olympic rapid fire; it beats the devil of over-shooting at eye-level targets.

How long does it take to learn point-shooting? The answer is a lifetime, and a long and happy one at that, for perfection is without limits in anything worth doing, or just fun doing, isn't it? And this is both!

As an example, my friend Glenn Seabright with his 3-inch barreled Hi-Standard .22 revolver was able to do a good, practical, double-action, defense sort of hitting after about two years of fairly steady week-end and occasional summer evening shooting. A cigarette butt at eight or ten feet isn't quite safe from him in unaimed, "point" firing. If the first shot misses, and the butt isn't splashed out of sight or effective range, the second is pretty sure to hit it or to chip it up and away like a mashie-struck golf ball.

Glenn is not a competitive revolver shot in slow, timed and rapid, although he's a high-grade competitive rifle shot. By natural implication this means that he's an excellent long-range game shot with a rifle. He does his best work with his own rifles, one in particular; but he's good with any rifle that is more than half decent.

As he has said, the rifle, not the pistol, is his weapon. My own opinion is that expertness with one of these two types of arm helps with the other; and the same goes for the easy and happy buildup of enthusiasm for them, too. It is true that when your ambition leads you toward highly specialized competition, it's a good idea to stick to the tools of that particular field, unless, that is, you now and then fire the other sorts of arms for relaxation and fun. Possibly some competitive shots have disregarded that angle, but then, it might not work at all for them.

Fast Double-Action Revolver Shooting

Without much doubt it is the most practical of all the kinds of fast handgun shooting described in this chapter. Learning to *use* the double-action feature built into most of our revolvers—and into most of the comparatively few current foreign ones, too—means quick let-off of the important, sometimes vitally important, first shot. Double-action naturally fits into the techniques of quick draw, hip shooting or point shooting, and extended-arm rapid fire at close quarters and under stress.

Probably most of us who own a revolver, or more than one, own a double-action. But it is perfectly plain that single-action .22s of various makes and grades have become extremely popular in the last few years—since the Ruger came out, in fact. Bigbore single-actions are selling well, too.

For a case history of single-action appeal, here's my friend Mike Robinson. A few months ago he qualified as Expert Junior Rifleman, N.R.A., with his Model 52 Winchester .22 on our club range; last Friday evening he was three-quarters through Distinguished, which is not quite kid stuff! Mike is only 15 years old, but he's gunwise and careful. He's been permitted to buy his first handgun. (He claims his father's handguns as his own, but I never look hard at him when he says that!) By the way, he earned the money for his 52 and the pistol that's coming up. He has fired a good many double-actions and autoloaders, but now there's no doubt in his mind that he wants a single-action Ruger .22, and the standard-weight, not the light one.

Why? Mike goes to school and he is at least average in sociability. He has heard the other boys talk guns, and he has contributed his share of talk, which I think must be considerable! He also watches TV, including Westerns, frequently, for he gets good school grades without having to kill himself. So for him the single-action is it, and for a great many others, too.

However, I maintain, perhaps bullheadedly, that the double-action is still the more popular; and it certainly comes in many more models—including two made to look like a single-action, the Hi-Standard and the Harrington & Richardson. Few of us use the d.a. as a d.a., as every handgun shooter knows. "You can't hit anything with it, that way."

You can learn, but it takes a great deal of time, ammo and will-power. Aimed, slow-fire, double-action shooting is entirely different from the fast sort, or it can be. This method uses a deliberate trigger pull. Even with a fine d.a. lock mechanism, the pull is heavy, say ten pounds or more, and it seems to get heavier as the hammer creeps back. Actually, it may not grow heavier, but the finger seems to want to cry quits, at least during early trials. The last bit of weight should go on, of course, when the sight picture is good. With the thumb held low in double-action, as it usually is, it may serve as an indicator to the trigger finger that the point of discharge is at hand.

The old Smith & Wesson hammerless .32s and .38s, using the short S. & W. cartridges, had a perceptible stop or pause at that point. On the Iver Johnson hammerless, a cheaper gun, less finely finished and sometimes passed by inspectors with a more obvious barrel-cylinder gap, that stop was especially noticeable. Our hammer revolvers, made for more all-round service, have no such stop. But who would want it?

No one, it's sure, would want it for rapid fire. Smoothness of pull is preferable then, at least to most of us. Although a few skilled shooters use d.a. for very accurate slow-fire, they are really few. It takes a long time to get there.

For rapid, the pull-through of the trigger finger is usually smooth, unhalted and fast. Ed McGivern was the king of that country. His record of plunking five .38 bullets into the area of a standard playing-card at 15 feet in two-fifths of a second is amazing, but it did happen so. McGivern was strictly honest.

He and Mrs. McGivern were the subjects of an article by Chad Wallin in the 1959 *Gun Digest*. It's a short article, necessarily, but it seems to give the main points, personal and technical. Reference is made, as it should be, to McGivern's book on *Fast and Fancy Revolver Shooting*.

You will note in the illustrations for that article that McGivern stood up straight—no crouch. He did, in following moving targets' rise or fall, bend his body slightly. Slip shooting and fanning both got a good workout in his lifelong investigations, and in the latter he made the remarkable playing-card-size group of five shots in 1⅕ seconds, one-third as fast, you notice, as his double-action record. He also tried semi-automatic pistols, but found, as some of our fastest shotgun users have found, that the self-loading action, a mere flash in time though it is, was slower than his trigger finger. He went back to double-action revolvers. Oh yes, he did two-gun work also. He was, all in all, more than a specialist in fast (and accurate) double-action shooting. He was a truly scientific investigator.

Somewhere there must be someone who in time can equal or even better McGivern's work, and the fine old man would have been delighted, for he was, we know, the impartial, unselfish scientist. But to come so near to perfection is, really, unnecessary. What I do think necessary is that everyone who uses a double-action revolver should shoot it occasionally as a double-action. That means getting the first shot off fast, the chief advantage—next to reliability, usually we can say with truth—of the revolver over the usual autoloader. So it seems wise to master that advantage, at least to a better than hopeless degree! It could pay off.

Let the shooting be single shots at first, and let there be plenty of patience and some experimenting with different holds. Grip the gun rather hard, and don't dally with the trigger travel, which should be steady, and not slow. Perhaps a foot-square mark at ten feet is small and distant enough. To hit one fast and surely might sometime save your life. Or you could modify this to less speed and more accuracy; the start just mentioned is a bit of an exaggeration, though for almost everyone double-action is terribly discouraging at first.

It *is* discouraging, but it is interesting, too. Stick with with it long enough to get the thrill of two consecutive hits just about right, under not too difficult conditions. Then keep what you've gained, and perhaps add to it, by an occasional practice gunful on trips afield or to the range.

If your gun is an autoloader you needn't worry so much about fast shooting *after* that still important first shot has gone. The auto shucks out empty and slams in loaded brass quite fast enough, and its trigger travel is short. Few of us could balk it if we tried.

Fast, accurate shooting is easier with the auto than with the revolver *unless* we put time and effort into either prompt thumb-cocking or double-action trigger work. Both are hard to learn, but full of rewards. Only recently has d.a. shooting had much of a trial in formal rapid-fire courses, which *are* practical in a real though not all-inclusive way.

Let us learn, finally, to shoot quickly and well from almost any position, even from a crawl under barbed wire, a stoop below overhanging branches, or getting into or out of a low-slung automobile. And let's include the positions for deliberate slow-fire accuracy, the prone, sitting, leaning, slouching and so on.

The deadliness of our handgun cartridges depends upon their built-in killing power, our accurate placement of hits, and sometimes on the speed of delivery of those hits. These are the things we can do about our practical effectiveness with a pistol. Sometimes two, or even one, will make up for deficiencies of the others; but not always.

Discussion of handgun cartridge deadliness can and does flow on forever, like the River that flowed out of Eden. It's fun, for all of us can contribute something gleaned from experience or from theoretical pondering in the stillness of late townside nights or in the quiet of the woods. The cartridge's own killing power is a particularly rich and satisfying lode to dig into, although it's a bit impersonal except in cases of specially prepared ammunition. By contrast, our personal accuracy and speed of fire can be embarrassing topics! However, we do learn from others' experience as well as from our own; and we *are* determined to learn and improve.

Another factor is personal courage. Nearly all of us have it when we need it, although its possession may come as something of a surprise.

Sometimes raw courage alone will do it, with no real weapon to help.

One of my friends was fly-fishing for trout, accompanied by his very young son, who was wisely aware of the back-cast. I know that part of the stream, and the beautiful, semi-wooded country it winds through. It was a happy day until a bull pushed out of the brush and bellowed at them from across the not very deep brook, pulling up divots with his hoofs. Under quiet orders the boy went *slowly* to the fence and climbed it to safety, while his father held that big, ugly animal off by cracking the leader and flies in its very face. The brute never did charge, for the man—and what a man he was!—covered his own retreat with the snapping of that flimsy tackle.

Another friend had an almost identical experience, except that there was no water barrier, frail though it was for the former fellow, with the fence only a few yards behind it. His weapon was more potent, though not much, one of the early Colt Woodsman .22 autoloaders stuffed with the old low-velocity, Lesmok powder long-rifles. But then, would you expect to stop a charging bull with a clipful of high-velocity long-rifles?

This bull kept coming, but slowly; he didn't break into a charge because he didn't quite dare to. Bullets from the little pistol kept kicking up the dust in front of his hoofs, and one of them actually hit a hoof! At that he fairly roared, but he didn't put down his big, horned head and plunge forward. The eleven-shot gun was nearly empty by the time his two human enemies had got back across the fence.

Before I heard of these incidents, I hadn't thought of either of these friends as courageous, or as not courageous. They were just my friends, and that was plenty. Like millions of other quiet, easy-going people, they proved that bravery can flash up at an instant's need.

CHAPTER 11

RIMFIRE CARTRIDGES

PROBABLY the .22 short and .22 long-rifle rounds give us pistol and rifle cranks more shooting fun than all other calibers added together. In the manufacture of American centerfire ammunition, two additional components are needed, compared to the rimfire. They are the primer cup and the anvil against which the explosive in that cup is smashed by the firing pin or the hammer nose. European centerfire cases, as a rule, have no separate anvil component assembled into the primer; it is built into the cartridge case. The priming composition of the rimfire is smeared around the hollow rim of the case or "shell." So unless we reload our centerfire brass—and percentagewise, few of us do—it's the rimfires that give us cheap, abundant shooting.

We can't reload a rimfire for economy or to change its ballistics to suit our need or whim—not safely, that is, though experimenters have tried it. Less than a half-century ago, at least one of our biggest companies offered bullets and primed rimfire cases for sale. Some people must have used them with their own ideas of powder charge. All that has "gone down the stream of time," along with other now unheard of availabilities, some useful, some plain crazy.

We have the old, familiar Big Four makes of American rimfire ammunition: alphabetically, Peters, Remington, Western and Winchester. The first two and the second two are pairs, made under the same management and perhaps on the same machines, for often they appear to differ only in the headstamps on the brass cases. We have found Winchester and Western .22 long-rifles packed together and, long ago, Remington and Savage .25-20 High Velocity in the same box.

Evidently Remington had made those .25s for Savage, though still farther back, Savage made their own ammunition in various sizes. A new company, Federal Cartridge, has had a good many outside contracts in recent years. Their .22 short, long and long-rifle rounds have given excellent accuracy, to my knowledge and probably yours, too, in a considerable variety of arms. All that I have seen carry plain lead bullets, not plated with copper, cadmium or brass, and their design, formerly called "Airline," is distinctive. Only one narrow groove, cut, not milled like the edge of a dime, lies on the bore-bearing section. The single milled groove up front is on the ogive or curve; it could scarcely contact any rifling land in a barrel. The only criticism I have of Federal .22s, and I hope it is temporary, is that of insufficient lubrication. In good barrels, and even in one that came to me slightly pitted, Federal has given no lumpy leading to brush out; but in .22 revolvers with today's popular, deep, wide cone at the barrel breech, it's a different story entirely. One I know of was choked up badly. However, such barrels are liable to leading with any ammunition, even the .22 long-rifles with plated bullets. A factory "lot" or run of Feds I saw yesterday is well lubricated.

There has been comment that copper-plated bullets could cause rust in an uncleaned bore by way of electrolytic action. This seems a reasonable statement, but I've never known the thing to happen. It is noteworthy that in 1959 Remington began plating their Hi-Speed .22s with a substance that looks like brass. Except for a brief excursion into cadmium plating, this is, I believe, the first time they have used anything of the sort on .22s.

We can probably ignore the risk of rusting due to plating. One advantage these hard bullets have is that they seem to clean a bore that's just been fired with plain-lead ammo. Not a real cleaning, of course, but it shortens the pleasant job of giving the gun a real cleaning—which I do and enjoy, along with the small percentage of other hard-shells. These bullets also resist, to some extent, battering in a tubular rifle magazine, and that leads us to wonder whether they expand on game as well as lead does. The plating is thin, however, and on both wood and game it's hard to tell the difference. There are other factors, variations in bullet construction and in what the bullet hits!

High-velocity plated .22 bullets usually are lubricated with wax, which is less likely than grease to be rubbed off or to pick up dirt and grit in the pocket. That's where most .22s are carried, instead of in the belt or box or pouch, though they shouldn't be. Most target shooters prefer greased bullets for accuracy, perhaps for good reason or perhaps because they seem to be the proper thing. In hot weather, grease can melt and run, but on the range a seasoned shot keeps his ammunition shaded as well as he can, for heat raises pressures; and velocities tend to run ragged as the period of exposure goes on.

Reliability

To some of us who remember a few years back, it's amazing—but true—that today's rimfire ammo is practically as sure-fire as the centerfire stuff. A misfire is

183

news if the striker, firing pin or hammer nose strikes clear across the hollow rim that contains the priming, and hits it reasonably hard. Portions where the rim is unprimed are exceedingly rare in today's runs of production, though they used not to be. One or two misfires in a box of 50 weren't uncommon. We have short-throw strikers and hammers today, to speed the ignition of many target handguns and rifles; but speed itself is a factor in sure ignition, less effective than the weight of the blow, for sure, but still important. Our modern cases are of brass, not of soft copper as earlier, and some old guns, both rifles and pistols, do give trouble with the ammo we have now. Most of them, too, were built to fire black powder, or the later semi-smokeless formulas, which burned more cleanly, and both kinds are more easily ignited than smokeless, on an average.

There were outstandingly reliable gun-and-cartridge combinations in old days. For example, the Winchester Model 1890 (or 90) .22 WRF caliber rifle with ammunition of the same make almost never failed to fire, unless the stuff had been lying around for many years; and the Winchester 1903 (or 03) and Remington Model 16, semi-automatic rifles with their own special shapes of cartridges, were nearly as reliable in firing. They did, however, rather frequently fail to eject an empty and insert a fresh round, even when their actions were kept clean and oiled.

We have similar troubles today with some autoloading pistols, and rifles, too. Usually it is the fault of the gun, if the correct ammunition goes into it. Some pistols have recoil springs too strong for .22 long-rifle match ammunition loaded down to about 1120 f. s. velocity from rifles, such as Western Super-Match Mark III. That Mark III, as of right now, has performed the unusual feat of being a consistent winner in rifle matches for several years in succession. Its velocity is low, barely above the speed of sound, to give that accuracy. Consequently, some semi-automatics need to have the tension of their recoil springs altered to make them feed properly. When auto-pistols jam, it is usually because of bent magazine lips or a rough or poorly inclined bullet ramp leading from magazine to chamber. Lack of gun care can cause it, too, the arm being improperly lubricated, or lubricated not at all, or not kept clear of the carbon sludge that builds pretty much all around the breech of a .22 that uses either grease- or wax-lubricated cartridges.

Old and much deteriorated ammunition, rimfire or centerfire, can make trouble because it has lost its strength or the lube has caked up hard and flaky. A lot depends upon its storage conditions, hot humid weather posing the worst problems. Until recently, I thought that ten years' storage would cause accuracy, too, to deteriorate so much that the stuff wouldn't be worth using even for serious practice. I had had good luck with some six-year-old stuff in my Model 52 Winchester, though I hadn't expected it, for it had seen some pretty toasty summers, stored as well as I could

manage. The cellar was too damp, and was therefore out. Then Arthur Seabright gave me a box of 1941 Army Lot Western long-rifle, the low speed but not the Xpert type. I had his son Glenn fire it in his 52 because he shoots so much better than I. As I recall, he made a 98 or 99 at 50 feet with it instead of 100. Stupidly, I didn't think about trying some of it in an autoloader for functioning.

So as far as reliability of firing goes, we could today depend on rimfire ammunition for defense about as fondly as we could on centerfire. For feeding, it's reliable as a matter of course in revolvers, single shot rifles and pistols, and hand-operated repeating rifles. It is also trustworthy in a properly made and kept semi-automatic arm, although for this kind we ought to get fresh ammunition just on principle!

There is one serious hazard with the heel-type bulleted ammo, rimfire, or centerfiire like .32 and .38 Short Colt, but especially with the rimfires, I believe. These cartridges—BB and CB caps, .22 short, long and long-rifle, and .32 short and long—like the two old Colt types still made, have their bullets stepped down at the base to enter the brass. Case and bullet body are of about equal diameter. The heel is short, and the crimp varies a great deal in strength, all too often in cartridges from the same box. A loose crimp, or none at all in black or semi-smokeless powder loadings, often has been approved as contributing to .22 rimfire accuracy, but it can let oil seep back into the powder charge and even down to the primer composition. Then you get a squib or a misfire. So if a .22 auto-pistol is to be relied on for defense, its chamber should be either empty, or given but a trace of oil if loaded; and the revolver's chambers must be nearly dry, too. It seems not to be quite certain that even the most tightly crimped heel-bullet ammo is reliable in chambers swimming in oil. Sometimes just a few days' residence in a moderately oiled chamber can deactivate the powder and priming behind a bullet that is crimped in with about average strength—whatever that is; the variations are really tremendous.

Selection of a pistol or revolver depends largely on the ammunition it takes, and the .22 offers a wide choice to its owner. Although probably no other calibers of rimfire handguns roll off today's production lines, a great array of larger calibers was once made. Many still give satisfaction, depending upon ammunition supply.

Even yet, odd lots of long-discontinued sizes hang on in quantities that might be surprising. They are seldom for sale; they are hoarded! With new calibers coming out almost but not quite as frequently as they did —in rifle sizes, at least—in the 1880s and '90s, something's got to give, and it will be the old sizes.

This means everything above .22 long-rifle, except of course for the 1959 arrival, Winchester's .22 rimfire Magnum. The .25 Stevens went out a couple of years or so ago, and a fine cartridge it was. But not enough people bought it. It is still found at a few

From left: BB cap, CB cap, .22 short, .22 long, .22 long-rifle, .22 Remington Autoloading (see .22 W.R.F. chapter section), .22 extra long, .22 W.R.F., .22 Winchester Magnum Rim Fire, .25 Stevens short, .25 Stevens, .30, .32, .38 and .41 shorts and longs, .44 short blank cartridge. Note turn-over crimp, which holds the wad in place over the black powder. .44 Henry and Winchester, .46 short. Lamp photo, Winchester, Va.

dealers' and in some shooters' glory-boxes, for no cartridge disappears instantly. The .22 Remington Autoloading is in the same ghostly barge, plowing across the River Styx to oblivion. The .22 Winchester Automatic—not for pistols, though the Rem. 22 was a nice subload for .22 WRF or Special guns—is still precariously on the roster at this writing, and so are the .32 short and long. Their survival depends on how many rounds of them we buy per year, as a tangible factor, and on customer good-will, as an intangible. I've owned and liked guns for all of them; and any regrets you have, I share, too.

We just bow to the inevitable. Or most of us do. The .41 short rimfire was brought back because so many collectors who had derringers for it howled and howled until they got the ammunition.

BB and CB Caps

These are fairly recent casualties. First the "conical ball," then the "bulleted" or "bullet breech" caps fell off factory lists. They served special but limited purposes well.

BB caps are imported by Stoeger Arms, 45-18 Court Square, Long Island City 1, N. Y. They are made by the German Rheinische-Westphalische Sprengstoff firm, which began using non-corrosive priming in 1901. Packed in tin boxes of 100, they sell at present for the same money that buys two 50-round boxes of .22 shorts with solid bullets. Now we have also the Eley make of C B caps imported from England.

The BB cap dates back to about 1840, when it was simply a crimped percussion cap carrying a round ball. Later a black powder charge of about 1½ grains' weight was added; and some smokeless lots, I believe, have held powder, though usually there is none—just the priming as propellant. The round ball must have passed out of American production about 1900 or earlier. Few of us have seen one. For some years the BBs continued to be listed as "round ball," and for many succeeding years a good many shooters thought they were actually loaded with round balls. But a cylindrical bullet has long been standard. It is heeled

down at the base, of course; then there is a short bore-bearing section; and finally an abrupt taper into a short and timid little point.

The weight is from 18 to 20 grains. I've never seen one that was lubricated except with the copper-alloy "lubricating alloy" that Western Cartridge uses under the name Lubaloy. I have read catalogue listings of greased BB caps but never have had the fun of trying to load such short, slippery little rounds into my gun!

The front of the bullet is almost a true wadcutter, and it punches clean holes in tagboard targets and helps to reduce the danger range—a little; it isn't a toy cartridge. For snap-shooting at tin cans heaved almost straight up, it seems like a swell load, but its penetration is so low that if it hit the ribbed edge of the can it might come right back at us. We still must watch the background in spite of the fact that very light bullets, even the 40 grain .22 long-rifle, when fired vertically return to earth with hardly enough smack to break the wax on a document sealed by a Scottish lawyer. But it certainly could put out an eye, and ranging shots aloft are perilous except in real wilderness.

Shot from a rifle, the BB's velocity is 780 f. s., energy 24 foot pounds. For 100 yards, the figures given are 570 and 13, which sound reasonable. Some energy goes to waste in shoving the microscopically powered bullet through a long barrel; so a fairly short pistol should give it nearly equal power. It is too weak for any game except tiny frogs, too small to be killed for their little legs. The 25 foot N.R.A. pistol target seems practically made to order for it, and even in a handgun the report of the BB is light.

Probably no other cartridge profited as much from non-corrosive priming! The old potassium chlorate formulas made it the greatest barrel-eater of them all; and there was much talk, too, of how quickly BBs would lead a barrel. In my experience, they rarely lead a rifle barrel that is in gun-crank shape; and I recall a revolver, not throated out much at the barrel breech, that handled them cleanly. The old corrosively primed BB caps soon put a barrel out of gun-crank shape, and then of course the pits in the steel collected lead with great enthusiasm.

It seems best to clean and oil a gun after using modern BBs in it because priming, powder (if any), and bullet fouling, with no grease or wax to help, can't give quite the splendid anti-rust coating that modern ammo with lubricated lead bullets leaves in a firearm. This protection must be good—and usually it is—to carry the weapon unharmed through hot, humid spells, and days, months and even years of no-clean-um.

The CB, with 29 grain .22 short bullet—sometimes a little different in outline—has a rifle velocity of 720 f.s., energy of 33 f.p., with 100 yard figures of 605 and 24. Obviously, it has more paper power than the BB, though actual effects might tot up about the same, for one has a light but very blunt bullet, the other a heavier but more rounded one. In accuracy, it's an improvement on our oldest metallic cartridge still in use, the BB that Flobert, a pistol instructor in Paris, dreamed up for easy loading of target arms. It shoots better—or did when we still had it available—than the modernized BB. Some loadings did really nice work in rifles at the special National Rifle Association Junior distance of 25 feet, for these two cartridges and for rifled air or gas powered rifles. (The smoothbore airguns are eligible for 15 feet, and if your kids and the others on the block can't have a 50-foot range for "real .22s," wouldn't a 15 or 25 footer teach them much that might someday come in handy for life saving?) No apologies for that digression hooked in with parentheses. If the thought was new to you, you needed it.

Flobert rifles, and many others, commonly used both BB and CB caps, and some tubular magazine repeaters will feed them, a gunful or part of one. The chief advantages were economy and quiet shooting, later only the quietness, for the caps cost as much as .22 shorts.

A black powder charge of 1½ grains was standard for the CB, and I doubt that any "smokeless" rounds were put up in this size with no powder charge whatever. The greased and rounded profile of the bullet is less likely to lead a bore than the dry, bluff-nosed BB; but for quiet shooting the BB is preferable. Fired from a long-barrelled rifle, it sometimes makes no sound that you can hear, certainly, above the click of the hammer or striker; and in a well-built revolver with at least a 3 or 4 inch barrel, there is very little noise.

These little cartridges have given pleasure far out of proportion to their size. For firing in ancient .22 handguns like a pre-Civil War type of S. & W. seven-shooter chambered for shorts, or other finds that simply must be shot (if they will hang together under the strain), they are exactly right. But the gun *must* be in safe condition. In such old arms, we should be scared white to use modern .22 shorts, for most varieties have been hopped up 'way beyond the ballistics of the late 1850s. With power, pressure had to go up, too. So before firing, let a sensibly conservative gunsmith decide. Specimens of guns—and of gunsmiths, too—do vary a good bit! If the barrel hinge is weak, you know the gun is unsafe to fire as-is.

.22 SHORT

Bullet in grs.	F.S. vel. at muzzle	F.P. energy at muzzle	Bbl. length	Type
29	865	48	6″	Standard velocity
29	1035	69	6″	High velocity

Feet per second velocity and foot pounds energy for these two popular types of .22 shorts, fired from rifles, are considerably higher: 1045 and 1125 f.s. and 70 and 81 f.p., respectively. The amount of loss, from rifle to pistol, of the high velocity cartridge is surprisingly small. Still, the "low speed" is the short to choose for quiet shooting, and in most arms it is a little more accurate because the bullet isn't spun quite so fast. Over-stabilized, as a bullet is when it buzzes out at an excessive rate of spin, it is less accurate. And most arms taking the .22 short cartridge are rifled for the .22 long-rifle 40-grain bullet. To collect guns made for the .22 short only, with short chambers and rifling twist of from about 20 to 25 inches to a complete turn, or even to assemble data on such arms, would challenge a researcher. Yet the task might not be hopeless, at least with arms made during the 1900s, and certainly today very few indeed are built for the short exclusively.

There are several other kinds of .22 short loadings. The high velocity with 27 grain hollow point bullet is stocked by only a few dealers, comparatively; and its speed is so low, and the driving weight behind its hollow nose so small that it is only a little better killer than the solid-bullet, high-speed types. It does mushroom rather symmetrically. There is also the blank cartridge, sometimes loaded with black powder that lets us in for careful gun-cleaning, not only of the bore and chambers, but also of all the outer surfaces coated with the black residue.

And there are the plinking loads, more glance-proof than others—a standard velocity bullet of compressed lead dust and a very high velocity one of compressed iron dust—and the long-wanted 1959 match cartridge which sells at a premium price, too costly for plinking.

You know, this 1855 or '56 Smith & Wesson design has come a long way. How many others have appeared in new form a century and more after their birth? Except for the European-manufactured BB cap, and perhaps some BBs still made in Canada,* it must be our oldest metallic cartridge in common use. It sells by the million. And seven completely different factory loadings are a good spread for any cartridge; aren't they?

I think the first match-grade .22 short we ever had was the 1959 Western Super-Match Pistol, loaded to 1020 f.s. speed and 67 foot pounds, just under the high-velocity. It carries hard wax lubricant to help avoid gum-up in an auto's extractor cut and bolt face. Match ammo is specially inspected through the manu-

---

* Dominion Cartridge Co., Canadian Industries, Ltd., Box 10, Montreal, Quebec.

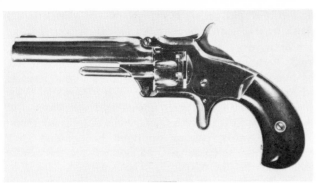

Smith & Wesson .22 short seven-shot revolver, Model No. 1, 3rd model. Courtesy Smith & Wesson.

facturing stages, and normally it *starts* as match stuff. Bullet, powder charge, priming and assembly all count in the reach toward perfection. Cases mean much, too. For years some top-flight marksmen have gauged rim thickness of long-rifle ammo they depended on for precision. A thick rim is positioned more snugly in the gun chamber than a thin one. It may even be oversize for a tightly breeched arm. A thin rim normally has too much head-space in the chamber. There's play that brings not quite perfect ignition. Segregate them according to thickness and you get more of the uniformity that makes accuracy. Excellent manufacture can lighten the exacting shooter's look-over job, or even eliminate it.

There are also such matters as evenness of lubrication, and too much or too little lube, though cartridges *are* expected to perform well both on dry, hot, summer days and on cold wintry ones! They must oblige. Crimp of the case-mouths must be even to make even "bullet pull," important to uniform velocities; and the crimp should be clean, with no fins of lead hanging down over the case metal. So it goes, and up goes the price of match stuff.

But it can be worth the price. Evidently these shorts were brought out with Olympic rapid fire competition largely in mind, though others of us use handguns specially chambered and rifled for .22 shorts. We want the best out of them at slow fire, too, at 50 feet and maybe at 50 yards on a nice, still day. For these, the match ammo would be worth trying, and so it would by owners of fine old single-shot rifles made for shorts. Here at last we might have ammunition that's worthy of those rifles, provided their stiff, heavy barrels "like" them. Rimfire .22 barrels are not standardized closely in bore and rifling groove dimensions, take them by and large. However, soft lead bullets are obliging in fitting them. To expect these match shorts, or any other shorts, to do well in quick-twist .22 long-rifle barrels is out. The short and the long-rifle are entirely different cartridges.

And the high-velocity, iron-dust bullet short is an entirely different short, too. March 1955 saw the marketing of the Remington Rocket, and all the big American companies now make this type. Present bal-

listics are a 15 grain bullet at 1710 f.s. velocity from a rifle, somewhat less from a pistol, but still outstandingly fast. The bullet is of sintered (powdered and compressed) iron, held together by a binder. You can pick these bullets up with a magnet. A somewhat similar bullet of compressed lead dust, usually lubricated, preceded the Rocket by several years. Velocity standards varied, but now it is rated along with the standard velocity .22 short.

The lead bullet loads, plain lead or lead plated with a harder metal, get the most use; and the solid bullet, high-velocity sort, can be bought almost anywhere that cartridges are sold. The quieter standard loads may be a bit hard to find, except in large cities, though the sintered iron rounds are common because they come in small boxes of 28 instead of 50 or more. They don't cost much, and they hardly sag a pocket. So why not have a little plinking?

These fastest of all rimfires, excepting the .22 Magnum, are *comparatively* safe to use afield. Their brittle bullets are less liable to ricochet than those made of solid, hollow-pointed, or even powdered and compressed lead. Direct hits on iron, stone and so forth of course break them into fragments too small to find, or to fly and do damage at any great distance. It has been claimed that a strike on steel at more than a 30-degree angle will not make them glance. But since some angling hits can make almost any bullet ricochet, and since straight-on smacks into oncoming lake waves can send a bullet right back toward the shooter, we can't say goodbye to common sense when we use them. Also, they have considerable range, for though they are light, these little fifteen-grainers, they are also fast.

They are brittle indeed! A trusted gunsmith friend of mine had a time with them when they were new. He was trying them in his long-chambered K-.22 Smith, which he thinks accounted for the arrival on target paper of two separate holes on one discharge. The bullet broke in two, amidships, and one of those holes was as cleancut as if a wadcutter had made it. This wad-cutting is normal with Rockets at rifle velocities: the bullet-holes in tagboard or even paper are punched out cleanly, partly because of the speed, partly because of the bullet's profile. We also get such holes with smoothly tapered bullets at really high speed, such as those of the .220 Swift, and others a good bit less fast.

The Rocket type loads make a sharp report, and a long muzzle flash adds to the general hilarity. Of course, they are horribly overstabilized by .22 long-rifle standard 16-inch rifling twist, but they are accurate enough for their purpose.

Compressed lead bullet shorts under such names as Kant-Splash, Krumble-Ball, Spatterless and Spatterpruf are for the plinker who hates to shoot iron bullets through his barrel; and a good many do, regardless of whether or not much actual harm is done by that metal to steel that even in .22 barrels is much harder. As a rule, they are lubricated; and since they are soft, they fill the rifling grooves on discharge and dam back the hot gases from cutting ahead and—to some slight extent even in a .22, probably—burning out the barrel. The report is low, like that of the standard .22 shorts. In my experience, in back-country where no harm could be done by a ricochet, they are slightly more likely to glance than the much faster iron-bullet rounds. In unventilated galleries—and perhaps under pretty good ventilation—the lead dust can irritate the lungs, and in fact do serious harm. This has cut their sales, and properly; but they are still made. For outdoor use, they are fine. I wish they were more easily available.

In Olympic rapid-fire at 25 meters, the short has its place because of its light recoil. To help further, many of the heavy .22 autoloaders made for this competition—it *is* a sport, but the competitive side is most important because of its magnified propaganda value —are equipped with muzzle brakes to reduce recoil still more. Five shots at five separate targets in eight seconds may not seem so fast to one well trained in Standard American fives in ten seconds on one target, but the succeeding Olympic stages of six and four seconds are different. It's a game we must master.

For 50-meter Olympic slow-fire, 60 shots in two hours at the very small-ringed target, the .22 long-rifle pays off especially in the greater wind-resistance of its 40-grain bullet. Under ideal conditions, cathedral-like calm, a .22 short gun, with correct chambering and rifling for the cartridge, can do well at 50 yards, or of course 50 meters. Even in a very good rifle, made for the long-rifle load as most of them unfortunately are, .22 shorts will just about cut the 50-foot rifle target's 8-ring, .817 inch in diameter, a shade over 13/16 inch. By the law of averages, some get into the 9 and 10 rings, but you find most junior-club shooters buying long-rifle ammo after their second or third attendance, if not before! The fine, well-preserved, old, and hard to locate .22 target rifles made for shorts are beyond their means; and few of them have heard of such arms. Perhaps, but not probably, some maker will oblige them. Twenty-two rifles must sell in multiple thousands.

Various foreign vest-pocket pistols are made for shorts, including the conversion for the Spanish-made Colt Junior .25 auto. There are some fairly heavy, long-barreled jobs, too, in low price ranges. But a great many more handgun-fired shorts go into revolvers, single-shot pistols, and single-loaded automatics chambered for long-rifle. In a single-shot like the Sheridan, for instance, the short is useful for plinking. It fouls a long-rifle chamber, and this black deposit can be hard to brush out. We had little or none of it in chlorate-priming days, but the shift to non-rusting ammo was worth it! As for erosion, probably several or many thousand could be fired

before it would occur. However, this is speculation; I don't care to ruin any chamber by experiment.

For most of us, the .22 short is out as a hunting load. Perhaps you, too, remember old gentlemen like Lyman Hall, who taught me so much about hunting when I was a little kid. His .22 short rifle was a Winchester Model 1890, peep-sighted and well cared for. With it, he killed woodchucks, reliably, up to about 35 or 40 yards, passing up those he couldn't stalk closer to. But he could shoot, and he placed those little bullets in the chuck's brain. The same went for gray squirrels, at proportionately shorter ranges. He was a sportsman, not a bungler.

Since most of us shoot little at game of any kind, compared to the rounds we expend in practice, the extra cost of long-rifles for a trip for frogs is justifiable. Sometimes the marshes and grass-bordered streams give us a shot at a crow, a harmful hawk (check your game laws on this), or tough snapping-turtle.

Under peculiar circumstances, the .22 short will do. One blowy, snowy day, when grownups in town scurried from one haven to the next, a youngster we know set off "up the crick" with hatchet, fish-line, hooks and bait in the pockets of his parka, also an ancient, nameless revolver loaded with thriftily bought shorts. Yes, the kid was "half Indian"; otherwise, he wouldn't have gone out at all.

Over a deep pothole he quietly chipped through the ice, baited up, and settled himself in a pose as motionless as the porkrind below the surface. Time went by, but the blood of youth kept him warm. Then came a crow, slanting down through the powdery spruces and alighting 20 or 25 feet away on the ice. His motive was unguessable (we all know the crow is an unpredictable bird) but it was his last flight. With infinite deliberation, the lad eased the little gun out of a side pocket and shot him dead. A lucky placement of the bullet? Of course.

.22 LONG

Bullet in grs.	F.S. vel. at muzzle	F.P. energy at muzzle	Bbl. length	Type
29	1095	77	6"	High velocity

This durable outcast is only 60 f.s. and 8 f.p. ahead of the high-velocity .22 short, but it fills chambers better. It is so much closer to the speed of sound (1100 f.s. or so, depending on the temperature) that it cracks much more sharply than a .22 short in pistol or rifle. Few, if any, .22 long-rifle auto-pistols function with it reliably, for the light bullet develops little recoil. Used as single-loaders, with longs, there is some danger of empties being extracted but not ejected, and then the slide or breech-block can slam down on them and possibly bend or break the extractor hook.

The .22 long has the case of the long-rifle and the

bullet, sometimes in modified shape, of the short. It is enormously popular and is likely to keep on being so. Here are some of its advantages.

1. Fodder for those who never heard of the fine long-rifle round.

2. Slightly lower price, by comparison to the l.-r.

3. Balm to the troubled soul a-dread lest shorts burn out his chamber, though blissfully regardless of the equally important leade or throat of the rifling in his single-shot or automatic—or his rifle.

4. A round-out of a cartridge collection. Many more useful loads have fallen away, but this one sells.

5. It is the correct round for a few foreign auto-pistols made for it alone, on the theory that the long is more formidable than the short. And it is, by a trifle. It's right, too, for old arms specially chambered and rifled for it, such as Colt 1887 (which functioned .22 shorts, too), Winchester 1890, and a few more modern Remington and Winchester single-shots sold at low prices. Here, too, as with special .22 short guns, the collector or recorder could get busy.

It's not as inaccurate in rifles made for the .22 l.-r. as the shooting family has been bred to believe. Some match rifles can take it and turn in nearly or quite perfect 50-foot gallery scores, five-shot strings, at least. At 50 yards, the results are likely to be sad, and at 100, terrible. Up to 50 feet, it should shoot rather well in single-shot pistols or semi-automatics, for their barrels are chambered. Revolver barrels aren't, and there's that jump from a .32 Long or .38 Special length chamber usually into a more or less gappy barrel throat. The much longer bullet of the long-rifle, with generous bearing surface, can slip through these handicaps so well that 10-shot, 50-yard groups may run as small as 1½ inches from the finest sixguns. The finest single-shots and automatics may do even better.

Practice should be serious, with confidence in gun and ammo. To do our best with each shot fired lays out and paves and maybe lines with hotdog stands the road to success. With any equipment, it's a long enough trip, but with good equipment—not necessarily the best, it can be a most joyous trip.

I rather regret that severity. Think of the fun the long, as well as the short, has given to millions of mighty nice people.

.22 LONG-RIFLE

Bullet in grs.	F.S. vel. at muzzle	F.P. energy at muzzle	Bbl. length	Type
40	950	80	6″	Standard velocity
40	1125	112	6″	High velocity

As of today, no compressed lead or iron dust bullet loads have been marketed in .22 l.-r. to prevent ricochets, and in the case of the latter, to permit extreme velocities. The .22 short, not the l.-r., is used in gallery shooting at 25 feet, and at twice that range there is little or no danger of splash-back of solid lead from well-made and well-set-up steel backstops. Such

backstops, in fact, are safe at 25 feet, but the lead-dust short was made for others not so good.

A sintered iron l.-r. bullet weighing perhaps 20 or 22 grains could be sent fast, but it would have little but sensational value. It would not expand on game, head shots alone could be taken, and even with excellent accuracy it would not extend the sure-killing range greatly by its flat trajectory. Cross-winds would push it off course, it's so light. To hollow-point it for killing power would be insane. Who wants to eat iron dust? In spite of printed warnings, some people would use it on game for the table, and what a field-day the newspapers would justly have with the law-suits that would come up!

Let us hope that the foregoing comments are as zany as they sound, and that no such l.-r. ammo ever is marketed. Seriously, the way to get a varmint cartridge is to buy something much more powerful. The only eligible .22 rimfire is the Winchester Magnum, and most of us with experience would call it the minimum even at rifle speeds.

The L.-R. on Small Game

Every type of long-rifle load has been used on small game, even the one loaded with Number 12 shot, about .05 inch in diameter and running a catalogued 2,385 to the ounce! This one is a prize punk. Rifled barrels scatter the pellets wildly, and the barrels lead up fast and take considerable brushing out before they are clean again. In smoothbore barrels specially made for them, these loads break small clay targets a few feet out and offer good practice, but under the best conditions they cripple about as many small birds as they kill outright. They are not much more than mouse loads, and except for clay practice we should forget them. Pattern, range, and penetration all are low.

The ballistics of .22 l.-r. rounds fired from rifles show how much power we sacrifice in using them in a handgun. Rifles with the standard load send the 40-grain bullet at 1145 f.s., with 116 foot pounds' energy. Figures for the high velocity 40 grain are 1335 and 158, and for the 36- or 37-grain hollow point, 1365 and 149—the last figure being the same for both weights of h. p. This indicates more fraternal agreement between manufacturers than regard for scientific accuracy!

Here, however, is a warning. Years ago, the old long-rifle—about 970-1000 f.s., not much over pistol ballistics of today's standard-speed rounds—was tested carefully and actually, not by theory alone, for extreme range with a rifle muzzle elevation of 17.8°. It made from 1300-1400 yards, just under .8 mile. If we check that .8 mile on our car speedometer, some day on a straight country road, we get a picture of the .22 pistol's dangerous range, and with low-speed long-rifles at that.

The long-rifle hollow-point, which we would choose for handgun hunting with this caliber—if we chose it at all—has just about the speed and effectiveness of the low velocity hollow point that was discontinued shortly before World War II. When that happened, there were howls from hunters who had used it, with good rifle marksmanship, on gray squirrels. They disliked the high velocity hollow-point because it was excessive. Well, so it sometimes is with body shots, usually raking shots; but at other times, it fails miserably. There isn't much resistance in a gray squirrel's body to upset a bullet, and only very good shooting makes it a good small game load. Cottontail rabbits, it's true, are killed rather easily, but most other small game is plenty tough. And even a wounded rabbit may run away and escape, to die later.

So with a .22 handgun using the most powerful l.-r. cartridge, we are limited by ballistics of 20 years ago, aren't we, by those of the obsolete low-speed hollow-point? That means we must really hunt, get within close range, and really shoot, place the bullet where it can kill and not cripple.

The L.-R. on Target

Even though most kinds of big game have been killed with pistols loaded with .22 l.-r. pills, and though a good many expert woodsmen rely on these arms for getting their camp meat on canoe trips and shoepac expeditions "back of beyond," where game is abundant and often pretty tame, this fine little pistol load isn't meant for killing.

Its field is target shooting, both training and competition. A whole series of courses leading to official qualifications, medals and eye-catching lapel buttons has been laid out for it. So we have "companion arms" like the Colt Official Police and Officer's Model and the S. & W. K-.22 as aiders and abettors to .38 Specials, and the Colt conversion unit as an understudy to the .38 and .45 autos with standard 5-inch barrels.

Weights, sights and balance are pretty similar; and if the marksman sees to it that trigger pulls are not over a quarter-pound apart, he has a team to work with. Theoretically this is so. Although many shooters find it absolutely so, many more, probably, prefer to have each gun reach their ideal for each class of shooting. The shooting case they carry to local, regional or national matches may contain, in addition to a small but weird collection of luck-bringing junk, a .38 Special target revolver, a .45 auto, and a heavy-barreled .22 automatic, with no similarity whatever in grip shape, weight, balance, or even in trigger pull. They don't feel handicapped, and probably they aren't.

There is special match ammunition that costs much more than the standard .22 long-rifles. It is worth the cost to some pistoleers of high ability. It has undergone still more rigorous factory inspections and tests. The rifleman often inspects it further, for evenness of crimp, for appearance—being horrified at seeing tiny fins of lead drooping down over a case mouth—and even for rim thickness to the ten-thousandth of an inch. Not all these niceties may bewitch the Pistol

Model "M," first issue, the Smith & Wesson seven-shot revolver with solid frame and swing-out cylinder, the type of gun for which the .22 S.&W. Long cartridge, a crimped .22 long-rifle, was introduced. Many earlier .22 l.-r.'s were uncrimped, for presumably better accuracy in single-shot target rifles. Courtesy Smith & Wesson.

Expert, but they can have real meaning to the rifleman.

Match loads used to come with light charges of Du Pont Lesmok semi-smokeless powder for 50- and 75-foot ranges, and with heavier doses for 100- or 200-yard work. These powders, including the Peters Semi-smokeless, which also was a fine formula for accuracy, are gone, and some of us still miss them. They ignited easily and uniformly in old arms with light hammer blow, and the sharp tang of their thin smoke was no annoyance outdoors.

We have two types of premium-price match loads, rifle and pistol, and so named by Remington and Peters. Winchester EZXS and Western Super-Match Mark III are for rifles. The new S-M Mark IV is for pistols, rated at standard 950 f.s. velocity, and carries hard wax lubricant like that of the Super-Match .22 short. Win now has a pistol load.

It pays to try all kinds in a match handgun, even the special rifle rounds, which may have slower burning powder than specialized pistol stuff. In some particular gun, for instance, the fit of certain bullet profiles might contribute much more to accuracy than the powder behind the lead. Guns like to be treated as individuals. Some shooters have found that some "pistol" load does best in their rifles. Actual trial may agree with theory, or beat the stuffing out of it. When we find the best load for our gun, we like to stock up on it—the same make, style, and factory lot, too. Under good care it lasts for years.

Some auto-pistols need to have their recoil spring tension eased up to handle reduced-velocity long-rifles reliably, as they must for peace of mind and happiness in timed and rapid fire events! Naturally we test for accuracy in slow fire before we adopt any load, and it helps to use both hands, with forearms rested, and the body comfortably planted down behind some sort of bench-rest.

Sometimes you hear a gun-crank name the .38 or .44 Special, according to his choice, as "the most accurate revolver cartridge ever made." He forgets the .22 long-rifle with its long, finely balanced bullet protruding from the case and trued up in the chamber —or in some match rifles and a few old target pistols, trued up also by the start of the rifling lands biting into it.

Compared to most other rimfires, it is young, three-score years and ten, plus a bit. It's an 1887 Peters and Stevens development, we have been told, though the late Walter Roper placed it at 1886 (as an arms designer he had material on a good many details in the gun and ammunition lines).

Many, if not most, early lots were uncrimped, to avoid bullet distortion. Along in 1903, at least in Winchester production, the *.22 S. & W. Long* variant came out with a good, strong crimp to hold the bullet in place against the jerk and pull of revolver recoil. Single-shots liked the uncrimped stuff very well at that time, even though sometimes the bullet would pull loose in a fouled chamber, or in a barrel throat, when an owner unloaded his gun. Oh well, save the spilled black powder for seasoning game; it tastes like salt and often served as such on trips 'way back in!

I think we'd best print a disclaimer of responsibility for that last comment. With pharmaceutical ads painting upset stomach as a major disaster, I'm sure we should!

.22 WINCHESTER RIM FIRE

Bullet in grs.	F.S. vel. at muzzle	F.P. energy at muzzle	Bbl. length	Type
45	1170	137	6″	High velocity
45	980	97	6″	Standard velocity, discontinued

Modern loadings, fired from a rifle, send the solid 45 grain .22 W.R.F. or .22 Remington Special bullet at 1450 f.s., with energy of 210 foot pounds. The 100-yard rifle figures are 1110 and 123. The discontinued hollow points, 40 and 45 grs., went at 1475 and 1450 f.s., respectively; and they were decidedly better killers than the solids.

This was the first really good .22 rimfire hunting load for rifles—and fairly good in pistols, too. The second was the .22 Magnum of 1959. The W.R.F. is an 1890 cartridge design.

Naturally, the W.R.F. has improved with time. The first loading seems to have been 7½ grains black powder behind that good old flat-nosed lead bullet, built for killing. Velocity claimed was 1125 f.s., as against 1107.3 (yes, figures used to be averaged down to the tenth, and you wonder what the actual dispersion was) for the later load of 7 grains black. Semi-smokeless and Lesmok powders did about the same, but old corrosively primed smokeless rounds, as usual in .22s, were a lot weaker.

The point of this is that today's high velocity rounds, even though the good hollow-points became practically unavailable soon after World War II, kill the least tough kinds of small game rather well, even at the pistol velocities which do little more than equal the old stuff. But they must be placed with rifle-like

accuracy. They are not kill-alls. It was decidedly noticeable from the first that the W.R.F. was a killer, especially with the hollow-points that came later.

Perhaps unfortunately, no handguns or rifles are made for it, the former going out of production before World War II, the rifles soon after it. But it is a hunting caliber for a good marksman and stalker, and to people like these it is more or less available in used rifles of many makes, and in used Colt Police Positive Target sixguns and a few Stevens single-shot pistols.

The .22 W. R. F. is among the most water-, and oil-proof of all cartridges. It is a rimfire, with no primer pocket in its base, such as centerfires have had since early days, except for various designs of "inside primers." (You may find one yet in .45 Colt or .45-70 Springfield calibers, for instance, and yet not have a rarity.) Its long, straight-sided bullet is seated deeply in the case, not heeled down to enter in .22 short, long, and long-rifle fashion. Others are the .25 Stevens of about the same 1890 date, and similar in proportions; the .25 Stevens short of 1902; the .32 long-rifle, much like our *centerfire* .32 Long Colt of today, about 1901; the .22 Winchester Automatic of 1903; .22 Remington Autoloading of 1914; and the .22 Winchester Magnum of 1959. The latter is the first common rimfire to have a jacketed bullet, though some .22 long-rifles were loaded so during World War II for use in survival-kit guns. Having lead bullets in your possession could lead to your execution if you were taken prisoner.

These tightly sealed rimfires pay off in arctic cold, or even in really cold weather in our northern states. They are lubricated inside in bullet grooves, or not lubed at all, like early lots of .22 Winchester Auto or the present gilding metal-jacketed Magnums. In a clean dry chamber, there is no external grease or wax to freeze, or at best, make extraction difficult. Users of the .22 long-rifle in auto-pistols have pointed out that it is well to rub the grease off the noses of the bullets in cold times. It helps them to find their way from magazine to chamber.

The W. R. F. is not a target favorite, but the modern high-speed loads in good rifles have grouped in about two inches at 50 yards, which is rather useful accuracy; and fine, old, single-shot, solid-frame, not takedown rifles ought to do even better. When .22 long-rifle velocities went to the highest ratings, accuracy suffered. With the .22 W. R. F., it was just the opposite, perhaps because of better manufacture; or was it the avoidance of the critical sound barrier until the bullet had gone nearly 100 yards? The .32-40 rifle bullet just about hits it at 200 yards, and it was a proved target favorite at that range, usually with heavier than the standard 165-grain bullets, which held their velocity well.

The clean, dry W. R. F. cartridge doesn't pick up grit to injure the bore, as greased long-rifles, for instance, do so eagerly. It has been a great outdoor favorite for that reason among others. But being something of a magnum, it needed understudy ammunition for plinking and perhaps for indoor practice, to reduce the noise. The old *.22 extra long* had them, from long-rifle down to BB caps, for it used a very long case of the same diameter and a standard or near-standard .22 long-rifle bullet.* In length, it almost filled the chambers of Colt Police Target and Smith .22-32 sixguns; and when we used black powder, its 7-grain charge was impressive, compared to the 5 of long or long-rifle, the 3 or 4 of the short, and the 1½ or what-have-you of the caps. It *was* effective, too, and some single-shot rifles were chambered for it. After it took on modern priming and smokeless powder, it was of value mostly to collectors. You can, though, use it as a rough gauge of the chambering and throating of a .22 l.-r. rifle. If it will take this round—some will—the tolerances are pretty generous! However, such a rifle may still be able to group into an inch at 50 yards. One I knew would put five long-rifles into ½ inch at that range. Strange? A shooter's life is full of unexplained mysteries—unless he knows too much for his own enjoyment.

Oldtimers used to cut noise and expense by firing an oversize .22 pistol cartridge in the W. R. F. This ".25" Bacon & Bliss load held 5 grains of black powder and 38 of lead, as compared with the 7 or 7½ and 45 of the W. R. F. The .25 B. & B. is obsolete; and so, unfortunately, is the .22 Remington Autoloading, though at this writing, I know where several .22 Rem. boxes are for sale! Some users of those Model 16 rifles have fired plain .22 longs in them with fair satisfaction, but we don't want to use an undersize case in a revolver for fear of gas-spit into the firing hand. The Remington rifle load was light, 950 f.s. for the 45-grain solid or hollow-point bullet, but with bullet weight equal to that of the W. R. F., it should print up pretty close to the sixgun's own ammunition at short ranges. Sometimes a fast bullet shoots lower, closeup, than a slow one of equal weight, because it gets out of the upward-recoiling barrel sooner.

On special order, Colt used to furnish interchangable .22 long-rifle and .22 W. R. F. cylinders, and then you had something, with the Police Target's adjustable sights. Apparently, rifling and bore dimensions were the same in these particular arms. The .22 W. R. F. bullet *is* oversize. Winchester rifling grooves for it have run to .226 inch as maximum, though in Stevens make the max is reported to have been .224, about the same as for .22 long-rifle. These rifles had a 14-inch twist to spin the long bullets, although the Remington Model 12-CS in W. R. F. or Rem. Special had only 16-inch spin, and shot very well indeed, using the fast modern cartridges. As speed goes up, the rifling twist can slow down, a little, and still keep the bullets point-on in flight.

I'm fond of the W. R. F. for the second rifle I owned chambered it; and the Colt and my share in the Rem-

ington pump that came later were fine, too. Experiences the Model 90 and I had would fill a book, though I doubt that anyone except our loving, patient, and so easily amused old dog Pepper would ever wade through it. I should hate to see the cartridge discontinued, as it will be if the demand falls low enough. But don't think that my affection for the W. R. F. has led to the following suggestion.

It should be a good subload for .22 Winchester Magnum rimfire rifles (perhaps only as single-loaders) and revolvers. Its bullet is of ample diameter for the .224-.225 inch Magnum rifling grooves. Magnum rifles with 16-inch twist do handle the long, 45-grain W. R. F. bullet well, although 14-inch was the rate in Winchester W. R. F. rifles, which of course were made for loads much slower than the Magnum. The August 1959 *American Rifleman* (p. 18) report on the Magnum showed good W. R. F. accuracy from the 14-inch Ruger Single-Six revolver; the 14-inch Colt revolver twist should do as well; and possibly the Smith & Wesson 10-inch spin would do even better.

Yes, the case is .04 inch shorter than Maggie's, .965 vs. 1.005. That means bullet jump into the chamber throats, wtih chamber erosion possible—after who knows how many thousand rounds?—and some loss of power and of at least theoretical accuracy. How terrible! But recall the good .38 Long Colt accuracy from .38 Special chambers, and that of .44 Russians in long-chambered .44 Special guns. All three combinations have the same type of loading, a deeply seated bullet with bearing surface covered by the case, not a heel-type bullet like that of the .22 long-rifle. The latter is more obliging with short subloads. Or is it?

Present prices of the loads are like this: .22 W. R. F., $2.00 per box of 50; Magnum, $2.60 for the same number. They add up when you shoot enough to master a gun. The W. R. F. is loud-cracking in a revolver, but the Magnum puts it to shame. You pay with muzzle blast for handgun bullet speed, but for certain purposes it is worth the cost. For many uses, it is not.

.22 WINCHESTER MAGNUM RIMFIRE

Bullet in grs.	F.S. vel. at muzzle	At 50 yds.	At 100 yds.	F.P. energy at muzzle	At 50 yds.	At 100 yds.
40	1550	1310	1130	210	150	115

	MR traj. At 50 yds.	At 100 yds.	Barrel length
	.5″	2.3″	6.5″

N. R. A. tests reported in *The American Rifleman* of August 1959 showed not quite six ⅞-inch soft pine boards, spaced the usual ⅞ inch apart, penetrated by the Magnum bullet fired from a 6-inch Smith & Wesson revolver, which has a 10-inch rifling twist. High bullet rotation helps to expand a fired slug, but in this case probably very little, compared to the spin from a 14-inch revolver twist—such as Ruger or Colt. The Winchester rifle twist is 16-inch, and the muzzle velocity of 2000 f.s. much higher. A well-cut Savage rifle barrel sent its bullet through six and one-half

---

*It seems that the first .22 extra longs carried a light bullet, similar to that of the .22 long, and we know that it came out at least eight years earlier than the long-rifle, in 1878.

boards which is understandable because a speeded-up expanding bullet sometimes penetrates less than an identical one at lower velocity. The fast bullet does more damage, of course, since it expands more widely.

The mid-range pistol trajectory figure of 2.3 inches at 100 yards shows the 6½-inch handgun beating the .25-20 rifle by .3 inch, or the .357 Magnum revolver by .1 inch at the shorter range of 50 yards. These decimals are drawn wire-fine, but they show tendencies.

Little Maggie responds about as we should expect to changes in handgun barrel length. Winchester lists 1420 f.s. velocity for a 4½-inch barrel and 1710 for a 10-inch. The latter should just about hit the long-barreled Colt Buntline's figure, or that of another one like it.

Velocity figures for a 24-inch barreled rifle (shorter tubes, down to 18 or 20 inches give microscopically more) are 2,000 f.s. at muzzle, 1660 at 50 yards, 1390 at 100, and 1180 at 150. Energy is 355 foot pounds at muzzle, 245 at 50 yards, 170 at 100, and 125 at 150. Mid-range trajectory is .03 inch at 50 yards, 1.6 at 100, and 3.7 at 150. The stubby, 40-grain bullet holds up well for what it is, a short-range "Express" type, really.

It was wise to call halt at 150 yards, for that would be a fair maximum of effective range on varmints when this class of rifle, tuned up perfectly and familiar to the shooter, is used by a really excellent shot of long experience in judging distances and wind—and in dealing with them. Up to 100 yards an only slightly less able operator should find the .22 Magnum rifle ready to back his ability to make sure, first-shot kills. At 150 yards the remaining velocity of 1180 f.s. might give but little expansion to the bullet, judging from experiences with the old standard velocity .22 W.R.F., soft-lead flat-point at extremely close ranges. The Magnum bullet would have to be placed almost perfectly to kill a woodchuck, for example.

Going at 1390 at 100 yards, it would cause a good bit of destruction and thus make the "bull's-eye" on the game somewhat larger for clean killing; but let's not count too much on this when the game is tough, as Chucky certainly is. At 50 yards (1660 f.s.) and a very little beyond, it should behave like a .22 Hornet centerfire at three times that distance; that is, it ought to show some explosive disruptive effect, especially in soft, watery animal tissues. As hunters know, all these are broad generalizations. The 150-yard stretch is about the Hornet's limit on woodchucks, although skill and/or luck have given longer kills. The lack of them has resulted in much shorter-range failures. It's an extremely unsportsmanlike thing to wound game or varmints and lose them, and we can be grateful to the Winchester folks for having used restraint in advertising this cartridge.

Handgun Killing Power

Fired from a 6½-inch barreled revolver, a popular and easily portable length, the .22 Mag's 50-yard velocity of 1310 f.s. should result in high destruction, though hardly true blow-up except in soft tissues.

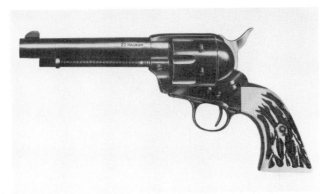

A great Western .22 Magnum revolver with 5½-inch barrel.

When we get into fairly high rifle velocities, about 2700 to 3,000 f.s. at the point of strike, the blow-up made by an expanding bullet, and sometimes by a hard-nosed military type, is so great that the load is *usually* unsuitable for any smallish game we plan to gather up and eat.

But all sorts of freak results come along, up and down the scale of destruction, as we know if we've hunted much, or even listened to a lot of truthful hunters. For instance, one time we shot a crow with a centerfire 2-R Lovell wildcat cartridge in a Winchester single-shot rifle, the soft point .22 bullet going at about 2700 f.s. when it arrived. It killed him instantly by merely creasing his neck. Not much blood came, and the bone wasn't broken. This was not blow-up effect in tissue, for hardly any tissue was affected, but a mysterious sort of killing power that occasionally comes from really high velocity. We should not expect it from a pistol, but it might occur.

At short woods ranges, a fast pistol bullet like this little 40-grain Magnum can be too rough on very small game we want for the cooking pot, and rough on some bigger varieties of small game, too. We don't ordinarily handload rimfires to suit our purposes as we do centerfires, but we *can* alter their exposed bullet profiles. With a .22 long-rifle we can split or file off or drill the bullet nose to make it more deadly, and some woods and mountain people do these things rather commonly. To reduce power with factory rimfires, we use shorter rounds, like the .22 short, or those with lower speed, like the standard velocity .22 long-rifle—though the solid-bullet high speed l.-r. isn't much more of a killer than the standard, except for its deeper penetration, seldom needed on .22 game.

The .22 Magnum is a killer as it comes from the factory box. To reduce power, we could use the .22 W.R.F. cartridge in its place, as mentioned in the foregoing chapter section. It should give us good accuracy and functioning in a revolver, though it would foul the long Magnum chambers and perhaps make extraction of Mag cases difficult until after we had cleaned those chambers.

It is speed, even more than the flat expanding bullet point, that makes the .22 Magnum round so deadly in a pistol. The .357 and .44 Magnums fire big-caliber, reasonably heavy bullets, well shaped to make big holes. Their muzzle velocities fall a bit below the 1550 f.s. of the .22 in a 6½-inch gun, being 1430 and 1470 with 158 and 240 grain bullets, respectively. These speeds come from 8⅜-inch .357 and 6½-inch .44 barrels. Cut down the speed of a tiny 40-grain bullet and you haven't much left. But at close range the .22 Mag would be a dreadful killer, turned against a human enemy. To compare its 210 foot pounds' energy with the old .38 S.&W. pocket-gun cartridge's smack of 173 f.p. is interesting, but we are thinking of what it would do in tearing tissue. The thought is gruesome. However, we read in almost any day's newspaper about much worse things happening to innocent, defenseless people—*unarmed people.* Pistol penetration of the .22 Mag is considerable; it tears through a half-dozen or so ⅞-inch pine boards. One or two mean a dangerous wound indeed, translated into killing, though not necessarily stopping, power.

The Magnum bullet is designed well for what it must do. A thin copper or gilding metal jacket, not a mere plating as on .22 rim-fires of lower power, allows it to take fairly quick-twist rifling without stripping in the grooves, and it keeps its expansion within reasonable bounds, for good penetration. One milled cannelure serves as a crimping groove to prevent the bullet from receding into the case under the pressure of some rifles' tubular-magazine springs, and though the bullet holds no lubricant, it should be about as water-proof as any others. It is seated more shallowly than the .22 W.R.F. bullet, with some of its bearing surface out front, which contributes to accuracy, at least in theory. It is a soft-point bullet with good lead exposure, and also up front there is a small hollow that undoubtedly adds to expansion without putting it in the destructive, blow-up class. At short pistol or rifle ranges, it ought to be almost glance-proof, though that is a quality that we can count on in mighty few bullets.

As far as recoil and average handgun weight go, the Mag is not too much for almost any grown person or for middle-teen kids. The muzzle crack is something else, but rubber, plastic or rolled-up cotton ear-plugs make a blessed difference. Target practice could be at first bearable for almost anyone in the family, and then quite a lot of fun. The 24,000 pounds pressure per square inch is surprisingly low—and some lots register even lower—but the Western Ball Powder helps to account for its pressure being in a class with .22 long-rifle high velocity stuff. Magnum pressure, however, has a longer peak, and the inside diameter of the case, down at the base, is larger than that of the long-rifle. Consequently, this cartridge just is not recommended for converted .22 long-rifle guns of a good many models. Another basis for this caution is the barrel's bore diameter of .224 inch, with groove diameter of .219, each some .002 inch larger than what we could call .22 long-rifle standard, though there are enormous variations—to put a fine point on it—

in the latter. There are some variations in .22 Magnum gun-barrels, but to gain good performance and safety, it seems likely that their standards will stay rather close.

Full .224-inch Magnum barrels could give accuracy with .22 long-rifle ammunition, selected for them, as these little, outside-lubricated bullets run a wide range in diameter. Some are as thick as .2255 inch, but others go much smaller; and even in match long-rifles there's quite a bit of latitude in bullets from the same cartridge box. For accuracy and for safety, we should need interchangeable long-rifle cylinders for our Magnum revolver, and perhaps they will become available. Magnum chamber diameters are much too big for .22 l.-r. rounds. The bullets wouldn't get a decent start for accuracy, and the loose-fitting cases, even though they would expand on firing, still could let quite an amount of gas escape backwards. Another hazard, pointed out in the *Rifleman* article, is that some tip-up breech actions could pinch the long-rifle case rim when they were closed, and thus fire the cartridge accidentally. These comments go for .22 shorts and longs, too.

But a special cylinder for selected long-rifle ammo, and for shooters who put a micrometer on their bullets, would afford not only a great deal of inexpensive practice with a target-sighted revolver but also convert it to a gun for very small game. I should still prefer .22 W.R.F. rounds in the Mag cylinder, even though the hollow points are long gone from production. The W.R.F. bullet is at least flat-pointed and faster than the long-rifle. The latter in the discontinued, hollow-point, standard-velocity loading wasn't much of a killer even when shot from rifles; and the present high-speed hollow-nose fired from 6-inch revolvers has just about the old standard rifle velocity just mentioned. I know that some shooters will say that the old, weak hollow-point was deadlier than a solid W.R.F. high-speed shot from either rifle *or* pistol. It just didn't seem so to me. All of us are entitled to our delusions; aren't we?

Background

Small but unusually potent .22 rifle cartridges are old stuff, as dates and data show.

There were two different .22 Maynard Extra Long centerfires, as James Grant noted in that old pet book on my shelf, *Single-Shot Rifles.* The 1873 with 1¼-inch case took 10 grains of black powder and a 45-grain flat-nosed lead bullet. The .22-8-45 of 1882 was only 1 5/32 inches in case length. Some had the No. 1 "small rifle" primer, and some had a still smaller No. O, no longer made. The short 1882 case is much like the foreign 5.5 mm. Velo Dog that carried a blunt, full-jacketed, 45-grain bullet for short-barreled revolvers. It wasn't powerful, but as rifle loads the Maynard .22s had a good reputation among old-time squirrel hunters.

The 1890 .22 Winchester Rim Fire was discussed before. It is the nearest thing today to the .22 Magnum. It followed the bottle-necked .22 Winchester Center

Fire, mostly for single-shot rifles, though I think some Winchester 1873s handled it. The overall would be just about right for that uncompromising repeater action—and of course for big, long, Colt New Service cylinders. With some minor changes, the .22 W.C.F. case became the .22 Hornet, and it was a good small-game cartridge in its own right, sending its flat-nosed, 45-grain, pure lead bullet along with from 13 to 15 grains of FFFG black powder. Velocities quoted were 1481, 1541 and 1563. We could compare them with those of the Magnum in pistols, recalling that this W.C.F. was known as a good squirrel and grouse cartridge—in little-hunted country the ruffed grouse is rifle game, law permitting it—but decidedly too weak for chucks and 'way below par for coyotes. Perhaps we need to think this over before hunting with a .22 Magnum pistol.

At the top of the pile of these once much-used, black-powder .22s was the .22-15-60 Stevens, which with its 2-inch, almost perfectly straight case was hardly adaptable to any standard metallic-cartridge revolver! But it was a finely accurate rifle round and a reliable small game killer. It sent the long, narrowly flat-pointed, lead bullet at about 1500 f.s., but still was rather quiet to shoot in the woodlots. We can duplicate it today in a .220 Swift rifle with a 55- to 60-grain cast bullet and 10 to 11 grains of Du Pont 4198.

In more modern times .22 Hornet pistols aren't new, the single-shot, Remington Rider, rolling-block, Navy and Army actions having been used by gunsmiths, and some .45-frame revolvers, too. Recently they have shortened the Hornet case to fit—overall when loaded with about a 40-grain bullet—S.&W. K-.22 cylinder length, and this gun alteration isn't terribly expensive, or the loads for it unproved. Velocities go up to about 2,000 f.s.; so it is in the .22 Magnum Rimfire *rifle* class, ballistically. Like straight Hornet pistols, which were commonly underloaded for safety with the full 45 or 46 grain bullets, it's a terror in sharp report, if you are sensitive to such things and do not plug your ears. But it does make a most interesting and useful handgun.

Add-up

The showing of the new .22 Magnum ammo at the March 1959 N.R.A. convention was rich in the tizzies it turned up, and that wasn't surprising. There followed a natural lag in production, and it seems that the first arms offered for it were the Savage .22-.410 over-and-under rifle and shotgun combination, the K-Smith, and the Ruger Single-Six.

It seems that the Rimfire Mag's chief values as a pistol round are that it is easily available—though not cheap, handloaders would say—and has enough power for many short and medium range handgun uses. It is sensational to the average shooter while it is new, but that enthusiasm won't last long. However, it is definitely serviceable, from plinking to defense. In the latter service, it might not have to draw blood. The sharp report and bright flash of one shot loosed off at the moon should put the average evil-thinker to flight. The guy or gal who fires that one is obviously *armed!*

We hope it sells well as a rifle load, too, and it should. No Hornet or Bee handloader who has experimented with reduced charges should doubt its accuracy. Not many small game hunters over 14 or 15 years old now use rifles, for we have come to worship success spelled this way, "$uccess." The full game-bag, you know, and for all but the skilled that means a shotgun. But maybe more will use a rifle, now that the .22 Mag is here, even though it can be rough on small game. It should be great fun for field shooting at inanimate marks, too, where its pretty bustible bullet can make that safe. It is a better than useless understudy, trajectory-wise, for rifles like the .30-30 Winchester and .35 Remington calibers with heavy-bullet factory loadings up to 100 yards and a bit more.

Elmer Keith, writing in *Guns,* saw it chiefly as a pistol cartridge, and his opinions carry deserved weight. However, possibly he does more hunting and shooting with handguns than with small game or short-range varmint rifles, and some of us do just the opposite. Any way you figure, it is more than just a new and interesting cartridge.

For years there had been talk of a high-speed .25 or a 7 mm. or .275 rimfire, and they would have had their points. Possibly .22 is better all-round, for both small game and close-up varmints. Either the .25 or the .275 could have been short enough for revolver cylinders, but they would have cost more to shoot than the .22. Still, they may come yet.

The best thing we could wish for any of the three would be that it would be used within its limits and thus not earn a reputation as a crippler. Doesn't that go for any cartridge?

.25 STEVENS SHORT AND LONG

The standard .25 Stevens, the long cartridge, dates back to about 1890 and looks like a large edition of the .22 Winchester Rim Fire of that year. The .25 Short, lowly in velocity and power, appeared about 1902 as an inexpensive subload, though possibly some handguns were chambered for it exclusively. Both are obsolete, the Long having been discontinued about 1958 and the peewee a bit earlier. Although the Long is almost impossible to find except in collectors' amounts, the Short is still advertised by some big ammunition houses.

The Long is a rifle cartridge famous for giving practical woods accuracy—and sometimes much better than that—with the right power to kill squirrels, rabbits and the rare woods grouse we catch sitting—kill them surely and without mutilation. In spite of velocity loss in a pistol barrel, its flat-pointed bullet of 65 or 67 grains has the stuff that handgun lead needs for killing power, weight and width as compared to the .22 long-rifle and the .22 W.R.F. It was a common caliber for Stevens single-shot pistols, and .22 revolvers have been converted to shoot it. Some Stevens and Wesson pocket rifles, pistols with barrels about 18 inches long and fitted with detachable skeleton stocks of steel rod, took this size. They appealed to voyageurs who penetrated regions where trail travel or canoe portage was exacting and game was abundant and unsophisticated.

There is a way of getting .25 Stevens ballistics with the reloading advantages of a centerfire case. Herbert Longo described it many years ago in *The American Rifleman*. Shortened and mouth-expanded .22 Hornet brass did it. This is a custom, not a cheap, way out; but it could mean even more to the pistol shooter than to the rifleman in working up an ideal small game load. He could bring pistol power up to the equivalent of .25 Stevens rifle power, so highly desirable and a good place to stop, as indicated before. About 15 years ago, perhaps farther back, one or more factories did load .25 Stevens high velocity rounds. In rifles, the speed developed by these experimental and never generally issued rounds must have been around 1500 f.s. or a little less; and the .25 Stevens still wasn't a long or even medium range varmint cartridge at that rate, or anything near it. But in a six-inch revolver, these rounds must have paralleled the standard stuff fired from rifles, and so well proved on game. The .22 W.R.F. rifle speed of 1450 f.s. drops to 1170 f.s. in the handgun; so the speeded-up .25 would have dropped, presumably, to about that figure in the pistol. It would be near-duplication of .25 Stevens standard-issue rifle rates, which varied from 1130 to 1180.

Not so many years ago, all .22 rimfires except the BB and CB caps and the Extra Long could be had in hollow-point styles. The .25 Stevens got the treatment, too, and the short as well as the long, though its standard solid-bullet round had only 945 f.s. muzzle velocity, fired from a rifle; and scooping out five grains of lead to make it an "Express" bullet couldn't have speeded it up very much!

With any loading of ancient or late-lamented rounds, the .25 Stevens was a quiet rifle load to shoot in woods full of squirrels. Black, semi-smokeless and Lesmok powder made a light, flat report; and the smokeless that came in with non-corrosive priming wasn't at all sharp. Shorts were not much more than the snap of your fingers! Short pistol barrels increased the report, but not excessively, even in smokeless loadings, as compared to the mid-range .38 Special, for instance. Standard rifle energies of the long cartridge ran from about 190 to 208 foot pounds, with the bumbling short turning up a surprising 130 or so. But we figure killing power more on what a bullet will do than on its listed foot poundage. We know that a light, flat-pointed .25 caliber lead bullet at a little above the speed of sound, starting velocity, does clean, humane work on small game up to about 50 yards or so—when we place it right. It needs definitely less exact placement than any of the .22 rimfires except the Magnum—that is,

it can get along with less when it must. Naturally we do our best on each shot.

.32 SHORT AND LONG

For generations, the .32 was so accepted that those numerals inspired confidence, at least among the not too exacting. It was a standard size and much like the .31 cap-and-ball caliber of the Colt Wells Fargo or Baby Dragoon. The adult Dragoon was a .44.

The good accuracy of the .32 Long as a rifle cartridge isn't well-known. It is built much in .22 long-rifle proportions, with long bearing for the rifling grooves, and in some recent lots it has done extremely well. Some shooters perhaps got better accuracy with black powder lots, which haven't been made regularly for over 30 years and hardly could do much now. But smokeless, noncorrosive rounds have the advantage of modern manufacturing techniques, which *can* produce 10-ring 50-foot accuracy in the much-belabored *.22* long; and some fine .32 lots come through.

Just now, both .32 Short and Long are still catalogued. Since some sort of .32 rimfire came out as far back as 1861, we naturally hope the size will round out its century, and even have "many happy returns" in addition. But hope is an eternal spring.

There were other .32 rimfires: Extra Short, Long-Rifle, Extra Long, a black powder Short blank, and shot cartridges in Long.

The first held six grains of black powder and 55 of blunt lead. In form and grace, it resembled the .22 BB Cap and was fired mostly in pocket arms like the Protector repeating pistol. Picture an old-style automatic trout reel, not a spinning reel of any kind, with a short tube projecting out front and a squeezer lever at the rear, and you have it. It enclosed a revolving magazine and was meant to be shot from the hip or through a pocket. The type was called "palm pistol," for you held it almost concealed in your hand and squeezed to fire it. Later the .32 Extra Short came in smokeless, corrosive primer loading, the only .32 rimfire of the kind I ever heard of. A still weaker .32 Protector centerfire took only four grains of black powder and 40 of lead; the .22 long-rifle had five and 40. Both rounds were of the variety that one of the late Stewart Edward White's westerners would describe, in sharper language than used here, as irritating no-end if you were shot with it and found it out the same day.

The Extra Long took the standard 90-grain Long bullet and a husky 20 grain black powder dose; so it was close to the .32-20-100, a variant of the original .32-20-115. The blank Shorts went into celebrating and race-starting pistols, and a lot of them into small Remington single-shot rifles for the smallest boys at military schools. Longs loaded with no. 10 shot were of two kinds. Both used the regular Long copper case of those days. One had wadding and a heavy crimp;

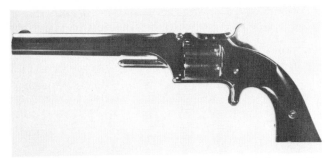

A long-barreled .32 rimfire Smith & Wesson sixshooter, the Model No. 2, Old Model. Cylinder is plain, not fluted. Some of these guns are still in use, and if they are in absolutely sound condition, particularly if the barrel hinge just ahead of the cylinder is still strong, not weakened by rust or wear, they can be considered safe with modern .32 short and long ammunition. These two have not been stepped up in power as the current .22 rimfires have been. Photo courtesy of Smith & Wesson.

the other set a greased, bullet-shaped shot-holder in the case to prevent rifling lands from being fouled with lead. These ill-patterning loads could kill small birds up to perhaps 20 feet, cleanly, too, by great luck. This sort of junk should not have been made.

Modern rifle ballistics are 945 f.s. for both short and long, with 158 and 179 f.p. energies. Short bullets go 80 grains, longs 89 or 90, and all have rounded points that usually aren't too rough on even small game. They're still used in many rifles, including the 1892 Marlin lever-action repeater, and in pistols, some made for shorts only.

The '92 Marlin, like some single-shots, had an interchangeable firing pin system to give choice of rim- or centerfire. Evidently, the Short and Long rimfire —and the little-known *Long-Rifle,* too—were parents of Colt centerfires. Outside lubricated, heel-type bullets run from about .310- to .315-inch diameters, for the guns and cartridges were not sharply standardized until later years. Powder and lead rations were nearly identical. The centerfire *Long-Rifle* (or "Interior Lubrication") Colt is the .32 Long Colt as still made, using the same old pointed, inside-lube bullet with deep hollow base that, backed by black powder, swelled the much undersize lead to fill rifling grooves. With modern smokeless, it hasn't the sudden blow to upset the lead so well; and if the barrel is much over-bored, results show it. Much the same type of bullet goes into modern .38 Long Colt rounds; but .38 Special revolvers, which fire the majority of these cartridges, have smaller barrel diameters than the old Colt service sixguns for which the inside-lube Long was designed. It seems to have replaced the outside-greased, heel-bullet Long in a hurry, much sooner than this happened in .32 centerfire Colt.

A .32 rimfire handgun is certainly better than none at all when you need a pistol for defense. Unless it is very short-barreled and loaded with shorts instead of longs, it should be more potent than most .22s. It has bullet weight and width, and fair penetration. If the cartridges go off the market, most guns could be con-

verted to centerfire Colt .32; and if those too become unavailable, the .32 Smith & Wesson Short and Long are likely to stick around for some time. Rechambering, with the approval of an honest and informed gunsmith, would allow us to use these S. & W. sizes. A Marlin '92 rifle I know did excellent work after Charlie Canoll of Waverly, N. Y., rechambered it for the stronger, more reloadable Smith cases.

.41 Short and Long

The Long, with 16 grains of black powder and blunt-nosed 130-grain bullet, much like that of the 160-grain .41 Short Colt centerfire, is gone. Apparently, all the "National, Williamson, Colt, Remington, Southerner, Derringer, Ballard, Forehand & Wadsworth, and Frank Wesson Pistols"—quoting an old Winchester catalogue—took it, for it is listed as "Adapted to all Pistols of this Caliber."

Compared to the Short, with 10 or 13 grains of black powder behind a pointed 130-grain bullet, it was rather effective; but like other useful loadings, such as the old flat-nosed .38 Colt Special and the little .38 S. & W. Short with U.S.-made 200 grain blunt-point bullet, it didn't get around enough to become well-known and popular. The .41 Long rimfire was far less effective than the .41 Long centerfire, with 21 grains of black powder behind a similarly bluff-fronted 200-grain bullet, which we still have available in smokeless, non-corrosive.

Bullet diameters of .41 rimfires go about .402 to .405 inch, much like the centerfires and a pistol-size "Eley's Needle Gun Cartridge" in my collection, with thin, brass-sided, unrimmed case, and a base that I'm not going to stick a needle into.

The .41s were gone for some years, even the Short, which in one of its last listings as a smokeless, non-corrosive round sent a 129-grain pointed bullet at 520 f.s. velocity for 78 foot pounds' energy, one pound over that of the .22 long fired from a six-inch revolver. Derringer barrel length was usually about three inches, and the tiny, curved-grip guns tended to kick loose in your hand. So the light powder charges made some sense, after all. Now we have similar pistols for the .38 Special, a much heavier round; but folks have use for them as hide-away pistols just as before, and they buy them. So many .41 rimfire pocket pistols—single-shot, double-barrel, and revolvers— were made and given reasonable care from the first, that collectors have a fine array of them.

It was at the urging of Philip J. Medicus, it seems, of 18 Fletcher St., New York 38, that Remington revived the caliber; and now you can buy modern, non-corrosive .41 Shorts again. Medicus has served shooters well with his supplies of obsolete, foreign, and generally hard-to-get ammo, and he handles the usual standard line, too. The firm name is changed to Male-Town, Inc., and the address to White Plains, N. Y.

Most .41 rimfire pistols with small, saw-handle or

bird's-head grips sling their bullets high and wide when you fire them at arm's length, though from the hip you could hit a man across a poker table. That was their job, though some were carried in a boot-leg or up a sleeve or in a vest pocket in the hope of having some sort of gat left if your adult-size sixgun or automatic were taken from you. And they still are hidden away like that, with good sense.

Other Old-Timers

To make the rimfire pistol cartridge picture a bit clearer, we should look at a few others so old that they have become more or less collectors' items.

There were various sizes between the popular .22 and .32, and one of the best liked was the .30. It was chosen by many who liked to have a gun around the house or in the pocket, and, not being accustomed to shooting, wanted something mild but satisfying. The bullets were shaped like those of the .22 short, stubby and round-nosed, like most of the rimfires above .25, though a few were flat-pointed, like some .38 Longs, the .44 for Henry and Winchester rifles as well as Colt revolvers, and the .50 Navy. Bullet diameter of the .30 was about .292 inch, and Winchester used a 55-grain in both Short and Long, the black powder recipes being six and nine grains. The Remington .30 Short topped the six grains of black with a 58-grain bullet, but Mr. Blackman and I couldn't tell the difference between the two makes. Old "Uncle Dan," as he was familiarly and lovingly called, gave me the first pistol shooting I remember having, and to my lasting gratitude. Such things were "unconsidered trifles," mere phone-poles, not milestones, in his long life. He and Mrs. Blackman were as happy as anyone —or any two—else I can remember. Had you known them, you would forgive this digression.

His .30 revolver was a five-shot Remington with small "bird's-head" grip, but there were others in this caliber, including Colts, and single-shot pistols, too, like the Stevens Tip-Up.

There was a .35 Allen & Wheelock .35 rimfire, but all I know about this cartridge is that A. & W. made their own ammo in this size. The same goes for the .42 Forehand & Wadsworth, for which the ammunition was made by U. M. C. (The Union Metallic Cartridge Company joined with Remington Arms at least as early as 1910, with the "Remington-UMC" trademark familiar by 1912, anyway, and in 1934 Du Pont took them over from Hartley & Graham along with Peters Cartridge and the great old Parker shotgun firm.) Real collectors can tell you of other odd rimfire sizes. I have been collecting since about fourth or fifth school grade, I suppose, but not avidly. I seem to be unable to take pride in my ignorance, and that's too bad, for I know that to do so is a great consolation.

.38 Rimfires

These were respectable in their time, and they derive more or less from the .36 cap-and-ball caliber so famous in Civil War times. In Shorts, both Remington and Winchester used the same load in rim- and centerfire: Rem, 15 grains black powder, 125, lead; Win, 18 and 130. In Longs, the Rem ration was 18 and 150 rimfire, 18 and 152 centerfire, the Win equivalents 21 and 148, and 19 and 150. Plainly, the rimfires gave rise to the Colt centerfires, which are still on hand. Rimfire .38 bullets are outside lubricated and measure around .370 inch diameter, varying a good deal. Some 9 mm. pinfires I have are about the same.

The .38 Extra Long, for rifles such as Ballard, Remington and Wesson, had the 38-grain black powder charge standard for Winchester-made .38-40 W.C.F. cartridges, but its bullet was no 180-grainer; it was the 148 as used in the .38 Long rimfire. You and I know that, in the nature of things, many fine big-game trophies must have been brought down by piffling single-shot rifle ammunition such as this slim, approximately 2½-inch-overall .38. It seems a safe fifty-fifty bet that the percentage of wounded and lost game was no higher than in, say, the 1950s, with so many 3,000 f.s. bullets slapped out of lever, pump and semi-automatic rifles in three- to six-round bursts.

.44 Rimfires

There were powerful rimfires, with killing power due to their big bullets, for handguns of the past. The .44 Short, for stubby-barreled pocket guns of bull-dog type, including the Remington, had from 15 to a respectable 21 grains of black powder behind its rounded or flat-nosed 200-grain bullet. The thin rimfire case held powder compactly, and it was still a short and handily packed round.

A much wider flat usually went on the point of the .44 Henry and Winchester rifle cartridge, used also in Colt revolvers; but on the special .44 Pointed cartridge for the same guns the flat was narrow, to increase penetration by a bit. For the lever action rifles, these cartridges had to be of almost equal length; so the Pointed's powder charge was cut from 27 or 28 grains to 26. A special .44 Henry centerfire was made, but it never became very popular. Bullet diameters of the .44 rimfires ran about .436 inch, and the slugs were outside-lubricated. At one time this .44 rimfire caliber was a great favorite out in Indian country. Rifle and revolver took the same loads, just as similar two-gun matings did after the .44-40 Winchester centerfire, a longer and considerably more powerful cartridge, came in 1873.

There were long .44 rimfire cartridges for single-shot rifles. Best known were the .44-28-220 Long, sometimes called the Ballard, with 1 1/16-inch or shorter case, and the .44-30-220 Extra Long, sometimes called the Howard, with 1 34/64 inch case. It seems that Ballard, Howard, Remington, Robinson and Wesson rifles used both lengths, and there were other rifle makes, too.

.46 and .50 Rimfires

The .46 Short, a powerful load for Remington, Smith & Wesson, and other big army-type revolvers, had the well-balanced charge of 26 grains of black powder and a 230 grain bullet. Along with some .44 rimfires, it compared well with centerfires that came along, the .44-25-205 S.&W. American, .44-23-210 Colt, .44-23-246 S.&W. Russian and .44-26-246 S.&W. Special. The .46 Short's 230-grain bullet was actually about .45-inch caliber, and its exposed front taper and narrow flat on the point resembled, at least in some lots made, those of the 250- and 255-grain centerfire .45 Colt. This, with its big caliber, made it a good compromise form for penetration and shocking power.

There was also a .46-40-300 Long for Ballard and Remington rifles, and I have heard of a .46 Extra Long and a .46 Remington Carbine.

The first, half-inch, Remington, single-shot pistols for the Navy evidently took the rimfire .50-23-290, which was still available in the early 1900s, along with the centerfire .50s, which carried from 20 to 25 grains of black powder and a 300-grain bullet. Cases were straight or very slightly tapered, but the .50 Pistol round for the Army used a lightly bottle-necked case. Many of these early centerfires, pistol and rifle both, had inside primers, a system that hung on until .45 Colt and .45-70 Springfield had become much-used sizes.

Fifty-caliber rimfires were rather common: the .50-45 and .50-60 Peabody, and the much-used .50-70 Government were rifle rounds. A .52 Carbine and a .52-70 Sharps were, at least nominally, intermediates between the .50s and the big .58s, the .58 Carbine, Springfield, Gatling, Joslyn, and Roberts. Then there were the Spencers based on the almost straight .56-.56 case, the .56-.52, .56-.50, and .56-.46, the second numerals in the pairs indicating the rough diameter of the bullet seated in the tapered or necked-down cases. The same thing happened later with centerfire cartridges, the .38-40 Winchester case being a neck-down of the .44-40, the .25-20 W.C.F. coming from the .32-20, and so on—dozens of examples. There are literally hundreds of special "wildcat" rifle cartridges formed by necking down, necking up, blowing out, and merely shoulder-altering existing cases. Some of our best standard cartridges came from the work of experimenters not employed by the factories. A factory, however, is apt to change the forms slightly. Quite human!

Are Old Rimfires Useful?

A few boxes of time-seasoned rimfires still molder away on dealers' shelves or in cluttered attics of private homes. If their closely packed black powder has crumbled into dust, it will burn fast, provided that the old priming can light it off. Pressures may be too high for weak arms that chamber these sizes. Sometimes ancient priming can be rejuvenated by exposing the ammunition to temperatures that change considerably every day or so. J. V. K. Wagar, in a *Rifleman* article, seems to have been the first to record this often significant fact.

But there is also conversion of arms from rim- to centerfire, though it is attempted more rarely with old handguns than with old rifles. With reloadable centerfire brass, we can fit most chambers without too much sizing up or down. The bigbore rimfire pistols were built for black powder, not for any sort of smokeless loading. Attempted heat-treatment of their steels to hold anything like modern pressures seems almost insane, at least to this writer. Bigbores have a good deal of authority when loaded with the black powder and soft, more or less expandable lead for which they were made. They give both easy shooting and killing power. Report is low-pitched, and most of them are heavy enough to minimize recoil. But they aren't for Magnum conversion! Some were converted, themselves, from cap-and-ball to rim- or centerfire metallic ammunition.

Any mechanical alteration of an oldtimer, or even a change in the loading of it, is for the informed and the sensible. The firing pin, for instance, should be housed snugly in the frame of the gun, not permitted a free-for-all-disaster fit. Primers must be well backed up.

It is true that black powders now made are not "modernized" or increased in power; they are for old arms *in good condition*. But we mustn't use too fine a granulation. FFG is right for most pistol loadings, though the finer, faster-burning FFFG was used in .32 S.&W. Short and probably in .32 Short Colt; but these are light loadings since the cases are short, 9 grains in both, except for some S.&W.s with 10 grains.

But modern primers are more powerful than old corrosive types usually were. It's foolish to think that what is really a relic gun *must* be loaded to full, original capacity. All we should want is good, accurate shooting, not top permissible (*probably* safe) power.

Bullets mustn't be oversize. They should be no tighter than a push fit in chamber mouths, and that diameter mustn't be greatly over that of the barrel's rifling grooves. Sudden sizing-down of a bullet runs up pressures. An oversize barrel, compared to the chambers, is a handicap, of course, but soft lead expands rather obligingly from the blow of black powder, especially if it is hollow-based.

All we need do to enjoy shooting oldtimers is to use our heads and work along cautiously, and there is great satisfaction in firing them. To try for the understatement of the week: few of the big fellows, from the heavy, square-butt .32 Long rimfire S.&W. right on up, fit your hand poorly.

THESE are the well-liked centerfire calibers. It is granted that probably more civilian handguns fire .22 rimfires than any half-dozen centerfire cartridges added together. Most .22 ammunition is cheap, makes comparatively little noise, and requires a less rugged backstop to catch its bullets. Good but inexpensive .22 revolvers and automatics, and at least one model of single-shot, the Sheridan, still are made, and some old single-shots and others sell at reasonable "used gun" prices. We must admit that ancient, pot-metal, potentially dangerous handguns are used by youngsters, and by adults who should know better. Since the .22 doesn't look formidable except in big, heavy models, it is likely to ride in the tenderfoot's pocket when he takes a whirl up the river, or over the hills, to break into short-gun shooting. The new Savage single-shot has the length and weight to make it a good trainer.

Even when the beginner gets the ideal start, firing under the eye and hand of a sympathetic but strict coach, he's almost sure to launch out with a .22. In fact, he may never graduate from that class, or want to. He can go on using the tiny rounds in a gun, or several guns, of his own, and do at least as well, have as much fun, and earn nearly as many medals as the targeteer who enters the "centerfire" (usually the .38 Special) and the .45 games. Among those who have shot their way to the top or near it, we shall find that the highest scorers used a .22. It is easier, in most ways.

Yet the Dream Gun may be a centerfire, and most likely one of moderate power. For target shooting, for small game hunting, or just as a companion in familiar or "unexplored" country, the bigger calibers have an appeal that no .22—except possibly the .22 Winchester Magnum—can quite match.

So the tyro struggles to perfect his technique with the smallbore, saves his money for a .38 or perhaps a .32—.44s and .45s may still seem too big a bite—and keeps on hoping and honing. He wants a good one, when he does buy it.

More power to him, for we remember so well our first centerfires. We can't recall any other thrill quite like the one he'll get when he winds his sweating fingers around the butt of that first "business gun" of his very own and spills out of the heavy, oblong box a handful of those shiny, strongly made centerfire cartridges. No wonder shooters live a hundred per cent alive and keep happy!

But of course, he may not be a target shot at all. Plinking or woods-wandering may be his fare. For small game hunting or for home and family protection he may want something well above .22 long-rifle rimfire power. Let's hope that he does! Most of the light and medium calibers, from the tiny .25 Auto up to and including the standard .38 Special, are not much harder for him to take in his stride than a .22, when gun weight is mated rather closely to the recoil of the loads. There will be more recoil, naturally; but the .22, ex-

CHAPTER 12

LIGHT AND MEDIUM CENTERFIRE CARTRIDGES

cept in pin-weight arms, has almost none to annoy a beginner. He or she starts from a point of near-zero recoil. Two or three shots, and the tyro disregards .22 lift and shove. If the report is troublesome, ear-plugs go in and dull it—or they should. The initial dread of a handgun is overcome, and therein lies one great advantage of the .22 as a trainer. There are others; but which do you think is the biggest?

With the centerfire, however, our rather new shooter gets obliging ammunition. It can give him power far above that of the garden-variety .22, and just possibly a tiny bit more of sure-fire reliability. The old-time wide gap between rim- and centerfire trustworthiness, in this respect, has been narrowing for approximately 40 years. There's not much left.

But centerfire ammunition is obliging, compared to rimfire, in that it can be reloaded, not only for economy that rivals the rimfire's, but also to give exactly the sort of performance we can reasonably want. Powder charges and bullet weights and designs offer limitless variety for experiment—*and for practical uses*. True, handloading is not for a careless person, but neither are guns.

We might say—I think it's true—that centerfire ammo is obliging because it gives us a kick in the pants, and says, "Why don't you reload my brass and really get to know your gun—and learn something about ballistics, too?" Or am I being too fantastic for words that go into print?

Ballistic tables, given for many cartridges in this

From left: .25 Auto, old soft point load; .30 Luger; sub-caliber, round-ball cartridge for use in Luger insert barrels before the current Erma .22 long-rifle conversion came in; .30 Mauser; .32 S.&W.; .32 S.&W. Long, old metal-point, lead bearing bullet; .32 Colt New Police or Police Positive; .320 British as once made by Winchester; .32 Short Colt; modern .32 Long Colt; old outside-lubricated .32 Long Colt (note shorter case but same overall length); old .32-44 S.&W.; .32 Auto; .32-20; .30 M1 carbine; .35 S.&W. Auto, metal-point, lead bearing; .38 S.&W.; .38 Colt New Police or Police Positive; old 200-grain bullet from .38 S.&W. cartridge; Kynoch-made .380 British; .38 Short Colt; modern .38 Long Colt; old outside-lubricated .38 Long Colt; .38 Special; old .38-44 S.&W.; 9mm. Luger with early type of truncated-cone bullet; modern shape of 9mm. Luger; .380 Auto; .38 Auto; old outside-lubricated .41 Short Colt, its lube dried up and useless, as happens after many years of storage; modern .41 Long Colt. Lamp photo, Winchester, Va.

chapter, report the familiar feet per second of bullet velocity and its energy in foot-pounds, which as we have noted mean less in killing power than its shape, diameter and construction. They list also the trajectory rise of the bullet over the line of sight, we could say, at the middle of a certain range, as at 25 yards when we are shooting at 50—though actually the highest point is a bit beyond midway, much as with a base-ball or golf-ball. The barrel length of a factory's test gun is given, and the penetration in the long-standard ⅞-inch soft, dry pine boards, spaced ⅞-inch apart, at 15 feet from the muzzle. This is a rather important figure, although, like the other figures, it is only a guide, since guns are individuals and vary much in chambering, boring and rifling sizes and quality. To the barrel length of a revolver, we could add the cylinder length, if we cared to be theoretical. Actually, the same cartridge may give either more or less velocity from a revolver than from an autoloading pistol, with its chamber included in the barrel length. There are not only the variations in snugness of chambering and boring to affect velocity, but also the close or far-too-gappy joint between a revolver's cylinder and barrel, and the amount of throating-out given the barrel breech. Only actual testing, not theory, can determine the velocity of a certain gun and load setup. This means chronograph tests, not penetration contests, un-less both types of handgun fire bullets so hard that they don't expand. The faster an expanding bullet goes, the more it distorts or "mushrooms" itself in the testing material, and its enlarged diameter makes the going rough.

.25 COLT AUTOMATIC

In Europe, this cartridge is known as the 6.35 mm. Browning, like its bigger brothers, the .32 and .380 Colt Auto, the 7.65 mm. Browning and 9 mm. Browning Short.

Bullet in grs.	F.S. vel. at muzzle	At 50 yds.	F.P. energy at muzzle	At 50 yds.	M.R. traj. at 50 yds.	Bbl. length
50	810	755	73	63	1.8″	2″

Penetration ⅞″ soft pine boards at 15 ft., 3

In good hands, a gun firing this weak cartridge can

do the business. Among the fellows around a poker table in New York City, sat a man well-known among his friends as a gun-crank, a licensed pistol carrier who liked to fire his guns as well as cuddle them. He had practiced. No doubt he had taken some ribbing about this hobby.

There was a good deal of money on the game, and things looked bad when the apartment door burst open and two holdup men muscled in with drawn pistols. Onlookers saw a flash of blued steel, a darting jet of flame, heard a resounding roar in that "smoke-filled room," then the crash of a body on the floor. Two more shots from the .25, and the jangle of breaking glass. In the succeeding quiet, they took stock. The first hoodlum had been drilled through the forehead, and the City would not need to bear the expense of his trial. The second had been winged as he dashed into a bedroom to break through a window leading to the fire escape. He got away, leaving no blood trail. The .25 isn't famous for laying one.

Was he apprehended later? I don't know. Newspaper follow-ups to some stories are tantalizingly absent, or of necessity delayed.

To handle this little hunk of dynamite—and the .25 can be just that when the chips are down and courage and skill are high—a great variety of foreign automatic pistols has been made, including some old, especially unreliable, and positively dangerous, unsafe imitations of the Colt and Browning brothers. A 2-inch barrel is about standard, but the Hercules Bullseye type of powder commonly used in the .25 comes close to burning completely in the short furnace. There were short Mausers, of course, and other Mausers equally well-known here, not so many years ago, with barrels about 3½ inches long.

A few revolvers were made for the .25, and multi-barreled pistols, also double-barrel pistols with rotat-able four-round chambering, for the case is not rimless, but semi-rimmed (or semi-rimless, if you prefer) with a flange to headspace it in the chamber. The .32 and .38 Auto Colt are of this sort, too, and have been used in other arms than semi-auto pistols. Most of the non-self-loading .25 pistols should be far more reliable than the autoloaders. In this caliber, the latter have a pretty bad reputation for jamming, even with fresh, strong ammunition.

A .25 A.C.P. auxiliary cartridge holder has been made, and may still be available, to permit firing this Auto Colt Pistol round in .250-3000 rifles. It is not a happy combination, as so many have been, for the Colt is the smallest of all .25s, with .250- or .251-inch bullet diameter, instead of the .257 which is standard for other .25s, including the obsolete .25 Stevens rimfire. Its hard little jacketed bullet, driven by a small powder charge, can scarcely upset to fill .257-inch rifling grooves as we should want it to. But it could pot a grouse or a rabbit at very short woods ranges, if handled right; it is not a good small-game caliber except with perfect placement, which is hard to manage with either pistol or rifle! The .25 Stevens Short cartridge, which some adapters used to take, is not manufactured any more. After all, the .25 Colt caliber is chosen primarily for short, flat, handy auto-pistols that can go almost anywhere with us.

It isn't the smallest standard centerfire automatic cartridge ever made. There was the similarly proportioned 4.25 mm. for German Lilliput pistols, years ago. Its 11- to 14-grain jacketed bullet was approximately .167 inch in diameter. Tested by the H. P. White Laboratories at Bel Air, Maryland, it gave a surprising 776 f.s. instrumental velocity at 15 feet. This potentially deadly little freak was described briefly in the chapter on foreign pistols. We still think the .25, or possibly the .22 Short rimfire, is the smallest vest-pocket gun caliber that is practical except in cloak-and-dagger work. And wouldn't the dagger do much better, if you could thrust or throw it?

The .25, a 6.35 mm., is weak enough, with its ho-hum 810 f.s. velocity and its energy of 73 foot-pounds, less than that of a standard velocity .22 Long-rifle fired from a 6-inch revolver. The .22 high-velocity hollow-point is deadlier than this smooth, hard bullet of greater caliber and weight. But sometimes the mere display of a gun discourages would-be assailants, provided that a glint in your eye shows your willingness to fire if pressure is brought to a peak.

We could compare the .25 to a very different pistol cartridge, the 5.5 mm. rimmed Velo Dog, a straight-cased .22 centerfire for short-barreled pocket revolvers almost never seen here. Winchester and Remington made it, and the full-jacketed version of its extremely blunt 45-grain bullet helped to develop the .22 Hornet round, which started as a wildcat, not as a factory load. Fine accuracy those pellets gave in Hornets and .218 Bees, handloaded as issued. At short ranges, the full velocities could upset them a little on impact. Turned end-for-end and swaged into soft-nosed bullets, with the lead exposed at the former base sticking out, they were deadly on varmints at moderate ranges.

Smallbore High Velocities

We cannot compare the slow .25 Colt to high-velocity pistol cartridges also of small or smaller diameter, the .22 Winchester rimfire Magnum, or the Hornets or altered Hornets, or even the .25-20 Winchester repeating rifle cartridge for which a very few revolvers have been adapted. The Hornet types have speed that makes them deadly by comparison.

In the nature of things, we shall have more of the same, factory and wildcat cartridges. A caliber of .30 is not too high to go to, as we know from the pistols that have been made for the Army M1 (or M-one) carbine loads. But considering the weight and bulk of a pistol that most outdoorsmen are willing to tote for practical purposes, the .25 seems at the moment to be a good top limit. The .25-20's 60-grain hollow-point steps out from a rifle at more than 2,200 f.s. velocity, at least when temperatures run about 70° Fahrenheit. Its pressure lies below that which a strongly built handgun, of good size, can stand. By contrast, the .32-20's 80-grain, a very stubby and underweight bullet indeed, develops about 2,000 f.s. We can expect to lose around 25% velocity in a pistol, when loaded with just about the best powder available for this sort of handgun job.

Short, fast, small caliber bullets built for quick expansion do kill varmints at proper pistol ranges. These ranges depend much more on the handgunner's marksmanship than on the speed and smack and flat trajectory of his loads. That's an understatement that rates some sort of metal badge, though it needn't be of precious metal. However, some people do have the skill that makes such now "freak" handgun rounds useful to them, and the good sportsmanship to use them decently. For defense against some vicious human enemy —oh my, oh my! Results would be ghastly, but they would save the day.

They are also fascinating to tinker with, the zippy handgun rounds. Right now, such investigation draws much interest. So, I'm sure, did the development of .30 caliber military rifle cartridges in the 1890s. But the crop proved to be practical; didn't it? What armies now use .45 caliber lead bullets by preference? The .30s do the job, and the scope of the job has grown far beyond belief, the belief of men who lived so many years ago.

Is the .25 Practical?

In speaking of the .25 Colt, we'll forget about game shooting—in spite of an early advertisement that showed a black bear just above cub size laid out with the 13-ounce gun. It's a prize poor game combination, a light, short-barreled, sketchily sighted, heavy-triggered pistol with a grip for one and a half fingers, and firing a non-expandable 50-grain bullet at such modest pistol velocity. Soft points once were made for it, for many years before World War II; but they didn't expand farther down than the front edge of the jacket. The roughened noses were deadlier than smooth ones, at least in profile, but not by much in actual results. Unless the soft-point cartridges were handled through the gun a number of times, the noses stood up to the battering and seldom were responsible for a jammed action. The .32 and .380 Autos also came in soft-point, little, if at all, more expansible, but the velocity of the good old .38 Auto sometimes mushroomed such bullets, except those with short lead exposure. Luger and Mauser .30s were worth-while in soft point, too. The hollow-point 9 mm. Luger, like the later hollow-point .38, was pretty hopeless, and the soft-point 9 mm. was a scarce item indeed. Norma now imports .30 and 9 mm. Luger soft-points for handloading.

All this U. S. factory-made expanding auto-pistol stuff has gone down the river of past time. Handloads with blunt or semi-wadcutter soft-lead bullets in the bigger calibers are more deadly on most game than any old factory charges ever were. One would have enjoyed trying soft-points in the original 1300 f.s. loading of the Super-.38, but the factories handicapped that one with a much too toughly jacketed hollow-point.

Since the .25 Colt is a cartridge for infrequent use, it almost never has been handloaded. It is doubtful that tools are available except as custom products, though Lyman-Ideal used to list a "special order" mold for a .252-inch 51-grain pellet mistakenly labeled ".22," with code number 252435. Someone must have reloaded the .25; and the molds may still be available from the factory, for it has made, or will make, practically any sort that's wanted.

We have heard of a .25 Colt pistol fitted with target sights and dressed-down trigger pull that shot quite well. The old .25s were assembled no more loosely (for surer functioning despite lack of care, including a drop or two of oil where needed) than other guns of the type. Is *any* cartridge, in itself, inaccurate in a good arm that is built for it? I think the answer is a carefully qualified "No."

But I remember a good pistol shot sitting in the door of my tent and missing a fish-eating heron (legal to kill, then) that stood perhaps twenty yards away in river shallows. The bullet struck two or possibly three feet short, and the .25 that fired it was one of the guns that he used probably two or three times a month. With Stan's much more familiar Colt target revolver lined up on him, that bird would have stood no chance. As it was, off he flew, disgusted and insulting. No one could blame him.

For protection, though, the .25 Colt is quite different. The twenty-yard shot rather seldom is called for; it's more likely to be five or six, if one has to fire at all, since he's obviously armed with a gun that *can* kill. Placed right, the little bullet does the work; it has done it hundreds if not thousands of times, as newspaper readers know. Yes, it kills by chance, we could almost say; it has about the lowest rating in stopping power. But most of the guns, foreign or old American, that fire this cartridge are scarcely burdensome to carry, except perhaps in a swim suit. They can be with us, if we remember to pack them and can do so legally.

April 1961 Arrivals

April, 1961, brought three important announcements to handgunners. Surely least sensational, but perhaps most significant to the majority, was Ruger's Convertible Single-Six revolver, although the Remington .22 Jet and Winchester .256 Magnum cartridges are a long stride forward in handgun ammunition.

The convertible Ruger has interchangeable cylinders, one for .22 short, long and long-rifle—or for the imported BB and CB caps—and one for the .22 Rimfire Magnum. Pulling out and replacing the cylinder pin for the conversion is easy and quick. The sights are fixed, non-adjustable except that the rear sight can be driven to and fro for an individual's windage adjustment, but this fact hasn't hurt the long-established Single-Six's popularity very much. The rear sight can be filed down to lower bullet impact, or replaced with a higher one, should that be necessary, to raise it. The careful shooter would sight in for the cartridge and range that are most useful to him.

This Ruger comes with 4⅝, 5½ or 6½ inch barrel, with a 9½ at extra cost. The first advertisement carried the not surprising announcement that "This feature cannot be incorporated into guns now in the field." Such conversion work would swamp a factory's service department! However, the important news is that what was long wanted is here, and it's almost certain that other firms will follow suit.

Here are the factory figures for the new centerfire magnum cartridges, the .22 Remington Jet and the .256 Winchester Magnum, the .22 with a 40-grain bullet, the .256 with a 60-grain, both soft point, jacketed. The .22 used an 8⅜-inch barrel, the .256 an 8-inch. Note: Not all have proved up.

The Remington.—Velocity at muzzle and at 50, 100, 200 and 300 yards: 2460, 2100, 1780, 1280 and 1020 f.s. Energy at these ranges: 535, 390, 280, 150 and 90 f.p. Mid-range trajectory heights at 50, 100, 200 and 300 yards are .2, 1.0, 5.7 and 18 inches.

The Winchester.—Velocity at muzzle and at 50, 100 and 150 yards: 2200, 1890, 1630 and 1420 f.s. Energy at these ranges: 650, 480, 350 and 270 f.p.

Winchester-Western also gives bullet drop figures of .9, 4.4 and 10.9 inches at 50, 100 and 150 yards, as compared to 2.5, 10.4 and 25.7 for the .357 Magnum, and 2.2, 9.8 and 23.9 for the .44 Magnum. The free recoil for these three calibers is stated as 3.3, 7.0 and 18.9 foot pounds from 44-ounce guns. Half the recoil of the .357 certainly would affect few shooters in the field, and the .22 Jet's recoil should be noticeably lighter than that of the .256, with only two thirds of the latter's bullet weight. The Jet's higher velocity should bring a definitely sharper report to one shooting both guns side by side, though much depends on the snugness of the joint between barrel and cylinder. As much as .010 inch could be pretty bad, for these new cartridges are ear-ringers, at the best, when fired from handguns or even from custom-made single-shots to be expected, with no barrel-cylinder joint at all. Almost any shooter would wear ear-plugs when firing them at target, and maybe in the field. If he shoots right-handed and one-handed, the right ear would take the worst of the blast, but in two-handed shooting he's going to get slapped down, anyway, if he doesn't wear the plugs. However, some people can take the racket far better than others, still do good shooting, and still hear conversation—a day or two later, perhaps!

I realize that I'm overdoing this topic, but I don't relish my own deafness except in heavy street or road traffic, in some factories, under the smashing roar of jet plane, or among a whole lot of children with unin-

The .22 Remington Jet.

hibited egos. Much good shooting has been done with .22 Hornet and similar handguns, and it will be done with these Jet and .256 revolvers, just as it was with the .220 Swift rifle and the .357 revolver, which also were considered ear-busters, on their 1935 arrival. People got used to them.

Air resistance does more than gravity to reduce a high-speed bullet's long-range efficiency, at least when that bullet's weight is low for its caliber. Both Jet and .256 bullets are light, riflewise, and these bullets approach or even reach the rifle class. They are jacketed for easy expansion, quick breakup, but even so, small caliber bullets must have explosive effect to kill varmints surely and humanely. And we must never forget

that it's from five to ten times as hard to place a bullet from a pistol as from a rifle!

Being at heart a conservationist as much as a hunter, I'm conservative about the killing power of sporting arms. I hate to have animals or birds escape wounded, to die later, and miserably. A varmint deserves as fair treatment as game does, and by that statement I'll stand till there's skating in hell, every Saturday night, if one gets time off then. Sure, I'm enthusiastic about these new cartridges, but only when they're used effectively.

In considering them we can draw on past experiences with small rifle cartridges. The high velocity .25-20 60-grain bullet at from 2200 to 2250 f.s. muzzle velocity showed blow-up effect on woodchucks at short ranges, and it was effective on them, *when well placed,* up to about 100 yards. The original .22 Hornet 45-grain at 2350 f.s.—2400 when the non-mercuric feature was added to its already non-corrosive primer—extended the sure killing range perhaps 50 yards. It's faster now, but still our lightest acceptable woodchuck cartridge except for the very best shots, or at shorter distances—and perhaps except for the easily wind-blown .177 custom jobs. On animals as heavy as coyotes the .25-20 probably was more deadly than the Hornet, though neither is first choice, by any means.

We can translate these findings into Jet and .256 evaluations, considering our individual handgun abilities, and come out correct or very close to it. The Jet's bullet is five or six grains lighter than factory Hornet bullets now made, and that doesn't help it to hang on to its velocity or to fight wind. Still, it should do as well as the early Hornet, or better, in fact, within a full 100 yards. And *that* distance is only for the most capable handgunners.

Against human enemies both Jet and .256 would be terrific at short ranges. Far out, their flat trajectories would make hitting easier than with other handgun rounds, unless the wind blew very hard, and tagging the enemy would be enough, usually to put him out of action. It might be infinitely better than killing him.

At this time Colt ".357," Python and Single Action Army .256 revolvers are planned for summer, 1961 sales, and there may be Ruger models, too. The Smith & Wesson gun for the Jet already is pictured in advertising. It looks like a K-.22 with the long cylinder (.357 length) and shortened barrel breech extension of the Combat Magnum.

With the S.&W. come chamber inserts for .22 long-rifle or shorter rimfires, and the firing pin is instantly adjustable from rim- to centerfire. On special order there's an auxiliary cylinder, complete with ejector, for the rimfires. The inserts remind us of the old Winchester "Supplemental Chambers" that let us fire pistol cartridges in rifles, .32 S.&W. in .30-30, .38 S.&W. in .35 Win., and so on. There's a good deal of latitude in the Smith's rear sight adjustments.

The new cartridges are based on .357 Magnum

brass, and no doubt they'll be used in rifles. The Jet, long-shouldered and short-bodied, reminds us of the old .32-40-150 Bullard black powder rifle round, not the .32-40-165 *Ballard* that was taken up by Winchester, Savage and Marlin and survives in smokeless powder, soft-point bullet loading. It is subject to much blowing-out to increase powder capacity, this Jet, for use in good, strong rifles. The .256 is more conventionally shaped, a good bit like the .218 Bee. Both have enough taper for easy extraction from their own, individual guns when reloaded but not full-length re-sized, especially the Jet. Enlarging either case's body or shoulder to hold more powder for pistol use is distinctly for specialists, if for anyone. They're good as they are, and enough, don't you think?

.30 or 7.65 MM. LUGER

Bullet in grs.	F.S. vel. at muzzle	At 50 yds.	F.P. energy at muzzle	At 50 yds.	M.R. traj. at 50 yds.	Bbl. length
93	1220	1110	307	254	.9″	4½″

Penetration ⅞″ soft pine boards at 15 ft., 11

This small, bottle-necked, high-pressure pistol cartridge has enjoyed world-wide renown for some sixty years. The .25 Colt (6.35 mm. Browning) was new in this country in 1908, but at that time the Luger .30 was fairly well established here. You could buy the guns and their ammunition.

Since World War II, it has been eclipsed in popularity by the straight-cased 9 mm. Luger, a somewhat later cartridge. But the .30 caliber ammo is still easy to find in our sporting goods stores, even though 9 mm. pistols in use must outnumber the .30s by twenty to one—at a rough guess.

The high-velocity flat-shooting .30 has been a favorite on exploring trips by land or over the seven seas. Its sharp little bark has sounded, too, in lonely outposts of the "civilization" we have carried, mostly for our own ends, to far places with queer-sounding names. It has had its share of wanderings through our own wild places, east and west. It has given its due of pioneering service—in its own peculiar fashion.

For killing power, it depends almost entirely on its deep penetration. The shooter must place his hits. Old soft-point bullets expanded a bit, though jackets were tougher than necessary to prevent the bullets' "stripping"—ripping straight through the bore without proper rotation, and of course without accuracy. Hollow-points were distorted but little when they hit. Sometimes they were flattened lengthwise, like the long, 160-grain, *full-jacketed*, 6.5 mm., Mannlicher Schoenauer rifle bullets, instead of being flattened at the nose when they struck tough resistance. Except for their sawed-off points, flattened narrowly in manufacture, they were not much more killing than the round-nosed jacketed .30s.

But the penetration of eleven of those almost classic "⅞-inch dry pine boards" is equaled, generally speaking, only by the .30 Mauser and the .38 Special and .45 Auto metal-piercing, and beaten only by the factory Magnums and some custom jobs.

Deep-penetrating bullets usually can carry damage into vital organs and leave a long narrow wound on their way, if the aim is true and no heavy resistance deflects them. So even the little navy-bean .30 pellets can kill big game, and they have been used a good bit to finish off large animals knocked out by rifle bullets, which are more expensive to buy and heavier to pack. The approximate two pounds of a Luger and about as much additional weight in its compact ammunition have seemed worth-while in the woodsman's load, to supplement the rifle on big game and small. But even on small game, the little bullet simply must be placed well. Time and again, it has failed from so-so shooting, and about that there's nothing in the least surprising.

Luger deadliness is entirely different from the smash of a .44 or .45 that gives shallower penetration. In war, hits as they come, seldom perhaps in instantly disabling spots, are more effective from big, comparatively slow bullets. For a gun-fight, even the 9 mm. Luger, approximately a .35, is preferable to the spectacular .30. And in penetration and flat trajectory the .30 still *is* rather spectacular among standard factory cartridges.

This high-velocity load is fascinating to shoot, with light recoil and a sharp, distinctive bark, which is not unpleasant as it "blats" forth from a 4⅝-inch or longer barrel. It can be reloaded with bullets of standard or slightly greater weight. An excellent barrel should handle them in soft alloy, perhaps in pure lead, without troublesome fouling being piled up in the grooves. The full velocity is actually low, under that of the .32-20 rifle, which often is loaded with soft lead. If the pistol's faster twist fouls up with such bullets, or if jams occur, it is time enough to put a little solder, tin or antimony into the melting pot.

Since the cartridge is truly rimless, in reloading it we must be aware of headspace, that close tolerance between the head of the fully chambered brass and the face of the breech-block. Fired from the same gun, cases should be a good fit, the shoulder behind the short Luger neck preventing the cartridge from entering too far into the chamber. But we mustn't set this shoulder back in case-neck sizing, an operation not absolutely necessary in reloading all pistol rounds, but advisable with this one and the .30 Mauser, which also is bottle-necked.

Among other truly rimless cartridges, are the .380 and .45 Auto Colt and the 9 mm. Luger. Their cases get headspace on their thick mouths, which should be neither crimped over the cast lead nor even beveled too freely in order to allow us to seat it. Tight fit of a bullet in a case expanded by previous firing is secured by neck or by full-length case sizing. The .25 .32 and .38 Automatics are semi-rimmed. They sit on that flange and enter a properly breeched gun just far enough.

Such a variety of German-made ammunition, military and sporting, has leaked into our country "through channels" not always approved by commanding officers that it is hard to say just what types are safe in pistols, and what most decidedly are not. Lugers vary a good deal in quality and strength, too, for many firms have made them, and under greatly different manufacturing conditions. Even though the .30 calibers have been mostly commercial jobs, at least for the German armed forces, some poor ones got out in the years right after World War I. Some really "super" ammunition has been loaded for 9 mm. "burp guns," sub-machine guns or "machine pistols" of many sorts; and some later, stronger pistols than the Lugers *may* handle them perfectly, with no trouble except, perhaps, a gradual wear and loosening-up. A lot of fellows seem to take pride in the fact that their post-World War II handguns will fire these almost proof loads (considering pistol strength as compared to that of burp guns) and still stay in one piece. This really isn't bright. A few hundred extra foot-seconds' velocity mean little in killing power, if anything at all, when the bullet is full-jacketed, and not much in the flattening of trajectory that the average fine shot can really *use*. Unless foreign ammo is in the original unbroken carton and we can read the labels, it may be risky to take the chance of firing it.

The .30 Luger Carbine round, seldom seen here, is heavily loaded. Usually it has blackened cartridge cases, for sure identification. Long-barreled carbines, 16 or 18 inches or so, gave close to 2,000 f.s. velocity with it, and pressures ran about 40,000 pounds per square inch, like those of the .30-30 rifle cartridge when it sent its 170-grain bullet at about 2,000 f.s. instead of the 2200-odd it has now. The Luger carbine was used for hunting medium- and fairly large-sized game in German preserves. Over here, a few woodsmen used it for similar purposes. It was light to pack along on a hard trip, and so was its ammunition, which of course could be had with expanding bullets. The Luger barrel moves backward in recoil, locked to the breech-block, for a quarter inch or so. Nicely shaped wooden forestocks were commonly fitted to the carbines; they helped in holding for steady aim.

Any such pistol, stocked for two-hand hold, is now a "firearm" under Federal law, just as a Thompson sub-machine gun is. It is subject to a heavy tax. But few of us would want one, at any rate. Even the old single-shot "pocket rifles" in rimfire calibers come under the same classification if they are in shooting condition.

.30 OR 7.63 MM. MAUSER

Bullet in grs.	F.S. vel. at muzzle	At 50 yds.	F.P. energy at muzzle	At 50 yds.	M.R. traj. at 50 yds.	Bbl. length
85 or 86	1410	1210	375	276	.6″	5½″
Penetration ⅞″ soft pine boards at 15 ft., 11						

It is similar to the .30 Luger, but more so! A longer bottlenecked case holds more powder, and the lighter bullet goes faster. Penetration runs somewhere about

the same, because extra speed is counterbalanced by lack of the weight that keeps the bullet driving on through. Some of the old .30 Mauser bullets, particularly as made by Remington, had unusually long-exposed soft-lead points. They should have expanded as well as or better than, the 100- or old 115-grain .32-20 soft-points as fired from a rifle. That is competent expansion on medium-sized game at ranges up to 50 or perhaps a full 75 yards. The hollow-point and full-jacketed bullets behaved about like .30 Lugers of these kinds.

There are some .30 caliber cartridges closely similar to this Mauser round. The 1893 7.65 mm. Borchardt is for what has been called the first successful auto-pistol, invented by a Connecticut Yankee of that name. The 1901 7.63 for the clip-loaded Mannlicher pistol never was well known here, though Borchardt ammunition came from one or more of our factories. The Russian military 7.62 Tokarev is a close copy of the Mauser. There is some interchangeability, at least between Mauser and Tokarev. The 7.65 Mannlicher under D.W.M. (Deutsche Waffen und Munitionen Fabriken—German Arms and Ammo Manufacture) code number 466 is a shorter and straight-cased cartridge. It has been reported by W. H. B. Smith, in *Small Arms of the World,* that the 1901 Mannlicher ammo was obtainable only from Austria. Few of these .30s except the Mauser (and of course the shorter Luger) would have much practical use for us here, and few others would be easy to get.

The .30 Mauser pistol is used all over the world, rather generally, except right here in the United States. In spite of this lack of popularity, which has been relieved a bit recently by one or more importing houses, our factories still load the commercial full-jacketed ammunition. The 1896 Mauser pistol has been changed through the years. In 1932, some became early burp guns, switchable from semi- to full-automatic fire; and detachable, not built-in, magazines were furnished in 20- as well as the old 10-shot capacity. Now the cartridge is used far more . . . in sub-machine guns than in one-hand pistols.

There are imitations of the Model 1896, almost exact copies like the Chinese guns, some of which are made in scaled-up size for the .45 Auto Colt cartridge. Also there are, or have been, several Spanish modifications, not mechanical copies—some of them with a full-auto selective switch.

The Mauser military pistol, for the .30 cartridge, or for 9 mm. Mauser or 9 mm. Luger, never was easy to shoot well for anyone not long used to it. It is clumsy and heavy, around 45 ounces, and ill-balanced. The Luger .30 is a light gun; but even so, like the Mauser it has a moderate recoil, and with a barrel over 4⅝ inches, it is not extremely sharp-sounding. High velocity makes the Mauser speak right up. The rounded grip tends to turn in the shooter's hand; and this, along with the loud report, makes the Mauser freshman think he has something vicious to handle.

Well, he has. There are much more pleasant-shooting, more powerful pistols.

Like the Lugers, the Mauser pistols have barked their sharp commands in far wild places, in peace as well as in war. It was a Mauser automatic that Sir Winston Churchill, as a young man, carried in the 1898 cavalry charge at Omdurman in the Sudan. Back in our unspoiled American wilderness—of which we still have some—we would have encountered these guns perhaps more than occasionally, forty or fifty years ago. Now they are well outdated for such carrying and use.

Handloading

The 7.63 case is a strong one, thick-based like the Luger, and practically all auto-pistol brass as made now and for generations past. It can be handloaded, with quite a bit of lead bullet protruding from its short neck. There should be no attempt, I think, to go beyond standard velocities with this cartridge, and with semi-automatics in general. It is already a high-pressure round, geared rather closely to the safe working pressures its guns were meant to take. It is true that lead bullets slip through a barrel more easily than hard-jacketed ones, but let's not count too much on this fact.

If we were to use the 93-grain Norma soft-point Luger bullet in it, powder charges should be well cut down. Bullet weight, when the type of construction is the same, makes quite a difference; and even a strong gun like a good Mauser isn't to be overworked, or tempted to revolt! I have never handloaded this size, but if I were to do it I should begin by driving a .32 S.&W. or S.&W. Long lead bullet through the barrel to find the rifling groove diameter, and to get at least a fair visual idea of those grooves' depth, compared to those of familiar American barrels. Then for an 85- to 88-grain lead bullet, I should consider the .32 S.&W. Short factory product, or one I had hand-cast, or the heavier Ideal 308245—about 90 grains, really a gallery bullet for .30 caliber rifles, with a "dirt-catcher" groove up front, not to be lubricated—or the Ideal 308227 (formerly 308244), close to the same weight, and designed primarily for the Luger .30. I should weigh the bullets, in both soft lead and the lighter hard-alloyed, and take the results into consideration. Powder charges would start low and seldom, if ever, get much above those needed to operate the pistol's action with good reliability—for which the Mauser never has won many bright and highly engraved medals. Compared to our Colt .38s and .45s, it just doesn't compare, at least in many specimens.

First of all, I should want an accurate, pleasant-shooting load that wouldn't lead the barrel badly—I never had the least bit of trouble with this in my 9 mm. Luger. And then if solid lead wouldn't mushroom in slightly heavier field loads, I should hollow-point the bullet instead of piling on more coal.

If I had any of the old soft-point Mausers as loose

bullets, I should not have the heart to use them in the pistol. Too many friends would want to try them in their .30 caliber rifles. When they were available as "bullets only," they did quite a bit of varmint shooting in settled-up country. You couldn't and didn't need to send them fast—2,000 f.s. was enough to blow them up at short ranges. Except for the .32 Auto Colts, they must have been the lightest soft-point, jacketed bullets used in the Krags and Springfields by handloaders. Of course, they were wind-sensitive, and they lost their velocity fast; but somehow or other, in spite of their shortness for quick-twist rifle barrels (and the excess speed added to that, to drive their r.p.m.'s up to a horrifying rate), they were accurate enough at short, stalked-up ranges. Jim White, Warren Sherwood and I never heard one ricochet from anything, unless they were holding out on me. The nearest I ever came to this was the 60-grain hollow-point .25-20 in the .25-35 and in the .250-3000, too. Such rifle bullets often stay inside a woodchuck. The internal destruction gives him a quick death. "Painless?" I'd question that, too.

.32 SMITH & WESSON

Bullet in grs.	F.S. vel. at muzzle	At 50 yds.	F.P. energy at muzzle	At 50 yds.	M.R. traj. at 50 yds.	Bbl. length
85 or 88	705	670	97	88	2.6″	3″

Penetration ⅞″ soft pine boards at 15 ft., 3

Perhaps it should be called the ".32 S.&W. Short" to distinguish it from the Long, but it isn't so labeled on cartridge boxes.

The Winchester-Western bullet weighs 85 grains, the Remington-Peters 88; but the same muzzle velocity and energy figures are reported for both, fired from 3-inch barrel revolvers. This is really "togetherness"; isn't it?

Our little friend has seen an enormous amount of service, mostly in five-shot revolvers of excellent, good, and fair make; and he's still on the roster. Because he's a peewee, he has taken a lot of down-talk. Had he been human, he would have been frustrated long ago.

Less powerful than the .22 long-rifle high velocity, this .32 Short may be better suited to self-defense; and its bigger, heavier bullet, even though smoothly round-nosed, might kill small game more reliably, if we still had heavy, well-sighted guns especially built for it. But it is a pocket-gun cartridge, and the light revolvers that take it alone—won't chamber the S.&W. Long—are hard to shoot with any accuracy except mighty close-up. The .38 revolvers for the short S.&W. load are heavier, which helps.

Owners of the heavier, longer-cylindered sixshooters occasionally use it as .22 shorts are used in so many arms chambered for the .22 long-rifle, for plinking and even for killing extremely small animals. (Yes, we have all heard the stories, true and false, of .22 shorts' scuppering big game.) An old .32 S.&W. Short gallery load held 4½ grains of black powder, presumably the fast-burning FFFG, half the usual dose, and a 55-grain bullet. It needed special sight adjustment to bring it up to point of aim, or higher if the shooter used a six-o'clock hold at the bottom of the bull. However, it had real value for indoor work at 30 or 35 feet, and possibly farther. It could have paid off nicely in a target revolver chambered for the Long, even though its bullet would have had to skip through the over-bored section of chamber ahead of it, before hitting the neck-down at the Long's bullet seat; and then, somewhat mistreated during this two-stage journey, it would have smacked into the rifling throat. The .44 Russian gallery loads did all this in long .44 Special chambers and still shot nicely at ranges they were meant for. But big bullets can take more abuse and do rather well in spite of it.

Some of the very earliest Colt Police Positive Target sixguns, with 6-inch barrels and good sights for those times, were chambered for this cartridge only, as a choice from .32 Short and Long Colt. The great majority of these little Colts, made later, took the S.&W. Longs.

Remington produced a 46-grain round-ball gallery load, smokeless, as were some Winchester subloads with 55-grain lead. In black powder style, Remington put up a pretty good proposition, for those days of white smoke and a sharp smell that you love or loathe; the 46-grain ball over 4 grains of black powder in the .32 S.&W. *Long* caliber. They practically guaranteed its accuracy up to 12 yards! That was a standard target distance, for there were courses of fire very popular for pocket guns only. A fine idea it is, too.

Some people still shoot such courses, and you may remember that the first model of .22-.32 S&W. Kit Gun was offered with choice of straight-cut Patridge front sight or the "Pocket Revolver" type. The latter was a rounded half-moon blade, just like those on most service and police revolvers, except that just behind the top a little straight-down cut was made to give the eye a flat-faced section to aim with. The sharp corners of the adjustable rear sight were angled off; so the gun qualified for pocket class, since it had a barrel not over four inches long and sights that wouldn't readily snag in a pocket lining.

This "Defense" Doesn't "Rest"

Not all of the abuse the .32 S.&W. Short has taken lately is deserved. Much of the sadness of its reputation is due to many little old revolvers that still fire it, poorly bored and chambered, perhaps rusted out from neglect, and far too often slapped together, originally, with casual cylinder alignment and shocking "gaposis" (to use an old advertising term) between cylinder and barrel. A revolver so made, or in such condition, simply cannot give either the accuracy or power built into its amunition. And this cartridge, of 1877 or '78, for the S.&W. single-action, and for the 1880 double-action development, and so on down the decades of makes, styles and qualities, is of downright good design. In proportions of black powder and lead—9 and 85 grains, or 10 and 88 in some thin-walled cases—it is close to the .38 S.&W. Short with 14 and 145, or 15 and 146, and to the .44 S.&W. Russian with 23 and 246. All three have done accurate work, particularly the .44, partly because its big bullet chops larger, higher-scoring holes in target paper, and partly because such fine, heavy target guns, Colts as well as Smith, were chambered exclusively for it.

All three are short cartridges, built for compactness, and for compact revolvers, too, even the .44 tip-up, if it is short-barreled. These loads gave what was considered reasonable power in their day. As we should expect, hits with the .32 or even the .38 must be placed well to stop an opponent where he stands. Yet even the .32 has been used a great deal for defense. So many guns have been chambered for it, such as that great favorite in the South, the "squeeze-handle Smith" hammerless. that this cartridge should be on the market for a long time, even though few arms, or none at all, are turned out especially for it.

Think of the many times when a pocket-size .32— it is no fun to be hit with a bullet it squirts out—has saved the life of some decent, law-abiding person lucky enough or smart enough to have one handy when brutal forces threatened him, or her. Who can say that this pipsqueak cartridge—so soft and pleasant to shoot, you know—hasn't earned its place?

It is still useful for quiet shooting in a heavy long-cylindered modern revolver with 6-inch barrel. Then it sounds little louder than a .22 rimfire, and in fact it is less noisy than some. As for recoil, it is hardly any rougher in actual feel than a .22 with less than half its bullet weight.

.32 SMITH & WESSON LONG

Bullet in grs.	F.S. vel. at muzzle	At 50 yds.	F.P. energy at muzzle	At 50 yds.	M.R. traj. at 50 yds.	Bbl. length
98	780	740	132	119	1.9"	4¼"

Penetration ⅞" soft pine boards at 15 ft., 4

When you think it over, it seems possible that only for the .22 rimfires has a greater *variety* of American handguns been made than for the .32 Short and Long Smith & Wesson, and the New Police, which is Colt's round, identical to the Long except for the flat point of its bullet. Low pressures allowed manufacturers to use steel not of the highest grades; actions didn't need to be smooth to satisfy the average purchaser, and even straight-bored chambers got by, not throated down for the bullet seat. Prices stepped up as barrel lengths increased, or as butts were fitted with square instead of round-bottom side-plates, and these rises helped to pay the overhead. Few .32s except Colts and Smiths were of really high grade.

We could consider, too, the popularity of the .25, .32 and 380 Automatics, the .38 S.&W. Short, and the increasingly desired 9 mm. Luger or Parabellum, for which more American handguns seem likely to be made. In world-wide popularity, the 6.35, 7.65, and the 9 mm. Short—Browning equivalents of Colt Auto pocket-gun line—deserve careful consideration; but in the United States, the current models of .32 revolvers have been legion from the 1880s until recent years.

This caliber makes for easy shooting, generally much greater stopping power than that of the next popular step down, the .22, and certainly for much more reassurance to a defender of life and property. The .32 S.&W. Long is a little .38 Special, the two having had original black powder and gray lead weights in almost exactly equal proportions. It is a well-designed old-timer. It's little—no argument there—and the .38 Special is just about medium. Powder and lead ratios were 12 to 98 and 21 to 158, in grains.

This .32 cartridge was designed for the 1896 S.&W. Hand Ejector sixgun, still made in modernized form. Like the 1896 Colt New Police six-shooter, made until a few years ago as the up-to-date and slightly larger-framed Police Positive, the H. E. was, and is, a solid-frame, non-tip-up gun, with cylinder swinging out to the left for ejection and loading. Both makes are of essentially modern designs, hard to improve on except in minor ways. For many years they have been made with hammer-blocks that prevented accidental firing, if the gun fell and the hammer spur struck something hard and unyielding. Each make of gun takes either Colt or S.&W. cartridges, but not properly the Short Colt or the Long Colt. The former and sometimes the latter can be stuffed in, but the undersize cases may not expand enough on firing to block hot gases from coming back through the chamber, perhaps slapping the shooter's hand. Such rounds would be for emergency use except in their own guns.

Both cartridges, the New Police especially, are decreasing so fast in popularity that many shooters hardly known they exist. They are useful, and they don't deserve to be submerged by changing tastes. The way to keep them on factory loading lists—and so far they show little sign of wobbling off them—is to buy a box or two now and then.

Target Values

The .32 Long rates the attention of the targeteer who plans to step into "centerfire" classification. With it, he can compete in such matches, damping its light recoil with the weight of one of the lately discontinued but still available second-hand Colt .32 Officer's Model target guns, or a present-day K-32 Smith. These finely sighted, steadily balanced arms are slightly heavier than the early companion .38 Special models; there is less steel bored out of them.

Their weights are almost ideal for the marksman who shoots a good deal but doesn't train his muscles by daily snapping practice and at least weekly firing, to handle .38s on .45 frames, like the .38-.44 Smith Outdoorsman and the unfortunately discontinued Colt Shooting Master. Actually, these heavies never had great popularity among even the most earnest

and conscientious shooters, simply because they are a huge fistful and a great sag. However, the comparatively new Colt Python is no featherweight, and it is certainly well liked. Are times and tastes changing again? It is a long reel of time since .32s as light as the Colt Police Positive Target and the S.&W. Regulation Police Target, about a pound and a quarter apiece of good shooting, have figured importantly, in competition. But as woods guns they have what it takes, once you have learned to whip the wobble of their slim 6-inch barrels.

But back on target. The .32 handloads and factory fodder cost less than .38 ammo, though not much; they give less recoil and muzzle blast; with equally refined loading, they shoot with equal accuracy. Why, they might even have superior accuracy. The .25-35 rifle cartridge commonly beats the more powerful .30-30 in similar arms because of the heavier, less bored-out barrel, and the fact that it's such a soft little cuss to shoot. I think that the sticking point is the ammunition's quality. Thirty-two target guns are not just slopped through factory production, even though the size is not popular.

Except for the smaller holes that .32s cut in the target, and the little bullets' sensitivity to drift at 50 yards when a nice fresh breeze sweeps across the range, they are as reliable in scoring as the .38 Specials. But again, the ammo must be up to the need.

The factory wadcutter charge, sending a keg-shaped 98-grain bullet at 770 f.s., was dropped about 1957. It isn't likely to return unless the caliber regains the degree of popularity it once had—as the 28-gauge shotgun shell, for instance, certainly has done. You find those little fellows in a good many stores. No one calls them firecrackers any longer. The factory .32 wadcutter was fine for target work up to at least 25-yard range. Theoretically, the round-nosed standard Long is better at 50, if we believe in switching loads. Some of the best shots do not.

During the first 40 years of its life, the .32 S.&W. Long was known as a really fine target cartridge. It had done well even in the light target arms that long preceded the Officer's and the K-.32 in that caliber. A round-nosed bullet profile is one of the best for pistol wind-bucking and accuracy. Note those of the familiar .38 and .44 Specials.

Almost always some .32 Long reduced load has been factory-made. This indicates a cartridge's merit. Quite often we can pick up useful hints by studying old designs; so here goes for the .32.

There was the once-popular round ball eased out by some four grains of black powder, a serviceable squib up to about 30 feet. But 50 feet is a better range, if we can get it to use, and we could call it midrange for the .32. For some reason the factories chose the flat-pointed New Police bullets for midrange, with 7 grains of black powder instead of the full 13, or a light dip of smokeless. When "nitro," the latter class of powder, proved to burn none too well with so much air-space, the New Police bullet was set back, tightly fitted, with no crimp. It carried lubrication in its grooves, of course, but in some lots more grease was dribbled down over the bullet's ogive or forward curve. The lead sat about flush with the case-mouth. Only *light* charges of smokeless went in; consequently pressures stayed low in spite of this deep seating. All the nitro loads shot cleanly, and the reason for the extra grease I just don't know.

We could buy these loads—under New Police name, as I recall—when and if we had the money in the depressed late 1920s and early '30s, and we used them with great satisfaction. When factory wadcutters appeared, the heavy .32 guns had shot their ways to respect on the firing lines. Almost any good .32 Long or New Police rounds were accurate, and they should still be.

Oldtimers recall the Remington-U.M.C. attempt to gain sustained black powder accuracy with cartridges less fouling than the standard. The "Self-lubricating" .32 S.&W. Short and Long, .38 S.&W. and Special, and .44 S.&W. Russian bullets were hollow, filled with grease backed by a piston that squirted it out ahead of the bearing surfaces through small holes in the nose. Were they made at the instigation of Smith & Wesson?

Handloaders had been busy with reduced loads. Quick-burning Hercules Bullseye smokeless in 1½-grain charges under a deeply seated true wadcutter shoots well in most guns; but work *up,* not down, with any load for any individual gun, for safety. Don't start high. It's a pleasant load to fire, and it serves admirably for coaching a beginner in a gallery. Du Pont 5066 and the stronger 6 can be used, too; but with the deep seating I should not care to increase the load weight much, if any, though both are milder powder than Bull.

A great variety of molds can be used for the .32 Long. My own favorites have been the standard Long and New Police shapes and the Ideal semi-wadcutter 313445, which casts at about 93 grains. It has more bearing surface than the other two, and that could increase pressure as well as, possibly, the accuracy. Its sharp front shoulder did not lead the barrel throat of the Smith & Wesson I had then—or if it did the leading was so slight that I've forgotten the headache.

Now I use the Long bullet only. It serves my purposes with the small Colt Target—which I never fire at game.

Hunting Loads

There are slews of .32 Long handloads for hunting, and the uninitiated will be surprised at the power we can safely get from big-cylindered guns. But we needn't use heavy loads to make the .32 a satisfactory caliber for gray squirrels—when we can place hits with an extra degree of accuracy—or for rabbits of the Molly C. T. variety. The little pocket arms are all right for standard-power loads, but shouldn't be asked, I believe,

to handle much if anything more. They have thin-walled cylinders and thin barrel breeches, too, which sometimes are beveled at the rear for easy cleaning of that narrow space above them. Heavy .32s can take well-assembled loads up to about 1,000 f.s. velocity; but nothing makes the .32 Long a decent, sportsman-like woodchuck cartridge except when we are close up and can be absolutely sure of brain shots.

The as-issued Colt New Police with flat-nosed bullet actually seems to be at least as good as the much faster .30 Luger and Mauser with rounded, full-jacketed slugs, and perhaps better—as a small game cartridge, that is. Such hard bullets "scarcely get going before they're through"—and out beyond in the brush or dirt. But the best small-game .32 Long bullets, by far, are the hand-cast wadcutters like the Ideal, Belding & Mull, Cramer and other designs, some of them a bit heavier than standard. We are not, let us hope, planning to use this caliber for game at a long range. It's a woods cartridge, and that's it.

With the .32, the expert shot and handloader has more chance to do "original research" than with the thoroughly sown and cultivated .38 Special. Such a shooter is rather well armed for defense, using heavy loads in a heavy gun, and so are his wife and kids, if he will teach them. Yes, you and I know that the .32 is sub-marginal, but many old sheriffs and police officers would not have agreed with us, because they had found it adequate. Firing it is no punishment to anyone who gets the right start.

.32 COLT NEW POLICE OR POLICE POSITIVE

Bullet in grs.	F.S. vel. at muzzle	At 50 yds.	F.P. energy at muzzle	At 50 yds.	M.R. traj. at 50 yds.	Bbl. length
98 or 100	785	725	134	114	1.9″	4″

Penetration ⅞″ soft pine boards at 15 ft., 3

These figures are by Winchester. The 100-grain Remington bullet is credited with 137 foot-pounds, which seems logical. The 4-inch barrel was a popular Colt length; but the early S.&W. length nearest it was 4¼, as given in most .32 S.&W. Long ballistic tables.

Ballistic differences between these .32 Colt and Smith cartridges are so trivial that they are meaningless, except for the penetration. The flat-nosed Colt gives less because it can flatten still more in hard substances. In most .32 uses, that would add to its killing power. Even so, bullets of different makes are usually shaped a bit differently. The Long should shoot flatter, even at 50 yards, because of its rounded bullet point, but our figures for it are Winchester. The .32 Long bullets of that brand commonly are more bluntly rounded than those of Peters-Remington manufacture, just as they are in most .38 S.&W., .38 Special, and .44 Special lots. But these differences may be discontinued in future production.

The flat point of the New Police can mean something to the shooter who doesn't handload his ammunition, just as the flat point of the .38 Colt Special slug did, when that round was still made. True, the difference in effectiveness is small in such light calibers as these .32s. It should do a little better on small game. Naturally, there are many variations in substances that a bullet hits. But a flat-nosed pistol bullet pushes its way through resistance; it doesn't slide along like one with a gently tapered round point. At .32 S.&W. Long and New Police standard velocities, a bullet can't be expected to mushroom to any very helpful degree in small game, or in any living thing. They are just too slow. At the approximate 70 f.s. higher velocity of the standard .38 Special, there is little, if any, real flattening, too. We have to depend on bullet shape, which can include a hollow-point.

The .32 New Police never has been as well-known or popular as the .32 S.&W. Long. That is too bad. This cartridge may die off, like the .38 Colt Special. While it's around it's a better buy than the Long, as it has that slight edge in killing power; and it is probably just as accurate. Except at ranges too long for the .32, a round point does not add much, if anything, to target accuracy. It can help us place our hits, 'way out, if we judge by the preferences of most long-shooters when they punch target paper. But for long-range game, we still need a flat- or a hollow-point.

This cartridge, like nearly all other centerfire revolver rounds from .32 S.&W. Short to .45 Colt, once was furnished—when a store happened to handle them —with either full-metal patched or metal-point, lead-bearing bullets. The latter had a copper or gilding metal cap, usually tin-plated, over the nose to increase penetration; but little if any of this hard metal contacted the bore; and the seated portion of the bullet, soft lead, carried the usual grease grooves. We still have such bullets in .38 Special and .357 Magnum, the latter being a good one for stopping get-away cars.

A friend of mine once bought a bargain slew of hard-nosed .32 New Police, available because the police department in a neighboring village had found them ineffective in penetrating car metal. The mere dent wasn't enough! He used them up in a gun he didn't care greatly for, and though he isn't of Scottish descent —just plain Dutch, and a good steadying lot of it—it was a pleasing deal. He had the cases, too, for reloading. Each of us got a good big grin out of it, too. Fortunately, the officer or officers who had purchased this ammunition in the beginning never had a serious use for it. Probably that department has taken up the .38 Special as standard equipment by now.

The sharp-point, inside-lubricated, hollow-base bullet of the Long accounts for its 50-yard energy performance; and one would think it would shoot flatter than the Short at 50 yards and over.

These are Winchester figures. Remington .32 Long data are a hair different, an 80-grain bullet at 790 f.s.

Let's pick no more fractions, but be thankful that these two cartridges are still on loading lists, for their

.32 SHORT COLT

Bullet in grs.	F.S. vel. at muzzle	At 50 yds.	F.P. energy at muzzle	At 50 yds	M.R. traj. at 50 yds.
80	795	710	112	89	1.9"

Barrel length 4"
Penetration ⅞" soft pine boards at 15 ft., 3

.32 LONG COLT

Bullet in grs.	F.S. vel. at muzzle	At 50 yds.	F.P. energy at muzzle	At 50 yds.	M.R. traj. at 50 yds.
82	790	740	114	100	1.9"

Barrel length 4"
Penetration ⅞" soft pine boards at 15 ft., 3

cases run from about .314 to .318 inch ahead of the rim, with the outside lubricated Short bullet not much smaller in diameter. The .32 S.&W. Long brass goes from some .333 to .335 above the rim and should average a little shorter than .32 Long Colt, which has been made in various lengths, depending partly on whether the old outside-lube or the later and current inside-lube bullet was used, and to some extent on the makers' whims.

The bullet the S.&W. Long case houses is about .313 inch in diameter, so close to that of the Short Colt that rechambering a Colt for S.&W. cases is sensible. It has been done, at least on a Marlin lever-action repeating rifle that still shot beautifully after the change.

Colt .32 cartridges—Short, old greasy Long, and modern inside-lube Long—are so close to the .32 Short, Long and obsolete Long-Rifle rimfires that it might pay to have a .32 rimfire revolver, single-shot pistol, or rifle altered to center-fire to shoot the Colt sixgun rounds. No rechambering would be needed. Instead, the firing pin would be changed from rim- to centerfire, an old trick and one that makes sense to a handloader. Factory power and pressure of the .32 Colt centerfires and the .32 rimfires are much the same. A weak or doubtful gun would not be worth the conversion, anyway. In having this done, we should be betting on these centerfires' staying on the market long enough for us to stock up on reloadable brass, and quite a bit of it, too, for these Colt cases are thin and cannot be expected to last for—well, maybe more than a few dozen normal-power reloadings, if that many. If all this sounds zany, remember that numbers of people do love old, long-outdated, not-too-effective revolvers they happen to have, and they would like to keep them serviceable and fed for occasional use.

These cartridges have stayed in production all these years because many old guns still want them. The Colt single-action Bisley and the Army or Peacemaker took them. With the great barrel length and cylinder weight, and the trifling recoil, they were easy to shoot. As for accuracy, the outside-greased Long with finely tapered but still long-bearing bullet was close to the .22 long-rifle rimfire in build and proportions; and you could cast your own bullets and load them with care if you wanted precision. Tools were made to seat the heel-type bullets; and though they were simple tools, they were well made. They left the results up to the operator, and who would ask more?

Most of these little Colt .32s went into light pocket arms like the Colt New Line and the later Police guns, some of which came in target-sighted versions. Webley, Tranter and other revolvers took them, too. In fact, these cartridges are, or were, similar to Webley rounds. In 1919 and for a few years more, Winchester made .320 cartridges much like our Shorts, but still shorter overall.

The Short and Long go back to the 1870s, but about 1901 the Long was modernized with the same sort of hollow-based, inside-lube bullet it has today. Bullet weight dropped from 90 to 80 or 82 grains, but the black powder charge stayed at 12 grains. With this construction, the old Colt .32 revolvers at last had a water- and oil-proof cartridge. The sub-caliber bullet is too small for chamber and bore, but on discharge, powder gas rushes into the hollow base and expands it to a good, a fair, or a hardly acceptable fit. The system works well with soft lead and the quick-burning black powder (the fine-grained FFFG would do well here), and rather well with some of the faster smokeless powders.

The fact that no guns have been chambered for these cartridges for over 40 years needn't mean a thing. You can still have fun in learning to load and shoot these oldtime sizes. Except for the real gun-crank or the collector, a revolver in this size is no big bargain; but a person who owns *and* uses one needn't be ashamed of it. It was well made in a time when shooters were exacting and got the quality they wanted, or raised Cain about it. The lack of any stepdown from chamber to bullet seat makes the six holes in the cylinder easy to keep clean, and some of us like it that way.

The factory bullets are not shaped for killing, being round-pointed in .32 rimfire styles, the modern Long very sharp indeed. Ideal 299155 80-grain inside-lube Long does have a small flat at its point. Since it's a hollow-based bullet, the mold for it is of "point-cut-off" type; the nose, not the base, is next to the pouring hole. Some molds have been turned out like that for solid rifle bullets, because they make it easier to cast the lead with a full-formed base for accurate shooting. A great many old target bullets of cast lead had a narrow flat point because one school of thought preferred it to the round-point type.

We can convert any round-nosed revolver bullet made of lead into a so-so (at least) flat-point smacker by filing the front of it. This lightens the bullet and gives it a tendency to shoot low. It isn't hard to do this work uniformly, and for deadliness it can be most desirable. A few trial shots can tell us where to hold at a short range.

.32-.44 SMITH & WESSON

This cartridge is one for the book, for the researcher who loves practical old guns. It is not a powered-up modernization like the 1930 high velocity ".38-.44" version of the .38 Special. It's an old black powder round designed for supreme target accuracy, similar to the much longer and more powerful .38-.44 black powder cartridge. In the 1880s and '90s they were favorites of many shooters of the kind that never spare the horses when they're working for precision handloads. So this .32-.44 and the old, original medium-bore under the .38-.44 name ran along with rifle cartridges like the .22-15-60, .25-20-86, .25-21 and .25-25 86-grain, .28-30-120 and .32-25-150 Stevens. All are outstanding among the last and best efforts to make black powder shoot well in metallic cartridges of small or medium size, and the varieties of handloads for them were not to be counted in any one man's experience.

As a rule, those Stevens rifle cases (except the .25-20) held their bullets without a crimp. The idea was that turned-down brass could distort the lead, and black powder needs no decimal-second of time holdback to get burning as it should. Or so, at least, many people thought and still think.

These two S.&W. rounds also were uncrimped, perhaps for the rifle-shot's reason, and certainly for another and obvious one. The full-weight bullets were seated flush with the case-mouths, friction-tight down on the black powder. The .38-.44's long case reached to the end of the cylinder of the .44-frame, tip-up, single-action Smith guns used for both .32 and .38. This reduced the jump of the bullet into the bore to the shortest practical distance. The gun and cartridge were not freakish like the Russian Nagant setup that inserted the case-mouth into the barrel throat.

The .32-.44 case is much shorter than its cylinder, though it's larger and longer than the .32 S.&W. Long brass. It measures .347 inch ahead of its rim and it's about .970 to .971 in length, compared to the Long's approximate .334 and .906.

An unfired .32 Winchester Self-loading rifle case is is also .347 inch ahead of the rim and cannelure (it's semi-rimless)—give or take a mouse's hair—and if this brass that went out during or soon after World War II can be had; the .32-.44 handloader has only to shorten it. The .30 Army M-1 Carbine is truly rimless, giving no grip for the extractor, and it's big for a substitute, being about .352 ahead of the cannelure. It is actually about .002 inch larger at the rim than ahead of the cannelure groove. It is of thick brass—so is the .32 W.S.L.—and perhaps could be worked in the body. The rim, if left alone, might be large enough to give the extractor a hold. Then too, we aren't going to crimp any .32-.44 case-mouth; so the brass could headspace itself on the front of the chamber, probably, and we could poke out the empties with a stick. (I mean, of course, a nice, smooth rod, for these guns need and deserve the best treatment for what they've done and still could do.)

The .32-.44 factory full-charge was 10 grains of black and 85 of lead. It had to be fairly light so that the bullets would stay in place under the recoil of neighboring charges in the cylinder. The thick .32

Self-loading or .30 Carbine brass might require two or three grains' reduction of the black powder dose. I've never heard of these special S.&W. rounds' being loaded with smokeless; but probably Hercules Bullseye *could* be used, as it burns so well at moderate pressure. We'd definitely not use smokeless to increase velocities, but merely for cleanliness; and it might not burn well without a bullet crimp. The Bullseye charge shouldn't go over 2 grains. Yes, the guns have heavy cylinders of good, *old* steel, but this caliber and the .38-.44 oldtimer were built for accuracy, not for power.

The gallery charge was 4½ grains black powder and a 55-grain round ball seated clear down on the shiny kernels and held there by a smear of waxy grease, probably Japan wax, as used for old rifle bullets. This load was just a little above the .22 long-rifle in powder and lead supply. If we use smokeless like Bullseye under the round ball, or under almost any bullet, we should make sure that it isn't compressed. It normally needs a good amount of air-space to burn at reasonable pressures.

The .32-44 bullet diameter is unusual, about .323 inch, some .002 over .32-40 and .32 Special rifle standards and close to 7.9 mm. It seems probable that Lyman can supply the 32362 mold for it, casting an 83-grain bullet, and in soft lead this might weigh up to the 85-grain .32-.44 factory standard. Probably not all old S.&W. guns still available in this size have accompanying molds and loading tools. But without handloading, the caliber was expensive to shoot, over 50% more so than the black powder .32 S.&W. Long, and a bit over the .32 Automatic Colt. Then as now, most enthusiastic targeteers were handloaders.

I've had the luck to shoot two of these fine guns—never saw the Colt Single Action Army or Bisley in this size—one of them with handloads in factory cases, the other with black powder S.&W. Longs, which gave rather indifferent results even with the "soft coal's" effort to expand the lead to rifling groove size. It was an easy model for me to fire, with its long, ribbed barrel, small but reassuring grip, and clean, light trigger pull. Of course the report and recoil were almost nothing. Only the narrow sights condemned it as a target powerhouse, and very keen eyes could have used them.

For very small and easily killed game it should have been useful, for its conical bullet at least had a bluntly rounded point; and, as you know, a round ball has been called the killingest short-range chunk of lead there is, for its weight. Modern velocities negate that claim; and, of course, it isn't the shape for deep penetration. Under some circumstances it's doubtful that any round musket-ball could be as deadly as the 48-grain .220 Swift bullet, for instance. But at conventional pistol velocities a round ball delivers quite a shock.

There were some single-shot pistols in .32-44, I believe, although in them the deep seating of the bullet would have been a handicap, not a help towards accuracy. However, any cartridge famed for accuracy becomes popular among shooters; and it isn't invariably put into the sort of gun that's best for it!

But any .32-.44 in good condition should respond to careful handloading and careful shooting. Next the question comes up: would it pay to use .32-.44 loading technique with modern cartridges? The factories do employ flush seating of lead in .38 Special mid-range wad-cutters, but as far as I know there haven't been specially short-cylindered revolvers to shoot them, though a .38 Colt Super Automatic rebuilt to handle these loads could have its rifling throat right close to the front of the chamber, cutting bullet jump to an absolute minimum.* These custom arms use this particular .38 Special cartridge because it's short enough to fit their magazines. The flush seating of the factory—and other—mid-range bullets is really to reduce excess air-space for the reduced powder charges. Original .38 Special mid-range wad-cutters didn't have it. A bore-riding section of bullet stuck out of the case-mouth. Such rounds now are for collectors.

.32 COLT AUTOMATIC

Bullet in grs.	F.S. vel. at muzzle	At 50 yds.	F.P. energy at muzzle	At 50 yds.	M.R. traj. at 50 yds.
71	960	905	145	129	1.3″

Barrel length 4″

Penetration ⅞″ soft pine boards at 15 ft., 5

Known abroad as the 7.65 mm. Browning, it has been popular for well over a half-century. The Colt gun came out in 1903, in a different form from that of those that were cut out of production during World War II, never to return. The similar Browning arms seem to have started as far back as 1899.

The fast, full-jacketed bullet usually penetrates more deeply than that of the slower .32 S.&W. Longs; but its light weight prevents it from being, probably, as good an all-round cartridge for target, game and defense—not that either one could qualify as an all-rounder in serious service. A few foot-pounds of energy don't mean much.

There is little sense in substituting it for the long (if we have Longs in our possession) in revolvers made for that S.&W. and Colt sixgun size, unless we think we need a bit more penetration. Its tough-jacketed bullets can't expand to fit rifling grooves cut for the Long as well as soft lead can. We do lose some power as a result—and don't do our revolver any good. Gas gets by the bullet and shortens barrel life, rapidly or slowly, just as the ball bounces or the cat jumps. This comment seems worth its space because a good bit of this substitution has been done since, most likely, the earliest times.

As a grouse load for .30 caliber rifles the .32 Auto does well, with finely placed hits. Its bullet is held close

---

*The barrel of the 1961 Colt factory-made autoloader for the .38 special wadcutter cartridge is free-bored, cut smooth for over a half-inch between the front of the chamber and the start of the rifling to ease the bullet on its way.

to the rifling in Marble's steel auxiliary cartridges. I'd hate to have to use this combination for squirrel hunting at the average come-as-they-come ranges, for its accuracy isn't outstanding!

But in well made, snugly assembled semi-auto pistols made for it, the .32 Auto cartridge is accurate in a useful way. It's built much like the .38 Auto Colt, with much lower velocity, of course, to keep its pressure down for the blow-back, unlocked-breech guns it was designed for. Fine shooting is done right along with targetized .38 self-loaders firing standard factory ammunition and good handloads.

Many models of foreign autos have been made in this .32 or 7.65 mm. caliber; and our Colt, Savage, Remington, Smith & Wesson, Harrington & Richardson and other pistols have chambered it. Since its case is semi-rimmed, with rim diameter about .354 inch and body diameter just ahead of the cannelure around .333, it extracts well from revolvers' chambers, and a number of foreign revolvers have been made especially for it. This fairly fast little cartridge is well distributed, not only in Europe and over here, but pretty much over the world.

Handloading

The small, projecting rim positions the case in gun chambers, and for this reason the .32 is a simpler cartridge for the handloader to work with than true rimless rounds like the .380 and .45 Auto Colt and the 9 mm. Luger. These get their headspace in the chamber on the thick brass of the case-mouth, which abuts on the end of the chamber, and for that reason isn't to be crimped into a bullet groove. Slight variations in case length matter little in rim-positioned rounds like the .32, but they should be kept small indeed in true rimless brass of .45 Auto type.

The .32 Auto case has strong, heavy sides and the thick, flat-bottomed inside head construction that has been common to most centerfire auto-pistol hulls. From some guns having a considerable cut-out at the bottom of the barrel breech, to help ramp up the loads in magazine feeding, we do get rather badly swollen empties. These may have to be full-length resized to insure their getting back smoothly into the chamber after they have been reloaded! To do this complicates the job and shortens case life—both by a little. It is after all a common chore in handloading. Full-length resizing a rimless, straight-sided case can be as simple as driving it base first through a hole milled with great nicety through a flat piece of steel ⅜-inch thick or so. It works.

Since the .32 A.C.P. is an expensive cartridge, compared to .32 short and long revolver rounds, it's usually reloaded just for economy, to give lots of practice and shooting fun. Lead bullets cost little, once the casting equipment has been paid for; and a pound of metal, 7,000 grains, goes a long way in stock-piling such light little slugs as these, even after discounting the usual slag that oxidation forms in lead-cooking pots. Most if not all .32 autos have rifling grooves amply deep to

handle cast bullets nicely, just as revolvers do.

The 77-grain Ideal 308252 design is a really old one, resembling the factory bullet in shape, and having two grooves or cannelures, one for crimping, if desired, and one for lubricant. No sense lies in exceeding recommended loads. In fact, it's smart to cut them in first trials, for most of them go back to early times. Modern non-corrosive primers are husky, even in "small pistol" size and strength, compared to the early corrosive, potassium chlorate breeds.

It could be that the .32 is one of the nicest semi-automatic sizes to reload, for it's not only economical and pleasant to shoot on a casual holiday but also—and this can mean so much!—many of the pistols that fire it eject their cases to the right with fairly regular placement, not all over the lot, as some heavier calibers do. It is, of course, a mighty small case to look for in grass! Still, a blanket or a poncho spread out will catch most cases that are ejected on the firing line of our informal range.

Roundup

The full-jacketed bullet is a poor killer; and the long-discontinued soft points could expand hardly at all, short of hitting concrete or steel and the like, since they had little lead exposed and traveled slowly. The .32 S.&W. Long and Colt New Police are better, unless we need a bit more penetration for some obscure .32 caliber purpose. However, the autos hold more cartridges than the revolvers do, and they are quick to reload with a filled and ready spare magazine. The Colt, for example, held eight .32s in its magazine, and the Savage, ten. So shots could be rattled out faster and longer, and maybe wilder, than from a sixgun.

It is less the cartridge than the type of gun which is liked so well for pocket use on city streets and in the far wilderness. The auto is flatter, shorter and little if any heavier than most revolvers for the .32 Long. Its ammunition, too, is extremely compact. Many who would feel practically naked with a .25 Auto go their ways with minds set at rest by the slight additional weight of a .32 semi-automatic in pocket or holster. These guns are not just little city boys; they are country and backwoods boys, too.

The report is distinctive, sharper and more abrupt than those of most snugly fitted .32 Long revolvers. The light bullet makes recoil seem gentle to anyone who has fired half a boxful of these small rounds. Most .32 autos will chamber and extract the mild, less expensive .32 S.&W. Shorts as single-loaders, not using the magazines. These cartridges make rather useful loads for practice, though the heavier S.&W. bullets land high on a short-range target. Their bullets may appear much oversize for some .32 Auto barrels, but the low .32 Short factory pressures, with the softness of the almost pure lead bullets, take care of that.

.32-20 WINCHESTER

Probably because no standard revolvers have been made in .32-20 for years, the ballistic tables published for this round are "short and simple annals." However, they show that in long-barreled sixguns this 1882-issued Winchester rifle cartridge makes a handgun into a *useful* smallbore magnum.

Modern factory bullets weigh 100 grains in standard velocity loading—the original 115-grain Winchester was dropped soon after World War II—and leave a 6-inch barrel at 1030 f.s. for a muzzle energy of 271 foot-pounds. Penetration of 7/8-inch soft pine boards at 15 feet is listed as six for both plain lead and jacketed, soft-point bullets. We should expect more from the soft point because of the jacket reinforcement, even though .32-20 lead exposure is unusually long. This caliber of sixgun does normally expand its bullets in sizable game at moderate ranges; and our choice still would be the lead bullet, for a probable wider bullet expansion and for the longer barrel life it should give.

The full-metal patched bullets are out of production; and the 80-grain hollow-point high-velocity cartridges are "not for pistols," a printed warning that makes sense. Some people handload this bullet, with powder charges well below those for rifles using it, to gain speed. But such a short, light slug drops off so fast in velocity and power that it's worth little except at short range. It isn't particularly accurate when it's rotated as fast as revolver rifling twists send it, though it shoots rather well in slow-twist rifles in good shape.

There are plenty of molds available to cast solid or hollow-point lead, with or without gas-check cups on bullet bases to prevent lead fusion from hot powder gases and to help avoid leading the bore at standard or higher speeds. The bullet point is so wide and flat that some experienced woodsmen think that a hollow point isn't necessary for good expansion, at least on pretty sizable small game.

Some factories use a pistol primer in standard velocity .32-20 loads; some use a rifle primer for all types. The latter is normally hotter, and made with thicker metal in its cup, thus requiring a heavier firing-pin for good ignition. Practically any .32-20 revolver, even the little old Colt Police Positive Special, seems to have plenty of swat to fire the rifle primers surely and evenly, getting good ignition of powder even in this long, slim pistol case. The handloader would choose a pistol primer for pistol powders, and a rifle primer for rifle powders like Du Pont 4759. For Hercules Unique in the .32-20 it would seem to be a toss-up. As a rule, a rifle primer over-ignites pistol powder, adding something to pressure, of course, and tending to cause variable velocities that string the shotholes up and down on a target. This is easy to notice in rifle squib-loads when it occurs, and it usually does occur.

The foregoing suggestions are not of a directive nature! We all have to work out our best handloading formulas for our own guns.

The .32-20 is one of the most firmly established old cartridges for which no guns are now made. Winchester, Marlin, Savage, Colt and Remington repeating rifles still use it, as do a host of single-shot rifles, the

Colt and Smith & Wesson revolvers, and probably a few of the Harrington & Richardson single-shot pistols built for woodsmen, not for target shots. It does well in handguns, not losing a great amount of velocity in them, as compared to rifle speed, which is only 1290 f.s. with the 100-grain bullet. A 2100 f.s. rifle rate makes the 80-grain hollow point a pretty fair blow-up load up to 50 or 75 yards. There seems to be little sense in trying for such effects from a .32-20 handgun, for there are custom .22 centerfires—loaded-down .22 Hornets or shortened Hornets. In a single-action Colt .32-20 revolver, with heavy cylinder—and preferably *not* one of the oldtimers built for black powder!—we could come close to .22 Rimfire Magnum speed, though hardly with a full-weight 115-grain bullet. A lighter bullet should be used, such as a hollow point, and if it's lead, not jacketed, so much the better, pressure-wise. Naturally, the 1961 .256 Magnum makes earlier, pistol speeds seem poky, but a heavily loaded .32-20, safe in heavy guns, is easier on your ear-drums!

Probably all standard .32-20 revolvers except the Military & Police Target S.&W. and the Colt Army or Bisley Model in target form have fixed sights, adjusted at the factories for the 115-grain bullet that made a reputation among outdoorsmen for its flat shooting. This caliber still shoots flat enough for most pistolmen to use its trajectory with sure, well-placed hits on rather small game. Up to about 75 yards there's little drop. It's worth remembering that old Winchester catalogues consistently listed the 115-grain bullet for revolvers, even though the Company made 100-grain loads especially for the Marlin and Colt *rifles*. Back in the teens and twenties of this century there were factory-made 90- and 105-grain hollow point lead bullets as variations of the 100- and 115-grain solids. Demand was so small that they fell off the tree.

Load Variations

Handloading can speed up standard weights of bullets for revolver use in this caliber. The degree depends upon the gun. A thin-chambered Police Positive Special is a poor candidate for much acceleration; but we can do more with thicker-walled chambers in this increasing order: S.&W. Military & Police standard and Target, Colt Army Special and the later Official Police, Colt Single Action Army and Bisley. The vintage is important, for stronger and better-alloyed and heat-treated steels went into the later jobs. Here the handloader is much on his own, though factories can usually give the date of manufacture, based on the gun's serial number. However, it obviously isn't to their interest to plug for loads heavier than ammo-factory standards! The loader should follow recommendations cautiously, starting low and not necessarily getting to the top. Modern primers are husky, and many load recommendations were written long ago. After all, 100 f.s. extra velocity are expensive if they cost peace of mind, or a more or less worn or damaged gun!

Standard factory ammo, even from a 6-inch barrel, is noisy enough to be really painful to many folks with normal hearing. Fast .32 rounds can punish a person plenty, though they can be worth using for special purposes. Recoil from any of the three heavier old revolver types mentioned in the foregoing paragraph is mild compared to that of similar .38 Special guns with their much heavier bullets. It's a quick, snappy, rather enjoyable recoil—business-like. So unless the noise bothers you, the .32-20 is a pleasant-shooting handgun, and it could be called the very lightest caliber to rely on for defense. Its flat-nosed bullets are pretty effective. Many .32-20s, particularly the heavy models, have gone far into the woods and mountain country and got all sorts of camp meat, from venison on down, when held in steady, experienced hands. It is, of course, quite different from the .30 Luger and Mauser: it doesn't penetrate as they do, but it does more damage as it goes.

Because they had gobs of the stuff on hand and hated like sin to waste it, some shooters have fired the .30 M1 Carbine cartridges in .32-20 rifles and pistols. Sometimes they *will* chamber. The cases are too small except up front. Pressures are well above those thought safe in old .32-20 rifles, to say nothing of most of the handguns; and some lots of M1 production have given super-normal carbine pressure. It seems bright for all of us to continue passing around the word that this is DANGEROUS stuff to cram into a handgun, except one especially made for it by a reputable outfit.

At the other and pleasant end of the scale is the use of the .32 S.&W. Short and Long, and the .32 Colt New Police, as subloads in a .32-20. Beyond fouling chambers in rather ghastly fashion they do no harm, at least in the small number of rounds so fired. In a six-gun the Long and New Police could shoot to somewhat the same sighting as .32-20 stuff, for the bullets are of similar weight. They're slow, and slower still because some gas leaks ahead of them in the big, slightly tapered and bottle-necked .32-20 chambers. The .32-20 is actually a bottle-neck, although the shoulder is hard to see on some factory rounds, especially those that are cannelured right over that shoulder. The same is true of the .44-40, but the .38-40 is plainly bottle-necked.

Accuracy

Few shooters have considered the .32-20 as particularly accurate in handguns, though it's hard to see why, for it's a well-balanced load. Some very experienced shooters have rated it high, such as Chauncey Thomas, a practical outdoorsman and extremely able handloader who proved to some doubters that the heavy-duty .45 Colt and even the .44-40 Winchester were revolver cartridges of target grade or durn near it, when loaded and handled right. Factory .32-20s and .44-40s often have been loaded with what were essentially rifle powders, such as the old Hercules Sharpshooter. In a pistol that can make a difference, sometimes.

The .32-20 remains one of the cartridges that—except for the work of Chauncey Thomas and too few others like him—have never been given the accuracy research they deserved. So it is too long and slim in case shape for good combustion of handgun powders? The .357 Magnum is pretty long, too, but it has shot fine target groups with full and with moderate loadings. For long-range revolver work, which would you choose, a stubby, low-capacity case, or one that holds a good dose of not too dense powder that burns slowly enough not to boil up excessive handgun pressures in developing high velocities? If lighter loads don't burn well in the long .32-20 case, using pistol primers, we can go to the rifle primer, as some manufacturers do, anyway, in .32-20 and in .357 Magnum production.

It is true that some years ago there was talk of making just one strength in the small primer, but it seems that nothing came of it; and if so, that's good. Ignition problems vary quite a bit in cartridges ranging in size and power from the little .25 Colt Auto, .32 Short Colt and .32 S.&W. Short to the .222 Remington and .222 Rem Magnum rifle rounds! So do pressures that a primer must take without being ruptured.

Really, the .32-20 is a pretty modern sixgun case, a sort of "too early seen unknown, and known too late" magnum, though it doesn't need extremely heavy loading to burn its proper powders well. And neither do truly modern magnums.

.35 SMITH & WESSON AUTOMATIC

The actual caliber of this obsolete, hard-to-find cartridge is about .32-inch, as compared to about .310 for the .32 Colt Auto. Its body size is slightly larger than that of the Colt, being about .346 inch at rim and also above the rim and cannelure, as true a rimless as we can find. The .32 goes about .354. and .333, and it has been fired in these early S.&W. automatics, made from 1913 to 1921. In its own guns it's more powerful than the .35, but its smaller bullet has given it *some* leeway of safety when fired in that beautifully made, expensive Smith. Not a good practice. Case length of the two sizes is practically identical.

The 76-grain .35 bullet was of unusual but sensible design. The metal jacket covered only the point—or less than that in soft-nosed style—and the bore-bearing section was lubricated lead. The talking point was long barrel life, and that made sense. Except in barrels with special shallow rifling for jacketed bullets we can get useful pistol velocities with lead-bearing bullets, and good velocities, too. With them comes longer barrel accuracy life than we have with toughly jacketed bullets that can't upset to seal off the hot gases that try to cut past them. Such erosion wears barrels more or less rapidly, as .45 Auto shooters know.

The finest and ultimate way to get long barrel life with jacketed bullets was probably the method of A. O. Niedner, one of the very finest barrel-makers we ever had. On special jobs he cut rifle chambers so closely that they required brass cases lathed down to uniform wall thickness and loaded with two-diameter jacketed bullets, the fore-part of bore size, the rear large enough to fill the rifling grooves. Such cases needed no neck-sizing for reloading, for they were too tight to expand to a greater diameter than that to which they would immediately shrink back. I've had just one rifle chamber that tight, one cut by C. C. Johnson in a modern steel liner that went into the bored-out barrel of a Winchester single-shot. The caliber was .22 2-R Lovell, a wildcat case once well-known, a reforming of the obsolete .25-20 Single Shot brass. How would you like a centerfire revolver or single-shot pistol chambered that way? The system is for accuracy, not for top velocities.

S.&W. .38 and .38 Colt New Police

Back in 1956 the .38 S.&W. cartridge rounded out 80 years of life. It was designed on 1870 .44 S.&W. Russian lines, having much the same bullet shape and powder-and-lead ratios, for the 1876 single-action S.&W. pocket guns. This compact, strongly cased cartridge was inside-lubricated and water- and oil-proof, unlike the .38 Short and Long Colt as then made, with their case-diameter lead heeled into thin brass. It was more serviceable, and so promptly popular that there was no hesitancy about adapting the 1877 double-action Smith to it. And even then there was no sluggishness in bringing out new cartridge forms, whether to fill a need or to kick up trade.

The New Police round came later, the only important difference being the flat-nosed shape of its slightly heavier bullet. Both cartridges used a 14- or 15-grain black powder charge, according to manufacturers' fancy. They are interchangeable rounds, but the one that's preferable for serious business, the Colt, never touched the other in popularity. Now it seems even less well-known and distributed than it was 20 or 30 years ago. The Colt flat point is narrow, but it could help in stopping power.

These short .38s can't compete with .38 Special rounds in popularity now; but even so, a rather sensible viewpoint could class them as the smallest—except perhaps the .32-20—that are at all suitable for defense purposes. Time and again they have done a quick, thorough job when they were pointed right. To increase stopping power of this not-terribly-long-ago much-used police size, Western Cartridge designed

about ten years before World War II the Super-Police charge for the same brass. It sent a soft, bluntly rounded nosed, 200-grain bullet at 630 f.s. velocity from a 4-inch barrel. The energy was almost identical to that of the S.&W. bullet. These Supers penetrated an extra board of test pine. Weight drove the slower, heavier lead through. By actual proof in police line of duty, the Super was definitely more effective than standard loads, but we don't have it now because emphasis has gone to the .38 Special still furnished in that 200-grain weight; and rightly, too. For even the Special can lack the needed power.

A similar 200-grain, lead-bullet round went into the British service Enfield and Webley revolvers until the recent change to the 9 mm. Browning auto. However, during World War II it became necessary to jacket the British .380 bullet, lead having been outlawed on the grounds that it is inhumane; and the hard-nose military bullets ran from 176 to 181 grains. The pre-war theory had been that soldiers could learn much faster to shoot a .380 than a .455, and that the 200-grain lead was just about as deadly as the 265-grain .455. Hard to believe, but plausibility and credulity seem to be unmetered commodities.

Accuracy

The .38 S.&W. always was an accurate cartridge in good revolvers and in the few fine single-shot pistols that took it. Now it is probably never seen in any sort of close competition, though it certainly used to be—and could be again. There were target loads for it, including the 146-grain "self-lubricating" black powder round that squished the grease out ahead of the bullet bearing-surface, laying a smoother highway for its progress; and there were gallery doses. One took a 70-grain round ball over a light snifter of black or smokeless powder, and one that I never saw listed but happened to latch on to in New York—at Dannefelser's, I believe—had a smokeless charge behind a short, light cylinder of lead that was seated about flush with the case-mouth. I enjoyed shooting those loads in Francis Clarke's well-cared-for old S.&W. tip-up, but I lacked the sense to note down the bullet weight. They would have been fine in an indoor gallery, with adjustable

.38 SMITH & WESSON

Bullet in grs.	F.S. vel. at muzzle	At 50 yds.	At 100 yds.	F.P. energy at muzzle	At 50 yds.	At 100 yds.	M.R. Traj. at 50 yds.	At 100 yds.	Barrel Length
145 and 146	730	695	651	173	156	139	2.2″	9″	4″

Penetration ⅞″ soft pine boards at 15 ft.—4

.38 COLT NEW POLICE

Bullet in grs.	F.S. vel. at muzzle	At 50 yds.	At 100 yds.	F.P. energy at muzzle	At 50 yds.	At 100 yds.	M.R. Traj. at 50 yds.	At 100 yds.	Barrel Length
150	680	645	615	154	138	126	2.5″	10.5″	4″

Penetration ⅞″ soft pine boards at 15 ft.—4

sights to hike up to correct their low strike. But even without them we could still shoot for groups, not minding how far below the aiming point they formed. Further, we could nearly duplicate those rounds with handloads. By this time any reader should know that Stebbins—Heaven help him—is fond of the old kluck .38. In full charges it has fair power, and short cases do burn gallery powder pinches so nicely.

Many, many makes and models of pocket guns have been made in .38 S.&W. caliber, the solid-frame, side-ejection Colts and Smiths being the best American products—except perhaps the 1909-1920 Perfected tip-up Smith. That had both the top latch and the thumb-thrust cylinder rod lock of solid frame S.&W. type, and only its small round butt and sketchy sights made it hard to shoot. Some inexpensive old guns are pretty well fitted and triggered. A good one can give an investigative shooter lots of fun—and perhaps save his neck in a tight spot, since it throws heavy lead, though not the 200-grain, let's hope. That's rough on tip-up guns with small frames.

The 2-inch Terrier and 4-inch Regulation Police Smiths still are made with short cylinders (a scant 1¼ inches) for this cartridge, and at least in theory are preferable to guns with .38 Special-length cyls (about 1½ inches). However, those two above are light five-shot guns, and the Colt Police Positive Special and Detective Special, with long cylinders, are six-shooters and weigh important ounces more. Both makes need grip adapters or "fillers," the Colts especially, for without them these Colt .38s are knuckle-dusters.

On the Virginia farm the family did a nigh-enormous amount of shooting with the 4-inch Reg Police. None of us could tell the difference between S.&W. and New Police rounds at 50 feet. All seemed to strike about the same, giving us what we deserved. For hand-loading we liked the 150-grain Ideal 360271 semi-wadcutter, really a light .38 Special bullet, which fell from the bronze mold plenty big enough for this slightly larger-diametered .38 revolver barrel.

A vast number of fine Military & Police 5-inch six-guns have come back recently from England, relics of World War II; and British servicemen evidently were taught to care for their equipment. I've yet to see a poor one. The finish is gray, not lustrous blue, but the trigger pulls I've tried were perfectly smooth, double- or single-action. When you put an accurate cartridge like one of these short .38s into a well-made two-pound gun, fitted with an adapter if you need it, you have something. In spite of the long chambers the gun is worth custom adjustable sights. After all, many old Colt revolvers chambered for .44 Russian—not for the longer .44 Special that would have used nearly all the chamber length—shot pretty well. I seem to remember a world's record made by one, with hand-loaded ammo.

Chambering these ".380s" out for .38 Special is done; but usually the bore and rifling diameters are too large for factory Special bullets, requiring a fairly skilled job of handloading. Best leave the gun as-is, for it's a good one, shooting a good cartridge. Maybe it's close to ideal for family use, since its recoil and muzzle blast are so reasonable. Get the adapter, however, a reloading outfit for lots of low-cost shooting—including light charges for the beginners—and special sights later if you want them. Should the gun shoot low for you with issue sights, you could cut the front sight down, gradually, to raise the point of strike.

A rolling-block single-shot Remington pistol in this caliber would be a rare find now, but how shootable if still in good condition! The Enfield and Webley revolvers with spurred hammers for thumb-cocking are OK, and they might be available. A less expensively made but still satisfactory arm of good weight and size was the Harrington & Richardson Defender made for wartime guard duty, and a bit scarce on today's used-gun market.

Handloading

I wish that more people knew how fine this cartridge is to reload. The brass is heavy and long-lasting, yet easy to work even in light tong-type tools. Standard pressures are low and must be, for most of the vast number of revolvers that shoot this cartridge. Don't be tempted into magnumming any of the guns made for it. A little extra velocity doesn't mean much in killing power, but a little extra pressure can be dangerous. It's a spring tonic to see those big bullet-holes appear plainly on 50-foot target paper, especially from home-cast semi-wadcutters. Make sure of the weight and diameter of your cast bullets, and gauge powder charges accordingly.

.38 Short Colt and .38 Long Colt

These are nearly obsolete cartridges, adapted to double-action Colt revolvers that were adopted about 1892 for service use. Colt pump action rifles also took them, and so do modern sixguns.

The Philippine campaign following the 1898 war with Spain proved the .38's inability to stop courageous, determined fighters that a .45 almost certainly would have dropped. However, as late as World War I the old service .38s did some duty, at least for training Navy recruits.

These old service (and commercial) guns have un-throated chambers long enough to take even .357 Magnum rounds, which could be disastrous in spite of the large barrel diameters ahead of the cylinders. In good condition, they should fire the .38 Special *mid-range wadcutter* factory loads, or their equivalents, with complete safety. The deep hollow bases of factory wadcutter bullets—as made for many years and still made—once the early short, solid wadcutters had established the mid-range type, would give the lead some chance to upset and fill the oversize chambers and barrels. With black powder behind them they should do it easily.

The original .38 Long had an outside lubricated, heel bullet; and the .38 Short, like the .32 Short Colt, still is made in that way. These bullets fitted the bores

.38 SHORT COLT

Bullet in grs.	F. S. vel. at muzzle	At 50 yds.	At 100 yds.	F. P. energy at muzzle	At 50 yds.	At 100 yds.	MR Traj. at 50 yds.	At 100 yds.	Barrel Length
130 or 125	760	715	670	160	142	124	2.1″	8.7″	6″

Penetration ⅞″ soft pine boards at 15 ft.—4

.38 LONG COLT

Bullet in grs.	F. S. vel. at muzzle	At 50 yds.	At 100 yds.	F. P. energy at muzzle	At 50 yds.	At 100 yds.	MR Traj. at 50 yds.	At 100 yds.	Barrel Length
150	770	735	700	197	180	163	1.9″	8.1″	6″

Penetration ⅞″ soft pine boards at 15 ft.—6

and chambers. Specimens from the collection show the following bullet diameters: old .38 Long, .375 inch; Short, .373; British .380 (not quite as long a cartridge as our Short), .374. This .380, made by the great firm of Kynoch, is not to be confused with the World War II .380 Enfield round, which when made of unjacketed lead is inside lubricated like our .38 S.&W., and has the same case shape. The standard .38 Special and modern .38 Long Colt bullet diameter is .357-.358 inch. From 1919 on for a few years, Winchester made .380 British, outside-lube cartridges similar to the Kynoch. They are collector's items now.

Today's .38 Long still has a hollow in its base so that it has a chance to fill the old, oversize rifling grooves; but I think that some earlier caves were deeper. In black powder loading especially they did well in the big-bored service guns, and actually the .38 Long was one of our most painstakingly developed revolver rounds. Military sizes really get the treatment, and they should.

Practical Uses

There are good uses for these two Colt cartridges, even though we could make reloadable brass for them by shortening .38 Special, if we had to. That of course would be for only a few people, hand-loaders. They not only serve old revolvers and rifles with ready-made ammo, an important and appreciated favor, but they also oblige .38 Special owners as subloads.

The oversize Short bullet is safe to fire through the smaller-caliber .38 Special guns because it's very soft—both Short and Long were of pure lead in old Winchester loadings—and because pressures are very low. It did not lead up the barrels of the pre-war Specials I used it in. No doubt its heavy coating of grease helped.

In power and noise the Long lies between the Short and the standard Special, leaning a bit upwards in its racket. It is really mild, though. Thus we have three factory-made cartridges to go up the scale with, or four if we use high velocity Specials—and yes, five if our gun is made for .357 Magnum rounds. The lineup can be useful in early pistol practice or in later uses that call for more or less power under our trigger finger. For this we need adjustment in our rear sight; but so

we do, to some extent, with the array of .38 Special factory load variations.

We used to save rather important money by using Shorts and Longs, especially those good Frankford Arsenal Longs from the Director of Civilian Marksmanship; and we can still save a pocket-money bit if we shoot enough of them. When we began to *handload* rifle ammunition at the unsophisticated age of sixteen, we really saved the allowance silver and got much more shooting. We also began to learn what makes what.

The once-popular Long was factory-made in "mid-range" or "gallery" versions with reduced powder charges and full-weight bullets. Up to about 25 yards they had plenty of what's needed for accuracy. At that time, things weren't so congested, and 25 yards was probably the most common indoor gallery range for .22 rifles. With proper backstops and no one to fuss about noise, the pistols used that range, too. But there were short pistol distances, too, such as 12 yards, and shorter. We can still buy *25-foot* pistol targets, and they come in handy when it's legal to shoot down cellar, or in the woods when we take a handgun along for company.

It could pay to handload the Short when we want bullets big enough to fit the old guns, and no if-or-and about their expanding up to size. Lyman-Ideal molds should be available in this and in the Long weight. Either case would do, with a bullet-seating die for it. For gallery sport the Short would have less excess powder space.

Practically all Remington, Peters, Winchester and Western .38 Special loads now are standardized, except for the R.-P. high velocity, lead-bullet loads as noted under "Super-X" Remington 158 grain, high velocity is listed at 1,085 f.s. and the 110-grain zinc-alloy bullet rounds described here under "Hi-Way Master."

The .38 Special cartridge, originated about 1900 by Smith & Wesson, has marched a long way in its time, although from the first it seems to have been furnished in smokeless powder loading as well as with the 21- or 21½-grain rations of black powder behind its 158-grain round-nosed bullet. In powder-to-lead ratio it's close to the .32 S.&W. Long.

For some years this .38 has been the most popular centerfire revolver cartridge in our country. Binding the articles written about it, down through the years, would produce a chunky volume. It often has been called the best caliber for the one-gun shooter, except when noise and expense (not cut to a fraction by handloading) must be held low, or when top-rank stopping power is needed. That statement goes down pretty well.

But if you've been using a .44 or a .45 for a long while, to the exclusion of anything between it and .22, or even .32, the .38 gets to looking mighty small. After all, it's a .35, using about .356 to .358-inch bullets—bullets of .35 rifle caliber thickness.

Deadliness

Time and again the .38 Special has been cussed out as a weakling, 'way below a safe minimum when things get rough in city jungles, in woods or mountains, on the lonely and lovely plains, and on the still more fascinating sea—anywhere and anywhen a man's life or a woman's life depends not only on good straight shooting but also on the power that gives quick but final decision to marksmanship.

Let's consider first of all the factory loads. *The old Colt Special* is gone. It came out a bit later than the S.&W. Special, and like the .32 and .38 Colt Police Positive rounds, it had a flat-nosed bullet meant to give stopping power. After the high-speed .38 Specials came in with the 1930 model Smith .38-.44 Heavy Duty (at first only with 5-inch barrel, and still popular in that handy, *almost* all-round length), a few did show up with the Colt-type of bullet. But even the Colt Special is nearly forgotten as a cartridge name, for it's long-gone from production.

Standard velocity, round-nosed .38 Special cartridges vary slightly in their degree of bluntness up front, but scarcely enough to pin a thin hope upon. They're sharp enough to slip through flesh with little or, usually, no expansion. Even when they are speeded to 1100 f.s. or so, there's not much difference in this respect.

The metal-pointed bullets are meant to penetrate car bodies. For defense against human enemies they'd be less effective, almost surely, than the conventional round-nosed lead. Even a roughened point does more damage than a smooth one. However, like the .38

.38 SPECIAL—STANDARD CARTRIDGE

Bullet in grs.	F. S. vel. at muzzle	At 50 yds.	At 100 yds.	F. P. energy at muzzle	At 50 yds.	At 100 yds.	MR Traj. at 50 yds.	At 100 yds.	Barrel Length
158	855	820	790	256	236	219	1.6″	6.5″	6″

Penetration ⅞″ soft pine boards at 15 ft.—7.5

.38 SPECIAL—SUPER-X CARTRIDGE

Bullet in grs.	F. S. vel. at muzzle	At 50 yds.	At 100 yds.	F. P. energy at muzzle	At 50 yds.	At 100 yds.	MR Traj. at 50 yds.	At 100 yds.	Barrel Length
150	1065	985	915	377	323	297	1″	4.5″	5″

Penetration ⅞″ soft pine boards at 15 ft.—9, Lubolay coated lead; 11, metal-point.

REMINGTON HI-WAY MASTER CARTRIDGE

Bullet in grs.	F. S. vel. at muzzle	F. P. energy at muzzle	Barrel Length
110, zinc alloy	1330	433	5″

SUPER-POLICE CARTRIDGE

Bullet in grs.	F. S. vel. at muzzle	At 50 yds.	At 100 yds.	F. P. energy at muzzle	At 50 yds.	At 100 yds.	MR Traj. at 50 yds.	At 100 yds.	Barrel Length
200	730	695	665	230	214	196	2.2″	9″	6″

Penetration ⅞″ soft pine boards at 15 ft.—7.5

MID-RANGE WADCUTTER TARGET LOAD

Bullet in grs.	F. S. vel. at muzzle	At 50 yds.	At 100 yds.	F. P. energy at muzzle	At 50 yds.	At 100 yds.	MR Traj. at 50 yds.
148	770	655	560	195	141	103	2.1″

Note: Penetration not listed. Wadcutters are designed to punch easily scored holes in target paper. They soon give up in hard substances, and they seldom are accurate much beyond 50 yards; but they make big holes, within their limitations!

Auto Colt, the 9-mm. Luger, and other fast, hard bullets, they just could be life-savers when survival depended on penetration of a substantial amount of living tissue, a farmyard bull's massive forehead, for instance. Naturally they need a good velocity to go deep. The 110-grain zinc bullet is tough, too. Against heavy animals it should be in about the same class as the metal-point, and fully as good for stopping a hoodlum's car. All these deep-penetrating slugs are specially for police use. The average sportsman has about as much use for them as a cat has for a self-flushing toilet.

The Super-Police 200 grain, taken up by all the factories after Western had pioneered it, has a good reputation as a stopper. Its rounded nose is rather blunt. I think that in early lots it was blunter still. Naturally it "throws high," quite noticeably so at 50 feet; but sometimes you live or you die by what happens at ten feet or even closer, don't you? It's one of the best factory .38 Specials for defense—though hardly easy to shoot in a light pocket gun!—but a flat and-or hollow point could improve it or any other similarly shaped handgun bullet.

Then we come to the wadcutter, the most lightly loaded of all .38 Specials except the blanks and the gas cartridges. It's a target round that some shooters don't quite trust at 50 yards if there's a wind to push it off course. They like it at 25 yards, unless a hurricane blows up and all hands take to the cellar. *This* bullet is shaped to kill, not to puncture deeply into big beasts but to stop a man. It makes a real .35-caliber hole; it doesn't ease through. Sure, it lacks speed. And the old full-charge wadcutter sending a 148-grain spool of lead at 870 f.s. was discontinued because of trouble in old guns whose worn ratchets failed to line up their cylinders precisely. It was a much-too-fast, square and uncompromising thing to send ripping into a barrel breech that tended to "shave lead" from even a tapered-profile bullet. It wasn't a safe load to market, for shaved lead hurled out by powder blast can injure bystanders very seriously indeed. When a gnat gets into your eye, it hurts. Lead is worse. In a well-conditioned, properly lined-up gun, that heavy Western load gave no trouble; and it shot, as I recall, very close to standard velocity, 158-grain impact at 20 yards or so.

But it's gone, and for the best in .38 Special effectiveness—as in so many other calibers—we depend upon handloading. We shape and power the bullet to our needs. If you have a mold for the flat-nosed Colt Special or the hollow-based, factory-type wadcutter—which itself came from a handloader's mold design, the Ed McGivern bullet under Ideal number 358395, a 148-grain—you have the makings for your bullet. There are better shapes, of course, that come from molds, but these two are good, if you want standard shapes. The Colt Special can give lots of penetration with some destructive power; and the wadcutter, loaded

rear end to, is a real mushroomer. Since loading it so puts the hollow up front, we have less air-space for the powder, and charges shouldn't be heavy.

Availability

The .38 Special's ammunition is available almost everywhere in the Western hemisphere—not on the tip of Cape Horn, I daresay, or even near the remote fastnesses of Jackson Pond, Chenango County, New York, where sunfish and "grass pickerel" draw few fishermen! But pretty generally it's easy to get. What dealer "hasn't heard of it"? Most gun-stores have at least one or two kinds, and your choice in used revolvers in this caliber is wide if you look for them.

Some of us who are N.R.A. members can buy the standard lead-bullet ammo from the D.C.M. at most attractive prices. As yet, we can't buy the primers unless we have some of those cases that took the "large pistol" or "caliber .45" size instead of the small, which is now almost 100% .38 Special factory standard if not a full century per cent. The D.C.M. has those, and the large rifle size, but no pistol powder at present or in the likely future because, as was said truly, pistol powder isn't expensive. A can of it goes far unless we spill it—or smoke when we are hand-loading. In 1961 the D.C.M. announced that its primer sales would be discontinued.

Right now the D.C.M. has some World War II type .38 Specials with copper-coated *steel jackets*. They are not the full-weight jacketed jobs that factories used to sell, with copper jackets with or without a tin wash, in place of the metal-point, lead-bearing varieties, but sub-weights. A jacketed bullet has a hard time in sealing the bore against powder gases, at least until it's well on its way from cylinder and forcing cone into the rifling grooves; but a metal-point, even if the copper or gilding metal nose contacts rifling lands, wears the barrel little because the cylinder of soft, lubricated lead behind it upsets to fill the grooves. There are special uses for full-jacketed bullets in handguns, though metal-points do the same thing—give penetration.

It looks as though the .38 Special's day were still at high noon. The .357 Magnum has a great hold, but many of these guns shoot their share of Specials as subloads. If you don't object to the weight and size of revolvers that are comfortable with the .357, that caliber is a far better all-rounder than the .38.

The gas cartridge should be mentioned, now that we're on rather odd .38 Special rounds. It's primarily for law-enforcement officers. One I know keeps his service revolver loaded with this kind at all times, a practice that I for one find hard to approve. When you fire it you hear a weak little pop and see a cloud of tear-gas bloom out, preferably down-wind! Some have been made with 1⅜-inch cases instead of the 1.16-inch .38 Special standard, for use in single-shot "fountain pen guns." These are supposed to be safe with this weak charge, and are safe, at least in my extensive experience of two rounds fired in such a gadget. After all, the pressure must be as low as that of any other metallic cartridge commonly to be had. The charge has to drive almost no real weight or bore-resistance out of the muzzle.

The gas loads don't stand up to storage as really truly cartridges do. After a time the gas loses its potency and all you get is a white cloud of practically non-irritating smoke—not to be rated with the aroma of burning cedar or birch logs, but we've smelled many things that were worse.

A Wadcutter Biography

Ballistic principles used in developing the wadcutter bullet are interesting, and they may be helpful to the handloader. In the second decade of this century the load became popular, though its accuracy lay below that of today's product. Short, solid bullets were used, in 120- and 123-grain weights. Nearly half the lead protruded from the case; and this section was of bore diameter, or near it, to ride on the rifling lands and thus align the projectile in the barrel. A splendid principle, except that .38 Special and other barrels vary a good deal in land and groove diameters. Then too, the unusually large powder space didn't burn smokeless any too evenly. Now the land-riding feature has been sacrificed to seating depth which reduces empty space. To cramp the powder still further into reasonable limits, a heavier, much longer bullet is used, with a hollow base to assist prompt expansion to fill the rifling grooves. The great length of the modern bullet adds to bore resistance, too, and in that way helps to burn the light powder charge more completely and uniformly.

These loads shoot like nobody's hard luck, and there are molds to cast dead ringers of the factory job, after we've mastered the accomplishment of making excellent bullets. At present only the .38 Special seems to be factory-made in wad-cutter style. But long ago, in the dark ages before we knew about great depressions and world wars that repeat themselves, there were .44 Special and .44 Russian wadcutters of a light 145-grains weight—those .44 standards were 246-grain round-points—that also were advertised for 20-yard target. Modern .38 cutters shoot accurately much farther than that.

A couple of short-lived wad-cutter rounds were smallbores, Remington's Hi-Speed .22 long-rifle and the .32 S.&W. Long that all the big four factories made. The .22 undoubtedly was intended to be a target cartridge, for its bullet ended in a pimpled, flat-faced snub like that of today's .38. At that time, high velocity .22 rimfires had a poor (and generally deserved) reputation for accuracy, though we now find factory lots that shoot possibles from good rifles that like them. Perhaps the Hi-Speed loading was chosen in order to appeal to two markets, for hunters as well as target shots used these cartridges while they were current. That, however, wasn't for long. As I recall, some auto-pistols would handle them, and some wouldn't.

The .32 wadcutter was around for several years when that cartridge was enjoying one of the spells of popularity it has had. Some called it the most accurate of all factory .32 Longs, but guns differ and so do shooters. When the .32 sank back into comparative oblivion as a target caliber, the wadcutter for it sank, too, and almost without a trace. You seldom see any of them around now.

Being a .32 fan, I didn't get any charge of joy in writing the above paragraph.

Last Round-up

Modern Colt .38 Special revolvers are described as being safe for the high-velocity cartridges of factory make, but Smith & Wesson recommend them only for their .44-frame guns, the .38-.44 Heavy Duty and the Outdoorsman. Of course they can be fired in .357 Magnum arms. It seems decidedly risky to fire modern, speeded-up cartridges in old revolvers with cylinders of plain, non-heat-treated steel.

Unquestionably the Special is a useful and practical gun. It is so much fun to shoot, too, that its cartridge is reloaded more than any other handgun size. Each year police departments and match-ambitious clubs load it by the multiple thousands for practice and competitive firing. The lone shooter loads it by the hundreds for his own delight. They employ powders and bullets in endless combinations. For heavy field duty the Keith semi-wadcutter is a favorite in overweight, solid design of 173 grains, and in near-standard 160-grain hollow base or hollow point. One could wish that the latter had a straight-sided instead of a tapering, more easily cast cavity shape. The old straight-cave Express rifle bullets of .40, .45 and .50 calibers left no doubt as to their expansive qualities, but velocities ran from about 1500 to nearly 1800 f.s.

Other semi-wadcutter bullets with a short guiding section ahead of the crimping groove are liked, too, such as Ideal 357443, an early 165-grain .357 Magnum, and those worked out long ago by such shooters as J. B. Crabtree with his 115-grain 360345 for target use up to about 25 yards. So it goes up and down the line, the lightest lead bullet being either a round ball of about 70 grains or the old Ideal 360363-S, a conical one of the same weight.

The ball could be a 000 (three-oh) buckshot of more or less .36-inch diameter, if we could find any; but for many years this size for 10-gauge shells has been out of production. Buckshot vary so much in diameter that many would be culls, but molds can drop uniform bullets. About 1½ grains of pistol powder is enough, or possibly almost twice that weight of Du Pont *Bulk* Shotgun Smokeless. The ball is held by friction at the case-mouth, or down near but not compressing the powder, and held there by a smear of stiff grease. For handling, this makes a better load than the ball set in the mouth and greased externally. We can, though, set a stiff grease-wad like one made of Ipco lube just under it, and that stuff is so adhesive that it normally stays in place, even during hot weather. Such loads *can* be fairly accurate at 20 feet or so. A lot of us have used the inexpensive buckshot just for plinking fun, and with the light powder charges there's very little noise. But there is some danger of any such low velocity bullet's bouncing back at us from a log or dead tree that it can only dent, not penetrate. There just isn't any gun or load for careless shooters, is there? We have to know the answers and take all precautions.

Factories used to load a .38 Special round-ball gallery cartridge with seven grains of black powder or a lighter smokeless charge to equal it. There were also much more accurate mid-range smokeless rounds with 104- and 130-grain round-nosed lead bullets. If wadcutter bullets tend to lead our gun's barrel throat, and we still want really light charges for short-range practice or for very small game, a revival of these two factory rounds could well be just the thing.

By far the greatest number of 25- and even 50-yard (and shorter) .38 Special handloads for practice and for match use must be those carrying some sort of full- or semi-wadcutter bullets. The clean-scoring value of "leather-punch" bullets is a big thing. These flat-fronted bullets do well for small and medium game shooting, too, and for defense. A good many of us must have guns for which we've bought only a wadcutter type mold—and really want no other.

At any rate, a .38 Special revolver of any weight or size "deserves to be shot," and it isn't complete without a loading set. This gives us the chance to work up combinations that fill our various needs, our highly practical purposes.

.38-.44 SMITH & WESSON

We mean the old one, not the modern high-velocity .38 Special that sometimes goes under that label. Both were named for .38 revolvers made on a .44 Smith & Wesson frame. The modern gun is the double-action, solid-frame Military; the oldie is the single-action tip-up.

This now rare .38 cartridge has a $1^{15}/_{32}$-inch case to fill its revolvers' chambers to the brink, a successful accuracy design at least with black powder. Above the rim, its case measures about .384 inch in diameter, compared to the .38 Special's approximate .378. The difference in diameters is about half that between the .32 S.&W. Long and the .32-.44.

The .38-.44's 20-grain black powder charge gave unusual old-time velocity to the 146-grain bullet, similar in weight to that of the .38 S.&W. Short, but blunter in nose shape. The light bullet kept recoil low, as was proper, for these bullets weren't crimped in the case. Only friction fit kept them from jumping forward under recoil and locking the cylinder's revolution. We have seen, with sorrow, .38 Special bullets held in place not only by a case-mouth crimp but also by a

deep cannelure grooved into the brass right over the bullet. This mutilates the lead. But for service use it's justified, we must admit. Sometimes even factory bullets will break their crimp under recoil, though that would be rare in loads as light as any standard .38 Special. However, a light gun bounces back harder than a full service weight arm; and such guns sometimes must be just as life-savingly reliable as any others.

But the old .38-.44 gun and its cartridges were built for accuracy, and no such mutilation of lead would have ben tolerated. It seems that the chambers of .32-.44 and .38-.44 S.&W. guns were cut with closer tolerances than those of most other revolvers. They were of high quality, of course. It has seemed desirable to prevent fired brass from expanding so much that case resizing would be needed. This part of a hand-loading job is by comparison fairly new. Cases swollen to fit their chambers snugly do line up their hand-loaded bullets well and truly with the bore, compared to loose brass. Oldtimers realized this advantage and could make use of it because, as a rule, a good crimp holds a lead revolver bullet in place against the pull of moderate recoil. Also they needed no cannelure *behind* a bullet to keep it from receding into the case— even when the rounds were stuffed into a rifle's long tubular magazine—because that case was crammed tension-tight full of black powder.

These accurate target revolvers had sights that were adjustable, though crudely, by our standards; and a .38-.44 gallery load of 5½ grains black and a 70-grain round ball was sold at a reduced price. However, the long brass cases made even these subloads more costly than the best .38 Specials available then.

But many of these easy-to-shoot target Smiths were in constant use—some still talk to targets. Molds to drop a variety of about .360-inch bullets for them should still be available. Because of the comparatively light "bullet pull"—the grasp of the case on the bullet, really—it would not seem practical to use anything over the old standard factory weight of 146 grains. A .38 S.&W. Short bullet has about the right weight; and it might be of the right diameter unsized, as it comes from the mold. It isn't necessary to use the full black powder charge to get good shooting. Smokeless loads just might be asking too much of the old guns, strong though they were by black powder standards, with thick chamber walls and barrel breeches. Smokeless might, too, give a quicker, sharper recoil than that of black powder—though it would feel lighter, in loads of equal power—and thus tend to loosen the unfired bullets in the cylinder.

Unfired cases are really hard to find, and old ones do wear out even when they are washed and dried after each black powder use. F. H. Miles, "The Gunsmith," Box 324, Bedford, Virginia, can make almost any sort of cartridge cases to order. Those upstairs that I bought from him are good. At least fair results

9 MM. LUGER OR PARABELLUM

Bullet in grs.	F. S. vel. at muzzle	At 50 yds.	At 100 yds.	F. P. energy at muzzle	At 50 yds.	At 100 yds.	M. R. Traj. at 50 yds.	At 100 yds.	Barrel Length
115	1140	1035	965	332	274	237	.9"	4"	4"

Penetration ⅞" soft pine boards at 15 ft.—10

could be had with unfired .351 Winchester Self-loading rifle brass, still factory-made, though it's only about 1¾ inches long. That makes it some 3/32-inch too short to deliver .38-.44 bullets from case-mouths into barrel, with no bridge of chamber to skip across. The .351 is a little small, too, above the rim and cannelure (it's semi-rimless), by about .007 inch; but that's nothing dreadful at black powder pressures. Cases might swell on being fired, but not much, for .351 brass is thick and heavy at the base and pretty well above it.

The black powder capacity in thick .351 cases might be cut by a few grains, even with bullets set out ahead of the case-mouths as far as they could be and still give leeway to the cylinder's turning. The strength of modern primers (small pistol size for the .38-.44) could make up the difference in powder charge, for they're more energetic than the old No. 1 and No. 1½ that were made to light off black powder.

For smokeless loadings, which should be kept mild if used at all, .351 cases should be better than the original .38-.44s. To revive this fine old caliber, to make it shoot as well as it ever did, 50 years and more ago, is a worthy ambition for a pistol shot with an interest in painstaking—and perhaps illuminating—research; but to revive needn't be quite the same as to modernize. I hope someone will do it. Advertising, if not just a long reading of for-sale ads, ought to turn up a .38-.44 Smith & Wesson revolver.

Almost certainly the black powder to use would be the FFG granulation. Under it, and subtracting the amount from the black powder dosages, it should be safe to use two grains of Du Pont Bulk Shotgun Smokeless—five grains by black powder measure. That would make a cleaner-shooting load, and be appreciated, for the standard .38-.44 load of 20 grains of black for a 146 grain bullet means a rather heavy powder ration, which in turn means a fast foul-up of barrel grooves. We'd like to be able to fire at least ten target rounds without cleaning; and with straight black we mightn't be able to, and still keep accuracy. Never compress Bulk Shotgun heavily. Even a fairly mild compression, under long storage, can break the soft grains. Then they burn much faster, and with higher pressures.

Good shooting to you, whoever you are, who do this research job so badly needed!

The Remington-Peters loads give 124 grain bullets 1120 f.s. velocity and 345 foot-pounds energy at the muzzle of a 4 inch barrel test gun. This weight of bullet, or 125 grains, was the old, familiar standard; but during World War II Winchester began turning out a load with sharply rounded 115 grain bullet in quantities for our allies. Since their present commercial round keeps to this low-weight and really moderate-velocity standard, it would seem to be just about perfect for pre-1908 Lugers with flat, not coiled, recoil springs. These rare pistols have thumb-and-finger grips on the breech-block's toggle joint that are milled only at the front, not in a complete circle. They should be humored.

At least as early as World War I the foreign-made 9 mm. Luger bullets began to appear with sharply rounded point in place of the old flat-nose with long bearing exposed ahead of the case-mouth, ending in a sharp conical taper that led to the flat up front. It seems possible that in guns *adapted* to the Luger 9 mm., such as the Mauser Military, and in Lugers, too, the sharp-nose should have been a more reliable feeder. Some slight degree of killing power was lost by the change, and the sharp bullets proved more likely to glance off hard objects struck on a slant; but even our own cartridge companies adopted the change a few years after the 1914-18 war was over.

Seasoned woodsmen who had relied on their Lugers for killing deer and even bigger game—close up, for they knew how to stalk—may and probably did find that the better-balanced flat-point had plowed a straighter path in really deep penetration. But the flat-point is gone, along with the hollow point, which seldom amounted to anything as an expander, though now we have become able to buy imported Norma 116-grain soft points for handloading.

Actually the Luger 9 is a good lead-bullet cartridge, and gun. Rifling lands, if still in good condition, are generally high enough to get a good bite into the lead, unlike those of some .45 Auto caliber barrels, and there's a good choice in molds.

The truncated-cone, nose-chopped-off-square, lead bullets I cast in a Lyman-Ideal 356402 mold did excellent work and took standard or near-standard velocities nicely. The more or less soft lead helped to keep pressures nice and low, compared to jacketed stuff. Luger barrels do vary widely in diameter, and the first of the molds sent me was much too small. The factory made a prompt exchange.

If you want a round-nosed bullet, there's the .38 Auto Colt mold No. 358242, a 125 grain; but the rounded-nose shape is blunter than those of current factory rounds—and in general a good thing, too. Various other 9 mm. or .38 revolver-type bullets of this weight or below it can be used, some too blunt for magazine feeding but perhaps very fine (or even the best) for single-loaded practice firing. Bullets over 125 grains or so are for advanced handloaders who make careful allowance against pressure increase by cutting powder charges or going to a definitely slower powder.

I didn't have to full-length resize my cases for reliable feeding, though I see now that I should have done it for greater accuracy. I merely neck-sized them in my light Belding & Mull bench tool—if you can speak of a practically straight, untapered and not bottle-necked case as having a neck! The bullets were held firmly; but the case "necks" were off-center enough to see with a hard pitiless look. I wasn't nearly good enough with that 4-inch gun to see any ill effects from the bullets' being delivered in sneaky, sidling fashion into the finely cut rifling that received them.

Gun and Ammo Variety

There has been a host of guns and loadings in this caliber, and more are due.

At the start, let's beware of using *any* true 9 mm. Luger loadings in 1910 Glisenti army models and 1915 Berettas made for the standard Italian short case.

There are auto-pistol cartridges too long to fit a standard Luger, our own .38 Auto Colt, and several foreigners that are seldom seen here. These include the 9 mm. Bergmann and Steyr (much alike; the former was a Spanish military caliber), the old Mannlicher, and the military Mauser also, the 9 mm. Browning Long that sends a 110-grain bullet at 1083 f.s. velocity

So many foreign pistols for the 9 mm. Luger came here after V. E. and V. J. days that for many months after the end of World War II our factory ammunition often was "on back order." Now we have the light Colt Commander and the Smith & Wesson autos, and we can expect more American-made arms in this caliber.

There is danger in using some foreign ammunition that fits a Luger 9, much military stuff having been loaded for rugged sub-machine guns, with velocities up to 1600 f.s. and perhaps higher, as fired from the long-barreled burp-guns. (The name is appropriate; it suggests the sustained *brrrp* that, as kids, some of us hauled up from our stomachs when called upon to "do the double-drag.") There is much more over-loaded 9 mm. Luger stuff still floating around than there is for the .30 Luger. Some Walther P-38s and other one-hand pistols have fired the rough rations and got away with it, but it's a risky and a pointless business. Off and on since World War I there have been Lugers that were shoddy in material and assembly, and the wartime P-38s are not a tribe of 100% perfect specimens, either.

American factory loads are strong enough to function most pistol actions. Only *unusually* good Lugers, with reasonably fresh and capable ammunition, are reliable to the extent of giving no more than one jam in, say, a thousand shots. Lugers, Mausers and almost all

centerfire autoloaders except the .38 and .45 Colts of nearly any vintage, and the 9 mm. Smiths, have a rather dusky reputation for absolute reliability, although they're interesting to shoot. The Luger points like your finger, provided that your hand is big enough for it. Of course there are exceptions, on both sides of the fence, to that sweeping statement.

It might be correct to classify the Luger 9 as a pocket-gun cartridge, even though it gives superior ballistics in a six- or eight-inch barrel and has had an enormous amount of frontier use all over the world, in a wide variety of guns—mostly Lugers, until the later years. But it is a short-cased round, and under permissible pressures the .38 Auto Colt is the more powerful load of the two. The Colt is still short and slim enough to allow its pistols to hold a compact single-column magazine for seven, eight or even nine cartridges. Such a gun can still fit a rather small hand and a not too big pocket. The old Pocket and Military Model Colts felt good in my grasp, but the big Super-.38 and 1911 .45 grips are rather a stretch for me. Certainly the modern Smith & Wesson 9 mm. could qualify as a pocket arm, and in the type fitted with double-action trigger it's quick to get into action. But a much larger cartridge means a bigger fore-and-aft grip, and who today wants any style of auto-pistol with its magazine out ahead of the trigger guard? To put up with that you would have to be a Mauser Military fan.

Popularity

The 9 mm. Luger is an excellent medium-bore, high-velocity cartridge, fast growing in popularity here; but let us hope it won't eclipse the .38 Auto. When velocities, gun weights and builds, and barrel lengths are about the same, the .38 is nearly as pleasant to shoot as the 9. Differences are so small that you must look for them. But it's a question as to which caliber will stay more easily available in the years to come.

A great many people admire compactness in a pistol cartridge, and both rounds have it. The Luger is shorter, and with factory ammunition, which most people shoot, it's practically as effective in spite of its lighter, slower and more pointed bullet. For some odd reason it costs, just now, two pennies more per shot than the .38; but this means almost nothing to the very great number of people who do only occasional shooting with a handgun. If they do enough to keep up a reasonable amount of skill and familiarity, that's fine. Just reasonable ability could be a life-saver—for themselves and for whoever may happen to depend on them, if and when things get rough on a small or on a nation-wide scale. Either way, as loyal and law-abiding citizens, they are an asset to our Country. And they are, too, on the side of those of us who burn up hundreds or thousands of rounds of ammunition a year. Having guns, and liking and depending on them to some extent, they aren't going to accept proposed anti-gun legislation calmly!

They are heavy buyers of the war-relic weapons,

.380 COLT AUTOMATIC OR 9 MM. BROWNING SHORT

Bullet in grs.	F. S. vel. at muzzle	At 50 yds.	At 100 yds.	F. P. energy at muzzle	At 50 yds.	At 100 yds.	M. R. Traj. at 50 yds.	At 100 yds.	Barrel Length
95	955	865	785	192	158	130	1.4″	5.9″	3.75″

Penetration ⅞″ soft pine boards at 15 ft.—5.5

some good and some not so good, that get, mostly, only occasional use. As the supply of these arms diminishes there should be more demand for American-made 9 mm. pistols such as the present Colt and Smith, with other makes presumably coming up. This Luger caliber is likely to remain popular for a long time. It has a good deal to offer, including a not too terrific muzzle blast when fired in guns with barrels nicely over four inches in length. As a pretty powerful centerfire it isn't hard to master.

Perhaps you have to be a gun-crank to prefer the .38 Auto. With cast-lead bullets, shaped or even hollow-pointed for deadliness, you have much more to work with. There's more powder space in the .38.

Ballistic figures beyond 50 yards mean little with this stubby cartridge, for 50 is a long, long shot with a little pocket automatic. At such a range the discontinued Hi-Standard .380, a heavy gun with five-inch barrel, would be quite different!

In Europe this cartridge is known as the Browning, and it is decidedly popular. Here it's a rather expensive and not really common little trick, an ear-ringer, compared to the .32 Auto, in the short-barreled old Colts, Remingtons and Savages that handle it, and in the almost countless small imported types.

It is, or used to be, definitely more walloping than the ubiquitous .32 Automatic. But like the 9 mm. Luger bullet, its slug has had the tranquillizing treatment. At first made with a bluff, almost semi-spherical nose; it now is sharpened down, at least in some makes, to allow it to feed more reliably in the host of good, fair and downright poor foreign pistols that have crossed the sea and settled here. It's true that the old American .380 pistols had, as a rule, a less charming reputation for gobbling their rations with nary a choke than the corresponding .32s had. This may have been partly due to the blunt bullet noses, and perhaps in part to the case-mouths, which are not, normally, crimped over the bullets.

For the .380, like the .45 Auto and 9 mm. Luger, has a truly rimless case, the flange at the bottom being not appreciably bigger than the body just above the extracting groove or cannelure. So the case gets its headspace in the chamber from its thick, uncrimped brass up front. To hold the bullet from being driven in on the powder charge, some straight, truly rimless, uncrimped cases have another cannelure, a little one, just behind the bullet. It can be useful when—and almost only when—a cartridge is cocked bullet-upward in the filling of the magazine and the mag follower's retaining button (if it has one) slips from the thumb and drives the bullet up into the magazine lips. Since

Luger mags have such a button, and Colt centerfires do not,* the cannelure behind the bullet is not so useful in .38 and .45 unless the ammo gets some other kind of abuse. Perhaps from the start, most rifle cases originally meant for black powder, which left no free air-space in full-charge loadings, had cannelures behind the bullets when smokeless came along. We still see them in the .32-20, .32-40, .38-55, .45-70 and others, though not in .25-20 Repeater cases.

Does the .45 Colt commonly fail to feed because of that square, abrupt lip at the case-mouth? You know the answer as well as I do, or better: the .45 is a superbly designed, locked-breech gun handling powerful cartridges; and it scarcely ever fails for any reason short of having an absolute moron as its master.

As with the Luger and the rest of the semi-automatic pistol rounds, the .380's expanding bullets have gone down the river of time. Perhaps they seemed gangsterish. But we can cast lead bullets for it, such as the Ideal 358242 in short (not .38 Auto) form. Since weights from 95 to 107 grains have been listed for it, we should do well to weigh some samples, or have them weighed, before even starting to think about powder charges. The .380, used almost exclusively in light-weight, blow-back action arms, is not meant to be a high-pressure round.

The loss of soft point .380s called for no long, wet weep. They may have looked good, but they were a delusion. At the low velocities they didn't mushroom. I once saw one that some vandal had shot through the water in an almost submerged but still serviceable row-boat. Except for the rifling marks it looked like an unfired bullet. Those marks were sharp and clean enough to indicate that the bore was still in condition to develop standard or near-standard speed. They weren't sketchy.

The low-pressure .380 works as a single-shot sub-load in some 9 mm. Luger caliber pistols. (I never tried one in the .38 auto Colt.) In such makeshift use the extractor hooks grip the rim hard enough for the firing pin to give the primer a strategic kick, and thar she blows! Headspacing is practically unlimited, but the mild backthrust permits us to get by with this tomfoolery.

In reloading the .380 we must make sure of the headspacing in its own guns by not crimping the case-mouth. Neck-resizing should be enough to hold the bullet securely in place.

If you shoot it much it saves big money to hand-load this cartridge, which costs a bit more than stand-

---

*Colt's 1961 Gold Cup .38 Special auto has a pair of these buttons.

.38 COLT AUTOMATIC—HIGH VELOCITY LOADING

Bullet in grs.	F. S. vel. at muzzle	At 50 yds.	At 100 yds.	F. P. energy at muzzle	At 50 yds.	At 100 yds.	M. R. Traj. at 50 yds.	At 100 yds.	Barrel Length
130	1275	1140	1050	469	375	318	.8"	3.4"	5"

Penetration ⅞" soft pine boards at 15 ft.—10

.38 COLT AUTOMATIC—"OLD-TIME" LOADING

Bullet in grs.	F. S. vel. at muzzle	At 50 yds	At 100 yds.	F. P. energy at muzzle	At 50 yds.	At 100 yds.	M. R. Traj. at 50 yds.	At 100 yds.	Barrel Length
130	1040	980	925	312	277	247	1"	4.7"	4½"

Penetration ⅞" soft pine boards at 15 ft.—9

ard .38 Special rounds and takes so much less powder and lead for full velocities. It is not a caliber to sneer at, although the size, shape, weight and hardness of its factory bullet make its foot-pounds rating mean little as compared to some that ring the energy bell less loudly, such as the .38 Colt New Police. The .38 Special mid-range wadcutter, which has only three foot-pounds more of energy in print, is a vastly superior stopper, unless we are shooting something that is pretty hard-shelled and we place the .380 bullet exactly where it is going to damage the critter most.

But a .380 pocket gun is so small and flat that it can go with us where bigger ordnance couldn't go conveniently. There would be less temptation to leave it behind the oatmeal sack in camp or in the bureau drawer at home. These little gats hold a spate of cartridges, too, ten in the Savage, eight in the Colt.

Its reliability as compared to that of a revolver or a big-caliber Colt or Smith auto? The question is in order. None of us, I'm sure, would care to stake everything on one almost 100% sure shot, followed by a jam.

Almost since the 1900 or 1902 initial guns, this formidable load has been a favorite of outdoorsmen. It has yelped its sharp cry in far-off places. In the same general ballistic class as the .30 Mauser and .30 and 9 mm. Luger—all much used here, too—it goes to the head of that class, giving similar penetration, and a fairly wide and weighty bullet.

Although its guns never have been sold in huge quantities, they are something like the old Model 1886 Winchester rifles in various .38, .40, .45 and .50 calibers, and, of course, in the later .33 high-power. Most people who bought them were experienced.

Two .38 A.C.P. loads are still marketed at this writing; and if the lighter one became unavailable, we handloaders probably could get new, empty factory cases—or resize old ones—and jacketed bullets. We could adjust our powder charges to the old guns. Though many may be collectors' items and never fired, many others do live an active life. People who don't handload would be out of luck, as they so frequently if not consistently are!

The old load, practically duplicated by the modern light one except for the type of powder, has been cut from (on paper) 1070 to 1040 f.s., as fired from the

4½-inch Pocket Model; but it should still come fairly close to 1100 from the 6-inch Military and the earlier Sporting Models. The high-velocity Super-.38 Auto claimed 1300 f.s. when it appeared in 1930 for the 5-inch Colt on the 1911 .45 frame. Now it's listed at 1275, a difference that you *might* get in cartridges from the same factory box. It would not be surprising or disgraceful if you did.

Use of Super ammo in earlier Colts is annoying if not dangerous. The magazine is pretty sure to be "ejected" and perhaps swelled out of shape, and the thin slide may be cracked. Most Super-.38 pistols handle the milder factory cartridges with certainty. After belting a few gunfuls of this ammo at target we are less likely to be saying, "Huh?" and "Whazzat?" on our return home than if we had used the business stuff.

With its strong, semi-rimmed brass, having a definite rim to position the case in the chamber, and quite a few suitable molds, this .38 is splendid for reloading. It can almost qualify as an all-round size. If a fellow uses a lead bullet weighing between 125 and 130 grains he can make good target rounds for a fixed-sighted arm. Clean-cutting, semi-wadcutter lead like Ideal 360271 in 125-grain works well through most actions—better than 99% perfectly through my 6-inch Military. It is fine on target and more deadly on small game, by far, than the round-nosed variety, such as the 125-grain 358242 or the factory full-jacketed. Hollow the point of that round-nosed lead pill and it's deadlier yet on small stuff that is big enough to offer some resistance.

Powder charges as soft as 1½ grains of Hercules Bullseye will do rather well with cast bullets—not the jacketed, which might even stick in the bore with so little push behind them—on a 50-foot range. They cut the report below that of a standard .32 revolver cartridge, almost to that of .22 rimfire volume. Bullets do whack against the steel backstop with considerable enthusiasm, and that will scare some people who aren't range-hardened. Empties are not ejected; they are little more than loosened and slid back and forth in the chamber. So they are easy to find, unlike full-charged cases flipped seven ways from Sunday, and sometimes clear off the poncho spread to receive them.

Medium and full-power loads with this semi-wad-cutter bullet operate most actions reliably. The full (but not overloaded, please) rounds can make bigger wounds than factory bullets do, by far, though of course much less deep wounds in sizable animals. Bert Shay likes the 145-grain 12-S Hensley semi-wadcutter, and some shooters have used standard-weight .38 Special lead in this case. For bullets over 130 grains the powder charges should be cut, even though plain, lubricated lead gets through a barrel more easily and with less pressure than jacketed lead does.

Hollow-pointing a lead pistol bullet, even a round-nosed one, adds to its moderate-penetration killing power; and the good velocities available in .38 Auto help the mushrooming. With the discontinued factory soft points, some of which had long lead exposure up front, this .38 was one of the few pistol sizes that could open such bullets on game; but with hollow-nosed, not too hard lead it can do even better. The good soft points give way to hollow points when the high velocity loads came in, but these bullets were disappointing. The jackets needed to be thinned down plenty at the front, but they weren't. Soon after their arrival, all American-made expanding pistol bullets except the .22 rimfires went off the market. At that time a wave of gangsterism was sweeping the country.

Is It an All-Round Caliber?

For some of us the .38 could be the all-round semi-automatic pistol if we don't expect to need the much superior knockout power of the .45. Now the 9 mm. in Colt, Smith & Wesson, and imported makes is close on its heels or maybe trampling its neck in the matter of popularity. The Luger ammo costs more but certainly isn't worth more, at least to most of us who know the two equally well through shooting and handloading.

A little extra available power in any all-round weapon does no harm, at least when it can be had in a gun and ammo of such little additional bulk and weight as the .38 compared to the 9 mm. In squib loads, which are so necessary to most of us whose shooting often is restricted by what other people think about noise, there's little difference between these two cases. Both can burn small charges of powder well.

So my vote, for whatever it's worth, goes to the .38. I honestly can't remember which cartridge I began using first. I like them both; and by clearing my head of gun-crank ideas I'd come, it seems sure, to the conclusion that the two aren't so tremendously different.

But even with any specially worked up loading, these two can't equal a .45 Auto for defense purposes, the .45 being similarly handloaded. There is an *unless:* unless you need deep penetration into some big, heavy animal. Both .38 and 9 mm. have been taken to big game countries because they have the deep reach into living tissues. Sometimes they finish the work of a rifle; sometimes they do it all on their own.

For a one and only gun choice no bigbore is really common, though the reasons for this may not amount to much. One sensible reason is that most wives and youngsters as beginners, and most men as beginners, learn much faster with a medium-bore. But is this really sensible when the owner of the gun, whom we shall assume, perhaps unthinkingly, to be the Mister, is a handloader? One of the biggest advantages in handloading is that it allows us to mild down the ammunition to what we want, then build it up when we want more authority in it.

But except for the competitive target shooter, the .38 Auto can be *almost* as completely useful, with handloading of course, as that great vote-getter, the .38 Special. However, we were talking about an all-round semi-automatic pistol, not a revolver. The Webley revolver has been chambered for .38 Auto, but who of us would prefer that caliber to .38 Special, if our first choice was a revolver, not an autoloader? Certainly the Special is a better all-round cartridge than the Auto, but it's a revolver cartridge except in limited use.

And that use is not so limited, at least on competitive firing lines. There seems to be no waning of enthusiasms for the .38 Super Colts that have been custom-altered to fire the .38 Special wadcutter round. If that 1911 .45 Model frame fits your hand and the pull is good, this sort of job eliminates thumb-cocking in rapid fire, or the much more difficult mastery of accurate, fast, double-action revolver firing—which we rarely see on a firing line. Colt made a safe bet in bringing out the 1961 target autoloader in .38 Special.

The overall length of the factory-style wadcutter Special is the overall length of its case. So, magazines can hold these rounds and still be fitted into a Colt auto's grip. With its good weight and reasonable velocity the .38 wadcutter is superior for match use to bullets we should be likely to load into the short Auto brass. When a stiff wind crosses the 50-yard range we might prefer to have in our hand an unaltered .38 Auto with bullets shaped to buck wind much better than the square-fronted wadcutters do. Or we might not, everything else being equal.

The 100-yard energy figure looks questionable, compared to the record of less blunt bullets, which it apparently couldn't equal in holding striking power. But it is close to the 200-grain .38 Special in its ballistics. Heavy bullets of good length retain their velocity and energy well. Note the figures for the standard .38 Special with 158-grain bullet, which has a much more streamlined nose shape.

The .41's penetration is small and it is meant to be. This bullet's job is to make a wider wound path than one would expect, judging from its medium caliber and rather low speed.

The Remington-Peters 195-grain plain lead bullet —the 200-grain Western is Lubaloy coated, like most lead bullets of that brand, except the standard velocity .22s and larger caliber match bullets—is credited with

.41 LONG COLT

Bullet in grs.	F. S. vel. at muzzle	At 50 yds.	At 100 yds.	F. P. energy at muzzle	At 50 yds.	At 100 yds.	M. R. Traj. at 50 yds.	At 100 yds.	Barrel Length
200	730	705	680	231	207	200	2.2"	8.8"	6"

Penetration ⅞" soft pine boards at 15 ft.—3

exactly the same muzzle energy and velocity as the 200-grain Western. We grow accustomed to such phenomena, don't we? There must be a most kindly spirit among the members of the Sporting Arms and Ammunition Manufacturers' Institute. Who'd be so unfeeling as to criticize such friendliness? Seriously, they're on our side: they don't like antigun legislation any better than we do. Many of them are shooters, too.

The .41 centerfires seem to have been designed as much for gun-fighting as any pistol cartridge we ever had. In one form or another they date back to about 1876, when the West was in its heyday of adventure. Or was it the struggle of constructive men against twisted and evil men, and against a relentless wilderness, too? The 1875 Colt New Line revolvers came along to take .41 Short and Long rim- and centerfire cartridges, though we'd hardly consider these rather small five-shot guns as true frontier arms. They were made without trigger guard loop, the "sheath trigger" being housed in nearly a straight-down projection of the frame.

But the Colt Lightning double-action .38 and .41 of 1877 became extremely popular in the West. It was slow to reload because it had the rod ejector and loading-gate system of the 1873 Single Action Army. The 1878* Army and Frontier double-action of similar type was for big cartridges like the .38-40, .44-40 and .45 Colt; but it seems to have been chambered for additional big and small rounds: .32-20, .41, and the .450, .455 and .476 Eley. Sometimes it is called the Bird's-Head because of the way its rounded grip appears when you hold the gun upside-down. Then, of course, the Army and Bisley single-actions were made commonly in .41, and the medium-weight, modern-design, streamlined, double-action Army Special, which became the Official Police of today, or as near it as never mind. For this reason, you often hear our latest Official Police and Officer's Model Target arms described as "built on a .41 caliber frame." Their frames and cylinders are a trifle larger than those of the S.&W. Military & Police and K-Target guns, which in the beginning were built to handle .38s.

A big advantage of the .41 centerfire—which many of the old Western gunmen must have appreciated—was that a medium-weight, medium-size revolver could handle it. With it, you still had a pretty formidable arm, easy to pack, easy to hide in short-barrel styles, and light in recoil. The ammunition, too, was lighter

and less expensive than large bores with heavy bullets and twice its dose of powder. It was really not a good cartridge for game as large as deer. It had good bullet weight and width, but not much penetration. This fact did not prevent numbers of far-traveling old prospectors—and Eastern woodsmen, too—from choosing it.

Large-frame revolvers took all three types of .41 centerfire rounds, the Short and Long and the 1878 Winchester design, called simply ".41." This carried a light 130-grain bullet backed by a stiff powder charge of 20 grains of black—just one grain under the .38 Special's ration. The rim of this speeded-up cartridge was wider than those of the Short and Long; and, as I recall, only three rounds could be loaded into an Army Special's thin-walled cylinder. Every other chamber had to be empty.

That odd cartridge, like the .41 Short as always made and the Long as made in the beginning, had an outside lubricated bullet heeled down at the base to go into the thin brass and be crimped in place there. The Short's rations were 14 grains of black and 160 of greasy lead, or 15 and 163, and probably other combinations, according to make. I do not know the load of the .41 Long with its early outside-lube bullet; but the inside job, which we have today in smokeless, had recipes of 21 and 200, and 22 and 195. Both Short and Long were furnished in smokeless loading for many years, long before and long after non-corrosive priming came in. Even with black powder the Short gave very little recoil, and with smokeless it was almost a gallery charge. Painstaking manufacture could have made it accurate, too, for its full-sized bullet fitted the unthroated chambers and the rifling diameter of about .401 inch. The inside-lubricated Long bullets had to be undersized to seat in the brass, but their hollow bases permitted the quick blow of black powder to expand them to fit.

Accuracy

The straight-bored, unthroated .41 chambers are easy to keep clean; and these revolvers can give good shooting with well-made, heel-type bullets that fit them snugly and are delivered smoothly into a fine barrel. There is no jinx on the .41 if it's handled right.

If we want the convenience of inside-lubricated bullets, so clean and so waterproof, we can load them in .41 Long hollow-base design, such as Ideal 386178. This is a 190-grain, with wide V-shaped base cavity and the usual bluff, uncompromising point. To get proper expansion in chamber and barrel, we may have to go to black powder loading. Now, outside-lube ammunition is a nuisance to prepare, by hand work; but we might be glad that Ideal bullets 386176, a 155-

---

* Or 1877, as given in Colt's centennial booklet, *A Century of Achievement, 1836-1936,* page 21. Here the big .45 is listed as Colt's first double-action.

grain .41 Short, and 386177, a 190-grain Long, are still on the mold list.

Such bullets are easy enough to cast, their slightly rounded bases simplifying the job of casting as well as of seating them in the brass. But we do not ordinarily grease and size them, simultaneously, in a machine. In fact, we probably wouldn't size them at all. We can lubricate them by pressing in the grease with a fingertip, a simple skill to master, or by dipping the loaded cartridges into a pan of melted lube. Pure, soft lead would be the metal, the better to seal the bore with either black or smokeless, in this low-pressure caliber.

The .41 cases as long made take small-size pistol primers, though the old, wide-rimmed Winchester job used the large pistol size, for some strange reason. Ignition is no problem in these small-capacity cases; and the modern pistol primer is strong enough. A .41 handloader advanced enough to use Du Pont 4759 rifle powder in the Long might go to the stronger small rifle primer, cautiously, to get better combustion of this big-grained propellant.

Does the heel of an outside-lubricated, soft-lead bullet expand to take the rifling, thus in effect adding to the bore-bearing length? It certainly does, and very evenly too, in .22 rimfire style. It should in the .41 Long, too, except perhaps when low powder charges make our loads squibs.

If the barrel of our old .41 is badly pitted we may never be able to get decent shooting from it. However, if the bullets we cast are truly full-size for that particular barrel, or a bit oversize, we can try something that often helps barrels that are only "rough," not badly pitted. That is simply to harden the lead. You may get something of this effect by dropping the newly cast bullets straight from the mold into cold water. This really does toughen their skin. Another way is to use tin, antimony or even solder in a mixture of metal. Jacketed bullets often shoot remarkably fine groups from barrels that would be condemned on sight; but none, it seems, have ever been made in this pistol caliber. With handmade and expensive dies, they could be made, but few shooters would care to go that far with a caliber that has such a poor reputation for accuracy. I never heard of anyone attending a match with a .41; did you? We *could* use .38-40 pills.

However, not all of us care to accept everything that's told us. If you have a .41 in good condition and with at least a four-inch barrel, let's say, and a total weight of around 30 ounces or more, you have the start for experiments that might open many sophisticated eyes. It would be a fairly long trip at the very least, but interesting.

Using a 10 to 15% booster of smokeless like the mild Du Pont *Bulk* Shotgun under black powder is OK for many old bigbore rifles. We can use a slightly larger percentage for smallbores like the .32-20, in rifles. I just should not care to try it in many pistols, and particularly not in the .41, which in Army Specials

has such thin chamber walls. The heavier, old-time sixguns in this caliber seem mostly to be of early vintage. Their steels may be what we should call today deficient in margin of strength. This sort of loading cuts black powder fouling helpfully, allowing us to fire longer strings without field cleaning; but it does raise pressures. Then too, the .41s are crimped cases, unlike the old special target .38-.44s. Ordinarily black powder is loaded into them with considerable compression, for the crimp will hold the works together. This type of Shotgun Smokeless is soft. It will crumble under storage when it's compressed, and then its pressures go up.

A Modernized .41?

The blunt .41 Long bullet shows one of the best factory designs ever dreamed up as a man-stopper. Few if any factory-loaded .38 Specials are as good. Guns handling it could be either heavy or medium-weight, for belt holster or for the pocket. They've been great favorites on the Western frontier as well as down South. They can be hard to find today, or at least hard to buy. Dick West, over downtown, is a typical owner: He just smiles and says, "I guess not" to a tentative buyer. I admire him for it.

The 200-grain .38 Special Super-Police is quite a fair killer. This oldtimer has nearly identical paper ballistics, plus a fired-bullet diameter of about .40-inch as compared to a skinny .35. Only by a little does it miss having the punch of cartridges combed out for the following chapter.

With better factory loading and in guns with close chambering and boring, the modern-type .41 Long could have been the most useful medium caliber. However, barreling it for that cartridge would have made it about a .386. It did behave courteously in easily carried two-pound guns. Lots of wood-hicks and less seasoned outdoorsmen have discussed the might-have-been quality of the .41, as the open fire danced or the rusty stove cracked its aged joints in happy activity.

So far, we have only experimental or custom-made revivals. Gordon C. Boser (of Springville, N. Y., as I recall) designed Ideal bullet No. 401452, a 206-grain semi-wadcutter for a .41 caliber revolver. For cases he used reworked .401 Winchester Self-loading brass, semi-rimless and thick and strong at the base, which now is difficult to find or to duplicate. Perhaps shortened .303 Savage cases could be adapted. Mr. Boser's was a worthy modernization of the .41 caliber; and naturally we hope that we will see other active interest along this line. The gap between .38 and .44 in popular factory sizes is wide enough to be ridiculous. It needs to be filled, a need beyond that of a temporary sales appeal.

This adapted .401 case is of larger diameter than the .41 Long, for .401 brass goes about .428 inch at the base, just above the rim and the extracting groove, as compared to some .407 above the .41's rim. It's for large, heavy-cylindered revolvers that we should ordinarily load for considerable velocity and power. I should not have called the Boser round a revival, except of the caliber in general. Compared to the Colt cartridge it's a magnum. Handgun magnums are all-round useful, aren't they, with their wide range of power?

But we may have to come to a .41 Colt revival, whether we like it or not. Our present small-capacity .41 Long ammunition may be taken from us by the streamlining of production. Then we should need substitute brass. The .25-35 Winchester rifle cases, thick and strong at the base, would be promising. They run about .410 inch just above the rim and the tiny cannelure that so many rimmed cases now have—though they used not to—and that's not far from .41—.407 inch. (We mustn't confuse this case with the rimless .25 Remington Auto, which is around .415 above the big cannelure.)

Our .25-35 rim would need narrowing, at least for medium-sized cylinders, and thinning, too, from the top. It should not be thinned from the bottom, because we don't want to weaken the primer pocket's perforated web by deepening it. That we should have to do if we ground away at the bottom of the case. It's true that some, if not all, large pistol primers aren't as "tall" as large rifle primers, but the difference is small, perhaps .005 inch.

The inside of the .25 case may need considerable reaming out to let us seat inside-lubricated .41 bullets properly. We must cut smokeless loads 'way down, then work up slowly, because the thick rifle brass gives less air-space for the powder.

If .25-35 ammo goes off the market and becomes almost impossible to find, we could, with still more work, probably make do with .30-30 cases. That size should hang on! It's both under-rated and over-rated, if you see what I mean. But when it's given a fair chance it can do surprisingly well.

.41 Caliber Stand-ins

The .41 cartridges have been fired as subloads in .38-55 rifles, and Winchester once made a "supplemental chamber" to accommodate them in the .405 moose and big bear gun. In that big barrel the bullets had lots of room in which to skitter around, for .405 rifling groove diameter is about .413 inch. This chamber took the .41 Short with its approximately .40-inch bullet. I presume that some pretty close grouse and rabbit shots must have been missed by the setup.

In the .38-55 rifle, without any adapter, the .41 rim positions it in the chamber, though the extractor isn't likely to work. With Winchester, Savage and Marlin repeaters, it was possible to get in with a small screw-driver or a knife-point and pull fired brass; but it was not so easy with the Winchester single-shot. When its breech is open, the extractor is still up front, and more or less in the way of a prying blade. It was J. V. K. Wagar, I think, who in a *Rifleman* article told of cutting a groove in the top of the barrel—it could do no harm, for the old single-shot seats its cases in deep, flush with the face of the barrel—so that the brass could be pried out.

The .41 Colt pressures are so low that brass wouldn't swell excessively at the first firing, and they are too short to get much grip on the rifle's chamber wall. The modern .41 Long bullet isn't greatly oversize for the .379-inch .38-55 rifling groove diameter; and the large .41 Short bullets are soft and of course powered with very low pressures. Either subload should be safe, but the Long should give by far the better accuracy.

You and I both realize that the .41 Colt cartridges and the .38-55 see little use today. We know, too, that both calibers are useful indeed in their particular line of country, and interesting to load and fire. Accuracy of the .38-55 in fixed ammunition style, as we buy it or usually handload it, and in separate bullet and powder-charged-case gun-loading, is well proved and generally known. But .41 caliber accuracy, as far as I know, never has been proved since smokeless powder came into wide use. It is doubtful that any specially refined, target-sighted revolvers were made in .41 except perhaps a few early Bisley or Single Action Army Colts. Sights could be made and fitted. The rest of the proof—and it should not be a tiresome "burden of proof"—is a challenge to some investigative handloader and shooter. I hope that this challenge will be taken up. After all, who has heard of a revolver cartridge that was, in itself, inaccurate, especially one firing a reasonably long bullet at moderate velocity? Naturally a blunt-nosed slug like the .41 isn't built for more than about 50-yard 10-ring punching—so far as we know today. Or am I wrong? Anyway, we should hardly expect it to make necessary the manufacture of 100- and 200-yard official pistol targets.

Since I wrote the foregoing relative to the .256 Magnum cartridge, Western has informed me that the ballistic qualities and perhaps even the form of the cartridge have not been definitely decided upon.

I T IS QUITE possible that few of us often need a bigbore handgun, but its power makes it fascinating. Anyway, we might be thankful, some grim day, for the wallop of a .357, .38-40, .44 or .45. Big bullets put down an enemy sooner than small ones.

A lot of us enjoy using big guns. Pound for pound of powder and lead expended in a bigbore gives us as much pleasure as the same amounts dribbled out in a longer series of pops or cracks from a .32 or a .38. Those gaping holes in paper or tin-can targets, the heavy blast and heaving upsurge of the muzzle, the drag on the holster belt or shoulder yoke, and the chest swelling with pride in the possession—sometimes the mastery, too!—of a bigbore: such details make the punkin-roller what he is, crazy as a June loon, maybe, but a happy sort of guy.

And some plainly need a big gat. Those fortunate enough to spend time in wild, remote sections often choose a large caliber for game killing. When a deer must be bagged for camp meat, the medium power loads are far less satisfactory, with equally good placement of shots, than the big fellows. And deer are not the biggest and toughest game that's killed with handguns. The occasions have been rare and are continuously becoming less common, when firearm-carrying man must defend himself against animal. When that time does come, no caliber seems excessive, no pistol weight in the hand seems too heavy for reassurance.

A Secret Service friend who served in the once-famous Grover Cleveland Bergdoll case told me that he and his associates commonly toted .38 Specials on the job, but that when unusual difficulty was foreseen the .45 was first choice. So too, against savages in that British Empire on which the sun never set, the bigbore proved not only desirable but also downright essential. Officers carried handguns of various types up to .50, .60 and still larger caliber—the .450 and then the .455 revolvers being standard while those wars were on.

True enough, in World War II the British .380 with slow 176- to 200-grain bullet handled most emergencies in which a handgun was of material help. But at times many of "the Master Race" were ripe for surrender when the going became tougher than the Fuehrer had led them to expect. Seldom does civilized man fight with the fanaticism of the savage. That the Russians use a version of the .30 Mauser cartridge proves little about stopping power. To the Kremlin mind, Russian lives are cheap. A snootful of bullets from a burp gun is entirely different from one or two, probably not vitally placed, from a pistol. Most men or women who may fight for their lives, or for still more precious stakes, want power at each squeeze of the trigger.

Cartridges assigned to this chapter are regarded, more or less generally, as right for deer killing. Their mass or else their velocity produces that "knockdown" effect we have a right to expect *at short range and with well placed hits.* For some shooters the ranges haven't been short at all, but those occasions came through necessity. After all, a big, heavy, reasonably long lead bullet

CHAPTER 13

HEAVY CENTERFIRE CARTRIDGES

doesn't need a great deal of residual velocity to get into the works and kill—if it's well aimed. A few woodsmen of great experience hunt deer for sport with a pistol; and nearly all of them choose a bigbore, usually with handloads more effective than factory rounds that must be held down to pressures that the weakest guns chambering them will stand. But these people don't want their skill in bush-craft and marksmanship negated by weapons of inadequate power. There are exceptions when heavy trophies are taken neatly and humanely by pipsqueak guns in cool and steady hands. Exceptions make news. In the shooting world there are many of them, but only a few of the failures with popguns get into print or even are confided to trustworthy friends. They make an intelligent and decent person feel sick and ashamed.

It's true that some experienced outdoorsmen are opposed to deer hunting with any handgun. Too many bunglers take to the woods with pistols when such hunting is legal. Even a marksmanship test before licensing wouldn't weed out all those who were likely to wound rather than kill. There's the matter of buck fever, which comes from lack of confidence. Which shakes confidence more, a paper target or a fine game trophy?

The .357 Magnum hasn't shrunk, now that there's a .44 Magnum! It's still a powerful load, also it's an exception in being a medium caliber boosted to good, average or better bigbore efficiency by high velocity and an ideal bullet contour. That 158-grain semi-wadcutter, like the 240-grain .44 Mag, is the best factory design, coupled with plenty of speed, for all-

233

.357 MAGNUM

Bullet in grs.	F. S. vel. at muzzle	At 50 yds.	At 100 yds.	F. P. energy at muzzle	At 50 yds.	At 100 yds.	M. R. Traj. at 50 yds.	At 100 yds	Barrel Length
158	1430	1255	1130	717	551	447	.6″	2.8″	8⅜″

Penetration ⅞-inch soft pine boards at 15 ft.—12

around use on targets and game. Its shoulder cuts a clean hole in tagboard, a messy one in flesh and bone. There's enough tapered flattened point to guide it accurately up to 200 yards and even more. It's a favorite of "long shooters" who pit their handgun skill against that of neophyte offhand riflemen, or each other's. For this, we can handload with a round-nosed bullet set as far out of the case as the cylinder allows.

I was wrong in saying the .357 hadn't shrunk. It isn't Sanforized. Since the 1935 beginning the velocity figure has dropped from 1510 f.s. to the present 1430. Other Magnums, and other cartridges not Magnums, have suffered a great sea-change from the wear and wash of time. It's a fact that some production lots of cartridges, rifle rounds at least, have been recalled because their pressures were just too high. Later the advertised ballistics dropped, too. In the case of the .357, the original 1510 f.s. came from an 8¾-inch barrel; the modern 1430 comes from an 8⅜-inch, which of course wouldn't cost any 80 f.s., or anywhere near it. The long barrel was an oversight. The slightly shorter one we now have as standard maximum puts the barrel-and-cylinder total within the ten inches permissible in Standard American target competition.

The caliber name of .357 is correct, the fractional inch diameter of most inside-lubricated revolver bullets we call .38s. The .38 Special is a development of the .38 Long Colt, with more powder room and a bullet not greatly different. And Maggie is a big, healthy child of the Special, about 1/10-inch longer in brass and loaded to much higher pressures. Calling her ".357" helped discourage .38 owners from thinking they could safely fire this blockbuster in their guns by the simple expedient of having the chambers reamed out a leetle mite.

Only guns originally made, and stamped, for the .357 should fire that load. It has been safely used in rifles, like Remington rolling-block single-shots of good weight and tough steel, rebarreled by gunsmiths who appreciated the some 42,000 pounds per square inch of strain. Many .38-40 and .44-40 Winchester Model 1892 or 92—not 1873, let's hope—lever action repeaters have been converted to .357, and some to .44 Magnum. How a .357 Mag. rifle could be deadlier than a heavily but safely handloaded .38-40 or .44-40, it's hard to see. But no gun-crank in his right mind (plain nuts, did someone say?) would question the interest and fun of playing with such a musketoon.

An All-Round Caliber?

The .357 *is* the all-around caliber for many shooters who sometimes want, or might want, great power without handloading. Most .38 Special factory rounds give accuracy in Magnum revolvers. For less smack and greater economy the .38 Short Colt can be used without the slightest heart-flutter of apprehension over harming a fine gun. Its over-sized bullet, even though it's heavily smeared with grease, may lead the barrel-breech; but so do other loads in this and other calibers using soft lead-alloy bullets. Most of us now accept this, and brush out the leading when it gets too bad, though special loading or a lucky correlation between gun and ammo may prevent this fouling. The revolver, with its throated and sometimes much too throated or ill-polished barrel-breech is the big offender. Many .38 Special handloads suit the Magnum. Its own strong case is of course a honey to reload unless you want less air-space for squib loads. Most factory .357s lead barrels rather badly, but cast bullets with gas-checks may shoot pretty cleanly.

From left: .357 Magnum, early form of Winchester loading; .38-40; .44-40; .44 S.&W. Russian; .44 Special; .44 Magnum, Remington load; .44 Bull Dog; .44 Webley; .450 British as once loaded by Winchester; .45 Webley; .44 Colt; .45 S.&W. Schofield; .44 S.&W. American; .45 Auto; .45 Auto-Rim; .45 Auto-Rim, old Peters load with 250-grain flat-point bullet; .45 Colt; .455 Long Colt; .455 Mark II; .44 Shay Magnum on .30-06 brass. Lamp photo, Winchester, Va.

Any way you shake it down, a good pistol or rifle deserves carefully handloaded ammunition. With the .357 we have more working space than we have with the enormously popular .38 Special, for which millions of handloads must be put up every year; and its guns are made to take higher pressures. They have to be, even the lighter ones, but that doesn't mean we can't blow up a Magnum with kluck loading. We can, and most of us know we can.

If we don't like to scrub out the carbon fouling rings from our sixgun chambers, down below the throats, we can still use Magnum brass exclusively, even for squib stuff or near it. It's possible to use several tight-fitting cardboard wads—target tagboard is good—under the bullet, *not* pressed down on the powder, and make squibs that burn powder more cleanly than when there's lots of air-space for the powder to shuck around in. This calls for slow and cautious experiment. Since the powder is more confined than it is without the wads, we get higher velocities with the same charges. Consequently, we use less powder, such as 2 grains Bullseye in the .357. Felt wads might be better, though I've not yet tried them in pistol cartridges. With the wads we finally hit a happy medium where report and velocity are both very low. By starting low we do risk having a bullet stuck in the bore; so we watch for bullet strike on our backstop or target. If the bullet is not excessively hard or oversize, it isn't difficult to drive it out from the muzzle. Some barrels are tapered from breech to muzzle, and that helps. If we try to shoot the bullet out, we put a ring in the barrel. Now, I've heard of a bulged .22 rimfire barrel that won a New York Metropolitan rifle match, and I had a Springfield M-II .22 barrel that was so bulged that the cleaning patch took a merry jump whenever it hit that free-up, but I prefer barrels that aren't bulged. I hope I'm not eccentric in feeling so. The Springfield would shoot into a half-inch at 50 yards, and that's as much as I expect to do with any rifle, though hope is not dead.

Only rather recently have prescriptions exceeding factory power been well-known to shooters, but they could come in handy in heavy .357 guns. A March, 1951 *American Rifleman* article on the subject was prepared by the late Al Barr and the H. P. White Company. It's authoritative. *All* the data are important—on powders, primers, cases, bullets, and in particular on the seating depth of bullets; which must be of correct diameter for the bore, not oversize, which runs up pressures. The factory-rated 1430 f.s. velocity gives excellent killing power for almost all needs, but some loaders prefer a hollow point unless they need great penetration. The 156- or 158-grain Ray Thompson solid-point, gas-check bullet is a big favorite (Ideal 358156) with those who like a copper cup on the bullet's base, in spite of the higher pressures it causes when the rifling must cut it. For a hollow point there's the Keith 155-grain, Ideal 358439. But there are dozens of good .38 Special and .357 Mag. bullets we

could use, including cast round balls (just one in a cartridge, normally, two for experiment) in squib charges to shoot indoors.

There are jacketed soft-point bullets, custom made, to stand high velocities without metal-fouling the bore. The .357 is really a fouler with most soft or rather soft-lead bullets. A recent *Rifleman* ad from Walnut Spring Custom Loads, Route 1, Fayetteville, Arkansas, lists swaged soft-point bullets in .357 caliber, also in

The .357 Magnum looks small beside the .44 Magnum, but it's still a competent cartridge. Photo courtesy Remington Arms Company.

.429-inch for .44 Specials and Magnums and .454 for .45 Colt. This is only a sample mention.

But to qualify as an all-rounder, a sixgun may have to be fairly light to carry. The big Magnums, suitable for the heavy sort of handloads, are inconvenient for some of us to tote. The smaller-frame Colts and Smiths aren't much bulkier than average .38 Special police guns, and with them you still have the advantage of factory .357 power if and when you need it. Of course they recoil heavily with those rounds. But they are better guns than over-loaded .38 Specials because they *are* safe with factory .357 Mags.

Game-Killing Power

The Western moose and elk killed with the Magnum in early days fell to standard cartridges, I believe, probably one of the pioneer Winchester lots that sent the 158-grain lead bullet at 1510 f.s. velocity for an energy of 800 foot-pounds.

Let's consider a couple of discontinued Winchester self-loading rifles. The Model 1905 .35 fired a 180-grain soft-point bullet, heavier than the Magnum's, and toughened for reasonable penetration by means of a thin copper jacket. Velocity was 1400 f.s. and energy 785 f.p. The Model 1907 or 07 .351 sent a 180 grain, with rounded instead of flat point, at 1850 f.s. velocity and 1370 f.p. energy. Penetration was through 9 and 13 ⅞-inch pine boards, respectively, with the Magnum making about 12. Before the .35 was announced, Harry Payne Whitney, a noted sportsman, tried a pilot model in the Arctic and found it light, much like the .38-40 rifle in power.

Even the .351 is not a "good" deer gun. It's marginal, like the .25-35 and the .25 Remington, with just enough power under ideal conditions. Yet it's ahead of the .357 revolver, and the rifle can hit more difficult targets. Three- or 4-inch, 100-yard, ten-shot groups—measured in the usual modern way, from center to center of the two shot-holes farthest apart—sometimes can be made with a .351. How many can do this with the Magnum sixgun, firing two-handed from prone or sitting, or slumped over or against a convenient stump, log or rock? The .357 is accurate, hardly second to the renowned .38 Special. However, it isn't the choice of top-rank target shooters, because they don't need its flat trajectory at a mere 50 yards. But to speak of it or any other pistol as an excellent substitute for a big game rifle is ridiculous. Both figures and shooting show it to be inferior in knockout punch to outmoded deer rifles, which rather uncommonly make clean, one-shot kills on the white-tails, except when really good hunters and game-shots are using them.

However, the pistol can be much more useful in close cover than a rifle or even a carbine. The .44 Magnum sixgun is far more deadly than the .357, and some .44 Special, .45 Colt and similar handloads can beat the .357, too. The latter now seems outdated as a revolver cartridge for big game, just as the light Win. self-loaders are, though the 1910 .401 Win. was one of the best woods cartridges for deer and black bear. If a fellow is to hunt deer with a handgun, he'd best master a bigbore. None of these remarks applies to those who have had long-continued success with the .357 class of arm. A couple of hunters I've known were perfectly satisfied with the little Winchester .35. There must be others of their kind, even today, who perhaps have gone to heavier rifles simply because they can't get the .35 Self-loading rounds.

Barrel Length

The original S.&W. folder told us that about 40 f.s. velocity went down the spout with each inch of barrel lopped off, down to six inches. From there to 3½ we subtract 50 f.s. per inch. Starting from the 1510 f.s. then given for the 8¾-inch, it works out to 1275 for the 3½. Tests made later showed that the old folder had been just about right, when the original, powerful, 1935 Winchester ammunition was used. Since that time much less powerful lots have been marketed in some makes. It seems that all the factories have re-duced their .357 velocities. The same thing has happened in some other calibers. In general, it's been done in the interests of safety. However, the formidable shape of the .357 lead or Lubaloy coated lead bullet adds points to its stopping power. Velocity is probably the chief factor that makes its 158-grain metal-tipped bullets chew through steel as they do.

But guns and factory lots of ammunition vary. Primers and powders change, in general for better all-round performance. Loading companies often alter their velocity standards, up or down, as seems best.

Later tests run at the H. P. White Laboratory, Bel Air, Maryland were reported by Major General Julian S. Hatcher, U.S.A. (Retired), known to most of us as technical editor of *The American Rifleman*. The November, 1954 issue carried the story.

The Potter counter chronograph was used, with its first screen 10 feet from the muzzle, the second out at 20 feet. This recorded velocities at 15 feet, which would be about 13 f.s. less than muzzle velocity for the .357, 5 less for the high-speed .38 Special, and 3 less for the standard Special. Two guns were used, Colt and Smith, with barrels cut off as the various stages came up. The Colt, a "Three Fifty Seven," started with a 6-inch barrel. Differences in velocities between the two guns were small. Here are some figures for the S.&W. barrel:

Western Lubaloy Magnum: 8⅜, 1328; 6½, 1270; 5, 1232; 3½, 1185. Remington loads used then gave less, such as 1183 in the 8⅜ and 928 in 2-inch. They also gave more muzzle flash, which wasn't noticeable in the Westerns that were fired.

Remington .38 Special, standard: 8⅜, 802; 6½, 785; 6, 784; 5, 773; 3½, 740; 2, 691.

Peters .38 Special High Velocity: 8⅜, 953; 6½, 960; 6, 952; 3½, 887; 2, 794.

Short cartridges lose speed in a long, throated chamber.

Why Choose a .357?

The .357 Mag. is noisy, even with long barrels, and recoil and upchuck aren't trifling. A standard .44 Special or .45 Colt kicks a bit, and heavy but sometimes useful handloads bark and rear a good deal like the .357. The latter naturally has lost much of its terrors with the coming of the .44 Mag., which is still something for a few of us to say, "I don't want one about."

But with the .357 you get more versatility of loads, from handrolled gallery stuff to factory and own-make rounds that are nearly, if not quite, as heavy as most of us are likely to need. Vital to some handloaders is the fact that a cake of lead bought at the hardware store, or a section of filthy old drainpipe bestowed on us by a friend who's renewing his plumbing, casts a lot more .357s than .44s and .45s. If brass is scarce we *can* adapt .351 rifle empties to .357 handloading, checking the comparative powder capacity. This just might come up sometime.

Furthermore, medium caliber ammunition doesn't bag out the hunting coat pockets or sag down an already heavy belt as the thick stuff does. And if we must have a medium-weight gun we can get it in .357. This kind didn't come out until late, but it does have its uses. Compare the available power with that of a similar .38 Special revolver. Arms like the Colt "Three Fifty Seven" and the S.&W. .357 Combat Magnum, about 2¼ pounds each, have their places.

.38-40 WINCHESTER

Bullet in grs.	F. S. vel. at muzzle	F. P. energy at muzzle	Barrel length
180	975	380	5"

Penetration ⅞-inch soft pine boards at 15 ft.—6

It is refreshing to turn from a highly popular cartridge to an old favorite, nearly forgotten, and needing a little defense! This 1879 design for the famous 1873 Winchester rifle has seen service in far country as well as in nearby woodlots and "up-along the crick." In really old Smith & Wessons, and in Colt single-actions and double-actions made for it up into the 1930s or 1940s, it's been an outdoorsman's favorite.

It is the smallest of the heavy bigbores, rifling groove diameter going about .401 inch, like that of the .41 Colt. Interchangeable sixgun cylinders for these two cartridges have been fitted to serve the same barrel; and this has been done in .44-40 and .44 Special, too. In the latter combination the barrel groove diameter may not be so obliging, for early .44-40 Colt barrels can be as small as .424 inch, although later ones went to the .427, which is about .44 Special standard, give a thousandth or two.

In power, the .38-40 revolver load has been likened to the .44 Special. Its flat-nosed bullet has greater velocity, energy and penetration than the Special, but 66 grains' weight of additional lead in the .44 could sometimes make a difference. If we need to make large wounds, the .38's lack of bullet width is compensated by its bluff point. We can't expect a great deal of mushrooming—if any—of the .38 jacketed, soft-nosed bullet at standard pistol velocities; but at least it tears rather than drills. A soft-lead hollow point like the Ideal 168-grain 40043 could do some damage, but this pistol cartridge isn't well adapted to much speeding up. It is bottlenecked, and that increases pressure somewhat, when the same powder is used as in a straight case. Its body, just above the rim, is .0075 inch larger than that of the .44 Special and only .016 smaller than the .45 Colt's. The .44-40 runs about .002 inch larger than the .38-40, down there at the base. These figures from cartridges in the collection may not agree with others taken, and indeed they hardly could, for there are always variations in production. They do explain why the .44 Special is and deserves to be a favorite for heavy loads, and why .44 caliber was chosen for the Magnum round. Then too, the Special is comparatively new—compared

to the .38-40—and even the early S.&W. Triple Locks that introduced it were pretty strong guns. A great many .38-40, .44-40 and .45 Colt caliber revolvers are old. The earliest single-actions are for black powder only, in full-power loads or anything near them.

But with standard-velocity ammunition the .38-40 revolver did well in the wilderness. Though it never was a target favorite, it isn't inaccurate with proper loading. It carries up well over distances at which the average good handgunner is likely to fire. The comparatively light bullet makes recoil moderate, and a .38-40 with 7½-inch barrel is a mighty pleasant big gun to shoot. Even in the narrow-gripped Colt New Service, it's comfortable; and in the Single Action Army and the Bisley, stocked very differently but both easy to shoot, the recoil is not a bit unpleasant. Black powder loads give a boom that's dull, at least as compared to full-charge smokeless, which cracks pretty sharply and seems to be quicker, though lighter, in kick.

Definitely, it needs handloading if we're to get the best from it. The soft-point smokeless factory loads, the only ones now made, are accurate enough except possibly in overbored barrels that might come along now and then. But the jackets of even these low-power bullets are a little too heavy to expand promptly in the bore and seal off the gases. They do shorten barrel life. Reduced loads are easy if we have even the simplest tools. For them we'd use smokeless in light charges in any sound .38-40, making sure that our cast bullets were of full rifling groove diameter. Remington once put up a light load of 28 grains FFG black, with lead bullet of standard weight, in this case and in the .44-40. However, without some filler over loose black powder the fouling is pretty bad. It builds up fast enough, anyway! There were a dozen or so other .38-40 factory loads, all of standard revolver power or beyond it, and more in the .44-40 if you count the round-ball Marble Game Getter offerings of various types which could be used in .44-40 arms, and were. But "Never again!" was the prompt decision after the owner had labored at scrubbing the lead out of rifling grooves, as he more often than not had to— at least when the twist was of fast revolver standard, one turn in 16 inches. The 36-inch twist of Winchester rifles did well with some Game Getters; but with others it was a mess in fouling, and, of course, in wild shooting.

Probably all High Velocity rounds with full-weight bullets in .32-20, .38-40 and .44-40 are in collectors' hands, and the High Speeds, too, with sub-weight, hollow-point, jacketed bullets—except for the .32-20s, still made with those stubby 80-grain bullets, which do shoot well at short range in some rifles. None of these loads is for a revolver. They have been so used, but it's dangerous practice. Factories do *not* replace, free of charge, cylinders blown open by such ammunition, or by handloads.

Only one handloading difficulty is likely to plague the owner of a .38-40 sixgun, provided that he uses his good commonsense. Some chambers are reamed out so liberally, up front, that fired brass comes out with practically no neck-length left on it. Then neck-sizing is necessary, of course, and lots of it. This wears cases rather fast. The normal neck is just long enough to house the borebearing part of the regular 180-grain bullet, which we'd choose—except possibly for a hollow point of similar lines—because we should not expect to find one of these sixguns with adjustable sights. But still, such sights could be custom fitted; and they do belong on an outdoorsman's pistol, which a .38-40 is, exactly.

.44-40 WINCHESTER

Bullet in grs.	F. S. vel. at muzzle	F. P. energy at muzzle	Barrel length
200	975	422	7½″

Penetration ⅞-inch soft pine boards at 15 ft.—6

Many who ought to know considered this 1873 rifle cartridge the best handgun load that factories supplied for big game hunting. That was long before the .44 Magnum. The bluff, flat-nosed bullet at good velocity needed no "modernization" to give it killing power at moderate ranges. Its only serious rival, in this particular field, was the .45 Colt. Comparison is interesting.

The 255-grain .45 starts at 870 f.s. from a 5½-inch barrel and sweats up 429 foot pounds energy. The .44 figures, for a longer barrel, are given at the head of this section. Both penetrate six ⅞-inch boards on factory test, though we could expect the Colt to show up better in flesh and bone because of its sharper point and greater weight. Old factory .44-40 and .38-40 bullets were of pure lead; the .45 bullets were hardened, one part tin to twenty parts lead. That could mean a little. The jacket of the modern .44-40 soft-point bullet resists expansion pretty strictly at revolver velocities, but the bullet nose is wide and flat to start with, and some .45 factory slugs have hardly any flat at all. So we should expect the .44 to make a bigger, but less deep, wound, even in jacketed type, the only factory bullet left in this and many other old sizes. The natural remedy is handloading, as suggested in the .38-40 section, with cast-lead bullets.

The .45, with long bearing surface, a sharp front profile, and steady balance, has better sustained energy and usually somewhat superior accuracy, other things being equal. Both, when well loaded for the individual gun, give greater precision than the skill of all but really good shots can use. The lighter .44 bullet gives less recoil, and its higher velocity comes along with a sharper crack in smokeless loadings. We could just about notice these differences if we looked for them.

Both cartridges ought to stay on the market for a long time. No .44-40 guns seem to be made now, but the caliber was even more popular than the .38-40.

The .44 ammunition still goes to far parts of the earth, and some that are not far but are decidedly different from the mainland U.S.A. It still is used in South America and the West Indies, and to some extent abroad. At times it saw military service, as in Winchester carbines, rifles and muskets.

For fixed-sight guns the 200- or 210-grain cast bullets are right, and revolvers target-sighted for the .44-40 are certainly rare. If we want to use different bullet weights, there are .44 Special molds that drop lead above and below .44-40 standard, and only some sizing-down, if necessary, adapts them to .44-40 barrels. Oldtimers remember the 217-grain lead bullets that Winchester loaded into .44-40 Marlin and Colt Lightning Magazine Rifle (a pump gun) rounds, also the 115-grain round ball for the smooth shotgun bore of the Marble Game Getter over-and-under .22 and .44.

Although the .44-40, like the .38-40, repays handloading, it is seldom the choice of a shooter who has much interest in target. He almost always picks a .44 Special, .45 Auto, or possibly a .44 Magnum as his bigbore arm. But hundreds if not thousands of .44-40 sixguns must still travel too far for their users to tote tools, molds, and ammunition components. Unlike the Special as always made, this .44 is *not* underloaded by the factories. It should be easier to find, even today, in stores or trading posts that edge the wilderness. With a .44-40 and ready-made hulls a pistolman is pretty well armed.

.44 SMITH & WESSON RUSSIAN

Bullet in grs.	F. S. vel. at muzzle	F. P. energy at muzzle	Barrel length
246	770	324	6½″

Penetration ⅞-inch soft pine boards at 15 ft.—4

Those figures are probably the highest claimed for the .44 Russian cartridge before it was discontinued in 1955. Present .44 Special ratings, also from a 6½-inch barreled revolver, are 755 f.s. and 311 f.p., unimportant differences. They were taken, presumably, at about 70° Fahrenheit. My 5-inch Smith gave factory-load velocity of around 690 f.s. at 32° F. The loss due to cold air and short barrel seemed to be about normal.

In the beginning the Russian with 23 grains of black powder and 246-grain bullet turned up a little less velocity than the .44 Special with 26 grains and the same bullet. Smokeless loads, as generally in revolver cartridges then using this propellant, fell a little below the black in velocity. For a long while there was a notably superior black powder difference in the .45 Colt. In more modern times the 770 f.s. rate held for both .44 Russian and .44 Special. The natural and correct conclusion is that the factory smokeless loading of .44 Specials is too economical in the use of powder. But it always has been a fine target cartridge, especially for long-range use. So has the Russian, though its

First model Smith & Wesson single-action revolver, which introduced the fine 44 S.&W. Russian cartridge. Courtesy Smith & Wesson.

smaller powder capacity limits the handloader as to velocities.

History and Design

The Russian of 1870 origin, built for the Tsar's government, was probably our first American-made pistol cartridge with inside lubrication. This may help a little in cold weather; and it certainly helps in hot: the grease doesn't goo off the bullets or pick up grit from your pocket. It's generally much more evenly distributed lube, too.

The Russian followed the outside lubricated .44 S.&W. American of 1869; and both were used, not interchangeably, in various models of Smith & Wesson revolvers. The inside-lube Russian was adopted shortly by Colt sixguns; and even after the .44 Special came in 1907 many of those short cartridges were used in their own guns as well as in long-chambered Specials. Sometimes, when they had lower velocity than the Specials, they outshot those rounds in the same revolver. A lot of gallery marksmen used Russian brass for light handloads in their Special guns because the greater density of powder loading seemed to give better accuracy. Probably they still would if they could get the cases. They can make them by shortening the Specials to about .965 inch, and so of course can owners of .44 Russian caliber arms. Some modern Specials have a cannelure to get in the way, and that's too bad. It isn't needed on a revolver cartridge now that we don't have to tell the difference between black and smokeless factory loads by any method other than looking for a "smokeless" primer stamped U, W, US or P, that is, by the ring in the brass behind the bullet's base. They are all smokeless now in ball loading, and the primers are non-corrosive and without initials.

The early temper of the Russian bullet was one to 40, tin and lead, which is soft, though .25-20, .25-21 and .25-25 bullets were one to 60, hardly worth the fluxing. Generally Russian and Special bullets have a hollow base to assure prompt upsetting in the bore. Most guns made for these rounds had or have such close tolerances that this feature isn't likely to run up pressure, as it can when a barrel diameter is 'way below that of the cylinder mouths behind it. Most of us would like about one to 15 temper now for our .44 bullets, give or grab a little either way, to help keep lead fouling down.

But the shape of the rather long-nosed rounded bullet (varying a good bit now in different makes) and the 23- to 246-grains proportion of black powder and lead worked up into a highly accurate load. Popular frontier sizes like the .44 American and especially the .38-40, .44-40 and .45 Colt, favored a heavier powder-to-lead proportion for more velocity, though it's doubtful that the American got it. Its smokeless rating was only 695 f.s. from a 6½-inch barrel. The short heel of the bullet inside the case offered little resistance compared with the long sections of the inside-lube jobs. By and large, smokeless loads need a crimp for good combusion.

The .32 S.&W. Short of 1877 and the .38 S.&W. Short of 1876 were close to the Russian in powder-to-lead ratio, the .38 almost exactly the same. Bullet contours weren't much different, which hardly seems accidental. When the .32 S.&W. Long of 1896—13 and 98 grains—proved to be very accurate, too, it was natural that the .38 Special of about 1900—21 and 158—should be like it. The round-nose bullet hung on in S.&W. design, having started with the .22 Short of 1855 or '56, until the .357 Magnum came in 1935 and the .44 in '55. By that time most informed handgunners liked the semi-wadcutter nose shape right well for general use, including target—with good reason.

Old though they are, these S.&W. cartridges commonly rate as the highest, commercial, centerfire, accuracy developments of revolver ammunition, excepting only the Magnums. There could be exceptions, of course, such as the flat-pointed .32 and .38 Colt New Police and .38 Colt Special—the latter no longer made for lack of intelligent demand—which shoot with nearly equal accuracy. And some of the countless .45 Auto loadings, worked over exhaustively by the War (or Army) Department's experts, have given almost incredible accuracy in test guns. Some of them, but not all by any means, have short heavy barrels backed up by rifle-type bolt actions.

Factory Variants

We can learn something from history if we open our minds. That goes for such a trivial subject (a non-shooter could say without being committed to the booby-hatch) as handgun loads. The Russian cartridge is gone, speaking practically, but the .44 Special still gets rung up on cash registers. It and even the Magnum inherit some of the good things that belonged to the .44 Russian.

Factory production of the Russian was no slouch in either quality or variety. The 246-grain Russian bullet came in plain lead, hollowed and "Self-Lubricating" lead for special black-powder rounds, full metal

.44 SPECIAL

Bullet in grs.	F. S. vel. at muzzle	At 50 yds.	At 100 yds.	F. P. energy at muzzle	At 50 yds.	At 100 yds.	M. R. Traj. at 50 yds.	At 100 yds.	Barrel Length
246	755	725	695	311	283	264	2.2"	8.3"	6½"

Penetration ⅞-inch soft pine boards at 15 ft.—4

patched, and metal-pointed with lead bearing for the rifling grooves. These were for full-power rounds.

For gallery work there were a 105-grain round-ball load and a 115-grain conical. About 50 feet was their working range for accuracy. But a flat-faced wadcutter with just a little pimple of lead up front—to look like a steering device, perhaps—weighed 145 grains, used smokeless powder only, and was recommended for 20 yards. It should have done well up to 25, at least. The black powder dose for the 105- and 115-grain bullets was only six grains, either FFG or FFFG, I don't know which.

The .44 Special inherited some of these loads, and in the way of hand-cast bullets it inherited much more.

The .44 Special case accommodates heavier loads than the short .44 Russian, having a black powder capacity of 26 grains as compared to 23, both compressed, of course. Late factory runs of Special brass have solid heads; they are flat at the bottom instead of being belled up into a form of "balloon" primer pocket, or "semi-balloon" we should say. The brass below the bulge was thinner on the earliest forms of centerfire cases, as we can see by looking at an empty used for almost any old rifle cartridge that was loaded with black powder and paper-patched lead bullet. This modern solid-head case holds less powder than the earlier and still pretty common .44 Specials. We couldn't expect to pack 26 grains of black into it.

"Solid head" has a new meaning now—still referring to cartridge cases. It implies the thick, flat-bottomed brass being used in more and more revolver cartridges, even in the tiny .32 S.&W. Short. It has been standard for auto-pistol and modern high-power rifle cases right along. The original meaning distinguished the cases that were milled out brass, body and rim both, from those more easily manufactured, the "folded head" sort, the rim being not milled but folded into form. They were really weak, though for black powder reloading the good ones stand up pretty well. I never had a failure with one. A file cut can show that the inside is actually a bit hollow around the circumference, though not so much so as on a rimfire, which holds its priming charge in that hollow, ready for the hammer or firing pin to compress it.

Solid-head cases are important in .44 Special, which is used so much for heavy handloads. They call for a reduction of stiff smokeless powder charges. As an example, Elmer Keith, in *Sixguns,* page 272, lists a .44 Special charge of 18.5 grains of Hercules 2400 in the semi-balloon cases, but only 17.5 grains of that powder in the solid-head type. The bullets advised are his own design of Ideal 250-grain solid or 235-grain

hollow base or hollow point. He explains, too, that cases must be in good shape and bullets sized to fit the rifling groove diameter, not oversize. These are heavy .44 Special loads for use in strong guns, and essentially they are specialist's loads in preparation and in purposes.

It's a common saying among mountaineers, plainsmen, woods loafers and swamp angels that the factory cartridge is shamefully underloaded and always has been, with smokeless. They are right, for their statement refers to killing power. Even in penetration the factory Special is nothing wonderful, and its sharply rounded bullet point isn't meant for tearing.

Target Use

That bullet contour, like the other S.&W. designs except the Magnums and perhaps the .22 Short, seems to have been for target accuracy first of all. A bullet punches a hole, doesn't it, and the bigger punch you need, the bigger bullet you select? Only in rather recent years has the shape of bullet point for killing received as much attention as it needed, though of course it got some long ago.

The .38 Special, and the much heavier and somewhat less wind-sensitive .44 Special, prove to do remarkably fine work at ranges four, five and six times the official 50-yard. The rounded points helped. The .44 became known as "the most accurate revolver cartridge ever made," the .22 Long-rifle having been conveniently forgotten. Naturally, it was far more dependable at 50 yards than any little .22 or .32 bullet, when wind whipped across the range.

The fine target revolvers for the .44 Special were heavy, by oldtime standards when barrels were slim and sometimes as thin as a shotgun's tube at the muzzle; but shooters liked the weight after getting used to it. So the .44s went to indoor ranges, too, where on the smaller targets their big bullets cut ambitiously into higher-scoring rings than a smallbore with the same placement could clip. A great variety of molds were cut to make sub-weight bullets for the .44. Even around 170 grains weight there were plenty to choose from, a 173 wadcutter, a 175 semi-wadcutter with long lean point extending from its front shelf, and a conventional but still well-liked 175 round-nose. This should do nicely up to 50-yard target range and not badly in the rather light game-hunting field. It was listed as suitable for velocities up to 1200 f.s., in .44-40 cases, not in Specials, though probably it could have come fairly well up to it, at that. But it was really for light recoiling target loads, and unless you wanted a wad-cutter type it would have been an all-purpose paper-punching bullet from 50 feet to 50 yards, give plenty on both sides.

There are heavy wadcutters, from 245 to 260 grains. The Ideal 429352 245-grain, with land-riding front section and groove-filling rear, starts at about 930 f.s. when pushed by 7.8 grains of Hercules Unique —out of the old semi-balloon cases, for it's a stiff charge. Few of us would find it pleasant on the target range, or pleasant anywhere, if we hadn't sized our bullets to rifling groove diameter to keep pressures where they belonged. A hollow point would add little if anything to its deadliness, for wad-cutters mushroom widely if they're fast and not too hard, not under 16 to one, lead and tin, let's say. If velocity is wanted, a 173-grain wadcutter can be expressed at 1170 f.s. via 10.3 grains of Unique, and plenty of know-how in the assembling. Sure, such loads are more than just likely to lead the barrel breech, for wadcutters are good at that. But the stuff can be brushed out, and should be, if only for safety, if it builds up big. They are special-purpose charges, and for short ranges because keg-shaped lead has a tough time in plowing through the air.

But already we have got into

Hunting Use

because stiff loads wear down our stamina in the abundance of shooting we do on the target range. We don't need them there, at any rate. Certainly some specialized target rounds fit well into use in the field, depending on the amount and kind of killing power we need there. The regular factory cartridge, with its more or less sharply rounded bullet-nose, can kill medium-sized small game, and probably even turkeys, if one of those birds ever forgot his parents' training and blundered into range, which some do. It can kill them well with correct placement of the hit, and still not ruin the creature for the dinner-table celebration of the hunter's skill. This bullet, speeded up, would be about the .44 Special's best for deep penetration. The factory slug is soft, as practically all are but a mold to duplicate it can be filled with a harder mixture.

Few of us need super-loads, which in time loosen cylinder alignments faster than standard stuff does, and can, when factors do not work together as they should, bend or crack the top-strap, burst the cylinder, and even do serious injury to those who stand by, if not to ourselves. Seldom, however, is the shooter hurt. Justice enjoys an occasional nap.

The .22 caliber 2-R Lovell, made from the long, gently bottle-necked old .25-20 single Shot case, long "obsolete," must have been the most commonly overloaded of all small rifle cartridges. Some folks tried to make it into a .219 Zipper or even a .220 Swift! But that was long ago. Now we have full information on the. 44 Special in loading books and booklets. We do need to remember, in all our handloading, that many recommendations were based on older and weaker primers, on more capacious semi-balloon primer pocket cases, and on old powders like Du Pont No. 5

(which does *not* duplicate modern 5066). Case inspection, bullet sizing and seating depth, knowledge of our own gun's strength and dimensions—all those things aren't nuisances but our protection.

The hollow-point bullets are for mushrooming when velocity still is pretty high; the flat-fronted solids for penetration combined with high destructive effect, compared to that of the round-points; and the subweight bullets, those under 200 grain in the Special, for smaller animals. For defense against an inhuman human the full-flat .44 wadcutter is a smacking bullet. I'd trust my life to it if I had to, at short ranges, of course. Indoors, it penetrates fewer walls and partitions than a round-nose, and that might mean everything.

Until the .44 Magnum came, the .44 Special was the finest large caliber for the handloader to prospect with, having good smokeless powder capacity and a case that requires less boring-out of cylinders than the thicker .38-40, .44-40 and .45. It is still good. For many of us it's as big and long as we should ever want, maybe too much so. With the Magnum so popular— Ruger didn't even bother to produce a .44 Special for his lineup—fewer .44 Special guns are likely to be sold; but many are in use, and highly prized. Some .44 Special rounds are sold for use in Magnums, of course —especially to those who don't handload and who've decided to put off getting used to the Mags. for a while. Special owners buy a box or two now and then, either to get the brass or to have a little of the shooting they enjoy. The cartridge is far from being unpopular, comparatively speaking. It never was a

The .44 Magnum and its 240-grain semi-wadcutter bullet. The deep copper or gilding metal gas-check cup is crimped into the lower grease groove so that it won't be shed on firing, as some are. The Hornady is perhaps the only gas-check sold to handloaders that is made to crimp into the lead, well below the grease groove, but it stays put. Photo courtesy Remington Arms Company.

.44 MAGNUM

Bullet in grs.	F. S. vel. at muzzle	At 50 yds.	At 100 yds.	F. P. energy at muzzle	At 50 yds.	At 100 yds.	M. R. Traj. at 50 yds.	At 100 yds.	Barrel Length
240	1470	1275	1120	1150	870	670	.6"	2.7"	6½"

Pentration not given at this writing, but high velocity and consequent rapid bullet expansion would limit it. Perhaps a metal-point bullet like that of the .357 will be made for it. In 1961, factory loaded soft points came along.

record-breaker in sales; its chart line must have run pretty steadily through the years. For a half-century-old round it's doing nicely. Actually it's a *late* revolver round. In such development—of cartridge cases, at least—1907 is hardly much farther back than last Thursday's meeting of the home-town service club.

The Western Cartridge figures for the Lubaloy coated Magnum bullet are shown in the table above.

Sometimes this 1955 cartridge is called the ".44 Remington Magnum" because of the cooperation of that firm with Smith & Wesson in designing it. The first .357 rounds came from Winchester. It seems that Elmer Keith had much to do with the .44's start, and Phil Sharpe with the .357's. Probably both would say that the big thing is that shooters have these cartridges.

I know of no experimenter who used .351 Winchester brass to develop a super .38 (.357-inch) revolver round; but some may have before any factory became interested. There have been experimental .44s, as a rule on .30-06 brass to get the strength. One of Bert Shay's goes some 1%₃₂ inches in case length, a scant 1⅝ overall with a 260-grain wadcutter seated. It's not only too long for a .44 Special chamber, but also too fat, being about .466 inch just ahead of the cannelure. The Special goes about .455 ahead of its rim. A gun factory can lengthen its chambers, but a gunsmith usually stops with reaming existing chambers, in length and sometimes in diameter too as for this job.

Even heavily loaded .44 Special revolvers can be unpleasant in recoil. When they're altered as just described to take still more powerful charges, they naturally come back harder. The .44 Magnum revolvers with standard factory rounds are, without any argument, too unpleasant for some shooters to accept. There is a jolting effect, the hand holding the gun is lifted high in the air, and checkered stocks may rasp the hand uncomfortably. However, all the factory revolvers now made in .44 Mag. either have smooth wooden grips as standard or can be fitted easily with such grips as factory-made. Almost any shooter, if he really needs one of these arms, can master it in spite of its recoil, and in spite of its muzzle blast, too. We can use ear-plugs for at least 95% of our shooting, as owners of .220 Swift and high-velocity 6 mm. rifles would tell us.

Two things must have been expected when the gun and cartridge were designed: bore leading and near-excessive handloads! The gas-check on the Remington bullet and the Lubaloy coating of the Western are to reduce or even eliminate leading. The design of the first .44 Magnum revolver, the Smith & Wesson, was for

strength to withstand heavy loads. The cylinder is long, and the barrel breech is consequently short—less liable to bulging from an oversize bullet ripping into it at high speed. The whole gun is strong, and so are the others made for this cartridge. We could compare the short barrel-breech to those of five-shot pocket Smiths in .38 Special caliber, the Chief's Special, the semi-hammerless Bodyguard, and the hammerless Centennial. It was inevitable that some owners would use high-velocity Specials in these arms, even though the factory does not advise doing so.

Game-Killing

The long-range effectiveness of the factory .44 Magnum cartridge is lessened by its flat point, but it's needed for killing. Heavy revolver bullets penetrate well on fairly distant game, even at their reduced speeds, because of their weight and their *lack* of velocity. Speed mushrooms the usual run of expanding, high-velocity rifle bullets so much that sometimes—at close ranges, anyway—they don't equal long, heavy sixgun slugs in penetration. They do make bigger wounds by their expansion, and their shock and laceration are greater. But a well-placed large-caliber bullet needn't mushroom much to kill promptly. The hard job is to place it right, and this becomes so much more difficult as the range lengthens that this kind of shooting is only for the expert. But long-range shooting at any kind of game, with rifles or with handguns, can be a ghastly inhuman thing. It's nothing to do for brag, but sometimes it becomes necessary. Often an experienced hunter, armed with a gun somewhat inferior for distance work, has stopped the escape of game that a less able though better equipped companion has wounded. This goes for short ranges, too. Time and again the .44-40 rifle or carbine—distinctly sub-marginal, we'd call that caliber today—has put a neat end to a job that some poor bungler had started.

At all practical ranges the .44 Magnum obviously has more stopping power loaded into it than any other current factory round. There are special jobs like .45-70 revolvers, which we should be foolish to call useless, for almost any well-stocked handgun's recoil is bearable. The gun lifts, rears up; it doesn't send, say 80%, of its recoil straight back against the shooter in rifle or shotgun fashion.

For deep penetration on big game, combined with destruction, we'd use heavy bullets in the .44 Mag. The 240-grain factory slug isn't exactly stubby, for a handgun bullet, though it's shorter than the six-grain-heavier .44 Special with long, tapered point. It's a well-designed, well-built bullet. Elmer Keith has used his own design of 250-grain semi-wadcutter bullet, Ideal

429241, in the Magnum with husky charges of Hercules 2400 rifle powder. It is a plain lead-alloy bullet with no gas-check, jacket, or hard metal base to increase pressures. Then there's his 235-grain hollow point when less penetration is needed. Almost any cast bullet can be hollowed up front by tools if not in a mold we happen to have. The 1961 soft-point, 240-grain factory round, for rifles and carbines, is safe in revolvers, as the factories load it. It has good lead exposure and a thin jacket.

At the other end of the long line are light bullets that the Magnum can use for high velocity and considerable destruction on varmints—not including black bear, as some rate that fascinating animal. He can, we'll admit, fail utterly to fit into the human scale of things, but who would class him with human hoodlums?

In January, 1957 and October, '58 issues of *Precision Shooting,* Kent Bellah discussed high-velocity loads with sub-weight bullets. Now, the factory-load velocity from a 6½-inch barrel is given as 1470 f. s., though early lots or at least early figures went higher. Bellah rated the following handload at 1700: 220-grain lightly jacketed Jugular bullet, 26 grains 2400 powder, primer not stated, as I recall, but presumably Cascade No. 300, a good one, which he seems to like very much. This bullet is not much under factory weight; it's a soft-point, and the thin jacket stiffens it for velocity and penetration as well as preventing lead fouling. Then there's his 170-grain Jugular load, the bullet hollow-pointed, with 27.2 grains 2400, for a speed of 2,000 f. s. The publishers and this writer take no responsibility for these or any other handload recommendations and their use, for components and loading methods vary widely.

Bellah's figures suggest that the zinc-based Prot-X-bore bullets develop more friction and pressure than the lightly jacketed Jugulars, and this we should expect. The thick, hard zinc washer or other form of base at the bottom of the bullet does wipe out leading or other old fouling. In standard or reduced loads such bullets have their points and do not seem to cause undue barrel wear, for they seal off the gases well, if they fit the individual barrel correctly. This they're pretty sure to do. Harvey Prot-X-bore zinc-base bullets weigh 158, 170 and 220 grains. There are .357s, too.

In a September, 1958 *Precision Shooting* story Bellah tells of Mason Williams' (Stanfordville, New York) 242.6-grain .4297-inch .44 bullet with rounded, soft-nosed lead core swaged into heavy custom-made jacket—not the thin .44-40 factory jacket—to give deep penetration on game. This it should do, though jacket stiffness, or any jacket at all except the lightest, calls for a reduction in powder charge in the interests of safety.

Target Use

Some can handle the big Magnum revolvers with little effort. For long-range competition, they have flat trajectory and some advantage in bucking wind, even though blunt bullets lose velocity fast and this loss or "lag" makes a bullet more susceptible to wind-drift. Smallbore riflemen choose the low velocity .22 long-rifle cartridge in preference to the high speed, not only because in most arms it's more accurate but also because it's a better wind-fighter. However, the fast .22 Rimfire Magnum beats any .22 1-r in a breeze.

Still, we aren't confined to flat-nosed .44 Mag. bullets if we hand-load. Few bigbore target shots don't reload their empty pistol cases if they shoot extensively and realize what home-rolling can do for their scores. It can fit the ammo to their own guns.

There's a great variety of .429-inch bullets (approximate figure) to fit their individual handguns, and some are round-pointed. This brings us into the matter of cartridge overall, which could be too great for the cylinder to accept. But there are short-point, round-nosed bullets like the Ideal 429106 and 429478, 175 and 205 grain, as well as more tapered points like the quite different Winchester and Remington designs of "standard" 246-grain, and the old-time Ideal 429383 and 429251 240 and 250 grain, or 244 and 253 as catalogued long ago. (Much depends on the hardness of the bullet, for tin and/or antimony lighten it.)

Since the really long-range revolver competition—200 or 300 yards—is slow-fire, we might benefit from a freak load. That is, we could handload long-pointed full-weight bullets for single-shot use only, employing the chamber-filling unaltered Magnum case, but seating the lead deeply enough to accommodate chamber length. This could be below the crimping groove in the bullet; but most of them have at least a slight shoulder above it, over which the brass could be turned. Whether or not this crimping, combined with snug case-sizing, would burn 2400 powder properly for accuracy would be the only problem. We must remember, of course, that seating any bullet below normal depth decreases powder space and calls for reduction of heavy charges. Certainly we could duplicate the Ideal .44 Special recommendation of 7.8 grains of Unique for a 245- to 250-grain bullet, with velocities well over 900 f. s.—and a bigger, more comfortable gun to shoot it in. But lightly crimped loads, even when not very heavy often permit bullets to jump far enough forward from recoil to protrude from chamber mouths and lock the cylinder's rotation. For timed or rapid fire or for any practical purpose (except single-shot use) our revolver bullets have to stay put under the recoil of neighboring rounds.

And the Magnum can be loaded down for 25- and 50-yard target use, and for gallery, the latter even in close to .44 Special manner in spite of its greater powder capacity. The guns that use it are heavy, but some shooters do their target best with arms of such weight. Recoil, at least, seldom adds to their fatigue in long sessions when they shoot light charges in heavy revolvers.

An All-Round Gun?

Perhaps this depends on where you live and what you do, the details that Alice's White Knight in Wonderland wanted to know about the "aged, aged man, a-sitting on a gate."

A fellow living in wilderness where he might need the ultimate in standard handgun killing power could appreciate it as his one and only pistol. His wife and even his rather young children could fire it two-handed in spite of its weight and kick. He would shoot it in the same fashion, afield, to get the best hitting out of it. Perhaps he would have little use for subloads; but a townie would, and he, too, could be armed in practical fashion with this caliber and no other.

I've always had sympathy with vagrants, being one myself whenever I get the chance to leave houses and roads and smoke-stained skies behind. But some of the tribe aren't too nice. All you need do to discourage such a wanderer, if you live where you can cut loose with artillery, is to fire one shot at a stump, can, rotten tomato or other low-value inanimate target with a big handgun. The blast of a magnum puts the message in big type.

Some Obsolete .44 and .45 Calibers

Although the bigbore handgun probably won't have had its day until ray-guns are catalogued, it has reached the era of specialization. Barely a half-dozen such calibers hang on in common use, and the guns that fire them are large and heavy. Well into the second decade of this century a wider choice had us wishing. There were target and service models, still with us in altered or new forms; *and* there were the bulldogs. These short, light, handy pups slung lead in generous installments. Now the pocket gun is a .38 or thereabout, its usually light bullet speeded by dense and comparatively high-pressure loading of smokeless. In a pinch we might have to shoot straighter, no longer hauling from overcoat or britches pocket the potential deadliness of a bigbore.

None of the cartridges briefly described here are still made by American companies. Most of them use black powder in thin brass cases that stand a few firings but are hard to replace after they have split. A few, like the .45 S.&W. are of great promise because the reloader can cut down current brass, in this instance the .45 Colt. When no way out occurs, there is long and patient search, by advertising in *Shotgun News* or *The American Rifleman* or other gun magazines; or a personal look through gun and hardware stores, the longer established the better; gun repair shops; pawnshops; the marvelous Bannerman's army goods house in New York; and even through the material or memories of shooting friends. Some of the fellows may recall having seen the stuff. The guy was going to break it down for scrap lead for his .38 Special, but he's had the measles and may not have got around to it yet. Pistol and rifle club members gladly help if they can. Sometimes an oldtimer, a non-member who drifts in to see the boys and girls fire and to revive ancient sagas of achievement, can steer you to a forgotten supply depot. There's fun as well as exasperation in these searches.

Many old guns are distinctly worth fooling with. We learn something from every caliber we load and fire. Tools in some obsolete sizes can be had, particularly in the Ideal line, and an amazing variety of molds. Many a genius has made his own tools or adapted others. Molds that drop too heavy a slug have been filed away at the base, shortening the bullet by one groove and one bearing band. Most oversized bullets can be slimmed in a die and still have enough groove depth to carry grease; or you can load a grease wad behind the bullet, separating it from the black powder with a cardboard wad. Don't overlook rifle bullets if the molds can be shortened to give you the weight you want. And don't be suspicious of long-discontinued tools and molds of Ideal, Winchester and Smith & Wesson make.

For loading data and to give an index to wallop, seldom the equal of the standard .44 Special, it seems well to list factory black powder and lead formulas. Also, we should suggest that using smokeless in some of these arms either borders or steps right into serious risk if we insist on having full power ammo. Pure-lead bullets were in general use in the lowest power smallbores like the .32 and .38 Colts and in short bigbores such as the .44 Webley, .44 Bulldog, .45 Webley and .50 U. S. Government Pistol. But later or more powerful sizes like the Smith & Wesson .32s and .38s, Colt .44, .44 Russian, .44-30-220 Merwin & Hulbert, .45 S.&W. and .45 Colt used tempers of one to 20 or one to 40 tin and lead. Of course we should experiment with our own mixtures, keeping them soft if barrel grooves weren't a tight fit for the bullet we had to use.

You could classify bulldog bigbore cartridges as using no more than about 20 grains of black powder. The *.44 Bulldog* for British Webley and our own H.&R. guns took 15 grains of powder and 168 of lead. For guns with cylinders long enough to accept it, there was the *.44 Webley* with either 18 or 19 grains of black and a 200-grain bullet. The *.450-13-226* was a slow, light military cartridge. Various Webleys and others used it, also our Colt New Service double-action and Army and Bisley single-actions. Somewhat similar was the *.45-20-230* Webley, once used a good bit here.

We might handload some or all of these short old cartridges, even to forming the brass we'd use. The .44 Bulldog and Webley measure about .455 inch above the rim, much like the Krag .30-40 rifle cartridge. Converting such heavy rifle brass to handgun use calls for narrowing the wide rim and, for such thin-rimmed cases as these two, for reducing the thickness of the rifle case rim. If we file down the head of the case we make the primer pocket too shallow for safety—primers might protrude and be fired in chambers not under the hammer by the recoil of another round. To deepen the web or bottom of the pocket could make it too frail to stand up. So we would trim off the top of the rim, with a simple file, probably.

The .44 Bulldog case is about .555 inch long, and the Webley .683. I measure cartridges I have, and find in these old sizes, as well as in a few current ones, some variation as to make and lot. These two .44 bullets are of about .432 inch largest diameter, and they're heeled down at the base to enter the thin brass. They could, if we had to, use a straight-sided inside-lubricated bullet. If we do, it should be hollow-based (like modern .32 and .38 Long Colts) to let the powder, which should be black FFG or possibly the faster-burning FFFG, have a chance to upset the undersized lead to fit the rifling grooves.

Heavier .45 Bulldogs, used in service-weight guns as well as in pocket shorties of B.D. type, are the short .450 British and the somewhat longer .45 Webley. For their brass, which goes some .4775 inch at base, we can shorten .45 Colt cases to .694 inch for the .450 and to .830 for the .45 Webley. Colt rims may have to be thinned, but hardly narrowed a bit. These two British loads took outside-lube, heel-type, .457-inch bullets, or at least close to .457, since guns and cartridges in the same caliber do vary.

Two well-known .44 holster gun cartridges were not hard to buy before World War II. For muzzle-loading cap-and-ball revolvers "transformed" (as was commonly done in the old days) to fire metallic cartridges, there was the *.44-23-210 Colt* with a slightly hardened "1-40" tin-and-lead bullet, heel type and about .443 inch diameter. Ideal mold No. 430185 was made to cast it and may still be available. The .44 Colt cases are 1 1/16 inch long and .461 inch diameter just above the rim. So we might try reforming .38-40 or .44-40 brass, or shorten the .006-inch undersized .44 Special cases and use them. It seems that some of the .44 Colt bullets were outside-lubricated; but a Remington specimen shows a neater trick, a grease wad under the dry bullet. With a card wad under the lube, to prevent it from contaminating black powder, this should work OK. Hard, high-melting-point lube like Ipco does not harm loose smokeless powder in a case, so far as I've been able to determine in rifle ammunition.

The *.44 S.&W. American* has an outside-lubricated bullet of about .435-inch maximum diameter, the same as the diameter just above the case rim. Case length is .940 inch. We could try .438-inch .303 Savage rifle brass for our cases, but there would probably be not only rim work but also some reaming out of the case mouth, when shortened, to allow us to seat a .44 bullet. Such reaming is a fairly common necessity when we convert high-power rifle brass to pistol use. It decreases our powder capacity; but we gladly trade that decrease for the longer life of strong, thick case metal, which early handgun cartridges seldom possessed. Once popular, the .44 S.&W. has

been factory-loaded with a round ball set down on a light whiff of black powder.

The *.45 S.&W. Schofield,* once an Army cartridge used also in long-cylindered Colt Single Actions chambered for .45 Colt—and how disgusted those hawg-leg Colts must have been!—is by comparison to the foregoing rounds a cinch to handload. We simply shorten the 1.28-inch Colt cases to not quite 1 1/8 and use .45 Colt cast bullets. An old bullet formula for both S.&W. and Colt .45s was a fairly hard 1-20 ratio of tin and lead. Many factory bullets were hollow-based, but a flat-based cast bullet of a size to fit the gun's own barrel is all we want. We have seen—and probably you have, too—the S.&W. case headstamped ".45 Colt" after "someone had blundered" at the factory.

These fine old S.&W. .45s deserve to be used. Some of us may find that they fit our hand extremely well for a bigbore revolver and are surprisingly easy to shoot. It's doubtful that factories loaded smokeless powder rounds for them, and I don't believe that we should in anything near full-power recipe. Factory black powder loads were .45-30-250.

.45 COLT AUTO

The Colt's magazine almost fills the grip, and the grip generously fills a medium or outsized hand. So the .45 Auto cartridge is a shorty, with small powder space according to sixgun standards. It's efficient with stubby, light bullets that help to hold pressures within the rugged limits of the action. John M. Browning did experiment with a rimless type of .45 (long) Colt cartridge for a semi-automatic pistol design. But military requirements naturally are for compact ammunition and guns that almost any soldier can learn to shoot. How much pistol practice the average recruit gets and how much regard some military minds hold for the combat value of handguns are other matters—matters which need more attention. But you don't need much formal range practice to be able to hit an enemy soldier three feet from your fox-hole. If you hit him about right with a .45 Auto, round-nosed and hard-jacketed though it is, he's likely to subside.

The 1911 gun and its cartridge have a 1640-yard reach with a muzzle elevation of 30°, it's been said. They should pinpoint a small village at that distance, if the sights could be correctly aligned on it. The big bullet should make a distinct and perhaps terrifying thud when it landed! Obviously the .45 combination of gun and load are not a substitute for artillery; they are for close, fast fighting. Sometimes a good dishout of penetration can help—and they have it in fair-enough degree. The .45 in good hands and even in just fairly able hands has proved so deadly that it has been terrifying, and nothing less, to enemy soldiers. Up close, in battle or in unpeaceful civil events, its big muzzle is a frightening thing to look into.

Perhaps our .45 Auto Colt is the best middle-of-the-road service pistol cartridge for war or navy departments that still have the good sense to favor a

.45 COLT AUTOMATIC—WESTERN SUPER-MATCH WITH JACKETED BULLET

Bullet in grs.	F. S. vel. at muzzle	At 50 yds.	At 100 yds.	F. P. energy at muzzle	At 50 yds.	At 100 yds.	M. R. Traj. at 50 yds.	At 100 yds.	Barrel Length
230	740	710	680	280	258	236	2.1"	8.7"	5"

Penetration ⅞-inch soft pine boards at 15 ft.-5. There are also Remington and Western 185-grain, semi-wadcutter, jacketed loads giving 775 f.s. speed and 247 f.p. energy.

.45 COLT AUTOMATIC—WESTERN METAL-PIERCING SUPER-X

Bullet in grs.	F. S. vel. at muzzle	At 50 yds.	At 100 yds.	F. P. energy at muzzle	At 50 yds.	At 100 yds.	M. R. Traj. at 50 yds.	At 100 yds.	Barrel Length
230, semi pointed	945	890	835	456	404	356	1.3"	5.4"	5"

Penetration ⅞-inch soft pine boards at 15 ft.—11

NOTE: Remington Metal-Penetrating Hi-Way Master sends a 173-grain, special composition (mainly zinc-) bullet at 1140 f. s. velocity for 500 foot pounds of energy, the usual 5-inch auto-pistol barrel being used in the tests.

.45 COLT AUTOMATIC—STANDARD CARTRIDGE

Bullet in grs.	F. S. vel. at muzzle	At 50 yds.	At 100 yds.	F. P. energy at muzzle	At 50 yds.	At 100 yds.	M. R. Traj. at 50 yds.	At 100 yds.	Barrel Length
230	850	810	775	369	335	307	1.6"	6.5"	5"

Penetration ⅞-inch soft pine boards at 15 ft.—6

.45 COLT AUTOMATIC—WESTERN SUPER-MATCH SEMI-WADCUTTER

Bullet in grs.	F. S. vel. at muzzle	At 50 yds.	At 100 yds.	F. P. energy at muzzle	At 50 yds.	At 100 yds.	M. R. Traj. at 50 yds.	At 100 yds.	Barrel Length
210 lead	710	650	595	235	197	165	2.3"	11.5"	5"

Penetration not important and not listed.

bigbore that will stop a man right there, and without ten-ring accuracy of delivery. It was a long time in the making and it's almost the only one left in circulation. *American Rifleman* "Dope Bag" columns have told us of others. The Mars .45s, both short and long, were extremely powerful, blunt-nosed brutes, and the Roth .45 was no midget. There was a Bergmann .43, and an experimental *.41* Colt tried to make a compromise between the rejected .38 and the desirable .45, along about 1903. Who shoots them now?

In our Government's experiments, Frankford Arsenal made up a rather long-cased .45 carrying a 230-grain bullet. But it seems that the first commercial .45 Auto, for the 1905 Colt which was sold for some few years from 1906 on, took a shorter case holding a 200-grain bullet. This had a much more tapered nose than the almost semi-circular snoot of the Frankford 230-grain.

The modern 230-grain cartridge, which we call the Model 1911, began with a Union Metallic Cartridge Company issue in 1907. I think that this round, or one like it, was in the hard grasp of the eagle that drew attention to the first advertisement of the 1911 pistol in commercial form. Some of you should remember the right of it; I'm just guessing. It was advanced in having a gilding metal jacket washed with tin—the old white bullets were common until the middle 1920s—instead of the cupro-nickel jacket that Frankford used in .30 caliber rifle ammo. Some makers called this 230-grain the "Government Model" to distinguish it from the 200-grain, which hung on for years and is the correct formula for such smooth-lined 1905 pistols are still used. Velocity of the 200-grain

was about 900 f.s. Plenty of us 1911 Colt shooters liked it for its zip, when we could get it. Sometimes that light bullet was given more bore-bearing surface by a deep hollow base. So were some of the squatty but darned efficient 200-grain bullets for the .401 Winchester auto-rifle for use in the woods. It's a common method, after all, to use in lengthening a bullet.

Handloads and D.C.M. Ammunition

The semi-wadcutter shape of bullet, with a flat, clean-cutting shelf well below its flat point, had been cast and used by target shooters long before the Remington jacketed and Western lead semis were marketed. Weight reduction means lighter recoil, which helps so much in timed and rapid fire events. Some customized .45 auto-pistols have been geared especially to lighter-than-standard ammunition. Probably most target shots use their own cast-lead bullets, except in matches that allow only full-power, service-type stuff. A hard one-to-ten alloy of tin and lead usually takes narrow rifling grooves well and does its part toward achieving accuracy, as well as contributing to long barrel life.

Many civilian forty-fivers at some time or other clasp to their hearts big or little booty in the form of Government ammunition. As National Rifle Association members we are entitled to buy it from the Army's Director of Civilian Marksmanship. I have never known the D.C.M. to ship out poor stuff in any type or caliber, and usually it's extra good. At this writing the available .45 Auto fodder includes loaded rounds, 234-grain jacketed bullets, and primers, all of them at prices well under retail. The D.C.M.'s aim is to encourage marksmanship; and he knows that some of us handload. In 1961 the D.C.M. announced that bullet and primer sales would be discontinued after all stocks had been sold.

For some years, Government ammo has been non-corrosive, but old stocks of the chlorate-primed stuff remain. That means little to a careful shooter, who is aware of the tenacious copper deposit left in his .45 barrel by most jacketed bullets. He'll clean that bore, anyway. Corrosive ammo only makes it more essential that he doesn't let the sun go down on the wrathy mess it leaves.

Until recent years, Government .45s used primers smaller than our "large pistol," .204-inch instead of .210-inch. The cases have been so good that handloaders often reamed out the sub-size pockets to .210. Some World War II rounds had steel bullet jackets, copper washed, which at least theoretically increase barrel wear, or steel cases that seldom delight a handloader. A magnet is useful! But almost all .45 Auto cases are strong and long-lasting, and with solid heads, as a matter of course. Frankford Arsenal and commercial loading companies have proved that this caliber of handgun ammunition can be made to shoot about as accurately as any other, but all good ammo needs a good gun to team up with it. A loosely fitted autoloader isn't for target victories, but it can function under conditions of mud and dust that would put a superbly fitted pistol out of action, or at least make it unreliable. A military handgun must function surely, and the big Colt has a reputation for doing so.

Primers now sold are non-mercuric and non-corrosive. It was not so when the first non-corrosives appeared, nor was it generally known that mercuric residue makes brass brittle—except when the fouling of black powder blocks it off from the brass. Well do I remember one of my handloads with this priming of the middle 1920s. A hunk of brass just above the extracting cannelure broke out, there was a peculiar report, the magazine, blown into uselessness, clattered on the dry stones of the river bed, and blood ran freely from a gash over my shooting eye. The rest of those loads, their Frankford Arsenal jacketed bullets seated with normal—and considerable—tightness, later swirled down into the unplumbed center of Plymouth Pond.

But all sorts of .45 loads, including light target rounds with cast-lead bullets, are easy to assemble. They are perfect for short-range practice and it's surprising what short rations of powder with full-weight bullets will operate the semi-automatic action. Whisper loads in any gun with jacketed bullets are hardly practical, though I've had pretty decent 50-foot accuracy with them in a .220 Swift rifle more to prove that it could be done than for any sensible reason! Make any such loads low enough and the bullet decides to sleep in—right there in the bore. Lead bullets can be very easy to drive out with a cleaning rod, but jacketed ones could be terrible! So far—and I trust from now on out—I've had only one stick, and that responded readily, being about .0015 inch undersize.

Rimless .45 cases do need attention, more than many others. The cartridge gets its headspace on the thick, *uncrimped* mouth of its case, which abuts on the head of the chamber. So to get even and safe results, the cases need to be uniform in length. Nearly all of them are finely made, but it pays to gauge them, for sizing and neck-expanding a case can lengthen it.

Summary

The .45 is powerful, satisfactory in standard-velocity loading for a variety of tommy-guns. All sorts of big game have been killed with it, fired from handguns, all over the world. Penetration is quite good, and the shocking power of the big, slow bullet is formidable. Handloads with cast bullets of standard weight and bore-bearing surface (which also affects pressure) can take on increased velocity if that is wanted, with Hercules Unique powder, good in the short case. A fairly soft lead bullet is a trifle more deadly and less subject to glancing off the line of fire than a full jacketed one. Blunter bullet points can increase killing power, at some expense of penetration.

It seems that the .45 Auto never has been furnished with soft-point jacketed bullets. It's a military caliber, and expanding bullets are ruled out for war; but practically all other auto-pistol sizes have been made commercially with soft-point bullets. Standard .45 Auto velocity is low, well under the rates of the little .32 and .380. We know that those two, and the .25, amounted to near-zero as expanders with the soft points that once were furnished and easy to get. With an extremely thin jacket, and with the really long lead exposure up front which hardly any pistol bullets except some runs of .38 Colt and .30 Luger and Mauser ever had, the .45 might become a better game cartridge. Frank A. Hemstead, Box 171, Culver City, California, did make .38 Special and .45 Auto bullets with long-exposed soft points, and perhaps still does. But velocity under 900 f.s. isn't a promising characteristic, though such bullets would be more effective than full metal cased ones.

"You can get .45 Auto ammunition almost anywhere." It's like the .30-06 rifle round in that respect. Both are likely to hang around for a long time ahead, even if they become completely demilitarized. And a pistol cartridge with about half of its bulk in bullet is nothing if not compact in pocket or pack-sack.

The report and recoil have an undeservedly bad reputation because so many of us begin our bigbore shooting with .45 Auto ammunition. Compared to more powerful factory and handloaded calibers, the report is neither sharp nor great in its volume. Recoil is not severe, either—the bullet is so light for its diameter—but in the semi-automatic pistol it can get your hand to shaking after as few as ten full-charged rounds have been eased off at target. In field use, when few shots are fired at a time, the comeback is almost mild, considering what comes out at the muzzle end. It's the repeated slam-back of the action that the untrained hand objects to. Lighter loads reduce this reaction considerably. Except in matches in which the service ammunition is required, you find competitive shooters favoring mild loadings, pretty generally, up to a full 50 yards.

Alone with the .38 Special, the .45 Automatic comes in factory production—which just about has to pay its way—in three general loadings. There are the standard cartridge, the light-bullet target round, and the heavy metal-piercer for police use, especially designed to drill through car metal. There are more varieties in .38, but any strictly handgun cartridge that's supplied in two or more commercial varieties is a winner in popularity contests. Both of these much-used calibers have been turned out in special military loadings, such as the tracer .45 and the full metal patched .38. The former type, especially, is hard on a handgun's barrel. Both of them are special-purpose jobs that the average civilian wouldn't be likely to choose for any purpose. No matter: enough bushels of standard ammo are bought right along to keep both rounds on the loading lists! It seems that no other handgun calibers except the .22 rimfires have so long a life expectancy.

And let's remember that the .45 is, even yet, our Service cartridge. In case of national emergency—which could mean all-out war—it should be available to the right kind of Americans. Some acquaintance with it and with the guns that fire it effectively, would be just that much more contribution to a thing that we now accept perhaps too easily and unthinkingly. It's freedom.

.45 AUTO-RIM

Bullet in grs.	F. S. vel. at muzzle	F. P. energy at muzzle	Barrel length
230	805	331	5½″
Penetration ⅞-inch soft pine boards at 15 ft.—6			

This excellent cartridge for Government 1917 Model Colts and Smith & Wessons, and for the 1950 Model S.&W., was made commercially as early as in 1931, perhaps earlier. For a long while both lead and full metal patched bullets were supplied in 230-grain weights. There was also a rather fascinating Peters load with 250-grain, flat-nosed lead bullet, practically a .45 Colt Peacemaker slug and almost as effective, because the velocity was not much under that of some smokeless Colt rounds made then. Being a heavy-bullet round, it shot high at close ranges; but how much would this matter in the average gun-fight? However, it passed out after some years; and soon after the end of World War II, the full-jacketed 230-grain went, too. Most shooters prefer to use lead bullets in their revolvers, though they may find that a harder alloy than the factory reduces fouling and gives better results, except, perhaps, in killing power. Of course

the Auto-rim bullet is round-nosed and pretty slow, but a hand-cast, flat-pointed bullet in the same brass can be made very deadly indeed.

Auto-rim cartridges are not for military use. First, they're loaded with lead bullets which, even in pistols, are now ag'in' the rules—rules which are odd and grim and not to be understood by a logical mind, are they? Then too, if you use Auto-rims, you throw away the advantage, after the gun is empty, of reloading with rimless .45 Auto rounds in three-shot clips. With these half-moon—or is it last quarter?—clips, two drops fill the cylinder. Some of us learn to be handy, quick, and *almost* unhurriedly sure in dropping two or even three separate cartridges into place, provided we don't use full-faced wadcutters. But it takes a lot of practice; and when our hands are cold it's never easy.

Clips are made of stamped steel and sold by Smith & Wesson and who knows how many gun supply houses. They are strong and reasonably uniform in thickness. However, the rims or extracting flanges of Auto-rim cases are more even; so we get more exact headspacing with these rounds than with the rimless cartridges held in clips. Better, more uniform ignition is likely to result; and for precision shooting this pays off.

Rimless ammo without clips can be used, and very commonly is, in revolvers chambered for it and for the Auto-rim, except for early Colt 1917 issues that have chambers bored straight through the cylinder, with no stepdown for the bullet seat. Those arms, now scarce, require clips or Auto-rim cases. The other 1917 guns, and the S.&W. 1950 Army, are so chambered that the end of the chamber stops the thick, uncrimped .45 Auto brass from entering too far, thus getting their headspace as similar cartridges do in autoloaders, the various .380s, and arms for the 9 mm. Luger, being examples.

To extract unclipped rimless brass from a 1917-type revolver, you simply pry it out with a finger-nail, and usually this is no trouble unless the cases have been swelled by previous firing, and not resized. If the hulls stick, a pencil or even a fair-sized stick should eject them.

Of course the Auto-rim is not for the autoloading pistol. The extractor would righteously object to riding over that big, thick rim with no restful reward of settling into a deep cannelure beyond the rim. The rim has to be abnormally thick, for it replaces the rather thin rim of the .45 Auto case, and adds the thickness of the clip. So the result is a sturdy-looking case that stands up well to many reloadings. Since it headspaces on its rim, not on its mouth, the matter of case length isn't nearly as vital as it is with the .45 Auto.

Those who want a little extra power can get it by handloading with Hercules Unique powder, commonsense, and a set of scales for weighing each charge. Cylinder walls are thinner and less strong, than those of the .44 Special and .44 Magnum.

The factory load sends its 230-grain lead bullet at

.45 COLT

Bullet in grs.	F. S. vel. at muzzle	At 50 yds.	At 100 yds.	F. P. energy at muzzle	At 50 yds.	At 100 yds.	M. R. Traj. at 50 yds.	At 100 yds.	Barrel Length
255	855	815	775	405	368	333	1.6"	6.6"	5½"

Penetration ⅞-inch soft pine boards at 15 ft.—6

Note: The same muzzle velocity and energy figures are given for the Remington .45 Colt cartridge with 250-grain bullet, fired from a 5½-inch barreled revolver.

805 f.s. velocity, though a few feet more used to be catalogued. The present 45 f.s. differential between this cartridge and the .45 Automatic (in auto-pistols) should be noted and then forgotten. Different lots of the same cartridge could show nearly, if not quite, as big a difference. And a good 1917 or 1950 barrel will outshoot a worn, pitted 1911 tube.

In some arms and in some calibers the difference in velocities between revolvers and semi-automatic pistols is at times quite considerable. Usually it's not great in handguns of such quality as most of these .45s have. To the revolver's barrel length, we add the length of the cylinder—and subtract plenty of velocity if the gap between them is wide! It usually isn't, in these weapons. Owners of early '17 Colts with no step-down to the chambers might do well to buy a new cylinder. This would eliminate most of the gas-cutting past the bullet, and the consequent loss of power and accuracy.

Converted .45 Sixguns

Before leaving this .45 Auto-rim discussion we should look at some of the conversions that have been inflicted on good military revolvers. Yes, it's true that conversion can bring gains in convenience or in power.

Reaming out 1917 chambers to take the long .45 Colt cartridge is, or at least used to be, common. It's difficult to do exactly right, for the long case depends for headspace on its rim. This is lost in the shuffle when one of these cylinders, located so far from the breech-face to take the clip plus rim of .45 Auto brass, is reamed out. The crimped mouth of the Peacemaker case tries to abut on the stop of a lengthened chamber with the sureness of the thick, uncrimped mouth of the Auto cartridge in its original chamber. It sometimes has a hard time in trying to oblige. Endplay, or excess headspace, increases the cartridge's backthrust, which might be heavy, anyway, in some handloads. If it's grossly excessive we may hear the mocking click of a misfire. We are almost certain-sure not to get good even ignition, anyway.

A better way is to send the gun to the factory for a .45 Colt caliber cylinder. On both Colt and Smith left-hand side-plates, there is a little, precisely made projection to contact the rear of the cylinder and limit its rearward travel. This must be correctly located for the length of the cylinder involved. When our conversion is made, we still have the problem of sighting. Full-weight .45 Colt bullets, 250 or 255 grains, are going to shoot higher than 230-grain stuff except at some point well out. Beyond that they are likely to print lower. Handloading with lighter bullets can

correct that, if our particular practical use of the gun demands it. It might not so demand.

Some pretty nice British guns, and some American ones, too, have been altered from the rimmed .455 British to .45 Auto rimless by grinding away enough of the cylinder breech to accommodate clipped .45s. To some of us, this is sad. We can make .455 brass for handloading by shortening the easy-to-get .45 Colt Peacemaker, the long Colt, as explained in the .455 section ahead. Thus, we can avoid using the too-light, undersized .45 Auto jacketed bullet, which just doesn't set up to seal a good-sized .455 bore. By careful handloading we could make these Webleys, in good condition, shoot very well. Yes, we could use .45 Auto Colt brass for our handloading, expanding it if needed to take full-sized lead bullets. But with our thinner adapted brass we should have more powder space and still enough strength in the crimping to hold bullets in place. Of course we couldn't profitably use the adapted .45 Colt Peacemaker brass if someone had already cut off the rear of the original .455 cylinder. We should have to use the crimped case-mouth for headspacing; and that would be too bad. Unless the grinder had borne down too enthusiastically on his work, the headspace of the altered .455 British gun should be OK for .45 Auto-rim cases.

Stores and trading posts almost all over the world, from big-city shops to the most remote and colorful emporiums, carry the 1873 Colt .45 in stock for folks who may use a handgun as an almost daily tool. These people want power, and no fooling with molds and dies and levers. For more years than most shooters can remember they have been buying it in those

The 1877 Army and Frontier Model was Colt's first double-action revolver for the already popular .45 Colt cartridge. It has the "bird's-head" type of grip. Turn the picture upside down and with some luck and sympathy you may see the resemblance. Photo courtesy Colt's Patent Fire Arms.

heavy, oblong packages. Or mebbe just a gunful at a time, and thankful to get that. Of course there are deadlier modern factory and handloaded rounds, but the storied Colt. 45 has as much in it as is usually needed.

Historians debate the question as to whether the ammo stuffed into the first Single Action Army guns was .44-40 Winchester or .45 Colt. No matter: both have *made* history. From the early 1870's until shortly before the 1898 Spanish-American War, the .45 Colt —with some interludes of the shorter, less powerful .45 S.&W. round—was the service sidearm caliber. The old gun rode ten thousands of miles over the endless plains alongside the cavalryman's yellow trousers-piping; and in thousands of desperate fights it spoke its verdict of finality. Against man or beast, civilians trusted their lives to its smashing, penetrating power. When the .38 Long failed in the Philippine Campaign, the old .45 was called in from the bench. Though in altered form—some military bullets were full-jacketed at about this time, as I remember—it did what the .38 just couldn't do.

Since the .45 was a Government cartridge, much experimental work was done on it. It seems that the factories never produced full-jacketed bullets for it, though Remington loaded some hard metal tipped (250 grain) slugs over smokeless powder in this pistol caliber, as in so many others. Gallery loads usually were for the handloader, who could and can choose from many molds; but somewhat reduced black powder charges of 28 and 35 grains behind standard bullets came from the factories. Their heaviest loads were the 38-grain dose with 255-grain bullet, and the 40-250 combination, long regarded as the top cream. Western Cartridge was the first, or near it, to produce smokeless powder rounds with similar velocity packed into them.

Collectors value old Frankford Arsenal rounds like the copper-case cartridge resembling a rimfire, but with inside primer set in a battery cup held in place by grooves in the side wall of the thin shell. Similar ammunition once came in .45-70, .50-70, and .58 Musket and Carbine sizes.

Only a few years ago, factory ballistic sheets credited the 250- and 255-grain bullets, over smokeless powder, with 870 f.s. velocity from 5½-inch guns, a trifling 25 f.s. over today's ratings. Reliable lists show more potent handloads, for use *only* in modern heat-treated cylinders. With cylinder walls so thin compared to those of .44 Special guns of the same make and model, we must be extra careful to use for such loads only bullets that have been sized to fit the individual barrel. Cylinder throats ahead of the chambers must not be oversized, compared to barrel dimensions, for they allow soft lead and some not so soft to expand under the powder blow. Rifling is not the correct die to use for bullet sizing when velocities are near the top! A great many good guns that have seen a lot of service have been fitted with new cylinders and/or barrels;

and the two may not be matched as they should be. For an extra heavy bullet with unusually wide flat point, Elmer Keith experimented with 300-grain .45-90 Winchester rifle slugs sized down from about .457- to .454-inch diameter. This left enough grooving in the lead to carry lubricant. He backed these bullets with black powder. As usual with revolver cartridges for heavy duty that includes a good bit of penetration, the shape and weight of the bullet make for killing power rather than the mere velocity. All this is within sensible limits, naturally. For expansion at some cost of penetration, there's the hollow-pointing of bullets. Velocities of .45 Colt handloads can approach and sometimes equal those of home-rolled .44 Specials. The greater powder space of the .45 is on our side, if we attempt this. Against us are the thinner cylinder walls and the greater likelihood that the Special will be a newer gun, though of course there are strong, modern .45s, too.

The targeteer can prepare light stuff, even round-ball cellar loads. Many .45 Colt target guns have been made with competent adjustable sights, in spite of a mistaken under-rating of the cartridge's accuracy. Bisley and Army single-actions as well as New Service and Shooting Master double-actions have worn factory or custom adjustable sights; and there have been old and modern Smith & Wessons, too. It can't in the least detract from what many come right out and call the "glory" of the old .45, to state impartially that most shooters who itch to develop the heaviest (sometimes the goofiest) handloads, or those most accurate on the range, choose the .44 Special—or did, before the .44 Mag. appeared. The thicker steel of .44 Special chambers, compared to the .45's, has tempted a number of us to load to destruction. Some folks learned from these mishaps, and what's more, publicized them for the benefit of other shooters. Some kept still. Progress seldom is smooth sailing under a friendly sky. Was the sea charted without even the grinding of a keel?

Modern Appraisal

For the moment let's consider the .45 Colt without regard to its history or its handloading possibilities, simply as a factory-issued cartridge. It is well distributed, and in some backwoods stores, almost or completely within hollering distance of game trails, it may be easier to find than some much more modern rounds.

Many old and recent guns are available for it, and at least two standard, not special-order, jobs are made right now, the Colt and Great Western single-actions. Are revolvers in this caliber a perfectly sensible, not romantic or screen-inspired choice?

It's a big cartridge, rougher to master than the .44-40, .44 Special or .45 Auto, but very much less rough than the .44 Magnum. It has two sorts of killing power, penetration and smash, neither in super quality, but good. With that small flat, sometimes almost non-existent, on its bullet point, it penetrates pretty deeply;

but it doesn't swamp out a full-caliber hole as blunter pistol bullets can do. It has always been an efficient sort of compromise, though some wouldn't call it a compromise at all. They would say it was all you would ever be likely to need.

We know from its military and civilian record that few men hit solidly with it went on fighting, though of course there are much surer and deadlier loads than this factory job. We also know that it has done well in the wilderness, being very authoritative, for a pistol round, on big game. Out there, the .45 and the .44-40 were the big favorites. Mid-twentieth century men average bigger than those of the late nineteenth, but have wilderness animals changed much?

For anyone needing a large-caliber handgun, made today and easily available, the .45 Colt size fits in nicely between the .44 Special and .45 Auto, and the .44 Magnum, which is decidedly more a specialist's chambering. What about the .357 Magnum with its high velocity and energy? You don't have to be a smallbore crank to choose that excellent cartridge. I shan't say that it would help to be, for that I don't believe. But it does seem to me that the heavy bullet of the .45 is a positive factor, and that handgun velocity is not even yet in such a bracket, though sometimes it comes near it. A shooter sensitive to muzzle blast will do better with the .45 than with the .357.

I confess that I've got myself between a rock and a hard place: the decision between the two is difficult. For a back-packing trip of considerable duration I would take the .357 for its much lighter ammunition. Water-borne, in a canoe, the .45 would be likely to go aboard. At this particular landing place, I'm convinced that the .45 remains a good and not "dated" choice in factory ammunition, and in handloads, too.

THREE .455s

This was a standard British caliber and at least three types have been made and widely used, though but little in this country. Unlike a trio of John Bull's sporting rifle children, the .275, .300 and .375 Holland & Holland Magnums, they offer us no special advantages. They are good military cartridges, well proved. The two revolver rounds are so short that cylinder lengths can be moderate and increase the guns' compactness. Most American shooters favor longer cartridge cases for greater powder capacity and higher velocity. So far, the compactness of a short-cylindered revolver doesn't mean much to us. For example, most of our .22 revolvers' cylinders are long enough to accept .32 S.&W. Longs; and some, though they are on small guns, would take the .22 Rimfire Magnum.

The *.455 Canadian, Long, or Colt* has about a .91-inch case (which we could make from .45 Colt brass by shortening it and by thinning its rim if that proved necessary). It was manufactured here by Winchester from the early 1900s until the 1930s. Seventeen grains

of black powder gave a leisurely amble to the 265-grain lead bullet with very deep hollow base. The point was rounded much in .44 S.&W. Russian or .44 Special fashion. Later, smokeless powder went in, and finally there was a smokeless, non-corrosive loading. The streamlined bullet contour produced good target results. Although by modern standards it was not shaped for killing, the Canadian Mounted Police and others who used it, instead of the also well-distributed .45 Colt, probably didn't go hungry in good game country because it was too feeble to knock down deer and even larger animals. Bullet weight itself gave considerable power, though penetration wasn't its long suit. The Dominion Cartridge Company, Canadian Industries, Limited, Box 10, Montreal, Quebec, loads the 265-grain bullet to 770 f.s. velocity, and real power, more than its 349 foot pounds sound like.

Compared to the .45 Auto or Auto-rim, the old Winchy loads were inexpensive, especially in black powder. Some of us found that they fitted S.&W. 1917 45, head-spacing on the bullet ogive. The big bullets flew mighty high at short ranges, but it was a jolt of delight to see them smack a soft or breakable target. This glorified plinking was worth the price of a boxful or two. Those who owned .455 revolvers could get American-made tools and molds, and the thin cases stood up for a few firings. The adapted .45 Colt brass should do better, at least in the latest solid-head type.

The shorter *.455 Webley Mark II* was used by the British in World War I, extensively, and to a considerable extent in World War II. It has about a .76-inch case, similar in other dimensions to .455 Long brass, and like it, very thin by our standards. It was made commercially here until about 1940. Apparently it was never loaded with black powder. The smokeless charge is dense, giving about 600 f.s. speed to the 265-grain lead bullet when fired from a 6- or 6½-inch barreled revolver, for an energy of some 220 foot pounds. Some loadings were more powerful, and for many years Remington used a 275-grain lead bullet.

Webley, Colt, Smith & Wesson and other revolvers handled the Mark II, and so did that almost unique six-shooter, the Webley-Fosbery *automatic revolver,* an arm that usually exists only in unlettered minds! This ingenious weapon was less reliable in warfare than the standard double-action. On firing, the barrel, cylinder, and top part of the frame recoiled backward, cocking the hammer and ratcheting the cylinder around for the next shot. The gun worked pretty well when it was clean and when the shooter gripped it tightly. Some thought that this acrobatic recoil was less disturbing than the slam of the .45 Colt automatic with its much lighter bullet. Some thought it was terrible. A few of these Fosberys were made in .38 Auto Colt caliber. They should have been much nicer to shoot, though far less deadly except when deep penetration helped.

The Mark II lead bullet was peculiar, but ingenious, even demoniac, in its deadliness. Its point was long and tapered; and its base less deeply hollowed than that of the .455 Long, at least in some production. Anyway, when the point, almost sharp and well ahead of the center of gravity, struck flesh there was a tendency for the bullet to go giddy and turn sidewise. The same "barbarous" action showed in .303 British Mark VII rifle bullets. They were full jacketed for war use, with a clay, wooden, fiber, or aluminum plug in the tip of the sharp nose, the rear part of the jacket being filled with the usual lead. It was a long bullet, replacing the long, heavy, round-nosed 215-grain Mark VI. The Mark VI was stable under almost any condition, being rather blunt up front and having its center of gravity where we'd expect it to be.

Humanitarians condemned the tippy bullets. Those who knew war were not surprised or perhaps even shocked. Soon after the Spanish-American conflict, we too had come up against savage men, fighting for their Philippine homeland. Our men *then* had a doubly distasteful job of the sort which had been in the British line of duty for generations. "To be shot with explosive bullets, or wretchedly starve and die" is a line I recall from childhood days, printed before the British had been our very *active* allies. You can tell the Anglophobes that it makes a mighty difference, whose ox is being gored.

The Mark VI full-jacketed .455, interchangeable with the Mark II, was legal ammunition in World War II, because the bullet wasn't made of lead. It seems to have been made in 255- and 265-grain weights, full-jacketed.

Many .455 revolvers take either the long Canadian or the short Mark II and Mark IV cartridges, though the Webley-Fosbery was short-cylindered for the latter types. Just lately, numbers of Webley .455 revolvers have been imported, and most of them seem to have had their rear cylinder faces ground off to accept the .45 Auto rounds in three-shot clips. Rifling groove diameter for .455s has been stated as .454 inch, but some British barrels are larger. In wartime production, especially, we aren't surprised to find considerable latitude. Boring and rifling tools start big and wear down, as always, and under the stress of "emergency" manufacture, replacements may be slow to come by. The .45 Auto Colt jacketed bullet can run as small as .451 or .452 inch. One picked up at the range and handed to me showed practically no rifling cuts at all on one side. It had come from a .455 Webley in good condition. This gun has its drawbacks, as all do; but it deserves fitted bullets. The Webley's grip is narrow, less comfortable than the wide S.&W. Magnum type of handle, but at least it is stuck on well. It comes low enough so that no filler or adapter is needed in the top of that space between trigger guard and grip.

The *.455 Webley Automatic* cartridge, apparently never made commercially here, was officially beyond reproach as a service round. It fires a 220-grain full-jacketed bullet at 750 f.s. muzzle velocity, with energy of 270 foot pounds.

But that hard bullet has a bluntly rounded nose, almost a "man-stopper" in design, as some of the earliest, experimental .45 Auto Colts had. During World War I the Royal Navy used this gun to some extent. It's so square-built and ugly that it looks a bit like something whittled lazily out of a two-by-four. Actually, it is nearly as pleasing to handle and shoot as our Model 1911 Colt, except for the lack of muzzle weight. It hasn't the long, barrel-enclosing slide of Browning type.

Few of these pistols ever got here, and ammunition for them would be scarce and costly, if it could be had at all. A handloader might be able to adapt .45 Auto brass; and then sensible powder charges behind a medium weight cast bullet, not too soft, ought to give him fine shooting. The gun is a good one. A number of our Colt 1911 models were made in its .455 caliber for wartime use.

There are several Ideal mold designs for .455 revolver cartridges, such as the 190-grain 456401 semiwadcutter and the long-established 295-grain 457196, with deep, wide hollow base. But I doubt that half a dozen people, if that many, have reloaded the .455 Auto round in this country. Ideal 457127, formerly listed as 210-grain but now as 195, has much of the rounded front profile of the Webley automatic's service bullet. Both weights are below the 220 grains of the British jacketed bullet, and the flat recoil spring of the Webley is less amenable to lightening than a coiled spring, of course. The old .45 Colt Auto bullet, Ideal 452374 225 or 230 grain, and the new gas-checked 452484 220 grain have more tapered bullet ogives than the British service issue. They are longer bullets that would reduce powder space. The five or ten grains extra weight of the former should be allowed for, too, in loading, even though lead bullets produce lower pressures than hard jacketed ones, other things being equal. First we should have to measure the rifling groove diameter; and if it were down near .450 inch, which seems unlikely, we should select a bullet that could be sized down without losing enough depth of cannelures or grooves to carry a good amount of lubricant. It's difficult, too, to size a bullet down a whole lot and still keep it evenly squinched slimmer all around its diameter.

REALLY BIG BORES

But not boresome to contemplate! On the contrary, there is no end of fun, for a guncrank, in monkeying with any of them. They have power, too.

The *.476 Eley* was a medium-length black powder cartridge that offered more life-insuring power than .450 and .455 British rounds, because its 270-grain lead bullet was blunt and big, and some 20 grains of black powder booted it out fast enough to do what it had to do in close in-fighting. The case was of the thin folded-head design, about .475-inch in outside diameter, like its heel bullet. If we could get the gun, and the mold, we might be able to work down .45-70 brass to fit the chambers. But .38-56 Winchester rifle cases (not the straight-cased .38-55s, but bottle-necked) would make the job easier; and perhaps the thick .33 Winchester hulls would, too. Both .38-56 and .33 are obsolete, but not yet hopelessly scarce.

The .476 cartridge resembles a .41 Long Colt, magnified a good bit. So we know that it would be quite an awesome creature in spite of low velocity. Colt single- and double-action revolvers chambered it. They could be had until the first decade of this century. American catalogues listed them, although the sales must have been small.

At least some .476 bullets had an expansion plug in the hollow base to make the lead fill rifling grooves promptly. This had been done in the Minie ball, and some other muzzle-loaded bullets used the system. A bullet could be small enough to ram down a somewhat fouled barrel, yet when it was fired it took the slow spin of the rifling. Later it was found that a plug was unnecessary.

Single-shot Remington handguns for the *.50 Government Pistol* cartridges were Navy and (to some extent) Army sidearms in years immediately following the Civil War. There is good comment on their ammunition in James Grant's book, *Single-Shot Rifles,* and in some old catalogues. The first round seems to have been a rimfire, as we should expect, the .50-23-290 with 55/64-inch case length. In center-fire the standard case length was ⅞-inch, the load being 25 grains of black powder and a soft lead 300-grain bullet with a narrow flat on its point. U.M.C. used a 20-grain charge of black, at least for a while. Such formulas are a far cry from those of today's .220 Swift rifle cartridge, in which some recommended feedings of high-pressure smokeless are more than 91 per cent of the bullet's weight. And super-.220's take even more!

Cases were straight, or just mildly tapered, except for that of the .50 Army, which was slightly bottle-necked. The specimen Grant shows has a blunt rounded point instead of the usual slow or sharp taper to a small flat. It seems that bullets were inside-lubricated, as a general thing. I don't know about the earliest issues. If they were, the 1870 .44 S.&W. Russian would lose its place as our first American handgun cartridge with this style of lubrication. "Firsts" are hard to track down in gun and ammunition history, and in quite a few other achievement records, too! At any rate, we can be thankful for what we have today, the really good developments, that is, and for what is presumably in the works.

There's a great deal of fun in working with old calibers; and the .50 deserves a trial if we can get one before it has been converted, by rebarreling or by barrel lining, to some small-bore modern size. Few .50 pistols are extant, and the cartridge itself is rare enough to draw a yelp of joy from a collector—or a grim and covetous silence, beetle-browed. Because of the good gun weight, reasonably strong action (though it's for black powder), and nice fit of the grip, many .50s have become .22 Long-Rifle, .32 S.&W. Long, .38 S.&W., .38 Special or .44 Russian in caliber. Long ago, Remington made a target model in .44 Russian. There were plenty of slow-fire shooters.

Adapted brass might be the easily available .348 Winchester, a heavy, body-tapered, bottle-necked case derived from the old, thin-walled .50-110-300 and .50-100-450 Win. sizes. The latter are hard to find in quantity. Lyman .50 caliber molds drop bullets of widely varying weights and diameters, but some too-large bullets can be sized down considerably. My father's .50-95 Winchester-made mold cast a three-groove bullet of about .512-inch diameter, and when the hollow-pointing plug was not in place the weight went to about the standard solid-bullet heft of 312 grains. It had fairly deep, rounded grooves for lubricant.

An idle and perhaps silly thought is: how would the .50 Pistol stack up against the .44 Magnum in stopping power, with little penetration needed? A 300-grain bullet is heavy, and half-inch caliber is big. The .44 has velocity that, after some penetration, expands its 240-grain, wide-fronted, soft-lead bullet to much more than .50 caliber—to say nothing of some hand-cast designs. The old .50 bullet is too slow and a little too pointy to flatten much, if any. The .44 has deep penetration; but then, except on pretty fair-sized animals, both calibers would have that to contribute. Also the .50 is a single-shot, though possibly some double- or multi-barrel guns came in this size. If the .50 fitted your hand the better, and thus permitted you to get the important first shot off sooner and straighter, it certainly would have some edge on the big sixgun. But few of us would care to depend on a single-shot arm of any sort for defense. It has been done, but it's outmoded!

Larger-caliber modern handguns have been made in this country. Tear-gas pistols of *28 gauge, about .55 caliber,* are police and plant guard equipment. Some are of larger caliber. Flare pistols for the sailor or airman yawn good and wide at the muzzle. Shot pistols were liked, and legal, for small game hunting, and for protection, in the past. Now they are "firearms," and subject to light Federal tax. The Ithaca Auto and Burglar Gun, a *20-gauge* double, was rather popular for many years. In size and recoil it made a good place to stop, for practical and then-legal uses.

Wildcat Cartridges

Several hundred special, non-factory rifle cartridges have appeared in the last three or four decades in .177, .22, .24, .25, .256, .270, .275, .30, .333, .35, .40, .45 and other sizes. They still appear in new or partly new versions. Excellent, impractical, many downright dangerous (like others) when overloaded, they all in common contributed to the body of knowl-

Recovered bullets, mostly from soft wood backstops. From left: evenly mushroomed .22 short Super-X hollow point and the same brand in solid, both from 4-inch barrel; .22 long-rifle Remington Hi-Speed hollow point (plain lead, not coated) from 3-inch barrel; .32 S.&W. Long from 3¾-inch barrel; sidewise views of .30 Luger hollow point and full-patched solid from 4⅝-inch barrel; .38 Auto full-patch from 6-inch barrel; .38 Special 173-grain Keith solid at about 800 f.s. velocity from 6-inch barrel, across the grain of oak; same load, endwise into the oak, showing almost perfectly even mushrooming (which might contribute to straight-line penetration in game); .44 Special factory load from 5-inch barrel; same, but with bullet point filed off to .44-40 shape; old metal-point, lead bearing .44 Special from same gun, the point slightly flattened; .45 Auto Colt recovered from shale, its jacket half-engraved by rifling lands of a .455 Webley barrel that was oversize for it; .44 Special Ideal hand-cast wadcutter recovered when the deep snows finally melted on Last Frontier farm in New York state, and in mint condition as it had left the barrel (you may be able to see the right-hand pitch of the rifling mark and also note how it's wider up top, where the bullet first contacted the lands and tried for an instant to go straight through without rotating, as revolver bullets do; base of .45 Colt case, originally fired with a mercuric primer (death on brass) and reloaded several times before a final round of normal power sheared it off from the case body—that wart sticking up is the old type of semi-balloon primer pocket, now fast going out of use. Lamp photo, Winchester, Va.

edge about ballistics. Such factory rounds as the .22 Hornet, .218 Bee, .219 Zipper, .220 Swift, .257 Roberts, the 6 mm. .243 and .244, and even the old and nearly forgotten .25-20 Single Shot took on their first life in the hands of private investigators. Factory executives usually were quick to see the flowering and reap commercial profit from what these fellows had done for pure love of the game. We are thankful that they did! The fact that they almost invariably altered wildcat case shapes meant nothing to the great majority of us who use standard case shapes exclusively.

Few wildcat pistol cartridges have been worked up. Until the recent .22 Hornet kitty came out, shortened for .38-Special-length cylinders, hardly any of them have been popular. But now there are more shooters, more spending money, and more interest in high velocities that come with light recoil—though they never do come silently!

For years many practical handgunners have entertained a growing belief—and have been happily entertained, themselves, bless them—that the caliber for the deadliest, not-too-big, and entirely practical cartridge is around .40, about midway between the .38s and the big .44s and .45s. In this caliber we can have either heavy cylinder walls (the revolver, not the sensitive automatic, is the subject for experiment) or thick brass to help hold the pressure. We can strike an efficient balance between velocity and the weight and width of bullets, and still have a not very heavy or bulky gun if we want it so limited.

Although this uncharted field is expensive to wander in, it's inviting. There have been shining rewards at

the end of the rainbow. We have mentioned Gordon Boser's use of the now-scarce .401 Winchester Self-loading case and the Lyman 200 grain 401452 bullet, which has wide bearing bands to stand high velocity without stripping. Compare this with the standard .38-40-180 of closely similar bullet diameter, and the heavy case with the rather thin, bottle-necked .38, and possibilities loom up.

There are also the wildcat .44 Magnums. Bert Shay's we have mentioned before, and that of "Pop" Eimer, a gunsmith of Joplin, Missouri. His .430 Magnum in converted .44 Special guns sends a 230-grain bullet at some 1500 f.s. Twenty grains of Hercules 2400 was the charge, at least in pre-war lots of that powder, and pressures play around 25,000 and 30,000 pounds per square inch. Cases are hand worked from .30-06 brass, shortened and reamed. Nothing less, he said, can take it. Since such loading calls for exact knowledge of what makes what, and for long experience, we do not recommend or guarantee any heavy charges in this book.

Some say, "You can have your Magnums. I'll take a milder load, as accurate and easier to handle, and try to place my shots a little better because of it." Yet many hunters know that in the woods and mountains all theories take wings, that there's no substitute for maximum power at the tip of the forefinger, that no charge we can school ourselves to shoot with precision is too heavy when events turn out according to nature's caprice, and not as we should have reason to expect. A .22 pistol in a berry-patch you share with a black bear that may nourish a grouch is *really* a smallbore!

The cap-and-ball or the flintlock enthusiast is a handloader in the nature of things. Being an enthusiast, he enjoys the loading process almost as much as the shooting. We could compare him to the trout fisherman who finds the darkest winter months brightened with a glow to the east, that promise, invisible to some of us, that spring is mustering her forces for the grand march. He's busy with fly-tying, rod-winding and reel-tuning—or he is if he likes to do things for himself.

No less hopelessly hobby-gripped is the pistol shooter who handloads. The gleaming empty centerfire cases flung through the ejector port of his semi-automatic or punched from the cylinder of his sixgun are "golden numbers" in their promise of enjoyment ahead. At times, some of us have shot mainly for empties to reload!

It's fun, and it's healthful relaxation, this careful, unhurried handling of the components—cases, bullets, powders and primers. Bigtime match shooters and those on their way to such skill have complained about the labor involved, even when they used quantity-production tools. To me, some of those wails lacked the ring of sincerity. I pitied the winners equally for the toil of keeping their long rows of medals bright and shiny! One evening I put up several hundred .32 S.&W. Longs with a slow old tong or nutcracker tool. Plain honesty now recreates this chore as having ninety per cent pleasure.

Handloading is economical: the tools pay for themselves in a few hundred rounds, unless our eyes are bigger than our stomachs and we buy a more elaborate outfit than our amount of shooting will justify. Unless the tools are downright poor—and few are—their design and weight and power mean very much less in quality production than the skill and the care we use when operating them. We can develop the skill, and without the care we have no right to use them at all. Any gun accident affects not only the shooter who is guilty of it, and perhaps innocent bystanders, too, but also our whole tribe. Accidents get publicity, and almost everyone reads a newspaper. Accidents give us shooters a bad name.

There are less tangible though more weighty values in handloading than economy, though it's true that most of us wouldn't shoot nearly as much if we had to buy every centerfire round brand-new! The loader fits the load to the gun for accuracy, and to the job, too, from gallery squibbing to game or defense shooting. He can feed obsolete or foreign arms for which special ammunition is non-existent in the quantities he needs. With any centerfire caliber, he gets the ample firing that helps to make him an effective pistolman.

Much has been written about handloading, most of it reliably, although with modern components some old advice is no longer even safe. J. R. Mattern laid the groundwork for us in *Handloading Ammunition.* It's out of print, deals with a bygone series of primers and powders, but is worth hunting down for its de-

CHAPTER 14

BASIC HANDLOADING

tailed and interestingly written information, much of it still basic. Phil Sharpe's *Complete Guide to Handloading* and Earl Naramore's *Principles and Practice of Loading Ammunition* are later and larger books. Inexpensive handbooks like the Ideal from Lyman Gun Sight Corporation, Middlefield, Connecticut, the Speer Products manuals from Lewiston, Idaho, and the one from Belding & Mull, Philipsburg, Pennsylvania, give valuable information. *The American Rifleman,* 1600 Rhode Island Avenue, Washington 6, D. C., and *Precision Shooting,* St. Johnsbury, Vermont, carry the latest findings and theories in their monthly issues. I think that no shooter with an inquiring mind should be without them. The latter is *not* exclusively a magazine for bench riflemen, though at first it seems to have had that reputation, and still carries a great deal of information that bench-resters want and need. There are, of course, other outdoor magazines. Almost every one has its shooting editor who gives advice on handloading and many other activities. Years ago, some load recommendations did horrify some of my friends —and me, too—but I think that the advice given now is sound.

But when we consider handloads we consider our particular gun, too, or we should! Vintages, makes and models vary in strength and in inner dimensions. Mistakes, including misprints, do get into almost any printed matter, as we all know. It's only horse-sense to *compare* data carefully, even in the same book or booklet. You may, or may not, find some surprising discrepancies. When doubt exists, forget the ambition to put up the most powerful load possible for your gun. That is a pretty good thing to forget, anyway. There's a temptation among some shooters to make headlines, metaphorically speaking, by using and ad-

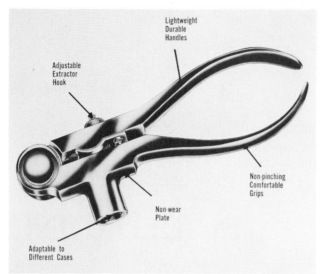

Lightweight
Durable
Handles

Adjustable
Extractor
Hook

Non-pinching
Comfortable
Grips

Non-wear
Plate

Adaptable to
Different Cases

Lyman-Ideal No. 310 tong tool handles take dies for bullet sizing, case working and priming, and final cartridge assembly. Being modern, they have wide interchangeability of calibers. They're a long step from early Ideal and other tools that loaded one cartridge just so, with no adjustments, but sometimes with an integral bullet mold to give complete service except for lubricating the bullet and measuring the powder. Some did size the bullet, after a fashion. Actually, the "crude" old tools turned out pretty good ammunition, for they were well made. Sure, standards have advanced.

vising hot loads. It's unfortunate. (There goes the understatement of the week, or at least a husky candidate for that rating.)

TOOLS

Tong tools like the modern Ideal 310 do well with pistol cartridges. So do some oldies like Winchester and Smith & Wesson, and later ones of this type, such as the Modern-Bond. To repeat, the payoff comes from the care, skill and downright intelligence (when it's used) of the loader. The oldest tools seldom if ever have means to resize case-necks to hold bullets tightly against the shuck-forward of recoil. But almost all of them made for pistol cartridges do crimp case-mouths hard enough into grooved or ungrooved lead to hold bullets against the recoil of loads these particular tools were intended to put up. Some without crimping adjustment don't handle anything but stand-

ard-length brass correctly, and case-length does vary a little in production, though more, I think, in rifle than in pistol sizes.

A step up in price from the usual tong tool is the Belding & Mull Straightline, which can be screwed to a bench, laid on a table, or held in the lap. As you throw the lever the case-holder goes straight forward toward the cap-extractor, brass-working dies, or bullet seater. The tong tool is hinged ahead of its dies, and the pressure on the work is angled down. But probably too much is made of that fact. The tong tool— as far as *it's* concerned—is able and willing to put up first-class ammunition, at least when it works on brass as short and thin as that of most sixgun and some auto-pistol rounds. Time and again this nutcracker type of tool has loaded minute-of-angle .22 Hornet and .218 Bee rifle ammo, able to shoot into an inch at 100 yards.

Belding & Mull Model 26 bullet-seater belongs to that rather large family of die-and-plunger persuasion. It is a separate tool, for bullet-seating only. You set the primed and powder-charged case into the breech of the die and push the bullet down through the muzzle. Then whack the head of the plunger to set the crimp. If the fit is tight, the bullet goes straight down into the brass, which of course should be belled or expanded enough to allow the lead to enter without getting a shave. This makes for great accuracy. My only criticism of this seater is that there is no provision for varying case length, at least in theory, although there's little if any trouble until the angle that forms the crimp has become worn. It may, after thousands of rounds loaded. Then the remedy would be to have the die shortened at the breech, and the counterbore there, for the case's rim, deepened a trifle.

By far the great majority of tools now are of heavy, bench-type persuasion. The Pacific, Hollywood, Schmitt, R.C.B.S., Herter, C-H, Potter, Lyman, Grigsby and many others old and new do have power and they save time in more than just a few gunfuls' production. Prices vary greatly, and so do size, strength and general adaptability. Some have conversion parts for shotgun shell loading. Some have the power for making jacketed rifle or pistol bullets easily. Just about every tool now made, except the simplest fist-grip size variety, will take dies for cartridges of almost any sort.

Belding & Mull (Philipsburg, Pennsylvania) Model 28 Straightline set up for case-neck sizing and expanding. Primer ejecting punch, or decapper, and bullet seating die and punch are shown with it.

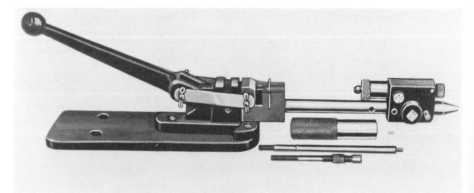

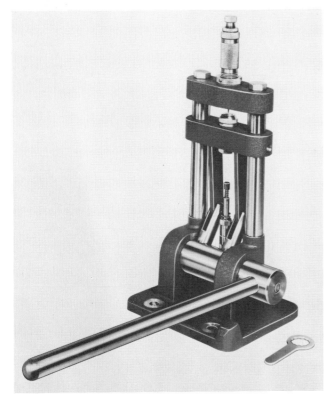

Heavy loading press from C.-H. Die Co., Box 3284, Terminal Annex, Los Angeles 54, California.

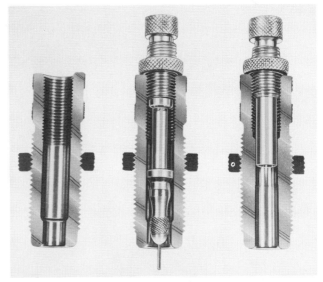

Dies for C.-H. tool.

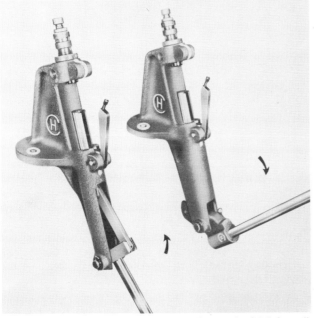

A very moderately priced C.-H. loading tool of "C-frame" type, which can be had to operate with either up or down stroke of lever.

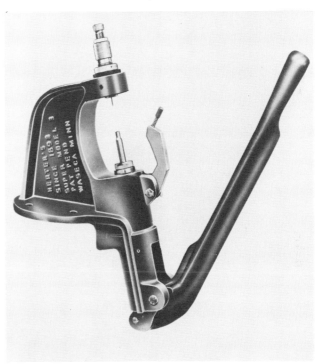

Herter's Model 3 Super is a heavy C-frame tool that can be adapted to practically any sort of metallic pistol or rifle cartridges, and to shot-shells. It operates on the down-stroke of the lever and is inexpensive. From Herter's, Inc., Waseca, Minnesota.

This is important when tools are as elaborate and expensive as most of them are now, and when we load for different calibers—including guns we don't keep long enough to become acquainted with before they're traded off for something different!

If we want the quality that care *and* a leisurely approach can put into ammunition, the biggest tools may lose their advantage of speed compared to the slow rate of hand tools. We might, for instance, want to scrape primer pockets clean before we reprime. The gritty or even the finely pulverized ash—it comes from some Cascade primers—from the last discharge can cushion the hammer's blow or, possibly, make fresh primers protrude dangerously. Some of us find it easier to seat primers with careful feeling for the bottom of the primer pocket when we use hand or

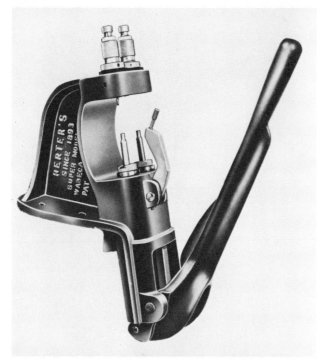

Herter's Model 81 resembles Model 3 but has two stations.

Hollywood Super Turret is a heavy tool for quantity production, with great power and easy to operate.

Hollywood Senior, from Hollywood Gun Shop, 6116 Hollywood Blvd., Hollywood 28, California, is a heavy, powerful tool, widely known and used.

tong tools than with heavy bench tools. And numbers of us like to inspect every case, as we work it through the stages, for signs of any weakness. Yes, we can still do these things with any tools, if we will take the time.

Molds

Bullet molds need care. Perhaps the only non-specialist alteration, not always needed by any means, is lapping them. Bullets just cast may stick in them because of rough surfaces which an ordinary magnifying glass would show. Since lapping is only for smoothness, not to enlarge the cavity, we should use a fine compound and turn the cast lap—a bullet with a gripping "handle" in its base—slowly, at first not closing the mold jaws fully.

You can get fine bullets, very often, without any such refinement; but it is true that hard tapping with a stick of wood, to loosen the cast bullets, can distort them and even the mold itself. It's best to form the habit of never tapping the mold; instead, tap the joint, or one of the handles near the joint, or even the end of a handle. Most new molds need breaking in before they'll drop their bullets, anyway.

Some molds can be shortened at the top to cast lighter bullets, a precise job in leveling off the top truly. With a base-cut-off mold, not a point-cut-off

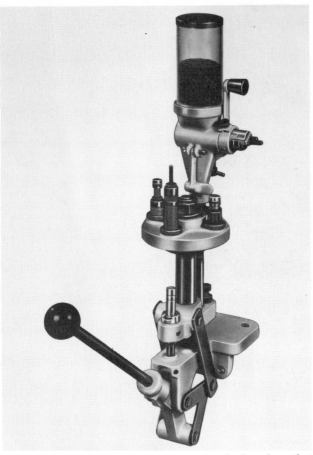

Lyman-Ideal turret-type press is one of the class that process a case without any need to remove it from the holder. Handle reversible for up or down stroke, as wanted. Picture shows powder measure in place.

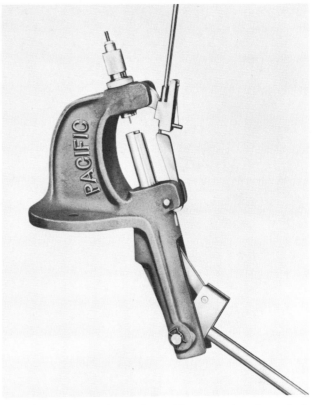

Pacific Super Tool complete with automatic primer feed. From Pacific Gun Sight Co., Inc., 2901 El Camino Real, Palo Alto, Calif.

Pacific three-die pistol set replaces former two-die set and sells at same price. No. 1 die sizes lubricated cases full-length, also holds them ready for trimming to uniform length, if necessary. No. 2 die expels fired primers, expands cases, and flares or bells their mouths for insertion of cast bullets without snaving them. No. 3 die seats bullets and crimps the case-mouths to a degree that is adjustable. It contacts more than 60% of a tapered bullet's nose.

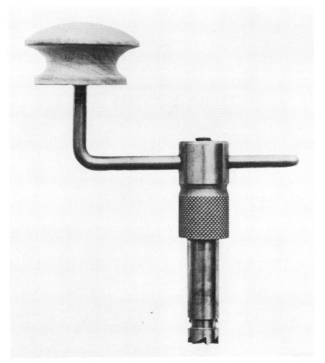

Pacific case trimmer for use with the No. 1 die, at the top of the resizing stroke. Insert it in the die opening, and turn.

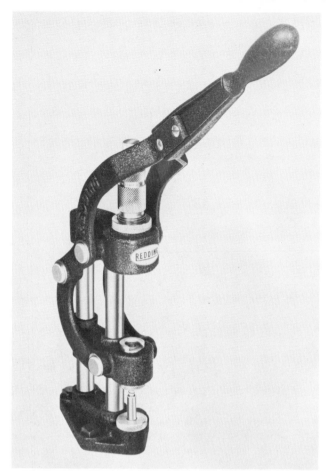

Moderately priced Redding-Hunter (112 Starr Road, Cortland, N. Y.) joins the powder measure and scale in the R.-H. line.

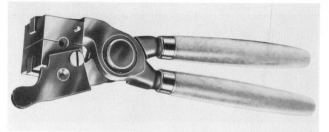

An old standby for the average shooter, Lyman-Ideal single cavity mold. Other singles by Lyman fit the same handles, though the old fixed-block Ideals, Winchesters, etc. lacked this convenience, common to Lymans made now.

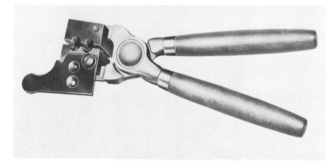

Lyman double-cavity mold.

mold—which is uncommon now except for hollowed bullets—we must be sure to leave a lower band on the bullet wide enough to prevent fusion on firing. Molds come in such a variety of styles and weights that tinkering with them in this way is scarcely justified. Cutting off some of the plug for making the hollow-base form of the Keith-Ideal .38 Special mold was easy, when I found that the bullet as cast was too light to hit where I wanted it to from an S.&W. Military & Police I had. Cutting off the base of the Lyman 360271 mold to reduce the bullet weight from about 155 to 125 grains, to convert it from .38 Special to .38 Auto, was more than I dared to try. My friend John Robinson, then president of our old Lynchburg Rifle & Pistol Club, did it for me, a very fine and satistactory job indeed.

Lyman puts out several hundred molds for old and new type bullets. They are good molds, as made now probably averaging better than older ones of this and other makes, including the Winchester. This comment may go down hard with some shooters who had or still have molds cut long ago that they'd never willingly turn loose. We have made great strides in the manufacture of jacketed rifle bullets, thanks mainly to the bench-rest shooters. But cast-bullet accuracy is by comparison a red-headed stepchild. It shouldn't be.

Some prefer single-cavity molds for uniformity, and a few oldtime riflemen even fired bullets in the order in which they were cast. Hensley & Gibbs, 2692 E Street, San Diego 2, California, make expensive, high-quality multiple molds, the four-cavity being popular. But remember that these things weigh plenty and are slow to warm up for good production. We cast our best bullets before we get tired; so we should gear our choice to our strength. As for uniformity, the really good multiple molds seem to do just as good work as the singles. They do help in big production, which some of us simply must have.

H.&G. and Lyman also make the molds for Harvey Prot-X-bore bullets of "S.F.M." type. Shoot as cast from mold; don't size the bullets first. From H.&G.,

Lyman-Ideal p r i m e r pocket reamer cleans out the residue of firing. It comes for large and small size pockets.

most important for accuracy. The three preceding have quality we can count on. They are manufactured for us; we have little control over them. And we don't need to, although, as time goes on, they're bound to continue to be improved.

Powders

Since straight pistol powders are highly condensed, we need a mechanical powder measure, not a scoop or dipper as often used with black powder, for anything like normally full loads. It can be built into the bench tool assembly or used separately. Ideal, Hollywood, R.C.B.S., Belding & Mull, Redding, Saeco, and Lachmiller are among the standard makes. Excellent scales such as the Pacific or Redding check the measure and should be used for each maximum charge that goes into primed brass. Some shooters economize by buying only scales, not a measure, and thus are equipped with the most precise means of rationing powder. When they enjoy their handloading, the loss of time in weighing each charge, light or heavy, doesn't mean a thing.

On the other hand, if the loader doesn't insist on being ready to put up top loads, he can get on nicely

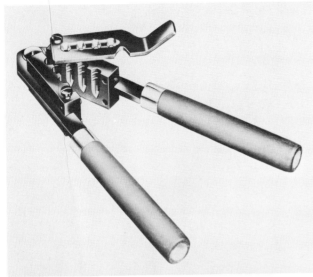

Lyman four-cavity mold—for rifle bullets, as shown here.

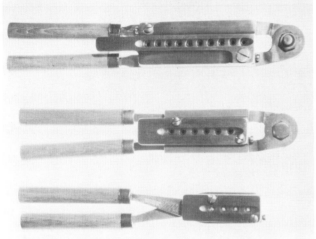

Hensley & Gibbs ten, six, and four-cavity molds. Note the forward hinging of the big ones. The four-cavity mold contains bullets.

too, come the core molds for Harvey Jugular jacketed bullets, also sold by Lakeville Arms, Lakeville, Connecticut.

Yes, molds deserve care. The inner surfaces must be kept from abuse, and so in fact must the outer. They aren't for cracking walnuts or tightening bolts, though no doubt they've done such things and *possibly* have survived still useful. Bronze molds can't rust, of course, but steel or iron can. They should be stored in wooden boxes, unlined. I leave an oiled bullet in the cavity. Oil must be cleaned out before we start to cast bullets again. If not, a long series of wrinkled slugs will drop before good bullets come. Burning the oil out of the mold—that's what it amounts to—is likely to leave a carbon deposit in the cavity that makes Grade A bullets impossible to get.

AMMUNITION COMPONENTS

Of all these parts of a modern cartridge—powder, primer, case, and bullet—the last is almost always the

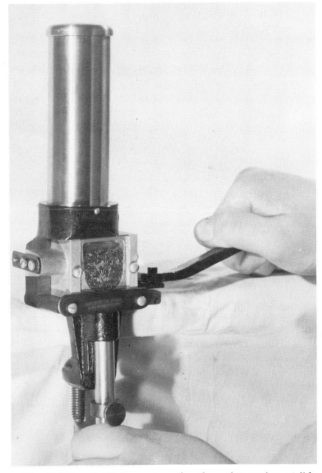

The Belding & Mull measure is of an interesting visible type, showing the powder down at the bottom of the reservoir. It can be had with micrometer-set chamber for the powder charges.

with only a measure. By keeping to mild loads he can do without ever weighing a charge, first having his measure's rationing verified by the druggist—long-suffering friend of all the world!—or by a handloader who owns scales.

Measuring powder is simple. The main thing, for accuracy, is to keep jolts, jars or any sort of ruction from affecting the measure's amazingly exact work, just as we avoid drafts and wheezes when we use scales. For reasons of health we make dog-goned sure that the measure is set correctly. Pistol powders are concentrated energy. About the only duplex load we should be apt to drop into a handgun case is a priming of black powder with bulk smokeless. Wider development may come—well, it has, already—to short-gun ammunition, as it has to rifle stuff. Both are for the long-initiated.

Shooters' Accessory Supply, Box 205, North Bend, Oregon, has specialties for powder measuring. The Little Dripper came first, it seems. It speeds powder weighing for those who use this specialist's method. You set the mechanical measure to throw a slight

Redding-Hunter measure with micro-set chamber for the powder.

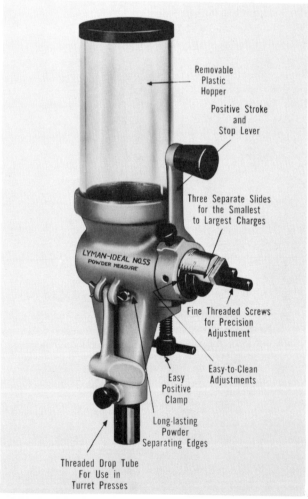

Lyman-Ideal No. 55 powder measure is a refined form of the long-familiar old No. 5. The hopper or reservoir is of transparent plastic. Chamber setting is finely adjustable.

Removable Plastic Hopper

Positive Stroke and Stop Lever

Three Separate Slides for the Smallest to Largest Charges

LYMAN-IDEAL NO.55 POWDER MEASURE

Fine Threaded Screws for Precision Adjustment

Easy-to-Clean Adjustments

Easy Positive Clamp

Long-lasting Powder Separating Edges

Threaded Drop Tube For Use in Turret Presses

undercharge, pour this dose into the scale's pan, then drip in enough kernels to teeter the balance. The Mez-u-rite kit has an adjustable charge cup and serves the small-lot reloader well, incidentally costing but little. The Multi-Mezur is for speed. A plywood box holds 20 cases and a slip-over tray of transparent plastic does the rest. Just one load weight, of course. Phil Teachout, editor of *Precision Shooting* (formerly *Shooter's News*) likes it, made extra blocks, and could charge 100 cases in two or three minutes. The company now furnishes extras. This little trick is accurate, and fascinating, too!

The Electric Dripper followed the Little Dripper. Originally for finishing sub-measured charges, it can drop full charges also, and speed is adjustable. It works by vibration and is highly useful with pistol powders like Hercules Bullseye, which tend to gall in a mechanical measure.

Powder Types

A careful loader can use several different kinds of powder for a pistol cartridge, especially a big one. The fact that some, like Hercules Bullseye and Unique, contain nitroglycerine never was as important to the pistolman as it was to the rifleman, for most handgun heats are low by comparison. We have non-corrosive primers now. For example, the old Hercules Sharp-

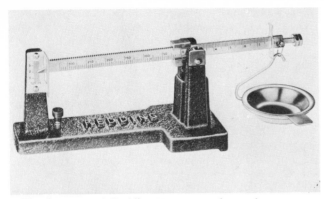

The long-proved Redding-Hunter powder scale now contains an oil damper to shorten the settling time.

shooter, once a factory and pretty much a handloading standard for cartridges like the .25-20 and .32-20, was sure and not too slow death to rifles in these and similar calibers. But when the clean primers came in, it lost most of its terrors.

"Bull" is the most concentrated pistol powder available. It does well in most standard and practically all light loads and is a great favorite for such rounds. It burns cleanly even in very small charges and has contributed to fine accuracy. It never had any serious reputation for eroding handgun barrels. Because it's so economical, it's been used for thousands of round per gun. A slight overcharge is just a little more serious than with less condensed powders; but a handloader must be careful with any load, mustn't he?

I did see one gun blown up with it in a rather peculiar way, but it could have happened with slightly slower and less concentrated powders. This Bisley Colt .45 was an old one. The shooter saw that one of his bullets had moved forward from the case, under the recoil of other rounds, and he pushed the lead back in with his finger, well beyond the normal seating depth. Firing that round blew the chamber apart and bent the top-strap above it. A new, modern cylinder went in, and a skilled gunsmith bent the top strap back into exact line. What's more, the top-strap stayed straight when shooting was resumed.

Hercules Unique is of a coarser cut than Bull. It gives much higher velocities at safe pressures; yet it burns pretty cleanly in cases as small as even the .32 S.&W. Long. Hercules 2400 is "strictly" a rifle powder but it can be used, with know-how, for powerful loads in big cases. At standard pistol velocities it doesn't burn well in handguns.

Du Pont 4227 rifle powder, of nitrocellulose type, is a working partner of 2400's, both giving full velocities in small cartridges like the .22 Hornet and .218 Bee, and doing well for light loads in almost all large rifle cartridges. It is less concentrated than 2400 and requires a higher weight of charge for similar results; yet it has been used to some extent in big handgun cases.

Du Pont 5066 seems to be the only straight pistol powder left in that make. It's nitrocellulose, like Du

Pont's big rifle powders, though the No. 6 that was discontinued only recently was of double-base type like Hercules Bullseye. No. 6 was denser than 5066, with more power to its volume, and more clean-burning in most loads. With 5066 we use heavier charges than with Bull, to get like results; so it stacks up slightly higher in the case. Both of them are great favorites for standard-velocity handgun loads, with Bull perhaps more favored for extremely light charges. Powder does not have to burn completely in the bore to give useful accuracy. Some of the brotherhood take pride in swinging out a cylinder, putting a fingernail down below the barrel breech to act as a reflector, and saying, "Just take a look. Pretty clean-burning charge, isn't it?"

With any pistol powder it's only good sense to direct a flashlight beam into each powder-charged case to make sure that a double hasn't sneaked in. In the machine-like routine of some bench tools there's actually little if any likelihood of such a disaster—for disaster it could easily be. Sometimes an old measure will slip, too. It pays to throw a double charge to see what one looks like, then dump it, of course.

Du Pont 4759 replaced that old favorite of a generation or more, No. 80, to the regret of many careful loaders, for 4759 is coarse and less easy to measure

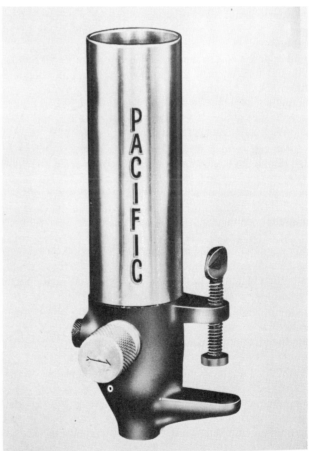

Pacific powder measure has no top, as it's meant to be kept full to produce even metering of powder. And after all, why smoke when you're handling powder with *any* device?

with great precision. But it stacks up beautifully and is cool—so cool that it often fails to burn cleanly (but need it?) in a handgun or even in some rifle loads. Yet it gives accurate results and is a fine high-velocity pistol powder in many large calibers and some not so large. But we use it, too, with care.

Black powder coarser than FFG granulation isn't useful in most handgun rounds except the large, practically frontier sizes. This FG is for big rifles, mainly, though some shooters have preferred it to FFG in loads as light as 30 grains' weight. The coarser we can use, the less heavy the fouling is likely to be. The fine FFFG is for few calibers except the tiny .32 S.&W. and Colt Shorts, the old .22 Winchester Center Fire rifle round that fathered the Hornet, the still less capacious .22 Maynard rifle sizes, and so on. But for priming flintlocks this size and still finer granulations have advantages, as they ignite and burn easily.

So most of our pistol-type black powder loads would probably use FFG. All black powders are dirty, requiring prompt cleaning of both gun and cases we want to keep from corroding. However, in revolvers it often gives safe power above factory loadings. For use in old guns it's the safest propellant we can get, short of Hercules Sharpshooter, perhaps, which is obsolete and was made for rifle cartridges, anyway. Unlike Sharpshooter and practically all other smokeless powders, black is loaded in full-case capacity. That is, it's normally compressed by the bullet above it, though excessive compression and long storage can pulverize its grains and raise its pressure dangerously. Almost any ancient primer with a spark of life will fire black powder. In thunderstormy weather it's actually dangerous to shake a canful of it. Glass makes a good container for home storage. But do not leave it where light can strike it.

We can reduce its fouling with a priming charge of Du Pont Bulk Shotgun Powder—no dense variety, though smokeless pistol powders are used right along for this purpose in strongly built black powder rifles—set in the bottom of the case and held there by a slightly compressed load of black powder over it. This prevents sifting of the two, which could be dangerous. About 10% by bulk measure, not by weight, is enough to use in priming handgun loads, and I'd hate to do this for old guns like the Bisley mentioned in the third paragraph of this "Powder Types" section.

With this duplex loading we might get long-sustained accuracy from black powder. Straight black loads, especially heavy ones in proportion to bullet weight, foul some barrels so fast that shots may go wild before we've finished even a ten-shot target string.

After the shooting, the cleaning of guns and cases used with black is really no terrible chore. Water, cold or hot, washes away the sludge fast from barrel and chambers and all those odd corners where sixgun fouling goes. Hot water, almost any kitchen detergent, and a bristle brush clean the cases. One washing does it, followed by a rinse in hot water, and drying in the sun or almost any place that's cat- and dog-proof. (They like to play with these things, and so, of course, do we; only we're privileged.) Use the brush in both washing and rinsing, and one of the same "caliber" as your handgun is correct.

We can use Du Pont Bulk Shotgun by itself as a pistol powder; but there is little advantage in doing so, as Bullseye and 5066 go farther and we know what we are loading, with them. Dense, high-pressure shotgun powders like the old Du Pont MX or the new PB, or other old smoothbore standards like Hercules Infallible and Red Dot, are almost last-ditch material for the pistol loader. In the past, Infallible proved to be an excellent fodder for automatic pistols; but it was loaded mainly by ammunition companies, who have every means of determining what is and what never ought to be. Most of us shooters have neither pressure-gun equipment, nor hands and guns to spare. If shotgun-powder loads are ever used, they should start light and be built up with awareness of pressure signs: flattened or pierced primers, unearthly sharp report, smearing of lead across the cylinder face, and extraction that's even a little bit difficult.

For like reasons we don't use powder salvaged from blank cartridges or from foreign cartridges. Blank powder goes bang with a minimum of confinement and barrel resistance. Even the black powder in some specimens is so fine that its burning rate is terrific. *Never* use it to push any bullet or charge of shot.

Here is a tale of an unfortunate misunderstanding of print. A really rifle-wise friend had heard of the old Du Pont No. 1 Rifle Powder which, for rifle use, could be loaded bulk-for-bulk with black: same powder scoop or measure setting, same everything except that the soft grains crumbled pretty fast under tight compression. (Du Pont Bulk Shotgun resembles it in use, but for shot-shell loading only, and wads plus shot are more easly shoved through a smoothbore barrel than a bullet through a rifled barrel.)

He loaded his 1886 Model .45-70 Winchester with one round of bulk-for-bulk with the Bulk Shotgun and about a 405-grain lead bullet. The report was indescribable and best forgotten and the breech was almost wedged shut. It took a hard haul on the lever of the sound, modern-steel Winchy to open it. Pressures must have been close to the limit, whatever that is, and who wants to find out?

Primers

Primers are even more sensitive souls than powders, I suppose; but fortunately it's less easy for us to misuse them. Those we buy now are—almost certainly unless they are ancient—non-corrosive and non-mercuric. The first quality obviates prompt bore cleaning if we have used smokeless, not black powder. Firing these primers with smokeless powder and lubricated lead bullets builds up rust resistance, as many canoemen and salt-water beach-combers know. But their long-term protection is just a little debatable, especially if we've mixed brands of primers, as compositions still vary, here and there. I know I'm being over-cautious. But right now, in the hot and humid summer, two of our .22 rimfire rifles upstairs have been left deliberately uncleaned after one or more target sessions. Sure, the *outsides* are oiled against rust. We aren't bone-lazy, I should kindly hope.

The non-mercuric feature means more: long life under dry, cool storage, and long life for reloaded cases, too. Firing just one mercuric primer makes a case brittle, except with the overlaid fouling of black or the regrettably obsolete semi-smokeless powder. (We mean King's Semi, not Du Pont Lesmok, which wasn't for handloaders, though it was splendid in just about every rim- or centerfire pistol size cartridge when some of the factories used it.) A case made brittle, or "rotted," by meruric priming fired in it may, in times, split lengthwise, burst or partly break off at the head, or give way in its primer pocket. A burst is particularly nasty in an auto-pistol with the rear of its chamber beveled down to form a loading ramp for cartridges hustling out of the magazine. Before warnings against this primer poison were printed we had to find out for ourselves. It was a brisk and sometimes startling discovery.

Among commercial primers the .175-inch or small pistol size goes into most old or new cases up to and usually including the .38 Special and the .41, and some big ones, too, such as .38-40, .44-40 and .455 varieties. When shortages compel us, we can substitute the thicker-cupped and hotter .175-inch rifle primers, cutting the powder charge for safety. Unless our handgun has a heavy hammer, we may get a few misfires or hangfires. Rifle primers can damage a revolver's recoil plate through which the firing pin hole is drilled. With them we're more likely to find evidence of ragged uneven ignition in the gun's tendency to string shots up and down on the target. Likewise, when we must, we can set the large .210-inch rifle primers in cases meant for the thinner, weaker, less "tall" .210 pistol primers. Here we run the risk of having protruding primers that might be fired accidentally. Pistol cases

used extensively with these primers have their pockets permanently deepened. With hot .210 rifle primers even black powder can be over-ignited, and it seems certain that old, soft steel barrels have been eroded by just a few hundred rounds of such stuff.

But sometimes supplies *are* short and we may want to hoard our best components for serious use. Probably I've pleased my Scottish ancestors and certainly I've had fun in thus using Frankford Arsenal .30 caliber rifle primers—the obsolete, comparatively mild, corrosive No. 26 with the No. 70 Potassium chlorate composition—in a .44 Special Smith. Since its light hammer fall, unlike that of the Colt single-action's "thumb-buster," gave frequent misfires with these toughies, I often got nearly double the practice I would have had with pistol primers. I would hold back on the trigger to prevent the cylinder from turning, recock the hammer, and squeeze off another "shot." But I used such primers sparingly, and now not at all, in handguns. Erosion might show up, though my powder charges are usually mild. The recoil plate got by unharmed, thanks to no intelligence on my part, but by good luck. A worn firing pin hole through it can let primer metal flow back in and lock the cylinder. The ultimate purpose of a handgun is protection we can count on, isn't it?

The old .204-inch F.A. primer, corrosive but not mercuric, was for many .45 Auto cases made by or for the Government. Most wartime cases made by Winchester, and some from other plants, accept standard .210s. The .204 pockets can be reamed up, for the .45 case-head is solid.

For years we had only five standard United States makes of primer: Peters, Remington, U. S. Cartridge Company, Western, and Winchester. The U.S. dropped out, and later Peters and Remington twinned up, and Western and Winchester, too. The Big Five or the Big Four had become the Big Two, except for packaging. That has come along in the W-W brand. Federal Cartridge went into the primer business; and this brand was easy to get, a few years past, when Big

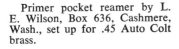

Primer pocket reamer by L. E. Wilson, Box 636, Cashmere, Wash., set up for .45 Auto Colt brass.

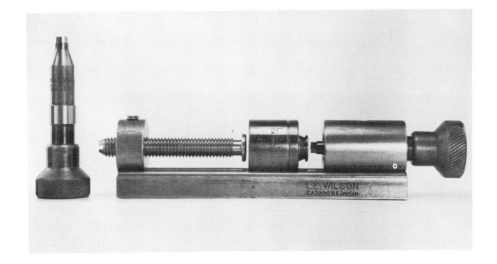

The Fitz primer flipper turns primers right side up for easy pickup and use. From Fitz Custom Grips, Box 49702, Los Angeles 49, Calif.

Fours were a bit scarce in some stores. Federal became established as quite OK, and then a new brand, Cascade Cartridge, Inc. (at first called "Speer"), appeared at a reduced retail price. This, too, proved up, and for some months now, all of them have been selling at C.C.I. prices. There are other makes, such as the East German R.W.S. Sinoxid, also non-mercuric and non-corrosive as a matter of course.

As for quality, there shouldn't be much sensible choice. All are good. But different makes, or even different lots, vary in hardness. Just now, Remington and Peters are among the toughest, and C.C.I. about the softest. Most good handguns will take any of them, and do well. If you seat primers fully and without distorting them, and still get hangfires or misfires, the remedy could be a softer primer. If soft primers back up into a worn firing pin hole and lock the revolver, or shave off in an automatic, something harder is needed.

Cases

A rifleman loading for accuracy sorts cases as to number of firings, make, and even the factory lot. (This number, if it appears at all, is stamped, not printed, on the cartridge box.) Such nicety can repay the pistolman.

Our commercial cases are now so alike in shape and depth of primer pocket, though not always in powder capacity, that we no longer need stick to corresponding brands of brass and primer. And almost no mercuric primed rounds remain to be bought, anywhere.

Very tight cases, not resized after firings, grip unoiled cylinder walls and allow primers to back up when charges are very light. Sometimes this locks the cylinder, though it can be turned by hand, with considerable force and with loss of time that might be

serious. Moderately tight fired cases do align bullets with the bore axis, just as in a rifle. Such cartridges can't slump down to the bottom of the chamber. In handguns this advantage is perhaps more theoretical than in rifles.

Sometimes the rifleman buys new empty cases for heavy loads or other special uses, but the pistoleer less often does. For stiff loads in either arm, I prefer cases that have gone through the firing of factory doses, which show up most defects in brass. I never had a soft-headed case, which literally flows under stress, blowing its primer, and can let gas fairly flood back through the action. The few cracked or broken-off heads I've experienced were in much reloaded brass. A new .250 Savage and a new .351 Winchester case split almost full-length above the heavy bases or heads. But the Model 54 Winchester bolt action proved more gas-proof than I had believed possible. The self-loader is hammerless and would almost hold the flood of a summer thunderstorm! Burst cases in revolvers seldom if ever injure the shooter unless the gun is weak or the loads excessive.

During the Great Change in American primers, some of us bought new, unprimed cases when nearly all factory ammo contained mercuric non-corrosive primers. Then we used the old chlorate primers and a cleaning rod. Mercury certainly can affect pistol cases, the straight ones as well as the bottle-necked variety. Sometimes it merely splits a case; sometimes it takes its head off. A reloaded, swelled case body in a chamber could be hard to remove; but you had the other five chambers to use, with luck! Torn-off or ruptured heads in an auto-pistol were liable to be mean. They opened a way for gas to get into the action and the magazine; and sometimes a brass fragment or two would be hurled back at the shooter.

The young shooter has much to feel good about, but one who has been through the transition stage of primers has the real relish of the good stuff we have now.

Modern pistol brass is almost uniformly good. Extruded big-rifle brass may not have the long strong life of the drawn stuff; but failures due to the metal itself, not to the handloading, are infrequent. Incidentally, when we compare the quality of World War I and World War II cases, the later usually is well on top. It has had enough storage, and active use too, to make that evident. Of course exceptions always exist. We are speaking of American material only.

BULLETS

Most of us cast our own lead or lead-alloy bullets and lubricate them with a formula we like. That may be Ideal, Ipco or some other commercial make, or an oldtime or newly thought-up recipe for our own mixing or straight use. Hard, auto water-pump grease costs little, or maybe nothing if you smile; and for standard-velocity loads, it does well in most guns. You don't melt it; you put it in the bullet grooves as-is.

Ipco has done well for me in all sorts of weather, and in some guns—rifles, not handguns—has cured leading troubles that nothing else seemed able to. This is strictly personal and limited experience, as I do not shop around and try every lube I hear of. In your guns, this black, hard, adhesive stuff might not suit you at all. But I still use Ideal, too, without the graphite incorporation that Ippy has, for practical reasons and not merely in gratitude for the many happy years of service it has given me.

The Director of Civilian Marksmanship offers us N.R.A. members full-jacketed, 234-grain, .45 Auto bullets at a mouth-watering price, and they are quality stuff.* The copper or even the wartime steel-jacketed

erosion, if they are soft enough to upset and fill the grooves promptly. They can be constructed and powered to expand on game that's big enough to offer resistance. Also they are less likely to glance in field shooting, at game or inanimate targets, though we can't depend much on this unless speeds start, and stay, in high rifle brackets.

We can buy factory full-jacketed bullets in the auto-pistol sizes, and jacketed soft points in .32-20, .38-40 and .44-40. The last is likely to be undersized for most .44 Special barrels. A hard subsized bullet is poor for a revolver, or for any pistol. Bench-rest rifle shooters have found that undersized jacketed bullets sometimes give unusual accuracy, maybe the best; but as a rule

Norma-Precision (South Lansing, N. Y.) Luger bullets, full patched and soft point. The .30s are .307-inch, the 9s .355. Hollow bases help the 9s to expand to fit .38 Special and .357 Magnum barrels, when loaded to the high velocities these bullets can give. The copper or gilding metal plated soft steel jackets of the soft points are thinned at the front to give better expansion at pistol velocities. Another use for these soft points is in .30 and .35 caliber rifles, at muzzle velocities of about 2500 f.s., for short-range varmint shooting when it's essential to run *no* risk of ricochets. Dependent on many rifle and ammo details, satisfactory 100-yard accuracy often is obtained.

bullets can be a bit less rough on an auto-pistol barrel cut snugly for them than some of us think. If they're of full barrel-groove diameter the destructive cutting of gas ahead of them, as they squeeze into the bore, isn't really excessive. My pre-1914 .30 Luger took 2,000 such factory loads, both non-corrosive and chlorate primed, and showed no trace of rifling throat erosion. I didn't do much rapid fire, but used the handy little gun mostly in the woods at slow fire, plinking, and hunting. Bert Shay's experiences with the .45 Auto and jacketed bullets tops this record considerably. A revolver is more subject to gas-cutting than an automatic is, because of the long space between the chamber throats and the start of the rifling. Exceptions: the old .38-.44 S.&W. target guns and the 7.62 mm. Nagant and others like it. They practically spoon-feed bullets into the rifling.

But if the auto handles lead bullets reliably and accurately, as so many do, we prefer them for most purposes, as in the sixgun. They give less barrel wear from friction, probably, and very much less from gas

these jackets aren't especially tough. In 1961 the 240-grain soft point, jacketed .44 Magnum came along.

There are imported Norma 93-grain .30 and 116-grain 9 mm. Luger bullets, soft point or full patch, with thin steel jackets. The 9 can be used in .38 Specials and .357 Magnums as a light, high velocity bullet, though it may be small for some barrels. But the big news about these bullets, I think, is that they come in expanding type for autoloaders in these calibers. No American stuff like them has been made for many years. Our old hollow-points in .30 (or 7.65) and 9 gave almost no expansion in game, though the soft point .30 was at least fair. Soft-point 9s were almost never seen, at least in U. S. makes. These Norma bullets have given match-grade accuracy. We need not shy away from the copper-plated steel jackets, which I understand are really iron, and thin, too. But look at the next .30-06 rifle bullet you recover from a backstop, and you may see how narrow the streaks are that were polished by the rifling *grooves*, not the raised lands. The high .30-caliber velocities demand fairly thick strong jackets; and if some bullets do not completely seal the barrel, why, that goes with the type

---

*These .45 bullet sales will be discontinued after stocks on hand are exhausted.

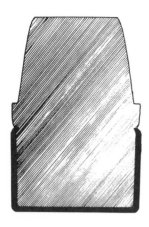
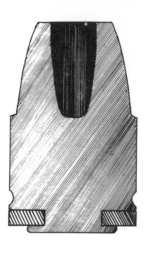

Drawing of sectioned half-jacket Jugular bullet (left) and Prot-X-Bore with zinc base sealed on by the lead, Harvey-designed. Courtesy Jim Harvey, Lakeville, Conn., and Kent Bellah, Saint Jo, Texas.

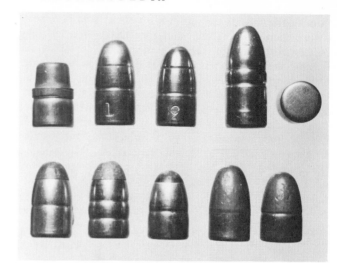

Top left, the .44 Jugular jacketed that sparked development of Bigbore Harvey Maglaska rifles. Others in this row are of two-stage type worked up by Harvey for high velocity big bore rifles. Bottom row, experimental bullets not tough enough for the high speeds. Courtesy Jim Harvey and Kent Bellah.

of arm and ammunition. It seems to me that in any personal pistol that does nearly everything that needs to be done with lead-alloy bullets, the use of metal-jacketed bullets is just for special purposes.

How about the .22 Rimfire Magnum? Well, its jacket is thin and the bullet is made full-size for arms correctly bored and rifled for it. Some of its rifling twists are steep, and its starting velocities are high. A gas-check on a fairly hard lead-alloy bullet probably would have done nicely for this little Mag, but that would have called for deep hollow-pointing to make it expand, and the overall bullet length would have been greater. The thin jacket was sure to work, and it seems to have been the right solution. Even revolvers should have long barrel life with this moderately-

pressured round. Rifle barrels should go deep into the tens of thousands.

"Jugular" bullets were described by Kent Bellah in the October 1956 *Precision Shooting*. They come from Jim Harvey, Lakeville Arms, Inc., Lakeville, Connecticut, and sometimes are called "half jacketed." Jackets are thin, about .014 inch, and the lead enclosed is soft for quick expansion. For contrast and comparison; the very heavy, gilding-metal-coated steel jacket of the .458 Winchester Magnum full-patched elephant bullet is about .10 inch at the nose and .067 along the sides, whereas, the cover page of the August, 1959 *American Rifleman* is some .004 inch, and six inner sheets around .014. One of the first Jugulars was a .357, for the Mag-

Powder charge, bullet and case of that popular high velocity revolver cartridge, the wildcat or custom-job (not factory-made) .22 Harvey Kay-Chuk, as contrasted to the makin's of the .22 long-rifle round. Courtesy Jim Harvey and Kent Bellah.

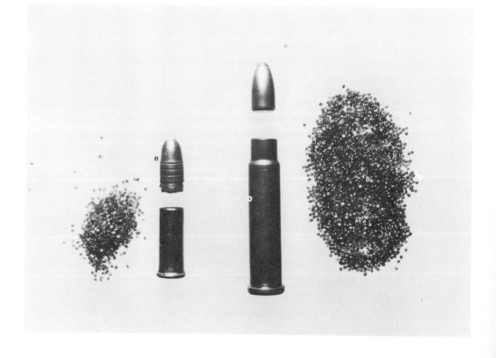

num or the .38 Special, in 127 grain solid or 114 grain with conical hollow point. Heavy loads with such light bullets give a sharp report, and usually considerable muzzle flash; but they have an explosive effect on small or medium sized varmints, while velocity remains high. Of course, they shoot flat. Accuracy is reported good up to 50 yards at least (that is a long varmint-pistol range for really good shots who want quick and sure kills); though very light, slow loads aren't so good. Of course this bullet type isn't made for squib or even small shooting, the restful kind that seems to teach us

New Harvey lever ejection swaging dies are inexpensive, fast, and simple to operate.

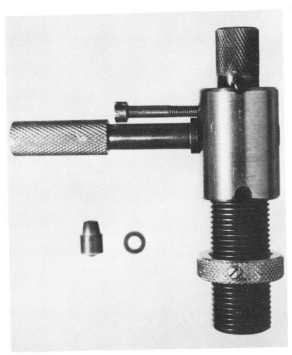

Harvey bolt action die for swaging Jugular or Prot-X-Bore type bullets.

Harvey cannelure dies with interchangeable collet bullet holders for .38, .357 and .44 caliber bullets. These crimp jackets or gas-checks on bullets to prevent their being shed in flight.

as much basic marksmanship as anything else. Such short and light bullets aren't to be trusted for deer hunting. Some shooters would pass up a pistol caliber as little as .357, no matter what the loading. There are heavy Jugulars, too, like the 265-grain .44.

Some years ago, Frank A. Hemstead, Box 171, Culver City, California, put out jacketed .38 Special and .45 Auto bullets, really long-exposed soft points. You crimp your case over the top edge of the jacket, into the soft lead. This system works well, for it gives the clean shooting of a jacket and a good solid crimp to hold the bullet in place against the jarring recoil of neighboring rounds. Some people had always wanted a soft-nosed .45 Auto bullet.

Mason Williams described swaged handgun bullets in the May, 1958 *Precision Shooting*. He referred to the Harvey lead type with zinc washer base, and to the jacketed. Both shoot cleanly without lubrication, as we should expect. Zinc polishes a bore, removing old leading at least from all portions that the zinc washer can reach. It is more the common rimfire .22s

—many of them, for sure—than the bigbores that are throated out excessively at the barrel-breech. Harvey swaging dies come in Bolt Action and in Ejection types, the latter being for quantity production.

Lead cores for the jacketed bullets can be cast in molds, but undersize lead wire is said to be better. For .38 use .312-inch wire, for .44 and .45 use .348-inch. The swaging is *up*, not down as with earlier varieties of swaged soft-lead bullets. This method ought to eliminate air pockets. An accurate, properly adjusted, lead wire cutter is needed.

Swaging dies are three-part: body, nose die, and ram. The nose die determines the weight and shape of the bullet, once the correct body bearing is fixed upon. These Harvey bullets rather typically have short bearing surfaces to reduce friction in the bore and permit high velocities—something like the .44-40-200 as compared to the .44 Special 246-grain. Excess lead is bled off at the junction of nose and body dies; and there isn't much, if cores have been cut right from the lead wire. Swaged jacketed bullets at very high

The Hollywood Super turret tool set for bullet swaging. One pin on each side can be re-positioned for normal stroke in cam arm.

The Hollywood Senior is another of the rather large number of tools with the strength to swage bullets.

The latest Hollywood Senior steel tool with Hollywood lead core cutter in place.

Close-up of Hollywood Senior set up for core cutting. Wire alloyed one part tin to ten parts lead is really hard, but it's used for some jacketed-bullet cores.

speed can shed their jackets on impact or even in flight. So Harvey has designed a jacket crimper for use in the regular swaging tool.

A good bit of force is needed, and that means soft, not hardened lead, and a heavy bench tool like the Pacific Super or Hollywood Super, to ease and speed the work.

In loading, bell the case-mouth and see that it's reamed; also size the case body, or at least the neck, for the bullet. Do not seat the bullet and crimp the case-month in one operation, for this forces the lead forward, as the crimper goes to work. Then the excess-lead ring ahead of the case-month is likely to be shaved off and spattered back, on firing, by the barrel's leade (or forcing cone or throat—we have wide latitude in christening that ream-out at the breech). What's more, a build-up of lead can in time lock the cylinder. I had one .38 Special Single Action Colt that refused to handle semi-wadcutter cast bullets for more than a few shots before freezing up in this way. A gunsmith could have fixed that, but there was none near me then. I sold or traded the rebuilt job without further ado.

All sorts of dies, some of them similar to those just mentioned, come from the Bahler Die Shop, 1500 Thompson Road, Coos Bay, Oregon. Among them is a hollow-pointing nose die for RCBS Models A, B and Junior, C-H Magnum, Hollywood, Pacific, and probably others. Calibers included are 9 mm. Luger, .38 and .357, .44 Special, .45 Auto, and .45 Colt. Bullets themselves can be swaged instead of cast, and at an even faster rate, if that matters. Lakeville Arms jackets can be used. Bahler will make up special shapes or calibers on order.

The specialists and their work just mentioned are only a sampling. A lot of fine amateur work is done, too, and more purposes and more methods to achieve them can be expected right along because we Americans are treated pretty liberally in our use of arms. We must see to it that we stay so! Horrible examples of anti-gun legislation do exist in our country, like weeds in a fine, fair garden, and what to do about them is obvious. Congressmen are inclined to read even postcards. They don't understand everything, but most of them welcome information that is presented sanely and courteously.

Lead Bullets

Perhaps the first bullets were stones—selected and backed with wadding, we hope—but lead won this land and this freedom, and it is still useful. For most of us handgunners who reload our centerfire cases, a bullet mold, lead pot, dipper, and some source of generous but directed heat become our bullet factory. Swaged bullets are more likely than cast ones to be free from bubbles, full-weight, full-formed, and accurate. But in casting we learn to look for defective bullets, even those little spots on the bases that show as soon as the cut-off has been tapped over. If a small punch will tear into them, we know we've got air-pockets in

the lead. Weighing, too, will sort out the culls. With everything hot, and a good head of lead-weight above the mold's pouring hole, we should get steady acceptable production with a broken-in mold. Now and then a mold doesn't need much breaking-in.

If our gun has non-adjustable sights we are wise in choosing a mold that drops bullets close to factory weight. The usual rule is that heavy bullets fly high, light ones low, at distances where most of us find it practical to shoot—not that the silvery bulls-eye of a moonlight night doesn't tempt even sober men. Heavy powder charges may send bullets high, though the quick barrel time of a fast load may get the slug out of the barrel before it's kicked up to the point at which a slow one escapes.

Sixguns often corrugate some people's foreheads by a tendency to lead at the barrel-breech. This pile-up of metal looks terrible, detracts somewhat from accuracy and, you'd perhaps think, imprisons under itself the fouling of corrosive primers. This last I've been spared. A gunsmith can smooth out a barrel throat, and there are special throat-cleaners, as described in the "Care" chapter.

Anyway, Ray Thompson of Grand Marais, Minnesota, is so keen a pistol shot that he designed some .38 and .44 Special gas-check bullet molds. That little copper cup on the bullet's behind, familiar to riflemen, evidently does expand somewhat to check the weaseling of gas as well as to reduce base fusion of hot loads. More important, it reduces or eliminates throat leading. There are other gas-check mold designs, and the .32-20 Ideal 110-grain, No. 311316, is an oldtimer.

Harvey's zinc gas-check washers, mentioned in the foregoing comment on jacketed bullets along with other Harvey bullets, are either cast on or sealed on with an extruded lead pimple. The molds came first; the swaging outfit hit the market in the summer of 1955.

These are mostly light bullets except for the 124-grain 9 mm. Luger or .38 Auto. The .357 or .38 caliber come in 135-grain solid and 125-grain hollow point. The .44 goes 220 grains, the .45 Auto 190. With these bullets a gun may lead at first, but usually they clean out a leaded bore. The zinc base can't fall off, as some gas-check cups do in flight. It does the same job of helping soft lead to hold the rifling at high speed. Swaged soft lead is dense and about as uniform as it's possible to get that metal. However, a good share of the remarkable, old, bench-rest and offhand rifle records were made with cast bullets, carefully selected, loaded and fired. It was years before modern bench-resters with jacketed bullets could beat them at all consistently.

The use of the auto-pistol and the tendency of many revolvers to lead has caused us to lean a little too hard, possibly, on tough cast-bullet alloys. Some you can't scratch with a thumbnail. How could those bullets mushroom on game or expand to fit an over-size barrel? They glance more readily than soft bullets, and some are actually so light with tin, antimony, linotype metal or solder that they don't shoot quite to zero with the standard soft alloys that factories use. If the auto handles fairly soft lead and the revolver doesn't foul too badly with it, many of us like to use that kind. But the rather hard one-to-16 or one-to-17 tin and lead alloy or their equivalents are good practical favorites. In handloading you fit your cartridges to your gun, and maybe to your notions, too.

Copper-coated .22 long-rifle bullets came out in the 1920s, as I recall, at first over semi-smokeless powder charges. In some guns this coat or wash reduced leading, and still does. Machine-cast slugs of the type come from Cladaloy Bullet Company, Box 643, North Hollywood, California; and they are popular.

Sometimes lead is a Precious Metal! Kirksite "A" zinc-alloy is a way out of lead scarcity. Since its weight is about two-thirds that of lead, generous handgun sight elevation is called for. It's so hard that it scarcely shows marks from worn rifling that would still leave good tracks on lead, but it seems not to have worn out barrels. Lightness makes it wind-sensitive and poor in holding velocity; and it doesn't mushroom, though it might break up quite well in hollow-point style, even at handgun velocities. Yet when lead is scarce we might be thankful for it. It needs a new or a very clean mold, for it doesn't mix congenially with lead traces.

Leather and Wax Bullets

My stepfather used to rid the barn of rats with a .36 caliber cap-and-ball sixgun, loaded with a fair dose of black powder and full wadcutter-style bullets punched out of heavy harness leather. Smack, not deep penetration, did the work. The stock and the human family were safe. It took some stalking, waiting and shooting, and even in the usual refreshing variety of farm jobs it must have been a welcome interlude. No doubt it helped in the development of the first-class still-hunter of Adirondack deer that he later became.

These loads had some punch. A *Rifleman* article by James F. Brady described the use of wax bullets, case-mouth punched out of a block of paraffin, powered by primers alone, the flash-holes in the brass enlarged to increase that power. These bullets of course shoot low, but a double target can be used, one bull for aiming, a lower bull to mark the bullet strike. Noise would be very low, and recoil non-existent, but no gun and load are for fooling.

THE JOB

So far we've talked mostly about equipment. The job should be pure fun. Enjoy it by taking it easy. Deliberation can avoid almost any possibility of a careless mistake—and why not enjoy life, anyway?

Next to safety comes uniformity, in components and in our way of assembling them: the firm but not excessive forming of brass and seating of primers, the even, sure stroke of the powder measure's handle, the true lining-up of bullets in case-mouths.

Brass

Before we decap our empties we inspect them. Split case-mouths can take a crimp and hold bullets after a fashion, but hardly with uniform tension. Since brass intended to carry lead bullets should be reamed at the mouth to avoid mutilating that lead, there's a tendency for thin pistol cases to crack there after much crimping to hold the bullets, and expanding or belling, before that, to allow us to get them in. Blowing off of case-heads is now happily rare, and nearly always we get advance warning in dark crosswise lines above the rims.

With most handgun ammunition developing low pressures, excess head-space, or too free play of the cartridge back and forth in the chamber, seldom need whip up much worry. There must be some leeway in

A simple, light, but efficient case-trimmer furnished by Lyman-Ideal. Setup shown is for .375 Holland & Holland Magnum rifle brass.

the head-spacing of revolver brass. Some auto-pistol cartridges go into the chamber just far enough because they're positioned by a bottle-neck or by a semi-rim on the head. The .380 and .45 Colt and the 9 mm. Luger are examples of the truly rimless, with little difference (if any) between the diameters of the rim and of the brass just above the extracting cannelure. They get their head-space seat against the front of the chamber, on which the square uncrimped mouth of the case must abut firmly. If too short, they have excess head-space; if greatly over-long, they could keep the breech from closing fully. I've never hand-loaded the .380, but the other two gave me no trouble in a good bit of use. Still, it can happen. For target accuracy in the .45 autoloader, or the revolver when loaded without clips, cases should be of correct uniform length to get even ignition of primer and powder.

When a fired primer is punched out with unusual ease, the pocket in that case can be considered oversize, made so, or expanded by use. Such brass should go out; and creeks, catch-alls, or junior collectors might welcome it, with the understanding that it shouldn't be reloaded. A loose live primer may be driven back against the breech-frame of some revolvers, when we fire another cartridge in the cylinder. Few sixguns are constructed for safe multiple fire of that sort! Our inspection should check flash-hole size in the primer pockets. Slight variations may cause almost no change in velocities, other things being equal, but now and then a flash-hole breaks out a little to the side. Such cases are for discard.

Many of us put up good lead-bullet ammunition and never size the brass to fit the bullet snugly, relying on crimp to hold the lead. This is an economy measure, of tools or of time. For accurate work we value the uniform bullet pull that sizing both brass and lead can give, the more water- and oil-proof effect, and the certainty that our loads will fit all standard arms of the same caliber. They will, if we resize the brass full-length, not merely the section that holds the lead. Jacketed bullets always need neck-sized cases except in unusually tight chambers, generally those of rifles made to special order long ago. However, pinched case-necks have held rifle bullets well enough to give

good shooting; but this expedient would hardly do in a revolver, with its recoil, or in the feeding process of an auto-pistol.

One easy way to size straight, rimless cases full-length is to send them base first through a die. A flat bar of steel about ⅜-inch thick, with a hole bored precisely through it, did well for a .45 Auto I had. It was so finely made that it seemed not to affect the evenness of case-wall thickness, one of the factors that make for accuracy. Most people who size handgun cases use a regular commercial tool with dies to reduce the brass, and expanding plugs to open it again to a smaller but even diameter. Specially hardened parts last a long time. Their price spells economy for those who handload in large quantities.

Crimping revolver case-mouths on the lead is almost invariably necessary. A crimp helps powder burn well and, more important, ought to prevent a bullet from being shucked forward out of its case by recoil. If the bullet nose sticks out the front of the cylinder, the gun is locked when that round comes up. In heavily charged sixguns, some of the standard factory ammo has had its bullets unseated by recoil, and heavier crimping has had to be used. One method used for a time was to turn a cannelure or groove in the case, right over the midsection of the bullet. Such grooves don't "shoot out" on the first discharge, and the mutilation of lead doesn't help accuracy a bit. However, the cartridges were reliable in light, alloy-frame guns which were meant for serious duty and accurate shooting.

Rifle and pistol zinc-alloy bullets from Cladaloy Bullet Co., Box 643, North Hollywood, Calif. Round-nosed, .45 Auto and wadcutter .38 at top, semi-wadcutter .44 at bottom, with round-nosed .44 and .38 to its left. At extreme right is a flat-nosed .44-40 or .45 Colt—can't tell for sure—and the rifle bullets seem to run from .25 to .35 —or maybe .375—and .45. Photo courtesy New Jersey Zinc Co., 160 Front St., New York 38, New York.

Bullet-Casting

Bullet-casting is fun after we have learned the trick, though to learn it with a brand-new mold can be fun and games for a while. It's better to have the metal too hot than too cold, for the rather contradictory "frosted" color of lead cast at excess heat seems not to harm the product. Molds can be cooled, if you like, and the best way I know is to hold them in the flow of an electric fan. Another method, which I'm too superstitious and backward to try, is to dip the mold into water, not empty, but with a bullet in it.

The bright, silvery slugs of normal casting delight the eye of anyone from two years old to ninety-plus. To avoid marring their beautiful contours, we pad the table or bench that catches them, for dented marred bases don't make for precision shooting. Gas gets past them unevenly at the muzzle, and this can and usually will tip them. Even well broken-in molds generally need to be warmed by rejected bullets before dependable production starts. Some of us are perfectionists, rejecting every not quite right bullet. Others save all except those with unfilled bases and use the culls for plinking, or for aerial practice—if they can get to a place where that fascinating sport is safe.

Electric melting pots draw the lead from the bottom of the mass, where it's under pressure from above and free from dross that may have escaped our skimming. But if the electric pot is small, skimming is much harder to do than with an open pot with the heat below it. Most cookstoves give enough heat—they heat the kitchen plenty, too! One hot day in western Tennessee I built a little soft-coal fire outdoors in the shade and cast some perfectly usable .38 Specials. If we wanted wax bullets, as were fired in the old Gastinne-Renette gallery in Paris, we shouldn't need anything hotter than a pair of young ardent hands. Or did last night's passing glance at TV affect my judgment?

The big ammunition factories sell lead and jacketed bullets, and there are dozens and scores of custom makers. Practically all lead bullets sold are sized and lubricated, ready to load, though some with metal bases aren't designed for lubrication and don't need it. "Perfecast" are cast, as the name implies; Speer has swaged lead bullets; Cladaloys are plated; and so on. But the majority are lubed and sized lead-alloys. There are all sorts of shapes, weights, and designs, including hollow-points, of course, and bullets with beveled bases, easy to load without shaving. But some people wouldn't trust them not to let gas cut ahead, as the old Frankford Arsenal, 173-grain .30-06 M1, jacketed boat-tails did to some extent. But M1s were superb at long range, and their barrel erosion compared to that of the flat-based 150-grain bullets was not excessive.* The sides of a jacketed aren't fused by cutting gas, as lead is. Still, a lot of capable pistolmen like a beveled-base lead bullet, and shoot high scores with that type.

*Late reports cast doubt on what we formerly accepted as the excessive bore wear of the boat-tailed 173-grain bullets.

Molds should be kept clean, and free from the pitting of even the slightest rust. Crumbs of lead between the jaws yield to a carefully steered razor-blade, and a carbon solvent helps in maintenance work, too. Most of us seem to like to heat a mold simply by casting bullets in it till they come smooth. By alternating two molds we avoid over-heating. Casting shouldn't be a race against time, anyway. It does no harm to set the mold alongside the pot, but not too near. An open dipper, not a snouted one, is correct for multi-cavity molds with a trough to receive the lead.

To flux the alloys and make the metal flow better, we used to drop in a piece of beeswax or bullet lube about a half-inch in diameter, stir it up, dodge the smoke, and then skim the pot. Printers employ special fluxes for their type-metal casting, and can give good advice. A big pot is nice for working up a good supply of evenly alloyed metal, and from it we can cast ingots in trays. They come of a size to put into smaller and handier electric furnaces to use for bullet casting.

For heavy loads, bullets should not be over .001 inch above rifling groove diameter of the gun they're meant for, and smaller, down to exact diameter, are all right. They too can help in getting target accuracy. The main thing is not to have them too big. As always for accurate, medium-power loads, it pays to experiment. Weighing and sorting bullets take time, but for precision target work it's well-spent time.

Most experienced target shots favor what might seem to be low powder charges in .38 Special, and in .45 Auto, too. They reduce fatigue. You will read more about this, if you like, in Bert Shay's chapter following this one. A very light charge can fail to give 50-yard accuracy, and one slightly above it can be wind-sensitive. Long bullets of course hold their velocity better than short ones of similar design, and the cross-wind has a harder time in shoving them around. But some bullets must be rather short, like those for the .45 Auto. Yet that stubby cartridge does splendid work on target, as well as on more serious work assignments; and few 50-yard shooters would go to a heavier one such as the .44 Special. Except for .45 matches, the rather small .38 Special cartridge remains the great favorite. It will take bullets heavy enough to fight wind. You know, too, that it *has* served for 200- and even 300-yard target, though hardly as an equal of big calibers.

A mechanical bullet sizer and lubricator like the Meepos, Pacific, Ideal, Cramer and others does quick and usually precise work. But if we lubricate bullets months before we load them, we should check to see if the lube has flaked or started to melt. It may stay on for years, as I've had buck tallow do, without caking into uselessness.

Hand lubrication is slow but can be uniform and full enough for practically top accuracy. Did all the fine old bench-rest rifle shots use machines? Set in a pan with melted lube around them, bullets are picked out with a headless cartridge case that trims off excess lube, or we can chill the pan and break out the bullets rather well. The fingertip method is less trouble for a few bullets. You learn to peel pretty uniform chunks off the stick of lube and press them into the grooves with your forefinger as you rotate the bullet. Some use grease wads under the bullet, especially in rifle cartridges, old paper-patched slugs and so on to modern jacketed pills. They reduce powder space and increase loading density and pressure, for which you allow. Industrial Products Company's Ipco (Box 14, Wakefield, Massachusetts) is graphited and especially made—or it was in the beginning—just for this purpose, under jacketed bullets. Without any card wad under it, it seems not to pollute the kernels of rifle powders in any way, but I am not so sure of its effect on pistol powders, at least in hot weather. Probably I'm wrong, and it may not do the least harm. I have used this kind of lubrication only, with lead rifle bullets, leaving the grooves unfilled; but this method was not for hot loads or much of anything else except to see if it would work. It did; and then some other aberration claimed me.

Measuring Bores

It's really the barrel's rifling groove diameter, not its bore diameter, that we want to know for selecting a bullet that's full-size for it, or perhaps a thousandth-inch over. To measure the barrel of an auto-pistol or a top-break revolver is easy. We start a slightly oversize bullet in the breech and drive it on through, catching it when it comes out, that so that it won't fall and be dented. Soft lead does well, and a little oil in the bore does no harm. Even a round bullet can be used, but a straight-sided conical one is easier to measure with the micrometer.

All clear, so far, but how do you drive a bullet through a solid frame revolver's barrel without dismounting the gun? You start at the muzzle, which certainly isn't throated out as most barrel-breeches are; and then too, some Smith & Wesson barrels, and no doubt others, are taper-bored, tighter at muzzle than at breech.

The other day my wife and I measured a .44 Special Smith bore, using a bullet that could have been made to order for the project, Ideal 245-grain wadcutter No. 429352. It has a long, straight forward section that rides on the rifling lands—is imprinted by them when it's fired—one wide grease groove and one narrow crimping groove with a short, full-size band above it. Glen cut the bullet in two with a hacksaw, neatly, and the base part was allocated to the lead-pot. I filed off a bit of the remaining wide band under the crimp groove, and beveled it so that no big lead fins would flow back when we drove it through the barrel. While I held the gun muzzle-up and with the cylinder swung out she started the bullet, its wadcutter point first, driving it flush with the muzzle by tapping a hardwood stick with a tack-hammer. Then she traded the stick for a section of steel cleaning rod, being careful to center it so as not to mar the barrel; and from there

on, it was easy. I caught the bullet in my hand, and the engraving of the barrel lands stood up in beautiful, clean-cut ridges. A perfect specimen to measure.

Then I remembered something well-known but forgotten in the enthusiasm: this is a five-groove barrel! There were no directly opposite ridges to lay the micrometer across, but these S.&W. lands and grooves are of just about equal width. By squinting and trying and breathing hard, I got a full .428-inch measurement, which should be close to right. The .429-inch bullets are as thick as it should use for any heavy load, and .428 perhaps are even better.

Use of Powders

This has been described in the Ammunition Components section preceding this one. Here only a reminder to take caution seems necessary. Any standard-velocity or hotter pistol load is critical, even more so than most rifle rounds, because case capacities are relatively small and practically any powder we should use, except black, is concentrated. Du Pont No. 4759, a midrange rifle powder which is good for full loads, too, in little cartridges like the .25-20, could be another exception. It's rather cool-burning, and with light charges of it we have difficulty in making it burn at all thoroughly in handgun and small rifle brass. But it can be overloaded, naturally, and now it seems to have become less popular for pistol use. I've used it in large and small pistol and rifle cases and still keep it on hand for rifle use. I shouldn't hesitate to use it again for the short-guns, if I needed to. Loads would still start small and never become ambitious. Friends who have used it for pistols still like it and load it commonly. Perhaps I've been missing a good thing lately.

We must always keep in mind factors that affect pressures: bullet seating depth, bullet diameter, weight, hardness and barrel-bearing length; primer strength; case capacity, strength and condition; and the individual gun. A weak length can break the chain of safe loading. As we gain experience we can, if we like, go on to heavier loads than we started with, but hardly, I think, on the say-so of anyone else. Guns vary in original strength, condition, and inner dimensions of barrels and chambers. Some chamber walls are so thin that they never should be asked to hold any load above factory standard pressure. And components vary, too, even from lot to lot of the same make and type, though but little here, as a rule. Some old recommendations that were sound with primers and powders as made at the time just wouldn't do now. Case capacities have been reduced in some sizes by the adoption of solid-head construction.

Bullet Seating

Except for the wipe-off, final inspection, the packing, and the charge-labeling and dating of the container, this is usually the last step in handloading. Then, often enough, we wish we had more loading to do!

If the bullet is seated and the case-mouth crimped on it at the same time, there is some liability of minute

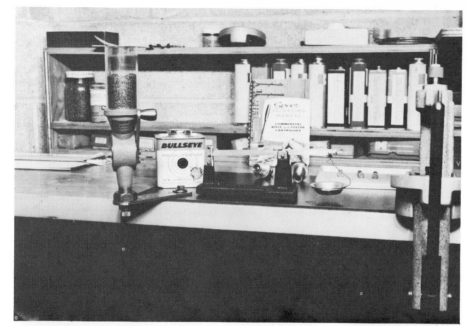

Loading bench and equipment to load a .38 Special cartridge: powder measure, can of powder, Redding-Hunter scale, Speer's *Reloading Manual,* set of dies, lube pad, and R. C. B. S. Junior tool. This series of photographs was prepared for us by Fred T. Huntington of R. C. B. S. Gun & Die Shop, P. O. Box 729, Oroville, Calif.

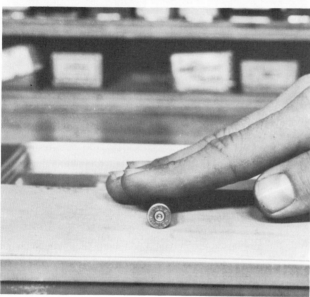

Necessary operation No. 1: proper lubrication of case with R. C. B. S. lubricating oil and a Carter's 4 x 8-inch uninked pad. Apply oil to pad, let it soak in, and roll cases on pad.

Operation No. 2: sizing case in sizer only in R. C. B. S. three-die set.

particles of lead being forced or cut off, and these of course tend to foul the bore. James E. Clark, an outstanding pistolsmith (Box 4248, Shreveport, Louisiana) has written interestingly of his loading methods in *The American Rifleman,* and in that fine little paperback, *Gil Hebard Guns.* He is nationally famous as a pistol shot, as well as a .45 Auto accurizer and handloader. A bullet-seating method he favors is to both crimp and swage the case around the cast bullet, first seating the bullet as a preliminary separate operation. One way is to back out the seating die so its crimping shoulder cannot touch the brass, but still have the seating punch down where it can do its work. A special taper-crimping die from Gil Hebard (Knoxville,

Illinois) removes the belling of the case-mouth, put there to avoid lead-shaving, and swages and crimps the brass around the bullet to about one-fourth its length. This can also be done with the cartridge's own case-sizing die, the shoulder at its mouth crimping and swaging the previously seated bullet in place. If the sizing die works the brass for much over one-half or at most two-thirds the bullet's length, the case may spring away from the bullet, and you don't get a secure crimp. Before I had .25-20 tools, I used to crimp the case-mouths with a .220 Swift neckdie, not as an accuracy refinement but to hold the bullets in place under the thrust of a tubular magazine spring. It was a makeshift measure, but it worked. Some loads happened to shoot very nice groups. It was possible to get a nice, even, symmetrical crimp.

There is a special crimp-size die, Mr. Clark reported in a *Rifleman* article, that comes from John E. Giles, another .45 specialist, at 1504-R South Highland Avenue, Clearwater, Florida.

James Clark finds that his own .45 handloads will group in less than three inches at 50 yards, from an accurized auto-pistol, and in less than two inches, from a heavy-barreled 1955 Model Smith & Wesson target revolver. About the best claimed by any factory is 1½ inches, from target guns using such target-type ammo as the .22 long-rifle, .38 Special, or .44 Special.

As Fred T. Huntington of the R.C.B.S. Gun & Die Shop, Oroville, California, pointed out, many shooters of .357 and .44 Magnum sixguns like the separate seating and crimping system, because its avoidance of lead shaving reduces the tendency to foul or lead the

Operation No. 3: expanding and decapping. Proper expanding and slight bell-mouthing of case let the reloader seat lead or lead-alloy bullets without shaving them. R. C. B. S. originated the three-die sets, at no additional cost to the buyer.

Operation No. 4: place bullet on top of case-mouth in preparation for seating and crimping. R. C. B. S. crimpers are built into the die, being ground on to the chamber reamer; so the crimp is in a straight line with the sidewall of the case.

An operation in conjunction with expanding is priming, shown here. Note the removable shell holder that lets the loader change easily and quickly from one caliber to another.

The bullet is in place, ready to be raised into the seater die for seating and crimping.

The completed cartridge.

point shooting. I suppose it would take thousands of such pistol loads to contribute noticeably to chamber erosion. They aren't in a class with split-neck, high-power rifle cases, which in time can harm a chamber.

Records

It pays to keep some records of loads, for memory is fallible. Sometime we might want to know—and perhaps recommend or warn against—formulas that were either excellent or execrable. (That word hurts my throat. How's yours?)

When we use, regularly, two or three different loads, some of us make easy identification by the shape of the bullets, the make of the cases, or the color of the primers—white, yellow, or gold. Even so, a dated load memo packed into each box of cartridges can avoid much frowning and bewilderment.

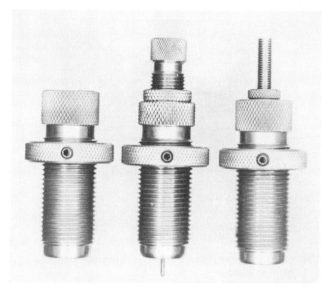

The regular R. C. B. S. three-die set.

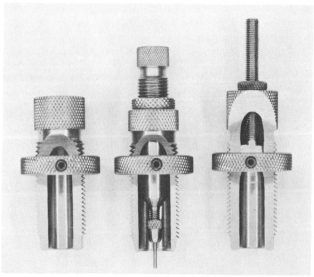

Cut-away view of R. C. B. S. three-die set.

bore. (These high velocity sizes can be pestiferous in this respect.) Fred has made four-die sets for Jim Harvey of Lakeville Arms. Under this system one die sizes the brass, the second expands it, the third seats the bullet, and the fourth crimps the case-neck around the seated bullet. As Fred points out, some folks have difficulty in adjusting a seater die to seat at the right depth and *also* crimp correctly; consequently, a quadruple set is a time-saver. It can avoid frustration and getting all shook up, as you and I can plainly see.

We are indebted to Mr. Huntington for his series of photographs that track through the process of loading a .38 Special cartridge. He made a nice job of it.

A straightline tool, as most of them are now, seats bullets well if tolerances are close and we do our part. Lead bullets, and those with short conventional gas-checks, need belled or expanded case-mouths when they're seated, if they aren't to be shaved. Reaming the case-mouth thin is hardly enough with full-sized bullets, provided the brass has been resized. Perhaps the best method is a short neck-expanding to start the bullet smoothly into the case. For most bullets a quarter-inch or so is plenty. Jacketed bullets seldom require even case-mouth reaming, though it does no harm if the work is performed consistently. Uniformity is the big component of accurately loaded and accurately shooting ammunition.

Belling case-mouths requires no special expanding plug or button. We can use a tapered steel rod or even a ball-bearing. But belling the mouth and then sharply turning it in with a crimp wears the already reamed mouth in double time, or near it. Soon cracks appear, and the brass is ready for discard or for more or less no-account loads, not accurate because crimp strength varies. They do all right for plinking, aerial work, or

Substitutes

From time to time loading supplies are short. A careful skilled handloader sometimes can find make-dos and substitutes. Naturally, that kind is careful.

Black powder immediately pops into the mind, for almost any old primers that go wink will fire it. Match-heads have done that, set inside re-formed primer cups, without the anvil, as space was at a premium. Various smokeless rifle powders, powder salvaged

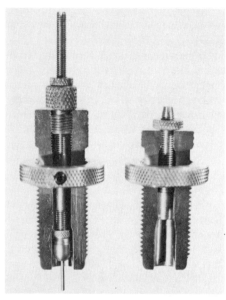

Cut-away view of R. C. B. S. two-die pistol set for .30 Luger, .30 Mauser, or any other bottle-necked pistol case.

from ancient loads with dead primers, and even shot-shell powders can be shoved into service if a loader knows his stuff and *still* is cautious.

Kirksite and other zinc alloys pinch-hit for lead. Odd calibers sometimes can be fitted with brass: cut-off .32 Winchester Self-loading cases for the .32-.44 S.&W.; .351 Win. for the very long .38-.44 S.&W.; reworked .25-35 or .30-30 hulls for the .41 Colt; .35 or .351 Win. S.L. for .38 Auto or Special, and so on. A micrometer and old cartridge catalogues help, and many a veteran handgun pressed into service has delighted a pistoleer. At least he avoided being shortaged into the stone-throwing brigade.

Safety

Always we must keep alert and thoughtful to avoid trouble, though handloading and the shooting of home-rolled ammo needn't be dangerous sports! Factory labels warn us against firing high-velocity .32-20s in revolvers. A few fast .38-40 and .44-40 rounds must remain unfired and shouldn't be turned loose in six-gun chambers. Most of these .32, .38 and .44 stingers have light, hollow-point, jacketed bullets. The older soft-point or full-patched high-velocity cartridges used full-weight slugs and in these sizes normally were headstamped "H.V."

At the other end of the scale, black powder loaded under compression and stored for years can crumble into dust that generates pressures too high for sound arms. Often such oldtimers are just weak and smoky. Most smokeless powders lose strength, gradually, unless they've been stored near excessive heat.

Large rifle primers, taller than pistol primers, may be distorted if seated flush with pistol case-heads. Such maltreatment can cause misfires from breaking and displacement of the primer's pellet. Also it can make a primer too sensitive. Heavy-hammered guns like most big single-actions fire rifle primers reliably, as a rule, when we have to make them do it. Such primers are hard on the recoil plate in the revolver's breech.

Extremely light loads serve in the gallery or wherever we don't want to chase auto-pistol cases around the lot. Bottle-necked rimless cases used for squib loads in rifles commonly have their shoulders set back by the force of the primers. This gives them increased head-space. Bottle-necked pistol brass like .30 Luger, Mauser and Borchardt possibly would get the same treatment, with very light powder charges, even though small pistol primers aren't very strong. However, the large pistol primer, which we use in squib-loaded rifle cases to avoid over-ignition of fast powders, has plenty of strength to shorten heavy bottle-necked brass that head-spaces on its shoulder, not on a rim or belt.

Lightly powered bullets can stick in a barrel. A second load rings the barrel and may or may not dislodge the first bullet. One winter evening we stopped a visitor at the range from ruining his Savage .32 automatic. It had "sounded queer." No wonder: the bullet of an old, perhaps oil-soaked, cartridge was peeping out of the muzzle.

Deeply seated bullets raise pressures, often seriously with pistol powders. Many an uncrimped auto-pistol bullet has been manhandled down into its case. Better not fire such stuff.

Know your gun. Bullets should not fit extremely tightly in chamber mouths or barrel grooves. If chamber mouths are smaller than barrel groove diameter, the lead must be soft indeed to expand to fill the grooves and deliver power and accuracy. A new barrel or a cylinder reaming job is needed.

Bullets with long bearing, as well as those that are oversize, tend to raise pressures. A bullet oversize for your gun may be just right for a friend's barrel, or the opposite.

Some of us haven't the time or facilities for handloading, even though the wish may be there. Here are a few custom loaders, picked somewhat at random, but with regard to their reliability. Bob Moody, at Helena, Montana, specializes in heavy, Keith-bullet loads in .38-.44 High Velocity, .357 Magnum, .44 Special and so on. Fred M. Seguin, 2218 Tower Avenue, Superior, Wisconsin, often has contributed his experiences to *The American Rifleman*. Paul G.

Mansfield, New Boston, New Hampshire, must have had enough snowed-in time to work out a good many projects. One is his 8 mm. Japanese in .30 Luger cases, powering 85-grain, .321-inch lead bullets. Look under "Ammunition (Custom)" in "Directory of the Arms Trade" near the back of John Amber's *Gun Digest* annual for many others. But no listing can include all the good ones, and the poor ones you try just once.

If you're in doubt of the quality, at least see if the reloads you've bought will chamber. Some won't. Two of my friends, before they got tooled up for these sizes, had .222 Remington and .32-40 loads they couldn't use—unless they'd had their guns rechambered to a hell's delight to accept that horribly mistreated brass. Seemed as though .32 Special dies had been used for the .32-40s, but what loused up the .222s I still can't figure. However, there are ways . . .

In other words, ingenuity is unlimited!

The following comment from old friends fits so aptly into current discussion of cast-bullet deficiencies, some rather difficult to observe or to avoid, that we are happy to include it in this chapter. Even though bullets swaged from extruded lead wire are growing in popularity, and justly so, most of us who make our own still cast our own. Here is definitive advice.

MATCH QUALITY .38 SPECIAL WADCUTTER BULLETS

By THOMAS C. FLORICH *and* THOMAS C. FLORICH, JR.

It is likely that .38 Special midrange wadcutter handloads exceed in amount all other handloads in all calibers. These loads of about 750 f.s. muzzle velocity are not too noisy in gallery ranges, and they do nicely for fine 50-yard work outdoors. Pistol clubs, police departments and individual shooters use them for instructional firing, routine practice and match work. The clean, round, easily scored holes they make in target paper appeal to shooters and especially to scorers.

Having loaded them for many years, originally with bullets cast with dipper and lead-pot, and more recently with an electric, bottom-feed pot, we have observed some details which spell the difference between good ammunition and match quality loads. The series of articles on "Cast Bullet Rifle Loads" by Colonel Harrison in the December, 1957 to March, 1958 *American Rifleman* gave clues to details which, applied to revolver ammunition, resulted in superb loads.

There are two types of wadcutters, and weights vary with the alloys used. One form is the wadcutter of 150 grains' nominal weight. It is a plain cylinder for about half its length, which is seated out of the case. Below a crimping cannelure in the middle of the bullet are the grease grooves. This type is used much less than the other, but fine-grouping loads are made with it. Most used are bullets from molds nominally called 146- or 148-grain wadcutters, which are seated, all or

nearly so, in the case, as in factory midrange loads. This form of bullet has four driving bands with three grease grooves between them, and a crimping cannelure just under a "dirt-scraping band" that is quite thin or narrow. It, too, is loaded to give fine-grouping ammunition, both by factories and handloaders.

The advantage of the former, half-cylinder-exposed type is that it can be cast with fewer imperfect-looking bullets. The slight disadvantage is that being less deeply seated than the multigrooved type, a little more powder is needed to get the 750 f.s. muzzle velocity. About 2.7 to 2.9 grains of Bullseye are used with it.

The multi-grooved type, which gives the 750 f.s. with 2.5 grains Bulleye or 3.1 of No. 5066, has the drawback of more imperfect-looking bullets cast, particularly up front where that thin dirt-scraping band is not always perfectly filled out. Sometimes it shows just a tiny nick or two. Often about half of the dirt-scraping band appears filled, resulting in an obviously defective-looking bullet.

Cases: Sort them by makes, number and location of cannelures, and keep them separate right through all loading operations into cartons of finished cartridges. After many loadings, cases develop mouth-cracks from the constant working of the brass in belling out and then crimping. Discard all such.

Alloys Used: Keep various lots separate. Lead pipe scrap from old plumbing systems, with some wiped joints, usually has enough tin in those joints to make it flow well in casting. The "wiping solder" used on these joints originally contained 33⅓% to 40% of tin. Sheet lead used in roofing work or shower stalls has no tin in it, but contains anywhere up to 6% antimony, and a little tin added makes a good revolver alloy. Battery metal, plates or straps, contains various amounts of antimony, up to 13%, and sweetened up with some tin makes a good revolver bullet alloy. Cable sheathing varies. Some has up to 5% antimony; less is usual. Sweetened up with tin, it too runs good bullets. Most unplated .22 rimfire bullets are of nearly pure lead. But any alloy with an appreciable percentage of aluminum, zinc or magnesium, as sometimes used for cable sheathing, won't cast for sour apples. Avoid all such. Whatever alloy you use, pure lead and tin, or a suitable scrap alloy with tin added, be sure that there is just about 3% tin in the mix, and you'll find the percentage of perfect-looking bullets much greater than without the tin. If you choose commercial "pure lead," for each pound of it use one ounce of 50-50 solder, which the trade calls "common solder," or one-half ounce of pure tin, and you'll have just over a 3% tin alloy to work with. More tin does no harm but is unnecessary and wasteful for these revolver bullets.

Working with a three-cavity, 146-grain, Cramer wadcutter mold and a Saeco ten-pound, electric, bottom-feed pot, with sheet lead scrap plus 3% tin, gives bullets that weigh 144 grains mean. This mold of ours drops them .3595-inch diameter and they're sized to

.357-inch. The alloy is pre-mixed, well fluxed, and stirred before casting into little ingots of about one pound each. In bullet casting, you can work with five pounds or so in the pot, adding ingots as needed without slowing down the casting. Pre-heat ingots on the edge of the pot. Stir that pot frequently, but flux sparingly in bullet casting, as excessive fluxing promotes bubbles in bullets. These spell trouble.

Being deliberate, we take a slow pace, and about three hours at the casting pot are enough for a session. In that time about 12 pounds of ingots have made some 600 bullets. When the sprue cutter plate is knocked aside, look at the bases for holes or bubbles. Discard such bullets. In slow, steady casting at even heat they rarely show up.

Inspection: Examine bullets individually. Later, examine them every time you handle them preparatory to loading. Look at bases, sides, and noses. Keep in one lot all those that look normal in all respects, and in another lot those with tiny dents, base holes or swirls, or bands with wrinkles. It takes about 1½ hours to check 600 visually. If your casting went smoothly you'll find about 80% normal-looking and the rest with slight defects—using the multi-grooved type of wadcutter mold. For weight check determine the mean weight of normal-looking bullets, which was 144 grains with the mix used. Setting the scale—in this case a Brown & Sharpe yarn or roving scale sensitive to one-tenth grain—at 144 grains, a one-eighth inch oscillation above or below the index line on the long end of the beam insures the selection of bullets from 143.5 minimum to 144.5 maximum for 50-yard match loading. None of these normal-looking bullets went above 145 grains, and but few approached this weight.*

Here is the detail of 11 pounds, 13 ounces of one casting—about 590 bullets.

Nine showed gross defects not noticed when dropped from the mold. They were discarded in the visual check.

Of 581 bullets visually acceptable 120 showed minor defects; set them aside for weighing and use in gallery practice.

The 461 bullets left as normal-appearing were weighed. Thirteen weighed too light (142.5 to 143 grains) and were cut apart to see if any bubbles were inside. (See later notes on this point.)

The other 448 weighed from 143.5 to 144.5 grains. These were lubricated and set aside for 50-yard loading.

Of the 120 showing minor visible effects, when weighed, 86 ran 143.5 to 144.5 (most of them close to 143.5). 34 ran 142.5 to 143.5 (most of them close to 143). These were used for gallery practice.

In a previous casting that did not go too smoothly, and when more than the usual few with base holes were found, with 15 such discarded after visual inspection:

382 looked normal and ran 143.5 to 144.5. 48 with small defects ran 143.5 to 144.5. 83 with small defects ran 142.5 to 143.5. 4 with small defects ran under 142 and were discarded. 2 looked normal but were well under 142 and had holes inside when cut apart, as later referred to.

Weighing bullets is a slow operation. It takes three or more hours to weigh 600 when everything goes nicely; so there is an inclination to depend on visual examination alone. Do not. In the past several years of casting and loading some nine to ten thousand bullets and originally just sorting them visually, there would be, in 50-yard shooting, a rare wide shot. These unaccountables, which were sevens or sixes and once or twice not even on the target—with all others eights, nines or tens—were traced down, by weighing, to big holes inside the bullets, and the reason for the unaccountables became obvious. By using an awl in visual inspection, you'll find it possible to insert its point into a seeming pinhole in a base, up to an eighth or a quarter inch. That's a big hole, and fatal to accuracy. Only weighing after visual sorting eliminates all such hard-to-spot defects.

Since weighing the bullets, we've had every call give us full value of that call on the target without a single wide or unaccountable shot. This is all that the best of factory match ammo does for the shooter! Weigh them for 50-yard work.

In recent years, close examination of factory match loadings shows a rather light crimp on these midrange cartridges; and on our following this lead, a light crimp caused no problems of bullet creep (breaking forward out of the crimp, under recoil of neighboring rounds). Consequently we use such a crimp. On full service loads a good, strong crimp is essential.

In the bullets set aside for 50-yard work, which are normal in appearance and run uniform in weight, from 143.5 to 144.5 grains, we have observed a condition of which no handloading text or manual we have read makes any mention. Cutting these in half down their center lines we found that about 85% of them disclose an axial cavity running from about ⅛ inch above the base for about ⅛ inch upward. This cavity is long, narrow, and usually well centered. It has a quite different appearance from the bubbles which occur almost always in bullets under our minimum of 143.5 grains for 50-yard use. Since these segregated bullets group well, the axial cavities either have no adverse unbalancing effect or are so uniform a condition that they seem harmless as far as grouping is concerned.

A possible reason for these cavities comes from pure conjecture on our part. It is a condition that Dr. Franklin W. Mann and his associates observed, over

---

* The rare one of 145 grains' weight seems to result when the sprue cut-off plate screw loosens. It is tightened at once, of course. So the rare 145-grain bullet is heavier than the mean, we judge, because its base is thicker owing to that loose plate!

Bullet No. 1 (at left): As cast, not sized. Visually acceptable and weighs 143.5 grains.

Bullet No. 2: As cast. Set aside on visual inspection. Dirt-scraping band at top is not filled out fully. Weighs 142.5 grains.

Bullet No. 3: Normal-looking but light bullet cut in halves, disclosing a hole, not a shrinkage cavity. Weighs 141 grains and is under the 142.5 grains acceptable by weight for gallery practice. Note the clean bubble appearance. Axial cavities have a frosty, crystalline look.

Bullet No. 4: Typical axial cavity found in from 75 to 80 percent of normal bullets. Cavity has frosty appearance and is well centered. Such bullets group well, give full value of the calls, and make clean, round prints. Seven of these bullets, sectioned, ran in weight from 143.5 to 144.5 grains and all were visually acceptable.

Bullet No. 5: Visually acceptable, but weighed light. Defects: hole near outside edge, close to base, also an axial cavity, which account for the abnormally light weight. Photo by Lamp, Winchester, Va.

50 years ago, as rather common in cast lead bullets. Dr. Mann called them blow-holes or trapped air. May they possibly be shrinkage holes—a vacuum formed as the bullet cools and the mass of it shrinks in cooling? The uniform shape and location of these shrinkage cavities are apparently a coincidence due to the use of the bottom-feed, electric pot. To insure proper feeding of a mold from such a pot, the mold must be held perpendicular to the feed nozzle at the sprue hole. These cavities occur along the center line of the bullets.

When the 13 bullets mentioned above, normal in appearance but light—only 142.5 to 143 grains—were cut apart, "bubbles" were disclosed in six, so-called to differentiate these imperfections from axial cavities. Three had axial holes much larger than those of acceptable-weight bullets—irregular in shape and either longer or wider than those in the 50-yard segregation. Although the remaining four were cut into as many as seven pieces each, we could locate no holes. Further efforts in cutting the pieces became impractical, but probably there are holes in one of another of those fragments. At any rate, the six with bubbles which were not axially located, and the four with the large axial cavities, deviated from the location of the cavities found in acceptable-weight bullets. The nearer a hole is to the outside of a bullet, the greater its unbalancing effect on the bullet's flight.

Finally, these rare bullets encountered in weighing, which were even lighter than the 13 above, when cut apart showed holes that were larger, and well removed from the axis. They were bubbles, not the axial cavities of acceptable bullets. Such imperfections seem to be due to excessive fluxing of the pot during casting, as bubbles of similar appearance have showed up at random on the outside of bullets right after fluxing the pot. These bubbles occur in the bases, bands, or grooves, or as swirls almost anywhere. Light fluxing minimizes the number of discards after resuming casting from a fluxed pot.

In checking some nine to ten thousand of these multi-grooved wadcutters, which are not as easy to cast as larger, smooth-sided bullets for rifle work, or the round-nosed revolver or pistol bullets, we found it obvious that we must follow careful visual inspection by weighing to eliminate the unacccountable shots that show on the target when only visual sorting is done. It may sound discouraging, but the only dependable bullet is one that looks normal and runs uniform in weight.

Factories swage their lead-alloy bullets, but unfortunately in both swaging and casting there are always particular problems. For match work, the factories keep the weights of such bullets uniform. Only weighing assures uniformity, regardless of the technique of forming that bullet.

Our observation of hundreds of ten-shot targets, fired from a forearm rest to run down the unaccountables, showed up a fact that may interest the student of Dr. Mann's work, *The Bullet's Flight from Powder to Target*. It should help him to run down the X and Y errors in rifles, as the doctor called these aberrations.

Bullets rigidly sorted by weight and visual inspection seem fully capable of possibles when shot from the forearm rest at 50 yards. These groups, which form away from the normal off-hand zero, would when centered on a bull's-eye score 96 to 98 quite regularly. In outdoor handgun work of this kind, we find two very real problems. Changes of light and shadow give the widening effect to groups that are normal with open sights, even when they are well blackened. The other problem in this sort of work is that the effort to get a uniform sight picture (with revolver sights) for a good hold, trigger release, and call of the shot, is very tiring on even young and healthy eyes.

In spite of these handicaps we found, quite early in this work, that good calls went into very small groups, except for the unaccountables. All the good calls in the small groups gave clean, round prints, whereas the unaccountables out of the group showed more or less elliptical (tipping) prints. Using the rigidly sorted and weighed bullets, we noted no tipping bullet-prints, and those bullets have given full value of the calls. Although there is a vast difference between Dr. Mann's rifle technique and ours with revolvers, the results verify his findings so precisely that they are startling.

CHAPTER 15

HANDLOADING FOR SPECIAL PURPOSES

BY ALBERT J. E. SHAY

PISTOL ammunition can be handloaded in many ways, from the ice-pick and bottle-capper stage to the modern straightline bench-tool method. In spite of the help given by precisely made tools, good ammunition depends mostly on the time, care and horse-sense spent on the job. Whether you go after bull's-eyes, small game or big game, a good pistol can turn in an amazing performance with some study, measurements, and simple precautions in assembling its fodder.

New and perhaps better tools are advertised, particularly in *The American Rifleman* and *Precision Shooting.* I've loaded with practically all of them, but my stand-by since 1930 has been the Pacific. Many of the others work with a down stroke of the operating handle, but the Pacific does it with a lift. What is discussed in this chapter was done with the Pacific.

I used the automatic primer feed in its early days but discarded it as a nuisance. A test of fully preparing 500 .38 Special empties showed not ten minutes saved by the auto primer.

In the late 1920s, with free lead for the taking from the ranges, we figured the cost of .38 handloads at about 35 cents per 100 rounds. In this day of atoms and jets, lead has risen out of the mire and slime of base metals to a place in the sun. So firms like Cladaloy Bullet Company, Box 643, North Hollywood, California, are coming up with ready cast, sized and lubricated zinc-alloy bullets for a price almost as low as the lead, were you to buy the pure lead to make them. These light bullets proved accurate in a couple of guns tried. They need a greatly higher sight setting. Few guns of today have enough latitude in elevation to put them in the bull with a normal point of aim. A much higher rear or a much lower front sight does it. They will take lots of velocity, but they deposit a bore fouling all their own.

In computing the cost of, say 10,000 rounds, add up the cost of lead, a suitable pot for casting, mold, lubricator and sizer, and the lube. When you approach the top target brackets you need 10,000 shots a year to keep your end up. If you'll cast your own, cultivate the acquaintance of a few plumbers and telephone linemen. It may pay off with lead and lead-alloy, most of it ready for casting just as it is. If you live and breathe in an electrified area, note the fine electric melting pots. Their convenience, cleanliness, and above all their ease of casting *better* bullets are juicy items. Many molds that you fret and cuss over for hours with the snouted pouring ladles—and the kitchen range too hot or too cold—come down to earth and produce good bullets at once via the electric pot. The weight of metal forced into the sprue of the mold acts to drive out the air, and the uniform heat is just right.

The Saeco, from Santa Anita Engineering Company, 2451 East Colorado Street, Pasadena 8, California, is ideal with its rheostat control. Incidentally, this firm has taken over the entire line of *Cramer molds.* The less expensive job from Potter Engineering Company, 1410 Santa Ana Drive, Dunedin, Florida, has cast me over a half million bullets, and their double element variety does well with three- and four-cavity molds.

What bullet for target shooting? There must be nearly 100 different .38 Special molds from the chief makers, Ideal, Bond, Cramer, and Hensley & Gibbs. Up to now, nothing quite equals the deep-seated wadcutter with three grease grooves, Hensley 50 and Cramer 16 H, nearly identical, and identical in performance. In the middle '30s, while I was president of the Brooklyn Rifle and Revolver Club, we had several members belonging also to the New York City Police Pistol Team. Practically all were handloaders, and one a close neighbor of mine. Earle W. Rowe, Patrick O'Neill and I set up a machine rest in a 50-yard indoor Police range—ideal for a test. Pooling our equipment and knowledge, we loaded 14 different .38 Special bullets with several different charges and powders. The best place to set up the target for the gun to print from rest was 56 yards from the muzzle. The Cramer 16 H gave the best accuracy. I still have a 56-yard group, fired from my then new Officer's Model Colt with heavy Single Action Army barrel installed by George Hyde, with six shots in 1¼ inches. This cylinderful helped select the bullet we've been using since then for match shooting!

Precision Bullets

The sizer and lubricator must have the right size die for *our* gun. The Ideal Handbook lists .38 Special Colt barrels with .354-inch groove diameter, Smiths with .357. You can bet that these figures are close to the truth, but to be sure, take your beautiful blue darling and slug the bore with a cast bullet .002 or .003 inch oversize. How?

For .38s an $^{11}\!/_{32}$ inch drill rod is about the closest you can come, nominally .3437. These are pretty smooth steel and require little work except with a hacksaw. Cut off a section about two inches longer than your barrel. Grind or file a slight bevel on the end you'll insert in the barrel; then spin it smooth with fine emery cloth. See if it will slide into the barrel, all the way. If not, go back to the emery cloth. Wipe it clean, brush out your barrel, leaving the tiniest bit of oil inside. Start the bullet in the muzzle, point first, with light blows from a bronze or copper hammer. When it's nearly all inside, use a short rod, *smaller* than the bore, to get it fully inside. From here use the drill rod, as close to size and as smooth as you can get it, and hammer it gently all the way through the barrel, with cylinder open or removed. When it's near the breech, hold your gun close down over a cushion and let the slug fall softly.

Look to see that both lands and grooves have left their imprints, and use your micrometer. Unless the thing has five grooves you can easily measure the groove diameter of your pizzle. If she mikes within a half-thousandth inch either side of standard, forget it. For low and medium velocity target loads you order your sizing die in even thousandths, not over .003 inch larger than groove diameter. You'll see why, later.

We discuss the bullet and its accessories first because it *is* first. Casting and processing consume the most time in handloading. There are many sizer and lubricator designs, the oldest probably being the Ideal, now revamped. And there are the late Pacific, the Cramer and others—and the Star. To my mind, this one, costing more than the others, is worth every penny. I don't see how I got along without it for so many years. It's at least four times as fast as the usual push-in, push-out types, as good as any and better than some. Each diameter of bullet with grooves differently spaced requires another die, in this machine, but they are less expensive than some for the other makes.

Always, when you order your sizer and lubricator, send a sample of the bullet you intend to use. Even if the tool will lubricate any amount of grooves, the top punch to fit your bullet nose is important. There's no surer sign of a green handloader than a misfit top punch that mars the pristine beauty of the bullet. And it's just as important to send a sample bullet to the loading tool maker, too.

No doubt you have ordered your sizer and lubricator for .358-inch bullets. Remember this when you order your loading tool. The expander plug for case-necks should be exactly of that diameter, too. (Don't forget the spring-back of brass.) We now have bullets cast, sized and prepared, and our loading tool arrives. We're all of a twitter to get some loads done and see how they perform. OK, but let's go on with bullets.

Many loaders arrange tools for use while they stand up. Me, I was born lazy, or too close to the ground. You take a long session more easily sitting. Perhaps with tools that work on the down stroke you must stand to apply pressure. Anchor the tool to a solid bench, lagscrewed to the floor, or rigged so you can stack enough bullets on the shelves to hold it in place.

A good place to keep processed bullets free from dust and injury is in undented movie tins. It may take leg-work to find them, but so what? Since they're limber when filled, I find an uncreased piece of corrugated paper box, lay the uncovered tin upside down on it, and scribe the circle with a pencil. With a sharp knife I cut to the line. This is large, but the bulge around the inside will take care of that. Press it in without bending and you have a stiff dust-tight tin. I used to stack bullets in layers, but this seemed superfluous with the Star. I counted a neatly layered boxful, then spied me a counter in a junk hardware store window and spent $1.49 on it. It was easy to rig it to the Star to count for me. When bullets dumped in helter-skelter and shaken down added up with those in shining rows, was I surprised! Rough on the bullet bases? I wasn't going to fire them in a bench-rest rifle match!

Pulling Bullets

Here's another gadget. Harry Stebbins suggested extracting bullets from pistol cartridges with some of the pullers offered to the handloader. I can't. I have a good puller that has done at least 50,000 rifle jobs, but not one pistol cartridge could I make it perform on, though I wanted to: .45 Auto, .38 Special with steel jackets, 9 mm. Luger for sub-machine guns, and .30 M1 carbine ammunition. The thing just slipped gently off the end of lead bullets, and those jacketed ones were tapered right from the casemouth—no old truncated-cone Luger bullets among them—and gave no grip. Powdered resin? No use. All this was before pullers like the R.C.B.S. came into use.

We set a load on the Pacific shell holder, ran it all the way up with no die in the frame, and tried to grab it with pliers. Not enough room for pliers and not enough to grab. Well, make it show up above the frame of the tool. We removed the operating handle with toggle and link, inspected it. The link was of ¼-inch flat stock ⅝ inch wide, and a part of it ground out to let it pass up into the guide frame. Maybe if this link were longer it would push the cartridge farther up through the frame when the handle was lifted. We came up with a length of flat stock ¼ x ⅝ inch, and laying a regular Pacific link on it, we marked and cut off a section long enough to allow an inch more between the holes for the pins in each end of the link. We drilled and reamed a hole near each end to ¼ inch, the diameter measurement of the pins. Laying on the original link, we scribed the curved outline on the flat stock and took it to the grinding wheel. When we had it down to the mark we tremblingly hurried to the tool, fitted the shell holder and link to the toggle, and tried. She wouldnt go up!

Now what? The part ground away wasn't deep or long enough. So it was grind a little and try. By lengthening a lot and thinning the link a lot more than the original we finally made it pass up the guide, and lo! the top of the shell holder almost stuck out the top of the frame. The pliers again! They wouldn't take enough hold, not even big gas pliers.

Then came inspiration. Remembering Grandpa's tool chest, we frantically rummaged through and dug up a pair of shoemaker's nippers. We didn't intend to *salvage* bullets, but just get them out. At that, jacketed .45s, 9 mm.s, .38s and .30 M1s, some of them steel jacketed, weren't marred out of accuracy. The carbine slugs made an inch group at 100 yards in the D.C.M. Springfield sporter. Want more?

Cases

We have saved our empties and gathered some from the range where less frugal souls fling them at the trash-box. Watch out, for soon you'll be initiated into that bane of all things made of steel, scratches. One tiny grain of sand, concrete, ashes or other grit will scratch your die, and forever after the mark will show on your resized cases. I used to wash brass and store it in closed boxes; yet the most I ever got from a steel die with pistol cases was 30,000. Then it had worn out.

Along came Mr. Paul Knepp with dies lined with Carbaloy, of cemented carbide. These Lifetyme Dies come from Carbide Die & Manufacturing Company, Box 226, Covina, California. They're made for most tools for straight-sided pistol cases. They size, decap and expand, your tool doing the priming. With one for your most used caliber, your worries are over. They just wipe off grit and sand, and the brass comes up smiling, as bright or brighter than new. Some have processed a million rounds. I wore out at least six regular dies before I bought one, and I had lost money. They pay in quantity loading!

Rig your tool to a bench where you can sit comfortably. Dig up a swivel chair without arms and raise the tool high enough for the handle to pass between your knees. If you have any regard for the floor you need a primer catcher. The Potter provides for this, but no other tool I recall except the Star loading machine, and one for the Pacific from Frank Foster, Box 983, Clovis, New Mexico.

We assume you're right-handed, but if not, you can go into reverse. Put a shallow box or tin within easy reach on the left. I use camp stools, one on either side. On the right we place the loading block, really a counting block because I put primed cases mouth down in it, ready for me to inspect for high primers. They can lock a sixgun, cause misfires, or convert an autoloader into a machine gun as the slide slams down on them!

On the left of the tool, on the bench, I put a tin can lid, usually with rolled edge, and with enough lead poured in to cover the bottom and give it weight. After you've caught your fingernail on the edge of this tray, full of primers, and the whole shebang has cascaded to the floor, you'll approve of ballast.

Learn to roll a primer with the forefinger so that the anvil side is up, and to caress a seated primer with that digit to be sure it's fully in. When the block is filled, a quick rub-over with a dry cloth removes all traces of oil from the cartridge bases. Soon it's no trick to completely process 250 to 300 cases an hour, ready for powder and bullet. But do it s-l-o-w the first thousand times, keeping alert to rub out false motions.

Most sizing dies come with case expanders with a beveling attachment on the expander plug, though they formerly didn't! This bells the case-mouth to permit you to start the bullet, but the angle makes it still hard to get the bullet perpendicularly into the brass. After years of battle we requisitioned the services of a machinist with a lathe. By removing the bullet seater of the early type Pacific seating die, a plug was threaded to insert in its place, the lower end turned down to about .004 or .005 inch larger than bullet diameter. Setting the seating die in the tool with this plug inserted, screw it in by trial until the tapered point enters the case-mouth about ⅛ inch.

Run through all your primed cases, placing them on your left as for fired ones. Pass them to your right with the right hand as you would in decapping, sizing and priming the empties at first; but this time you need only a receptacle for them, as they are counted. When all are opened up, replace the opener with the original bullet seater. The R.C.B.S. Gun and Die Shop, Oro Dam Boulevard, Oroville, California, in their new line of dies for all ⅞ x 14 thread loading tools, incorporated some such ideas into their *three-die* sets for straight pistol cases, and current Ideal expanders have a shoulder portion to do the trick.

Full-Length Sizing

Semi-balloon primer pocket cases fired in other guns than yours may be bulged too much, close to the rim, to fit your weapon. Full-length sizing in Pacific type tools didn't iron out the bulge. This meant buying an Ideal or other make of full-length die for arbor press use. They said you can use a vise, but try it if you want to. After the arbor had put a few thousand .45 Colt cases through the die, I put the skull to work and came up with a Brooklyn Bridge affair for my Pacific.

The only part for which I had to get machinist help was that taking the place of the shell holder. In place of the end to hold the case-head, it was turned down to ¾ inch and threaded a short distance, the top end being left smooth. I scrounged around and got three pieces of flat stock. For the bottom it took 1¾ x 4½ x 5/16 inch thick, the top 1 x 4½ x ¼, and the center 1¼ x 4½ x ⅛. Clamping all these together, drill a ¼-inch hole in the exact center of the flat. Then ½ inch from each end, drill a ⅜-inch hole through all three. Open out the largest bottom piece to a ¾-inch hole and the thin center piece to a ⅞-inch hole. Leave the top bar with its ¼-inch hole. Cut two pieces of ⅜-inch drill rod to 8-inch length. Thread both ends and have eight hex nuts to fit. Try to thread these the same amount so the nuts will set up even. Run the first two nuts up as far as they will go, place the two rods through the bottom heavy stock, and run the other two nuts up to hold rigid. Now run the thin piece down part way on the rods where they are smooth. Run two more nuts, one each down to the end of threads on the other end of the rods, place the bottom plate over the shell holder you have made with upper end set in the tool frame, and run the ¾-inch

nut down to finger tight. With the thin plate just on top of the frame where you screw in your resizing die, take this die and remove the expander from it, and screw it down to hold the center plate. Now with the top bar slipped over the two ends of the side rods, and a plunger threaded for some distance on one end for adjustment, made of ¼-inch drill rod and with a nut on either side of the top plate, draw down the two nuts to hold the top plate in position without any play.

Now you are ready to full-length resize, right up to the head, the cases your die is meant for. Adjust this plunger rod so there's room for you to set the case on the flat shell holder or ram and lock the *bottom* nut there; then proceed. Guide the case to the entrance of the die, or you'll crush it as sure as shooting. But you can full-length size all your cases with one-tenth the time and one-fifth the labor of the arbor press, and do it sitting down. A spare movie tin with a piece of felt cut to fit the bottom, and saturated not too heavily with sperm oil, is a big help in lubrication. Just roll

Paging Rube Goldberg. The Brooklyn Bridge on the Pacific is my dream of a gadget to full-length resize pistol cases right up to the hilt. Gunsmith Russ Carpenter of Plattekill, N. Y., made the ram; the rest I made at home. Machinist Hans Seiber showed me how to get all three cross-pieces centered, and let me use his slow drill-press to drill the ⅞ and ¾-inch holes. You remove the decapping punch from a Pacific-type die, take off the top bar with suitable *floating* push-out rod, oil your cases and go to work. After this, such ornery cusses as .45 Colt, .44-40, .32-20 and .32 S.&W. Long drop into the chambers like new brass. It's worth the effort. Background shows the Star sizer and lubricator, and some of the racks of Pacific dies. Both these Pacific tools have been broken and repaired. One is kept set for small primers, the other for large primers and used exclusively for pistol loading.—Bert Shay.

your cases with your left hand before you pick them up. I hope the unions don't get after me and my labor-saver!

This Annealing Business

Various good articles have been published about annealing brass cartridge cases. For the casual handloader's own work, any of them do nicely. But if you hanker to hire out your handloading to discriminating customers, something less technical, and faster, seems in order. Or you may have a variety of calibers to make or alter cases for, and you may want more than 20 rounds to load at one sitting.

Right after World War II, a myriad of strange, sometimes awesome cartridges and guns found their way here via the G.I. souvenir route. Many of these arms were without even a fired case to go by. Most bolt action, military-type guns accepted some type of case made from existing American brass, except the exotic long cases out of Germany. But the rimmed variety of single-shot, over-and-under, and three-barreled *Drillings* posed problems, some possible to solve, and a lot impossible.

When you spend several hours with a machinist and lathe to trim down rim thickness and rim diameter on a .30-40 Krag case, for instance, to make it chamber in an 8 x 57 JR over-and-under, you get quite a pain if the case splits at the neck on the first firing. If a customer is paying for the time, there's often quite a loud squawk about the price. I don't blame him.

So I looked around for a means of annealing casenecks, not by buying a tank of gas and a special torch to burn said gas, but seeing if what I had would do. The sole item was a lowly gasoline blow-torch.

First, it was evident that heat doesn't travel as fast in brass as in copper. To find out how fast, we lit the torch, got up good pressure, and with a can of water handy, took a .30-06 in our fingers, first decapping it. Knowing heat travels up more easily than down, we held the case-neck under the flame about 1½ inches from the mouth of the torch, right at the point of the "blue," and kept it there until the neck began to glow red. It was still not too hot to hold, but we dropped it into the can of water. After a half-dozen of these we graduated to shorter ones, the .257 Roberts, then the Krag, and finally the .250 Savage. They became warm in the fingers, but not too hot to hold until the neck became red; and dunking in water instantly stopped the spreading of heat. It was no trick to dry them in the sun or in the oven of the kitchen range. And, Mister, when dry they looked a lot like nice, fresh Frankford Arsenal cases, but for the shine. Don't take my word; try it.

Next, to do it faster and without the personal touch of fingers. Finding a No. 10 can exactly the same height as a No. 5 (tall cans of fruit juice come this way), we filled the No. 10 seven-eighths full of water and set it in front of the torch. With two No. 5s flanking it, a bridge of old steel plate was set across on which to stand two cases at a time before the flame. A ten-inch length of 1½ x 16-inch flat stock served as handle, and by arranging cases handy to the left, one picks up a pair at a time, sets them carefully together on the $\frac{1}{16}$-inch flat handle and slides them to place in the flame. Stop-watch timing showed only six to seven seconds needed to heat necks red. Then a tip of the handle dropped them into the No. 10 can of water. When the can is full, or the lot finished, borrow the "Boss'" kitchen colander, set it over a bucket and dump the lot. Shake the excess water out and spread the cases to dry. I usually pick a sunny day and spread them on the roof, where they never get too hot, but dry quickly and cleanly.

If what follows sounds fantastic, I can corroborate, and demonstrate if there are doubts. My friend of long standing, Tom Florich, once bought some 800 Norma 9.3 x 74 R cartridges, all with split necks. We loaded bullets and powder we salvaged into 9.3 x 62 cases made from .30-06 brass for rimless rounds, and then cut off 300 of the old 74 mm. long cases to 60 mm., rimmed as originally made. These we necked to 8 x 60 R for Tom's beautiful, scoped single-shot rifle. The rest of the 74s we cut to 57 mm. and with the same die necked them to 8 x 57 JR (Infantry, Rimmed), some for my Gebruder Merkel over-and-under and some for his *Drilling,* same caliber. Shortening had taken all the splits off the necks.

Now, these Norma cases were Berdan primed, and we felt it was far-fetched to decap them for neck anneal! I remembered a trick learned in a country schoolhouse in Michigan, where we found we couldn't fill a water glass by inserting it mouth down in a bucket of water. Why not anneal the necks with primers in place?

I lit the torch while Tom prepared the No. 10 can with water, and with pliers in hand and goggles in place held the necks in the flame till they were red. Two-thirds of their length into water they were plunged, neck down, and Tom picked them up in his fingers and set them neck down in a loading block. Their warmth dried them quickly. We loaded the half-dozen annealed and fired them in the Merkel without a hitch. They grouped, too. We were in!

With about 800 to anneal, this method looked tiresome. I bored a couple of $\frac{7}{16}$-inch holes side by side at one end of the $\frac{1}{16}$ x 1½-inch flat stock, and from there on dropped a pair of cases into those holes, heated them, dunked them in water, and bounced them out on a turkish towel. Team-mate Tom promptly picked them up and set them in the wooden loading block to dry. Up to now, at least 500 have been fired with original primers, with no fizzle or even a hangfire. With a Berdan decapper and new Norma primers, a few hundred have been reloaded and fired some more. No split necks, either.

This led to annealing pistol cases. Many .45 Colt cases started splitting at the neck on the second reload, and .44-40s were as bad or worse. When we had several hundred .45s to load with shot, tests showed that a freshly annealed neck gave a 10% better pattern by actual shot count than one crimped without anneal. Less resistance in unfolding the crimp probably caused this. Annealing these in the regular way was feasible; but here the heat traveled too fast, and about 5% shed their primers after these mild shot loads.

I had an idea, but not the means or ability to work it out. With the aid of my friend Gil Hussner, who dabbles in metalsmith work, solution was easy. He narrowed one end of a strip of stainless steel 2 x 12 x ³/₃₂-inch to one inch for a handle, bent it somewhat like a trowel, and on the other end fashioned a 1½ x 2-inch metal box, ½ inch deep, and soft-soldered it to the flat. When it arrived it took at least five minutes to get it into action, I was that anxious.

The blow-torch lit, the can of water ready, and a few .30 Luger decapped cases at hand, we started, thinking we might as well go all the way to see if it would do *any* kind of case. By dipping the metal box in water and spilling a bit out you regulate the amount you need. For the taller .44s and .45s the box can be nearly full. Little cusses like Lugers and even shorter ones take just about enough water to cover the bottom of the box. Set it with two cases in place, at the proper place of the flame, and when they reach the desired temperature, flip it over, spilling them into the water. With the same motion pick up a new puddle for the next time.

This was as far as I could go. Perhaps some meticulous brethren won't trust rifle cases annealed by the earlier dry-bottom method. So just make yourself an outfit like this and you can set any two rifle cases in the water and do likewise. Either way is good, and your cases last—and last. That's what annealing does.

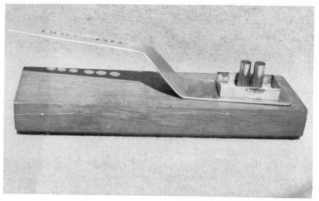

The handle for the water-cooled method.

A pair of .45 Colt cases being annealed. Note color change of upper third of cases above water. These were heated slightly more to make color change stand out before turning the little pan of water to drop them into the cooling can.— Photos by A. C. Smith.

Measuring Powders

With at least half a dozen good powder measures, some better than others for pistol, there's an outstanding one for fool-proof speed. This Pacific is the cheapest of all for *one* load. It has a cast iron base, with brass hopper and brass drum machined to fit, and a pocket drilled in the drum, with stops set so it can rotate the pocket up under the hopper, then down to the drop orifice. Extra drums are inexpensive. You order one for the minimum charge of 2 grains Bullseye and with hand drill or drill press enlarge or deepen

The only thing missing here is the water in No. 10 can. Wish I'd thought of it, but could you rig up to anneal from this pic?

it to the capacity you want. You check with scales and take out only a shaving at a time, for Bull is pretty heavy. Du Pont 5066 is bulkier, and so was their No. 6. Once set, this measure doesn't change and can't get out of adjustment. Speed is due primarily to its having no handle, just a knurled enlargement of the drum. Only short motions rotate it up to fill and down to empty.

Clamp it on a small projection just to the left of the loading tool. It has no cover, is to be filled and left open so you can watch it. Smoke if you must, but my advice is "Don't!" Normally it holds enough for 100 medium power rounds, is then about half empty, and should be refilled. If you have more than one kind of powder around when you fill it, put the others out of sight. Then you won't forget what's in the measure. But when loading is done, dump all powder back into its own can. Bull, especially, settles in a measure. Next day, start to load this settled flake powder and probably you'll get from five to ten loads with no powder or only a little. Of such things are bulged barrels made, unwittingly trying to shoot an extra bullet out of the bore—also unkind remarks when your gun goes *phutt* and a slug rolls free of the muzzle, or sticks. Du Pont 5066 and 6, differently shaped and dry running, don't pack and bridge so easily; but they shouldn't be left in a measure.

Quantity Loading for Target

With prepared cases on your left side, if you're right-handed, your tin of readied bullets on your right, powder measure full, and bullet seater adjusted to depth and crimp, you rotate the powder measure's knob, stop *one second* at this position, and rotate it to the stop, with a snap that jars it a bit. Dump the first four or five charges back into the measure until the powder has settled; then gaze into a charged case to get an idea of how full it looks. Go ahead with the time-saving system I described in the chapter on choosing the target gun, or work out your own.

Watch crimping. You should *feel* it after the bullet is seated home. Fold the crimp into the space or groove made for it on the bullet; it won't bite into the lead, with no place to go. Your case just buckles and probably won't chamber. Crimp *must* be uniform, too.

Make a place for your fired cases and number the containers so you can go all through the cases before a second loading. We bum those five-quart oil cans from gas stations, cut the tops out neatly with a can-opener, fill them up, and tie a piece of wrapping paper over the top to keep out dust.

If your ammo boxes aren't compartmented like those for wadcutter rounds, you may find difficulty in stacking loads. We took a small piece of four-inch board, sawed off about 2½ inches, square, and turning it at right angles, screwed it fast across the end. This made the board sit up at about 30 degrees. We mitred a short piece of quarter-round molding, and setting it at an angle also to the flat upper surface, screwed it fast.

This formed a corner nest that slanted toward you and to the right. Loaded cartridges stacked in stayed put until the box was full.

Game Loads

Here are brief general comments. There are others, pretty much throughout this book, including this chapter.

Remember that bore-size bullet sizer for the heavier loads you'll want? It's to keep pressures down. But squirrel hunting is one of the first things I learned the pistol was good for. There's no need to change from your target wadcutter load, except that you'll want to resight for just over the front sight impact if you've been holding at six o'clock, the bottom of the black bull's-eye, to hit center. The .38 wadcutter will slap a squirrel silly from the tallest tree I'd expect to hit him in. A neat shot can lift him right out of that crotch he settles into so cannily. You must see them first, but your target gun and sights are right for squirrels. My favorite for target and game is the old King ramped red reflector front sight, always showing well. Under some lights, the color may change from one side to the other; but you see the whole of the square bead, not just one side of it. That's essential.

But when you hunt such game as woodchucks at up to 50 yards, or maybe hanker to try your skill on a deer, you need two more kinds of bullets and a heavier gun to fire them. Although you can put up, intelligently, stiff loads within the safety limits of the target arm, they cause it to shoot loose in short order. For the chuck, jack-rabbit, fox, coyote and such sorts of pests the high-velocity hollow point is right. You want quick sure kills and you aren't afraid of spoiling meat. A hollow point, well placed, at something over 1,000 f.s. in a pistol executes them neatly. But 1100 and over is better, though few normal-weight pistol bullets except the Magnums get far over 1200. A fast hollow point can be self-defeating in deer hunting: you may not get a shot where only a little penetration will do the job. However, *all* this hunting with handguns requires the sportsmanship to pass up too uncertain chances. If sportsmanship flagrantly fails to take hold, legislation probably will. Most game laws were motivated by game-hogs, and by others of their tribe.

Guns have almost human differences. What is good for ours may be poison for yours. A modern-steel Single Action Colt in .32-20, .38 or .44 Special, .38-40, .44-40 or .45 gives you a working basis, as does the heavy Smith & Wesson line, the .38-44 Outdoorsman, and the .357 and .44 Magnums. There are also the fine, modern Rugers and the recent and current issues of Great Western. These stand pretty stiff loads without coming apart.

Get a sizer and lubricator that are only .001 inch over rifling groove diameter at the most. Select a hollow point, or a solid, that seats out of the case in normal manner. You need powder room. Be sure to get good, strong cases to hold the powder and lead. Old, weak, soft or brittle ones aren't up to handling heavy loads.

.32 Colt Automatic

Naturally, heavy .32 Long handloads are not for light revolvers, but the sound ones fire the .32 Auto ammo safely. A .32 S.&W. Long sizing die does for the .32 Auto case, although you may need a different bullet-seating die if you own a good Colt, Mauser, Walther or other make of .32 autoloader and wisely decide to reload. Pacific made me a seating die with built-in crimp, a fine job, and I use the .30 Luger hollow point cast bullet and Ideal 308252 .32 Auto of about 77 grains. Mine is an old one, with just one grease groove. I should carry my Colt afield more if it weren't for losing ejected cases.

For over ten years I thought of the Dumond 6-inch barrel and new sights. Then in 1945 I searched back through *Rifleman* files for his ad, located him near Hartford, ordered the job and waited less time than on some gunsmiths I could name! Ten bucks, and I had the barrel, a beautiful gold bead front sight, and a rear to match. They can't be had now. Mr. Dumond has gone to his reward, a first-class conscientious gunsmith.

Out ran a target before the 25-yard bullet catcher and the Luger hollow point and 2 grains of Bull began to talk. That long-nosed little rascal put five consecutive shots *in the figure 9* at nine o'clock on the Standard American rapid fire paper. I never equaled it again, but sight correction to the right made punching the 10-ring monotonous. I'd got used to the trigger pull and couldn't touch 'em off so carefully. With a strange gun, you often get your *best* groups, your shots leaving at some unexpected instant.

.32 Smith & Wesson Long

Come the time and the chance, perhaps, to buy a fine small-caliber gun. Perhaps the best is the .32 S.&W. Long, as accurate as any cartridge. The K-.32 S.&W. and old Officer's Models are its target arms of good weight, and some useful little sixguns take it, too. Don't sneer at its power. A plainclothesman friend of mine from a big city visits me about once a year, gets me to load two boxes for him with a bit of extra zoop for his business gun, in which he has great faith. Bond wadcutter D-314-528, 109 grains, gives 900 to 1,000 f.s. with 2½ grains of Bullseye. *His* load for *his* gun. It could be too rough for some.

A big guy ran amok at a large resort and had to be pacified with a shoulder shot. The little slug spun him around and sat him down with all rough ideas subdued. It wasted no energy in passing through, just slapped, and that was that.

Bullseye powder is fine for short barrels, and accurate in 1½-grain sniffs, too. In a 6-inch .32 the slower 5066, 6, and Unique are right. Use a wadcutter bullet set partly out of the case, for powder room Hercules' old booklet lists a 98-grain round-nose at 1010 f.s. with 4.3 of Unique—and of course the older and milder primers, an item to bear in mind. My Officer's Models like that little wonder of mine, the 75-grain hollow point for the Luger, and 2.7 of Bull. These stiff loads aren't for general recommendation.

With those Officer's Models I've equaled my best 50-yard scores, over 95. Two grains of Bull do well with the Hensley & Gibbs 98-grain No. 66, the deep-seated 95-grain wadcutter 52 B by Cramer, and the Bond D 314528 ground off to cast 101 grains. With their great economy, practically .22 long-rifle recoil and report, these two Colts lead plenty of the brethren to attempt the impossible—to buy them.

.32-20 Winchester

The neglected .32-20 is a fine pistol cartridge in heavy guns like Colt Single Actions. Look at the metal in their cylinders, but don't be too sure! It might be a pre-1900 gun of "black-powder steel." Medium-weight Army Special and Official Police Colts came in .32-20 and the S.&W. Military & Police, the latter the only Smith I found comfortable with stiff loads as it came from the factory—no Magna grips then, of course. These guns look reasonably strong in .32-20, but mine were Single Actions, which took thousands of handloads and did some hunting.

I shook down to Bond C-311655, 120 grains from my mold, accurate in pistol and rifle, and no short-range slug. Medium target loads gave me 94x100 at 50 yards on the Standard American target, and some hotter loads chronographed at Phil Sharpe's in 1951 in a 7½-inch Colt made a 100-yard group of 2½ inches, five shots, from arm rest. DuPont 4759 was the powder.

The standard flat-point lead bullet penetrates and mushrooms well. It knocks a gray squirrel out of a tree as well as the .38 Special, in actual trials. With 5.1 grains of Unique, listed in old booklets at 1080 f.s., a bullet from an 18-pound raccoon showed as remarkable mushrooming as if it had been shot against a steel plate. Two chucks, fairly close by, and a porcupine have fallen to my 5½-inch Single Action, which seems to have the accuracy of any comparable handgun—if the .32-20 is loaded properly. The bullet is well suited to hollow-pointing and about 1100 f.s. velocity, but it seems to me that the regular flat-point solid does well enough.

But I had a machinist make a hollow-pointing attachment for a .30 Luger, Ideal 308244 (now 308227) mold, and the mushroom bullet drops out at 75 grains. In the .32-20 it shows little if any more "explosive" effect than the standard soft-lead bullet.

Here's a phase of ballistics that has rated little thought, the pitch of rifling twist. This hollow point from a 10-inch twist probably would be much more destructive because of rotational speed. But fast pistol twists aren't deemed necessary, 16-inch being common, though the S.&W. .32-20 twist was 12.

Factory High Velocity loads aren't for the .32-20 revolver, but their solid-head cases are. A box of Remington lead-bullet loads purchased a few years ago were of semi-balloon type, less desirable in spite of slightly greater powder space.

.38 Special and .38 Auto

These .38s give snappy velocity and exceptional accuracy with 125- to 130-grain bullets; they do well on the smaller varmints, though they can't buck the wind well. The 145 to 150 grainers get their best velocity from powders like Unique and 2400, DuPont 4759, or even the old Hercules Sharpshooter. The February, 1951 *Rifleman* listed good loads—and pressures with modern primers and powders. See also the N.R.A. handloading booklets reprinting such articles.

I found the round-nosed 125-grain Ideal 358242 for the .38 Auto an ideal all-round bullet in that size, doing finely in the .38 Special too, and functioning most arms for the 9 mm. Luger. Hollow-point it for hunting; leave it solid for target. In my Officer's Model .38 Special, it has won me many medals, using 2½ grains of Bullseye. It suits the short .38 S.&W. cartridge also, except for some guns with fixed sights, which might shoot low with it.

The Cramer 24 C hollow point goes 145 grains as cast, is highly accurate, and stands high velocity. I've tried all the loads in that *Rifleman* article up to and including 12½ grains of 2400 in the .38 Special. Sized .356, this Cramer gave fine accuracy in my Colt. Read the pressure data and decide whether you wish to use the loads in your gun. Many factors raise pressure, and slightly different tolerances in your gun from the pressure gun's measurements might boost it from 5,000 to 10,000 pounds additional. You don't want your shiny blue darling coming apart in your hand.

Most loaders advise new cases for heavy loads; yet a previous firing constitutes a test, and some new ones come apart on their first use. The law of averages indicates that new cases are best. Check old ones for unusual bulge from former use. Ironed out in the sizing die, that part is brittle. Somewhere in Phil Sharpe's *Complete Guide to Handloading,* in Ideal or Belding & Mull handbooks, or elsewhere, is the load for your gun. The .38 Special loads can scarcely be counted. Pick your bullet and try its nearest counterpart's advised charges, remembering diameter and seating depth as well as weight.

For deer a heavy wadcutter or semi-wadcutter seems preferable to a hollow point, giving more of the penetration often needed. It's not unlikely that a soft-footed hunter may come on a deer in the brush and have time for a quick shot at 20 paces or less. He *must place* a small bullet right, in neck, head or heart, or let the chance go if he can't be sure. A 150-grain lead pellet can make a nasty wound; and, if not planted well, it might take the lordly buck three days to die, or three months to recover. Picture yourself in those circumstances and without the aid of medicine or hospital. Then see if you don't care whether or not you just wound.

Bond D-358582, 150 grains from my mold, shoots well in the Special with all the powder I care to put behind it. Ideal 358416's flat point copies the old factory .38 Colt Special, and Ideal-Keith 358429, rated at 173 grains (or later, 165), might reach 1200 f.s. in some guns, but that figure should be approached circumspectly. There's a lot of lead—and barrel resistance—in it.

.38 Special Squibs

"I dot it, I dot it!" cried the little boy, running to his grandma the first time he learned to button his own pants. You think I don't remember the incident? Well, I do, and it was *me.*

That's how I feel about this light load. I woke up from a nap the other afternoon with this idea of 1.5 grains Bullseye on my mind: ram a real strong wad on the powder as I do in shot loads, about 10-15 pounds' pressure. Tough Kraft paper or paraffined milk cartons will do, but spongy gray card, as from suit boxes, doesn't. The 126-grain Cramer worked, but the 146 Cramer and 150 Bond showed lobbing on the 20-yard target. Too long to stabilize at this speed? I used both large and small pistol primers, the former in some large primer pocket Peters cases I had. The loads really perked in two guns, but not in my 7½-inch Officer's Model with barrel free-bored at the breech.

For scores I jacked up the King rear sight 12 clicks and got 82 and 84 slow-fire. All those out were my fault. Loaded this way, they all have the 10-ring address if held right. This system worked in the *.32 S.&W. Long,* too, with 1.2 grains 5066, the 95-grain Cramer bullet, and no sight change at all. Good cellar loads, for they sound just about like a .22 long-rifle cartridge fired in a rifle. I felt there *must* be a way, and this is it.

Some .44 Calibers

Now we move into the "bellerin' forties," skipping the .38-40 partly from lack of experience but mostly because few old Colts and others remain to fire it today. Elmer Keith says in one of his writings that one of his guns shot the 210-grain Ideal .40-60 Winchester Model 1876 rifle bullet beautifully. It was sized to fit.

I own and shoot an early S.&W. .44 Special, the New Century fondly called the "Triple Lock." With a pair of built-up stocks to fill that vacant space behind the hump of the frame it would be comfortable to shoot. It's beautifully accurate and has the fine old action that clicks like the balance wheel of a good watch. A couple of Colt single-actions—.44 Special and .44-40 with interchangeable cylinders and a new factory barrel fitted to one with a gunsmith's help— have 5½- and 7½-inch barrels and give me plenty of experimentation in these interesting calibers. The .44-40's large case gives real velocity with 200-220-grain bullets, and care. Powder room keeps pressures from rising as fast as in the stronger Special case. But brass from most rifle chambers has a risk-incurring bulge near the head, where it most needs strength. New cases work well in the neatly chambered Colt: no apparent expansion. The case is larger-bodied than the Special; consequently, its chamber walls are thinner.

My 214-grain Ideal 42498 uses either Du Pont 4759 or Hercules Sharpshooter in 19½-grain charges, enough for my purposes. Even then the Single Action performs a 90-degree arc and enthusiastically points at the firmament, seemingly at the instant of trigger release; and such loads aren't for "black powder steel" guns of early vintage.

Velocities with the Potter chronograph at Phil Sharpe's, distance 25 feet, were 1073 f.s. from the 5½-inch barrel and 1150 from the 7½. We used 4759 powder and bullets sized .427 for .4265 grooves. If you use the full range of available .44 bullets, you'll need *plenty* of sight adjustment. There's a foot difference in impact at 25 yards from the 173-grain Ideal to the old Ideal-Heath that casts 255 in my mold. The beautiful 260-grain Cramer is useful, too. Ballistics can duplicate those of the .44 Special, most likely; but solid-sighted guns marked ".44 W.C.F." won't be too useful with the heaviest slugs.

The Special was designed for smokeless, with well balanced bullet weight and powder space. It will stand more crowding than the .44-40 and is more economical to use. In mine, 16.2 grains of 4759 burned well and gave 1075 f.s. with 5½-inch barrel spinning the Cramer No. 7 of 241 grains from my three-cavity mold. Sized to .427, those bullets were exceptionally accurate. Hollow points are used a great deal, but blunt solids should perform yeoman service on any flesh you'd think it safe to approach with a handgun under .44 Magnum, let's say. You must speed the hollow point above 1,000 f.s. to make it do its stuff.

My old friend and shipmate, J. Bushnell Smith, now gone to the Happy Hunting Grounds, told me that *any* good bullet, properly hollow-pointed, was more accurate than before. I tried this in both .30 caliber rifle and .38 Special sixgun and found it to be true. But I just can't hold better than the groups these .44s give me. The Colt once put five shots in a rosette, all touching, at 25 yards for me.

Casting hollow points takes time. Cramer molds have a clever attachment that stays with the mold, is just gently nudged with the mallet used for the sprue cutter.

Paging Jack Henniger. Jack went with the purchase of Cramer products to Saeco, then in Santa Anita. You want to get acquainted with him if you plan hotter than normal loads in your sixgun. His stunt saves wear and tear on many fine pistols; it's called "torque relieved barrels." He can fix your pet so that stiff doses put less strain on the action; and by our tests improve accuracy and practically eliminate boreleading, common with fast loads. Tell him I sent you, and for no commercial reasons. He's a fine, earnest fellow.

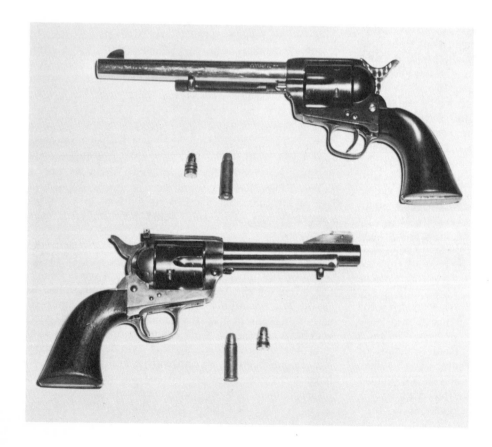

The Roaring Forty-Fours. Upper: Built-up Single Action Army with new nickeled barrel from Colt, marked ".44 Russian and Special." Fitted to .002-inch clearance from cylinder. One-piece thumb-rest stock of Circassian walnut by Joe Barnes. Action smoothed, hammer engine-turned, over-size base pin and bushing installed by Bert Shay. As tight as they come. Lower: Another S. A. A. built up by Colt in early 1930s. Two cylinders furnished and fitted. That is how we could make the two guns use .44-40 and .44 Special cases interchangeably. Upper cartridge and bullet: .44-40 and 255-grain Ideal. Lower: .44 Special and 244-grain Cramer. A load of 16.2 grains of Du Pont 4759 gives exactly 1075 f.s. instrumental velocity at 25 feet. Both guns are more accurate than I can hold. More than 500 heavy loads through each have failed to show any loosening of parts. —Bert Shay.

.44 Shay Magnum

Before factories gave us .44 Remington or Smith & Wesson Magnum cartridges and guns, a number of us tried various ways to increase powder capacity behind .44 caliber bullets. Safe heavy loading of the .44 Special wasn't enough. Furthermore, if solid-head Special cases had been available before this project started, we might never have started at all!

The case is .30-06 brass, preferably new, trimmed in Wilson trimmer used in drill press. First cut: maximum travel of cutter, with shortened bearing. Second: to about 1.330 inch. Expand with R.C.B.S. .44-40 intermediate die, with .427 expander. Remove decapping pin and replace with .410 to .412-inch expander button for guide to keep expansion centered. After expansion, trim to 1.315 inch and load with six grains Du Pont 6 (or 5066) and any 240 to 255 grain bullet. Don't crimp. Oil cases and fire them to make them cylindrical and fully formed. For ordinary use, load with standard charges of any pistol powder. Case should be mouth-annealed for longer life.

Have your gunsmith make you a seating die with crimper, using same reamer as for use on cylinder of gun. Old type Pacific dies have removable crimper and bullet seating punch. Take .45 Auto seater die, remove bullet seater and crimper, and substitute seater and crimper from a .44 Special Pacific die. For full-length sizing die use a rifle die like one for Ackley's almost straight-sided .30-06 Improved or .257 Improved. Brass not overworked should last for 30 to 50 loadings, which is good.

All bullets for Colt revolvers to be converted in this way should be sized no larger than .427 inch. The largest Colt .44 barrels I've slugged are .4265 and no more. But slug any barrel that is to use heavy loads, as a matter of principle. Bond bullet 429655 full wadcutter seems best, as it can be crimped in the groove provided and has shorter bearing surface to raise pressure than Ideal-Heath 429336. The latter, and Saeco No. 7, should be crimped above the shoulder to hold them under heavy recoil. Other .44 Special bullets not too long to clear the cylinder length when fully seated can be used, also the 210-214 grain .44-40, which can be crimped in the top groove and ought to hit very high velocity, safely.

The chamber reamer should be ground to .468 inch with clean, sharp cutting edge at *front,* and designed so that a close-fitting, *smooth* pilot can be inserted to fit the cylinder leade neatly, making the reamer run true. A slightly tapered "roughing reamer" should start the chambers in the cylinder to allow the .468 reamer to run true. First see that the cylinder fits the frame of your gun, then ream so that a case trimmed to 1.310 inch will insert and just clear the rear of the gun's frame and turn freely. Try it often in the gun, when reaming, so as not to overdo it. The 1.315-inch case with light crimp will then run freely for cylinder rotation.

With cylinder depth reached and firing begun, you'll notice small lead slivers peeled back about the case-mouths. Use a No. 8 taper pin reamer, spiral fluted preferred, and shave about $1/16$ inch of the *inside* edge of the leade, entering the taper pin reamer from the rear. This will stop the lead peeling.

Case weights ran like these: Magnum made from Frankford 1938 .30-06 brass, 145 grains; W.R.A. .44 Special solid-head, 99.8; Western semi-balloon, 78; Remington semi-balloon, 75.2.

Capacities of fired brass poured heaping full of Hercules 2400 powder and struck off level were 30.9 grains for the Magnum, 30.1 for the solid-head Winchester, and 31.3 for the Remington.

A great many loads were tried and chronographed, as we had interchangeable cylinders, and the strong solid-head Specials fell over 100 f. s. below the much stronger Shay Mags with Hercules 2400. The 17-grain load gave 1153 instrumental velocity, at 25 feet, with the 250-grain Bond C-429-655 bullet (perhaps still available from Modern-Bond Corporation in Wilmington, Delaware) weighing 250 grains, in Magnum brass, and only 1021 f. s. with a harder 245-grain bullet-mix in the Special. With 17.5 grains of 2400 the comparative figures were 1172 and 1061. But 17 grains is a heavy load; and, as you know, pressures depend on many variables and shouldn't be taken for granted. Hercules Unique in 9.4-grain charges sent the 245-grain Bond at 1107 f.s. from Magnum brass, and at 985 from Winchester.

A dual load for W.R.A. solid-head .44 Special cases set 1.5 grains Bullseye on the primer, with 15 grains 4759 above it, with graphite wad for lubrication, and Ideal 429336 semi-wadcutter alloyed to weigh 250 grains on the nose. It's accurate, having made a ragged-hole group at 25 yards. Powder is slightly compressed, can't shift, and burns without the obnoxious flash of 2400 loads. This bullet is too long for the Magnum with a proper crimp. Bond C-429-655 is a favorite because of its compactness and well shaped crimping groove. It's a most accurate true wadcutter, as thousands of shots have proved.

.44 S.&W. Magnum

In this case, and in the guns for it, we have what shooters have longed for. Remington and Smith & Wesson did the development work, and Elmer Keith probably deserves more credit for the prodding than anyone else. Numerous loads for it have been published; and more will come up, in the nature of things. But just as with any other load and type and quality of arms, may we invite your attention to the remarks closing this chapter?

Oddly enough, case lengths of this cartridge and of the wildcat or what-you-will Magnum just discussed are about identical. Of course the factory case has more powder room, although it is strengthened where strength is needed. We experimenters are limited in what we can do.

.45 Colt

The grand old .45, apparently born with the Single Action Army about 1872, still goes strong. It looks a bit like a slim, short brother of the .45-70. I'm told that once the latter was tried in a specially made pistol—and of course lately some big revolvers have been hand-made for it. The idea is not zany at all, when you think of killing power that might be needed in a handgun. A gullible soldier shot the Army thing, or maybe did it on pain of court-martial. The exact record dims in my memory but the gist was: just one shot! The one-hand nightmare of this preview landed some 40 feet behind the dumfounded soldier and was promptly snaffled by some institution organized to preserve relics of the past, working models or not.

Today's .45 kicks enough to satisfy most shooters, and it performs *most* of the stunts ever ascribed to it. Even back when—Sam Colt and his cohorts understood the shape of handguns. After he died, those who carried on forgot some fundamentals. Take one shot with a heavily loaded Single Action and one with a New Service. That N.S. kicks, with a soul-jarring punch down to your boot-soles. The S.A.A. curls in your mitt and points heavenward. After the smoke clears you can spot your shot!

I've loaded and shot black powder in several calibers, and how oldtimers made long runs of bull's-eyes with it I'll never know. Ten through my .45 and I can't find rifling lands any more. Where there isn't enough drinking water, let alone some to wash in, fellers that play with that stuff must look a sight after a day's shooting. I can't keep dainty using it in *cartridge* guns, to say nothing of those old heroes that drink it in at the business end.

But if you own an S.A.A. .45 don't hesitate to shoot it, with sensible loads. Chambers aren't always neat, and semi-balloon cases are thin clear down to the rim. Among some York State range loot we once found just 49 solid-head Westerns, apparently the only ones known to Science. One short of a boxful, and collectors had to have their cut. I hid some, especially for my hog-leg Colt.

Out of storage came 270-grain bullets of my own design, Bond F 454-625, catalogued at 258 grains. The shorter Bond goes 243 and is meant for the Auto case in sixguns. My .38 Special experiments had indicated that a long cylindrical section makes a bullet easier to stabilize, and gives the most weight with minimum seating in the case if you want lots of powder room.

In the .45 Colt case the 243-grain and 4 grains of Bull, 5 of No. 6, or 6 of No. 5 or No. 5066 give accuracy and light recoil even in a New Service. At 25 yards for revolvers for the Auto case, 2½ grains of Bull is nice, 3½ of 5 or 5066 perhaps better but less economical. Five of 5066 or 4 of Bull roll her right along. Though primers are flattened, pressures don't seem high. The Auto case has sliding room in the chamber. Naturally we took all loading precautions.

In the middle 1930s I sent Charles Askins, Jr., some with 3 of Bull, and some with 5 of No. 5, for 50-yard work in his Colt Shooting Master. He wrote that they gave the greatest percentage of kills on big Western hawks for any ammo so far tried, and that the 3 of Bull turned in the best rapid fire scores he'd made with that Shooting Master, to date.

My first big gun, about 1923, was a New Service Target with 7½-inch barrel and rosewood stocks, a thing of awe. In active duty on a battleship, I wanted it adapted to the Auto case, with all that free ammunition slipping by, and trips ashore necessary to buy .45 Colt stuff. I pestered Colt every year till about 1930, when they gave up and fitted a cylinder and crane, also a 6-inch barrel. When this gun was allowed, a lot of matches were won, or the daylights scared out of the winner when I was runner-up. Both barrels are still bright and spotless inside, can make the 10-ring holler quits at 50 yards. I wish I had had a short action put in! It's still in its prime of life.

Bond B-454-510 goes 190 grains, shoots well, and is about the lightest for the Peacemaker. Bond wadcutter D-454-713, of 255 grains but base-ground to 235, needed deep seating for the auto pistol. It took the lightest load that would work my many-times-rebuilt Colt Auto of 1914 with full recoil spring, only 2.3 of Bull. Chronographing at Phil Sharp's in 1949 showed 621 f.s. A belt-buckle puncher!

I've had the heads of 12 out of 50 once-fired .45 Colt cases pull off in full-length resizing. Look lovingly at your .45; measure the thickness of even the New Service's cylinder walls, and consider the few thousandths of an inch of steel between the cartridge and fresh air at the cylinder's bolt-cuts right over the chambers. Factory loaded .45s give a healthy smack. If you must speed up, lighten the bullet and get some not too sudden powder, like Unique. I've used about all the Du Pont 4759 I could seat the 235-grain bullet against, but I've yet to see the chronograph wink out 1,000 f.s. The fastest in an old Hercules booklet reads: "235 grain lead, square shoulder, hollow base, 10.7 grains Unique, 1050 f.s., pressure 15,000 pounds, seating depth .444 inch." I haven't clocked it.

From facts Phil Sharpe told me about hollow bases' greatly increasing pressure *without* raising velocity I want no truck with them. They're a nuisance to cast, too. The .45 Colt has so much powder space that a fairly sassy load is needed to burn the powder, and cases must be sized to a tight friction fit and given a husky crimp. So keep your dies fairly small.

.45 Colt Automatic

Reloading the .45 A.C.P. has been discussed in masterly fashion by nationally famous shots, with many differences in opinion. I didn't handload for my Model 1911 until after I'd left active duty in the Navy —and free ammunition—in 1927. Then I needed to, but I never ran into half the difficulties predicted. The first "must," hard bullet metal, slid under the table.

Shape and overall length meant more, as I found at the cost of nine molds.

Also I found, again, that each gun was an individual. Many hopefuls came to me for handloading lessons, and what would feed through my gun and make bull's-eyes wouldn't always perform so sedately in others. In interior finish a fine early commercial gun had something on later ones—and a lot on guns made for the Government. But I sailed on, loading cast bullets to near-factory velocity, till one sad evening a cracked slide caught my eye. Colt made that good, with their compliments, but I changed from 4 grains of Bull and a 246-grain Bond to the idea of using as *little* powder as would work satisfactorily. A *Rifleman* article had indicated how the light barrel resistance of a cast bullet, passing up the bore, allowed it to get out of the muzzle so fast that the slide slammed back with excessive speed—and stresses.

Lighter recoil permits anyone to score higher. The Crawford design of Cramer 200- to 210-grain bullet caused dubious club discussions, confounded most of us by its reliability of feeding, accuracy, *and* shooting to the sights at both 25 and 50 yards. After some 18 years' service it's still to be found seated in about a dozen different ways and depths. Many a long breathhold I had, wondering why she wouldn't go off; then a look at the slide would show a tiny bit protruding back of the frame. A slap of the hand would seat the cartridge, but that ruined rapid fire; so back I went to seating its shoulder just below the case-mouth. Brass opened for bullet starting could be forced gently back to place by setting the crimper, not to crimp, but barely to engage the case lip.

In 1945 I sent my two .45 Autos to A. E. Berdon for his accuracy tuneup, anti-slap trigger, roughing of the front grip strap, also reblueing of the 1914 gun, then with snow in its hair. It already had King sights, and the pull was to be 2¾ pounds. The National Match pistol was to lift a four-pound trigger weight. With them went selected barels graciously given me by that grand old pistolman, John Henry Fitzgerald of Colt's. They came back so easy to get bull's-eyes with that they almost scared me! Aging muscles and dimming eyes proved that no matter how much accuracy the Old Maestro puts into a gun, someone must bring it out. They are relics of a day when 90 or better at 50 yards was no dream but a frequent reality.

Nickeled cases seem thinner than the old brass, and chambers now run tighter. Loading the time-tried Cramer 5 C and 3 grains of Bull, I had to switch from a .454 to a .453 bullet sizing die. That easy-seating, bevel-based bullet, its shoulder set flush with the case-mouth, made a customer's .45 tick like a Waltham. But the .453 bullets seated all too easily in the once-fired cases, and some day we shall run into trouble again.

You can load plenty of lead and zip into the rimless .45 for sixgun use, with no fear of cracking slides, but when fingernail extraction of cases becomes hard, back down a bit. This of course is only a rough gauge of pressure, but it's to be observed and acted upon. The case is one of the strongest, but flattened or pierced primers show that discretion has been flung out the window. With Bond F 454-570, 243 grains from my mold, 2½ grains of Bullseye make a nice target load even in the S.&W. 1917 revolver. In the Colt, only, I used 5 grains of old No. 5 for a heavy load. A special Providence watches over my Single Action with interchangeable Auto and .45 Colt cylinders. With its fixed sights that baby keeps her point of impact at 25 yards with bullets from the 220-grain Bond to the 255-grain Bond D 454-713. She would be the next to the last I'd part with; the last would be that flat hunk of comfort, my 1914 .45 Auto.

You must crimp revolver cases; and you'd think that three generations of handloading lead bullets and smokeless for handguns would have taught bullet designers how to make a crimping groove. A freshly annealed .45 case used for shot, no bullet interfering, will *almost* bend at right angles, but try crimping it into one of those narrow slots cast in most sixgun bullets. I designed my crimping groove with a 45-degree slope from the base of the bullet and a 90-degree angle from the point. With it I've yet to see lead hop forward and try to lock the gun from the heaviest .45 Long Colt recoil. A halfbreed grease and/or crimping groove won't do, nor will a narrow slot. After four or five loadings, .44 Special case lips don't wanna bend at all; but I fixed them, by gum, by annealing the front of the brass. When shekels get heavy in my pocket I want a Bond C 429-655, a weighty .44 with short bearing surface, full wadcutter, *and* a decent crimping groove. All it lacks is a *round-bottom* grease groove for nice casting and the elimination of that miserably narrow band ahead of that groove. Look at Bond F 454 if you'd like to see where I got the inspiration for my bullet.

The Cramer 5 C 210-grain for the Auto seems to do well in sixguns, too. It saves lead, cuts recoil, but needs elevation in most guns. Only 2.8 grains of Bull and no doctoring of the recoil spring make it reliable in my Berdonized .45s, and 3 of Bull make it right for 50 yards.

7 mm. Japanese Nambu Automatic

This cute little cuss which fits the hand so nicely is rare in the United States, and the ammo for it still rarer. But if you have one, all is not lost. Cases can be made from .30 M1 carbine brass, new or fired.

Up to now, we've made respectable loads for four different Nambu 7s, including our own, and though the weak mainsprings give misfires with U. S. primers, we found the flat-faced Remington No. 1½ the most reliable, easier to dent than convex primers. We had not tried the the Cascade 500, which at least in some lots is soft.

From left: rectangular steel block, with nest; shell holder, special for 7mm. Nambu; holder for use in reaming.— These photos by A. C. Smith.

Wilson shell trimmer rigged on drill-press and set for trimming the formed case. *One* operation.

Drill-press running and cutter trimming. See the brass shavings fly.

Shell holder in clamp ready for reaming. Drill "I" in place, first cut. Drills "J" and "K" lying on nest block.

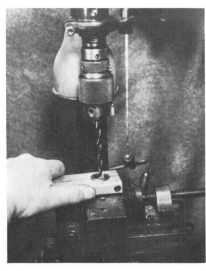

Shell holder in clamp, case seated centered under drill by "nest," and drill ready to ream first cut.

Rig for annealing cases: Burns-O-Matic torch; two No. 5 cans inverted; one No. 10 can with water; plates as bridge and to build to height; hand-made "dipper" for water to set base of case in while heating its mouth. When mouth begins to turn red, flip to left, dropping hot case into water. Dip dipper again for more water, very fast.

If you're equipped with some of the gadgets necessary for a thorough job in other handloading, you're not too badly off to start on 7 mm.

The bullet problem was solved by Hensley & Gibbs. I wrote Mr. Gibbs, sending him a bullet pulled from a Japanese service round and asked him to make a mold cherry maintaining contour and length, and leave it to size to .283 inch, with one lube groove. We determined this by slugging the barrel, which seems tapered its entire length, and we then thought the bullet should measure maximum groove diameter. After a lot of sweat

and blood this proved to be wrong. They worked better at .280. The H.&G. mold is No. 134.

Mr. H. Nelson Busick of Baltimore first approached me on this work. He'd done the ground-work of finding that carbine brass would form the basic case, and he'd inveigled Fred Huntington of R.C.B.S. Gun and Die Shop, Oroville, California, into making loading dies for use on the Pacific or any tool with ⅞ x 14-inch threads. For a shell holder I found that my old .25-20 Single Shot part would do, as made for the .22-3000 Lovell. We had an L. E. Wilson case trimmer, from

Cashmere, Washington; and we made it work, on the drill press.

This very short case needs a very short holder for the Wilson trimmer but any machinist with lathe can make it for you with a ¾-inch length of one-inch round stock. It should be counterbored on the upper end for at least $^3/_{16}$ inch, as the overall of the finished case is only 0.772 inch. By careful manipulation of a taper pin reamer from the base end it can be finished so that the full-length resized case will allow the base of the case to stick out ⅛ inch.

Now get three *letter size* drills, preferably sharp, clean and new: letter I .272-inch; letter J .277; and letter K .281. These are to ream or drill out the inside of the necks after forming, as there's a great deal too much metal left to hold the bullet and allow chambering.

For reaming with drill press and letter drills you need—and I do mean need—another item, a holder for the shell holder. These little cases get gosh-awful *hot* with the drill reaming. The holder's holder can be made with a sound piece of hardwood ½ inch thick, 1¾ inches wide, and 6 inches long. About ¾ inch from one end on the flat side, drill a clean 1-inch hole for the shell holder. From this end make a clean saw cut right through the center of the flat and hole drilled, back to within 2½ inches from the other end. Now drill edgewise through the *short* end with a ¼-inch spur bit, all the way through, get a ¼-inch carriage bolt and small wing-nut, slip your shell holder through the 1-inch hole about even both sides, and tighten the wing-nut. Here you have a "holder for the shell holder."

Next you need a gasoline blow-torch or one of those little Burns-O-Matic affairs with a tank of Propane gas. After all this work on the brass it must be annealed, or it will split at the neck the first time you fire it! Before you begin, cases must be decapped, if they are new and already capped, or "primed," as we usually say. But punch out fired primers, too. To anneal, set the bases in about ¼ inch of water (we use the shallow, pressed tin lid of a metal box to hold the water), and heat the neck portion till it starts to glow, then dump into a nearby No. 10 can of water. You can heat two cases at a time, as described in the "Annealing" section in this chapter.

Better start with 120 to 130 empty carbine cases, as you're likely to have some spoiled cases along the line, and we assume you'd like to end with 100 loadable cases. So we begin the process.

Before full-length sizing, *remove the neck-expanding plug in the die.* Otherwise you'll have a squeezed-down case *locked in the die,* and the die would be ruined in getting it out.

Lightly oil the cases and seat the .30 M1 brass all the way home. It will come out with a long bottle-neck. Rig the shell trimmer in the drill press, for this amount of work in using it by hand will tire you out in about two cutoffs. Use a drill vise, chuck the threaded end of the Wilson cutter in the drill chuck so that at its

The 7mm. Japanese Nambu officers' pistol. Below, from left: .30 carbine case; the case formed in R. C. B. S. full-length sizing die *without* decapper; case trimmed to .772-inch length, and a lubricated cast bullet shown above it; the case loaded with cast bullet after reaming three times, annealing, resizing, deburring, and priming; an original Japanese round, for comparison.

upper travel the teeth will *not* withdraw into the bushing. The machinist can shorten the Wilson bushing by ¼ inch or more on each end, thus allowing you more cutter travel. Now, with the formed case bumped firmly to seat in the shell holder and your trimmer stop run 'way up, make a trial cut. Make sure also that the travel of your drill spindle is stopped *before* the chuck makes contact with the Wilson bushing. Set the drill stop to avoid this.

Now adjust the cutter to trim the case to .772 inch on the nose. Trim all your shaped cases to this. You are now almost ready to begin reaming necks. Although it isn't absolutely necessary, a big help for centering necks under the drill is what the machinist calls a "nest." A rectangular block of metal which will clamp squarely in the drill vise is center punched; and a letter-T drill, or a 23/64-inch drill, is started in the block just enough so the very shallow hole has square sides. Jockey this around, or better still, leave it in the vise as drilled as a device to set the base end of your formed and trimmed cases into, so the drills used for reaming will kinda automatically center in the neck.

Now lock your shell holder, the Wilson type, into the wood holder good and tight; enter a trimmed, formed case from the solid end; and ream all the cases that have reached this stage. The first drill to use is the letter I, .272 inch. After all are reamed once, change to the J drill, .277, and go through the same process, leaving your "nest" centered. Next the K drill, .281, and, if you're not too tired, sit down and deburr, inside and out, all your cases.

After standing at the drill press for these operations

you'd like to sit a while. So rig your annealing setup and go ahead, or cast your bullets of about 1 to 15 tin and lead alloy. After annealing, we dump the brass into a purloined kitchen colander set in a water bucket, shake well to get most of the water out, and set in the sun to dry. If it's winter, and most likely it will be, set them in a cookie tin on the radiator, and watch them.

With bullets cast and lubricated, and sized to .280 inch, the same as usually supplied by Ideal for .270 Winchester cast bullets, you are close to the big, final step. First run all your cases through the sizing die again, this time with a neat .280-inch expander plug in place, and prime them with the primers you choose, such as the flat-faced Remington or Peters, or some make that you know to be softer. For off-center firing pins that aren't too strong, some of us like primers with three-pronged anvils instead of the bar type.

Set the powder measure to throw 2.6 grains of Du Pont 5066, slightly bell the case-mouths before you charge the brass, and jockey the bullet seater to give an overall cartridge length of 1.056 inches.

Load, wipe and inspect the product, and then: "Commence firing."

Don't expect a world-beater group; but at 50 feet on the Standard American we were able to keep them in the black, even with the very poor sights.

Watch where your empties fall. They're kinda valuable! You can easily save them, when squib loads do all you want done, by underloading so that empties are not ejected by recoil.

9 mm. Luger Automatic

The 9 mm. cartridge has plenty of eye appeal and is coming to the fore in our country. A fine gun, I think, is the Belgian Browning, with the same comforting feel as the Government .45, and actually easier to shoot. Colt .38 Auto tools suggested themselves, but to get the short case up inside the seating die wasn't easy. Grinding off, from the *bottom* of the seating die only, enough to let it seat the bullet worked, and so did Ideal bullet 358242 hollow-pointed, the .38 Auto cast bullet. In one or two Lugers we got about 5% feeding trouble, but fine accuracy. I ask Jack Henninger if they could make Cramer 31, catalogued at 136 grains, weigh 124, Luger standard. Well, it went 124.1. Jack brushed this favor off; just one of the things they do for shooters. Now, how would the 136 have functioned in a Luger, with a lighter powder charge?

Lugers are fascinating, in both .30 and 9 mm. calibers. These pistols, of many makes and vintages, vary greatly in both quality and strength. Any loads I list could apply only to the guns I used. They could be unsatisfactory or actually unsafe in some others; so do *not* take the following data as recommended. Every gun must be fitted with its own correct charges. This rule applies particularly here.

In two 8-inch .30s, two 8-inch 9s, a 6½-inch .30, and an original 6-inch Navy 9, I expended about 5,000 primers in a couple of years, learning about Lugers,

especially those with heavy barrels. I have several pages of loading data, much of it chronographed, all with lead bullets. Their versatility is amazing. One 9 mm. takes from 30 to 50% more powder to function than normal weight barrels; yet it shows no tendency to be overloaded, no primer pressure. I load bullets all the way from 116 to 166 grains, even Hensley semi-wad-cutters, which function *and* make bull's-eyes all day. They also make beautiful targets with very light loads, even at 50 yards.

Then, when I ran into trouble from leading with too hot loads (enough to function them), using pistol powder, I went to "duplex" loads and ran into amazing performance in both calibers. It also stopped the leading, by using a small charge of Bullseye, or sometimes No. 6, against the primer, then 4759 on top. There must be enough to pack a bit; so the two don't mix. Velocities to 1400 f.s. instrumental (less than computed "muzzle" velocities) are attained without fouling, and with amazing accuracy. As you know, a properly fitted and loaded lead-alloy bullet gets through a barrel more easily than a jacketed one does. In one load with the 148-grain Hensley & Gibbs semi-wadcutter .38 Special bullet, the chronograph recorded five shots with an extreme variation of only 6 feet per second, and still they tell me it's "wrong." I learned long ago that theory is only theory until it's been proved; then it's fact.

The 9 mm. Luger is the *one* case I've been able to fill up to a standard weight *cast* bullet (not jacketed) with Bullseye. Don't *ever* try it with any other, and don't try this on my say-so. If your Luger perks with less than 4 grains in 9 mm., better do it that way, or lighter. Some are sloppily chambered, and the lower part of the chamber breech is cut out for feeding and can't support the brass above the thick base. An ironed-out bulge once let go through a hole about the size of a six-penny nail. Extractor and a piece of breech-block on each side of that extractor blew to hellangone off the gun. I had one set of spares, but now I load a little under and save the gun for the future.

Old discontinued Du Pont No. 5 works well, stands some crowding in the 9 mm. case, but I've found 5066 a bit more dense, more brash. A .38 Special zeroed in at 50 yards with 2.8 grains of 5, 146-grain Cramer deep-seated wadcutter, in Peters 20X large-primer cases only, made 7s at 12 o'clock with a like amount of 5066. Du Pont No. 6 doesn't like crowding, and spills pressures over fast if you use too much. In my *.30 caliber* Lugers, the fast Bullseye and No. 6 didn't give me accuracy with jacketed bullets, and they were worse with lead-alloy. No. 5 and 5066 are fine. The bottle-neck? Or am I dreaming?

Here are some fundamental "laws" dictated by conscience and the realization that pistol loading is only for the careful:

1. Don't crowd pistol powders except as mentioned just above, and then at your own risk. Go *slowly,* always, and consider the strength of your gun.

2. Inspect each case for a double charge if you want to keep your gun and yourself safe and healthy.

3. Keep supplied with neck-dies that hold bullets friction-tight in all calibers.

4. Crimp revolver cases, but not true rimless auto cases.

5. Inspect all brass reloaded more than twice for splits and cracks near the head. They take guns apart.

6. Check for high primers, not fully seated. In the revolver they cause hangfires or prevent the cylinder from turning. An autoloader's breech-block chambering such a load can set it off. It's been done.

7. Find a way to start lead bullets into cases straight and not shaved.

8. If your guns leads excessively, change powders. This may help.

9. Slug the bores of your handguns and get bullets to *fit*, not just anything that's foisted upon you.

10. If you *must* speed them up, keep bullets to not more than one-thousandth inch over rifling groove diameter and don't seat them deeply, reducing powder space. Again, the publisher and we writers cannot be responsible for the results from *any* of the loads mentioned in this book. There are just too many variables in guns, ammunition, and loading procedures.

You'll never know peace and contentment again after handloading your own. The investigative bug gets you.

THERE are gun fads, national, local, and some that are plumb loco. About 1910 a craze for short-barreled, takedown big game rifles swept the country; and .22s followed suit. Most of them were featherweights, and all were easy to carry and to take apart for cleaning, inspection and packing. Their trifling handicap to the hunter was the fact that he couldn't rely on sure-kill hits on deer much over 75 yards away, or on small game beyond about 30. These oldtimers still show up in brush country, where they have their points.

Factories don't always give us what we want; so in tune-up as well as in repair or adjustment of extras, the gunsmith can make our dreams become real. It pays to get a squint at work in process or completed for another customer, for some irresponsible jobs are done. Men named here are believed to be reliable, and others, too, as good or perhaps better, ply this exacting trade in honorable fashion—but anyone can slip, sometimes. The good ones stand back of their work and correct any mistakes they might make.

The big thing is to be sure that we'll like and profit from the alteration by better shooting and greater satisfaction in ownership. Up in Waverly, New York, Charley Canoll turned out excellent work. His ideas are sound, but he must execute his patrons' orders, provided that the results are safe. One winter saw a furore of barrel-shortening. Revolvers crowded in to have their 5- or 6-inch barrels lopped to 4-, 3- or even 2-inch pocket or waistband "belly gun" style. I wondered how many Robespierres who had sent their gats to the guillotine really needed a snub-nosed roscoe or could hit with it. The shifter-shooter rarely keeps a gun long enough to master it, and these chopped-down blasters certainly must have felt new! Oh yes, snubbies have their points. One man I know scores high at pretty hot local matches with his 2-inch .38 Special. An exception!

Gunsmithing can be desirable or whimsical, and there's a whale of a difference. A passing fancy, even well executed, may be an eyesore, a handicap after the work is done and irrevocable. A smoothed or lightened trigger pull can build up our skill, but to do this job well or even assemble a revolver's complicated mechanism after trying it requires more skill than many of us have. It's sensible to call on the smith rather than fail wretchedly and perhaps ruin costly or hard-to-get parts.

Just as with rifles and shotguns, there are handguns that we can rightly call "custom jobs." They may be built almost from scratch, or factory models altered and/or refined by gunsmiths, or strictly amateur jobs. To me at least, these classifications don't mean a thing in relative values. The criterion is simple: does the job give us greater pleasure, or better shooting? Or does it give both? One could be enough, so long as we get what we want. Engraving, for instance, hardly improves a gun's grouping ability; but if we like it and consider it beautiful, we've got what we want. A finely tuned

CHAPTER 16

GUNSMITHING AND ACCESSORIES

action or a beautifully lapped barrel hardly changes the outside appearance, but either one can help us to better shooting. I tend to like people who like guns, for they belong to the brotherhood and most of them are assets to our country. If their tastes aren't mine, what do I care? I can still learn something from them, I hope.

GUNSMITHING

Under this heading we include both complete arms and work done on such handguns to adapt them to special requirements. The discussion suggests some of the things that can be done; it can't cover this almost illimitable and constantly growing field. Many refinements that once were special custom work have been incorporated into standard production of ready-made pistols because of their evident value. Wide grooved triggers and hammer spurs, refined sights, built-in grip adapters, oversize target stocks, muzzle brakes to hold down the upchuck of recoil, and detachable barrel weights are typical improvements that have become standard on some of the more expensive and more or less special-purpose handguns that factories put out.

The Dardick Gun

At this writing the Dardick is still in the custom-built, prototype stage, with standard production guns and ammunition scheduled for 1960. The unusual, interesting, and truly significant details about the Dardick are that it is what is called a "chamberless" arm and that the rounds (called "trounds," as they are in the form of rounded-off triangles in cross-section) have plastic cases. Plastic has only begun to do duty in gun

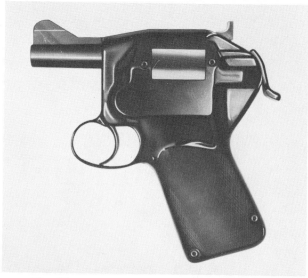

The 25-ounce, 11-shot Dardick Series 1100 pistol.

The 34-ounce, 15-shot Dardick Series 1500. Detached barrel and views of its plastic-cased, triangular cartridge also shown.

and six or eight other people, still clean barrels). The mechanism is comparatively simple, and the magazine is loaded with single trounds or with a strip clip in Springfield .30 caliber rifle or Mauser Military auto-pistol style. Present capacities are 15 .38s in the 1500 model and 11 in the 1100. Calibers are .38 S.&W., .38 Special, .38 Auto, and 9 mm. Luger, and there are .22 rimfire adapters and quick-change barrels for small shooting. A safety device prevents firing a .38 or 9mm. bullet into the .22 caliber barrel; so that hazard is eliminated! Sure, the Dardick is safe and well engineered. It is strong, and so are its trounds.

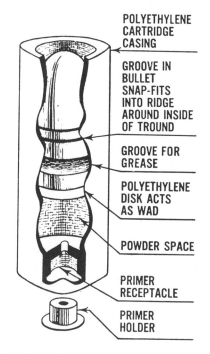

POLYETHYLENE CARTRIDGE CASING

GROOVE IN BULLET SNAP-FITS INTO RIDGE AROUND INSIDE OF TROUND

GROOVE FOR GREASE

POLYETHYLENE DISK ACTS AS WAD

POWDER SPACE

PRIMER RECEPTACLE

PRIMER HOLDER

Drawing of sectioned Dardick cartridge.

manufacture, as in the no longer startling but now well-proved Remington Nylon 66 .22 Auto-rifle. Although cartridge cases of rubber, for instance, have been used in the past, the employment of modern high-strength plastics is only entering its world of possibilities. By 1960, plastic shotgun shell cases had become common.

The gun is chamberless in that three triangular receptacles, open on one side, closed on two, handle the cartridges. The ammo goes in at an open side, in loading, and out at the same open side, in ejection; it is not pushed in and pulled out as in conventional arms from single-shots to automatics. The three-stage cycle, 120° each, is trigger-operated as in a double-action revolver; but the hammer can be cocked by hand, as in most d. a. revolvers. So the practical result is the high speed of fire that a double-action revolver gives, no slamming back and forth of a semi-auto's breech-block, and the large magazine capacity and automatic tossing-out of empties of a semi-auto pistol. There are no chambers to clean, only the barrel (for those who, like this writer

Cartridge cases are of Fortiflex plastic made by the Celanese Corporation of America, and molded by the Rogers Manufacturing Company of Middletown, Connecticut. This rigid polyethylene is much lighter than brass, smooth feeding, free from corrosion danger, and able to expand against the barrel face to seal in gases. And it's a non-strategic, manufactured material, not like a metal. It can be, and sometimes is, colored for identification of different loadings.

The cases serve as containers for factory or hand-loaded cartridges, or as cases in themselves. The latter, as the .38 Dardick Special, has taken normal and much higher pressures safely through the strength and resilience of the plastic. A polyethylene disc or wad separates powder and bullet and helps to seal the powder gas behind that bullet until it's got well into the rifling. In this, the case helps, too.

For its barrel lengths, the Dardick is unusually short, with most of the weight of the gun in and above the hand. Large magazine capacity makes its grip big, in size and slant much like that of the Colt .45 Auto. At first you might think of it as mainly for police and service use, since it holds so many cartridges and fires them so fast. It looks odd, barrel-light, and far from streamlined. Any such criticisms are temporary and trivial, I think. It is the principles of the gun and its ammunition that count. Few two-inch-barreled, heavy-frame .38 Special sixguns are downright beautiful, but in six-inch target style they are.

The Dardick can be converted into a rifle with stock and carbine-type barrel, 16 inches or over in centerfire, or 16 or over in .22 rimfire. This could mean something to police departments that don't need and in fact don't want a shoulder arm with long range and deep penetration.

Factory Custom Work

Some factories furnish special handguns—about as much now as in the past—to suit individual customers. Engraving, plating, color finishes, special stocking or mechanical tune-up, and even non-standard barrel lengths are typical requests.

As an example of tune-up there's the custom short-action Colt Officer's Match .38 Special as made for and catalogued by Gil Hebard Guns, Knoxville, Illinois. It has a specially made hammer and trigger, with a stop on a skeletonized part of the hammer to end the thumb-cocking action at just the right time against the easy resistance of the hammer spring. Some of us remember reading how Stewart Edward White had his .45 New Service Colt converted to single-action for surer and easier field shooting. This Colt has had similar treatment: a long pull on the trigger does not cock and drop the hammer, although it does turn the cylinder one chamber space.

Mr. Hebard states that the work is done by the factory's custom repair department, with Mr. Arnold Goodwin responsible for its quality. Easy handling and no tendency toward misfires are claimed, and all this sounds reasonable. If by "custom gun" you mean one made specifically for one individual, this offering probably wouldn't qualify, as catalogued; and would that matter? Custom stocks made to fit a particular (and we do mean particular) hand are something, but this Colt as illustrated in the catalogue doesn't have them. It has the mechanical quality, and that too counts in its own department.

.22 Hornet Handguns

This type of high-speed, smallbore handgun isn't new, or supposed to be. Reduced handloads in .22 Hornet rifle brass have been used off and on for years in big heavy guns custom-built for them, such as the .476-caliber frame Colt New Service. We can call the NS that because it and the Colt Single Actions too handle that thick, rather stubby black powder round as well as the .45. But the popular modern Hornet pistol takes shortened Hornet brass, cut off .05 inch, necked, and blown out to give greater powder capacity. Jim Harvey of Lakeville Arms, Lakeville, Connecticut,

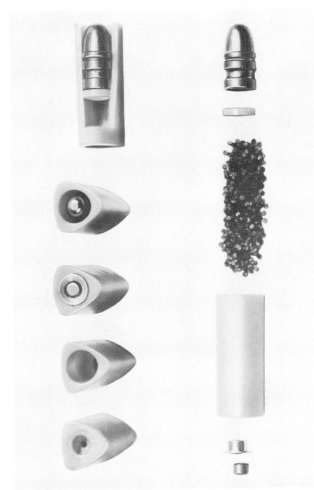

Views of Dardick cartridge components: bullet, wad, powder charge, case, battery cup for primer, and the standard small pistol size primer that's used.

and Kent Bellah, gun editor and writer, worked it up for K-.22 Smiths with rechambered cylinders and firing pins altered to centerfire. So far as I know, the .177 caliber hasn't been applied to high-velocity pistol use. It could be, but unless the velocities of the little 25- to 30-grain pills were substantially higher than those of the Bellah-Harvey Kay-Chuk there'd be no gain in killing power by what we call explosive effect. Plenty of .177 wildcat rifle cases have been made—and used with considerable satisfaction—on .22 Hornet, .218 Bee, .22 R2 Lovell, and .222 Remington brass. The first two are short enough to have sixgun possibilities.

Kay-Chuk velocities up to 2200 f.s. are listed, and penetration of 1/8-inch cold rolled steel. Speed puts a jacketed bullet through steel, but parts of that jacket—if any at all—may not go through, but instead, come back toward the shooter. One of my best friends took a hot piece of .250 Savage jacket that had come back 35 or 40 yards to tag him in the chest. It hurt, but the wound wasn't serious. If it had hit an eye, that eye would have been put out.

K-C bullets include a special 37-grain Sisk soft point, a s.p. 40-grain Sierra, and a Lyman 34-grain cast, No.

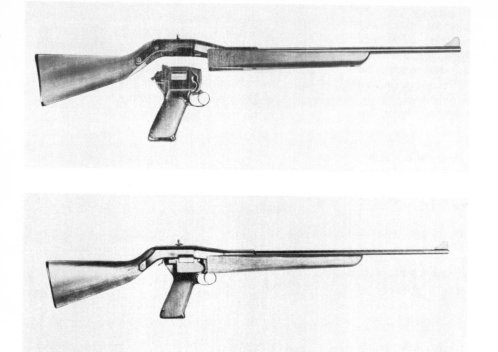

The Dardick pistol action fits into the Dardick rifle's receiver.

Dardick rifle—or is it a carbine?—completely assembled.

225107, hollow-pointed. The special Sisk preceded announcement of the .22 Winchester Magnum bullet, but they are somewhat alike: wide, flat soft point, hollowed.

Powders are the usual pistol line, plus Hercules Unique and 2400, which are becoming part-time pistol propellants as well as rifle powders, though Unique has been used a long, long time in handgun cases. Primers are pistol, which do the ignition and help lower pressures, and brass is Remington because it's relatively thin in Hornet size. Cast bullets are fairly hard, for the rather quick twist, and bullets over .224-inch diameter are too thick. For a moderate load Bellah recommends 8 grains 2400 and the pistol primer. Velocity would run about 1800 f.s. with bullets under the 40-grain that seems to be an advised and sensible maximum. That is above .22 Rimfire Mag sixgun speed. With handloading you play up and down the scale to your satisfaction, get what you want, and save money.

The only objection to this type of pistol is its sharp report with fast loads. Ear-plugs help, and if your .22 high-speed sixgun carries a scope sight with rather short eye-relief, as some do, the plugs would be what the Army calls "mandatory!"

Kimball .30 Semi-Automatic

This high-velocity pistol seems to fall between big-time and custom production, but it should have a future. The address is J. Kimball Arms Company, Box 41, Detroit 23, Michigan. It is an expensive, hand-fitted gun for the .30 M1 Carbine cartridge, with .38 Special and .357 Magnum (interchangeable by merely swapping magazines) contemplated.

The standard service .30 cartridge is rated at over 1500 f.s. velocity from the 5-inch barrel, and it can of course be handloaded with soft- or hollow-point bullets. There are six rifling grooves, with 12-inch twist, and magazine capacity is seven rounds, or six in .38. Since this is not a pocket gun, but rather for field use, the Micro-Click rear sight is set well back. A good grip-slant and fair muzzle-weight should help in accurate shooting. The general appearance of the pistol is attractive.

Being a blow-back, not a locked-breech autoloader, the Kimball has few parts. On firing, the barrel goes back with the case for a short distance, against the brake of the recoil spring. Tool-marks intentionally left in the chamber (except up top, where they could cause feeding troubles) slow the blow-back action by holding the fired case in the chamber for a split-instant.

"Pistol into Rifle"

Colonel Ward O. Betz wrote up his experiments with a wildcat pistol cartridge in the August, 1956 *Guns*. He formed a quarter-inch long .30-caliber neck on .357 Mag. brass and had a 1917 Colt .45 A.C.P. revolver's chambers bushed for the cartridge, using an 8 15/16-inch length of .30-30 rifle barrel, 12-inch twist. Les Lindahl of Central City, Nebraska, did the work, screwing and pinning the barrel in place—S.&W. fashion.

The Colonel worked up loads cautiously, using the 93-grain .30 Luger jacketed bullet. Up to 700 yards' target range his sixgun did right well, for a pistol. He reported good killing effects on jack-rabbits at 200 paces and over, the soft-point bullet evidently holding its velocity well, when started at near-maximum safe speed. We mention his work to illustrate, in general, what is being done about high handgun velocities with bullets weighing well above those used in smaller bores

—probably close to 1,900 or 2,000 f.s. with this .30, or possibly higher. They are strictly for the most capable experimenters and, in the hunting field, for those with high shooting skill and the unwillingness to take on chances more likely to result in wounding than in clean killing.

At the other extreme, Elmer Keith has written in *Guns* about really big sixguns using heavy bullets of good diameter, and at high speed, too. These hand-made jobs weigh six pounds or so and are much heavier than old Colt Walker or Dragoon cap-and-ball revolvers; and they follow the graceful lines of modern Colt, Great Western, and Ruger single-actions.

Cases are the .45-70, also the bigger-based .348 opened to .43 (.44 Special) for a 250-grain bullet of the familiar semi-wadcutter Keith design. With this bullet, velocity of about 2,000 f.s. has been attained. Such huge pistols are not impractical; they could be life-savers. Their weight keeps recoil bearable, more than we can say for some featherweight custom rifles; but even with those, good stock design and being recoil-hardened can make for profit, not misery.

SOME CUSTOM REFINEMENTS

The foregoing is but a brief sketch, a sampling, of what can be done in the realm of special custom-made handguns. There are far fewer of them than of custom rifles. The field of invention is hardly scratched, and perhaps current emphasis falls on speed of bullet, not on shootability, the gun's back-up of our skill in placing shots where we want them, on paper targets or on game. Oh yes, stocks to fit the hand, sights to suit the eyesight, and weight and balance to cooperate with hand and arm muscles, all these get attention, and they have for a long time. All are strictly individual, or should be!

Here is a cursory look at custom work that can be applied to as-issued handguns or thereabouts.

Colt .45 Auto

This intensely practical gun is popular, at least with those who shoot it well. In time, the pounding of recoil destroys its accuracy, loosening the fit of barrel and slide. The *finest* shooting often must be gunsmithed into it to start with, for issue .45s are and must be loose in order to function under rough service conditions. Tight tolerances don't go well with dust, mud, sand and grit.

Among match shooters the name of A. E. Berdon, Lakeland, Florida, is revered, as it should be. His work added points to a score by snug barrel fit and an anti-slap or anti-backlash trigger that gives a clean pull that quits when the hammer has been released. Other men do fine accuracy jobs, or have in the past, such as Jesse Harpe, 913 Tampa Street, Tampa; Alton S. Dinan, Jr., Box 674, Canaan, Connecticut; Giles' .45 Shop, Rt. 1, Box 41-A, Odessa, Florida; F. Bob Chow, 3185 Mission Street, San Francisco 10; American Gun Works, 10348 Columbus, San Fernando, California;

A Pachmayr accuracy job on the .45 Auto. From Pachmayr Gun Works, 1220 S. Grand Ave., Los Angeles, Calif.

Accuratized .45 Auto by George Elliason, Precision Arms & Tool Co., 31528 Groesbeck Highway, Fraser, Mich. Slide is tightened to the receiver, barrel bushing fitted snugly in the slide and to the barrel, and the barrel built up at two points to position it the same for each shot. The trigger is built up in height and width for close fit, and given a spring stop. Oversize hammer and sear pins are fitted, and hammer notch is adjusted to give the desired weight of a smooth pull. Front strap of grip and arched mainspring housing at the rear are stippled for grasp.

Eliason Arms, 1225 Webb, Detroit; R. L. Shockey, Box 795, El Reno, Oklahoma; Pachmayr Gun Works, 1220 South Grand, Los Angeles; Gil Hebard Guns, Knoxville, Illinois; C. R. McCasland, Box 57, Hinton, West Virginia; and still others, for this is but a sampling. James E. Clark of Shreveport, Louisiana, Box 4248, is a top-ranker in both gunsmithing and match shooting.

For years *The American Rifleman* has been a clearing-house for gunsmithing ideas on this and many other small-arms. See for spot examples the January '44, April '49 and January '52 issues, and back, forward and through these dates. Personal advice to N.R.A. members comes from the *Rifleman* staff, too, and at one time or another many of us have taken advantage of that service. Your .45 Auto should feed reliably,

The .45 Auto barrel bushing and recoil buffer from Beckelhymer's, 513 Salinas Ave., Laredo, Texas.

even with cast lead bullets of reasonable profile up front, its trigger should behave *almost* as well as that of a good revolver, its accuracy should not handicap your ability, and so on. In short, it should be a good target gun if it has the necessary time, money and effort spent on it. And it should still be a formidable fighting gun, except under the roughest conditions, if need comes up.

Accurized .45 Autos, with some restrictions, are now "legal" in Service pistol and of course in centerfire matches. Tight slides help, like snug barrel bushings up front, and rear barrel links that reduce vertical barrel movement when the action closes. Good trigger pulls help, and the reduced play of the trig in *any* direction. A trigger shoe makes the pull *seem* lighter, and gives better control. Recoil effect can be modified, and close headspacing of barrel and breech adds to ammunition accuracy.

Hand-fitting grips are fine, but not allowed in the National Trophy Individual Match. In military service a fighter may have to use any weapon he can get, and using the grip of someone else can be like wearing his shoes!

So it goes. The .45 *can* be a most accurate and individualized arm, and most of us who own one would find it right for nearly any service. We owe most of all, perhaps, to Mr. Berdon. He died in Lakeland on December 4, 1958. As the following February's *Rifleman* obituary said, he was a Purdue electrical engineering graduate, who began .45 accurizing in 1934. His best-known patent, the obituary stated, was for his "mouse-trap" device, to keep the barrel's muzzle and breech always in a uniform position. We can be thankful that to his technical training was joined an under-

standing of what .45 targetmen want from their big handguns.

.38 Special Auto

It was inevitable that .38 Special conversions of Super-.38 Colt auto-pistols should come for target shots who don't want to thumb a sixgun's hammer or use it double-action in rapid fire, five shots in ten seconds. Factory or handloaded .38 Special wadcutters are short in overall, accurate, and pleasant to shoot. The .38 Auto is or can be made an accurate cartridge, too, but its report and brisk recoil are sharper than those of the mid-range Special. Accurized by nice fitting, a .38 Special auto helps in short-time stages, and the blunt lead wadcutter bullet, though slow, is normally a better man-stopper than the hard rounded Automatic.

Some who make these conversions are William Vonella, 884 Broadway, West Long Branch, New Jersey; American Gun Works, mentioned in the preceding .45 section; and R. L. Shockey, also mentioned there, who uses the feeding ramp patented by J. E. Clark, Box 4248, Shreveport, Louisiana. The work has given 1¾-inch groups at 25 yards.

A heavy-slide .45 from Giles' .45 Shop, Rt. 1, Box 41-A, Odessa, Fla. Also available with extension rib to set front sight farther ahead and give an 8-inch sight radius.

Giles Super-.38 conversion to .38 Special. This, too, can have the extension rib for the front sight.

Colt Single-Action

American Gun Works, also J. L. Nagorski, Upper Black Eddy, Penna., have converted single-action Colts to .22 rimfire. This grand old gun has an undeniable reputation for breaking down, at least in not too careful hands. Both Colt and the Christy Gun Works, 875 57th Street, Sacramento 16, rebuild it on your frame and straps, and recase-harden frames. Christy revitalizes Colt New Service double-actions to .38 and up, with cylinders and barrels made there. A tricky piece, the combined firing pin and ejector for a Remington Model 12 .22 pump gun, which they supplied to me, is standing up finely.

John Lochuk's May '45 *Rifleman* article on "Smithing the Colt Single Action" describes a short hammer-fall. This would help on target paper; but some recall using tough rifle primers in the S. A., when they had to. The whack of the long-swinging hammer gave almost 100% sure ignition, but a shooter can find it disconcerting.

The S. A.'s firing pin can break, though rarely. Christy and the Dem-Bart Company, Box 700, Tacoma, have a floating firing pin assembly to replace the original pin and the recoil plate in the breech-face. The most used, best loved guns, like the S. A. and the .45 Auto, see so much service that weaknesses become apparent and may be magnified out of actual importance. If so, lay this blow-up to dear old human nature, like your own faults.

Fast Double-Action Fire

This requires a gun in good shape. Ed McGivern with a K-.38 S.&W. let off five rounds in ⅖ second, *and grouped 'em.* For this speed, a gun surely has to respond!

Mr. McGivern's obituary in the February '58 *Rifleman* shows his perseverance in learning. His book, *Fast and Fancy Revolver Shooting,* 1938, reissued in 1957, scarcely can help reflecting it—it was so apparent in spite of his unpretentiousness. In 1904, at about the age of 30, he began it, in Montana. His best in consistent, combined speed and accuracy came in the 1930s. He could put six bullets into a thrown tin can before it fell to earth.

For fast work the double-action trigger pull and the trigger return spring must be well matched. The trigger must return forward promptly, but not so energetically as to throw the gun out of alignment for the next shot.

Precision Shooting of January, 1959, carried William E. Peterson's "Double-Action for Accuracy," well worth study. Finger movement may be as much as ¾ inch, and the position of the trigger acts "like the indicator of a pressure gauge." A custom grip with projection to notify the finger that the hammer is about to fall can help a small hand, though pull is, ideally, straight through without a pause, even in deliberate double-action firing. On some guns you get the advantage of an unchanging pull straight through, not a build-up. The S.&W. is a general favorite, for its cylinder is turned and locked while the hammer is still rising, and the final pull is therefore smooth. Peterson says we can back off the S.&W. mainspring strain screw, down near the bottom of the butt, and even cut off the hammer spur—first, to lighten the pull; and second, to reduce its inertia at the start. (Soft primers, like some Cascades I've used, could be reliable.) Check for sidewise drag of the firing pin, and fit a new one if necessary. We may be able to cut off a turn or two of the S.&W. rebound spring inside the square block above the trigger. Sliding surfaces should be polished.

Peterson says that 100 rounds could tell if this double-action shooting has possibilities for you. Start with slow fire and work up to, say, five shots in 20 seconds—"Timed fire," as we know it on the range. Curl the finger around the trigger and let it follow the frame of the gun above it as the finger goes back.

Elmer Keith in *Sixguns* gives much helpful detail on fast d. a. shooting. "Get your hand squarely behind the gun," he says, "and grip it like closing your fist, with the first finger independent but toward the thumb. Grip hard and uniformly, and strengthen your hand to do it." The cylinder must move smoothly, and the inertia of a big heavy one helps, as gun weight itself does. He finds the flat mainsprings in the big Smiths smoother than the coil springs in little ones like the Centennial and Chief's Special, those small, five-shot .38 Specials.

Barrels and Cylinders

Most of us use these as they come. Long ago, The Niedner Rifle Corporation did furnish .38 and .44 target revolver barrels, on a par with their superb rifle barrels, and now the American Gun Works supply custom tubes for Colts and Smiths, smoothly lapped, a finish that we'd expect would give us greater accuracy and ease of cleaning, and sometimes higher velocity. Alas, too many top-grade factory revolver barrels do need lapping at their breech-throats (forcing cones), as excessive leading built up there may

Giles heavy-barrel Ruger .22 auto has match grade barrel with polished chamber and cartridge feeding ramp. A bolt stop magazine follower holds breech open after the last shot. Giles rear sight has close, exact adjustments for target use. Hammer, trigger, and sear have special oversize pins to give a crisp 2 to 2½ pound pull. Note the special stocks on this gun.

Giles heavy-barrel Hi-Standard. Rear sight is mounted on the rear extension of the barrel rib, doing away with the variations in position that are possible when a rear sight is mounted on a recoiling slide.

This Remington rolling-block single-shot pistol was rebarreled to .22 long-rifle by A. O. Niedner and stocked by Thomas Shelhamer of Dowagiac, Michigan, Special sights, the front sight mounted on a barrel-band base. From long-time experience in using the work of these men I can vouch for its absolutely top quality. They represent the best of an earlier generation, and they are not forgotten. The old Niedner Rifle Corporation is no more, and Mr. Shelhamer makes but a few stocks now.

or may not indicate. Some bullet profiles and lead alloys will foul up almost any throats—while some, by great good fortune, won't.

Rifling twists of one turn in 15 inches are from about 1 to 5 inches faster than some factory jobs. A quick spin suits long bullets, and possibly standard twists are slow for standard ammunition, such as long-sided wadcutters, at least. For these, the Colt Officer's Model took on in recent years a steeper pitch of rifling, 14 inches. If ammo isn't up to scratch, a fast twist usually helps. Such details are a headache for a perfectionist, like the clearance between cylinder and barrel. Too much, and we get fireworks, blast, and power loss unless the barrel is stubby indeed. Too little—and this is rare—and lead shaved off wadcutters from a not quite perfectly lined-up chamber may halt the cylinder's revolution as abruptly as a loosely crimped-in bullet can. Phil Sharpe once said that from .002- to .010-inch clearance will do, and that sounds exactly right. Some factory guns have as much as .013 or even more, and they aren't really nice in their way of talking. A smith can correct "gaposis," setting some barrels back if that seems best, and inexact or wobbly line-up, too, or perhaps even a bent ejector rod or a warped crane, the part that carries the swing-out cylinder and ejector. He can cut back a battered muzzle, if the gun is worth it. Another type of gunsmith or dealer might try to sell a weapon with filed-off serial numbers or "United States Property" marking. Modern science can read such legends still, and we might not care to be mixed up with the previous owner!

Spare Parts

Spare parts may replace broken ones, or improve on originals. We can list only a few of many specialists. B. K. Wingate, Box 154, Carlisle, Penna., is one, and so is James E. Serven, 1028 Oak Street, Santa Ana, California, who also offers bits and pieces for Remington and Colt cap-and-ball revolvers. Ralph Pike, Kalispell, Montana, has unbreakable bolt and trigger springs for the S. A. Colts. American Gun Works make and install its parts, as well as furnishing a short hammer-fall action for big S.&W.s. Some find that unaltered oldtimers cock a little hard by thumb, or by forefinger in double-action work. (In rapid fire, some of us learned to press on the trigger as we started the hammer back by thumb, but this requires a lot of

The fine shaping, checkering and finish of wood appears also in this Shelhamer stocked Winchester Model 70 rifle. It is difficult to form a rifle stock with a full, face-supporting cheek-piece and a Monte Carlo comb rise so that it is both a real help in marksmanship and still a beautiful thing to look at, but Mr. Shelhamer obviously succeeded.

empty-gun practice, in the interest of safety, before we try it with loaded rounds.)

Since any gun can break down, there are many parts purveyors. Joseph Scaramuzzo & Sons, 601 South Halstead Avenue, Chicago 7, and Firearms International, 4837 Kerby Hill Road, Washington 22, D.C., are well patronized, the latter specializing in foreign arms. Western Gun Exchange, Whittier, California, has new parts, especially for Lugers, Walthers, and big Mausers, and the N. F. Strebe shop, 6215 R Street, Washington, does maintenance work on foreigners. The Kenfix Company, 3706 Florida Avenue, Tampa, works on old revolvers and foreigners, and tries to stock all Thompson sub-machine gun parts, which law officers, with all their sleuthing skill, possibly might find hard to run to earth. Do not forget Christy Gun, just mentioned under "Colt Single-Action."

Broken springs may be difficult to replace. Russ Carpenter, Plattekill, and Charles Moore, Delhi, both in York State, as is Victor Pearsall of Mount Upton, are specialists. Flat springs are broken most commonly, but they're pretty rugged, at that. Frequently they serve for 75 years or more, like one upstairs that powers the heavy hammer of a steadily used Remington rolling-block .40-50 single-shot rifle.

Engraving, Inlaying and Plating

Some of us like guns dressed fit to go to a West Indian governor's reception—which can be a most human and happy occasion, though we *don't* commonly attend with arms—and some of us like them plain and straight businesslike. Good appearance, in itself, never hurt any gun's shooting, but tastes vary as to what good looks are. Decoration can please, or insult, almost any taste, for it varies from florid to restrained, and so do tastes vary. "There is no accounting for taste," and I don't quite see that a person should be either proud or ashamed of his taste. He is what he is, he likes what he likes, and his individuality is to be respected.

As for any gun decoration at all, I can only say that I've enjoyed hunting and target work with both plain and beautifully (I thought) decorated arms, and countless others have had the same experience. I like almost all guns and almost all shooters, whether or not they resemble my guns or me! This too must be a common feeling.

Colt and Smith & Wesson have done and still do some engraving and special stocking of their own arms. In any recent issue of John Amber's *Gun Digest* you can find a list of engravers in an arms trade directory at the end of the book. It isn't and obviously cannot be complete, but it's a good one. We are showing a few specimens of engraving and other decoration, merely representative of what this big and interesting field covers.

Many of us know that engraved gun steel continues to look good—if it looked good to start with—after long miles of carrying. Artistry still stands out and even is enhanced. Plain steel, worn by use and not

abuse, takes on a nickel color, neither bright white nor blue; and it doesn't add to a gun's resale value! This off-white color can be proof of the miles and hours of happiness that gun has given us, and as for selling that arm, why, it would be last-ditch need that would demand it. We want to keep it, and signs of honest wear belong on it: they are valued. That's how some gun-lovers feel. Good friends have offered in all kindness to reblue my guns, and I've been grateful for

Work done by Arnold Griebel, 4724 N. Keystone Ave., Chicago 30, Ill., for the late King Faisal of Iraq. Note realistic portrayal of the ibex.

the offers but haven't accepted them. These people understand. Friends do.

Engraving can tell a story, at least of a simple incident or situation, or it can simply present a view of something in nature or in the imagination. The approach, or the viewpoint, can range from the comic to the classical. But let's have the subject one of which we shan't tire. Can't it be as important as the gun's caliber, action type, weight, balance, and so on? We want to own our gun until, and after, it has become a

Cap-and-ball Colt work by E. C. Prudhomme, 305 Ward Bldg., Shreveport, La. See also his work on a Borchardt pistol, shown in the Luger section of the chapter on foreign handguns.

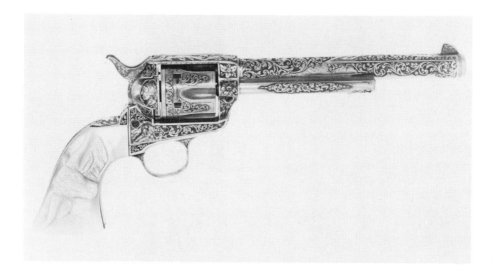

Prudhomme work on a Colt Single Action Army.

Engraving and inlay by Prudhomme on .45 Auto Colt accurized by James E. Clark, Box 4248, Shreveport. Note how Mr. Prudhomme caught the straining of the oxen pulling the covered wagon. A gun for both long-time admiration and high scores.

Beautiful work by Smith & Wesson on the single-action model that introduced the short .32 S.&W. cartridge. This gun has a sheath-type trigger with no guard, as so many oldtimers had, and some modern pocket revolvers have had their guards cut away, up front, for speed work. Why not? Everyone should be extra careful with a pocket-size pistol; it's so easy to point it in the wrong direction

Here is the photograph of the Hoffbauer oil painting in the Smithsonian Institution, which Mr. Ward used as the design for his engraving of the cylinder of the 1860 Colt, doing this work for Mr. J. L. Rawls of the Department of Natural History at the Smithsonian. It shows Generals "Stonewall" Jackson and J. E. B. Stuart and some of their worn, devoted men. It should touch the heart, as well as stir the heart, of any American anywhere in this world.

part of us, an ally to back our skill. The less we shift guns, the better we shoot. So perhaps any decoration should come later, if at all. Lots of us like blued steel and brown wood, just as they are. Is this akin to a meat-and-potatoes taste?

We get about what we pay for in engraving and all that, though we shouldn't confuse quantity and quality. The cost can be hundreds of dollars, or only a few. Foreign labor costs run well below ours; but we may want American work of this kind, if we want any. In a trade-in or sale most "extras" don't bring what they should, as a rule. But work of this kind often does better, even though there are all sorts of tastes which dictate potential buyers' desire.

ACCESSORIES

This is an enormous field, with new entrants every month or oftener, it seems. Some are helpful; some

just relieve us of cash; and perhaps, as a kindly touch, of spring-fever, which comes when it's too late for snowshoes and too gummy and wet for anything but rubber boots, and a poncho in the pack-sack. At any time, long confinement in a city that has no indoor range can bring it on. Buying something in the gun line, when we're overstocked with essentials, can relieve it. We feel better then, and can feel foolish later, if we must.

Reading Matter

Books, magazines, catalogues, and newspapers' outdoor columns are seldom a waste of time! True, we outgrow, or think we do, some of them, but there are others more advanced; so we can keep on learning and enjoying.

We can list but a few, for totals are prodigious; and we can't corral all the good and worth-while specimens. Among pistol books there are Charles Askins, Jr.'s *Pistol Shooter's Book*, Julian S. Hatcher's *Pistols and Revolvers*, Elmer Keith's *Sixguns*, and Walter Roper's *Experiments of a Handgunner*. Also there are books on the history of handguns, and of their use, on gunsmithing, and on how to hunt and how to live in the wilderness. (Even though we may not care to hunt with any sort of pistol and any sort of pistol skill, it can be fun to have one along on new or old trails, for the little weapon is essentially companionable.)

The general outdoor magazines—on hunting, fishing, boating, camping and so on—have their gun editors, and each editor has his following. Each, I'm sure, tries to give impartial, unbiased advice, and with success. There are some 100%, or nearly, shooting magazines and annuals, big and little, with varying percentages of pictures and text. Here are a few of those I've enjoyed.

The American Rifleman long has been a champion of our right to own and bear arms, as others are, too, and as all ought to be—actively. As the National Rifle Association's biggest monthly publication it reaches thousands upon thousands by way of club and individual copies. N.R.A. members are warned of impending anti-gun legislation of local, state, or national type as well as staffmen or members can sniff the foul stuff out before it's too late to be opposed. There is considerable pistol information in the *Rifleman,* along with that on rifles, shotguns, collectors' interests, hunting, outdoor living, and so on. Life membership has manifold advantages. Address: 1600 Rhode Island Avenue, N.W., Washington 6, D. C.

Precision Shooting is edited by Phil Teachout, Lyndonville, Vermont. As far as I know, Phil is the most hard-working advocate of safe, accurate and legal shooting that we have; but he would object violently to this statement. In the nature of things there must be his equals. Let him resume his customary calm and friendly manner! *P.S.* has very few staff writers; its articles come from all sorts of shooters, some of them perhaps new to you, for awhile, or even not heard

The 1860 Colt engraved and gold inlaid by Woodie Ward, Box 5454, Beaumont, Texas.

A pair of Colt Single Actions engraved and inlaid by Woodie Ward for Mr. Mackey Coker of Dallas.

A much different type of work, also finely done, by Woodie Ward on a 5½-inch Colt S. A. A.

A 7½-inch Colt S. A. A. with Ward engraving.

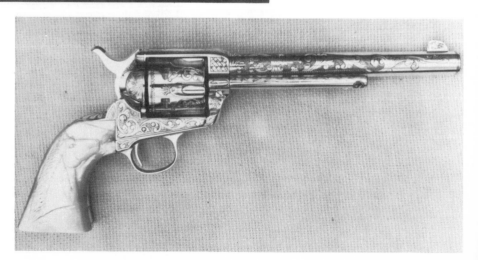

from again, once they've had their say. But all the stuff is solid meat, as is the makeup of the magazine itself, which has no big headlines or space-consuming decorations. I don't know any better source of useful practical information based on long experience and on the latest investigations, too.

John T. Amber edits the annual *Gun Digest,* which comes out in the fall and is available at sporting goods stores, bookstores, and newsstands all over the country. It's a big book, with over 300 pages of text. Its

Alvin A. White, 72 Verndale Ave., Attleboro, Mass., did this work on a 4¾-inch Single Action Colt. Gold line inlay decorates the borders of the engraving and runs around the edges of the cylinder flutes and through the scroll-work on the barrel and the ejector rod housing below it. On the loading gate a short-horn steer's head is inlaid in gold.

A 4¾-inch .44 Special Colt S. A. A. carrying Ward's floral and animal engraving.

Ward-engraved .357 S.&W. Magnum done for Mr. F. B. Fletcher of Bay City, Michigan.

Smith & Wesson .357 Magnum revolver engraved by J. Fugger. Note the realistic details of the moose portrait.

Another Ward-engraved short Magnum. It is in the Andy Palmer collection, Military Inn, Dearborn, Michigan.

Mr. Fugger's work on the other side of the same gun.

A Ballard rifle receiver engraved by J. Fugger of Griffin & Howe, Inc., 114 East 13th St., New York 3, N. Y. The portrait is of the late Harry Melville Pope, who was probably the greatest of all rifle barrel makers. His work went on Ballard, Stevens, Winchester and other single-shot actions, for the most exacting target shooting, and be rebarreled more modern types of arms, too.

A rifle's magazine floor-plate engraved by J. Fugger, showing the scrupulously exact details in its study of a Rocky Mountain ram.

articles come from both familiar and comparatively new writers. Almost every phase of guns and shooting is covered, and like the other monthly periodicals briefly described here, it is edited by a shooter. Articles may be and often are controversial; but they are edited for soundness, like those in the magazines we've chosen as examples of shooters' print. With so many writers represented, almost any reader learns something from a *Digest* issue, or at least is stimulated to consider other view points than his own. I think nearly all of us can stand some of that!

Guns is edited by Bill Edwards and is easy to find on newsstands if you don't subscribe to it, though many do subscribe. Bill, I should have said, is the technical editor, and he regularly contributes an article to it. There are some staff writers, well-known, and others who write for it. This magazine, like *Precision Shooting, Gun Digest* and the *Rifleman,* is definitely against those subversives and stooges who would disarm us. *Guns* appeals to the average guy or gal who might be interested in shooting. Its arrangement is catchy and convincing; and it's done a lot for the cause by snaffling the attention and the go-and-do-likewise spirit of many who would have, I believe, little interest in more solid-looking technical publications. However, Bill is a keen editor and has packed in solid stuff for his public. Easy reading needn't be frothy, as he has proved.

Shotgun News, Columbus, Nebraska, is typical of the best ad sheets. It costs little, comes every month, or oftener, and accepts and prints sell, trade and want advertisements in dozens of pages. Big-spread or column-width, many of these ads are downright interesting in what they tell about unusual arms, old or modern, whether or not they invite a change in your ready-money inventory.

Do not overlook newspaper stories and columns (especially anything to do with anti-gun legislation, which you should report promptly to the N.R.A. and to fellow-shooters). Do not overlook also the easy possibility of lifelong friendships which stem from casual correspondence. In this matter you can shorten your life, I suppose, by overwork, though most fellow-enthusiasts are understanding and put up with six-months-delayed answers when they must. Some of my finest friendships started with a postage stamp. I don't doubt that you've had the same experiences.

Sights

These may be accessories, though any pistol must have them unless it's for pull-and-point shooting, as so many oldtimers and some current jobs are. But we can't expect to hit what we can't properly aim at. Most factory sights are good as now made, square front and square-cut rear notch for the front to rest in, the tops even, except for holding over or under, and a strip of light on each side of the front sight as seen through the notch. These light- strips can be too fine for handicapped eyesight, or for good eyesight in poor light, as in shady woods, or early or late in the day. Wide ribbons seem just as accurate as narrow ones, to me, but each of us has his own vision to suit, and he must do exactly that.

Well-known to target shooters is the Merit optical attachment for shooting glasses or for all-day specs. Its adjustable-sized aperture, placed where we want it, sharpens most folks' vision. It comes from a store or from Merit Gun Sight Company, 6144 Monadnock Way, Oakland 5, California.

A micrometer adjustable sight for Colt and Hi-

Standard and other target arms comes from Gregoire Engineering Company in New Haven, and the Micro Sight Company is at 242 Harbor Boulevard, Belmont, California. Front sights slightly higher than factory issue may be needed. For the Colt Officer's Model a non-clicking rear sight was designed by the A. H. Gun Service people, 820 Main Street, Hackensack, New Jersey. King's full and semi ribs have been liked on fine barrels, with almost any color of front sight you'd want. The square, black, Patridge design is so close to universal in these days of more target and less hunting that few of us think we need a red, ivory or gold tip attached or inletted into our front sight. Yet red suits many eyes that look at (but shouldn't concentrate on) target paper, and gold can be smoked. Some remember the old Lyman system of an ivory bead front and a rear with ivory bars pointing at the wide aiming notch. Even in a cedar swamp they were quickly seen; and holding over or under the mark was easy, for this was a roomy rear indeed, like a hippo's. Stewart Edward White liked them and killed deer and African warthog with his New Service .45 thus equipped. At that time, few hunters seem to have emulated David and his sling against Goliath-sized game, though one old-timer, something better than legend has told us, jumped up on a cliff-side and slew a rhino with a geologist's pick as it charged blindly past. I think the hit was in the neck vertebrae.

A gun with fixed, semi-circular front sight becomes useful with various loads if adjustable sights climb on it. A windage and elevation adjustable front came, and may still come, from the Metro Firearms Company, 155 Canal Street, New York 13. Allen screws held it in place. A truly "long-range revolver sight" is that item from Firearms Development Laboratories, Box 25, Duarte, California. You attach it to big S.&W.s through the top screw-hole for the sideplate

Elliason rear sight from Precision Arms & Tool Co., 31528 Groesbeck Highway, Fraser, Mich., has wide-slotted windage and elevation screws with directional indicators. With sight radius increased to 6.85 inches, as done by this job on a .45 Auto Colt, each click of a screw gives about ½-inch correction at 50 yards. Similar pistol rear sights have been made, as by King and by Smith & Wesson, and the Colt Accro sight, also good, is similar in operation though not in design. An Elliason front sight is made of aircraft grade steel No. 4340, to resist the tendency of front sights on heavy-recoiling auto pistols to become broken or even to jump off and be lost. The Elliason front has a straight, serrated face, not undercut.

Inexpensive handgun scope and mount from Pan-Technics Ltd., Box 578, Encinitas, Calif. Magnifying power of 1.4 and 22-inch eye relief are listed, with perfect focus and maximum field from 5-inches to arm's length. Well aware of the interest in scoped revolvers, Maynard Buehler of Orinda, Calif., has produced a top-rib mount for big Smiths, Colts and Rugers, but at this writing there are few top quality long-relief scopes to use it. For two-hand shooting with or without a rest, conventional long-relief *rifle* scopes have given interesting and sometimes practical sixgun results.

Beckelhymer's sight mover for .38 and .45 Colt autoloaders lets you get exact windage adjustment on the drive-in, dovetail-type of standard service rear sight.

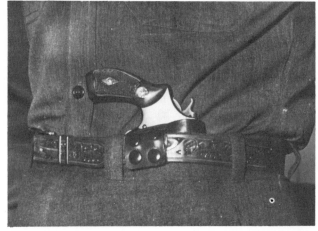

Pan-Technics scope on a Hi-Standard Sentinel .22 revolver. Double-action scoped firing is possible, but single-action is best for most of us, even with low-power scopes like this one. Like other low-cost outfits, the P-T will have faults, but do you remember what Weaver's inexpensive little .22 rifle scopes did to improve marksmanship in depression years? They weren't perfect either.

on the right, or have other guns drilled for it! It sits well behind the factory rear sight—target type or non-adjustable, either one. It has micrometer click windage and a pretty close setting system for elevation to distances over 200 yards, if you want that, or for light-bullet squib loads, close-up.

Colt and Smith have their own target sights, the latter's rear sight being much like the old King. Other companies have their designs, though some use the Micro-Click. It seems to be realized more fully now than ever before that even short-barreled, pocket-type arms need easy, sure sight adjustment instead of fixed hardware, and even some popular "snub barrel" models have them. They belong, except on strictly quick-draw guns that are for the pocket, not for the holster. They won't catch on a good holster, but they can in most pockets.

Holsters

Even the target shooter needs a holster unless he carries his gun in a kit-case. A fine holster for belt or shoulder churns up pride, whether or not it's carved or metal-studded for decoration. It lasts for decades if it's treated with neatsfoot oil when it needs it. Famous ones come from Berns-Martin, Calhoun City, Mississippi; Heiser Saddlery, 1024 Cherokee Street, Denver 4; the George Lawrence Company, 306 S.W. First Avenue, Portland 4, Oregon; the J. D. Myres Saddle Company, 5030 Alameda Boulevard, El Paso; and others, too. We cannot list them all. Even poorly tanned holsters should not rust a gun *if* we oil gun and leather well, but this is no guarantee. We have seen the results of neglect combined with cheap leather.

The upside-down Berns-Martin affords a good reach to either hand, a great advantage if you ever need it. A somewhat similar one comes from San Francisco Gun Exchange, 75 Fourth Street, S.F. 3. The old Audley belt holster's retaining spring engaged the trigger guard (marked it, in time) and yet was speedily released after some practice. Chic Gaylord, 312 West 47th Street, New York 36, has one something like it,

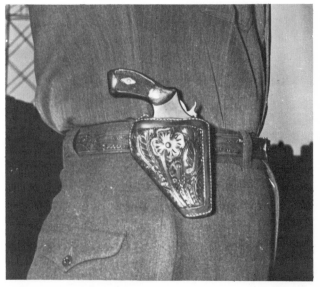

Berns-Martin "I. P." (inside pants) holster with a little five-shot S.&W. Chief's Special .38. Belt loop snaps are adjustable to 1-, 1¼-, and 1½-inches. A fine rig, most convenient for this sort of carry.

This "Lightnin" belt holster with 1-inch belt loop carrying a 2-inch barreled S.&W. Chief's Special comes from Berns-Martin, Calhoun City, Mississippi.

Hand-carved B.-M. "Speed" holster with S.&W. Combat Masterpiece .38 Special fitted with a grip adapter.

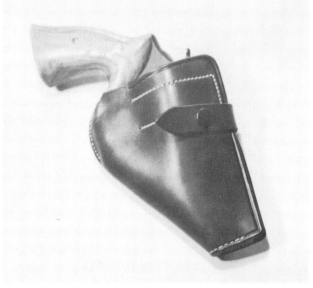

A plain finished Berns-Martin "Speed" holster carrying a 4-inch S.&W. .357 Magnum with factory-made rosewood stocks, not checkered.

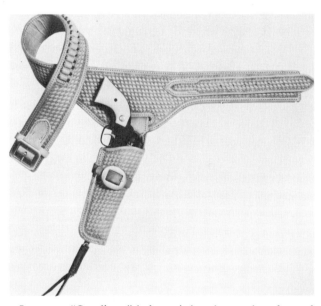

Lawrence "Gunslinger" holster pitches the gun butt forward for a quick side draw.

Hand-carved B.-M. "Speed" holster and 2½-inch belt for 5½-inch Colt Single Action Army.

The No. 7 shoulder holster from George Lawrence Co., 306 S.W. First Avenue, Portland 4, Oregon. Simple, service-able, well made for its job.

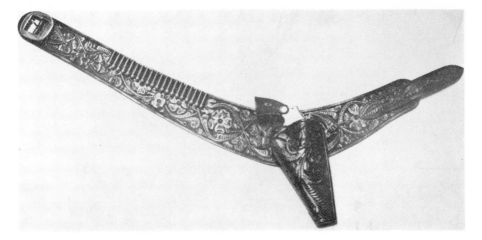

Berns-Martin "Speed" holster and single (one-gun) Buscadero belt, both hand-carved, with 6½-inch S.&W. Magnum.

Lawrence Regulation Police holster is pivoted to the cartridge-carrying belt slide, which can be slipped over a trousers belt.

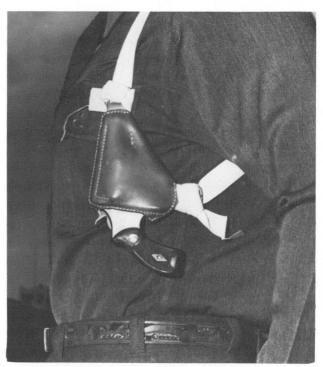

B.-M. "Lightnin" shoulder holster worn upside-down for quick draw of the small, short Chief's Special.

to prevent the gun's being pulled by a not-innocent bystander. It's reinforced inside, like some others, to give the smooth finish for a quick, sure draw. His combat model is hinged, a sound if not new idea, for cross-body draw, left side for a right-hander. You crouch forward, if you like that system, to speed the pull. Gun butts slanted forward help, too, of course. Target sights can be protected from blueing wear by a built-in protector, Lawrence fashion, or by the Berns-Martin front-opening method, a spring around the cylinder and the sights not touching the leather.

Stocks

Special stocks don't go on target guns only. Walter Roper, who was well-known as marksman, author and firearms designer, probably originated the modern popular use of custom stocks. Sanderson custom stocks are famous; they come from 17695 Fenton, Detroit. Bob Winger, 717 Broad Street, Montoursville, Penna., inlets and fits unfinished stocks, leaving the slow, careful workdown to the customer, as many prefer it. Hal Hartley, Lenoir, North Carolina, is an experienced artisan; and the Herrett Company, Box 741, Twin Falls, Idaho, tailors walnut to measure, with thumbrest, trigger guard space filler, a bulge for the empty-feeling palm, and a flare at the bottom for a secure and consistent hold.

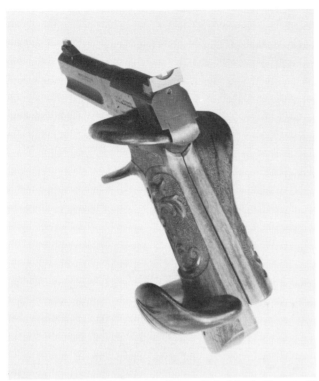

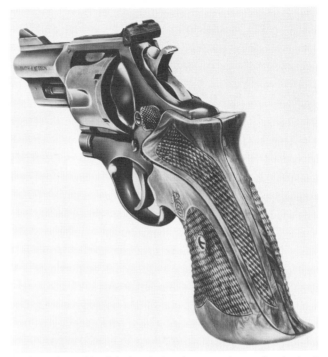

De luxe grade left-hand stocks on Colt Match Target .22 auto are made to fit the trigger finger, thumb, and heel of the hand. From Beckelhymer's, 513 Salinas Avenue, Laredo, Texas.

Fitz grips with right-hand thumb-rest and rest for heel of hand on a double-action S.&W. On this type of gun frame, most shooters like the sort of fill-in behind the trigger guard that these stocks have.

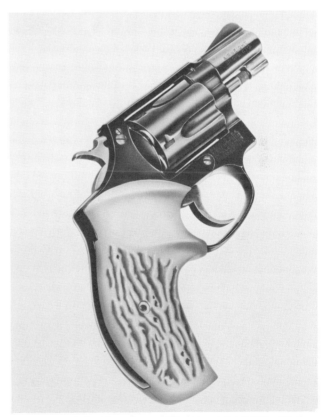

Finely decorated right-hand revolver stocks from Beckelhymer's.

Fitz "Gunfighter" stocks on this Airweight S.&W. .38 Special revolver reduce the shock of recoil, which is certainly noticeable even with standard-velocity factory loads fired from the as-issued gun. Grooves for right-hand trigger finger or left-hand thumb when it's held low in the pouplar double-action firing position.

Colt Single Action Army stocks from Fitz, Box 49702, Los Angeles 49, Calif. Note the fill-in behind the trigger guard, an unusual "extra" for this type of revolver frame.

Stocks with integral adapter or filler behind the trigger guard, from the Mershon Co., Inc., 1230 S. Grand Ave., Los Angeles 15, California.

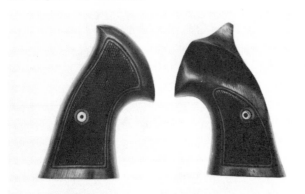

Mershon stocks as separate from gun.

Precision Shooting of September '56 tells of Gertrude Backstrom's target .38 by E. T. O'Dell, Raymond, Washington, a Chief's Special S.&W. chosen for its small grip, five-shot cylinder, with a Colt target barrel mounted, and some weight added here and there, as it helped her. Later she used a K-.38, and later still she tried and evidently liked a Colt Super-.38 Auto conversion to .38 Special.

Entirely different are pocket-gun stocks, for example the Fitz (Box 49702-R, Los Angeles 49) "Gun-

fighter" type. They reduce the recoil of light, small-gripped .38s and give you something to hang on to. They are grooved on each side for thumb and finger, right or left hand, and no difference. Although the filler behind the guard may make them sit high in the hand and thus increase muzzle upchuck, this is better than having your second finger chewed up by a recoiling guard.

There are other good plastic stocks, such as the Pointer, from Southwest Cutlery, 1309 Olympic Boulevard, Montebello, California, and the well-known Franzite. Pointer has or did have walnut, oversize, to be cut and polished to fit and feel natural, which is what any handgun grip simply must feel like. Much of this familiarity comes from long use, and from daily gripping of an empty gun, but some ought to be sort of bred into it.

Adapters and Color Schemes

Rubber adapters like the Pachmayr, Mershon, and the old Smith & Wesson fill unwanted space high up between guard and grip. For short-fingered shooters they sometimes make almost the best stock-fit possible. Ordinarily the small size is for the small hand, and it's true that some tiny grips are just too little for adapters. You need a three-finger hold, not a 2½! Most, but not quite all, shooters who have tried them on big-frame double-actions, not much different in feel from those of the 1890s, profit by them. At least the trigger finger doesn't' have to bow down to make contact. Short-fingered folks often find that target-stocked factory jobs may be fine for a hambone hand, but not for theirs. Usually these grips are checkered so beautifully that folks hesitate to sand them down to fit; so the search goes on. Magna stocks, full at the top but usually minus any filler or adapter, now go on even the little S.&W. pocket arms. They reduce recoil effect, as the type always does, and they give the hand a little more to grasp, which usually it welcomes.

Hard-rubber stocks are about gone, though most American standard-grade revolvers and small automatics had them. They warp rather easily, but filing

Adapter for .38-44 S.&W. Outdoorsman, from Pachmayr Gun Works, 1220 S. Grand Avenue, Los Angeles, California.

can cure that if you're careful on the job. Wood, usually walnut or rosewood, or something that looks like wood but isn't, is now the common and good material. It doesn't feel cold, is rarely slippery even when uncheckered. Ivory looks nice, feels nice when a raised steer-head or what-have-you helps fill the palm, and seldom gets slippery, as pearl is likely to do. Oil yellows ivory, but so what, unless it's a front sight bead? I've never seen the combination of a black adapter and ivory stocks, but it might be all right, at that. Ivory does preen up nicely with either a blue or a nickel finish.

Some Target Extras

These are legion, and again, like other accessories, some are worth-while to an individual and some are not.

Trigger shoes like the Henshaw from 818 Oakland Street, Pittsburgh 21, and the Ace, from Flaig's shop, Millvale, Penna., broaden the surface the forefinger works on, making the pull seem lighter and giving better control. If they increase the reach to the trigger, the difference is barely noticeable. A smooth, narrow trigger, especially on a gun that's too small for you, can be almost hopeless.

Muzzle brakes or compensators are common, appearing even on .22 short autoloaders for Olympic rapid fire that goes down to five shots in four seconds, on five different targets. They reduce recoil and muzzle upchuck, and many varieties are made. Some are integral, merely holes bored through the barrel, up front; some easily put on or taken off, like the Ruger Mark I, or the Top Shot, which comes from Lee Manufacturing Company, Wheelwright, Massachusetts, and is self-installed. A special front sight can increase sight radius. Well-known too is the H. C. Sorenson brake (Box 202, Beaverton, Oregon). There are numerous other good ones, and calibers accommodated go to the .45 Auto Colt Pistol, including S.&W.'s own brake for the 1955 Target revolver using .45 Auto and Auto-Rim loads.

Barrel weights add muzzle steadiness when it's wanted. Taped-on lead strips served well in earlier days. Some modern guns carry under-barrel tubes to load with weights, and some hang heavier weights out in plain view, to which there's no practical objection. Barrel ribs like the dural job by Dinan can carry special sights, or they can be heavy to add weight. (Alton S. Dinan, Jr., Box 674, Canaan, Conn.)

Hammer shoes or special wide hammer spurs make rapid fire cocking of a sixgun easier. With an offset shoe like Herrett's you needn't have your thumb straight in line. This can help.

A *variable-weight trigger pull* aids beginners and can refresh oldtimers by not letting them know when the shot will go. Less flinching and more attention to aim and hold result. Walter Roper described one in the March '48 *Rifleman,* worked up by Paul Palé.

Machine rests for testing guns and ammo can help with pistols, not only with rifles. Hobart S. White told of one in the May '47 *Rifleman.* Only dream castles come cheap today, but a handy fellow could build this rest. Even resting your forearm over a non-teetering stepladder is a help. There's the bench-rest, too; and the easy, relaxed, sitting positon, elbows on or over knees and back against a comfortable support, which Elmer Keith describes in *Sixguns.* He insists that long-range pistol accuracy proves pistol accuracy. This is sound comment even though some useful little handguns haven't the punch or trajectory for distance, as he well knows.

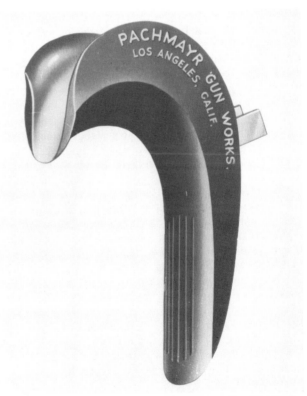

Detail of Pachmayr adapter for revolver grips. Metal clips go under the stocks, and as a refinement you can, if you like, carefully file the wood, plastic, or whatever, to give them freeway. I shouldn't call this necessary, except with problem stocks.

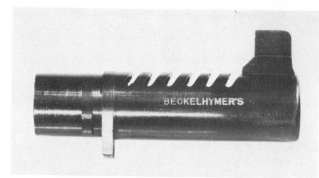

Beckelhymer's muzzle brake with front sight.

A Giles .45 recoil compensator barrel on a Mark I Ruger. Note special sights and trigger stop, also the neat stocks.

Bullet traps make shooting safer and amass surprising capital in castable lead. Many dealers carry the X-ring, and another good job comes from Detroit Bullet Trap, 8600 Lyndon Street, Detroit 21. Stops home-made of wood, packed earth or paper, and so on don't hand you the metal gratis, but they can and must be safe.

Timers for home or range practice run from stopwatches and kitchen clocks to elaborate electrical kinds. All pay off in dry or live-round shooting. Timed-Rite Products Company, 1518-R Welch Street, Houston 6, has a Dry Timer using 120-volt, 60-cycle household current. It shows a 25-foot reduction of the 25-yard target with black bull and the outer rings to allow you to call your shots. Switches give slow, timed, rapid and blinking signals for the readying commands. It can be used at less than 25 feet.

A clockwork timer from M. H. Rhodes, Inc., 30-R Bartholomew Avenue, Hartford 6, Connecticut, is pocket size, rings a bell for commands. The Mark Time is another, handled along with nearly everything else in pistol accessories by Gil Hebard of Knoxville, Illinois. Some clubs, like the one we had in Owego, New York, make their own timers; but small, home-useful types like those just listed are less common do-it-yourself projects.

Chronographs within the reach of some shooters record bullet velocities with useful precision. One comes from Hollywood Gun Shop, 6032 Hollywood Boulevard, H. (again), California. Other good instru-

ments are from Theodore M. Long, 40 South Bridge Street, Somerville, New Jersey; L. R. Wallack, Jr., Langhorne, Penna.; and Potter Instrument Company, 115 Cutter Hill Road, Great Neck, Long Island, N.Y.

Shot indicators for convenient, almost noiseless indoor practice are old hat, but good. As a little boy I had a chance to try the Hollifield Dotter, now almost forgotten, in a .38 Special S.&W. that seemed huge and unwieldy, though fascinating. You aimed at the top target, hoping to perforate the lower one, at a range of an inch or so. Out darted a rod to show what you'd done. This was for rifles, too. Today's Dri Shot Indicator, featured by Hebard, fits the .45 Auto and is not expensive or frail. A different method was developed by L. A. Vought, East Cleveland police instructor, the Gun-Lite for .38 Special revolvers. As the hammer falls, it spots a ray on the target, and this ray is adjustable to the gun's sighting. Batteries, lenses and frame weigh the same as a cylinderful of Specials. Address: 1588 East 133rd Street, East Cleveland 12, Ohio.

Targets

Some of us make our own. My friend Ray Reynolds of Winchester, Virginia's senior club toilsomely but happily draws his 50-foot reductions of the 50-meter

A 36-pound pistol rest designed by George Elliason and his associates comes from Precision Arms & Tool Co., 31528 Groesbeck Highway, Fraser, Mich. It tests the accuracy of pistols and their ammunition. Differently formed adapters for the holder at the top of the moving arm accommodate various models of handguns. A hand-operated cable release fires the weapon, and an air cylinder prevents the arm from slamming forward after the recoil. If a defective semi-automatic pistol goes full-automatic, a safety device limits the upward recoil. There are vertical and horizontal adjustments for getting on target. The rest must be bolted to a solid foundation. Gun shown is a .45 Auto-Colt with Elliason front and rear sights.

International slow-fire. If you plan to shoot small game at 50 feet or so, this one is a lot more revealing of your ability than the Standard American! Some of us use rifle targets easy to find in a rifle-shooting town, and at one-third rifle ranges they aren't hopelessly easy! Game targets on paper make sense, and for these you use a center hold, or else just under the desired spot, not covering it—for short ranges without overhold, of course.

The August '56 *Rifleman* neatly summarized ten- and outer-ring sizes of pistol targets.

Standard American:
50-foot slow, 10—.90 inch, 4—7.33 inches.
50-foot timed and rapid, 10—1.90 inch, 6—8.32 inches.
20-yard slow, 10—1.12 inches, 4—8.84 inches.
20-yard timed and rapid, 10—2.25 inches, 6—10.08 inches.
25-yard slow, 10—1.695 inches, 5—9.84 inches.
25 yard timed and rapid, 10—3.39 inches, 5—19.68 inches, with 1.695 inches X-ring, for deciding ties and to make life more interesting.
(Author's comment.) This one is used at 25-yard slow in Camp Perry course.
50-yard slow, same as above except that one more ring, the 8, is blacked to give better aiming point.

International:
50-meter slow, 10—1.9685 inches, 1—19.685 inches.
25-meter rapid, all-black, man-size silhouette, 5 feet, 3 inches tall, 1 foot, 5¾ inches wide, with ten elliptical scoring rings or part rings. Ten-ring, an ellipse, is 10 centimeters wide and 15 high, or 3.937x5.901 inches.

Air, Gas, and Rubber-Band Pistols

About every month a new air or gas pistol comes out, and they deserve popularity because of their practice value. European air-powered arms of considerable killing power are long-established, have been used in ultimate shooting, war; but they don't interest us here because we want safe practice and no hunting with these arms. I can be and probably am wrong, but that's my reaction. Every one here mentioned can do serious harm, can put out an eye; and most of them can give dangerous penetration in flesh or even in thin bone. They aren't toys!

Price and quality vary greatly. The Haemmerli .177 caliber Match was mentioned under "Haemmerli" in the "Foreign Pistols" chapter, and it ranks high. Daisy and Marksman types are for children, under strict supervision. They're popular, and good in their place.

The Plainsman CO_2, using that gas in a cylinder, is perhaps typical of pistols firing air rifle shot of about .175-inch diameter as compared to the .18-inch of BBs loaded in shotgun shells. It is built on Luger lines, but is still more light-barreled. It is accurate up to some 20 feet, easy to load or to adjust to low, medium or high speeds, but the trigger pull is long and heavy. Steel air rifle shot aren't for rifled arms, nor are darts. The latter are a little more accurate from a smoothbore, easy to pick out from a board and re-use, but perhaps more dangerous because they're so sharp. Hollow-based lead pellets are for precision work, by comparison. I know of no mold cut for them, but some handloaders who enjoy casting—as most of us do, I think—would welcome one. Fun and economy. A "Dope Bag" article in the October '57 *Rifleman* lists .177 pellet weight as about 8.2 grains, and .22 around 14, the latter with some 600 f.s. velocity from a *rifle* using CO_2 gas. Dropping to 387 f.s. at 50 yds. and to 250 at 100 yards, these rifle-slug-shaped pills lose pep fast but aren't foolproof. They can shatter window glass at 100 yards or crack auto safety glass at 50. Pistol velocities should be lower, but not much. Up to 25 feet and even farther, a good air or gas pistol should group into about two inches or better, and that's accuracy that is useful to a beginner. For aerial practice these guns have plenty of accuracy for most of us. However, since pellets may not even penetrate a tin can, there's a chance of their bouncing off such a target at a dangerous angle. Soft wood, really soft, is better. They are fun guns and good starters in training. Part of their training value is that they *aren't* harmless. And how many guns are harmless?

The Hy-Score is a revived German Haenel, once well-known here. It's a 30-ounce air pistol, also in gas model, with good pull for the type, and nice sights. The Schimel 30-ounce .22 uses gas, our familiar Crosmans come in both gas and air types, and the old Benjamin Company has gas pistols. The imported German Walther is a fine job. The Webley has typical British good quality and is much better stocked than the first early models from that plant, though they too were well made and finely accurate for the type.

Naturally we want accuracy better than the shooter's own holding and squeezing, though believe me there is plenty of long, sweating squeeze on most squiff-pistol triggers. Adjustable sights are fine velvet, and square-cut Patridge design is next door but a half-inch to mandatory. As to forward jump of air plungers, I'm undecided. It is no help, when at last the shot goes; but with powder pistols we get recoil, don't we? Do we want to iron out all hindrances?

I do think that good weight out front is something we should insist on in an air or gas pistol. A target gun needs it, even if we have to tape, solder, or sew it on! It seems indispensable.

This I say in spite of my fondness for the Bullseye rubber-band pistol which weighs, empty, about as much as a filled .45 Auto-Colt magazine. Rubber power is the thing for a slingshot, whether store-bought like the Wham-O or whittled from a sapling fork. It can be pretty fair power. BBs or Air Rifle are the usual bought ammo for it, though I remember using buckshot on an early-days toddle to the Black River in the Adirondacks. The way those No. 0 or 00 slugs

Walther LP Model 52 air pistol, 4.5mm. or .177-inch caliber. It resembles the Walther Olympia .22 auto in its lines, and it has good weight for steady holding. Sights are finely adjustable. From Interarmco, 10 Prince St., Alexandria, Virginia.

Webley Senior air pistol, .177 caliber.

Webley Mark I air pistol, .22 caliber. Grip slants on these Webleys are much greater than those on earlier Webley models, and to some of us may seem extreme. But most of us find that they pay off in shooting. These pictures by courtesy of Webley & Scott, Ltd., Park Lane, Handsworth, Birmingham 21, England, and Griffin & Howe, 114 E. 13th Street, New York 17, New York.

reached out into the broad stream and chunked up geysers when they quit was as heartening as my first 9 mm. Luger and .38 Auto Colt were, later. But the Bullseye (La Jolla, California) shoots No. 6 shot, of .11-inch thickness. It isn't even a sure killer on houseflies. It's for target, and at 8-foot range, the gun well adjusted, shots out of the quarter-inch bull are the shooter's fault. This gun will break a close-up, unwary light bulb; and it could put out a person's eye. Never fool with it.

Charles Askins has a fine chapter on these sub-power pistols in his *Pistol Shooter's Book*. It is not up to date on all the makes and models—and I didn't even try to be—but the little guns are so popular that only hot-cake publication every month could keep up with them. The principles in choosing are plain: you want one you can hit with, you'll want to shoot it a lot, and maybe the ammo cost will therefore figure. Shot is cheaper than pellets, and air costs less (even yet) than CO_2 gas.

Miscellanea

Gold old word! It sounds like the name of an insect tribe you might try to copy in a trout-fly, to be ready for the evening rise. But trout-fishing is selective, some

even calling it snobbish in their deep misunderstanding. This section is a catch-all, though it's a mere skim of the surface.

Special jackets styled a bit like skeet- or rifle-shooting coats, cartridge blocks to hold the right number of rounds for a course of fire, carrying cases

Ruger .22 auto magazine follower from Beckelhymer's holds breech-block back after the last shot has been fired.

to protect the guns and what-all and to mount the spotting scope: these may be scarcely more than basic. Powdered rosin to give a grip to a sweaty hand, sight blackening material squirted or painted on, or stunk on from a carbide lamp, a hat-brim to save your eyes and ear-plugs to save your hearing and help your concentration on what matters, a plug to score bullet-holes, and by all means a score-book for records that'll

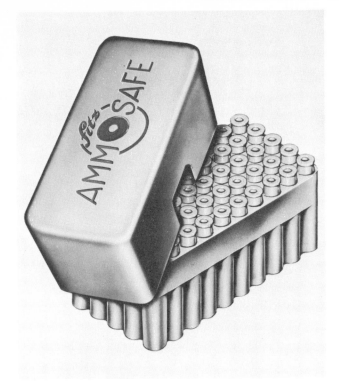

Fitz holder for cartridges, 50 rounds.

Sentry spotting scope is compact to fit into a pistol case, 13-inches long, 24 ounces. Retractable sun-shade up front, 50mm. objective lens, 20-power eyepieces. From D. P. Bushnell and Co., Inc., 41-43 East Green Street, Pasadena, 1, California.

help you in later matches—let's consider these, too.

Later another extra comes up, a display case for medals, and gunk to polish them with. We've come far from the hairy man who lashed a stone in a cleft stick and went out to battle for his dinner or for his life.

We have, haven't we? Or is there need of reassurance here?

For one, I doubt it. It is easy to ridicule target extras as non-essential impedimenta, excess duffle. But target is a game. Americans like games, and mostly we play to win as well as for the fun which never fails so long as we love the game for its own sake. Most target aids, and some target techniques we learn, fit into the field, too. There is only one danger, that pistol match shooting may become too expensive for a big following. That happened to offhand 200-yard Schuetzen rifle shooting. It might have happened to

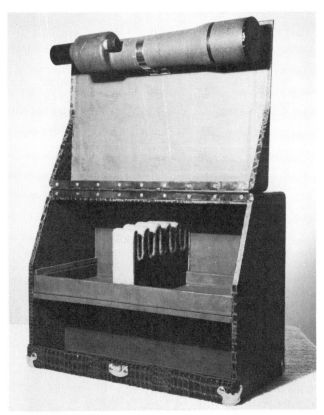

Pistol shooter's case by Beckelhymer's, a standard and popular type, with gun-rack, holder for shot-spotting scope (the raised cover brings it to about the right height), and a storage cellar for extras.

Big Bushnell Spacemaster spot-scope with 45-degree eyepiece that lets a rifle shooter use it without straining out of position—or anyway straining much. Powers from 15 to 60.

A pistol shooter's case by Pachmayr.

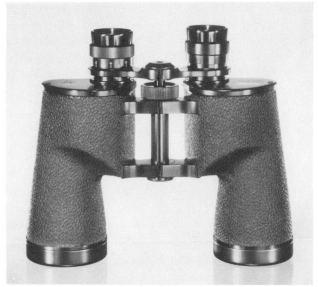

Bushnell 7x50

modern smallbore rifle if we hadn't had simplifications like N.R.A. Light Rifle, for which you can use a plinking arm and still win. Up to now, I don't think we've reached the danger point in pistol, but will someone please develop a democratic pistol game, just in case?

Certainly weapons belong in this savage mid-twentieth century world, and personal weapons, too, in spite of mass-slaughter techniques. The skilled, resolute, and armed individual still belongs. So gunsmiths are busy, and we can't have too many good ones.

Now there are schools of the craft. Typical are the Pennsylvania Gunsmith School, 100-A Western Avenue, Pittsburgh 12, and the Colorado School of Trades, 8797 West Colfax Avenue, Denver 12.

A Bushnell 7x35 (7 power, 35mm. objective lenses) Rangemaster binocular like this—also the standard 7x35, 7x50 and 8x40—were range-tested especially for us by factory personnel. Mounted on a tripod or a rest, all four spotted .22 caliber bullet-holes in the black at 50 yards. Except perhaps for the big 7x50 night-glass, all four are light and small enough for a hunter's use, too.

Bushnell 8x40

THE basic minimum care we give to a pistol to insure its functioning when we need it is one thing. Elaborate attention is something else. Those who really depend on a handgun lean toward fussiness rather than nonchalance. They're willing to do more than their part.

The chief enemy is rust. In tropical country that is damp, not those small islands of delight fanned by a gentle tradewind, rust finds its work easy and rewarding! It chews up bores and freezes actions tight. Ammo goes bad in that dampness, not quickly, not after any definite time, but too often when you least expect it. In our western deserts or in deep cold, rust has little chance. But drifting sand or flying, hard-freezing snow can lock an action as disastrously as rust can, if less tightly.

So there's practical protection, and sometimes apparently excessive care is good sense. The target gun isn't exactly coddled in its fitted and lined case; its sights need protection, and who will say that its lustrous blue finish doesn't, too?

The inside condition, that of chamber and bore, matter most to a real pistoleer, or to a potential buyer who knows the score. The fouling of non-corrosive primers, smokeless powder, and greased lead bullets is in itself highly rust-preventive. But different makes of primers may contain different chemicals, and a hodge-podge of their residue might cause rust. Copper plating or jacket on a bullet can rust steel through electrolytic action. These remote chances exist.

Many of us still clean our guns after every day's use, or at regular intervals, and aren't sorry to do it. There's satisfaction in gazing through bright steel tubes even if we know they need no inspection, and there's more fun in messing around with cleaning gear than in bending the spine in an easy chair and worrying about taxes. Some of the mental therapy we get from handloading enters into gun-swabbing. And some—who know—judge us by our gun's appearance, though perhaps less than by our skill with it, and far less than by our regard for safety in handling it.

Cleaning, so-called, can be not only a gesture but also worse than useless. I refer to the vile habit of dry-brushing chambers and bore after using non-corrosive ammo, wiping away part of the protective coating it has deposited. It pops your eyes to see otherwise well-informed shooters do it.

For a decent job we need certain materials, not necessarily expensive, and the knowhow of using them. Let's consider tools and methods together.

We want a rod. String cleaners or pull-throughs, weighted to fall through the barrel, do for field or emergency use. A good rod is thorough, lasts a generation or more, cleans up after hundreds or thousands of dollars' worth of cartridges.

Some call polished steel the best, like the Belding & Mull. It can't pick up grit, as scratched or battered brass, aluminum, hickory or walnut can. Held straight,

CHAPTER 17

THE CARE OF THE HANDGUN

to avoid excessive rubbing of muzzle or breech, it wears but little. It's strong. So is a celluloid-covered steel rod like the Parker-Hale, worthy of cleaning the finest. The Tri-Pak combination rod of light, strong duralumin has interchangeable tips, like some B.&M.s, for different calibers. For the barrel we want a knob or button tip. It distributes the cleaning patch's pressure evenly; and it's padded by the patch and thus is considerate of the recoil plate, that little round housing of the firing pin in the sixgun's breech-face. A properly tight patch is *forced* through. It pops out at the breech, the rod striking the recoil plate rather briskly, if you aren't careful.

But a slotted tip is right for a revolver's chambers. The patch stays on, and even on the drawback we clean to some extent. Best hold the cylinder firmly when cleaning its chambers, so that back-and-forth motion on its axis is cut to a minimum.

Occasionally a rod is stuck in a barrel. Dropping in oil along it, and from the other end, too, usually allows us to pull or push it out after it's soaked for twenty minutes or so.

Clean, strong cloth serves as patch material, canton flannel and unbleached muslin being favorites. You learn to shear different thicknesses and textures to correct size. Or you buy ready-cuts. Make the first patch small, for a dirty bore offers resistance. The last one, used to deposit a competent even layer of protective oil or grease, should be still more undersize. Some use a soft bristle brush, not the brass wire used for cleaning, to put in oil or grease. Bert Shay doesn't trust any but a free-flowing oil on a cloth patch to reach the corners of rifling grooves. "Ever notice a

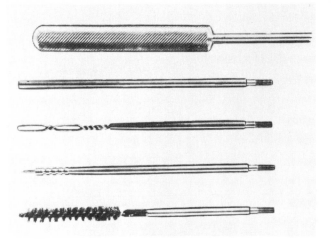

Belding & Mull (Philipsburg, Penna.) rifle rod handle and rod tips. The flat-ended tip next to the big, milled-steel handle is for calibrating barrels, pushing or driving a lead slug through them. Next is the slotted wire tip, more for oiling than for cleaning a revolver's chambers, for which we might want heavier metal. The needle on the button tip pierces a cleaning patch and is fine for bolt action rifles, though hardly for revolver or rifle barrels that we must clean from the muzzle. (Eventually I filed the needle off my B.&M.) The last tip is threaded for brass wire brushes of various calibers.

.45 A.C.P. just *slightly* neglected after using chlorate primed ammunition? Note where the first rust starts, right in those corners?" The deep-reaching though gentle scrape of a soft brass wire brush cleans a barrel well; so to preserve it his devotion to the soft hog-bristle brush is logical. I've rarely used one for this purpose. Perhaps I clean with unnecessary zeal. I could summon willing witnesses to say so, with emphasis and elaboration. Some oil barrels with a soft wool mop like the Parker-Hale. It should be rather small to do a good job.

Frankly, we hardly need a "powder solvent" for cleaning after most ammo we fire today. Water-soaked patches wipe out black powder sludge promptly, and warm water may shorten the job by a patch or two. Water dissolves the salty, corrosive fouling laid on by old-type primers, if no copper or lead plating keeps it from getting to the steel. Household ammonia, Chloroil and Fiendoil are copper solvents. The Army's Bore Cleaner is excellent, though it won't remove all the harmless sort of copper wash that ammonia does. Hoppe's No. 9 is a standby. I like it for most cleaning except the job exacted by a gang-up of chlorate priming and jacketed bullets (with no brush to help), or the easy chore that black powder and greased gray lead leave behind them.

But powder solvents do well after perhaps 95% of what we shoot, non-corrosive and smokeless, with no ferocious chemical foes lying in wait to assault an ill-cleaned bore. Gun oils do well, too, and high grade No. 10 or 20 motor oil.

The .45 Auto seems more difficult to rid of fouling than some others using jacketed bullets, such as the high-velocity Luger. Though a .45 barrel can be crusted with "coppering" and still shoot well, it doesn't look nice. A good method is to boil it in water, then get after it with a brass brush. Lots of us familiar with the 1903 Springfield and gray, cupro-nickel jacketed bullets of World War I type remember also Colonel Whelen's amonia bath that soaked the sticky dirt out of the bore. You powdered one ounce of ammonia persulphate and 200 grains of ammonia carbonate, dissolved them in four ounces of water, then added six ounces of 28% or "stronger" ammonia.

You put a rubber cork in the breech, slipped a rubber tube over the muzzle, and poured in enough of that terrific sniff to fill the bore and rise in the tube. After twenty minutes you upended the gun and poured out a bright blue, copper-rich solution. At once you put water-wet patches through the barrel, then plenty of dry ones, oiled it and set it away with a lily-white conscience. Once or twice I used a second application, probably unnecessary. This treatment should fumigate any pistol barrel so uncommonly unlucky as to need it.

It can't clean out rust or replace metal the rust has stolen. Gun companies furnish effective rust removers that aren't too rough on steel. These swabbing pastes have to take off blueing if rust lies deep. Stoeger's Rust-Off is similar except that you leave it on for several hours before rubbing it off. "Since time immemorial," kerosene has been used to scour off rust.

The best way to gun health is never to let rust get a bite. Good gun oils protect well except perhaps in long or particularly tough storage, but some "machine oils" are pretty thin. Riel & Fuller's Anti-Rust and Brownell's Sheath penetrate and flow obligingly, seem to me to rank with the best when salt air, incessant rain, or canoe camping sets up a problem. Anderol solutions are excellent. This list is merely a dip, not inclusive. The Army's "Oil, lubricating, preservative, special" spreads well, looks thin, shows hardly a trace of itself when you wipe the bore after several days' or weeks' storage. It's good. It lubricates the mechanism, too, and like some other thin oils (one must experiment), often is splendid for first-shot accuracy from an oiled barrel, having little tendency to sling that bullet wild. Many of us think too much of a gun to hunt with a clean, dry barrel, at least in a damp climate, but there are few guns that shoot through oil to the point of aim. Some really do.

For long storage there's grease for the bore. Gun companies naturally go whole hog and put out heavy greases. They're good; but easier and more effective as some of us use them are thinner pastes like Rig, Hoppe's grease, and the Birmingham Small Arms Safetipaste made in England. The latter has been tried and found effective for nearly fifty years. These need no thinning with oil for sure, even deposit in the bore, as some heavy greases do.

A barrel needn't be chuck full of grease, and it never should be plugged with a patch. That can cause rust by imprisoning damp air in the tube. Or you may forget the plug and shoot it out. Such traffic hazards, like a larding of grease, can "ring" or swell the barrel where pressure builds up, though a rubber cover over, and not *inside* the muzzle, can be shot through without harm to the bore. It's for hunting, not for gun storage. Use only light bore oil in shooting country, for it's enough.

Some handgun bores and chambers are so finely finished or use such well-fitted, perfectly contoured and lubricated bullets that cleaning them is easy. We shouldn't labor away until a tight patch shows no gray at all; we clean to remove powder and primer residue, mostly, and to reach a smooth, dry surface on which oil or grease can be laid. Too much cleaning does more harm than good, especially with poor equipment to clean with! But most guns shine more brightly inside and perhaps shoot better if a brass brush occasionally goes back and forth, full thrust, through their barrels and cylinders. These brushes, kept clean, can't harm steel unless we scrub inordinately, and they looosen obstinate fouling. A steel brush is a last resort after terrible neglect.

Some barrels and cylinders try to corner the lead market so greedily that they're almost impossible to clean with a brush used either dry or soaked with solvent. If they're free from the rust-pits of neglect, it's the throats that grab and hold the lead, as a rule. This condition looks serious and offends a normally crackpot shooter's eye.

It may detract comparatively little from accuracy; and reasonable cleaning with a brush and with good solvent on the patches seldom, if ever, leaves corrosive fouling under the lead, to work away like an underground saboteur. Special short brushes, like the Mill-Rose, for solid-frame revolver barrels, can be chosen oversize and threaded on the rod after it has been run down through the barrel. Such scrubbing should remove most barrel-throat fouling. L.E.M. Gun Specialties, Box 51, College Park, Georgia, sell a steel-handled, tapered brass tip for cleaning the throat, and rubber tips for cleaning cylinder and barrel. They carry bronze wire gauze discs. Mason Williams, Stanfordville, New York, has a de-leader for throats.

Liquid mercury rolled back and forth sucks up barrel leading. Smooth bullet contours, some lubricants, and a gas-check on a bullet base help to prevent it. If trouble persists, a gunsmith can polish the offending surface of steel, and many high grade handguns need it, even those made "in the good old days when workmanship was common."

But old or new, most of them in good shape respond well to the cleaning cycle: swabbing with alternate solvent-soaked and dry patches, brushing if needed, more wet and dry patches, then thorough drying before the preservative goes in. Many of us keep our gats in good shape with less effort, relying on the protection that ammo gives it. We clean now and then for a look-see or maybe when we shift to different loading components.

Yet even casual cleaning shouldn't skip some details. Sights need attention, for rust seldom improves their visibility, and hammer nose and firing pin hole should be clean. Bert tells of Lugers that would not fire because a speck of hard foreign matter was in the striker housing in the breech-block. I often checked mine, finding nothing; but all such finely machined, close-toleranced parts need watching. Firing dirties the outside surfaces of a revolver's cylinder, also the top strap, breech face and rear of the barrel. If the extractor, its stem, and its recessed seat in the cylinder go dirty, half-burned powder kernels can prevent the complete closing of a tight sixgun. Exposed working parts like cylinder ratchets, the hand that turns the cylinder, and the bolt that jumps up and locks it in line should be clean and lightly oiled to delay wear as much as possible. Some corners may need cleaning with a cloth on the end of a sharp stick. The crevice between barrel and top strap comes clean when we saw oiled strips of cloth back and forth through it. Wood stocks appreciate occasional oiling with linseed, and a soft old toothbrush cleans their checkering.

Blueing wears with use, and honest holster wear makes some of us proud—and why not? But silver-white sights aren't for precise shooting. We can black sights with smoke or liquid, a temporary but effective dressing up. Cold liquid blueing goes on easily and lasts rather well. It may not match the gun's hue, but it helps in aiming.

Perhaps once a year we *partly* dismount, clean and oil a much-used revolver. Complete, proper reassembling is difficult for some poor wights, including me. A bit of cloth on a toothpick helps clean, or a tiny paintbrush, or one of those little fellows made for whisking ground-up whiskers out of electric razors. The auto's slide runways should be clean and oily, its breech-face, loading ramp, and extractor cut (if any) in the frame looked after. If it's a .22 using greased or waxed bullets, the magazine tube gets pretty foul. Depress the follower, on which the first cartridge in the mag rests, hold it down with its button or with inserted cartridges, then keep the spring tensed by running a nail or two through the peepholes in the tube. I don't like to remove the bottom plate, preferring to have it stay as tight as factory assembly left it—unless of course it's designed for easy out and in. But I like to swab a magazine thoroughly, and a slotted rod tip helps.

Cold like that of the arctic can make reliability something to plan for. Ordinary oils go gummy or solid, though ice-machine oil may do if temperatures don't number too "high" below zero. It may be best to wash the action with gasoline, dry it, and dust in powdered graphite to prevent wear. Some guns function dry, and this could be the answer if lung-pinching cold service is to be short.

Steel doesn't rust in constantly sub-freezing cold. Poison primers then are harmless. But bringing a gun from such cold into a warm building makes it "sweat."

Soon moisture shows on its surface and it's wet inside, too. Wiping the outside and holding the dismounted gun over a hot stove will do wonders. Oscar Hammond advises the use of a gas-station air hose to dry a gun caught in rain or dropped in a fishing stream. There's a special nozzle for this. "Finish the drying over heat," he says, "and then oil it well." In cold weather it's best to leave the gun in the cold—not necessarily babysit with it—or to have kept it (law permitting) under our clothing so that it never got really chilled in the first place, or sweated up, either.

In long or short storage, guns and their fodder do best in dry, not too warm, air. Heat can make oil or grease flow off the job, or primers or some powders break down chemically. Twice a year should be enough to wipe out, inspect, and re-oil or re-grease firearms that are stored securely, and sometimes once in a decade is enough. But much depends on climate as, for instance, in jungle or on sea-girt islands. Shell Oil's VPI 260 powder is one of those that protect weapons stored in air-tight containers.

A leather holster isn't ideal for a pistol's long sleep unless it's of excellent material, and oiled or otherwise treated to fight off corrosion of steel. Stopping one night in the mountains, in preference to jolting another fifty miles to a good-sized town, I got into talk with the innkeeper—there were no moteliers, no motels. We had chewed guns only a few minutes before he brought out his .38 Colt Army Special. It almost stuck to its holster! Rust lay on all contact surfaces and its cylinder was lazy. The good guy admitted that he hadn't used or looked at it for quite a spell, and obviously he hadn't oiled or greased the ill-tanned leather.

Leather cartridge belts need such liniment, too, if they are to be comfortable to wear and slow in plating the brass with verdigris. Even wool-lined holsters make trouble unless they're rich in lanolin, processed to make the fuzz anhydrous, without the moisture natural to sheep's clothing.

I N THE short-gun clan, the plinking gun seems to give most people the most enjoyable and beneficial shooting. With it we get healthy outdoor exercise as well as valuable training for almost every type of practical handgunning. The plinker shoots at anything and everything, provided that it's safe and legitimate. His firing is varied, fast or slow, from the hip or from a rest, with right or left hand, or both, at stationary targets or at something swinging, floating, or thrown into the air. He learns, eventually, to draw from holster or pocket quickly and smoothly, without conscious effort, and to develop a trigger pull that "comes through" in less time than he ever thought possible during rapid fire on the pistol range. A noticeable improvement in his ability and an absorbing outdoor hobby build a combination that's hard to beat.

Any pistol or revolver can be useful for plinking. It may be of any caliber so long as we can afford to shoot it and will use it safely and without making a nuisance of ourselves. Bigbores may have to be handloaded for economy; and "danger distance" can be cut down, to some extent, by using light "whisper" loads. They may shoot lower than full-charge stuff, but we can raise a rear target sight or aim high with fixed sights, and this holding-over is worth learning for some time when a distant target may have to be hit without preliminary ranging shots. To reap the valuable harvest of plinking we're going to do a lot of shooting, not just fool around at it occasionally.

Barrel length may cut in anywhere between ultra short and extra long, though the medium to long seem to win most plinkers' votes. Grips are a matter of choice or may be "what you have." Somehow, most of them become adaptable and familiar after considerable use. Sometime, we may have to do business shooting with any handgun whose grip we can wrap our fingers around. Gun make is immaterial, unless we expect cheaper models to compete with world's-record makers.

We can even overlook gun condition in some ways if only we insist on safety. Pits in the barrel and roughness in the chambers (perhaps from shooting thousands of shorts or caps in a .22 long-rifle cylinder, or from careless cleaning) may mean little. Even slight wear resulting in imperfect alignment of cylinder and bore and the consequent shaving of bullets needn't be alarming—if the shooter wears glasses and doesn't allow others to stand too close to him. Split-hair accuracy isn't necessary to the plinker. There are hours of fun and extremely valuable practice in many an old gun, including the economically fed muzzle-loaders and cap-and-ball revolvers.

The average plinker prefers a .22 for economy and for greater safety, though its range can extend to nearly a mile. Low speed .22 shorts approach perfection for his first sessions. They make little noise, and they are the cheapest real cartridges on the market unless you handload centerfires and know how to cut all the corners. A little extra care of the chambers when

CHAPTER 18

PLINKING

BY OSCAR R. HAMMOND

cleaning the gun permits us to fire shorts in moderation and with a clear conscience. Sometimes they tend to leave chambers a bit rough after much use, and the ejection of long-rifle cases becomes difficult. Modern priming has cut this hazard considerably. The .22 long-rifle, a good plinker too, should be used farther from civilization; and high-velocity ammo shouldn't go into really old, small guns, as they weren't built to stand the gaff. They don't need to burst! The danger from split cartridge bases isn't pleasant to think of. I still wear a scar over one eye to back up that statement!

In plinking, safety and commonsense count more than in *any other brand of handgunning*. The target man is usually safety-minded because the virtue has been drummed into him since he first appeared on the range. He fires in only one direction—at fixed paper targets with a bullet-proof backstop! The Service man, policeman, detective and defense-gun man in general have had training in this department, too.

Gun Choice

Including used guns, the array of plinking pistols to choose from is enormous. Some rather new models of .22s appear to have been designed with this sport pretty thoughtfully considered.

Remember the old Stevens single-shot pistols? Various grades included some that stood up for a generation or more in the closest .22 rimfire target competition, slow-fire, of course. Others cost so little that the average farm or small-town boy could realize the dream of owning one. They were safe, reliable and accurate. So is today's Sheridan "Knocabout." Flat and short with its 5-inch barrel, this pound and a half of handiness is easy to carry, yet steady to hold. About the only criticism is that its trigger is so close to the grip that pressing it with the first joint of the finger is rather hard to do—and still have the hold feel natural. But it is more than low price that sells this gun. Another single-shot, the new Savage, has more sight radius, and the lines of a Colt Single Action.

An Italian Beretta .22 auto was deliberately named "Plinker." The Beretta Minx shoots shorts for economy, and so does the Astra Cub, which looks a bit like the old Colt .25 auto, though it has a Mauser-type hammer and sights that stand high enough to be seen easily.

The moderate price of the standard American Ruger .22 auto obviously brought competing models of good-sized plinking .22s to the market. Some shooters find the 4¾-inch barrel unsteady and short in sight radius. Late in 1954 the 6-inch came out, with barrel the same size at the muzzle; and it's a racy-looking gun, suggestive of an old Luger in 6-inch Navy model.

Hi-Standard's Flite-King shoots .22 shorts, and their newer Duramatic is engineered to do well in the low-price field. For instance, its cross-bolt safety also serves to lock the slide open. The gun's lines may look odd to you, but its grip is shaped to sit comfortably in your hand, and which counts more?

The Ruger Single-Six .22 made Colt Frontier-type single-action revolvers common in the moderately high-priced field. The Hi-Standard Sentinel double-action with Colt- or Smith-type swing-out cylinder took hold at once because of its low cost and its grip, which fits many hands—as does the Frontier sort of grip, too. Now there are many .22 revolvers of various makes, in these two classes, including double-action, Frontier-gripped guns with single poke-out or with simultaneous ejection of empties. The plinker has good choice in both revolvers and autoloaders.

Iver Johnson and Harrington & Richardson revolvers have been made from the old mite-size to some that would qualify in pretty close target competition, such as the recent I. J. Trailsman and the H.&R. Ultra Side-Kick.

How to Get Started

As this flock of new guns proves, most plinkers like .22s. Still, one usually must go a mile or so from settled areas to shoot, and he must look out for horses and cows, as well as humans. Safety comes first!

Bullets fired with good intentions often have a fool habit of glancing off a stone or bottle. Since they might hoard a residual killing-power unknown to ballistic science, they might leave us to pay for a farmer's valued cow. Even the mildest looking brook can kick a bullet from its surface, send it whining through the air and past (we hope!) the head of a distant passerby who'll complain about it—justifiably. Perhaps his hobby is chess, and if so, he certainly doesn't interfere with us plinkers. So let's grant *HIM* life, too!

These precautions discourage you? The country is full of safe places to plink. Once we're off the corporation and find a likely spot we can stop—and we'd better—to ask the owner's permission. He's likely to show us a good place, especially if we let him try a few shots and convince him that we're not desperados. If our gun doesn't make too much noise, that helps, for farm animals are used to quiet, and upset by undue ruction. And we might succeed in making a plinker bug of the farmer.

Targets come next. Tin cans, pieces of wood, soft clods of earth minus stones, corks, in fact any fairly soft material wins favor. *Don't* shoot at thick solid metal, rocks, or any other hard object. Bottles are fascinating, but please leave them alone! Bullets take great joy in glancing from their sides, and who wants to leave booby-traps of smashed glass for the good farmer's son to walk in? Though bottles are broken while floating in water, unless the slug ricochets off them—that boy might enjoy his barefoot wading more if he didn't have to do it in Indian-fakir style.

For the beginner, a good start is a row of tin cans, from large to fairly small, about 15 or 20 feet away on ground that has a backstop. Shoot slowly, squeezing the trigger instead of jerking it, and aiming low, high or dead-on as the sights, your hold, and the ammunition you use happen to demand. When smaller cans tumble consistently, you can get practice and fun in instinctive shooting. Extend the gun naturally toward the target just as you'd point your finger, then let go without deliberate aim. By this time you and the pistol should be rather well acquainted, and you'll be happy to see how close your first shots strike.

Then come more difficult targets. A can hung from a low tree limb, with a safe hill backstop behind it, and swung pendulum fashion is fun, and soon easy enough to hit as it reaches the end of the arc on either side and pauses while deciding which way to go! When it's thrown into the air the peak of its flight is the "cinch," for again it must hesitate, choosing between a journey into the clouds and a surrender to gravity. Aim at its lower part, or still lower, for its indecision is brief! And NEVER leave the background of your line of fire out of your calculations. Use light bullets and shoot almost straight up. Even a .22 slug can do bitter business at the end of a ranging flight that starts under a sixty-degree angle. Try to drop the lead into real wilderness of land or water. And make that trial a howling success. The life of the shooting game depends on *your* commonsense, too.

When you're really adept you can throw the can with your gun hand, the gun holstered, draw it, and fire one shot—and later, more. Remember the many self-inflicted wounds that have come recently from "quick-draw" that never got enough dry practice before live rounds were used. You don't want this kind of newspaper publicity, or the wound. At first it's disconcerting to see how darn fast that tin gets to ground. Even if it lands before a safe, high-angle shot can be got off, it can be plinked at once or twice for consolation!

But not on rocky ground, you bet! We just mustn't have ricochets in settled country.

Targets suspended on a pulley clothesline and jerked back and forth by a well-entrenched companion are wonderful post-grad practice for almost any type of defense work. They're lots of fun and their performance can be as varied as the imagination pictures. Bits of wood tumbling down fast water teach us lead and speed, both so necessary in pinning a running target. In really wild country that we know for sure is empty of human and animal life, these ricochets do no harm, for they fly away from the shooter unless he fires into an oncoming wave that may route the lead back to him. It can. *This* shooting is decidedly *not* for settled areas.

From here on, the plinker needs no more advice on targets and even on safety. Targets almost suggest themselves, and the shooter naturally promotes himself to the more and more difficult, including ranges and time limits tougher than he began with. Shooting against a companion of about equal skill, he gets the spice of competition. He may even build up the pressure that most match shots feel—and learn to control. Such coolness can pay off if he ever has to shoot for keeps.

A final wish before he goes on his happy way: let's hope he won't forget to clean up the debris at the end of the day's fun. Remember that grazing cattle can and do inhale empty cartridges, which don't do their stomachs any good.

WE DISREGARD well over 25 percent of our potential handgun enthusiasts, the women. This personal-opinion statement applies to formal match shooting, informal perforation of tagboard or paper targets, plinking, and—most serious of all—handgun training that builds sound confidence in a woman's ability to protect herself and her loved ones.

How did we win this particular stupidity award? Oh yes, most of us know that more American women now fire pistols, shotguns and rifles than ever before, that they compete and do well in matches and in less formal shooting. There are special ratings for them, like "Woman Champion" and "High Woman," in spite of which, now and then, one sails right up over all other contestants. These ratings encourage them, as they were meant to; but I've wondered if some women don't resent them. They might like to be classed with the men and have official distinctions junked formally and finally.

Only a few reach the top, you say, in pistol, rifle or shotgun competitions? Not many men do, either; and there are many more men on the firing lines. A couple of generations ago, very few women used any kind of target or hunting arm. Since then, we men have done much to encourage them; but we are still not awakened to the building-up of American shooting, so essential to our national (and local) freedoms. We've hardly begun to bat our eyes and stretch our toes.

Sure, there is "the battle between the sexes," and sometimes it's hard for even an intelligent man to free himself completely from its subtle heritage. There's the tendency to low-rate women in defense of his own sex. In business, professions, sports, and almost any activity you can name, the women are faster and faster becoming serious contestants. Well, let them. A slightly contemptuous attitude which a man may have, does him no good, and in the march of developing events isn't likely to hurt *her,* either! In short, this attitude is completely nuts.

Let's shuck any trace of it we have, and instead get going on practical lines. It's time we did. Already too many of us have reached a complete departure from the healthy team-up of pioneer days. Then, the man and the wife worked together because they straight-out had to. They made and improved their home and property, developing them as best they could into the dream they had cherished.

There was nothing child-like about the pioneer wife, except that almost universal feminine ability to see, as a child does, through the superfluous and the false into basic human realities. But let that pass.

The pioneer wife mastered the long and rather heavy Kentucky rifle, or the usually ungainly breechloaders that succeeded it, along with home and field work done faithfully and under the crudest conditions. No doubt she relished the thrill that comes with achieved marksmanship. Who wouldn't? But she

CHAPTER 19

MAMA SHOOTS A PISTOL

learned to shoot because she had to in order to do her part on the man-and-wife team, or to take over if he were absent, or wounded, or killed.

At this writing we have not quite such a close, ever-present threat of attack as these earlier Americans faced, but we could do with the sort of team-work and mutual reliance that they perfected.

The Start

The start is just about "everything." If it's right, she'll enjoy the handgun—and almost always more than she expected to—and will ask unashamed for the help you can give her. If the start is right, too, she'll go on to the stage where a shooter develops his own little techniques and licks his own little problems, and still has the kind of shooting "form" that makes hits.

I've had the most patient and understanding instructors in all my shooting, and probably you have, too. There's the hint, if it's needed. If not, I apologize.

Many inexperienced women dread a gun's noise and kick, and the chunk of steel feels heavy at first. Report is dulled by ear-plugs, which some women detest, and by light loads and by barrels beyond the "snub-nose" length. Standard velocity .22 shorts are fine for a start. Only the most powerful handguns, or pin-weights, give uncomfortable recoil; the usual kick is no punishment, but instead a mere lifting of the relaxed hand and arm. This becomes enjoyable, as we know, and after a very few shots, too. If a handgun feels just slightly heavy in early sessions of dry or live-round firing, that's all right. Your girl will learn soon that weight makes for steady hold as well as reducing recoil. One way for her to appreciate gun-weight is for her to fire at arm's length, to get the noise farther from her ears, with her wrist or lower forearm on a rest of correct height. Build it or use a stepladder. Then she can hold so steadily that "sight picture" means something, the lining-up of sights, top of front even with top of rear, just under the bull "at six o'clock," or in the middle if she prefers. Scour all slivers off the rest.

Since anyone likes to see the results of effort, tin cans might be the best first targets. Fill some with water and there's more to see! Paper targets come next, but not at regulation distances just yet. In your own beginnings didn't you ever sneak up on them? And was anyone else around to see? OK, *you're* understanding, *you're* helpful, and neither you nor she wants an audience for some time to come.

It will be a proud day when you take her to the club range, and it should be a proud one when she "takes" you in a match, formal or informal. How useful are you as a shooter if you can't coach well? You're just a unit. Training of others is what counts for the shooting game and for national security and national cleanup of crime. Violence does not flourish where there's the strength to resist it successfully.

You have a fine happy time ahead of you, with deep satisfaction that grows and grows. Go out and get it.

The Guns

These are chosen just as a man chooses, for type, caliber, weight, balance, fit, and sighting. The difference is that the girl has the benefit of your experience and of your understanding sympathy with her individual problems. It should definitely be *her* gun (or guns), chosen by her because she likes it. The half-dozen details listed at the top of this paragraph are essential, of course. Credit her with the good sense to see that they are. The gun can have them all and still be beautiful, and women are sensitive to beauty. Heres a runthrough of them.

Type. A revolver is simpler and safer for *any* beginner to handle than a semi-automatic is. But people vary in their understanding and use of mechanical things; so the auto isn't ruled out. At first it will be used as a single-loader, anyway, for safety and because there's no hurry in slow-fire shooting. Pausing to reload relaxes any buildup of mental tension. It may relax it completely, and the physical tension, too.

Caliber. The usual beginner's handgun, beyond air, gas, and rubberband pistols that are useful and fun for "home-work," is the common .22 rimfire, taking short, long and long-rifle cartridges, inexpensive and quiet, and almost without recoil in guns over two pounds' weight. In .32 and even in .38 calibers, a handloader can produce nearly the same obliging features, including even some saving of money. The second gun usually is a .38 Special, target or defense or all-round as the need or desire dictates. There is no particular top limit as experience grows, except that of commonsense—which intelligent women have,

though they may be too smart to make a feature display of it, men being what they are! It is sensible to use no caliber above what you can hit with.

Weight. Around 24 ounces isn't too much for the "average" woman to use for a start, and always a pistol of this weight will be useful on shooting holidays afield and in coaching youngsters. Much depends on balance and on fit in the hand, and we assume that the first gun will have at least a 4-inch barrel, revolver or automatic, to cut noise and to give a decent sighting plane. It's just too hard to align close-set sights accurately and as soon as she gets to paper targets a woman wants good grouping of the shots.

Balance can be right or horrible. Few small guns are too muzzle-heavy. The usual error is too much weight in the hand, not enough out front for steadiness. Remember that this steadiness isn't appreciated until after some shooting. If at first it seems a little too much, that impression will wear off fast. But note the *"little* too much." For hip or point shooting, we don't—most of us—want as much muzzle-weight as for field or target use.

Fit is of supreme importance. As separated from weight and balance it means the feel of the gun in the hand. And the hand isn't likely to change much in the next few years! Yes, it can adapt itself to almost any pair of stocks, but it shouldnt have to. The grip should feel right almost, if not quite, at the start, and after that it's going to be good right along. Since the gun, hand, wrist and arm (allowing for elbow bend, which may be different in some women from what seems right on a man!) should line up almost straight in firing position, the grip must be small enough to let the hand get behind it easily, or at least with little conscious effort. Even so, target shots carefully fit the pistol to the firing hand with the other hand before they loose off a round. They are right, for theirs is precision shooting, the kind we want our girl to master, too. It is not impractical; it can pay off. A too-small grip, if nothing better can be had, can be built up, somtimes by merely putting on an adapter or filler which so many revolvers need to fill unwanted space between trigger guard and front strap, the front of the grip frame. Cutting down an oversize frame is quite a production.

Sighting. The square-cut Patridge-type rear and front are almost general issue. It's high time that they were, because they are so exact and so easy to aim with. Adjustment for elevation and for side-to-side windage costs extra on almost all but the most expensive models. But money spent on sights is well spent if they help, as these do except on strictly pocket or on point-shooting guns which we'd never choose for learning. A shooter wants to hit what he aims at. The wonder of hitting what he (or she; male nature made me forget my topic, though I believe in it most deeply) aims offside to hit comes just too seldom! People aim and hold differently, because of differences in eyesight and physique. And different loads go into a deservedly much-used gun. So fixed sights are a handicap in learning to shoot, in competition, and in field work, also. We do put up with them on some good handguns that we use afield, or at target distances that don't vary much. Still, they are a second choice. It's mostly a long-held affection for guns that lack movable sights that keeps them in our possession. About them we stay pig-headed. Apologies to the pig, who has more sense than most other farm animals.

Safety

This we must have always, for an accident happens in an instant and leaves us the rest of our life to mourn it. Most women are extremely safety-conscious about guns before and after they are used to them. We could study this quality, as exemplified in women.

The first thing to do about any gun, familiar or unknown, is to ascertain whether or not it's loaded. That is almost always a woman's first question. "To inspire in the student the spirit of wanting to know is the teacher's most important task," said a history professor whose memory I revere. It is no task to teach a woman about gun-safety.

The two cardinal rules, almost all-inclusive when you think them over, are never to point any gun, loaded or empty or even a toy, at anything you wouldn't want to hit, and to make sure, always, of where the bullet (or shot charge) will come to rest. If you show her the gun-safety chapter at the end of this book, or one in another book, she will probably read it. We hope you will, too, even if you have read or will read nothing else here except that chapter and this paragraph.

Good luck to you both, but may neither of you ever need luck to make all your handling and use of firearms completely safe.

IT SEEMS reasonable to assume that at some time a handgun bug will have a golden opportunity to bring together a clean-cut young fellow and a well-kept pistol. Some of us who haven't given this matter quite a lot of thought might be confused by such questions as how to start, when, with what, and where.

Let's begin by imagining a young man, married, with a fair amount of plinking and target work under his belt, and a handgun or two of his own. Pretty soon a son appears. Pop has gone his unthinking way, merely keeping his guns locked away from the snoopy fingers that we all have in the house at times. I think he could continue this until his son (or daughter) has reached the age of about four years.

About then, cap-pistols and squirt-guns appear. Pop had better begin thinking about one of those small, light, automatic-pistol-shaped guns that propel a No. 6 shot by means of a trigger-released rubber band, as made by the Bullseye Manufacturing Corporation, La Jolla, California. They're so darned accurate at from eight to even fifteen feet that the old man may miss his pistol practice at the club some rainy night in order to play with the new gun. These pistols cost very little; they have a smooth, if long, trigger pull; and as far as I could ever tell they aren't dangerous unless one got a shot in the eye.

This brings up the main point I want to stress in the whole chapter. Let's be frank about it. No matter if you never teach *anyone anything else* about firearms, please, for the sake of all living things, pound into a beginner's head the fact that he should NEVER unintentionally point a gun at anything that would be damaged, to his sorrow, if the gun should be fired. Talk about the old-fashioned teacher's hickory stick; in this case you have my permission to use a hammer, if necessary! I don't mean this word-for-word, but I mean it!

Can you imagine a call from the Police? "We have your son here. Please come down as soon as possible!" So it turns out to be a shooting-scrape, and after endless questions your son says, "Dad never taught me anything about guns, and the gang had 'em."

I think you would sleep pretty damned poorly for a long time after that scene.

Now that I've blown the main-top, let's get back to the four-year-old stage. It seems that your own guns should still be left out of sight and locked up when they're not being used. Junior is probably running around at full speed and shooting up his playmates with his toy sixgun. BUT, let's remember, many gunwise parents won't let their children have anything to do with such toys, *except,* perhaps, when they are handled with exactly the same care that real guns rate. Such discipline isn't easy to instill and maintain when children are tiny, but it has been done. Such children aren't involved in tragedies with guns that "look like real," and are. Those who are allowed to "quick-draw" and "shoot it out" with each other get so awfully fast that you'd hate to face such speed with a real gun.

CHAPTER 20

HANDGUNS AND KIDS

BY OSCAR R. HAMMOND

Maybe they make you think. Anyway, somehow you feel a little older already.

Cheer up! That part will continue as time goes on. But will it hurt if it brings a safe and efficient pistolman into the family? He'd better be safe from the first; so if you put thumbs down on undisciplined play with toy guns, perhaps you're right, and most of the neighbors wrong!

But both of you can play with the rubber-band gun, which fires a projectile and *must* be handled safely. That will be at home, of course. Soon you both will graduate to an inexpensive air-pistol, accurate enough for fun and some instruction, and the whole family will join in. There's still no noise to disturb neighbors, but eyes and other tender places are *danger* spots. Junior's "Watch where you point it!" if needed, usually can have been brought to a fine polish by this time. Meanwhile, he's developed some trigger-control and become used to a heavier gun than the Bullseye pistol. Watch your own example!

School soon starts to bother the family (or relieve it!), but in a year or two maybe Pop had better let his target pistol show up. Start for the club range early enough to let Junior be shown the gun before he's pushed off to bed. Why not teach him to check to see if it's unloaded and, some other day, help clean it? (What better gift can you offer him than your time?) Don't go into over-much detail; but let him handle a real gun at home, under supervision. For comparison and instruction, tell him about football, baseball and other sports.

Possibly the pistol business should be soft-pedaled for the next few years unless he trends definitely in that direction. "Ramming a pistol down his throat" is a fine way to make him a gun-hater, even if you yourself love them, as no doubt you do.

Who can name an age when these youngsters will get the urge to become seriously acquainted with a handgun? But you can bet it will be before we older folks expect it.

If his interest stays high, expose him more and more to your own guns, making sure that they are unloaded and never pointed where they shouldn't. Dry shooting might be OK, but I can't make myself think that quick-draw should be done in any kid's presence. They see too much of it on the screens. If Dad does it, too, it must be all right, they will think. In his early years the boy thinks Pop is next to God, almost. Later, you must earn his devotion. Halos don't come cheaply.

Sometimes a boy is well into the teens before he shows real interest in guns. It may never come, but if it does, these suggestions based upon my own experience might help.

For a beginner I'd pick a light-weight .22, to be fired single-shot until he's used to it. This holds especially for automatics, which reload themselves in a flash, literally, after each shot. A too-heavy gun is discouraging to try to hold at arm's length, even for us older guys who may not be much on the muscle side. Of course grip size must suit the hand. Flinching comes quite surely from an over-heavy caliber. I knew one young lady whom some idiot talked into firing a .45 Auto, and she had never shot a pistol before. She didn't again, for a number of years.

Now as to "Where?" Well, few of us would care to fire on a range next to a kid who had had no preivous instruction! Let's find a good safe sandbank or steep soft ground for a backstop, out in the country and where the owner allows us. There should be no other people around, no animals, and no stones, rocks or metal to cause a ricochet. Those glancing pieces of lead can go almost anywhere.

Best start with large targets, close-up, and graduate to quart or smaller tin cans. Your garage-man usually will be glad to get rid of them. When cans begin to feel unsafe under Junior's fire, it's time to start on paper targets, not too small or far away. They show exactly where the hits are, and they make a definite numerical record of progress. A little later the larger guns may appear, if the time seems right.

At about this time we should take stock of ourselves. Are we so smart, after all? Lots of us have had, at one time or another, good instruction. But as years passed, we slipped into our own little habits, and scores slipped, too. We had excuses like "Bifocals," "Nervous work at the office," or just plain "Getting older." Maybe we should take the kid to the range and to a really good instructor. Then, the first thing you know, you may be competing against the boy some night and come out feeling worth two-bits less than nothing. It's been known, at this stage, for Pop to arrange different shooting dates for himself and the youngster! But you can pat your ego on the back by feeling that you gave him a fine start, anyway. He won't forget it; he'll be grateful.

Not all families will be like the imaginary one used as an example. "Junior" may be a girl, or there might be ten of them, or a variety. "Pop" could be a bachelor who has taken a friend's youngster under his wing. Does it matter?

In closing this chapter I'd suggest that you train just one kid at a time. Usually, after just a little instruction, *one* youngster will be pretty dependable. But as soon as you get a crowd around to prod him on, he's apt to blow his stack, get careless, and show off a bit. Even adults sometimes give in to such strange impulses!

As an add-up, it looks as though you should always set a good example, catch your pupil when he or she is really interested, start with the proper gun and ammo, finish with competent instruction—your own, sharpened up if need be, will do finely—and then stop worrying about Junior. By then he should be absolutely safe with a gun, and learning marksmanship so fast that, maybe, you'd better slick up your own laurels.

Good shooting to both of you!

THE NAME "target pistol" covers a multitude of sins. Experts and Masters are choosey.

First you decide what kind and how much paper shooting you will do. If it boils up to 500 .22s a year, and part of those at tin cans, you can be happy with an inexpensive gun. Of these, I've found the Harrington & Richardson Sportsman to be tops. It feels good and it's accurate. It stands a reasonable amount of abuse, and it has excellent sights. But it's more likely to break down at an early date than the best, the more costly arms. For competitive shooting you'd best get one of the American-made .22s used by most match shots over the country: Colt, Hi-Standard, Ruger, or Smith & Wesson automatic; Smith or Colt revolver. More later on the less popular .22 revolver.

There are three National Rifle Association classifications: .22 rimfire; centerfire such as .32, .38, .44 and .45; and the third and mostest, the .45 and no other. This can be a revolver, but the most used (and abused) is that old workhorse, the Colt .45 autoloading pistol, Government Model. In its various stages of accurization, or without, praised or damned by users, it presents the greatest challenge. Few reach Master with it, but once under control it produces amazing results. It also takes an amazing outlay of ammunition. Some may master its cantankerous disposition in a thousand shots, but I've never met any. Ten thousand, under expert coaching and with careful attention to detail, is a more likely figure.

You needn't own all of these guns to do serious target shooting. You can follow the game with only a .22, or a centerfire, or a .45—which would take in the centerfire, too.

To economize, the .22 is the gun to start with, and without previous knowledge or training it's *always* the gun to start with. When your knees don't knock together as you step to the firing line in competition, and after your boss has raised your pay, you might add another horse to your stable of handguns. Think well, and talk to lots of shooters, for when you shuck out some eighty bucks or more for the gun, and read the price of ammo on the dealer's shelf, you don't want to make mistakes. Once you've bought a gun you can't sell it for what you paid. Inflation has darned near made "lighter than air" craft out of firearms; they're so close to the sky. If, in the back of your head, you think you might eventually graduate to the .45, it could be the centerfire choice.

Consult a centerfire shooter, preferably half a dozen of them. Turn a jaundiced eye on the voluble brother who has "just what you want and will let you have it at a good price." The word should be "good and high," and probably it has some fault he'd be glad to get rid of. If you buy a new one and something goes haywire, you can fall back on the factory. Makers are cooperative, often making adjustments "with their compliments." Best take this advice to heart.

First look up a club in your vicinity. Go there when

CHAPTER 21

CHOOSING THE TARGET GUN

BY ALBERT J. E. SHAY

they are shooting, make yourself known, sit down and *watch* what goes on. Someone will notice you, for gunbugs are friendly. You needn't join—not right away. But talk guns and shooting, and see if someone is getting coached on the firing line. This, my friend, is it. Coaching! Don't start without it. With that new gun you learn more bad habits in a day than you can unlearn in a month of Sundays. There are uncountable wrong ways to hold it, handle the trigger, even to stand, and only one right way for you, which by yourself you stand a hundred-to-one chance of striking. It's harder to unlearn bad habits than to learn them. Can you quit smoking as easily as you started?

Autoloader or Revolver?

Perhaps you have decided to begin with the .22. Present trend runs to the autos, better and more reliable than ever, with four good target makes to choose from at this writing. Which fits your hand best? And how about the reach to the trigger? Some hands, like mine, won't accommodate themselves to a long reach. Consider barrel lengths and weights. Is there too much gun weight in the hand, not enough out on the front piazza, so that the muzzle wobbles about while you try to gently touch off a shot with your aim under the bull's-

343

eye? If you like a certain model, will it need a special heavy barrel? Probably club shooters will own most types and let you try them. *But let each owner coach you.* All should know some little tricks of handling their own.

Writing and rereading this makes me conclude that all is not right in this shooting game. Some store in each center of target activity should be issued a "try gun" for the known competitive shot to take to the range and find out about, before he lays down the lion's share of a hundred smackers for one that's unsuited to his purpose—or possibly his hand size, or temperament. I don't expect this day to come, but I have a right to think about it and put it on paper. Such a setup would have cut my stable of Colts by about 75%. Some fellows show up on the range with a new gun every season, having sold the old one. I do it differently. I still have the old ones and can't bear to drop them, especially with the licking one takes on selling a second-hand arm. Many of mine are better than when I took them home in the nice new box. I worked on them, and often some expensive gunsmith did, too. Added up, they come to a bright new penny. Even a bankrupt business should realize 25% on its investment, or am I dreaming?

Personally—and this is one man's opinion—I find the auto harder to learn to shoot than the revolver. It's the hang of the thing. My wrist is relaxed with the revolver, but the durned thing is in "neutral" with the auto. In this troublesome neutral position there's "no push, no pull" strain on wrist tendons, and in carefully calculated slow-fire shots, especially, nerve tension often causes a slight convulsive movement at the instant of let-off. It's almost too fast for the eye to catch on the sights, and one wonders why that shot was a 5, 'way out, when he was holding for a 10. These are called "unaccountables." They sure are! Only by dry fire with an empty gun can you catch that little sidewise slap of the front sight. This is fact, though I started with my own .45 auto in 1914.

But you have rapid fire to contend with. Unless you start with expert coaching and are willing to practice thumbing the hammer a half-hour a day for maybe a couple of years—to get the swing of five shots in ten seconds—the auto has the edge. With it you can squirt them out by just pulling the trigger for each shot. By the same token, you can squirt them all over the paper, or off it. Whichever gun you choose, you must do much rapid fire to acquire cadence and subconscious timing. Then you begin to click. You can dry fire the revolver to your heart's content, but not the hammerless automatic.

The .45 Colt auto is different. Rig a long strong cord, with a loop for the thumb of the non-firing hand—and possibly drill a small hole transversely through the hammer, though a good sailor can tie a knot that will do. Then extend the gun to shooting position, with the cord led up the firing arm, around the back of the neck, and down the other arm, the thumb loop

of the right length to cause no strain on the gun hand while snapping. Aim, squeeze off a simulated shot, and jerk the free hand to cock the hammer for the next shot. This may be the best of all guns to "fire" in this manner, with the added benefit that the piece seems to recoil as in actual firing. You can hardly overdo such practice. But wear a shirt! If the cord is strong enough it will probably be rough. A few shots may make you wonder whether you're lighting a fire or sawing your head off!

One other matter pesters the users of automatics. If your club includes hardy souls who shoot outdoors in winter, or even from indoors at targets outside, they find even the best .22s accumulating hard grease in the action. So malfunctions or misfires occur. Wax is stiffer than grease. With a good revolver you seldom have such trouble.

You choose between two pre-eminent weapons, the K-.22 Smith and the Colt Officer's Match. With care and proper upkeep either gives lifelong service. Choose by the all-important feel. Try the cocking action, ease of pointing and sight alignment, muzzle weight, and take no man's word for any. If some kind brother allows you to try his gun, *you* supply the ammo. He may be just able to scrape by with a couple of boxes a week. Don't be a borrower.

Competition

After you have the gun, do a little target shooting. From the start you need a spotting scope and the rig to hold it up for easy looking. With your longest shot-spotting range 50 yards or 50 meters, you don't need a $100 glass for pistol. A Mossberg or Saturn will do all you want.

To make scores you must know where shots strike, then correct your sights to get them as near the 10-ring as possible. Then learn to hit. This means slow fire, nothing else until you can keep all shots in the Standard American black. I trained one team for a full year, one night a week on slow fire only. Then a half year on timed fire, and another half on rapid. Finally we went to a match as a team. Everyone brought home at least one medal. We had developed the competitive spirit by shooting against each other in practice.

If you plan to compete, don't expect to step to the firing line the first time out and win the grand prize. It isn't in the cards. To become a competitive shot you *must* do lots of such shooting. You can practice at home till hell glares with ice, and make, perhaps, a world's record. It's different when you step up with forty other shooters all with the same idea, that of coming in first.

Be content to go to as many matches as possible and come back empty-handed for a year, maybe two. When you crowd the top three in your class you start to get confidence. Next time you may collect some hardware, perhaps even an "Oscar." From here on, it's attendance at lots of competitions, paying attention to details, and getting practice—and practice—preferably where others shoot.

Single-Shots

On some smallbore range you may meet an old-timer, or even one less seasoned, with his single-shot pistol. Some temperaments find deliberate fire just their meat. Usually they are phlegmatic, unhurried, easygoing. There's a place for such shooting, an art in itself, and it isn't just local. The United States Revolver Association (write to 59 Alvin Street, Springfield, Massachusetts) has slow-fire matches, with fine prizes the rule. Here the .22 single-shot shines.

In old days there were many single-shots to choose from. They went back to the later 1800s, the Stevens and Smith & Wessons. Then came the S.&W. Straightline, Colt Camp Perry and the H.&R. U.S.R.A. Nearly all are in use, or the treasured possessions of the "boys" who did use them. The '91 Smiths were about the lightest made for serious target work, and many had weight added to their barrels for better balance and trigger control. Some barrels were relined by the old master, Harry Pope, Lord rest his meticulous soul. To their owners they are priceless. There were fine Stevens models like the Conlin, Lord, and Gould.

Soon after World War I Colt marketed the Woodsman auto, which took the pistol world by storm. My first came in 1921, and how we all struggled to shoot this neat little squirt with its small grip and light barrel! But it hit where you pointed it. Smith answered with the Straightline single-shot. It had some aspects of the Colt but came with recess for the head of the hot, non-corrosive, smokeless .22 cartridge. There was also a finely fitted steel case for gun, cleaning gear, and all. Many were sold, but sooner or later they left most firing lines. My guess is that that same neutral wrist position showed that slow-fire guns need a bent-wrist grip.

Colt's Camp Perry looked and *felt* like a revolver, though both barrel and crane swung out for ejection and loading. First came a 10-inch barrel, then an 8, and a short hammer fall. Mine I have to this date, and it's still my best producer at slow fire. It has the Officer's Model frame, of course.

H.&R. made the U.S.R.A. first with a light 10-inch barrel; then a heavier one; then one still heavier; also a neat little 7-incher for a U.S.R.A. match where you drew from the holster and fired one shot in a given time. The last, just before World War II, was a heavy 8-inch, about the best balanced of all. H.&R.s were machine-rest tested and unquestionably had accuracy. Some S.&W. owners sneered at them, probably because the retail was once $22.50, but after a good American won the British Bisley with a 7-inch H.&R. the sneer twisted to the other side of the mouth.

The Tompkins from Springfield, Massachusetts, was of modern design, precision-made, and not priced for the casual shooter. Workmanship was like that on the best oldtimers. Its long, gently curved grip suggests the duelling pistol. Folks must have found that this helped in long gruelling slow fire at 20 yards indoors or 50 out, U.S.R.A. Some required 50 consecutive shots within a reasonable time limit.

Many slow-fire shots have tried the beautiful European Olympic single-shots, with set triggers, elaborate sights and stocks. Most of the fine shots I know who owned them seem to have set them aside for an American gun. Why? I guess it's scores. The better shots keep a scorebook for records. If the book says an Olympic model gave you five fewer points at 50 meters than an old doctored-up Smith or Stevens, you can figure what to use. But definitely this is for individual decision. We must start winning more International Matches again! Naturally the gun-handling techniques differ.

Reloading Your Ammunition

You heard about handloads before you took up centerfire. Sure, they're cheaper than factory stuff, if you "do it yourself." Don't expect anyone to furnish unlimited fodder at the cost of primers, powder and bullets. Time and costly equipment figure, and he must have an expensive outfit to roll enough for himself. To keep up your keen edge, once you've arrived, you need 100 rounds a week for home and club practice. There's no mystery to loading if you can follow instructions. But you must play it safe.

For uniformity you want a bullet mold—maybe one of more than one cavity,—a bullet sizer and lubricator, and a pot to cast from, preferably electric. You need a loading tool, preferably to full-length resize the brass, decap and reprime at *one* operation of the handle, and a powder measure. Pro-rate the cost over just two years of the shooting needed, compare the price of factory rounds, and you'll be out of the red. And, of course, don't change guns, even if you had planned to stick to one caliber. Know your gun and practice, practice, practice. It will pay off.

System helps. We first size, prime and fully prepare the cases. With my Pacific tool and measure I set the ready cases to my left, being right-handed. I use a stool. Between the cases and the tool, set up with bullet-seating die in place, I put the powder measure, making sure it contains powder! On another stool, at the right of the tool, I set sized and lubed bullets. Close to the tool on the bench, on the right, I rig an inclined wooden rack to hold the box for loaded rounds.

With my left hand I take the case, mouth up, hold it under the powder measure, then charge it with my right hand. Inserting a bullet *carefully* into its mouth, I place case and bullet on the shell holder with my left hand, reach for the handle with my right, and lift till the bullet is seated, slowly steering the case into the die, and not crimping these target loads too enthusiastically. I lower the handle, let go with my right, take off the loaded cartridge and place it in the box. Meanwhile the left hand picks up another prepared case.

Start slowly, weed out lost motions, and soon you'll do it nonchalantly and precisely. In this way anyone who applies his mind to the work can avoid *double charges*. And you needn't handle cartridges two or three times. Have labels ready, and label and date every box so you can use older loads first.

Caliber

What caliber for centerfire? Think well before you jump. The .32 S.&W. Long is known to be as accurate as the .38 Special. It's economical, costing less for brass, lead and powder. It gives less recoil—important in any target shooting. Perhaps unaware of it, you get nervous reactions in arm and shoulder, which your mind can't overcome. Our country's hot-shots use light handloads in .38 and .45 because of machine rest proved accuracy. With young eyes I could just about bet on hitting a postage stamp at 25 yards or even farther with a full load in my .45 auto, *on the first shot*. I couldn't hit it again in ten. The gun and load that give you the best accuracy with the least recoil pay in two ways—less powder, better scores.

If you decide to jump clear across the brook and take the .45 for a centerfire, killing two shooting needs with one gun, you're still in a quandary. Revolver or auto? If it's the auto, you can have a Super-.38 Colt altered to take .38 Special wadcutter cartridges. Except for slam it feels and acts like the .45 Auto, being fine for centerfire if you and this highly accurate custom job like each other. And of course it's a fine .45 understudy. Read the *Rifleman,* anyway, and see what the top .45 scorers use. There are good revolvers for the auto cartridge, but how many of the nation's top ten, or top fifty, choose them? Count up. The bugaboo of rapid fire enters. The .45 revolver frames must be big, so many shooters find them hard to handle. Try one if you like, but my personal feeling is that it's best to get the big bellerin' handful of .45 *auto* at the start. The sooner you begin, the sooner you learn. Naturally this one pays in handloading.

Barrel-Lengths and Sights

The barrel-length of a target gun sometimes becomes a problem. An inch or more under the usual six is offered on some target autos in .22 caliber but I've yet to see a top-notcher using such barrels. With Phil Sharpe's Hi-Standard .22 and its interchangeable barrels, I seemed to find that the 4½ wobbled back under the bull a bit faster in timed and rapid than the 6¾; but in the long run both gave my waning ability about equal scores. Greater sight radius makes the longer barrel guns easier to shoot, allowing more careful correction of aim. You observe your error better and more quickly. The sights are farther apart, like telephone poles compared to fence pickets. This can be overdone. I could score higher with an 8-inch single-shot than with a 10-inch. Inherent accuracy was the same. "Sight relationship," I call it. But an optical authority may say I'm wrong. It just happened to me.

Sights that come on some modern guns leave little to be desired but mink coats. They are well shaped and easy to adjust. The proportion of rear to front may not be right for your eyes, but you can file out this proportion with a bit of skilled work. Widened, the rear notch passes more light. You need some to correct alignment. At the club you can squint across the sights on the youngster's gun, and the oldtimer's, too, to help find out how sights should be balanced for *your* eyes.

Some fine gunsmiths undercut a front sight sharply, and at once you note an improvement. There's no glare from the sides, and the top outline is remarkably sharp and true. Factories must hit a happy mean. Some target gun owners want to use a holster! For that kind of carry, stick to factory sights and smoke them before you fire. They can rake enough leather as-is. The undercut type belongs in the shooting kit until you're on the range. Then the corners won't wear bright and annoy you in sunlight, and the holster will be happy, too.

Current trend seems to prove the manufacturers' conviction that few of us want short target barrels, though a generation ago the Colt Officer's Model, in .38, came in 4-, 4½-, 5-, 6- and 7½-inch lengths. Six inches is becoming standard on revolvers, with few but the large-frame S.&W.s carrying 6½ or more; and they aren't used much for target at 50 yards or under. Most people now skip the .44 Special for competition, as it's heavy compared to .32 and .38 guns in centerfire matches and can't enter the .45 classification. It had a grand reputation as the world's most accurate caliber, proved it in record competition, but you don't see it on firing lines at the Regionals.

Stocks

What you will see on many guns at the big matches are special handmade grips, properly called "stocks." Nearly half the shooters use some such stocks on their bull's-eye guns. Some are simple; some are a wonder to behold. Unquestionably they help many shooters, physically and psychologically. A man with a big hand feels he needs a big grip to fill it. One with a small hand sometimes whittles some off the one that came on his gun. Quite a few real craftsmen make and deserve a living at the business. Just one caution: don't throw away the factory stocks till you've shot the others a few months. Keep track of your scores, which could determine the final decision.

On both Colt and S.&W. revolvers I find the addition of a Pachmayr adapter *all* I can handle. We had stocks made for a .22 Colt Woodsman and a .38 Special revolver. Soon I put them out of sight and mind forever. But try special stocks if you wish. Convince yourself, either way. They could do wonders for you; they aren't just a fad.

Trigger Pulls

There are set rules for trigger-pull weight on both revolvers and autoloaders in N.R.A. and U.S.R.A. competition. If yours seems heavy—and you surely will reach that stage—have it weighed before altering. On centerfire revolvers both organizations allow 2½ pounds; so get yours slightly under 3. Best stick to a full 3 pounds on .22 autos, though 2 are allowed. If your .45 auto goes to the National Matches it must lift 4 pounds. These weights were arrived at through a strict sense of safety. If your trigger pull conforms and still seems heavy, even with a trigger shoe installed, put your jack-knife in your pants pocket and squeeze it with your free hand. You'll be surprised what company one hand can be to the other, even that far apart.

Target and competitive pistol shooting are among the keenest of sports and give relaxation (properly approached) all out of proportion to others. You *have* to relax, Bud, or you don't go far! Maybe you can tense muscles in baseball, football, tiddlywinks or even golf, but you must relax to make a one-hand smoke-stick behave. If you fight it and try to squeeze walnut sap out of the stocks, she'll fire, all right, but what you hit ain't fit to print. She has to be babied and coaxed and handled gently like a "colt" to perform up to snuff. Once you've learned the trick, she'll do almost unbelievable things, like ten tens in a row, timed fire, and all cuttin' each other up like a bunch of savages. Keep after it and you'll get there.

Whatever you've heard, pistol shots are made, not born. Some work harder than others, but all of them work. So do some pupils, to get through the eighth grade in school. Muscle and nerve control are the prerequisites, and a calm disposition helps. If you haven't got it, cultivate one. It can happen to anybody!

Don't start too big and don't hope for too much. Keep your scores, but don't argue with the scorer unless you're certain he's wrong. That is rare! He has scored a great many targets in his time.

W E SHALL assume that you have had considerable practice and some coaching by a trained shot before you go to the range to shoot against others. If the range provides a coach, and targets open for practice, this isn't necessary. You can learn the fundamentals of conduct that make for safety and pleasant relations with kindred souls that follow the sport.

But I insist that it's far better to get your first lessons privately. Firing line commands and the racket of pistols at a range don't help a beginner to concentrate on his problems. He can't shoot pistol and at the same time look at and listen to what goes on around him.

One of the first things to learn is a sort of subconscious concentration, hard to define. Disregard the annoying sounds of small-talk, which has no place during the firing, anyway. Shut your ears, or plug them, to others' firing, yet listen to the range officer's commands. Listen to what you should hear; skip the rest.

Cultivate an even temperament, and *never* flare up at anything said by the range officer or other officials. It will ruin your score and mark you as one for all others to see—and to watch. If you break a rule, consciously or not, and the officer must bawl you out, remember that you have it coming, and resolve to avoid any such future infraction at all costs. Be honest with yourself, and right then and there, not sometime later. Success is for the sensible, and so is the downright pleasure.

Private instruction pays, for a not too gentle instructor who "calls" you for your faults and explains them, goes far in keeping you straight when you get to the range. The officer there has no time to explain. He's busier than any human being should be. His eyes must be everywhere at once, his voice ready to snap like a whiplash to stop some thoughtless mug from leaving his gun loaded, pointing it at his neighbor, firing before the command, and so on. If he singles you out for some pointed remarks, why, they are impersonal. They have only to do with the conduct of his office.

N.R.A. and U.S.R.A.

Two governing bodies control our pistol competition: The National Rifle Association of America, 1600 Rhode Island Avenue, Washington 6, D. C.; and the United States Revolver Association, 59 Alvin Street, Springfield, Massachusetts. Membership in either or both supports the game and is a must if you wish to compete in open shoulder-to-shoulder matches and have recognized standing.

The N.R.A. conducts or sanctions local, state and regional competitions—the latter comprising a group of states—and also national competitions. Usually these include winners of regionals, gathered at a focal point once a year to fight it out for championships. Registered or unregistered tournaments are fired

CHAPTER 22

ON THE RANGE

BY ALBERT J. E. SHAY

shoulder-to-shoulder on an NRA-approved range, outdoors at 25 and 50 yards, indoors at 50 feet and 20 yards. Outdoor matches are generally conducted in daylight; indoor must be under artificial light.

Don't be diffident about entering. Shooters are nationally classified when, as N.R.A. members, they have fired three or more recorded match scores in registered tournaments or registered leagues. Ratings go from Marksman up through Sharpshooter, Expert, and Master. You enter your first competition as Expert, since your ability is unknown. Then after prompt classification you compete against those of about your own ability. Nationwide N.R.A. service carries your records and reclassifies you as you advance. Targets are scored, officially, at the range.

U.S.R.A. matches are also nationwide, though under different rules and classifications. Their predominant shooting is slow or "deliberate" fire; but they also conduct winter indoor leagues, not all slow fire, but over the course of slow, timed and rapid at 20 yards, under artificial light. This is fun, and it helps to build and maintain your skill. Both team and individual affairs run for ten straight weeks. You start from scratch, win classification by firing "rating" targets witnessed and certified by your local Governor or Deputy Governor. Then you send your targets to headquarters, at your own expense, for official scoring and your national rating of Novice, Senior, or Expert.

You start by firing 15 targets to get your Novice, then build up to more targets for higher echelons. You buy these targets from the Association, through your Governor.

Winter matches surely develop the competitive spirit. Teams are rated as beginners or Juniors, and on up to Seniors and Experts. They include ten competitors, and each week the five high scorers are that week's team. When all teams have submitted their season's targets and scores have been compiled, a bulletin informs each team of the league its standing. Included is each team member's individual standing, whether or not he made the first five.

An interesting outdoor schedule is run by the same standard, and only attending high officials do the scoring. It's mainly slow fire at 50 yards, though 50-meter matches are held to give the competitor an idea of his International ability. From these and similarly conducted N.R.A. matches the International and Olympic team candidates are selected and trained. And the U.S.R.A. conducts competitions with various types of handguns, stressing single-shots, pocket revolvers of certain calibers, weights and sights suitable for holster carry, and "free pistols," the highly specialized slow fire arms usually associated with European shooting. They cost plenty but are free from most restrictions.

Stance

Yes, there's such a thing in shooting a pistol, just as in hitting a golf ball or throwing the discus. It covers a lot, to say nothing of 90 degrees of arc! The 90° type sprang from duelling days, when you exposed your slimmest silhouette by standing edgewise, swinging the chin around to the shoulder, straightening the arm to the utmost, feet comfortably apart but not spraddled, the firing hand as far as possible from the eye. Some, like my friend Pat the policeman, might consider their slimmest alignment to be full-faced. But positions all the way around to full-faced can be used, though this puts the sights closest to the eye, which doesn't help in clear definition.

Somewhere between is right for you, so the gun will point naturally at the target, without the strain that you must shun. The bulky person who faces the target, his legs apart like those of the Colossus of Rhodes, defies anything to upset him. But find your stance and *make it* comfortable, from feet to neck muscles—and even eye muscles, for keeping both eyes open eliminates some strain. Don't asume one that twists your spine. That affects your whole body, tires you unduly—just what you want to avoid. On the range you see many positions, and you learn much by observing other people's faults.

Place your feet comfortably apart as if you would have to stand in that position for quite a spell. Settle all your bones, stiffen your arm out, *and then relax.* Close your eyes, point your gun at what you think is the target, open them and look at the sights. Unless they align on, or under, the bull's-eye, *shift your hind foot* till they do. Close your eyes, try again; then don't let anything move you from this position till your string of shots is fired. Don't bend your back to get on the bull. The strain will show in your score.

Don't ever make it hard work. Notice the fellow with knees bent in a crouch, his free forearm laid across the small of his back like one of the Three Musketeers crouched with a rapier in deadly duel? Yes, it's been done, and try that stance if you wish. Much better to stand naturally, the out-of-work hand in your trousers pocket. By relaxation are Champions made!

Holding

We are creatures of habit—good and bad habits. They come from cultivation, like smoking, or cracking your knuckles. The pistol being a small, wilful thing, compared to any rifle we would use for target, it gets much discipline from the human hand, applied in different ways.

All pistol shooters agree that the grip of the hand must be uniform in placement and in strength from shot to shot. Before any target string we *carefully* fit the stock to the hand so that the gun will be a sort of prolongation of arm and hand, free to recoil straight back, not offside. Base of thumb and the three lower fingers hold the gun, the No. 2 finger being a rest for it, on the guard or the adapter. Most of us relax the thumb alongside the hammer. Laying it down below the cylinder is more for double-action fire with a revolver. Some press the trigger with the first joint of the forefinger, some with its tip. Forcing the finger clear through the guard gets results for some shooters, though it's an old-fashioned method, like squeezing the whole hand to fire the piece, not squeezing or pressing the forefinger alone and independently.

We vary a lot in strength of grip, though no good shot grips the stocks so hard that his forefinger isn't able to do its own work, unimpeded, on the trigger. Probably a majority of our best shots now grip a pistol's stocks pretty hard. I can only state my own belief and practice, which have brought me good results. Maybe walnut has an affinity for the hand, but no pistols—and I mean *none* at all—insist that the hand be wrapped around them in a viselike grip to make them behave. For me, gentleness does it. Grip too hard and the gun fights back.

I really mean this. With any revolver—an adapter (if needed; few shooters need the buildup on a Colt Single Action Army type of frame) where the second finger can use it as a rest, and the sights adjusted for you—shoot ten 10-shot slow-fire strings over a period of days, letting it dangle on that finger, the others just gently curved around the stocks. Concentrate on a delicate trigger let-off with the sight picture as nearly perfect as possible, under the bull or in the center if you prefer. Record the ten scores.

Next time, grasp the gun as firmly as you can, without trembling, as though someone was going to take it away from you. Use the whole hand. See if it isn't harder to keep the sights aligned while squeezing the trigger. Fire ten more targets, compare the scores, *and* note carefully which method fatigues you more. You may be one of the many fine shots who make a gun perform by using a hard grip, but I think you might crack up sooner than the relaxed shooter. However, we must all find our own best ways, and what may tire one shooter may not affect another.

For cocking the hammer with the thumb in rapid or timed fire, some shooters curl the little finger under the bottom of the stocks. Most target revolvers made now have rather long stocks, even with an adapter applied or built in as part of the stocks. The wide and sometimes offset hammer spurs help in cocking, unless we are so used to earlier-style hammers that we don't welcome a change. Some undoubtedly feel that way, and do all right, too. Again, we must all choose our ways.

Many of our very *best* shots practice holding heavy objects and/or work on spring squeezers to develop strength in their shooting hand. Let the nature of your physique and your determination decide for you which hold you prefer, the relaxed or the rather hard. Either works, if you work with it. The relaxed hold, which I've always used, was taught by the "greats" in shooting of years ago, such men as Dr. I. R. Calkins and Roy D. Jones of the U.S.R.A., to say nothing of a host of others.

Breathing

No doubt you've learned to hold your breath while you squeeze the trigger. But how? Don't inhale a lungful and attempt to keep it as if you were going to try for a long-distance underwater record. Inhale deeply, let part of the air out; then your diaphragm feels comfortable, not distended. Hold it. You do this for one shot in slow fire and usually for the entire five in timed or rapid. If you tried to hold to full capacity for twenty seconds you might go purple in the face during the last five seconds! Blood pressure has no business to climb while you're trying to get off a shot.

Some shooters find it helpful to take several deep breaths, then about a normal one, before "Commence firing." Too many breaths don't work.

Sights and Aiming

Not all adjustable handgun sights suit the individual as they come. They may be wide and shaped right, but much depends on the eyesight. Most factory jobs I've seen during all my shooting lack one fundamental, proportion. If the front sight is ⅛ inch wide, the notch in the rear sight is also ⅛. Theoretically the greater distance of the front sight from your eye should allow you to fit it into the notch and have a bit of light on each side. Some eyes can do this, but ours never could.

The notch should be about 1½ times as deep as it is wide, the width may be only .010 or .012 inch more than the front sight. The deepening clears the picture, giving longer spaces for light on each side; so proper centering becomes much easier. It's like a booster clearing a weak picture on television, and less eyestrain and better scores result, particularly under artificial light. Though a good gunsmith does wonders

with a file, you may need higher sights to give him enough metal to work on.

There are custom sights like the old King, and the present Micro (Micro Sight Co., 242 Harbor Blvd., Belmont, Calif.) and Eliason (Precision Arms & Tool Co., 31528 Groesbeck Highway, Fraser, Mich.) as examples. But notice how many sights still have the square-cut Patridge notch, equal in width and height. It's like target revolvers with barrels heavy enough to counterbalance coming so late. We had the idea before 1930, but it took five years to find a gunsmith, George Hyde of Brooklyn, willing to fit a Colt Single Action barrel, cut to 6½ inches, on our .38 Special Official Police Colt with King sights. It fetched the weight up to 38½ ounces. This one is still our pet target gun.

No doubt undercutting (and reblueing) the front sight at a shallow V angle facing the eye helps eliminate sidelight and glare. But value that dull blue or matte finish on the tip. One day's holster wear removes it forever, gives you bright corners. Henceforth you must blacken your sights if you shoot outdoors, or indoors, if some light comes from behind, as it should. These tiny glinting corners can mean as much as 4 or 5 inches off at 50 yards. Even with perfectly black sights you may have to hold off, or adjust, to center your shots.

You seem to be unable to pin this down by a formula. Some shoot into the light, other folks away from it. You must find out for yourself. I never heard of anyone not being affected to some extent. With the service rifle at 600 yards, and the sun at one side, I had to correct two quarter-points of windage, equal to 12 inches on the target, to keep in the black. It seems still worse when sunlight comes from ahead of you. On the Poughkeepsie, N. Y., range, where you begin the day by firing into the eye of the sun at 8 a.m., it usually takes me the first ten shots to find where to aim. Then I'm too tired to care about the next ten shots, anyway!

First get acquainted with target sights. Read the instructions, if any, but find out. Some adjust elevation in the front sight. Lower it for more elevation, or the reverse. Other sights have both windage and elevation in the rear. Move it the way you want to hit. Some screws have right-hand thread that *pull* the sights; others push it. Use a screwdriver that fits both width and length of the screw slots, or make it so. Find by trial what gives when you turn a screw, then memorize. Nothing is more disconcerting on the firing line than to have a neighbor ask you, in a breathless pause, "Which way do you turn this thing? My shots are going low and left." The gun may be strange to you, and you may hate to show your ignorance; yet you don't wish to be rude. But looking at a screw can't tell you where it moves a sight when you turn it in.

Sight in on an overcast day when light is evenly distributed. Hold either at six o'clock or center, but be consistent. Focus on the sights, not on the bull 'way out there. Set your outdoor sights for 25 yard

Upper: "Slim," the .30 Luger-Springfield - Nickerson - Carpenter - Shay. The muzzle end of 8 inches of a .30-06 barrel was chambered and fitted by Ed Nickerson, collar made and spun on to abut against the receiver. Front sight, a Redfield Sourdough fitted to a cut-down military Mauser band by Russ Carpenter. Ideas by Bert Shay. Most accurate Luger we ever shot. Loads must be strong to work this action, even with two turns cut from recoil spring, for the heavy barrel assembly must move back the normal amount to "break" the breech block's toggle lock. Lower: Our number one target gun, top scorer for seventeen years and fitted with Berdon short action since 1947. Colt Official Police frame with Colt Single Action 7½-inch barrel cut to 6½-inches and fitted by George Hyde. King sights. Probably the first real heavy-barrel Colt ever dreamed up.—Bert Shay.

timed and rapid, centering the groups laterally. Then leave them alone is my advice. At 50 yards you *may* have to add two or three clicks or divisions on elevation. Learn this thoroughly and do nothing more to your target sights. If your lateral or windage is off, *hold off* to center. Monkey with windage, and when you come up for the next relay the sun may have shifted—and you forgot to go back to original windage. It's pitiable to see a person frantically fumbling with a screwdriver between strings.

Wind rarely affects you more than 2 or 3 inches, and you can fix that with a little "Kentucky windage," holding at five or seven o'clock below the bull. Your first string may be a little left; then you may pick up your gun for the second with a slightly different grip! Target sights take care of eyesight variations, trigger squeeze, canting the gun, and other personal variables. Once they're set, best leave them alone.

Trigger Control

Squeezing the whole hand to release the trigger is generally regarded as outmoded with either pistol or rifle. The grip force may change; so most of the successful shots cultivate an independence of the trigger finger, wanting it to do its own job all by itself!

With a rifle held steadily by the sling, or laid on a bench-rest's sandbags or what-have-you, an experienced shot eases on pressure whenever the sights look right, holds the pressure gained, and repeats until the shot goes. After longer experience he does "wish" the shot off, if he cares to, knowing just about when the rifle will fire. During World War II a training method was publicized by which the learner kept a steady pressure on the trigger until the piece fired. Not knowing when it would go, he could hardly flinch, and with fair holding ability his shots went pretty close.

A pistol is much lighter in proportion to its weight of trigger pull than any decently tuned-up rifle—except of course the Olympic pistols with set triggers. We must pull the handgun's trigger straight back, most carefully and consistently, or our forefinger alone will be responsible for wide shots. We choose the method of trigger pull that gives us the best results, as beginner or as accomplished shot. It is not properly a "pull" at all, and some don't like to call it a "squeeze." Maybe "press" is a better term. The main thing is to master this hardest of all details in rifle or pistol shooting, and that takes practice. Dry shooting may exceed live-ammo firing by a hundred to one or even more, by those who want to learn and to keep what they've learned.

Using the Spotting Scope

Any serious target shooter should get a spotting telescope. Small ones are convenient to carry and use, and to fit into your shooting case. Not over 20 power of magnification is needed.

When called to the firing line, place the glass where you can use it without moving your feet from shooting position. Keep them riveted to the spot selected by the shut-eye test. Focus the scope on *your* target. You're perfectly correct if you get a bit cranky when some brother next to you asks for a look through your glass. If you are phlegmatic enough, and full of the milk of human kindness, you can let him upset your position and focus, but your next shots may suffer accordingly.

Don't use a scope too much. In slow fire outdoors it may be wise to spot every shot. Changing light can move your group considerably, but correcting your hold will build up the total score. If tempted to inspect your first five in timed or rapid you'd often do well to check the impulse. In timed it isn't, after a while, too hard to get five straight tens, but to look and become elated can make you try too hard on the second string, get tightened up, and end with a mess of scattered eights. You may reach a stage where such things don't upset you, but spur you to greater heights.

More often they spur you, like a bronco, to "bucking." Speaking pistolwise, that means a little convulsive shove to the gun at the instant of let-off, and several timed or rapid shots low and a bit left.

At the Tournament

When you enter a tournament, go into all the matches for which your gun is eligible. There's no point in traveling miles to shoot 20 rounds slow fire, or even the slow, timed and rapid, plus the National Match course, then duck the grand aggregate to save a dollar or so. I almost had to club one pupil to get him to enter the grand. Some time ago, down South and out of my control, he attended a registered tournament. He ducked the grand. So he came in 50 points over other competitors in the aggregate, but didn't win a thing.

Do first things first at a match. Make your entries at the statistical office of the range, look over your stubs and carefully note what targets you'll be on and what relays you'll shoot. Then don't walk away and get stone deaf. Listen to announcements and be on hand when your relay comes.

Cultivate a normal life. Don't smoke three extra packs of cigarettes, or drink seven cups of coffee, or tank up on Cokes, just because they are available. Shun hard liquor, and even beer if it dulls your senses. Such things have no place on a range. You need all your faculties to remember which target to fire at and to listen for commands. Be as natural as you can; curb your fidgets if possible. Sit down, not too far away, and try almost to doze. This relaxes your nerves, and they will need it. Go to your firing point resolved to do your best but remembering that it won't matter if you don't even place. You'll have had your fun, anyway.

If your gun jams, come to "Raise pistol" or "Ready" and stay that way till the string is finished. Don't attempt to clear the jam, on the first interrupted string, or no alibi will be given you.

Don't argue with the range officer, or with the scorer unless he's made an obvious mistake. He knows how to score and will gauge a close one for you. Then let the matter drop. Sportsmanship pays.

If "Commence firing" and "Cease firing" are announced by a whistle, don't fire ahead of the first or after the second. If you do, and the range officer doesn't exactly catch you, but asks, speak up. You can be ashamed of it and admit it. You'll be thought a great deal more of for being honest.

Shots ahead of time disturb the whole line. There's considerable tenseness, even in some veterans. Always be considerate. If your target blows down, come to raise or ready and wait. You'll get another string.

Win if you can, but don't make a fetish of it. *Enjoy your shootin'!*

The Competitive Spirit

This is a game, and whether you win or lose is no life or death matter. So enjoy this sport that you actually take part in, don't just watch from a bench. You're more likely to win if you take it easy, although winning is incidental. Lots of us seldom if ever win, but we have fun, to say nothing of meeting interesting characters! And I'd say that more lasting friendships are made on the range than anywhere else in sport. With the right slant you'll get along famously.

Don't expect as good scores in competition as in home range practice. Something sets up a quiver the first few times we step to the firing line with strangers. Continued attendance wears off this surge of jitters, though a few never get rid of that creep up the spine, the slightly wobbling knees, and an unsteadiness of the gun's muzzle that wasn't there when they shot at home. Those hardy souls compete in spite of all this —they are the brave ones, deserving medals all their own. You may never get to know one, for they hide their light under a bushel.

A school magazine once carried the following bit of verse. For me the memorizing of it was practically semi-automatic.

LINES TO MY LADY .45

For wide open spaces the rifle's all right,
Where there's time, space and distance, and plenty
of light,
But for work on the instant, when shooting is tight,
You can't get the slant with a rifle.

So I'll say that at times it is all very well,
But for deviltry, death or the raising of hell
The Colt .45 is unusually swell
And will go where you can't with a rifle.

You can spatter a dollar at seventy feet
With a stunning precision that's pleasing and neat;
So I'll still make the claim that the Colt can't be beat
And will do what you can't with a rifle.

So when something is crashing the alders ahead,
And it's death to the brute, or you in its stead,
Let the Colt automat, the fist-filling gat, the chunky
blue cat,
Chuck its competent lead!

Spooked down from the hills by the slam-banging and view-halloos of mob hunters, the bewildered doe stopped and looked at me through a forty-foot screen of light willow and river-sedge. I didn't try to ease the .32 Colt target gun from its holster. I couldn't be sure of making a brain shot in the two or three seconds' time that I could naturally expect—and got; and an 800-foot velocity, 98-grain bullet is puny lead for smashing the spine or drilling through ribs and wrecking the heart. As a dry-ground trailer I don't live up to my legendary spoonful of ancient Red Indian blood. We waved at each other and she was gone.

The power of our handgun and our skill with it set up definite limitations in our hunting—or they should, in the interests of conservation and of common decency. Pioneers "learned on the game." There was a lot of it, and only a little ammunition to be expended. If they sweated along under the "smallbore fever" they did so to cut the burden of lead carried on far and sometimes perilous journeys. Few of us today have any such excuse for using sub-marginal calibers, or for going afield without skill previously developed on black-and-white, then game-colored targets.

As we master the woodcraft that brings us close to game, and the marksmanship that lands our bullets in those always small vital spots, we can, if we like, use less powerful calibers. But many of us don't. We get deeper satisfaction and more certain success from pretty heavy ordnance. Charles Askins, Jr., in his friendly, readable *Art of Handgun Shooting* and *Pistol*

CHAPTER 23

FAR FROM CHIMNEY-SMOKE

Shooter's Book, recommends the .38 Special midrange wadcutter for hunting gray squirrels. At first thought that seems rough. Then you consider that altogether disproportionate vitality of the gray compared to that of considerably heavier small game, the twigs that sometimes bar the line of fire—more surely cut by the flat-fronted wadcutter than by a round-nosed bullet—and that shooter's experience. So it goes, not forgetting the other side of the coin, the wood-hick who makes his living with a .22 rimfire, using mostly shorts, and the casual nature-boy who has lots of luck with a pea-shooter and forgets all the cripples.

Just the thought of leaving those crips in the woods can sour pistol-hunting for those who through long and happy experience have learned to fit into the outdoors and perhaps even to feel a kinship with its year-'round residents. When we arrive at the stage where we fire only when we're sure of a clean kill, and use a handgun fit for the work, we enjoy our slice of a sport that's second to none.

Few get that far, I'm afraid. But remember that it is not "sporting" to take on a difficult shot to make the going harder for yourself. If you cripple, you have made the going damnably hard for the animal, and by what species of logic can we justify *that?* Sometime, to save your own hide, you may *have* to make your first shot good; so learn to take cover and use it, as well as mastering the art of marksmanship.

"What you *will* see when you haven't got a gun!" Ah, but we have: it's the pistol in pocket or holster, or carried muzzle-down in the hand, the forefinger laid outside the trigger guard. If we glaze the glint in our eyes, walk casually and never directly toward our game, we may fool it. And if we don't—mind-reading means life, to most of the wild creatures—what of it?

355

Easy sport is no sport. At any rate, the pistol goes on many a trip the long gun never makes, and quite possibly it has barked in even more far-off places. The verse opening this chapter is not quite pure fantasy. Such moments have pounded like heart-beats in the past, and the past often lives again in only slightly different forms.

Small Game

But invariably there must be a beginning, and for the pistol hunter it is usually on the smallest and least challenging of game—and the hardest to hit right, too. Yet there's the challenge to known and trusted gun skill, and to clean sportsmanship which can say, when the odds are too great, "No. Don't." We have the stalk, the unobtrusive raising and silent cocking of the weapon, the aim, and the smooth, masterly trigger press. A scant forkful or two of wild meat may be at stake, or survival itself. What we learn in insuring the first can help us win the other when the grub-bag is limp and empty or the rarely challenged "majesty of man" is questioned by an animal.

"Silent cocking of the weapon"? It is not too hard to do with a rifle or shotgun having an exposed hammer, but practice it first with an empty gun and practice it again with any model that's unfamiliar, for hammer spurs, mainsprings, and triggers come in assorted forms! You hold the trigger back and thumb the hammer rearward as far as it will go, then release the trigger and let the hammer go forward that little distance into the full-cock notch. In the same way the actual cocking of a sixgun's hammer can be made noiseless, but the Colt's cylinder bolt still clicks, softly, and so does the Smith & Wesson's, twice, and still softly. The hammer of the .45, .38 or 9 mm. Colt auto is mounted so far to the rear that silent cocking is, for me at least, a two-hand job, calling for more motions. There are enough of them already to alarm game. Single-shot pistols with no provision for turning a cylinder can be really quiet to cock; but not many of us have either the skill or the desire to hunt with a one-shot weapon, and a pistol at that. They have been used a great deal in the past, in wildernesses where game was plentiful and tame.

Hunt the bullfrog, that gallant sentinel of the swamps, from the shore instead of from the silently gliding canoe and you find him a sharpener of skill. At the time when Du Pont Lesmok powder gave the .22 long-rifle bullet some 970 f.s. velocity from a 24-inch rifle barrel, we found that load, at first, excellent for frog-hunting. Later the hollow point seemed preferable, more quick and certain in killing, not too destructive when properly aimed, and much better medicine if a crow or hawk or snapping-turtle offered a safe and fair shot. Now the standard solid-bullet .22 long-rifles develop about that speed from a pistol barrel, and they are not excessive. I'm not tapping these typewriter keys to prove that you can get by with shorts or BB caps. Sometimes you can, but we are discussing loads

that are always adequate if you do your part, and that give some leeway if you don't quite. What the penny-wise or the would-be Slingshot Dave may have to say is not of interest to us. We've heard it. If hunting with .22 long-rifle ammo in the handgun is likely to bring you to game any tougher than a bullfrog, the load to use is the high-velocity type, hollow point or a solid with half the nose taper cut squarely off to keep it from slipping too easily through tissue. Never economize on hunting ammunition. Shots at game are *important*. Any expense or trouble we go to is worthwhile.

Around city dumps and ill-kept barnyards the big gray rat lives high. He takes a surprising lot of killing, resembles the fastidiously clean gray squirrel in this respect. But if shooting is allowed around his diggings, the shots will average shorter. He's a varmint of the worst sort, a disease-carrier, too, but he knows no better and deserves fair treatment. Take your choice, dime-hitting accuracy with a .22 long-rifle hollow point, or quarter-dollar precision with a much larger and deadlier bullet. We must get permission to do such shooting, and having got it we must do it safely.

A born woodsman, the kind who can finger a trout from under a bank when he needs food, sees many a cottontail rabbit crouched in his form. It is criminally unsportsmanlike to take him there with shotgun or rifle, but the beginner with a pistol can learn about buck fever by trying for him. To hit him running is a real accomplishment for the woods rifleman, often too easy for any but the greenhorn with a shotgun. Yet some pistoleers trip him now and then, and no one else finds his meat quite so tasty. The little guy gives up so easily that a .22 l-r hollow point, even from a handgun's short barrel, is heavy enough, I suppose. My own great admiration for the long-rifle is based on its target accuracy, not on its killing power in the game fields. Hold well ahead of the rabbit. It's no triumph to break down his hindquarters and have to pour in a finishing shot while he screams, and if you only break a leg you may lose him, though some varmint almost surely will find him later. He doesn't deserve that helpless wait for his death.

Squirrels are post-graduate pistol game except for those never-hunted fellows, 'way back in, who come and sit up at fifteen feet, wondering who you are. I've found the .30 Luger, even hollow-pointed at the factory, grossly inadequate. Why do we own a .38, anyway, or a .32 Long with wadcutter bullets of soft lead, if we want to cut it fine and make less noise in the woodlot? That same .32, speeded up by knowledgeable handloading of a keg-shaped bullet, does well on the tame, sitting grouse of the north. The sourdough's favorite gun for such enrichers of the pot used to be a .22 Hamilton single-shot rifle, with unshorn bronze-lined barrel about 15 inches long and its Baby Dumpling stock cut off to pistol contour and drilled for a carrying string. But all the advertising on slick paper, coupled with the defenses of the water-pistol clan, can't endear the .22 rimfire to a hardened pistoleer who hunts all kinds of small game for sport and still totes a serviceable conscience ticking away under his shirt. Sure, a grand old Westerner once killed a moose with a hatchet, when he had to. And so on, et cetera. But such people owned considerably more effective weapons and were proud to be seen carrying them.

For small game hunting with a pistol we want the best sights possible to help us guide the bullet. Those who hunt in shady woods may want an ivory, red or gold tipped front sight. In the open, unless light is really poor, the target-type black post does well when the notch of the rear sight behind it is wide enough. For the woods we can daub the black tip red with fingernail polish—and be careful not to rub it off. A pistolman afield requires an accurate outfit. His standing shots are harder—and his follow-up shots at wounded game infinitely harder—than those of a rifleman. No one else is so much obliged to make the first bullet kill.

Varmints

Of all the so-called varmints—none of which we'd want to see wiped off the face of our land—the woodchuck or groundhog is the easiest to hunt. He rates close to big game in being hard to kill outright. Skunks and porcupines are so serene in their built-in protection against most of the animal world that they offer no difficulty and therefore don't interest the sportsman. In tall grass the chuck can be stalked with enough difficulty to train the novice, and a woods-dwelling chuck is sporting enough for any of us. Woodchucks are so tough that the weakest satisfactory rifle load for them is the .22 Hornet, or custom-made .17s or .177s giving like velocities. Well placed, the fast "explosive" Hornet bullet is deadly up to 100 yards or a bit more. We refer to at least 95% clean one-shot kills.

A brain shot with a .22 rimfire is certain, but it's so hard to make with positiveness that many experienced chuckers want much more when they rely on a pistol. The most powerful handloaded combinations are none too deadly. Penetration isn't the problem, but rather the quick expansion of a fast hollow point of the softest lead that gives accuracy in our particular gun, such as a .357 or .44 Magnum, .44 Special, or .45 Colt. The short, speedy .38-40 and .44-40 hollow point slugs cast at home beat some other bigbores in prompt expansion—in relative freedom from ricochets, too, so important in the pastures. Some guns shoot them with the essential moderate-range accuracy. Remaining velocities much under 1,000 f.s. seldom upset lead properly in animal tissue, and the chuck offers little resistance. A bullet in the abdomen may or may not anchor a woodchuck; mighty few pistol bullets can do that, except really fast ones like the adapted .22 Hornet or Kay-Chuk Hornet, and then only at rather short ranges where velocity stays high. To count him

in the bag you must cut off his tail, not condemn him to slow death by fatal but nonetheless rotten shooting. When the expert pistol shot can be sure of a good, solid shoulder hit with one of the best loads, he can hunt chucks with a clear conscience. The new .22 Jet and .256 Magnum beat the Kay-Chuk, but let's not over-estimate them!

If you have never eaten woodchuck, start with the liver. Then, if you can, tell me of any more delicate meat. The quarters and even the back are delicious when tenderized by a first-class cook.

Semi-wadcutter bullets of the Elmer Keith or C. E. Heath designs are right for most game shooting with bigbores and .38 Specials, too. They have a wide flat point with a slight taper down to a sharp shoulder above the bearing surface. Hollow-pointing them for varmints is fine, though for deer we might prefer to have available the penetration of a solid. A hollow *based* bullet mushrooms when loaded and fired "wrong end to," and it prevents excessive gas-cutting and bore fouling if it's of the sharp, front shoulder type. Consider carefully the airspace left for the loading, and don't hesitate to cut velocity if your first handloads, lower than standard, show signs of excess pressure, like pierced or badly flattened primers, sticking cases, unusually sharp report, or lead smears across the face of the cylinder. They probably won't, with such moderate powder charges, but guns are individual things.

Anyone who hunts crows with a rifle and gets one occasionally should have little difficulty in stalking and killing mountain sheep or goat, or even antelope on the plains. Few crows fall to a pistol except those unsophisticated, not quite full-grown youths of early summer. Hawks and owls are stupid by comparison, but it takes a woodsman's eye to spot them at rest, before they become alarmed. Some should be killed, and some left alone for the good that they do. That's the consensus, though you'll find informed people that insist that all hawks should be spared. Check your state game laws, too.

Sometimes a coyote will weave up within handgun range or be run down by a horseman. A bobcat may be caught in the open, but more often he's treed by dogs, like the cougar, or met in thick woods, like the big Canadian lynx. For all such fellows we want the ultimate in pistol power. Skill may direct a .22 bullet to the brain, though it may not make a heart shot fatal soon enough, with almost any handgun lead. Shoot extra carefully at any of the big cats, for dogs deserve all the consideration we can give them. They give everything.

Deer

A few sportsmen hunt deer or even bigger game with a handgun. They know their business and have practiced hard with the powerful loads they use. Rifle hunting of such game can have taken on a sort of staleness. They really hunt, and they take short range shots only in the woods. Most of them use heavy bullets, but a very few rely on the .357 or even the .38 or 9 mm. automatics. Their hunting can be the acme of sport, but it is only for the truly expert in good country. Our deadliest handgun concoctions are not awfully far ahead of 1873 .44-40 rifle ballistics. Butchering an illegal, off-season deer with a tiny bullet and a big handout of luck goes into a different and smelly category.

Frankly, sub-marginal killing power calls for sportsmanship. Some shooters have it, but so few, I suppose, that I can't regard as cranky those who condemn all pistol and bow hunting. One of my friends up north has hunted deer for several seasons with bow and arrows, without success. I respect him because he governs himself by his knowledge that his broadhead must make a lung shot to be sure of a quick kill. This results when air gets in and collapses the lungs, and an arrow can do it. Deer turned into pin-cushions by ill-aimed shafts make him sick. They do me, too.

Many men who make their living in forest or mountain country kill big and small game with a pistol as a matter of course, and with about any type and caliber of gun their gnarled hands happen to grasp. They can and do get up close, or let the game do the approaching. Offer them the gun they would want—and lug the ammunition for them, too—and their ideas on ballistics would sort out into about two piles, the smash of a .44 or .45, and the long penetration of relatively small calibers like the two Lugers and the .38 Auto. The .44 Magnum and some less powerful wildcat bigbores have both qualities to a certain extent.

To make full use of any handgun caliber afield, as well as at target, we need sights that are sharply adjustable to different loads. Other essentials are an excellent trigger pull, not too light for a cold finger easing it off, stocks that fit *us,* and weight enough to make the gun hold well, even in a fair breeze, if we do our part.

Almost any reasonably penetrating load serves to finish game that has been downed by a rifle—when the latter's ammunition is scanty and precious. Few places in the world are safer than our northern woods, if a person knows their changing moods and how to meet them. There the .22 is a trapper's favorite. It is not for difficult shots, of course.

Seeing, Stalking, and Shooting

In our first woodlot, swamp and pasture hunting, we start with learning the ways of the game. Nothing beats all-year-'round exposure to the elements in building this stock of ever-fascinating knowledge—except the will and the ability to learn! We can't all have the airings we want.

But don't scorn the city park, for there we can develop the hunter's most valued skill, that of seeing small birds and animals before they move. As Stewart Edward White once said, it's a matter of disregarding what isn't game, and of seeing the game because it's different from its surroundings. But only to trained or greatly gifted eyes is it different. Such eyes pick up living details in the fleeting scenes from a train or automobile window, creatures that the average traveler doesn't see. To him that country is "desolate."

In pocket wildernesses that fringe our cities, as well as in their parks, we can learn to see by waiting. In spite of the usual twitches and jerks that long imprisonment over concrete and asphalt has put into our muscles, we'll see, after a few minutes of trying to sit still, small birds busy close around us. When we sit really still and have put more time into it, wilder creatures pass within sight or hearing. This is the easiest method of hunting squirrels, provided that we know actively used woods, recognizing them by the "sign" of freshly discarded nut shells or pine cones and the claw tracery on barkless old gray logs.

To hunt squirrels or other game while you are moving is a long step harder. In the woods a mile-an-hour gait is pretty fast. We must take time for long looks and listening from cover, go slowly to avoid noise. No hunting should be hurried, physically or mentally. The deliberate hunter is most successful, and most able to savor the enjoyment of the sport. Over-anxiety is a handicap and a mighty unhappy state of mind. Why hurry to "finish here and try Jim Smith's farm before it gets dark"? Could we expect better luck there, in quick-time step?

We handicap ourselves by choosing a pistol—when it's legal—to hunt with. And when we break any game law we're doing our best to ruin the legal tolerances and rights given to hunters. So because of the short-gun handicap we shoot as effectively as we can. For slow fire we use the two-hand hold rather than the method prescribed for the target range. It's steadier. One hand can cup the other, or support the wrist of the firing hand. Some rest the gun hand on the raised and bent forearm or elbow of the other hand, though this brings the sights so close that they may blur. Also, a revolver can burn the arm or the sleeve with its flame-spurt from cylinder and barrel joint, or an autoloader's slide may dart back dangerously, or disastrously, at the eye. Whatever hunting hold we use, we need to zero in at target with it. Bullet strike is likely to be different from that which target-shooting style gives.

We need practice in sitting and prone positions. Quite often we can assume them in the field, or we're already down and waiting, when game appears. Resting one or both arms over a log or rock, or draping the body over or against such natural bench-rests, is worth practicing before we go hunting—long before.

The six o'clock target aim, sights aligned evenly at the bottom of the big black bullseye, naturally gives way to a near-center hold. Most of us want the shots to hit just above the front sight so that we needn't cover the small vital spot we aim at. Some still prefer to use a small round front bead of the old Ira Paine target type for hunting, and to lay it on the exact spot. This does well at short range. At almost any distance a big-bead front, so held, hides too much of the game. Yet some like it for quick work or in poor light.

Few of us are sharp enough to try for moving game with the pistol, or to hunt them when visibility is decidedly poor. If we pistolmen were to get a reputation for wounding and losing most of the game we hit, conservation-minded legislators would be quite right in barring the handgun from the hunting fields. At least one state already bars it, strictly. Most of the pistol hunters I've known have been conscientious in this matter, sportsmen rather than exhibitionists. After all, sportsmanship isn't entirely a moral quality, though it certainly shows the living strength of self-restraint. But it is also the way to the fullest enjoyment of sport.

Shot Pistols

1960 changes in the Federal Firearms Act impose a tax of only $5 on the transfer or making of a shot pistol or revolver, also firearms with combination rifle and shotgun barrels between 12 and 18 inches long, and concealable firearms (except pistols and revolvers) such as burglar guns, cane guns, pen guns, etc.

A $200 transfer or manufacturing tax is imposed on all fully automatic firearms, all rifles with barrels under 16 inches, all shotguns with barrels under 18 inches, all firearms made from a rifle or shotgun and having an overall length under 26 inches, all pistols with shoulder stocks, all firearms with combination rifle and shotgun barrels under 12 inches, and all mufflers and silencers for firearms.

This is a considerable free-up or liberalizing of former provisions, from the hunter's viewpoint. It lets in some more or less useful sporting arms that previously must have been hidden, buried sadly in post-holes, or thrown into the ever-hungry maw of the sea.

Ithaca's old 20 gauge Auto and Burglar Gun, a hammerless double for one-hand use, slung lead pellets all over the place but was deadly on small game up to 15 or 20 yards, or a bit more. Harrington and Richardson's single-shot Handy Gun chambered for 2½-inch 28 gauge or .410 bore carried a rather awkward stock or "handle" with little back-slant and a wide lip to contact the web of the hand and thus help you hold down the bucking muzzle. But even in 28 the kick wasn't terrible, for the old short shell took only 1¾ drams powder and ⅝ ounce shot, or a half-ounce round ball. A similar .32-20 H.&R. still would be useful with the low-velocity factory rounds it was made for. The H.&R. shot pistol came in both 8- and 12½-inch barrel lengths, but I'd hesitate to have the 28 chambered out for modern 2¾-inch shells. To adapt the .410 to 3-inch shells should be all right.

A hand-made grip with considerable slant-back would improve the handling and shooting of these interesting little H.&R.s. So would a shoulder stock, if a $200 tax payment is chicken-feed. We'd still have annoying tremors in holding these light-barreled guns in deliberate fire, and we'd need more muzzle-weight, too, for quicker alignment or for steadier swing on moving game, but these little gas-pipes would have their points in go-light woods travel.

About the only readily available pistol cartridge loaded with shot is the .22 long-rifle. It's for miniature clay-bird shooting with smooth-bored "rifles," and it should never be used on any sort of game bigger than a mouse. Oh sure, it has killed rats and, no doubt, small game birds and animals, very close-up, but out beyond five yards or so it's a wounder more than a killer. Don't ever try it. When I remember the neat job my 28-gauge Parker, loaded with No. 9 shot to get a good packed pattern at forty feet or so, did on barnyard rats, the thought of using this rimfire junk on them makes me rather ill.

The long array of pistol and rifle shot cartridges is almost gone. Once practically every popular pistol cartridge, and many of the black powder rifle sizes, came in shot loading. The handgun line ran from the BB cap with a pinch of No. 12s to the .44-40 and .45 Colt with 8s or larger. Rifled barrels whirled out wretched patterns with such loads, and it was no fun to clean the almost soldered-down deposit from the grooves. Usually the tiny charge was loaded in a standard case, though some sizes, like the .44-40, which was standard, along with the round ball load, for the smooth-bored barrel of the Marble Game-Getter Gun, were obliged with special long brass. Remington-UMC shot loads above .22 generally rode in bullet-shaped wooden containers. They had an overall like that of ball cartridges and therefore could be fed through magazines. They couldn't lead the barrel; neither could they kill beyond the shortest ranges unless bullhead luck directed some part of their patchy patterns.

It was different when skilled handloaders assembled their own shot cartridges and fired them in specially smooth-bored handguns. They used pistol powders, which take so little room in the case. Wad pressure and crimping were experimented with to get the best safe results. Game as tough as coyotes—close by, of course—fell down dead to their product. Such guns and ammo could have served well in defense. For shooting in the dark, at the mere sound of a dangerous intruder, they certainly could have done the business. They could also have been gangsters' guns and loads, if such people had known about them, and maybe they did.

From this, my personal conclusion is that the use of shot in pistols is hardly worth-while for the majority of us shooters. We can load our standard rifled handguns with shot cartridges that we buy or put up for ourselves, but the patterns will be so erratic, almost surely, that we could hardly depend on them. A pistol with a barrel much over 12 inches in length is scarcely a "handy gun" for most purposes. It is true that shotguns were made in Spain, and perhaps else-where, with a length of rifling at the muzzle purposely to scatter the shot for short-range use. This of course they did. They aren't, however, to be confused with the British "Paradox Gun," meant for use in the colonies. This powerful weapon, commonly a 12 gauge, had a short length of rifling at the muzzles to spin a stubby express bullet, light and fast by black powder

standards. Some were hollow-pointed; others had a hardened tip, as I remember, to give a reasonable amount of penetration into fairly heavy game. Whether the name "Paradox"—which dictionaries define as an apparent contradiction—meant that the big gun killed game and also nearly killed you when you fired it, or whether it was just some wag's gag, I don't know. I never had a chance to fire one of them.

The following introductory note becomes necessary.

The father-and-son team who wrote this chapter has had, I calculate, about sixty years' combined and intensive shooting experience. In addition to military service it included big and small game hunting, target work and match competition, testing of arms and ammunition, and experimental loading and firing—all this extensively, as a major hobby and object of investigation. These men's acquaintance and friendship with nationally known shooters are broad, too.

The elder man's military experience began as a seventeen-year-old Tank Corps corporal in the A.E.F., 1918-19. In World War II he served as a second lieutenant, Infantry, New York Guard, executive officer, Co. G, and regimental ordnance officer and weapons instructor. Later, as a company commander and captain he was plans and training officer for the regiment, but still the regiment's ordnance and training officer.

His son, after four years of R.O.T.C. training, was commissioned as second lieutenant, Infantry, in 1949, joined the 77th Division (organized reserves), and at the outbreak of the Korean War spent six months as first lieutenant at the Infantry School at Fort Benning. After doing some specialized ordnance work at Tokyo Arsenal, he became a line officer in Korea as executive officer of Co. C, 35th Infantry, of the 25th or Lightning Division. He did regular tours with his outfit while it was in the line. When relieved, he was for two months executive officer at the division's corps school for non-coms, and during another relief his battalion did security guard on Cha Jo Du, the island some sixty miles south of Korea, where 6,000 hard-core commies were confined. On October 1, 1952, when prisoners on this island and on Kogi Du revolted, he happened to be officer of the day. There was plenty of shooting. In Korea he commanded his company while his C. O. attended a specialized school. Since he knew guns, he was always an instructor in their use —company, battalion or regimental. He taught all the Infantry weapons from pistols to .30 and .50 caliber machine guns and bazookas, and though mortars and recoil-less rifles are heavy weapons company arms, even these he knew.

H. M. S.

> *"Be not afraid of any man,*
> *No matter what his size.*
> *When trouble threatens, call on me,*
> *And I will equalize."*

The author of that doggerel is unknown. We do know, from Clyde Baker, the famous gunsmith, that the verse was carved in the grip of a Texas sheriff's Peacemaker; but the unfortunate soul left this vale of tears, not in a blaze of glory in a righteous gun-fight, but by the very prosaic process of turning his flivver over in a ditch and breaking his neck.

In the light of the above we feel that this is a

CHAPTER 24

THE PISTOL IN MILITARY SERVICE

BY THOMAS C. FLORICH
and THOMAS C. FLORICH, JR.

good place to remark that a pistol, like any other inanimate object, may be used properly and ever after have its praises sung, or may be used improperly and ever after be cursed for the barbaric action in which it was a directed participant. The intent and intelligence, or lack thereof, of the user is the accountable agent—not the pistol.

Here we may further clear the air by remarking that the authors of this chapter are riflemen by avocation, but with the magnanimity of all good riflemen they used handguns for their pleasure, always with the subconscious thought that, "If I'm ever in a sticky spot, this thing may come in handy." Each in his day when on military service made certain that there was a loaded handgun about his person. On many Army stations this is forbidden, but the attitude always has been, "If I get in a jam bad enough to need my pistol, I can always worry about regulations after I have survived!"

Bear in mind that guns first evolved as cannon. It is quite a tribute to the desirability of handguns that the design fast shrank from cannon to hand cannon. Further along in history, every step forward in ballistic and mechanical firearms design has found its way into handguns, immediately. Theoretical need or not, the real demand always has been there. Theorists have been knocking down handgun usefulness for centuries, and staff officers, officially armed with handguns, have been taking them away from GIs for just as long, and the ever practical fighting soldier has continued to beg, borrow or steal a handgun for his personal protection right up to this day. This is not the type of statement proved by accurate statistics. Soldiers have been forced to lie about this to all but their closest friends for just as long as they have been acquiring pistols.

The remarkable thing is just how often you can turn a soldier upside down, shake, and—whoops!—a loaded pistol falls out before the loaded dice, both being carried to glean some slight advantage from a not too munificent fate. Just let us reminisce for a moment and recall a few of the many, many instances. The BOQ neighbor expecting—and he was right—overseas orders as a 2nd Lt. Artillery Forward Observer, which job even the common Infantryman doesn't envy, one day palmed a small flat .25 auto, his "get-away" gun. This was shocking, for to have known him was to recognize a gent with absolutely no professional or amateur interest in firearms. His sole interest in life was women. The scholarly librarian whose only mechanical interest was printing presses—to my amazement he apologetically asked me to find him a gun. I scratched up a battered Luger for $30 and he carved replacements for the broken grips, himself, and asked me to coach him on his own time on Saturdays. Overseas he sold the gun for $75—when on his way home. The social butterfly I had known from fraternity parties and R.O.T.C. Summer Camp, to whom the Army was really just a joke in bad taste: overseas he tucked a light-weight .45 in his bosom. The highly competent Major whose advice and strong advocacy of the .45 Auto took my scores from miserable to an intermittent mediocre: he had helped rewrite the .45 manual, but on close questioning I discovered that he had a .38 revolver to keep under his arm when he went overseas. The affable Colonel with a .357 shoulder-holstered and neatly complemented under the other arm with a pouch that snapped open on the bottom for a fast reload. The time I got in bad for not drawing up charges on a GI who had pinched a .45: this was naive idealism on my part, for they threw the book at him, anyway. The three .45 autos bought personally and successively sold to persuasive chaps with overseas orders and less time left than I had. I finally gave up on the .45 and went to a .38 Special Combat Masterpiece as a matter of preference. The rich man who had a revolver made over for the .30 carbine cartridge, and the poor one who took a .32 auto with one magazine-load of ammo with him—and didn't waste a round. The slicked-over Chief's Special that was out of reach for many months only when I was under a shower in a shower point, and this was a rare treat, I assure you. The countless non-issue handguns revealed accidentally, casually, or more rarely, deliberately, while overseas, and the fantastic prices they brought, often proportionately higher than liquor.

What does this prove? Merely that tables of organization and equipment, military fads, theories and regu-

lations and the rest of it can go straight to hell! There is just no substitute for the old equalizer as the soldier's personal weapon.

Now let us clarify our position. A pistol is not the only weapon, a good substitute for other weapons, or even a good weapon as weapons go. It is really just the closest thing there is to an indispensable weapon for every soldier, regardless of his military job. It is the only means a soldier has for coming close to the Boy Scout ideal of always being prepared. With a pistol on his person he has an instantaneous means of delivering sudden death to his enemy from range zero to perhaps 200 yards (very good gun and shooter, and rare ideal circumstances). He has it with him night and day, in his sleeping bag, foxhole or latrine. It doesn't matter what he is carrying or how far he has walked or run. He can use it standing, sitting, lying down or crawling, with his hand in his pocket and with either hand. Even when he is caught with his pants down, the old equalizer is ready. And let's face it, surprise is a very big piece of the art and practice of war; so any fool should know enough to be prepared to be surprised sooner or later.

Having said all that, I must now add that as my primary weapon I'd select, and I list in order: an automatic rifle, a semi-automatic rifle, any old rifle, a carbine, a submachine gun, a shotgun, and last a pistol. It is also nice to have a couple of grenades to hand out big surprises, and a knife for quiet surprises. As you may have gathered by this time, I do believe in dressing up to the occasion.

Thus, if military authorities fail to realize that a handgun is the greatest single morale-building piece of living-insurance a soldier can be issued, he realizes it for himself. If the General Staff, Army Field Forces or his immediate Company officers do not recognize this, he takes care of himself as best he can so that when the chips are down the soldier's last-ditch defense and possible hope of survival are ready. The size, weight, caliber, type of action, and ballistics are arguable, and goodness knows these factors have been and still are being debated in minute detail. But until the individual soldier is provided with a handgun, any reasonable type handgun and the training to use it well, our military planners are failing miserably in their planning jobs.

Too radical a concept? Hardly. The lowest common denominator of war is one soldier imposing his will on one enemy, and this despite the air age, the nuclear age, the electronic age and every other type of variation in modern war. It doesn't make you any less dead to be killed in an old-fashioned obsolete way. And just look at your newspapers: there are still lots of primitive, obsolete, nasty people around that B-52s won't touch. So let's get off this routine about, "This is old stuff." People are getting killed every day by old stuff. I don't know where or when, but it will be so for us again. We should not stop planning and improving the lot of the soldier. T. O. & E.s provide for handguns for Field grade and Staff Officers, gun crews, communications men and so on; but they stopped short at the one group with the greatest need for a handgun—the Infantryman.

The bayonet has been reduced to the size of a heavy hunting knife, and bayonet practice is kept on the training schedule "as a morale-building factor." Now I ask you: throw a bayonet, scabbard, and the front stud from the end of your shoulder arm (if you didn't have a bayonet you wouldn't have that ungodly hunk of iron dangling from the front of your rifle barrel) on a scale and balance it against an S.&W. Chief's or a Colt Detective Special light-weight handgun—loaded, mind you—and I'll eat your hat if the hand gun doesn't weigh less. Remember, it contains five or six, respectively, instantaneous cures for "last-ditch" combat exigencies. I should like to see a vote among combat troops who have had enough pistol training to respect it, to find out just which hardware they would carry.

The weapon and the caliber:
During America's existence everything from the .22 short (during the Civil War "many officers felt themselves well equipped" with the breech-loading S.&W. model) to the 12-gauge single-barreled pistols (popular with the British against some of their more fanatic tribesmen) has been used effectively by men who learned to shoot the arm. Anyone who has seen a man shot by a .45 Auto knows that it is a good killer, and the .22 Woodsman, equipped with a silencer, did fine work for the O.S.S.

We have cited extremes. Let's get down to sensible criteria and perimeters within each criterion. I know that I shall be speaking dogmatically, but what I say is the most precise logic my mind can generate. Less would be hypocrisy indeed, when we are talking of saving and taking lives in war. Please note the numbers. They are not paragraph headings. They represent an order of priority I regard as a necessary sequence in evaluating any fighting handgun.

1. *Possession*. This is the first principle, the most important, and the one most overlooked. You must have your handgun on you at all times, and ready to shoot. The best made, most powerful, most accurate, fastest shooting gun is completely useless unless you have it on you. The best example of this sort of thing is a .44 Magnum. It is all the things mentioned in the previous sentence. It is also some 48 ounces unloaded, and almost a foot long, half a foot high and three inches thick! This makes it slightly handier to carry than an unabridged dictionary. Personally, if I carry a book, it fits into my pocket. There is just a slight chance (about 100 to 1) that I will leave my Webster's Unabridged on the shelf, but if you can carry it and use it, fine. However, I more than suggest, I insist, that any gun too bulky or heavy to have with you at all times is useless.

1. A. *Size*. What this means to me is that any revolver larger than a six-shot Combat Masterpiece or Trooper, or an auto bigger than a .45 (skeptic, don't scoff, they come bigger; try on a Navy Luger or one of those old Mausers with rifle-buttstock holster) is a total loss. They are not only too heavy but also too big. I know Canadian Mounties carried, and still do for all I know, a .455 on a New Service frame with 5½- or 6-inch barrel. Up to a couple of years ago the New York State Troopers had the same gun in .45 Colt, and now they carry 6-inch .38s. I also know the Armed Forces still carry the .45 Auto on the hip. I have only one answer. We are talking military use. The first time I barreled down a communication trench with a .45 on my hip I had the complete all-time cure for hip carrying. It took me fifteen minutes to clean out the mud, and at the time I didn't need the manual to strip a .45. Now it is possible that it might still have functioned, but I'm glad I didn't have to find out. As far as I am concerned, protective flap and all that hip holster is a frost. Also, I am not interested in large-frame revolvers with 6-inch barrels, since they are not comfortable in a shoulder holster. Further, I believe a gun must be readily accessible to either hand, and this means a cross-draw setup, either shoulder or waist. (You can carry a rig like the Border Patrol, a right-handed holster slung forward on the right side of the Sam Browne belts, but Sam Browne belts have been passé for some time in American military circles.) Until they redesign all the uniforms, you have too much on your waist, already. So it's a shoulder holster.

1. B. *Accessibility*. This means to both hands, and it needs emphasis. You and I don't know what we shall be doing when we need the old equalizer; but chances are good we shall be on our stomach or back or knees or climbing. And what's more, we shall be doing something with one hand—either hand—whether it be holding ourselves up or holding on to a weapon or a man or an ammo box that we cannot let go. It's a fifty-fifty chance the engaged side or hand will be the right one. If the handgun is on the right hip, getting into action from the left will be slow and awkward, or maybe just plain impossible. One thing I'm sure we shall not be doing is standing in the middle of an open spot like a TV Western hero with the hand ready and poised over the butt of the faithful six-shooter, waiting for a signal. The realistic approach is to hit the dirt low and fast, rolling as you hit, and keep rolling as you unlimber your weapon. A man flat on the ground and moving, is a tough target; and your opponent will be far enough off to have to pause to take a new and careful aim. When you stop rolling, aim and fire. Make your first shot good; that's all the time you've gained by your maneuver.

This points up the one criticism I have of the very excellent F.B.I. Practical Pistol Course. It is the best handgun training course I know. You fire at silhouettes from different positions, with either hand, at different ranges, but you carry and draw only from a high back-of-the-hip position, which is completely inaccessible to the other hand. This position has the advantages of terrific speed, of being safe to teach and use, and quite handy for the chap who is wearing a single-breasted business suit, but it is out of the question, in my book, when you have mud foxholes, barbed wire, etc., to negotiate.

Of equal importance in considering the type of gun you carry is the fact that you may not have the opportunity or desire to wear a gun rig, and your pet, if of reasonable size and weight, can be dropped into a pocket. Incidentally, a pocket is one of the nicest places in which to carry a gun. It has many virtues. Unless you're naked, you always have several available. Uniforms are thoughtfully provided with many large, accessible ones just about anywhere you look. In combat attire every GI bulges in all sorts of odd places, so another bump will scarcely be noticed by friend or foe. My favorite spots were the upper left-hand breast pocket of fatigues or combat jacket, for a small gun, and either of the lower front pockets of the latter, for any sized gun. Muff pockets on a parka are a one-handed proposition, but they're awfully fast. However, when you are moving around in a parka, it isn't zipped up all the way, and that upper breast pocket is handy. One further significant advantage in having a gun in or under clothing is the protection afforded it from low temperatures, mud, dust and wet. Don't forget that having a weapon that malfunctions is worse than having none. You usually find out about the malfunction at the worst possible moment; whereas, if you had had no weapon you would have been able to anticipate making other arrangements.

1. C. *Numbers*. I do not consider it illogical to carry two guns, the first to be as close and steady a companion as your skin. Necessarily this must be ultra-light and compact and concealable. This baby I consider a must. When all is said and done it is the only one you can be sure of having with you at all times. The other job would be a high-performance type (powerful, long range, good sights, etc.) and carried where concealment and lack of bulk and weight are not primary considerations. This second type is what most people think about when they discuss service guns, and I agree that they are great when you can afford to have one. This means your C.O. isn't regulation happy, you have the money and time to get a second gun and practice with it, and the thing doesn't get in your way on your primary job as it would if you were a rifleman. I'm thinking of crew-served weapons people, officers, and that sort of category.

2. *Safety*.

I humbly suggest that the man who carries a gun of such design as one likely or possibly certain to discharge accidentally is a damn fool. There are much easier ways to produce self-inflicted wounds. Among all the parts of a gun that I don't like, the one I don't like most is the safety. This is a complete misnomer. I believe that any gun that requires a safety is unsafe. If the safety can readily be put on and off on

purpose, the gun is usable because it is reasonably fast in getting off a first shot. Parenthetically, if you can't take the safety off fast the gun isn't very usable, for obvious reasons. Necessarily then, if the safety can readily be put on and off on purpose, it can be brushed off by accident in the normal course of actively carrying it on your person—remember, a soldier on active duty takes more and harder dives than a football player—leaving you with a loaded, cocked weapon very dangerous to you.

Specifically, I believe the conventional pattern double-action revolver to be the safest gun to carry. Remember the ad showing a claw hammer striking the revolver's hammer and the statement about a bar of steel between you and accidental discharge? Well, for once it wasn't mere advertising "puffing," as the British call it. The only way a double-action revolver is going to go off is by your cocking the hammer and pulling the trigger, or pulling the trigger through a long, heavy double-action pull. I think this is about as foolproof as you can get, and as safe as has been designed to date. The old-pattern single-action is safe only when the hammer is rested on an empty chamber, but I wouldn't be seen alive with one of those buckets of bolts. They tell me they were reliable, but so was the Model T Ford. As far as the centerfire Rugers of this pattern are concerned, I think we can all agree that Bill Ruger has very successfully used modern technology to re-engineer an obsolete design, thereby producing—an obsolete design. They are wonderful guns for sport and playing around, but for playing for keeps —NO! That design went out with the Pony Express.

The .45 Auto (this includes its brother the .38 Super and a variety of country cousins ranging from the 9 mm. Belgian Browning and the Polish Radom to an assortment of Spanish and South American copies of Browning's design in many calibers) is the safest automatic pistol I know. This is not for the reasons offered in the Field Manual about the grip safety and latch safety. Neither is it because of the firing pin, which is of inertia design, i. e., the distance from the face of the hammer to the primer is longer than the length of the firing pin itself, which is spring loaded away from the primer. What this means is that you can carry (and I do so) the .45 Auto with a round in the chamber and the hammer down. Needless to say, caution is exercised in lowering the hammer slowly, but once it's down you can whack that hammer spur with a carpenter's nail-driver to no avail. To fire, you must cock the hammer and pull the trigger.

Guns that I view with something less than enthusiasm (and as far as I know I am joined by every law enforcement agency in the country, for all of them use revolvers) are the run of the mill hammerless automatics. You either carry them with a loaded magazine and nothing in the chamber, in which case you are slow but safe, having to rack the slide back before firing, or you carry a round in the chamber with the safety on. The latter qualifies for the cartoon, run in a N. Y. daily, called "Inviting the Undertaker." I don't say you will have an accident with this genre, but you are like the fellow who does sixty through a school zone who hasn't hit a kid yet. It's really a matter of how long you can push your luck.

I regard the P-38 as a safe design but quite disconcerting unless you're used to it. When you put the safety on with the hammer up, it falls, but not on the firing pin. This really stops the music, the first time you see it. With a round in the chamber it is safe with the hammer down, as it has an inertia firing pin. It also has an indicator on the rear top of the slide to show when there's a round in the chamber. The S.&W. 9 mm. auto is another double-action design. This feature has been criticized as having limited value on automatics because of the sharp contrast between the first-shot long pull and the succeeding shots with short pull. This is true, but so what? If you are so needing of a first shot that you haven't time to cock the weapon, get the short pull, and take some sort of aim, the problem of the second shot can be relegated to the dim distant future after you have survived the first second or two. If you have lived that long you may well be in a position to take more deliberate aim on number two.

I consider the hammerless revolver the safest and most practical pocket gun going. By combining a grip safety with a long double-action pull it makes you really have to work at having an accidental discharge. The type also possesses the virtue of being very smooth and fast going in and out of pockets, as there is nothing to catch on clothes. Another favorable thing is that you can shoot from inside a pocket if things are desperate enough, and it will function. Any standard revolver, without a hammer shroud, will catch on the hammer. An auto likewise will catch as the slide goes back and forth.

A type of auto that is scarce these days came from Germany during World War II. These are the Sauer and Walther pocket guns, double-action for the first shot (therefore reasonably safe), quite compact, pointing well for autos, and accurate. They were available in .32 and .380, as a rule. I have little personal experience with them, but they should make first-class pocket guns.

3. *Shootability*.

Whatever features a weapon has or lacks, it is worth no more to you than your ability to make hits with it. If you are so ill-advised as to carry one you haven't made yourself sure of, Heaven help you.

Please do not allow yourself to be a victim of the warped psychology I have heard from otherwise intelligent people. This bit runs along the lines of "Oh! I know the recoil is heavy and I can't shoot a good score on a target, but it's plenty good enough to hit a man; and besides, under service conditions recoil doesn't bother you—you never even think of it—and you've got to have the knock-down power." Let's look at this piece by piece. First of all, we should make it

clear that at this point we are talking of high-performance type arms, and we'll get back to the pocket type later. Almost all the arms and cartridges in this category are capable of a very high order of accuracy in the right hands. My point is: are those hands yours? It is quite a common fallacy to think in terms of paper numbers and book ballistics. This really doesn't mean much to you because your big problem is not what is available, but what you can use best in what is available. Shooting is a manipulative art made by training a set of conditioned reflexes— a two-bit phrase for shooting habits. Don't kid yourself that when you're under pressure your shooting is going to be better than when you feel calm and relaxed and the target is not shooting at you. When you're under pressure those bad habits will be worse. The difference is that you will be too frightened to notice your flinch or bad sight picture. This is not an original thought. Here is the essential purpose of military training and discipline, namely, that when you are frightened to the point of near-panic you are carried through by the habits, training, conditioned reflexes— whatever you want to call them. The moral of this story is not to overgun yourself. The biggest is not the best. The best one for you is the one you have tried out and know you get the most hits with.

The foregoing material should be kept in mind regarding my pet peeve among service-type handguns, the .45 Auto. Briefly, the background on its cartridge is that the .38 revolver used as our service handgun in the Philippines did not stop some Moros after they were hit. Supposedly we performed autopsies on these Moros, and established that they had gone on to bolo some of our troops to death after they had been fatally shot through the heart by the inadequate .38 bullets. After the Philippine insurrection was over and it was reasonable to assume that we should not be fighting hopped-up fanatics of this type again (we haven't), the Army proceeded to make tests on steers in the Chicago stockyards. In these tests the .45 A.C.P. was quite impressive in knocking them over, and small calibers did not do as expeditious a job. Therefore, we had to have a service handgun of no less than .45 caliber. We have been cursed with it ever since. So far as I have heard, no one thought to ask himself how many Moros shot through the heart by the inadequate .38 revolver would have been missed completely if the solder had been equipped with a .45. Based on what I have seen, done, and heard others speak of on numbers of ranges, I should say that most of these Moros would not have been even scratched; also that a number of Moros just a little less hopped-up or farther away, who did not quite get to hacking distance, would have been missed and have got to bolo distance as well.

When all is said and done, the most powerful pistol cartridges are piddling compared to a moderate rifle cartridge; and we are all familiar with the ceaseless controversies over the merits of different rifle cartridges. Any normal man hit by a pistol bullet is going to be much more concerned about the present state of his health than about his erstwhile opponent's condition. If you are up against a tough customer, your best bet is trying to cut him down with an accurate shot to a vital or disabling spot from a weapon you can handle, rather than attempting to knock him down by an indiscriminate shot from a weapon you are not able to do your best shooting with. Under service conditions there are sufficient handicaps to good shooting without having two strikes on you, as is the case when you are overgunned. The .45 Auto Colt is generally accepted as the most difficult handgun there is to learn to shoot well.

You just cannot put the cart before the horse in picking a handgun as a weapon. First, you must have one of such configuration and caliber that you get hits with it. If you can't get hits, all else is dross. Only after you have selected such an arm, have you any right to pick and choose a caliber and bullet type that will kill things extra dead, extra fast, or extra far.

As a horrible example, the .45 illustrates other vital considerations. Before we go further, I should like you to know this is not pure blind prejudice or sour grapes. I'm of normal physique and I've never had any trouble in qualifying as expert over the Army course with the beast. But my standards are not only higher than those of the Armed Forces, but also different from them. If I am going to take the trouble to pack 39 ounces of gun, I demand sufficient accuracy to make consistent hits at 100 yards, and I mean accuracy I get with my skill out of a gun, not from a machine rest or in the hands of a really good shot. Such performance is readily available with a 9 mm. auto or an ordinary .38 revolver. That .45 is just too much gun. I fight a flinch from the first shot on. I don't develop a regular muscle fatigue in my arm; I develop a tremor from the pounding after the first few magaines. That excess recoil slows you down in rapid fire, too. Stand back of the firing line some day and watch how far down out of the sky the shooters have to pull that gun for every shot. Also watch how many reasonably well-trained shooters flinch, too.

The really unforgivable fault of the .45, and of most other automatic pistols, is that it doesn't point. I categorically state that any defense handgun that doesn't point is not a good defense gun. Try this for yourself. Set up a double sheet of newspaper or a silhouette, walk back five to ten paces, turn and fire without the sights. With nearly any revolver you will gets hits almost right from the start. I still can't get consistent hits with the .45, and Lord knows I've tried. I've read articles on how to do this, but the bloody thing still hits the dirt for me far too often, simply because the angle of the grip to the line of bore is not large enough. What that means to you and me in defending ourselves is that if we don't have time to use the sights with a .45, we stand a good chance of missing with that first snapshot.

Now the eventuality for which we carry a handgun is more likely to be one of those nose-to-nose, chest-to-chest foxhole propositions than potting some fool standing upright fifty yards away. This gives us the last big reason for not carrying a .45. Unless you carry it cocked with a round in the chamber and the safety on—we have already voiced an opinion on this —you have to take time to cock it, and a .45 is both slow and awkward to cock with one hand. I suspect you could empty a double-action revolver in less time than it takes to cock and fire the first shot with a .45, using one hand.

In passing, we should give the devil his due. The .45 has these not insignificant, but nevertheless secondary, virtues. In functioning, it is one of the most reliable handguns made; for its power it is quite flat and compact; you can get parts and ammunition almost anywhere.

You may have guessed by now that my nominee for a heavy service type, semi-concealable weapon is in the .38 Special or 9 mm. Luger category. The .357 Maggie I personally have reservations on. It is an awful lot of gun and it breeds flinching. If you practice sufficiently with full loads (you only kid yourself by using .38s in a .357) you may not be overgunned. However, after three years of playing around with it, I am overgunned, but I confess to still trying. Oddly enough, the one place where recoil is not bothersome, and does not slow you up, is in hip shooting. I suspect the angle of the arm to the shoulder, combined with the bent elbow, allows the recoil to move the gun straight back instead of upwards. I was quite surprised at how accurately I could pump out a cylinderful of .357s. Of course at the moment the .357 has a real virtue to me. After shooting it for a while, anything you put into a .38 feels moderate!

My choice of guns is either a Combat Masterpiece or Trooper equipped with factory target grips. Each make also comes in a police service version that is quite as good; they have standard-size stocks. On the S.&W. the regular Magna grips need a filler in the front, and when you attach a Pachmayr adapter the recoil with heavy loads pounds your middle finger against the trigger guard; whereas the target grips fill in the front of the frame while maintaining the desirable rear contour, affording the best compromise between first-class double-action performance and moderately good timed and rapid performance. I found that with my hands a target-type custom grip that follows the contour of the back of the frame but moves it rearward about a quarter-inch allows perfect hammer thumbing (you don't strain or break your grip). But it definitely is inaccurate in double-action because the trigger finger can't reach far enough to use the joint of the finger but rather is operating with the pad on the tip of the finger. Also, these custom target grips punish your hand more with magnum loads. On the Colt the ordinary grips with a Pachmayr filler are good, but I prefer the target grips with the raised checkering rasped off to reduce the diameter slightly. This minor change made a difference to me. With the larger grips I throw more bad shots.

A word on sights. Check them, and if there isn't plenty of light between front and rear in your sight picture, open up the rear notch. Speed is a must, and the light may not be always what you would like. Naturally, the front sight must be of the quick-draw variety. I've tried white, red, gold and black sights, using nail polish, luminous paint, mirrors, gold, ivory and plastic. They all end up worn and dirty, and the tricky ones broken to boot. These tricky sights lead to all sorts of unforeseen complications. When I obtained a quick-draw front with a piece of red plastic inlaid flush into it, I thought this was the last word. When I started to use it, it developed that unless it had considerable light on it, it might just as well have been black; but when the direct sun struck it, the glare was so bad it fuzzed out the sight picture seen through the rear notch. So I took out a match to blacken it, and I sure did—it burned up. Between wear and oil, all varieties of paint go pretty fast, and plastic and ivory are delicate. A mirror sight must be perpendicular, and the mirror really doesn't throw that much light; so they're out. What is best is some sort of sourdough gold bar, and I haven't found them any real asset if the rear notch is big enough; and if it isn't, you can't use the sights in bad light even if the front sight has a built-in neon sign. Remember that the best target-type rear sights are comparatively delicate, and high enough to catch on clothes. The only advantage they have comes when you change types of ammunition. If you can possibly standardize on one load and be sure of your re-supply of it, fixed sights, opened out, are the most desirable.

Ammunition: The best is none too good, and you want plenty of it. When the choice arises between extra hot performance and reliable functioning, the latter is the only logical choice. If you load your own, do a little oil-proofing of your own kind with some lacquer around the primer and the edge of the bullet. Bear in mind that here as elsewhere, moderation pays. The best is not necessarily the biggest. Let me illustrate three favorite forms of excess.

First, in working up handloads make sure that they are not so hot as to produce sticking cases, leading, and inaccuracy, as I found could be done by just following recommended loads in the .357. If you put up a good top load for your S.&W. .357 with a standard .3585-inch bullet and drop those hulls into a Colt, you will very likely get leading, inaccuracy, and sticky cases when you shoot them. Those Colts usually run .354-inch across the grooves, and bullets .004 oversize just do not perform well at those pressures. So work up carefully to your top loads.

Second, think twice about really fine loads that are outside the conventional pattern for that weapon and caliber. An example is a very fine, ultra-high-speed, metal-piercing load put out by a top firm in .45 Auto

Colt. The bullet is so light that ordinary guns are just barely on the target paper with it at 25 yards, and some movable sights do not have enough movement.

This means that you can't just do a minor operation on the fixed sights with a file. Either the front or the rear sight would have to be completely replaced, and if you ever run out of that brand of ammo you are out of luck. Any ordinary ammunition would be too far out with your extensively modified sights.

Third, the most powerful rounds your gun can handle may be too much for you to handle. No matter how hard I tried, I have never been able to hold an S.&W. Chief's hard enough to keep the web between thumb and forefinger from crawling over the hump on the frame after a couple of rounds of high speed .38s (158-grain at 1100 f.s.). This is not only inaccurate and slow; it would make a stone monkey flinch. The standard .38 Special load is really all that a light small gun like that can handle well—as far as the shooter is concerned—no matter how much the gun can take.

In the high-performance type weapon, I suggest that the most desirable load, disregarding the sighting problem, is a light bullet as fast as you can push it, rather than the classic school solution which calls for a big heavy bullet for maximum knock-down power. There is no question that this type has the maximum knock-down power, but I always prefer a weak hit to no hit at all. There is a triple disadvantage to the big heavy bullet in pistols. The heavy bullets give the most unpleasant recoil. (For some odd reason a top light-bullet load seems much milder to shoot than a top heavy-bullet load, regardless of the foot pounds of energy involved.) The heavy's trajectory is quite high for longer range shooting, and the penetration is poor through non-fleshy materials. This last point I consider quite important. Since the 1930s they have been proving the quality of bullet-proof vests by firing the .45 Auto at them. Personally, I think a .38 Super, or a .357 or .38 Special metal-piercing load will punch right through either the old steel-plate type or the modern fiber-glass. I do not know this for a fact because the only time vests were available they were scarce and valued items. I'm sure my thirst for knowledge would have been rewarded by a swift kick in the pants if I had punched a hole in one, even in the unoccupied state. Penetration does appear to be a function of velocity as well as of bullet construction, in pistol cartridges. Those metal-piercing loads are quite impressive on steel drums, auto bodies, etc. I feel this penetration subject to be important because if we have such vests our enemies will soon acquire some of ours or make their own in the next fracas. Further, it is nice to know you can reach somebody even though he's protected by lighter material like doors, furniture, auto bodies, etc.

Pocket guns are much maligned, and rightfully so, by target shooters. Remember, though, that this is the only one you will be sure of having with you *always*; so pick it first and with care. Personally, I should be much happier carrying the poorest, most awkward little .25 automatic ever made than none at all. The qualities we look for are compactness, lightness and smoothness—and a gun that will point. Accuracy and power are secondary. I suggest they rank in this order of desirability: a hammerless revolver, a revolver with a hammer shroud, a revolver with the hammer spur ground off (this is the part that catches most in coming out of your pocket), a revolver with a hammer, the small double-action automatics, and last the standard automatics. Please remember that very few automatic designs point. The revolvers that have shrouds or are hammerless can be fired from inside the pocket. This isn't a recommended procedure; but sometime it may be necessary. I have had no experience in carrying a revolver with a hammer shroud, but I suspect that it would be a lint, dust and dirt catcher when carried for any great length of time in the pocket.

Marksmanship. Instructions could fill several chapters, and there is a good deal of excellent material in this field. I want to make a few practical suggestions on your approach. Forget about target shooting. This is a game and has very little to do with practical military fighting with a handgun. The only place where hard holding and squeezing pay dividends is in deliberate sighting and aiming at longer ranges. Primarily your handgun is an emergency weapon for short ranges—and the faster the better. Practice on a man silhouette, and once you are familiar with the weapon put it away and take it out each time you shoot. Practice unlimbering it fast from wherever it is carried. Shoot from different positions at different ranges, and from both hands. You develop speed by analyzing in slow motion what are the necessary motions and eliminating the remainder, then gradually moving faster. I don't want you to think that the absolute top speed at which you can move your body is what you should be trying to achieve. What you are looking for is the top speed at which you can achieve hits. I too have tried to chase a stop-watch. It is the wrong approach. Concentrate on getting hits, not on who makes a bang first. Most of all, you not only have to burn up ammunition and find out just what YOU can do, you have to dry-fire with an empty gun, too. This will point up mistakes you can discover in no other way.

Take the time to learn to strip your gun. If you get a good dunking it will be necessary to strip it, or you risk malfunctions.

To sum it all up, ask yourself the following questions:

1. Am I going to be able to take this weapon everywhere with me—at all times?

2. Is it safe for me to carry?

3. Can I shoot it accurately enough to get hits—and fast?

With the preceding in mind, get yourself a gun, regardless of cost—remember it's not life-insurance payable when you are proved dead; it is living-insurance so they won't be able to pay off your life-insurance—and practice with it, at least a few hundred rounds, and take it with you, with enough ammunition. You can never have too much.

"Where men lived raw in the desert's maw,
And Hell was no place to shun,
Where they buried them deep without preacher or sheet
And wrote on their tombstone, crude but neat,
'This Jasper was slow with his gun.'"

CHAPTER 25

THE HANDGUN'S ULTIMATE PURPOSE

BY ALBERT J. E. SHAY

THIS may sound humorous, or romantic, or grim, but take it for fact that an assailant within pistol range of you belongs to the brute world. He may be an enlisted man or an inducted civilian, even an unwilling fighter; but if the chips are on his side of the table and he gets through to your womenfolk, he'll be brutal. Exceptions in our rough world of today are so few as to be nearly negligible. Therefore, be willing to shoot to kill. A "disabled" man may have strength enough left to stab or shoot you to death.

Perhaps every imaginative and virile American of our time who ever picked up any kind of pistol, fondled it, and unleashed his mind to roam, has had a solid secret conviction that with practice he could equal or beat the best of them in quick-draw. Fiction, song, movie and TV have led him on. He has thrilled to the writings of Clarence E. Mulford, B. M. Bower, W. C. Tuttle, Luke Short, Talbot Mundy, Stewart Edward White and others. He has taken from them what he hoped to find, including, sometimes, sound advice as well as wild enthusiasm for this typically American form of the duel.

Although some people have a peculiar aptitude and master this hand-and-eye magic more quickly than others, the through ticket is the determination that expresses itself in hundreds or thousands of hours of *practice*. Right in our times was the late Ed McGivern, his presumably unparalleled achievements still unobscured by the rosy mists of saga. Read his book, *Fast and Fancy Revolver Shooting,* and appreciate the time, effort and mentality that lie behind real mastery.

He demonstrated that the hard-to-shoot 2-inch barreled "belly gun" packed in the waistband is useful when time is of the essence, but he didn't need one. Much of his work was done with 6-inch, target-sighted arms, accurate work and breathtakingly fast. Records and recollections through the years show that few holster guns had barrels under 5½ inches, and the majority were 7½ or even 8. Remington and Colt single-action .44-40s seemed to need such lengths to burn black powder to the best handgun advantage. Two quick shots, and if the wind was right you were wreathed in a cloud of smoke! Quite possibly the intelligent gun-fighters of those days tried to maneuver their foes to windward, just as destroyers lay a smokescreen to hide the capital ships.

Though much of the shooting was at some ten or twenty feet, or less, it would be good to think you could draw and fire from the hip, and without conscious aim hit a man-sized mark at fifty yards! Try it sometime. If you climb to the consistency of placing nearly all your *deliberately* aimed shots in the black

of the Standard American at fifty yards, you have considerable defense ability and are in no way handicapped in learning the fast and short shooting, the other side of the medal of practical skill. Your enemy may be close, with an empty bayonetted rifle, or two hundred feet away, behind a barricade but exposing himself to fire.

Being preponderantly a target shooter, I've never tried conscientiously to master quick-draw except on rare occasions and mostly at inanimate objects. The half-dozen times I've stirred up small game close aboard and tried for it as it scurried for cover, the old gun came out and barked without any order from headquarters. Five of the six times were successful.

A recent incident is etched in my memory. Working in my garden, I usually carry a small sidearm to discourage small animals that destroy mainly the young fruit. A favorite is a Colt Police Positive Special .32-20 that perks beautifully with handloads for its 5-inch barrel. King installed their Police Night Sights, now perhaps unavailable, a ⅛-inch spherical gold bead and a white-outlined rear notch. You hold the bead on top of the notch, not carefully fitted into it. This makes it fast, and accurate with a center hold.

Wheelbarrow in both hands, I headed for the garden, and across a twenty-foot strip of lawn slithered a husky snake. I dropped the 'barrow handles, found the Colt in my hand, and thumbed two shots without conscious aim. Both holed him at the waterline. As he reached the stone wall he hesitated. So did I, long enough to aim this shot, and the snake lost interest in worldly things. This story goes in simply to suggest that perhaps half a million shots at target don't keep you from drawing quickly and firing without conscious aim. If I'd done *no* target shooting, that snake might have escaped with only such warning as his Paleozoic mind could have registered.

My accurized .38 Super automatic's hollow-point lead bullets blow up, safe from ricochets, when they strike a hard object. A couple of times they have crowded an extra large strawberry right down a ground-squirrel's throat as he sat up on the stone-pile and thumbed his nose at me. In the hunting field this gun is not so good if you want to save empty cases for reloading!

Holsters

Exponents of quick-draw are quite often nationally known target shots, like the justly famed Walter Walsh. To learn to let off a carefully aimed shot *and hit with it* is surely no hindrance to mastering speed *and* accuracy. We have to hit, just as the ancients had to with javelin or sling.

From old times on down, there have been innumerable holster designs for quick-draw, or no draw at all, with one shot through an open-end holster, or firing a hammerless revolver through the pocket. But the main trend was an individual fit for the weapon. They'd wet the leather and form it on the greased gun, then let it dry to hard, stiff shape. Now we have spring designs with leather-enclosed steel "fingers" that let us snap the gun out with a sharp pull, much quicker than the pouch holster. Heiser types are justly famous, and perhaps the most modern holster is the Berns-Martin by Johnny Martin of Calhoun City, Mississippi,

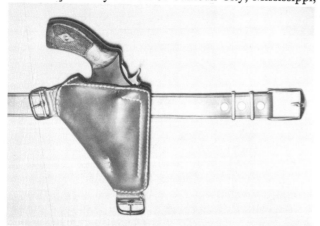

Berns-Martin "Lightnin" triple draw holster and one-inch belt, with shoulder strap removed, for right hip position. This triple-duty holster can also be worn forward of the left hip, for cross-draw, and with strap, upside-down as a shoulder holster that makes possible an extremely quick draw from that position.

Woman's light-weight, hand-carved Buscadero belt and holster by Lawrence. It makes for easy quick-draw and at present enjoys a wide revival. Many come in two-gun style, as do other holsters. This model, for women, is modified, using less leather. Some others are pretty heavy, and hot, if much walking is done, as a woodsman who's carried his home and household goods on his back could tell at a glance. But the stiff leather makes for a quick draw. Note the thong at the bottom of this holster, to go around the shooter's right thigh. It makes the leather stay put against the pull on the gun butt.

in both shoulder and belt types. His belt-riding "range holster" is open in front and lets you carry your target gun with blackened sights. John Berns and I went through training together in Newport in 1911, and Martin and I were on the All Navy Team squad in '26. Even then he was practicing quick-draw with belt holsters, and later at Camp Perry I saw him perform with upside-down shoulder holster and short-barreled belly gun. The great Henry Fitzgerald of Colt timed his split-second work. Johnny *hit*, too.

Decide where you want to tote your gun; get a good holster, and stick with it. Whistle up your will-power and drop all habits that slow your responses. Then practice (for a long time only with an empty gun, for your own safety) s-l-o-w and easylike, eliminating all flourishes and the lost endeavor of extra motions. A tall mirror helps.

Practice

Now the determination! Be ready to practice daily, thousands of hours all told, or the other bird will hang it on you for sure. Ed McGivern freely admitted that twenty years made his quick and easy road to success! Maybe you should become as good as you can, then tell yourself you *can* beat the other fellow. Losing their own nerve beats more people than the superior skill of an opponent does, in this business.

Back in 1925 aboard the *Wyoming,* we cruised the West Coast, my first visit there. I learned to carry my .22 Colt Woodsman in my waistband, without a holster. Shooting galleries were refined above the Coney Island and Norfolk type I'd seen. Most of them

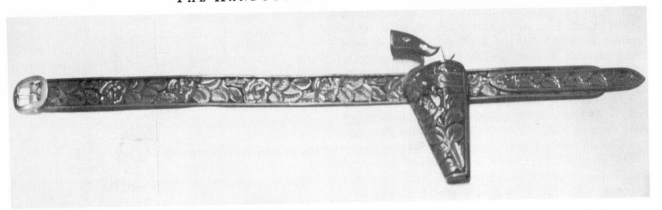

Berns-Martin "Speed" holster and belt, hand carved. This one carries a 6½-inch barreled Smith & Wesson .357 Magnum revolver.

had a two-inch iron ball hung from the ceiling at 20 feet or so, and all galleries had pistols, mostly Woodsmen with 12-inch barrels, the only ones I've seen. The idea was to start the ball swinging and keep it so till your ten-shot mag was empty. My gun, with its gold bead front, learned to hit nine times out of ten after a few hundred rounds, which eventually were free, for they drew a crowd. That was good for concentration, shooting "under pressure"; and the practice was fine for getting a lead on moving objects. Nowadays it wouldn't be considered safe practice at all, because of ricochets.

There is every possibility that any one of us may have to defend his home and family from a common enemy. The night marauder intent on the cash-box or silver, the sex-crazed lunatic or the sly saboteur, the enemy of society or of our Country—they are all alike. Everyone in the family should be familiar with the safe, effective use of a handgun. There mightn't be time for rifle or shotgun, or one hand might be out of commission. That suggests the wisdom of acquiring reasonable skill with either hand, well worth extra rounds allocated to it in practice.

An extra but inconspicuous gat around the premises, not far from your wife's usual haunts, can be something to thank God for if she has learned to use it. Even a .25 Auto bullet will penetrate almost any clothing and drill a neat, deep hole in the tissue beneath. You can fire an auto just once, for sure, from the pocket; and even a hammer revolver may hang up there after one round. That's what hammerless models and Colt hammer shrouds are for. But mostly there is time enough to draw the gun, and often the sight of it is enough of a persuader. Consider too the handy little .22s, those that are reliable, and they don't need the sharp-cracking high-velocity loads for penetration. The .22s are inviting for family practice, which can begin at ten yards or even six. What counts are hits in a man-sized area, sure and fairly quick, not tens in the center of the black. Shoot a piece of standard 8½x11-inch paper, then place it over your body anywhere and see how you'd like it. Try double-action if the revolver isn't easy for the pupil to cock, and he or she shies

away from the hours put in at learning to thumb a hammer, as he would in training for the National Matches. And don't forget *two-handed shooting,* and ear-plugs if wanted.

In standing off an enemy you don't expose yourself to give him an even break! Even on a desert without sagebrush there are friendly folds in the earth which can partly hide your body. The enemy uses all the cover he can find, you can bet.

You can fire from prone, sitting, kneeling, from behind a corner or a log or tree or rock. Try to keep the pistol at arm's length so the sights won't blur and your shots go wild. Two-handed shooting can boost accuracy at any range; so try it a lot on target paper. Before World War I our Navy included it in the use of the then new 1911 .45 Auto. One hand just steadied the other, didn't share in gripping; and you faced the target squarely with the pistol straight in front of you. With a sixgun the second hand must be really gentle, and kept away from the gun butt. Recoil must be natural, for accuracy. Some steady the wrist or even the elbow, instead. Try different ways.

When you fire from cover, never rest the gun on a log, rock or anything at all. She wouldn't hit to normal sighting. Maybe you'd sight in with the barrel supported on the starboard side, then *have* to shoot with a rest to port. Where would you be? Try these things to convince yourself.

Prone, and wanting to try for a careful shot, you can draw up your leg to a bent-knee position, lying partly on your side, and rest your wrist on or beside the knee, keeping your eye distance quite well. For a shot at game or anything not immediately threatening, you can sit with your back against a tree and use both hands, elbows on knees. The sights will be fuzzy unless your eyes have good accommodation, but lots of eyes do.

Long Range

You can do creditable 200- and 300-yard shooting with a gun with a 6-inch barrel, though more length certainly helps, with the extra sight radius—the distance between them that makes precision easier. At

Camp Perry I've often seen professionals and amateurs fire .38 Specials at 300-yard man-sized targets. Captain Hardy hit it with a cylinderful at 300 and used only one hand. It's interesting, and not too discouraging on a six-foot rifle target with round black bull, quite different from an object colored like the surrounding scenery, with no aiming point. To hit the latter you must cover it completely unless you've had installed a front sight with black and white bars across it, calibrated for different ranges. Then you run your front sight up to the proper bar and aim as at the usual six o'clock, just under the bottom of the bull.

I tried it once as we were about to leave the 300-yard rifle range for home. My .45 Auto was with me, naturally. We'd had to use 20-inch marking discs meant for 500- and 600-yard targets—but see you about those later. I called the pits, asked that one target be left standing, and found after three shots that a hold at the top of the six-foot paper would drop the .45s close to the center. The detail took down the target and returned, those discs racked up, plain against the hill background. There was a friendly challenge and I was keen to try, with the picture of a 2½-foot overhold sharp in my mind. A full magazine was let off and we needed no marker, for seven satisfying *clinks* came back to us. Later I regretted this vandalism, but then it was pleasant—and still is, in memory—to find seven large round holes in that rather heavy galvanized stuff, and made at that range.

Practicing with the All Navy Team at Annapolis, a couple of shipmates agreed to mark target for me at 600 yards while I shot my German Navy 9 mm. Luger with 6-inch barrel. From prone, with arms extended and wrists resting on a folded shooting coat, it took two of the old flat-nosed Winchester rounds to get on the 6x6-foot target. The sights went up to only 200 meters; so I had to hold high. After finding the paper I found it not too hard to keep them there, with about a third in the 20-inch bull's-eye.

Don't underestimate your pistol. It can send a .22 long-rifle bullet nearly a mile. The 158-grain .38 Special, well shaped and almost four times as heavy, might go—well, a mile and a half is a conservative guess. Even if it falls on you it has quite a punch. So has a .45! Firing over water, when it's safe, and using aiming points on a not too distant opposite shore, might be practice of untold advantage to you when the chips are down and you have to play your hand.

Know Your Gun

Range and speed and punch *sometimes* count, making it worth-while to have mastered a gun that has them. In training one of the "weaker" sex, you may find one who doesn't care for a little bit of lead-squirter. Years ago my life partner tried the Woodsman .22, now has one of her own; but she soon announced that it didn't give the proper thrill to shooting. Did I take her by easy stages to the .45 Auto? Not by a jugful! I *didn't* break her of the big-gun bug, either, and I'm glad. Do you hear? She took to Bellerin' Bess

and performed creditably from the start. Unless you're in Sharpshooter class or above, don't tangle with her in a .45 match. Even in slow fire she piles in the nineties and better all the time. She has her own .45 and a permit to carry it. Nuff sed?

I think that familiarity with your handgun is of prime importance. In hunting, fishing, or on countless other occasions, it's no good to you when it's home in a bureau drawer. You can pack it so its weight won't bother you. In all the years I wore the blue off my .45 Auto, I never seemed to notice its weight in shoulder or belt holster, or in the now defunct waistband, and I'm no big brute.

Keep this type of gun—a hammer autoloader with short or "flying" firing pin—always ready with the hammer fully down, the magazine filled, and *one in the chamber*. Empty-gun practice will teach you to cock it pretty fast. A double-action revolver or auto is faster for the first shot, but this neat, flat, easy-cuddling Colt is my choice, with its eight big bullets. Put it alongside a 4-inch .38 Special police revolver and measure for three dimensions. Count its weight against the revolver's six shots. Reliability? Stack it up against ANY OTHER GUN IN THE WORLD. Some have higher velocity; some have heavier bullets and more power—and believe me, more bulk. But for spitting them out, and reloading fast with extra magazines, I'll take the Service's choice any day.

A soldier goes into battle with his gun in his hand, and why shouldn't you? There's no faster "draw." So if it has to be, don't be squeamish; get your shot in first. You wouldn't walk up on a wounded grizzly with your gat buttoned down in a flap holster. All's fair in war, and war it is, whether it be against an enemy of society or an enemy of our Country and our way of life. Don't go out to fight it empty-handed. Even a pitchfork is a deadly weapon if it gets on target.

Whatever gun you choose, keep it working and cared for, not gathering rust or dust in a drawer or in a holster. You wouldn't keep a racehorse in stable for two years, then turn him out to win. A little practice as often as possible is the answer when ammunition or time is scarce. Handling, drawing, and perfecting the always smooth but gradually speeded-up trigger squeeze are answers, too. My ever-admired American, Theodore Roosevelt, said long ago when we were building up our Navy, "Only the shots that hit are the shots that count." That's as true now as it was in 1910, or in dates B. C. You can burn the air beside a determined enemy and he goes on, secure in his destiny. First learn to hit; then strive for speed.

There is something more that is fully as essential as the gun and our hitting ability. That is the inner fortress of resolution, the reasoned courage of a free soul who counts it better to die in defense of his freedom than to live as a slave. With this rampart against "the slings and arrows of outrageous Fortune" he can't altogether lose.

O DD things happen. Beginners get more than their share of these mischances, and the habitually careless get even more.

I knew better than to hunt with a cocked gun having no safety lock, but the striker of the Winchester Model 1904 single-shot was hard for a young fellow's finger and thumb to draw back. The folds in the sidehill I was working made favorite landing fields for early spring crows—good hunting if you could take a shot quickly. After a while that four-pound .22 rifle felt heavy. As I threw it across my arm a light pop sounded. No one in sight: what was it? I drew back the bolt and found an empty case. A crease in my canvas coat-sleeve had touched the light trigger. That was when I stopped being habitually careless.

We could hardly load a cartridge wrong-end-to into a pistol's box or clip magazine, as we could into most rifle mags of tubular type. Pistol mags with an outside button to depress the spring as we slide the rounds in are handy to load, maybe too handy. It's natural to depress the magazine follower far enough to drop in several cartridges at a time, but we must not. If the spring is strong and our thumb-hold on the button is weak, we can lose our grip, and then the follower, with or without a part cargo of loaded rounds, flies up most energetically. A rimfire or even a centerfire cartridge may be struck and discharged by a sharp bullet nose smacking strategically into it. This has happened at least once, and probably both you and I can recall times when it might have happened. Unconfined, as by a barrel, an exploding cartridge can't develop its full power; but it can be rough enough to hurt someone near by.

As a kid, I once built a driftwood fire, and after pretty fair coals had been built up I dropped a misfired .44-40 round into it and scurried behind a three-foot-thick tree-trunk. After the loud explosion and the scattering of ashes, I took stock. Both bullet and case had plowed deep paths along the earth. I was impressed. That must have been a black powder .44. Years later, up in the game country, I found a softpoint .30-30 bullet in the ruins of a burned camp. The lead nose was not even flattened. Still, I'd have hated to catch it as it left the case!

Yes, odd things happen. But nearly all accidents are explainable—afterwards—and caution or *precaution* prevents most of them. Don't let easy familiarity with a pistol or any other weapon make you lax in vigilance.

Especially to the beginner the little short handgun is dangerous, much more so than rifle or shotgun. It's so easily swung around and its muzzle is so eager to cover everything in sight! Coach that tyro with an unloaded pistol, teaching him the respect due to empty or supposedly empty guns, and then he'll do all right with loaded ones. Also teach him to let down the autoloader's hammer or slip on its safety after each slow-fire shot. It's so easy and natural for him to lower any handgun, after firing, while he gazes at the target in

CHAPTER 26

SAFETY MEASURES

hopeful search of a bullet-hole "close to the black"—bless his heart—that he'll endanger his own feet! If proper range rules are enforced, no such thing will happen, and enforced they must be, no matter how small and select the assembly is.

Good gun-handling isn't hard for anyone past the early teens to learn, and some learn it at much earlier ages, as a visit to an N.R.A. junior rifle club range can prove. But for a while most youngsters need to be reminded continually. They aren't quite to be blamed, for such is the butterfly character of their mental and emotional processes. In two years, or even less sometimes, intelligent and alert mid-teeners can become reliable range safety officers. Patience wins. Such patient instruction of any beginner, of any age, should start with *unloaded* guns—and the start shouldn't be too brief. Even an oldtimer must always and forever remember to handle every gun as though it were loaded—it might be!—by keeping its muzzle from pointing at anyone, and by swinging that muzzle up or down whenever someone blunders in front of it. He knows that odd things happen, but he's on his guard.

Bullet Travel

We need to watch the background of fire in target work, plinking, or hunting. Since handgun bullets often give amazing performance in penetration, target backstops must really stop bullets. The kind we sometimes build for outdoor use, a frame of logs filled with earth, is far from everlasting. Before the first season passes, it may develop leaks and need thorough overhauling and rebuilding. Take your lead pail along on this job. You'll pick up well-mushroomed slugs that show what lead pistol bullets do when they hit real resistance.

Some handgun bullets can range well over a mile and do plenty of business on arrival. A slow start doesn't necessarily mean a short flight, for weight and shape have much to do with carrying power. Even though ricochets travel only briefly, as a rule, their sound and fury account for many a "No Hunting" sign. The resentment they incur is justified, for when one of these end-over-end cartwheelers strikes a person it makes a nasty wound.

With the slow bullets from pistols being so prone to ricochet, the fellow who hunts woodchucks or other game with his handgun must be doubly careful. And in any hunting we must know positively what we shoot at. Is it game, or some domestic animal, or even a human being? Since the fool-with-a-gun doesn't bother about positive identification, many of us wear bright red or the still more visible yellow when hunting right out in the open as well as in the woods. The pistoleer who hunts at close ranges—he really has to hunt—must know how to stalk to certain, sportsmanlike hitting range; but in leafy woods even he must make sure of the background of his line of fire as well as identifying his target.

Safe Carries

The greatest reason for the pistol's popularity is its handiness, its easy portability. It can be carried as safely as a long gun, though it requires more sense to do so, more ingrained good habits, at least. It seldom drops out of a pocket, but it often falls from a holster if no retaining strap or spring or buttoned-down flap holds it in when we tumble. Then unpleasantness can arise most suddenly! Many hammerless automatics have no safety to lock the covered hammer or striker as positively as those on the old Savage and Luger do. A trigger safety can block the trigger effectively, but not necessarily the hammer. Safes that are smooth enough to be useful in anything like quick work occasionally shift off, "unbeknownst," in travel or in handling. Unless gun need is liable to be sudden, in which case we're alert enough, anyway, the best manner of toting a hammerless auto is with the chamber empty. If the gun is left cocked, the slide or the breech-block can be moved back and forth quickly and even rather quietly.

Early Colt autos with exposed hammer had no safety and seemed not to need one except for quick work. The hammer's half-cock was sturdy, though I have heard of one, on authority I wasn't personally acquainted with, that let go and fired the piece when it fell and the hammer spur struck a rock. The firing pin was too short (like that of modern hammer Colt autos) to touch the firing pin when the hammer was fully down, but when that hammer fell it booted the firing pin forward. A retaining spring held the pin back during the forward slam of the slide. So most of the informed users carry these guns with hammer all the way down, though it does seem unlikely that a fall from half-cock could fire the arm. But with the hammer fully down, these pistols are as safe as a fine

hammerless revolver, like the Smith & Wesson. For that matter, with little if any doubt, the long-discontinued Iver Johnson, Harrington & Richardson and other old hammerless revolvers are safe, too. After all, the covered hammers are cocked and released by a long pull on the trigger.

Bert Shay's .45 Colt Auto once fell on the highway and was run over by a six-wheeled truck. It didn't go off, and what's more, it wasn't harmed in any way.

A badly worn autoloader can "follow-through," go into machine-gun fire if its sear doesn't hold. Then the muzzle climbs—and fast!—sending the last shots high over any ordinary backstop, even the face of a pretty high cliff. No, we wouldn't deliberately fire into a cliff, begging for ricochets back toward us, but one makes extra insurance behind a good stop of earth, timber, or 45-degree slanted steel.

Some revolvers are safe in almost any rough usage. The break-open old Iver Johnson with hammer-the-hammer safety device could fall almost any distance and light on that hammer without firing. So could modern Colts, Smiths and others with positive hammer-blocks. Such guns lock the hammer at a sort of half-cock when their double-action triggers are forward. But some otherwise good revolvers have no such safety built into them. Single-actions are commonly carried with their hammers clear down on an empty chamber. With some of them, the fired primer of an empty case under the hammer nose will permit the cylinder to shift, bringing a live round into line.

An open-bottom holster doesn't hold dirt, pine needles or twigs to foul the muzzle, nor does it keep out snow or other dangerous plugs if we sit down deliberately or in unrehearsed fashion. Firing into such a plug usually bulges the barrel. In the canoe the holster's place is at the rear, hanging down like a dejected tail. And if the stern paddler is to have any sort of gun within reach he'd best be a cool customer. I've always felt secure as bow-paddler for my old friend Francis Clarke, and for one or two others who wanted a gun in the pilot's seat. Usually the "Guns up front" rule must be enforced.

Gun Strength

No matter how careful a shooter is, personally, he can get hold of a weak or dangerous gun. Smokeless powder probably has no place at all in any cap-and-ball or muzzle-loading pistol, or in Single Action Colts below the 160,000 serial number that still carry the old, original cylinders. Many Spanish copies of S.&W. or Colt guns, popular importations in the years between World Wars I and II, were unsafe with any factory loads. The .357 Magnum introduced the forty-odd thousand pounds per square-inch pressure to the American handgun world. It and the .44 Mag. are right only in guns made especially for them, and so stamped, such as Smiths, Colts, Great Westerns, Rugers, and a small stack of custom built rifles. The .357's .30-30 rifle pressure can be expected to blow up old .38 Long service revolvers whose unthroated chambers will take it. Dangerous too is the practice of rechambering .38 or .44 Specials for Magnum rounds. It may not be certain danger, but it's near enough.

Colt Woodsman guns under 83,790 serial were for low speed .22 long-rifles. They can and should be fitted with the newer, stronger mainspring housings, if high speed ammo is to be fired in them—and almost anyone may choose to fire it. The early housing is milled or cross-hatched at its curve, where you press in to dismount the gun. The later issues, different from modern post-war Woodsmen, have horizontal lines to distinguish them from the pioneers. Many fine old guns, like the Reising .22 auto, shouldn't be asked to digest the high-pressure rounds. They can give fine satisfaction, provided they're sound, with modern standard-velocity ammo, which is a little more powerful than the Lesmok and Semi-smokeless powder long-rifles they were made for.

Really dangerous is the use of factory High Velocity or High Speed cartridges in .32-20, .38-40 and .44-40 sixguns. Although only one variety is still loaded, the .32-20 with 80-grain hollow point, a few of the oldtimers remain unfired, just in the nature of things, and the Hercules Sharpshooter powder generally used in them stands up to ageing pretty well! The light bullets are or were hollow-pointed, the standard weights soft-nosed or full-metal-patched. "H.V." or "W.H.V." headstamps indicate probably all heavy-bullet super loadings; sometimes only the hollow point reveals the light-bullet type. Rifle handloads safe in these three calibers (or in some others, of course) may be entirely too rough for even a high-quality handgun.

We have stressed safety so much in our comments on handloading that little more seems necessary to say on the subject. Let's repeat just two warnings. Anything like heavy handloads are for just one individual gun until proved otherwise, for there are variations in interior and exterior dimensions, in vintage, quality, and design. If you want them you must feel your own way to them, taking no one's recommendations unless he's familiar with your particular gun. And components vary, the primer and even the powder, though both are held to close standardization unless the vintages are quite different. Most of all do bullets vary, though we'll naturally size or choose them to fit our guns and consider such details as weight, hardness, bearing surface, seating depth, and the particular lot of cases' own capacity.

A few old .22 revolvers and single-shot pistols of absolutely top original grade should be fired only with low or standard-velocity shorts, if at all. Typical is the neat little seven-shot "Ladysmith" S.&W. double-action which came in 3- and 3½-inch barrel lengths, or in 6-inch as a Münchkin-size target arm suitable in the dear old land of Oz, and hardly anywhere else.

The gun's condition is important, but A-1 shape doesn't necessarily mean strength. Many superb early Smith and Colt guns had thin barrel breeches facing their cylinders. Heavy loads can bulge them. Properly fed, these arms are undeniably useful, and deserving of use, but he who handloads for them should keep to low-pressure factory ballistics, or less, and avoid oversize and hard-alloyed bullets. They aren't for the latest hot loads.

Unfamiliar Guns—And Users

Any complicated or delicate mechanism calls for well-informed care in its use. The Walther P-38 wartime auto could be put together minus its locking assembly, still fire, and let the bolt slam against the stop lugs. This is decidedly unhealthy, and too few of us really know these arms. There are other attractive and mysterious strangers.

A person needn't be notoriously careless to "unload" an automatic by removing its magazine and forgetting to eject the cartridge from the chamber. Or he can empty the barrel first, then pull out the mag—and forget the round he has pumped into the chamber. So magazine safeties that disconnect or bar the trigger mechanism are pretty nice, unless you lose the magazine and thus perhaps go naked before "the bright face of danger." In 1947 the little hammerless Colts assumed these disconnectors, with serial 141,000 in the .25, 468,097 in the .32, and 98,894 in the .380 that by comparison seemed to cost so much more to shoot! Testing for such a safety is simple, with an empty gun: cock it, pull out the mag, and try to snap the hammer.

All of us must always know whether or not *any* gun near us contains a load. Last night at the range, Ray Reynolds and I discussed the liability of familiarity breeding carelessness. We think that the experienced, the long-time shooter should ask himself whether this particular hazard applies to him. Certainly it does apply to some.

We read too often of accidents incurred "while cleaning the gun." The terrible thing is that they *can* happen as accidents, though sometimes the account is hard to believe in spite of a kindly wish to accept it as truth. To prove it to myself I did manage to tear down and reassemble a Model 1911 Colt .45 Auto with a loaded round in its chamber—and was I muzzle-conscious! Sometimes "cleaning" consists of merely forcing a brush down the barrel and back. A cartridge could be left there, lying in wait. It must do as it's told, fire when its primer is indented.

Let all of us remember, beginner and old hand alike, that every firearms accident, like every shooter's act of vandalism or even of inconsiderate behavior afield, reflects upon the whole body of us who use and love guns. The shooting game's life depends upon public good-will, doesn't it? Put that burden of responsibility in your pocket, carry it proudly, and assume your part in spreading the safety message. Believe me, your part is important.

INDEX